A Coherent Splendor

The American Poetic Renaissance, 1910–1950

ALBERT GELPI
Stanford University

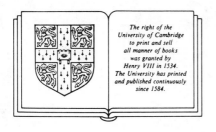

The right of the
University of Cambridge
to print and sell
all manner of books
was granted by
Henry VIII in 1534.
The University has printed
and published continuously
since 1584.

CAMBRIDGE UNIVERSITY PRESS

CAMBRIDGE

NEW YORK   NEW ROCHELLE   MELBOURNE   SYDNEY

Published by the Press Syndicate of the University of Cambridge
The Pitt Building, Trumpington Street, Cambridge CB2 1RP
32 East 57th Street, New York, NY 10022, USA
10 Stamford Road, Oakleigh, Melbourne 3166, Australia

First published 1987

Printed in the United States of America

Library of Congress Cataloging-in-Publication Data
Gelpi, Albert.
A coherent splendor.
1. American poetry – 20th century – History and
criticism.   2. Modernism (Literature) – United States.
3. Romanticism – United States.   I. Title.
PS324.G45   1987   811'.52'091   87–10876

British Library Cataloguing in Publication Data
Gelpi, Albert
A coherent splendor: the American poetic
renaissance, 1910–1950.
1. American poetry – 20th century –
History and criticism
I. Title
811'.52'09   PS323.5

ISBN 0 521 34533 2

Frontispiece: *Radiation* by Edward Bomberg

This book is for Barbara
and for Christopher and Adrienne
with much love

Contents

Acknowledgments

I want to thank several libraries for their help: the Berg Collection of the New York Public Library for allowing me to consult the unpublished poems of T. S. Eliot; the Beinecke Library at Yale and the Houghton Library at Harvard for the use of some unpublished H. D. materials in their collections; the Cecil H. Green Library at Stanford, and especially William Allan, then curator of English and American literature, for many instances of assistance. I am also very grateful to the Solomon R. Guggenheim Foundation for awarding me a fellowship which allowed me to draft three of the long central chapters of the book.

The scope of the undertaking has allowed me to acknowledge by name in the text and notes only those scholars and critics whose work my argument engaged explicitly, but I am acutely aware of, and grateful to, the many unnamed whose work has over the years helped to inform my understanding of the poets and the period. Many friends have generously given comments, encouragement, suggestions, and queries which have extended, challenged, clarified, and in all cases improved both the argument and the presentation. I have in mind and heart particularly (and alphabetically): George Dekker, William Everson, Susan Stanford Friedman, Robert Kiely, Denise Levertov, Herbert Lindenberger, Thomas Moser, Marjorie Perloff, Joel Porte, Adrienne Rich, Jonathan Veitch. Seth Magalaner served as keen-eyed research assistant at a crucial phase.

And of course the loving presence and active interest of my family I have relied upon throughout: my mother, who kept asking when I was going to finish the book, without once doubting that I would; my brother Don, an Americanist himself, always eager to hear me out on my poets both over the kitchen table and along the jogging trail; Barbara, ever my most enthusiastic and exacting critic, my companion in literary pursuits as in all other life commitments; and Christopher and Adrienne, who were fated to grow up with the book and came to view Papa's obsessions with H. D. and Pound and the others with a bracing blend of bemusement and curiosity.

ALBERT GELPI
June 4, 1987

ix

The greatest truth we could hope to discover, in whatever field we discovered it, is that man's truth is the final resolution of everything. Poets and painters alike today make that assumption and this is what gives them the validity and serious dignity that becomes them as among those that seek wisdom, seek understanding. I am elevating this a little, because I am trying to generalize and because it is incredible that one should speak of the aspirations of the last two or three generations without a degree of elevation.

WALLACE STEVENS
"The Relations Between Poetry and Painting"

i.e. it coheres all right
> even if my notes do not cohere.

EZRA POUND
Canto 116

Faas: A poet like Antin traces post-Modernism to the *Cantos* and *The Waste Land*.

Duncan: Well, I'm not a Modernist. He can do that. I read Modernism as Romanticism; and I finally begin to feel myself pretty much a 19th century mind.

Faas: Really!

Duncan: I don't feel out of my century, I like this century immensely. But my ties to Pound, Stein, Surrealism and so forth all seem to me entirely consequent to their unbroken continuity from the Romantic period.

ROBERT DUNCAN
"Interview" in Ekbert Faas, *Toward a New American Poetics*

Introduction

The Janus-Face of Romanticism and Modernism

> but gods always face two-ways....
> H. D., *The Walls Do Not Fall*

A Coherent Splendor is a companion volume to *The Tenth Muse* (1975). Although each book has its own integrity, together they comprise a single extensive essay on the American poetic tradition. *The Tenth Muse* traced the development of American Romantic poetry both out of and against its Calvinist source through chapters on five poets – Edward Taylor, Ralph Waldo Emerson, Edgar Allan Poe, Walt Whitman, and Emily Dickinson. *A Coherent Splendor* traces the development of American Modernist poetry both out of and against American Romanticism by focusing on a range of poets from that astonishing generation born in the final decades of the nineteenth century and coming to poetic maturity in the years just before and after World War I: Robert Frost, John Crowe Ransom, Wallace Stevens, T. S. Eliot, Ezra Pound, H. D., William Carlos Williams, Allen Tate, Hart Crane, Yvor Winters, Robinson Jeffers.

What distinguishes these two books from such excellent earlier studies as Roy Harvey Pearce's *Continuity of American Poetry* and Hyatt Waggoner's *American Poets* is the mounting of a literary-historical argument through the extended and detailed study of major representatives. The chapters aim at something of the comprehensiveness and depth of a monograph on the individual poets, while locating them in the broader cultural landscape. As in *The Tenth Muse*, then, my purpose here is double, at once historical and interpretive: to substantiate the argument about the tradition through detailed readings of important poems of the first half of this century. The historical argument provides the thread of continuity, and at the same time the explications are given such heft and force that they are never mere appendages to the discourse. The argument is less a clothesline for dangling scraps of illustrative literary laundry than a lifeline for entering and mapping the labyrinth and emerging enlightened.

Having spent more than ten years on the preparation of this book, I am acutely aware of the many distinguished scholars and critics who have written, often with assumptions and conclusions differing from my own and from one another's, about the period under discussion or about one of its poets. Nonetheless, I decided to omit references to other secondary works unless I was using or taking issue with a particular point or insight for the simple but compelling reason that in a book of this scope I could find no effective way to cite, much less to review, all of the pertinent commentary without doubling its size and cluttering and obscuring my own effort at clarification.

The book's title, adapted from Ezra Pound, evokes the Modernist goal: the imaginative fashioning of the unruly and resistant materials of experience through the expressive resources of the medium – paint, stone, language – into an autotelic work of coherent splendor. But the chapter titles, in deliberate contrast, all suggest the divisions, ambivalences, and conflicts which both necessitated and constrained, impelled and deconstructed the Modernist experiment at almost every point. The dissonance impelling the drive to consonance underlies the design of the chapters as well. This introduction sets up, for the subsequent chapters to substantiate and develop, the terms of the dissonance between Romanticism and Modernism and the terms of the dissonances within both Romanticism and Modernism which provide continuity between the two supposedly opposing ideologies which is deeper and more interesting than the initial points of contrast. The six central chapters, dealing with the careers of the major American Modernist poets, are framed: on the one side by a chapter on two pre-Modernists, Frost and Ransom, who anticipate some of the critical metaphysical and psychological dilemmas of the period without experimenting with aesthetic resolutions; and on the other side by a coda on two contrasting anti-Modernists, Winters and Jeffers, who define those same issues by contending against them from adversarial perspectives.

A number of commentators have accepted the Modernists' programmatic declaration that they defined their ideological positions in opposition to the Romantic advocacy of an Idealist metaphysics, a personalist psychology, and an intuitive epistemology. But I argue here for a subtler continuity between Romanticism and Modernism beneath the avowed discontinuity. Even more, I argue for a recognition that the epistemological, and so the aesthetic, divisions within Romanticism itself anticipate and lead to the divisions within Modernism, or, to turn the point around, that the dialectic within poetic Modernism, enacted in the interaction between its Symboliste and Imagist strains, extends and reconstitutes the epistemological and so the aesthetic issues that defined and then undermined Romanticism.

"Romanticism" and "Modernism" are, of course, slippery terms. Indeed, that slipperiness manifests itself in their ability to mask and unmask one another, to slide into one another only to polarize again; and that very slipperiness is the point of my argument. But let me begin with some broad and elementary remarks which will be both substantiated and complicated in the chapters to come. After the classical period of Greece and Rome, the history of the West has been read in terms of the consolidation of Christianity as the dominant cultural ideology during the Middle Ages and the gradual subversion or diffusion of that dominance beginning in the Renaissance. The Enlightenment, Romanticism, and Modernism mediate the dominant cultural ideologies of the eighteenth, nineteenth, and twentieth centuries, each transition pivoting conveniently at or near the turn of the century. These ideologies mark successive efforts to deal with the rising sense of threat and confusion at every level of life in the West, religious and psychological, philosophic and political: a sense of crisis intensified if not caused by the weakening authority of Christianity in all of those areas.

Where Modernism represented a reaction to Romanticism, Romanticism itself had represented a reaction to the rationalist, Neoclassical ideology of the eighteenth century. The Enlightenment sought in some instances to stem, in other instances to supplant, the ebbing of faith with the advance of reason, the decline of theology with the perfection of the empirical method, waning convictions about the sinner's membership in the community of saints with the fallible individual's normative socialization into secular institutions. But Rousseau initiated the transition to Romanticism by realizing that such rationalism repressed the individual's capacity to feel and denied those intimations of self and nature which, like the experience of grace for the Christian, locate the individual within a cosmic scheme. The effect of Cartesian empiricism, epitomized in the statement "I think, therefore I am," was to isolate the individual and then to divide the Christian-incarnational sense of self against itself, setting mind against and above body, subordinating feeling to reason. What's more, between Descartes and Hume, empirical analysis seemed to deconstruct the efficacy of reason itself, and by the end of the eighteenth century, the Romantics had defined themselves out of and against rationalism in the attempt to constitute a new incarnational holism on the basis of the individual's intuitional feeling outside ecclesiastical and civil structures.

This radical ideological shift elevated to primacy the individual's intrinsic capacity to perceive and participate in the organic interrelatedness of all forms of natural life and the individual's consequent capacity to intuit the metaphysical reality from which that natural harmony proceeds, which it manifests, and on which it depends. Assimilating gnostic Neoplatonism, German Idealism, and Oriental mysticism, the Romantic supplanted the right reason of the Renaissance and the logical reason of the Enlightenment with transcendental Reason, appropriately capitalized. Its flashes of intuitive perception superseded mere lowercase reason and revealed, in the contingencies of material existence, the indwelling essence of the Absolute.

In the aesthetic realm, transcendental Reason functions as the Imagination, and where the Neoclassical imagination had been charged with selecting and assembling expressive forms for the poet's thoughts, the Romantic Imagination assumed the awesome task of articulating those visionary spots of timeless time in an aesthetic form not only appropriate to but ideally unique to the personal experience being rendered. In English poetry this notion of an organic form turned the Romantics from the Neoclassical codification of genres and conventions to the more flexible possibilities of blank verse and the irregular ode stanza. The nascent American poetry, innocent of tradition and achievement, developed the Romantic notion further in the poetic prose of Emerson, the open form of Whitman, the verbal and metrical idiosyncrasies of Dickinson.

Romanticism, then, rested on the assumption that meaning – and therefore expression – proceeded from the momentary gestalt, wherein subject and object not merely encountered each other but completed, or at least potentially completed, each other. This personal and individual experience of potential correspondence was the source of Romantic psychology, Romantic politics, Romantic aesthetics. But it was also the source of Romantic instability and self-doubt, and so the genesis of Modernism. That epiphanic gestalt could not be invoked by the mechanics of thought or will; it could only be awaited and attended upon, and its occurrence was rare and fleeting. Romanticism made everything, including its anarchic politics, rest and pivot on such precarious moments in individual experience. No wonder that from the beginning, Romantic ecstasy was accompanied by Romantic angst; Romantic prophecy, by Romantic irony and skepticism. Literature and the arts operated in a state of crisis during the nineteenth century precisely because the moment of participative insight, in which the individual and the world were sealed in a revelation of cosmic and metaphysical harmony, became steadily more difficult to attain and to validate.

The deepening crisis in perception and signification, as the Romantic construct gave way through Victorian doubt to its *fin de siècle* decadence, set the agenda for Modernism. Farther along in the same ongoing process of cultural and social fragmentation that had impelled the Romantic to try a personalistic metaphysical solution, Modernism felt impelled, in turn, to assume a self-consciously anti-Romantic position. With reason long since deconstructed by the empiricists, and now with mystical intuition deconstructed by the Romantics and Victorians, the individual seemed left utterly alone with what the mind and will could make of the dilemma. World War I had swept away the last vestiges of the previous epoch and left a void: hollow men in a waste land.

For the Romantics, the Absolute was taken to be the farthest dimension of personal experience and so the supreme theme of art, though the formal and technical means of art could only imperfectly render the visionary moments which engendered and informed expression. Metaphysics determined – and exceeded – aesthetics as it did politics; failure to achieve aesthetic perfection, like failure to achieve utopia, testified to the paradoxical sublimity and impossibility of Romantic inspiration and aspiration. The Modernists proceeded from a skeptical, experimental, relativistic, even materialistic base to seek an absolute realization and expression which internal and external circumstances seemed to rule out. But for them the notion of the absolute functioned no longer as a measure of experience but as a measure of aesthetic performance. For the Romantics, absolute experience predicated aesthetic failure, but the Modernists could postulate the absolute only as an ultimate gauge of technical achievement. An aesthetic absolute was not a constituting cause but an experimental effect; its coherence was not referential, as the Romantics claimed, but self-referential; it inhered not in Nature, but in the work itself. Hence the salient characteristics of Modernism: complexity and abstraction, sophisticated technical invention and spatialized form, the conception of the artist as at once supremely self-conscious and supremely impersonal.

So in American poetry Emerson and Stevens, Whitman and Pound make Janus-faces, Romantic and Modernist, looking in opposite directions. But there are subtler understandings of the relation. The Romantics Emerson and Poe themselves make a Janus-face, as do Wordsworth and Byron; and Byron and Poe have been plausibly viewed as crypto-Modernists. By the same token, I would argue, Modernists like Stevens and Pound cannot be understood without reference to Romantic issues and allegiances, for the long shadow in the wake of the Romantic meteor has been starred again and again by bolts and flashes of the old incandescence. Modernists, for all of their loud inveighing against Romanticism, longed for and adopted positions that are unmistakably, though sometimes covertly, Romantic. In other words, the dialectic between Romanticism and Modernism resides in related dialectics within each which establish continuities between them more abiding and constitutive than the overt discontinuities. So Emerson and Stevens, Whitman and Pound – or Emerson and Pound, Whitman and Stevens – are Janus-faces that turn around and face each other.

The ways in which Janus-faces turn out also to be mirror images will, I hope, become fully apparent in the chapters to follow, which pursue these continuities and discontinuities through the interchange between Symbolisme and Imagism as the twinned generative strains of poetic Modernism. Symbolisme can be seen as signaling the disintegration of the Romantic epistemology into Modernism; and Imagism, as signaling the effort within Modernism to recover something of the Romantic epistemology. By the mid-nineteenth century, Charles Baudelaire had acknowledged Poe as the source of Symbolisme, and it flourished in France at the *fin de siècle* and after, with Stéphane Mallarmé and Paul Valéry as its central figures. The Symboliste influence came back into English-language poetry in the first decade of the twentieth century, largely through Arthur Symons' *Symbolist Movement in Literature* (1899), which, for example, transformed Eliot's poetry when he read it in 1908. A few years later, in 1912, Pound sought to sum up, with his friends Hilda Doolittle and Richard Aldington, the Modernist techniques for a "direct presentation of the 'thing,' " and he first labeled his axioms with the French spelling "Imagisme" to designate it as an alternative to "Symbolisme." Those two movements exerted a deep and abiding influence on twentieth-century poetry, precisely *because* they rest on contradictory notions of the poet's relation to language and of the nature and end of the poetic experience. That is to say, in poetry Romanticism evolved into Modernism, with Symbolisme and Imagism enacting the dissolution of the Romantic synthesis and constituting, broadly speaking, its subjective and objective epistemological poles: Symbolisme representing the mind's propensity to dissolve impressions of things into figures of its own processes, Imagism representing the mind's propensity to be shaped by its impressions of things.

As early as 1916, Eliot postulated the dilemma of the post-Romantic Modernist in terms of the subject–object split. The first of his six Oxford University Extension Lectures, entitled "The Origins: What Is Romanticism?," derides the old ideology: "Romanticism stands for *excess* in any direction. It splits up into two directions: escape from the world of fact, and devotion to brute fact....the two great currents of the nineteenth century – vague emotionality and the apotheosis of science (realism) alike spring from Rousseau."[1] At Harvard, Eliot had learned about the deleterious effects of Rousseau and Romanticism from Irving Babbitt, but here he had the prescience to present the dissolution of Romanticism into Modernism as a schism – "escape from the world of fact" and "devotion to brute fact" – that adumbrates (and caricatures) the Symboliste and Imagist alternatives. Reduced to the simplest terms, the historical argument of this book is that the epistemological tension within Romanticism diverged into Symbolisme and Imagism, and the interaction between those movements in turn defined the tension within poetic Modernism which made it as much a Janus-face as the Romanticism from which it evolved.

The poets discussed in these pages are all individualists, all white, educated, bourgeois, and all but a couple of them male. My commentary will call attention, from time to time, to the ways in which elitist, individualist assumptions about gender, race, and class limit and even distort the work under discussion. But I shall be more concerned with what the poetry *does* rather than with what it does not do – in part because the most illuminating criticism, in my view, arises and develops from the inside (that is, from inside the work and from inside the critic) and in part because this poetry, whatever its distortions and omissions, addresses issues critical to the psychological and moral life of those who wrote it and those who read it.

I have no naive illusions about the psychological and moral superiority of poets, but their power of articulation invests poetry with a special psychological and moral function: psychological in that it brings us to fuller, deeper consciousness of ourselves and our private and social lives, moral because that comprehension can then inform the discriminations and choices by which we sustain and determine our lives, individually and collectively. Reading the work from the inside does not mean reading uncritically; reckoning of the limitations and distortions is part of the complex process of discrimination which informs judgment and choice. To those who argue that Pound's poetry should not be read or studied because of the passages expressing misogyny, anti-Semitism, and fascist sympathies, Robert Duncan counters that Pound is the century's greatest poet precisely because he most fully and unsparingly, like it or not, represents us to ourselves. We need not agree with Duncan about Pound's preeminence to take his point: because poetry epitomizes and mediates the life of consciousness, it requires us – readers as well as poets – to know ourselves in searching and demanding ways, and so opens the possibility of being ourselves and of being something different and perhaps better. For all its personal idiosyncracies and elitist biases, then, Modernist poetry deserves the close and discriminating attention it demands because it constitutes an often valiant, sometimes last-ditch effort to validate poetry as a psychological and moral activity in an increasingly insane and amoral world.

The title of the book comes, as I have indicated, from Pound. Translating Sophocles in the government lunatic asylum where he had been confined as a psychotic, he made Herakles his hero and persona and exulted with Herakles in fate's despite:

what

SPLENDOUR,

IT ALL COHERES.[2]

Coherence was no longer to be assumed (with the Christians), defined (with the empiricists), received (with the Romantics); it was only to be wrought. To baffled readers of *The Waste Land* and *The Cantos*, Eliot and Pound spoke for their generation in voicing not coherence but confusion. Maybe never before had expression seemed so inchoate, so flauntingly exploitive of its need for coherence. By hindsight we can speculate that even more radically than the art of the previous centuries Modernist art manifested, even made a show of, its volatile contradictions: the artist perforce wore a Janus-mask. Nonetheless, despite doubts and self-doubts, against conflicts within and without, the Modernists relied on their prestidigitative agility in concocting an art object that would revolve like an unwobbling pivot on its own tensions.

The artists of this generation loom heroically larger than life, perhaps even more to us today than to their contemporaries, because of their determination to prove equal to the immensity of the task. Life at war set the terms of the imagination's survival; "the imagination pressing back against the pressure of reality" constitutes, in Stevens' words, "the violence from within that protects us from a violence without."[3] The splendor of what these poets managed in their "rage for order" is its own attestation: an eccentric and combustible coherence raying from and encircling the dark, violent center.

I

Robert Frost and John Crowe Ransom: Diptych of Ironists, the Woodsman and the Chevalier

The internationalist spirit of Modernism made its poets view Emerson and Poe, Whitman and Dickinson as quaint and provincial, in fact drew many of them – Pound, Eliot, H. D., Gertrude Stein – abroad to mingle with Old World expatriates like Joyce, Lawrence, Picasso, Stravinsky. Williams chose the local, but his locality allowed him to be part of the New York Vortex. Harriet Monroe's *Poetry* magazine was part of the Second City's attempt to prove itself a Midwestern Vortex, but Pound had grave doubts and Hart Crane gravitated from Ohio to the sophisticated New York scene rather than the Chicago Renaissance of Sandburg and Vachel Lindsay. So the calculated Yankee and southern regionalism, even provinciality, of Robert Frost and John Crowe Ransom represents as much an ideological and aesthetic stance as does the identification of Robinson Jeffers and Yvor Winters with California. The discussion of Frost and Ransom here and of Winters and Jeffers in the final chapter brackets and lends context to the consideration of the American Modernist poets in the body of the book.

Frost and Ransom, along with Stevens, seemed older in spirit than the others (though Ransom was in fact about the same age as Eliot and Pound). Ransom saw Frost as one of the poets who "are evidently influenced by modernism without caring to 'go modern' in the sense of joining the revolution,"[1] and he was in that group as surely as was Frost. Yet if their old-fashioned regionalism symbolizes their distance from avant-garde experimentation, their importance to the period provides not just a perspective on poetic Modernism but a way into the subject. Frost began his public career through the advocacy of Pound and at the end was the principal advocate for Pound's release from the asylum. And despite Ransom's personal taste for the seventeenth-century poets, his New Criticism popularized the Modernist notion of the autotelic integrity of the art object into a critical methodology that came to dominate the literary establishment of the middle decades of the century.

Though Ransom and Frost did not correspond much with each other and were not intimate friends, they enjoyed a long and mutually respectful association. As the reader who recommended Ransom's first book, *Poems*

About God, to his own publisher, Frost regarded Ransom as one of his discoveries. Though Ransom would disown most of those poems, Frost thought they had "the art, and...the tune," and the first reviewers tended to peg Ransom as a southern Frost. One anonymous reviewer pointed to the "colloquial manner" which linked the two; from the vantage point of the English tradition, Robert Graves saw in Ransom and Frost, as in Lindsay and Sandburg, a combination of colloquialism and provincialism; even fellow-southerner John Gould Fletcher called Ransom a "more urbane Frost."[2]

In the late 1930s it was Frost who, declining a regular faculty appointment at Kenyon College, recommended Ransom for the position from which he was to reign as teacher and editor of *The Kenyon Review*. The two poets maintained their acquaintance during Frost's almost annual periods of residence at Kenyon and during Ransom's frequent summer stints at the Bread Loaf School of English near Frost's Vermont home, which Frost lent to the Ransoms for the summer of 1942. During Frost's 1956 visit to Kenyon, he told the students that Ransom was "the greatest living American poet" – an accolade he did not easily confer on competitors, even for a moment's graciousness.[3] To Ransom much of Frost's poetry was "anything but pretentious," "trim and easy"[4] without the density and allusive complexity which the New Criticism would make hallmarks for judgment. Nonetheless, in a late *Kenyon Review* overview of the "Poetry of 1900-1950" he ranked Frost among the major poets of the period along with Hardy, Yeats, Robinson, and Eliot, but with his more Modernist contemporaries Williams, Pound, Moore, Cummings, Crane, and Tate classified as minor poets, and with Stevens suspended between major and minor rank.[5]

Frost and Ransom shared a commitment to revitalizing poetic diction and poetic form without violating them, and that commitment rested on a strain of irony that served as both defense and offense against desperate cosmological odds. Ransom described their particular sense of irony, its sources and ends, in an early essay on Frost:

> Irony may be regarded as the ultimate mode of the great minds – it presupposes the others. It implies first of all an honorable and strenuous period of romantic creation; it implies then a rejection of the romantic forms and formulas; but this rejection is so unwilling, and in its statements there lingers so much of the music and color and romantic mystery which is perhaps the absolute poetry, and this statement is attended by such a disarming rueful comic sense of the poet's own betrayal, that the fruit of it is wisdom and not bitterness, poetry and not prose, health and not suicide. Irony is the rarest of the states of mind, because it is the most inclusive; the whole mind has been active in arriving at it, both creation and criticism, both poetry and science. But this brief description is ridiculously inadequate for what is both exquisite and intricate.[6]

Frost's poetry, Ransom went on to say, is modern precisely because "its spirit transcends the Nineteenth Century mind and goes back to further places in the English tradition for its adult affiliations." If this sentence, written for *The*

Fugitive in 1925, sounds Eliotic, there is good reason, and irony inescapably permeates a century as conflicted as the twentieth.

But what makes poets not just modern but Modernist is the determination not to go back but to press beyond dualistic irony to rediscover the "music and color and romantic mystery" of "absolute poetry," to press beyond the defeated sense of betrayal in the conviction that the imagination, even without the Romantic props furnished by "the Nineteenth Century mind," was capacious enough, resilient enough, energetic enough to contend with its situation, maybe even to transform or transcend it. The lack of such determination and conviction is what distinguished Frost and Ransom from their Modernist contemporaries, even from Stevens, and made the risky experiment to reconstitute the language and form of poetry seem to them the folly of misguided youth.

I

1

Although William Prescott Frost of New Hampshire took his wife to San Francisco shortly after their marriage, and although he expressed his Copperhead sympathies by naming his son after the commander of the Confederate forces, the Frosts were tenaciously Yankee, and after returing to New England before the age of ten, Robert Lee Frost planted himself, body and spirit, in its rocky soil as a return to his sources. For good reason the poet chose throughout his life to play the farmer-woodsman of New Hampshire and Vermont.

To the Puritans, nature had first meant a savage and forbidding wilderness at the sight of which, Anne Bradstreet said, "My heart rose." New England culture began when these hard-pressed pioneers learned, as Frost put it in "The Gift Outright," to stop withholding themselves from the land and "found salvation in surrender."[7] Seventeenth-century diaries and journals begin to record quite early, despite the thinness of the soil and the harshness of the winters, a deepening sensitivity to nature, perceived no longer merely as the hostile environment which a civilized mind and Christian will must subdue but, quite the contrary, as the manifestation of the Creator in his creation. Edward Taylor and Jonathan Edwards expressed the generally accepted notion that the phenomena and events of everyday experience were types – that is, symbols ordained by God to reveal the workings of his gracious intentions in the natural order and in the lives of individuals and of the community. The transition to Romanticism can be summed up in Emerson's translation of Taylor's reading of nature as a panorama of types into a sense of nature as a kaleidoscope of symbols for the Oversoul. Frost was both Calvinist and Romantic – and neither; nature, he knew, was inhuman, but his hesitation about whether its inhumanity meant that nature was savage or divine made him wary both of finding salvation in surrender to the land and of "getting too transcended."[8] Frost characteristically wanted it both ways:

> May no fate willfully misunderstand me
> And half grant what I wish and snatch me away
> Not to return. Earth's the right place for love:
> I don't know where it's likely to go better.
> I'd like to go by climbing a birch tree,
> And climb black branches up a snow-white trunk
> *Toward* heaven, till the tree could bear no more,
> But dipped its top and set me down again.[9]

These familiar lines from "Birches" take on new interest when we see them as locating Frost's desired perspective: above but not beyond the

> pathless wood
> Where your face burns and tickles with the cobwebs
> Broken across it, and one eye is weeping
> From a twig's having lashed across it open.

"Burns," "broken," "weeping," "lashed": a grim typological lesson, and yet he is surer of earth, whatever its dangers, than of heaven. "Earth's the right place for love" is undercut by "I don't know where it's likely to go better."

Historically and intellectually, Emerson stood between Taylor and Frost. As the first recipient of the Emerson-Thoreau Medal of the American Academy of Arts and Sciences, Frost took the occasion to pay Emerson special homage. The four archetypal Americans were Washington the general and statesman, Jefferson the political thinker, Lincoln the martyr and savior, and Emerson the poet: "a poetic philosopher or...philosophical poet, my favorite kind of both." Frost's father was a flinty agnostic who read Darwin in place of the Bible, but he imbibed Emerson from his mother:

> [She] was fresh a Presbyterian from Scotland. The smart thing when she was young was to be reading Emerson and Poe as it is today to be reading St. John Perse or T. S. Eliot. Reading Emerson turned her into a Unitarian. That was about the time I came into the world; so I suppose I started a sort of Presbyterian-Unitarian. I was transitional. Reading on into Emerson, that is into "Representative Men" until she got to Swedenborg, the mystic, made her a Swedenborgian. I was brought up in all three of these religions, I suppose...it was pretty much under the auspices of Emerson. It was all very Emersonian.[10]

Under Emersonian auspices, Frost had recapitulated the religious development of New England from Calvinism to Unitarianism to Transcendentalism, and, nondenominational as it left him, it also left him with a compulsion to search nature for the proof of spirit. Frost excerpted the following lines from "Kitty Hawk" as the superscription for what he knew would be his last book, *In the Clearing*:

> But God's own descent
> Into flesh was meant
> As a demonstration
> That the supreme merit
> Lay in risking spirit

> In substantiation.
> Spirit enters flesh
> And for all it's worth
> Charges into earth
> In birth after birth
> Ever fresh and fresh.
> We may take the view
> That its derring-do
> Thought of in the large
> Is one mighty charge
> On our human part
> Of the soul's ethereal
> Into the material.[11]

These three jaunty sentences trace the transition of the incarnational sense from God's descent into history in the person of Jesus to a general Neoplatonic infusion of spirit into matter to the commitment of the human soul to its physical environment.

In fact, Frost argued, it was the willing and gutsy submission of spirit to the test of matter that marked the religious and moral superiority of the Western tradition to the Eastern, and his chief complaint about Emerson was that he too often fell prey to a false and simplistic Oriental Monism. What's more, Frost could not assume, with the idealist in Emerson, matter's receptivity and subjugation to mind. His father's Darwinism, like Robinson Jeffers', substituted for Calvinism as a materialist and scientific mode of predestination. At Harvard, Frost heard William James, who laid out the principles of pragmatism and the varieties of religious experience, and Charles Sanders Pierce, who wrote of the individual in a universe of chance. Nonetheless, he said in his remarks on Emerson, the pragmatist hero, open to whatever he might find and counting on nothing, dared "the descent of the spirit into the material-human at the risk of the spirit."[12] "Escapist-Never," published in Frost's last weeks, was still declaring: "His life is a pursuit of a pursuit forever."[13]

This humanistic sense of an errand to the wilderness made Frost (like Cooper and Thoreau and Faulkner) a chronicler of the individual in nature. Society smothered the spirit, and so whereas Eliot depicted the dingy sterility of Boston and London with helpless distaste, and whereas Sandburg struggled to resuscitate the Whitmanian vision in the teeming vulgarity of Chicago, Frost retired from the Machine Age to write poems *North of Boston*, where he tested again and again the typological proposition: does the woodsman encounter in the woods destruction or salvation, far-seeing Providence or blind Chance? Ransom said that it was the betrayal of a person's highest hopes and aspirations that made the ironist. In a 1917 letter written during one of the abject depressions that gripped Frost periodically throughout his life, he pushed his religious education past his mother's religious quest and his father's skepticism to admit the possibility of a final nihilism: "Presbyterian, Unitarian, Swedenborgian, Nothing."[14]

In "Once by the Pacific," Frost's earliest memories of the wild California coast turn Genesis into Apocalypse. Where Jeffers' Darwinian pantheism would exult in the extinction of the human consciousness and conscience in the amoral workings of physical forces, Frost's reaction is opposite: he psychologizes and humanizes the scene through his identification with the land in its elemental contention with the sea:

> The shattered water made a misty din.
> Great waves looked over other coming in,
> And thought of doing something to the shore
> That water never did to land before.
> The clouds were low and hairy in the skies,
> Like locks blown forward in the gleam of eyes.
> You could not tell, and yet it looked as if
> The shore was lucky in being backed by cliff,
> The cliff in being backed by continent;
> It looked as if a night of dark intent
> Was coming, and not only a night, an age.
> Someone had better be prepared for rage.
> There would be more than ocean-water broken
> Before God's last *Put out the light* was spoken.[15]

The water's being "shattered" and "broken" is a sign not of *its* vulnerability but, as it turns out, of the land's before the ocean's relentless onslaught. The first six lines repeatedly insinuate the possibility of the hostile forces' intelligent will: "waves looked... / And thought of doing something," clouds hung like hair, obscuring the heaven's eyes.

The succeeding eight lines address the land's and, by implication, the observer's vulnerability. Frost's response to the unleashed natural forces is to marshal his own verbal resources as tightly as he can: mostly end-stopped pentameters bound into couplets that work like a kind of topsy-turvy sonnet, sestet before octet. The word "lucky" hovers between "good fortune" and "chance": "You could not tell, and yet it looked as if / The shore was lucky in being backed by cliff." One of the few enjambments in the poems emphasizes "as if," and in contrast to the "like" in the previous line, "as if" functions not to introduce a simile but to pose a speculative hypothesis. "It looked as if" recurs a few lines later, as the octet toys with expanding possibilities. Frost's comment about Edwin Arlington Robinson's poetry applies equally to his own: "The play's the thing. Play's the thing. All virtue in 'as if.'"[16]

And as the threat of destruction mounts in the speaker's mind (a night, an age, the end of the world), the verbal play – doubling and repeating with a difference – suggests the pervasive uncertainty of things at the same time that it subjects that multivalence to the patterning of the observer's consciousness: the alliteration, assonance, and internal rhymes; the syllabic sequence of "like," "locks," "looked," "lucky," "looked"; the ironic pun on the Latin meaning of "continent" as "holding together"; the juggling of letters in the rhyming of "-tinent" with "intent"; the sound of "for rage" as "for age"; the recurrence of "looked" and "coming" from line two in the more ominous context of the octet; and, climactically, the inversion of God's command in Genesis into its decreative opposite, combined with the poker-faced speaker's anticlimactic understatement: "Someone [instead of "everyone"] had better be prepared....there would be more than ocean water [instead of "the entire world will be"] broken."

"The Fear of God"[17] warns against ever dropping a protective guard: "stay unassuming," and again Frost's characteristic way of punning makes a colloquial phrase take on a more troubling and sinister double meaning: not just "be modest, lie low," but "make and trust no assumptions whatsoever." "A Drumlin Woodchuck" presents the model; at his public readings, Frost would recite the concluding lines with rollicking emphasis, and the homophone "burrow/borough" concludes the parable:

> If I can with confidence say
> That still for another day,
> Or even another year,
> I will be there for you, my dear,
>
> It will be because, though small
> As measured against the All,
> I have been so instinctively thorough
> About my crevice and burrow.[18]

"One Step Backward Taken" shows Frost imitating the woodchuck in beating a "strategic retreat":

> Not only sands and gravels
> Were once more on their travels,
> But gulping muddy gallons
> Great boulders off their balance
> Bumped heads together dully
> And started down the gully.
> Whole capes caked off in slices.
> I felt my standpoint shaken
> In the universal crisis.
> But with one step backward taken
> I saved myself from going.
> A world torn loose went by me.
> Then the rain stopped and the blowing.
> And the sun came out to dry me.[19]

As before, the wit is double-edged; for all the relief it provides, it is a symptom of, and a defense against, Frost's insecurity, which reduces an overwhelming and inhuman threat to comic, human scale. Again Frost's observations about his fellow New Englander and fellow ironist Robinson are his indirect way of describing his own poetic strategy: "His theme was unhappiness itself, but his skill was as happy as it was playful...his art was more than playful; it was humorous." To Louis Untermeyer, Frost wrote, "many sensitive natures have plainly shown by their style that they took themselves lightly in self-defense. They are the ironists. . . . I own any form of humor shows fear and inferiority. Irony is simply a kind of guardedness." Frost's poetry, despite its personal voice, is not directly autobiographical, and the same is true of Robinson and Ransom as well. All three often chose a narrative or dramatic mode, and even their lyrics seldom, in Frost's phrase, "trench on" confidential or private matters. There were enough sufferings and tragedies in Frost's family life to make him want to keep them private, and he shared with most of his contemporaries the Modernist belief in the impersonality of art. The poem was itself a strategic retreat into expression without exposure, clarification without either self-indulgence or self-indictment:

> I grow surer that I don't want to search the poet's mind too seriously. . . . I have written to keep the over curious out of the secret places of my mind. . . . A subject has to be held clear outside of me with struts and as it were set up for an object. A subject must be an object. . . . The objective idea is all I ever cared about. . . . Art and wisdom with the body heat out of it.[20]

An unsettling shifting of scale runs through "One Step Backward Taken": "sands and gravels," "great boulders"; "my standpoint" (physical and metaphysical), "universal crisis"; "one step backward taken," "a world torn loose"; the effect is summed up in the delicious line "Whole capes caked off in slices," with "capes" reduced to "cake" and "whole" reduced to "slices." In fact, that line is the volta between the segments of another inverted sonnet, the sestet describing the threat and the octave describing the speaker's resourceful self-salvation, the usual five beats reduced to a brisker three, played out with all feminine rhymes, and funny ones at that: "gravels," "travels"; "gallons," "balance"; "dully," "gully"; "slices," "crisis."

The artful word play and gamesmanship were the equivalents of the disciplined grace under pressure which Hemingway prized in bullfighters and fishermen and Faulkner in hunters. Frost shared with them a need for man-made rules in a universe of chance, rules which turned the otherwise passive surrender to fate into a game wherein the player could test and prove his resistance to fate by playing within and against his self-imposed rules. In his famous old age, Frost wrote an essay on baseball for *Sports Illustrated* entitled "Perfect Day – a Day of Prowess"; the sportsman's virtues, he said, are prowess, justice, courage, and knowledge, but "prowess of course comes first" as "the ability to perform with success in games, in the arts, and, come right down to it, in battle."[21] For poetry, like sport, like life, was a game of battle against unknown odds.

Frost used to say that he got along well with Jesuit acquaintances because they perceived the underlying theological nature of his concerns. Was the notion of God compatible with a universe of chance? Was nature divine and moral, as Emerson claimed, or agnostic and amoral, as Darwin implied? Frost was hesitant about declaring the surmises of his worst moments. The sonnet "Design" was first sketched out under the title "In White" in 1912, a year before the publication of *A Boy's Will*, but did not appear until *American Poetry 1922: A Miscellany*; even then it was not included in a volume of his poems until the publication of *A Further Range* in 1936, and he never read it in public or recorded it:

> I found a dimpled spider, fat and white,
> On a white heal-all, holding up a moth
> Like a white piece of rigid satin cloth –
> Assorted characters of death and blight
> Mixed ready to begin the morning right,
> Like the ingredients of a witches' broth –
> A snow-drop spider, a flower like a froth,
> And dead wings carried like a paper kite.
>
> What had that flower to do with being white,
> The wayside blue and innocent heal-all?
> What brought the kindred spider to that height,
> Then steered the white moth thither in the night?
> What but design of darkness to appall? –
> If design govern in a thing so small.[22]

The poem is at once a terrifying version of the Greek and Christian arguments for God's existence by cosmological design, of Emerson's Neoplatonic theory of correspondences, and of Darwinian forces so chancy that they become biological necessity. If this least of events has its revelation, then is it not a type of divine indifference or malevolence? Almost every detail makes the reader do a double-take. The spider is dimpled, fat, and white, like an innocent babe, and the more obscene for these associations. The curative herb on which the white spider has killed the white moth is a heal-all, and not the usual blue heal-all but an odd and unnatural white, and the white satin of the moth's wings suggests a bassinette, baptismal or wedding dress, or coffin's lining. The metaphors in the aside of lines four through six restate the ironies wryly. The trio comprises the "assorted characters" of a little death drama, and "assorted," like the "found" of the opening phrase, "I found...," suggests both happenstance and purposefulness. For this assortment is no healthy breakfast cereal ("Mixed ready to begin the morning right") but a witches' brew for another kind of morning rite: baptism and marriage and funeral all in one. The octet closes by rehearsing the dramatis personae in a hideous little tableau: the spider like a lovely but chilling "snow-drop," the flower lacy but "like a froth" from "a witches' broth," the moth with wings kitelike in the stiffness of rigor mortis.

Usually the octet of a sonnet raises questions to be answered in the sestet, but here the opening drama raises the sestet's mounting sequence of three questions. The strong verbs of the second question, "brought" and "steered," draw out the implications of the first and lead in the third to the suggestion of a cosmic "design of darkness," all the darker for operating under the cover of night and in the deceptive guise of white. The word "appall" recalls a black funeral pall at the same time that it means "to turn pale or white with fright." The concluding couplet names Frost's worst fear, but it hedges by posing it as a question further qualified, after a comma break emphasized by a dash, by a conditional clause with a subjunctive verb: "What but design of darkness to appall? – / If design govern in a thing so small."

Frost could not, of course, have been unaware of the fascination of whiteness for Poe, Melville, and Dickinson. To Captain Ahab the whiteness of the whale represented his malevolence masked in the color of innocence, but to Ishmael it was the all-color, no-color whose ambiguity allowed him to affirm neither an Optimism nor a Pessimism but schooled him to be ready for either. In one poem Frost threatens to shove off for the white wastes of "snow and mist" at Hudson's Bay, ready to meet the "old captain's dark fate" in order to unriddle his cosmological questions; he imagines himself saying to Captain Hudson:

> "Better defeat almost,
> If seen clear,
> Than life's victories of doubt
> that need endless talk-talk
> To make them out."[23]

But Frost was honest enough to call this fantasy "An Empty Threat." No Ahab or Hudson, he chose the humbler heroism of the survivor; like Ishmael and Dickinson, he knew that the best strategy was to "stay unassuming" in manner and disposition. Even Melville, though he found it cathartic to imagine Ahab, framed the book with Ishmael. So it was the Ishmael in Frost who framed the white design of darkness as a question with a conditional clause.

Yvor Winters called Frost a spiritual drifter for refusing to take a metaphysical position, and other unsympathetic readers have accused him of coy perversity for hedging his bets and keeping his options open. "For Once, Then, Something," first published in *Harper's* in 1920, enunciates the open stance to which he stuck throughout his life:

> Others taunt me with having knelt at well-curbs
> Always wrong to the light, so never seeing
> Deeper down in the well than where the water
> Gives me back in a shining surface picture
> Me myself in the summer heaven, godlike,
> Looking out of a wreath of fern and cloud puffs.
> *Once*, when trying with chin against a well-curb,
> I discerned, as I thought, beyond the picture,
> Through the picture, a something white, uncertain,
> Something more of the depths – and then I lost it.
> Water came to rebuke the too clear water.
> One drop fell from a fern, and lo, a ripple
> Shook whatever it was lay there at bottom,
> Blurred it, blotted it out. What was that whiteness?
> Truth? A pebble of quartz? For once, then, something.[24]

Looking down a well becomes a conceit for peering into the mystery of nature. The poem acknowledges that "others" – believers, whether Christian or Transcendentalist – think that out of egotism he has deliberately positioned himself in relation to the light so that he cannot see into nature but instead sees only himself apotheosized in the surface reflection. Frost replied to the taunt only indirectly by giving an account of a quasiepiphany he did have *once*, the italics accentuating the uniqueness of the event. The halting, stop-and-start movement of the modifying phrases and clauses in the middle lines conveys the poet's hesitant straining for perception. Was "that whiteness" just a piece of quartz, or did that piece of quartz manifest a corresponding typological Truth? The Puritans read sermons in stones; Emerson preached that every natural fact is a symbol of a spiritual fact; Thoreau held each fact precious because it could flower into a truth. All Frost saw was "a something white, uncertain, / Something more of the depths," but whether of physical or metaphysical depths he could not determine. The complete, end-stopped pentameter sentence "Water came to rebuke the too clear water" interrupts the exploratory meandering. "For once, then, something": the concluding phrase both mocks itself for its inconclusiveness and records that "something" is far preferable to "Nothing." To his biographer Lawrence Thompson, however, Frost admitted his desire to keep both options in play:

> I doubt if I was ever religious in your sense of the word....I used to try to get up plausible theories about prayer like Emerson....I'm afraid I stay a semi detached villain. But only semi. My passion for theology must mean something....You can do some very objective figuring about man and the universe by taking God's name not altogether in vain.[25]

Frost's psychological ambivalence derived from his philosophical dualism. Of the poets he admired most, Emerson was an optimist and Robinson a pessimist, but Frost shared Ishmael's double vision:

> I am neither optimist nor pessimist. I never voted either ticket. If there is a universal unfitness and unconformity...I don't care to decide whether God did this for the fun of it or for the devil of it. (The two expressions come to practically the same thing anyway.)[26]

Frost attributed Emerson's optimism and Robinson's pessimism to their Platonism:

> I am not the Platonist Robinson was. By Platonist I mean one who believes what we have here is an imperfect copy of what is in heaven....Many of the world's greatest – maybe all of them – have been ranged on that romantic side. I am philosophically opposed to having one Iseult for my vocation and another for my avocation....A truly gallant Plantonist [sic] will remain a bachelor as Robinson did from unwillingness to reduce any woman to the condition of being used without being idealized.[27]

To Frost such Platonism smacked of Oriental gnosticism, which led Robinson and Emerson, from their different perspectives, to shy away from the engagement with matter. From Robinson, he said, he "only parted company on the badness of the world. He was cast in the mold of badness." On the other hand, "I am as strong on badness as I am on goodness," and Emerson was "probably too Platonic about evil": "He could see 'the good of evil born' but he couldn't bring himself to say the evil of good born." "I am a Dualist," Frost said, and as with Robinson, "Emerson's defect was that he was of the great tradition of Monists." Emerson's "Uriel" is based on the assumption that "unit and universe are round"; however, "another poem could be made from that, to the effect that ideally in thought only is a circle round. In practice, in nature, the circle becomes an oval. As a circle it has one center – Good. As an oval it has two centers – Good and Evil. Thence Monism versus Dualism."[28]

In view of his favoring Western, material ovals over Platonist, Oriental circles, it would be puzzling that Frost praised "Uriel" as "the best Western poem yet," except for the fact that Platonism remained a tempting possibility that he had to continue to toy with and fight against all his life. The Puritan and Romantic in him was willing to suppose that "there must be a whole realm or plane... – all sight and insight, perception, intuition, rapture," but the Darwinian in him saw nature as working by "the strife-method," so that faced with oppositions on every level of experience – "democracy monarchy; puritanism paganism; form content; conservatism radicalism; systole diastole; rustic urban; literary colloquial; work play" – "I should think too much of myself to let any teacher fool me into taking sides on any one of those oppositions."[29]

Frost's interspersing of aesthetic dualisms – "form content," "literary colloquial" – among the moral, social, and political dualisms indicates that poetry not only derived its content from "the strife-method" but exemplified it in its form and devices. If, as Frost observed of Robinson, "the style is the man. Rather say the style is the way the man takes himself,"[30] then Frost's style appropriately shows him as a dualist. That is to say, not only is the poetic form the way of holding thematic dualities in ironic tension, but also its formal devices themselves operate by creating a tension between elements which also makes the language ironic at every level. We have already noted the pervasiveness of punning and word play, and creative tension defines Frost's sense of prosody and metaphor as well.

As for prosody, from the beginning of his career Frost prided himself on being "one of the most notable craftsmen of my time." The excitement of the London publication of his first two books after a long and trying apprenticeship prompted some strutting to friends back home: "I am one of the few who have a theory of their own upon which all their work down to the least accent is done. I expect to do something to the present state of literature in America"; "I am possibly the only person going who works on any but a worn out theory (principle I had better say) of versification."[31] By this Frost did not mean flirting with *vers libre*, à la Pound and Eliot. In commending Robinson for being "content with the old-fashioned way to be new," Frost would ridicule the Modernist modes of Cummings and Eliot, Pound and Stevens:

> Poetry, for example, was tried without punctuation. It was tried without capital letters. It was tried without metric frame on which to measure the rhythm. It was tried without any images but those to the eye....It was tried

without content under the trade name of poesie pure. It was tried without phrase, epigram, coherence, logic and consistency. It was tried without ability.[32]

"The old-fashioned way to be new" was to quicken traditional forms with the authentic voice of one's time and place. The letters from London are filled with phrases describing this new principle of versification: "the sound of sense" (in contrast to Tennyson's and Swinburne's "music of words"), "the voice of the imagination," "the sentence-sound" "apprehended by the ear," "the audile [audial] imagination." For the sentence was both a syntactic structure and a rhythmic and sonic structure "on which other sounds called words may be strung." "The distinction between the grammatical sentence and the vital sentence" spoken in a narrative or dramatic or lyric situation created a double measure as "an everyday level of diction that even Wordsworth kept above" informed and realized the syntactic patterns and "the spaces of the footed line." Games require rules, and the player exhibits, even devises, his style by his performance within and against the rules of play. Free verse is flat and slack and boring because it forgoes the excitement and tension when a speaking voice conforms to and transforms the expectations and requirements of syntax and meter and rhyme:

> If one is to be a poet he must learn to get cadences by skillfully breaking the sounds of sense with all their irregularity of accent across the regular beat of the metre. . . . There are only two or three metres that are worth anything. We depend for variety on the infinite play of accents in the sound of sense. The high possibility of emotional expression all lets in this mingling of sound-sense and word accent.

This was written in 1913, and a quarter century later Frost was still saying to his avant-garde contemporaries, "The possibilities for tune from the dramatic tones of meaning struck across the rigidity of a limited meter are endless."[33]

Frost found in Emerson not the precursor of free verse, as Whitman had, but the writer of sound (in both senses of the word) sentences: "Some of my first thinking about my own language was certainly Emersonian. 'Cut these sentences and they bleed,' he says. I am not submissive enough to want to be a follower, but he had me there. I never got over that." To put it more precisely, Emerson crafted "sentences that may look tiresomely alike, short and with short words, yet turn out as calling for all sorts of ways of being said aloud or in the mind's ear. . . ." In fact, "I took Emerson's prose and verse as my illustration because writing is unboring to the extent that it is dramatic."[34]

Besides the tension between voice and the requirements of grammar and meter, there was the drama of metaphor. Emerson might have written these words instead of Frost: "all thinking, except mathematical thinking, is metaphorical"; "poetry is simply made of metaphor. . . . Every poem is a new metaphor inside or it is nothing." It is clear that Frost thought of metaphor not simply as a technique of "saying one thing and meaning another, saying one thing in terms of another" but as an epistemological principle. The following remarks echo Emerson's description of metaphor in "Merlin" as an aspect of a universal inclination to rhyme:

> That doubleness, like the singsong of meter, has something to do with how we are made as human beings. It is some essential part of how we think and are. . . . Man likes to bring two things together into one. . . . Not only rhymed couplets, but the coupling of all sorts of things that reason rhymes together. Rhymed couplets are the symbol of this tendency in man. He lives by making associations and he is doing well by himself and in himself when he thinks of something in connection with something else that no one else put with it before. That's what we call a metaphor. I couldn't do without that sense of two-ness.

As the way in which the individual accommodates a world of difference and indifference, metaphor is "life itself." In that sense, all particular metaphors "are the same old metaphor always," and "every poem is an epitome of the great predicament; a figure of the will braving alien entanglements." In lieu of metaphysical certitude, it is the "one permissible way" in which "to say matter in terms of spirit and spirit in terms of matter." In the end, therefore, "the only materialist. . . is the man who gets lost in his material without a gathering metaphor to throw it into shape and order. He is the lost soul."[35] Metaphor was not typological Truth, but it became Frost's characteristic mode of committing spirit to matter.

Still, for all our spirit's need of "establishing correspondence," "all metaphor breaks down somewhere," because material objects are not a perfect match. Circles, even circles with different diameters, can be concentric, but not ovals. If we press a metaphor beyond the limited terms of its statement, the differences between metaphorical elements circumscribe and imperil the area of connection or association. We cannot really compose the world by metaphor, nor can we dwell in a metaphor; still, with determination and skill, we can compose the poem by metaphor. Consequently, "the artist must value himself as he snatches a thing from some previous order in time and space into a new order with not so much as a ligature clinging to it of the old place where it was organic." The poem, then, is organic not to the natural process, as Emerson suggested, but to its own linguistic process of realization. Frost's well-known formulation is that the poem "begins in delight [that is, in some generative experience or emotion, "a lump in the throat, a sense of wrong, a home-sickness, a lovesickness"], it inclines to the impulse, it assumes direction with the first line laid down, it runs a course of lucky events, and ends in a clarification of life – not necessarily a great clarification, such as sects and cults are founded on, but in a momentary stay against confusion." "The Oven Bird" is the poet's totem; its plain song "knows in singing not to sing" and asks "what to make of a diminished thing." In letters and conversations Frost made the point repeatedly: "Each poem clarifies something," but "you've got to do it again. You can't get clarified to stay so"; "Living alone I am made aware of how regularly I am supposed to make up my bed fresh every day. Just so my mind."[36]

Yet there is compensation. The oven bird's very song is what has been made of a diminished world and a diminished mode of expression. If "the vast chaos of all I have lived through" merely provides the "raw material" of "life not yet worked up into form or at least not worked all the way up," still "a real artist delights in roughness for what he can do to it." In a 1935 open letter to the student newspaper at Amherst, where he spent part of each winter, Frost balanced the chaos of experience against the possibility of form: "There is at least so much good in the world that it admits of form and the making of form. And not only admits of it, but calls for it. In us nature reaches its height of form and through us exceeds itself." So, he concluded, "any little form I assert upon it is velvet, as the saying is, and to be considered for how much more it is than nothing. If I were a Platonist I should have to consider it, I suppose, for how much less it is than everything."[37] The "Kitty Hawk" poem, which provided the superscription to *In the Clearing* cited at the beginning of the chapter, went on toward its conclusion to postulate the quasi-theological "covenant" Frost took it that he had:

> But the comfort is
> In the covenant
> We may get control,
> If not of the whole,
> Of at least some part
> Where not too immense,
> So by craft or art
> We can give the part
> Wholeness in a sense.[38]

So Frost steered a course between Emerson's organicism and Poe's aestheticism. The poem "has an outcome that though unforeseen was predestined from the first image of the original mood – and indeed from the very mood." The poet must be attentive and responsive to the material as it "unfold[s] by surprise," for "it is but a trick poem and no poem at all if the best of it was thought of first and saved for the last,"[39] as Poe's "Philosophy of Composition" seemed to argue against Emerson's. At the same time, the revelation is a linguistic process. What the poet "can do to" the raw materials is to make them into the materials of his art, over which he has responsibility and control. Such clarifying connections as he can manage to produce result from his performance in the language game, rendering elements rescued from experience into phrases and composing the images into metaphors, articulated in a spoken or speakable voice which dramatizes and particularizes the linguistic conventions.

Frost's Emerson was less a Platonist of ideal circles than an existentialist in a universe of ovals:

> What Emerson was meaning in 'Give all to Love' was, Give all to Meaning. The freedom is ours to insist on meaning. . . . The one inalienable right is to go to destruction in your own way. What's worth living for is worth dying for. What's worth succeeding in is worth failing in.[40]

Self-reliance without reliance on the Oversoul; no wonder Frost confided to C. Day-Lewis: "It takes a hero to make a poem." Even an "unassuming" one in Yankee homespun: "I fight to be allowed to sit cross-legged on the old flint pile and flake a lump into an artifact."[41]

2

Frost's worldwide renown put him in an unusual and enviable position for a poet; an international celebrity, he hobnobbed not just with home-grown dignitaries and presidents but, by the end, even with the leader of the other great power, Premier Khrushchev. Throughout all that, and for all the pleasure Frost took in his fame, he sought to remain recalcitrantly, intransigently American. Something of a Darwinian in political as well as intellectual matters, he suspected any utopian internationalism which aimed at transcending the "strife-method" through which, he felt, nations, like individuals, sorted out their identities and tested their characters. We have heard him criticize the native strain of Emersonian idealism as "too transcended," and he challenged it with the law of nature: conflict based on self-preservation and the territorial imperative.

Both Emersonian nationalism and social Darwinism placed the person in his tribe; hence Frost's politics is inseparable from his poetics. He made the connection himself many times – for example, in a long inscription in *North of Boston* for Professor Regis Michaud of Smith College: "I am as sure that the colloquial is the root of every good poem as I am that the national is the root of all thought and art. . . . One half of individuality is locality; and I was about venturing to say the other half was colloquiality." The full inscription refers to a poem by Emerson, but the comment applies equally to his own poems. In an early letter he wondered whether an English critic could possibly comprehend the writings of Poe, Whitman, and, above all, Emerson ("so American, so original, especially in form"). When Ezra Pound championed him from London in 1913 and again in 1914 against those bourgeois American editors and publishers who had not recognized Frost's genius and forced him to find initial publication for his first two books in England, Frost seemed to resent Pound's slur against his countrymen almost as much as he was grateful for Pound's boost. In 1939 Frost took the occasion of receiving the Gold Medal of the National Institute of Arts and Letters to stake out his territory: "I should like to have it that your medal is a token of my having fitted, not into the nature of the Universe, but in some small way, at least, into the nature of Americans."[42] It is altogether understandable – and it was so to Frost himself – that he became in later years the popular figure of readings, interviews, even television appearances; he came closer than any other Amercian poet, except possibly Emerson and Whitman, to being a national poet, a laureate for all the people, Middle America included, as his participation in the presidential inauguration of John Kennedy dramatized.

For that proud event, Frost wrote a poem[43] dedicating the future to "a golden age of poetry and power," the alliteration again linking art and politics.

The poem traces out a "history in rhyme" which brings up to date Bishop Berkeley's eighteenth-century panegyric of America's beginning: "Westward the course of empire wends its way." If there is something uncomfortably imperialistic about such nationalism, as has become increasingly clear in the years since Frost's death, Frost would not have countenanced the objection; the strong ring of old-fashioned patriotism indicates how much of the nineteenth-century sense of America's manifest destiny Frost's mind and spirit had absorbed – the source of both his strengths and his limitations. He wanted to assert, against new-fangled collectivist ideals which seemed to be gathering momentum in the twentieth century, an individualism whose rugged spirit took the full measure of the material challenge nature presented. For Frost, America was the culmination of Western history, as Bishop Berkeley had foreseen, because it represented the fullest expression of Western individualism. At one point he planned to call his last volume *And All We Call American*.

The westward movement was not, for Frost, a passage to India, as it seemed to be for Emerson and Whitman, but a long, even violent engagement by the rugged newcomers with the rugged land across which they made their way. At the Kennedy inauguration he chose to read "The Gift Outright," which begins: "The land was ours before we were the land's. / She was our land more than a hundred years / Before we were her people."[44] If the frontier qualities with which we had transformed the land into our nation were lost, we would forfeit our chance to shine as the glory of Western history.

Frost did not want to believe that our individualism had deteriorated so dangerously, despite the incursions of socialism and communism since the Depression years. In his last volume, he turned Robinson Jeffers' prophecy of America's fall into a call to our ongoing manifest destiny. Jeffers' poem is "Shine, Perishing Republic"; citing Jeffers' title as an epigraph, Frost called his poem "Our Doom to Bloom." His fascination in old age with men like Kennedy and the Wright brothers stemmed from their extension of the frontiersman's daring into the Industrial and now the Space Age. It was only Kennedy's call to the "New Frontier" which reconciled Frost to the Democratic Party after decades of outspoken grumbling about New Deal welfare economics and one-world internationalism. The depersonalizing, emasculating circumstances of modern life made it imperative for Americans to touch earth again and to touch the grounds of their being again, not in naive pursuit of some false utopia but in an elemental contention with ourselves and our place. After all, the way west had been from the beginning a spiritual journey as well; the march toward the horizon proceeded from the psychic depths which it in turn mapped out.

If these remarks make Robert Frost sound like a New England version of Daniel Boone or Natty Bumppo, the poetry substantiates the image. The pioneer myth is the major myth of Frost's poetry, as of his politics, and the source of his controlling images and metaphors. "Into My Own," the very first poem of *A Boy's Will*, the first book, posits the myth:

One of my wishes is that those dark trees,
So old and firm they scarcely show the breeze,
Were not, as 'twere, the merest mask of gloom,
But stretched away unto the edge of doom.

I should not be withheld but that some day
Into their vastness I should steal away,
Fearless of ever finding open land,
Or highway where the slow wheel pours the sand.

I do not see why I should e'er turn back,
Or those should not set forth upon my track
To overtake me, who should miss me here
And long to know if still I held them dear.

They would not find me changed from him they knew –
Only more sure of all I thought was true.[45]

Where William Cullen Bryant's "Inscription for the Entrance to a Wood," written a century earlier, invites escape from the frets of the city to the quiet, serene woods, Frost's poem, published in the *New England Magazine* in 1909, initiates a lonely quest: "Into My Own," the thicketed tangle of nature and of our psyches. Those who follow will also move into the "vastness" of "those dark trees," "Fearless of ever finding open land, / Or highway." In "Birches," as we have seen, "life is too much like a pathless wood" from which the poet, "one eye...weeping / From a twig's having lashed across it open," seeks respite by climbing a tree; he must descend again to earth, with all its risks and dangers, but the pain makes the ascent as necessary as the return. "Stopping by Woods on a Snowy Evening" is not a charming poem about how fretful responsibilities sometimes distract us from a soothing excursion into nature. The woods are "lovely" *because* "dark and deep," and the poet poses that lurking mystery, as threatful as it is luring, against the round of activities which he invokes to deter him from it:

The woods are lovely, dark and deep,
But I have promises to keep,
And miles to go before I sleep,
And miles to go before I sleep.[46]

The New England woods were no longer, of course, the trackless wilderness which John Winthrop and Anne Bradstreet and Edward Taylor faced three centuries before, but they were still lonesome and scary, especially as a psychological landscape.

Often his errand leads Frost into the lovely, dark, deep woods. The beautiful description in "Spring Pools" changes rebirth into extinction, light into obscurity:

These pools that, though in forests, still reflect
The total sky almost without defect,
And like the flowers beside them, chill and shiver,
Will like the flowers beside them soon be gone,

And yet not out by any brook or river,
But up by roots to bring dark foliage on.

The trees that have it in their pent-up buds
To darken nature and be summer woods –
Let them think twice before they use their powers
To blot out and drink up and sweep away
These flowery waters and these watery flowers
From snow that melted only yesterday.[47]

The poem begins as winter revives in spring: a moment of Emersonian harmony; earth turns mirror with the just-melted snow and reflects "the total sky
almost without defect," so translucent that the heavens seem almost Heaven.
But the moment's vision is gone almost at once, sucked up by the roots "to
bring dark foliage on," "to darken nature and be summer woods." No pastoral
plenitude, the encroachment of nature obliterates the view of the sky as well
as the pools and wildflowers helpless beneath the overpowering trees. Frost
returned to this theme often: "Petals I may have once pursued. / Leaves are
all my darker mood" ("Leaves Compared with Flowers"); "The mountain
pushed us off her knees. / And now her lap is full of trees" ("The Birthplace");
"trees, seeing the opening, / March into a shadowy claim. / The trees are all
I'm afraid of" ("The Last Mowing"). As a poem, "The Oven Bird" is "a mid-
summer and a mid-wood bird."[48]

For the woodsman there is no safe season. In "Bereft" an autumn wind
swirls the leaves into a snake coiled to strike, and the poet knows his
vulnerability:

Something sinister in the tone
Told me my secret must be known:
Word I was in the house alone
Somehow must have gotten abroad,
Word I was in my life alone,
Word I had no one left but God.[49]

Year's end brings the anonymity of snow; even Thoreau felt effaced in winter woods without familiar markers. "Desert Places" depicts a waste of
"benighted snow" reminiscent of Stevens' "Snow Man," of Pym at the South
Pole, and of Dickinson's "White Sustenance – / Despair – ":

Snow falling and night falling fast, oh, fast
In a field I looked into going past,
And the ground almost covered smooth in snow,
But a few weeds and stubble showing last.

The woods around it have it – it is theirs.
All animals are smothered in their lairs.
I am too absent-spirited to count;
The loneliness includes me unawares.

And lonely as it is, that loneliness
Will be more lonely ere it will be less –
A blanker whiteness of benighted snow

With no expression, nothing to express.

They cannot scare me with their empty spaces
Between stars – on stars where no human race is.
I have it in me so much nearer home
To scare myself with my own desert places.[50]

Winter and summer, spring and fall, the relentless advance of nature moves against bewildered humankind, and the physically weaker woodsman can stave off annihilation only by using his wits and wiles to open and maintain a space for himself in the woods: a path, a road, a field, a house. In "The Wood-Pile" the poet, wandering through a "frozen swamp," "far from home" amid "tall slim trees / Too much alike to mark or name a place by," comes unexpectedly upon a moldering "cord of maple," symmetrically propped years before, still a witness to the person who once made his geometric mark there. Frost admires "the labor of his ax"; his contention with nature is a contention with his own wild and desert places.[51] "Beech," an epigraph for *A Witness Tree* (1942) facetiously signed "The Moodie Forester," is a witness both to the human effort to maintain clearings and to the advancing boundary of trees:

Where my imaginary line
Bends square in woods, an iron spine
And pile of real rocks have been founded.
And off this corner in the wild,
Where these are driven in and piled,
One tree, by being deeply wounded,
Has been impressed as Witness Tree
And made commit to memory
My proof of being not unbounded.
Thus truth's established and borne out,
Though circumstanced with dark and doubt –
Though by a world of doubt surrounded.[52]

In testimony to a long career of posting his place in nature, Frost called his last book *In the Clearing*.

Life's secret, dark and deep, is mortality; death lives in the woods. "The Draft Horse," a nightmare fantasy first published in *In the Clearing* but written many years before, presents the shocking alternative to riding home safely in "Stopping by Woods":

With a lantern that wouldn't burn
In too frail a buggy we drove
Behind too heavy a horse
Through a pitch-dark limitless grove.

And a man came out of the trees
And took our horse by the head
And reaching back to his ribs
Deliberately stabbed him dead.

The ponderous beast went down
With a crack of a broken shaft.

And the night drew through the trees
In one long invidious draft.

The most unquestioning pair
That ever accepted fate
And the least disposed to ascribe
Any more than we had to to hate,

We assumed that the man himself
Or someone he had to obey
Wanted us to get down
And walk the rest of the way.[53]

Frost's repertoire of verbal strategies – the disarmingly conversational pace, the prim pun on "draft," the tight-lipped tone – contrive to modulate the inexplicable violence to the range of human toleration, so that in the last ballad-quatrain Frost can ask a version of Ahab's vehement question – "Be the white whale principal or be the white whale agent. . ." – with Ishmael's rueful irony. Still, for all the poet's assumed stoicism, nature portends death – later for the man than for the horse, in this instance, but death nonetheless. Frost inscribed Bernard De Voto's copy of *A Witness Tree*: "There is no way out but through."

Sometimes the stars seemed to offer a superior view of the thicket below, as in "Come In":

As I came to the edge of the woods,
Thrush music–hark!
Now if it was dusk outside,
Inside it was dark.

.   .   .   .

Far in the pillared dark
Thrush music went –
Almost like a call to come in
To the dark and lament.

But no, I was out for stars:
I would not come in.
I meant not even if asked,
And I hadn't been.[54]

To Frost astronomy was more dependable than metaphysics. The "After-word" to the *Complete Poems* (1949) admonishes us to "take something like a star / To stay our minds on and be staid," since "it asks of us a certain height."[55] But when the poet asks the star to translate its mystery into speech which "we can learn / By heart and when alone repeat," it merely burns in silence. And since stellar time and stellar space afford perspective, not transcendence, sooner or later the pioneer must return to battle the elements. Clearing his place confirms his mastery of at least the immediate environs, psychological and circumstantial, and provides a framed patch of sky: horizons which he must guard against the trees' remorseless return.

American writers from James Fenimore Cooper to the present have lamented the violation of nature by Americans armed with an increasingly lethal technology. But the other side of this dilemma, intensified by the Calvinist influence North and South and recognized by many of these same writers, is the conviction that nature and human nature are, by their different natures, at odds, so that the woodsman approaches the inhuman woods as adversary, bringing to the conflict as his only advantage a consciousness which comprehends the conflict and his ultimate defeat. Therein lie his vindication if he contends with nature honorably. So the *Pequod* carries a representative crew against the whale. So Hemingway's old man says to the great marlin to which his line binds him: "Fish, I'll stay with you until I am dead"; "Fish, I love you and respect you very much. But I will kill you dead before this day ends"; and later, "I am glad we do not have to try to kill the stars."[56] So to Faulkner the hunt enacts a ritual in which men love the blood they spill and spill the blood in loving it. So, too, on a humbler scale, Frost's woodsmen open a space and turn the trees into a sheltering house where they can hole up for a while, perhaps with a wife and family.

In "Ghost House," "The Black Cottage," "The Birthplace," "Directive," and many other poems, ruined cottages and houses stand as mute reminders that life's cycle spells the individual's death. "The Need of Being Versed in Country Things" turns tears to irony at the prospect:

> The house had gone to bring again   ·
> To the midnight sky a sunset glow.
> Now the chimney was all of the house that stood,
> Like a pistil after the petals go.
>
> The barn opposed across the way,
> That would have joined the house in flame
> Had it been the will of the wind, was left
> To bear forsaken the place's name.
>
> No more it opened with all one end
> For teams that came by the stony road
> To drum on the floor with scurrying hoofs
> And brush the mow with the summer load.
>
> The birds that came to it through the air
> At broken windows flew out and in,
> Their murmur more like the sigh we sigh
> From too much dwelling on what has been.
>
> Yet for them the lilac renewed its leaf,
> And the aged elm, though touched with fire;
> And the dry pump flung up an awkward arm;
> And the fence post carried a strand of wire.
>
> For them there was really nothing sad.
> But though they rejoiced in the nest they kept,
> One had to be versed in country things
> Not to believe the phoebes wept.[57]

"Directive,"[58] one of the finest of Frost's later poems, seeks to press beyond irony to something like Emersonian acceptance of nature, though on naturalistic rather than transcendental grounds. The poem summons us to the source by losing us in the woods down a path overgrown but still showing wheel tracks across the glacier lines. Long, loose sentences of witty blank verse draw us back and back through geological aeons to "a house that is no more a house / Upon a farm that is no more a farm / And in a town that is no more a town," and beyond the clearing (soon to be no more a clearing) to a brook still flowing as it had and would: "Here are your waters and your watering place. / Drink and be whole again beyond confusion." No Heaven or Nirvana; no Platonic Idea or Paradise regained; but if we are strong enough at the end to retrace our steps – the hewn path and the brief clearing – we can comprehend the whole cycle from nature's vantage point as it flows on past and over us. Even in this extremity, however, consciousness equivocates. The final directive is not to drown in the flow but to sample the waters from a cup that belongs to the dead children's abandoned playhouse nearby. Acknowledging fate, Frost cannot help holding back.

Meanwhile, we have our clearings, sometimes even shared. Frost's world, like Cooper's, Hemingway's, and Faulkner's, is a lonesome man's world. Frost's few poems of love turn on the fragility of that relationship: "The Death of the Hired Man," "The Generations of Men," "Maple," "Two Look at Two," "Too Anxious for Rivers," "West-Running Brook." In "A Cabin in the Clearing," from which the title of the last volume was taken, a man and wife, snug in their covers, muffled by wood smoke and night mist, converse, raising together the questions they will never answer; they are left murmuring in the dark.

But there are few love poems in Frost's many volumes, and at its best, love is the meeting place of opposites – in "West-Running Brook,"[59] of opposite philosophies as well. To the wife, the stream is an "annunciation": "look, look, it's waving to us with a wave / To let us know it hears me." She was probably remembering Emerson's sense that an occult relation linked us and nature, so that we could nod to the vegetable and the vegetable could nod back in recognition. To her skeptical husband, matter moves by its own laws, but soon his hard-headed science gives way to a kind of philosophical poetry of his own. A wave, rising against the flow of the stream on a sunken rock, becomes for him a symbol of the individual's refusal to submit meekly to mortality:

> It is this backward motion toward the source,
> Against the stream, that most we see ourselves in,
> The tribute of the current to the source.
> It is from this in nature we are from.
> It is most us.

His wife is the Emersonian, but here he too comes to his own sense of correspondence with nature: paradoxically, a correspondence in universal resistance to fate. This is a different brook from the one in "Directive"; it draws the Transcendental and scientific views of nature which are the legacies of Frost's mother and father into an open-minded, loving dialogue as personae of his own masculine and feminine sides. Characteristically, there is no resolution. Neither view displaces the other, but both are accommodated in the agreement by husband and wife that "today will be the day of what we both said."

It is this saying, albeit a double saying, in which and through which we refuse "to fill the abyss's void with emptiness" without at least looking back to see the way we have come. Naming, especially the heightened and disciplined speech of poetry, runs counter to "the stream of everything that runs away," "the universal cataract of death that spends to nothingness," and thus language records for history and against time our brave, doomed opposition to annihilation. The poet is a woodsman clearing the words: "The background in hugeness and confusion shading away from where we stand into black and utter chaos; and against the background any small man-made figure of order and concentration."[60]

The unifying conception in Frost's poetry, closed in form but open-ended in meaning – all the way from "Into My Own" to the last poem of *In the Clearing* – is the pioneer myth. This last poem came unexpectedly and was written at one sitting, just before Frost mailed back the galley proofs for *In the Clearing*, and he forwarded it with the other poems. The preparation of his final book cleared the way for a summary word:

> In winter in the woods alone
> Against the trees I go.
> I mark a maple for my own
> And lay the maple low.
>
> At four o'clock I shoulder ax,
> And in the afterglow
> I link a line of shadowy tracks
> Across the tinted snow.
>
> I see for Nature no defeat
> In one tree's overthrow
> Or for myself in my retreat
> For yet another blow.[61]

In his late eighties, alone in the winter woods at sunset, Frost could relish a certain shrewd satisfaction in seeing the battle as still a standoff: neither victory yet for nature nor defeat yet for himself. The felled maple is another witness tree.

During the last months of Frost's life, I was seated next to him at a dinner before a *Harvard Advocate* reading. In the course of conversation, I proposed, no doubt haltingly and clumsily, a still fuzzy interpretation of his poetry in terms of the pioneer myth. As I should have known he would, he pooh-poohed the whole thing: critics, he said, like to make up patterns and read them back into the work; after all, "Stopping by Woods" and "The Draft Horse" were written years apart. But as he was preparing to leave the party after the reading, Frost asked to see me, and when I leaned down to his chair to thank him and say good-bye, he whispered in my ear, "Keep your eyes on those trees, boy." That was as far as he would go, but for me it was enough.

II

I

The gathering of poets, fiction writers, social and literary critics around the gentle, genteel, self-deprecating figure of John Crowe Ransom at Vanderbilt University during the 1920s was a cultural occurrence all the more remarkable for being unexpected, especially in what seemed to sophisticated New Yorkers and Chicagoans the unruffled backwater of Nashville, Tennessee.[62] The group included faculty colleagues like Donald Davidson and Andrew Lytle and handpicked students Allen Tate and Robert Penn Warren. The fortnightly meetings dissected the sad state of society and the arts and analyzed manuscripts submitted by the members to unsparing scrutiny. The group met for only a few years before Ransom and others took up faculty positions elsewhere, but their continued association and the tenacity of their intellectual and especially their literary views made an impact on the academic study of literature beyond their numbers.

The group's magazine, *The Fugitive*, edited by Ransom between 1922 and 1928, proclaimed them to be in flight from what they felt was the brutality and disease of modern society. Their prose rings with denunciations of the Industrial Revolution as an index of a failure of spirit. The consolidation of power in the bureaucracies of corporate enterprise and government destroyed the dignity of the individual's relationship to place and region, to family and neighbors, to morality, religion, and art. The result is the faceless masses huddling in squalid urban bondage to slave at the machinery of capitalist industry. The essays in the Fugitives' manifesto, *I'll Take My Stand: The South and the Agrarian Tradition by Twelve Southerners* (1930), attacked twentieth-century collectivism in the name of the individual's allegiance to soil and blood and to the hierarchical institutions and customs that supported those allegiances.

The enemy was Leviathan: the secular and materialistic state. Fascism was already established in Italy and communism in Russia; Nazism was around the corner. The United States was vibrating with the noise of various totalitarian ideologies, and when the New Deal arrived, it seemed to the Fugitives an alarming move toward socialism here at home. Their advocacy of a return to Jeffersonian agrarianism struck their opponents as elitist nostalgia for happy times on the old plantation, and the Fugitives accepted the "reactionary" label proudly for their politics. Nevertheless, they insisted that their regional outlook provided a profound insight into a fundamental cultural problem. Tate and Warren were among the contributors to *I'll Take My Stand* who wanted to indicate the broad intention of their criticism by calling the book *A Tract Against Communism*. Their opposition proceeded from a conviction that the agrarianism of the Old South, despite slavery, represented one of the last manifestations, however flawed and provincial, of the Christian humanism which had been the tradition of the West up to the modern period. Tate was later to claim, "I never thought of Agrarianism as a restoration of anything in the Old South. I saw it as something to be created not only in the South...but in the moral and religious outlook of Western man."[63] Ransom looked back at the agrarian venture, not without wistfulness, as "an escapade...the last fling of our intellectual youth," and went on to say: "Historically we were behind the times. But we were right in thinking that the times were bad, and even in thinking that they were desperately bad."[64]

This strong ideological position shaped Ransom's literary preferences and judgment, published in his *Fugitive* pieces (a few of which have been included in the recent *Selected Essays* [1984]) and in the essays collected in *The World's Body* (1938). The "Preface" warns the reader that the discussion of particular texts is aimed at a general theoretical understanding of how poetry works. The kind of poetry that interested Ransom was, he said, the response of an "adult," "fallen mind" to a postlapsarian world. To his mind, idealism was a neurotic symptom, and most of the poetry of the last hundred years or more exhibited a Romantic withdrawal from reality into adolescent fantasy. Such "heart's desire poetry," as Ransom sneeringly caricatured it, "denies the real world by idealizing it: the act of a sick mind....It indicates in the subject a poor adaptation to reality; a sub-normal equipment in animal courage; flight and escapism; furtive libido. It is only reasonable if such acts, even if they are performed in the name of poetry, should be treated under the pathological categories."[65] Paradoxically, the Fugitive opposed Romantic "flight and escapism," and to the insinuation that his agrarian dream showed his weakness for the old Confederate moonshine about Christian chevaliers and their ladies, Ransom was quick to point out that "Antique Harvesters" was his only poem about southern agrarianism. The rest of his verse "has no interest in improving or idealizing the world....It only wants to realize [it], to see it better."[66]

Nevertheless, this academically trained minister's son had enough of the would-be chevalier in him to view his less than ideal world with a sense of paradox and irony so consistent that it defined his psychological and moral stance as a poet and as the theoretician of the New Criticism:

> It is a paradox when you find something which in its bearing looks both ways, pro and con, good and bad; irony when you have something you thought was firmly established in the favorable sense, as good, and pro, but discover presently that it has gone bad for you, and is contra; the one is a pregnant ambiguity, the other is a radical yet slightly humorous sense of disappointment where you had least reason to expect it. The instances may be petty, and indeed the paradoxes may be only the accidents of words. But now and then there will be a paradox or an irony which is vivid, and crucial too, for great issues turn on it.[67]

A letter to Tate declared that art turned on antitheses and refused the imposition of Hegelian synthesis:

> Art is our refusal to yield to the blandishments of "constructive" philosophy and permit the poignant and actual Dichotomy to be dissipated in a Trichotomy; our rejection of Third Terms; our denial of Hegel's right to solve a pair of contradictions with a Triad. And here's a slogan: Give us a Dualism or we'll give you no art.[68]

From his minister father Ransom had heard about original sin, and his mostly narrative poems rehearse again and again the fall into consciousness of mortality. *Chills and Fever*, the title of one of his volumes of verse, provides a metaphor that runs through the poetry: a sickness that kills, sooner or later, through its violent alternations. Taken all in all, life, one way or another, comes to "six little spaces of chill, and six of burning."[69] Ransom's corpus of poems is thin, almost all written before he undertook *The Kenyon Review* (Frost wished that he would devote more time to poetry and less to criticism), and they cluster about a few interrelated themes. Many are about aging, among them: "In Process of a Noble Alliance," "Blue Girls" (which he once said, with only partly facetious gallantry, was the cruelest poem he ever wrote), "Piazza Piece," "Vaunting Oak," "Old Mansion," "Antique Harvesters." And many poems fix on the finality of death: "Bells for John Whiteside's Daughter," "Miriam Tazewell," "Here Lies a Lady," "Dead Boy," "Janet Waking," "Of Margaret." Usually the impersonal cruelty of death reveals itself most poignantly in a helpless victim: a flower, a leaf, a child, a girl, a woman. In a letter to Tate, Ransom finds in Poe a "very fine application of this principle – the lovely woman seen dead, etc."[70] Ransom's southern girls and ladies are presented with an ironic detachment that distinguishes them from Poe's melodramatic dream women, but Ransom's remark to Tate, who was himself fascinated with Poe, reflects his intuition that such anima figures function for male poets as projections of their anxieties about body and soul.

"Janet Waking" deserves extended explication as an illustration of the quality of Ransom's irony and paradox in treating mortality and as an illustration of the minute attention to language and technical devices which the New Criticism expected:

> Beautifully Janet slept
> Till it was deeply morning. She woke then
> And thought about her dainty-feathered hen,
> To see how it had kept.
>
> One kiss she gave her mother.
> Only a small one gave she to her daddy
> Who would have kissed each curl of his shining baby;
> No kiss at all for her brother.
>
> "Old Chucky, old Chucky!" she cried,
> Running across the world upon the grass
> To Chucky's house, and listening. But alas,
> Her Chucky had died.
>
> It was a transmogrifying bee
> Came droning down on Chucky's old bald head

And sat and put the poison. It scarcely bled,
But how exceedingly

And purply did the knot
Swell with the venom and communicate
Its rigor! Now the poor comb stood up straight
But Chucky did not.

So there was Janet
Kneeling on the wet grass, crying her brown hen
(Translated far beyond the daughters of men)
To rise and walk upon it.

And weeping fast as she had breath
Janet implored us, "Wake her from her sleep!"
And would not be instructed in how deep
Was the forgetful kingdom of death.[71]

Like virtually all of Ransom's poems, this one tells a story, and the narrative effect depends on the frequent and sometimes minor shifting of scale and pitch. The plot is simple: a young girl awakens from sleep's little death to discover that her pet hen has died during the night; but it is a good instance of what Ransom meant when he observed that apparently petty ironies often engage basic issues and problems. The intricate verbal play in the narrator's presentation is meant to keep us aware simultaneously of the smallness of the event and the enormity of its implications, so that we smile at Janet lest we weep with her. The mock-elegiac humor rescues the poem both from the disturbing grief of a lament like "Lycidas" or "In Memoriam" and from the bathetic sentimentality of a lament for a hen.

The first lines play with the ambiguities of sleeping and waking, and the pun on "morning" and "mourning" ("till it was deeply morning") anticipates the impending revelation. The object of the child's attention is introduced anticlimactically at the end of the third line, where "hen" rhymes flatly with "then" in the line above. Janet wonders how the hen has "kept," and the folksy "keep" as "preserve from spoiling" suggests slyly that all Janet's spoiling of the hen till now has not kept her from spoiling in that other sense of physical corruption. The full rhymes sound with a blunt finality ("slept-then-hen-kept," "breath-sleep-deep-death," most noticeably "knot, not"), but the feminine rhymes add comic touches ("daddy-baby," "-ing bee-ingly," "Janet-upon it"). The rhymes of the second stanza line up the family members as she rushes past them in a declension of affection ("one kiss," "only a small one," "no kiss at all") to look for her beloved Chucky. However, when her backyard is called "the world" ("Running across the world upon the grass"), bathos turns to hyperbole, and the imposition of the macrocosm on the microcosm intrudes on the levity just at the middle of the poem, when Janet wakens to death in her own little world. She calls Chucky "old" in affectionate familiarity, but she has in fact succumbed to age. The hen becomes Janet's surrogate and reveals her fate. The tragic shock (is it that? is it anything less?) drives her to seek escape and comfort in society; mortals are all kin. Suddenly wounded and grieving, she joins the human family for the first time, imploring "us" (including the speaker and the reader in the family tragedy) to "wake her from her sleep." The reader knows, better than Janet yet knows, that the feminine pronouns take in both her and Chucky, and that she is expending her breath in weeping for her own life. In the course of a few quatrains, her happy "cry" of greeting to Chucky has turned to a cry of sorrow; the grass is wet with the morning dew and the mourning tears.

Much of the fun of the language comes from the unstable juxtaposition of multisyllabic Latinate words and heavily consonantal, often monosyllabic words from Germanic roots. The Latinate words sound fussy, pedantic, arch, and the Saxon words lumpish and physical; the alternation makes for a quick elevation and deflation of tone. So, in the fourth stanza ("It was a transmogrifying bee / Came droning down on Chucky's old bald head / And sat and put the poison"), the fastidious and high-faluting "transmogrifying" jumps out of the statement "it was a bee" and contrasts with the ugly physical details of the heavily consonantal shorter words: "droning down," "old bald head," "sat-put-poison." The "poison" then becomes the fancier "venom," which Miltonically "communicated its rigor" to the chicken's comb; "rigor" also suggests "rigor mortis," a stiffness that paradoxically made "the poor comb [stand up] straight" while Chucky, alas, lay down. When the poem speaks of the hen as "translated far beyond the daughters of men," the Latinism of this phrase is a comically euphemistic universalization of her fate, which also calls attention to the narrator's language game at the same time that it retains its etymological meaning of "carried across." The biblical ring of "rise and walk" and "kingdom" is picked up in "instructed," but the religious message, like all the wit of the poem, is of no avail to Janet at this moment of disillusionment: she feels unable to forget "the forgetful kingdom of death."

"Janet Waking" is written in a meter regular enough to contain these shifts of tone and flexible enough to surprise with variations. The little narrative is spelled out in ballad quatrain, and the a-b-b-a rhymes reinforce the 3-5-5-3 sequence of feet in the lines while enhancing the ironic humor with the line breaks in the sentences. The expansion comes in the middle of the stanza, and the fourth line cinches the quatrain in tightly and sometimes comically, rhyming against the short first line and completing the stanza unit. The one run-on between stanzas occurs with the swelling of the purply bee bite. The narrowing constriction in the stanzas' closure (even when the trimeters become tetrameters in the pronouncements of the final stanza) conveys the sense of a falling off, a diminishment. By the end, the reader knows that the poem is not just about the death of poor old Chucky. Its irony encompasses Janet's betrayed simplicity and the bemused sadness of the older narrator, who empathizes with her fall from innocence but avoids betraying his own reserve.

In Ransom's world, the initiating betrayal puts everyone on guard. Anyone luckier than John Whiteside's daughter grows up in the knowledge that all things are vulnerable – especially human emotions. Men and women withhold themselves from contact or relinquish tenuous contact at the needful point.

Lovers lose one another in death, as in "Winter Remembered," or lacerate one another in an outburst that destroys their relationship, as in "Two in August." In "Old Man Pondered" and "Miriam Tazewell," withdrawal becomes a self-inflicted living death; "Emily Hardcastle" and "Hilda" are wedded in life to death; and "The Man Without Sense of Direction" is married to death more than to his wife. Characteristically, as in "The Equilibrists," the man and woman hang paralyzed, together but untouching, in a "torture of equilibrium" between head and heart, passion and consciousness.[72] Other poems of sexual tension include "Spectral Lovers," "Good Ships," "Eclogue," "Parting, Without a Sequel," and, perhaps the best of them, "Judith of Bethulia":

> Beautiful as the flying legend of some leopard
> She had not chosen yet her captain, nor Prince
> Depositary to her flesh, and our defense;
> A wandering beauty is a blade out of its scabbard.
> You know how dangerous, gentlemen of threescore?
> May you know it yet ten more.
>
> Nor by process of veiling she grew less fabulous.
> Grey or blue veils, we were desperate to study
> The invincible emanations of her white body,
> And the winds at her ordered raiment were ominous.
> Might she walk in the market, sit in the council of soldiers?
> Only of the extreme elders.
>
> But a rare chance was the girl's then, when the Invader
> Trumpeted from the South, and rumbled from the North,
> Beleaguered the city from four quarters of the earth,
> Our soldiery too craven and sick to aid her –
> Where were the arms could countervail this horde?
> Her beauty was the sword.
>
> She sat with the elders, and proved on their blear visage
> How bright was the weapon unrusted in her keeping,
> While he lay surfeiting on their harvest heaping
> Wasting the husbandry of their rarest vintage –
> And dreaming of the broad-breasted dames for concubine?
> These floated on his wine.
>
> He was lapped with bay-leaves, and grass and fumiter weed,
> And from under the wine-film encountered his mortal vision,
> For even within his tent she accomplished his derision,
> Loosing one veil and another, she stood unafraid;
> So he perished. Nor brushed her with even so much as a daisy?
> She found his destruction easy.
>
> The heathen have all perished. The victory was furnished.
> We smote them hiding in vineyards, barns, annexes,
> And now their white bones clutter the holes of foxes,
> And the chieftain's head, with grinning sockets, and varnished –
> Is it hung on the sky with a hideous epitaphy?
> No, the woman keeps the trophy.

May God send unto our virtuous lady her Prince!
It is stated she went reluctant to that orgy,
Yet a madness fevers our young men, and not the clergy
Nor the elders have turned them unto modesty since.
Inflamed by the thought of her nakedness with desire?
Yes, and chilled with fear and despair.[73]

In the biblical story, the Israelite woman Judith saves her town from its enemies by beheading their lustful commander, Holofernes, in his tent and opening their camp to the Israelite soldiers, but Ransom turns it into a parable of sexual ambivalence. His Judith is a figure of archetypal power whose feline sexuality threatens and overpowers the male weaklings of both camps. In contrast to the poems with female victims, chills and fever this time render the men physically weak and sexually impotent: "Inflamed by the thought of her nakedness with desire? / Yes, and chilled with fear and despair." It is she who has not yet chosen her mate, rather than vice versa, and in the "craven and sick" men's imaginations, her mate is a sacrificial adversary. Her very sexual attraction is their undoing: "A wandering beauty is a blade out of its scabbard"; "Her beauty was the sword." The prospect of impotence and castration makes her appear to them as a phallic yet castrating weapon. They read their fate in Holofernes'; his beheading is reduced to a bathetic sexual joke: "So he perished. Nor brushed her with even so much as a daisy? / She found his destruction easy."

Ransom employs his usual bag of tricks: the funny feminine rhymes ("leopard-scabbard," "Invader-to aid her," "daisy-easy," "orgy-clergy," "epitaphy-trophy"), the puns ("arms" as "weapons" and "embraces," "husbandry" as agricultural and sexual, "dames" as "ladies" and "concubines"), the elegant Latinate circumlocution (which, for example, turns the men's helpless horniness into "we were desperate to study / The invincible emanations of her white body"). The stanza combines an a-b-b-a quatrain with a concluding couplet, but again the last line effects anticlimactic closure, after the previous five-stress lines, by ramming the rhyme home with only three beats.

In Ransom's world, is any action possible outside the sexual arena to break the sense of male impotence? Captain Carpenter's quest for chivalric valor comes to an ignominious and comic conclusion; he is gradually hacked to pieces by a series of devilish enemies. Still, his intrepid refusal to give up and die makes him a kind of absurdist hero. Along with "Necrological," "Armageddon," and "First Travels of Max," "Captain Carpenter" dresses itself in the medieval convention both as a distancing device and as an ironic evocation of the knightly ideal of courageous action in the service of God and lady fair. If the ideal is there to be deflated, it is also there to comment unfavorably upon the contemporary decline of moral or religious values.

Like Eliot, Ransom usually treats contemporary society obliquely and unfavorably through the ironic filter of myth. In "Philomela" America is too "barbarous" and "democratic" (those positive words for Whitman) to receive the gift of song; the muse will not come to "a bantering breed sophistical and swarthy."[74] In "Prometheus in Straits" the titan who brought light to humankind now finds himself confounded by all phases of society and all the works of man. War poems like "Necrological" and "Puncture" (Ransom was an artillery officer in France during World War I) contrast the heat of carnage with the chill of corpses. In this muddled, warring world, religion has no redemptive efficacy. In "The Spiel of the Three Mountebanks" the charlatans preach caricatures of faith, hope, and love through their performing animals: Fides the dog, Humphrey the elephant, Agnes the lamb. In "Armageddon" Christ and Antichrist are arrayed in full battle array for Judgment Day, with the anti-Christians talking peace and the Christians calling for righteous bloodshed.

Viewed as a whole, the world of Ransom's poetry is so stripped of illusion, so incapable of amelioration and transcendence that paradox and irony become desperate and necessary stratagems of the spirit. "Desperate" is not too strong a word; Ransom uses it several times in crucial comments in discussing the function of poetry: "[Poetry] is a desperate ontological or metaphysical manoeuvre."[75] He was right in describing his poetry as the act of an adult mind looking at a fallen world. The themes which we have been discussing make the following configuration: mortality, age, death, alienation, the failure of love, division within the self, the "torture of equilibrium," the death-in-life of the isolated ego, the failure of action and of the heroic ideal, corruption and carnage in the social order, the inefficacy of religious virtue, the inoperancy of grace, the improbability of release from all these afflictions. Ransom's response was a "radical yet slightly humorous sense of disappointment." Disappointment, but not premature surrender. The humor is, as in Frost, the clue to the depth rather than the superficiality of his feelings. One of Ransom's last poems, "Master's in the Garden Again," which invokes both Hardy and Conrad as fellow pessimists, concludes: "But it's gay garden now, / Play sweeter than pray, that the darkened be gay."[76] In the third revision of the *Selected Poems*, he allowed himself a confidential moment not without its own sly evasiveness:

> At my age I do not mind at this point making a few personal remarks. During the *Fugitive* days of my fourth decade I was at great pains to suppress my feelings in what I wrote. I was both sensitive and sentimental as a boy; and I did not like that boyishness in my adult poems. My friends seemed to think that I managed it. But here I take pleasure in testifying that I could not easily control my feelings when I was finishing two very special poems ["Here Lies a Lady" and "Of Margaret"].... These are the poems which, as I finished them, wetted my cheeks. But I must add that they are fictions.[77]

Like Frost, he needed craft (in the sense of cunning as well as skill with words) to maneuver terror and grief, not so much out of bounds as within bounds. The poetic contrivance is a holding off, a clearing in the words, but also a verbal engagement, a commitment of spirit to matter. If the Yankee woodsman was a pioneer of sorts, the southern chevalier was a "Persistent Explorer" of sorts:

> The noise of water teased his literal ear
> Which heard the distant drumming, and so scored:
> "Water is falling – it fell – therefore it roared.
> Yet something else is there: is it cheer or fear?"
>
> He strode much faster, till on the dizzy brink
> His eye confirmed with vision what he'd heard:
> "A simple physical water." Again he demurred:
> "More than a roaring flashing water, I think."
>
> But listen as he might, look fast or slow,
> It was common water, millions of tons of it
> Gouging its gorge deeper, and every bit
> Was water, the insipid chemical H_2O.
>
> Its thunder smote him somewhat as the loud
> Words of the god that rang around a man
> Walking by the Mediterranean.
> Its cloud of froth was whiter than the cloud
>
> That clothed the goddess sliding down the air
> Unto a mountain shepherd, white as she
> That issues from the smoke refulgently.
> The cloud was, but the goddess was not there.
>
> Deafening was the sound, but never a voice
> That talked with him; spacious the spectacle
> But it spelled nothing; there was not any spell
> Whether to bid him cower or rejoice.
>
> What would he have it spell? He scarcely knew;
> Only that water and nothing but water filled
> His eyes and ears; only water that spilled;
> And if the smoke and rattle of water drew
>
> From the deep thickets of his mind the train,
> The fierce fauns and the timid tenants there
> That burst their bonds and rushed upon the air,
> Why, he must turn and beat them down again.
>
> So be it. And no unreasonable outcry
> The pilgrim made; only a rueful grin
> Spread over his lips until he drew them in;
> He would not sit upon a rock and die.
>
> Many are the ways of dying; witness, if he
> Commit himself to the water, and descend
> Wrapped in the water, turn water at the end,
> Part of a water rolling to the sea.
>
> But there were many ways of living, too,
> And let his enemies gibe, but let them say
> That he would throw this continent away
> And seek another country – as he would do.[78]

The setting of the poem summons Romantic precedents: Wordsworth crossing the Simplon Pass, Shelley on Mont Blanc, Manfred atop the cataract on the Jungfrau. In his strategically restrained manner, Ransom's persona also aspires to hear more in the waterfall than "the insipid chemical H_2O," to catch the voice of the god and the vision of the goddess veiled in vapor. But, empiricist by sad experience, he will not let imagination delude him. "The cloud was, but the goddess was not there": there was no magic "spell," the sense data "spelled nothing" beyond the chemical formula. The repetition indicates the chilling conclusion that there was "water," "only water," "nothing but water." If the mind's own fever seemed to invest the scene with mythic and numinous figures, "Why, he must turn and beat them down again" – but with no Byronic and "unreasonable outcry," "only a rueful grin." Ransom's description of irony in Frost, cited more fully at the beginning of the chapter, reads like a gloss on "Persistent Explorer":

> It implies then a rejection of the romantic forms and formulas; but this rejection is so unwilling, and in its statements there lingers so much of the music and color and romantic mystery which is perhaps the absolute poetry, and this statement is attended by such a disarming rueful comic sense of the poet's own betrayal, that the fruit of it is wisdom and not bitterness, poetry not prose, health not suicide.[79]

The ironist keeps from suicide by not abandoning the search for "another country" where fact and myth converge. For the ironist wears a Janus-face: the scientist-skeptic had no illusion about finding it, but the would-be believer persists in persisting (like Frost's "pursuit of a pursuit"). "Somewhere Is Such a Kingdom," another poem is entitled.

Somewhere quite else, it seemed. But maybe not so far, if the imagination attends to the world's body. "Painted Head" (1934) and "To the Scholars of Harvard" (1939) are Ransom's last poems before he turned in 1962, after retiring from teaching and editing, to the extensive revision and even rewriting of his poems in his last years. "Painted Head" represents the pinnacle of a career devoted to rejecting intellectual abstraction in favor of imaginative realization:

> By dark severance the apparition head
> Smiles from the air a capital on no
> Column or a Platonic perhaps head
> On a canvas sky depending from nothing;
>
> Stirs up an old illusion of grandeur
> By tickling the instinct of heads to be
> Absolute and to try decapitation
> And to play truant from the body bush;
>
> But too happy and beautiful for those sorts
> Of head (homekeeping heads are happiest)
> Discovers maybe thirty unwidowed years
> Of not dishonoring the faithful stem;
>
> Is nameless and has authored for the evil

Historian headhunters neither book
Nor state and is therefore distinct from tart
Heads with crowns and guilty gallery heads;

Wherefore the extravagant device of art
Unhousing by abstraction this once head
Was capital irony by a loving hand
That knew the no treason of a head like this;

Makes repentance in an unlovely head
For having vinegarly traduced the flesh
Till, the hurt flesh recusing, the hard egg
Is shrunken to its own deathlike surface;

And an image thus. The body bears the head
(So hardly one they terribly are two)
Feeds and obeys and unto please what end?
Not to the glory of tyrant head but to

The estate of body. Beauty is of body.
The flesh contouring shallowly on a head
Is a rock-garden needing body's love
And best bodiness to colorify

The big blue birds sitting and sea-shell flats
And caves, and on the iron acropolis
To spread the hyacinthine hair and rear
The olive garden for the nightingales.[80]

The first sentence is long (almost twenty-five of the forty-five lines in the poem) and deliberately difficult, its many clauses and phrases filled with abstractions and witticisms and stitched together by a string of puns on "head," "capital," "decapitation," "headhunting," and so on. It presents a cerebral maze through which the diagram of syntax leads logically: a single subject ("the apparition head") with a series of verbs ("smiles," "stirs," "discovers," "is nameless and has authored," "is distinct," "makes repentance"). This sentence describes a portrait of an anonymous young man whose appearance shows the healthy robustness of living fully in the body. But in showing only this ruddy, happy head against a dark background (in a Titian portrait, say, or a Rembrandt), the canvas betrays the vigor of the real man. The artwork has abstracted him from the process of living and growing and thus has succumbed to the intellect's universal but illusory desire to transcend mortal limits and be absolute. The bodiless head in the painting might seem thereby to have the Platonic "illusion of grandeur" in desiring such decapitation. But no; the image shows the opposite, shows that his was a homekeeping head, happy for its organic growth as stem of the "body bush." It was not the lively man in the painting but the artist who betrayed by the skill of his "loving hand" his subject's spirited body by decapitating the living head into a static and so dead image. Oddly enough, the head, impaled on the canvas at a hale and hearty thirty, becomes a death's head, congealed into paint. In retrospect the "unlovely" artist may repent "for having vinegarly traduced" the subject he loved. "Vinegarly," besides indicating the gall of betrayal, identifies the base of the tempura paint, and also of Easter egg dye, so that the abstracted skull has something as well of the hollow intellectuality of a colored egghead ("the hard egg...shrunken to its own deathlike surface").

At the same time, though in one sense art betrays life by fixing it, a further turn of the paradox is the fact that the abstracting portrait nonetheless attests to the essential realization that "the body bears the head / (So hardly one they terribly are two)" – "bears" in the sense of "carries" and "gives birth to." After the simple declarative sentence "Beauty is of body," the language of the poem changes dramatically. The duality of body and mind ("So hardly one they terribly are two") will come to reconciliation, if ever, if at all, not through the abstractions of the Platonic head but through the revelations of "best bodiness," and the medium itself will express the experience. For once, in Ransom, the two become one. The sensuous metaphors of the closing lines literally translate the abstraction "best bodiness" into an earthly paradise. The "rock-garden" on the skull's "iron acropolis" burgeons into the landscape of a living head: an "olive garden for the nightingales," adorned with the "big blue birds" of the eyes, the "sea-shell flats and caves" of the ears and nose and mouth, the tangles of "hyacinthine hair." Art written in recognition and realization of "best bodiness" results not in the decapitation of mind from body into dead image but instead in metaphor which joins head to body, grows mind in nature, nature in mind. Great art demonstrates that occasionally the persistent explorer can enter the world so spontaneously and frictionlessly that it expresses itself through him, in his medium. In such a miraculous instance, art offers paradise regained, all within the limits of mortality.

2

Quite expectedly, the kind of poetry which Ransom and his colleagues and students at Vanderbilt wrote was of a piece with the poetry they wrote about and with the theory behind the analytical explications of the New Criticism. When a number of them scattered to other campuses during the thirties, they continued to proselytize for the New Criticism in the classroom and in their publications, including the influential literary journals they founded and edited. After *The Fugitive* Ransom founded and edited *The Kenyon Review*, and Robert Lowell and Randall Jarrell were only the most famous of those who came to Kenyon College to study with him. Tate revamped *The Sewanee Review* on the *Kenyon Review* model, passing the editorship on after him to Andrew Lytle when his university career took him to Minnesota. Warren and Cleanth Brooks issued *The Southern Review* from Louisiana State University for a number of years before departing for Yale to turn its English Department into the academic command post for the New Criticism. Brooks and Warren's immensely popular textbooks, *An Approach to Literature* (1936, written with Jack Purser), *Understanding Poetry* (1938), and *Understanding Fiction* (1943), brought the methodology of the New Criticism, into classrooms across the country, and they have gone through many editions.

The World's Body (1938) anticipated *The New Criticism* (1941) in laying out a "poetic theory...in the constant company of the actual poems." The Romantic legacy made for an impressionistic, highly subjective and emotive criticism, but the "general principles" of the New Criticism would be worked out inductively and empirically through a close examination of texts. Ransom called for an approach that was "scientific," "precise and systematic," and "objective" in citing "the nature of the object rather than its effects upon the subject." A poem has an expressive function, but that is not the proper concern of criticism. What was new about the New Criticism in its literary-historical context was the focus on the poem as a "technical act, of extreme difficulty," which can be comprehended only through a detailed critique of the ways in which the medium has been made to operate. "The autonomy of the artist as one who interests himself in the artistic object in his own right, and likewise the autonomy of the work itself as existing for its own sake,"[81] demands a dispassionate focus on the mechanics of the artwork rather than on its expressive effects.

Even though Ransom and some of his associates disliked Modernist poets and preferred the seventeenth-century metaphysicals, their critical stance popularized and channeled into the academic study of literature during the 1940s and 1950s Modernist notions that the poets they disliked were working from two decades earlier. Within the academy, literary study meant scholarship, whether of a historical, philological, or ethical bent. "Criticism, Inc.," the last essay in *The World's Body*, flung down the gauntlet by distinguishing criticism from "1. Personal registrations, which are declarations of the effect of the art-work upon the critic as reader....2. Synopsis and paraphrase....3. Historical studies....4. Linguistic studies....5. Moral studies....6. Any other special studies which deal with some abstract or prose content taken out of the work," such as Shakespeare's attitude toward the law or Milton's geography.[82] The critic may sometimes consult the scholar or linguist or historian, but only for specialized knowledge needed to analyze the technical and structural properties which make the poem that poem.

The New Critics won the day, seized the initiative in literary study from the old-fashioned scholars, and their hegemony went virtually unchallenged until the arrival of the open-form poets of the late 1950s – the Beats, inspired by Whitman, and the Black Mountain poets, inspired by Williams and Pound – and the advent during the 1970s of critics of different ideological and methodological persuasions – Marxist, structuralist, feminist, deconstructionist. These new critical schools were quick to argue that the New Critics' supposed objectivity shrewdly masked their reactionary political and moral ideology. But for more than two decades their basic tenets, reiterated in *The New Criticism* and exemplified in their journals, held sway, and still inform the working habits of some who have gone on to other ideological and critical positions.

The New Criticism proceeds from the assumption that the kind of knowledge required for a *literary* judgment is "radically and ontologically distinct,"[83] particular to the nature of poetry and to the ontology of the poem being judged. The first three essays concern critics whose work opened the way for the new approach and exemplifies some aspect of it. But I. A. Richards and William Empson are psychological critics, Eliot the historical critic, and Yvor Winters the logical and moral critic, and Ransom finds each somewhat hampered by his bias. So the fourth and concluding essay is "Wanted: An Ontological Critic," and Ransom thought it so basic a position paper that he reprinted it at the beginning of his last book of essays, *Beating the Bushes* (1972).[84]

That essay first proposed the categories for analyzing the ontology of the poem which Ransom would continue to refine and reformulate for the rest of his career and which entered the vocabulary of a generation of critics. His dualism led him to construe poetic language into two aspects – semantics and phonetics – each of which itself has two aspects. On the semantic level, language combines logic – that is, syntax, theme, argument, plot, which comprise "the prose of the poem" – and texture – that is, the suggestive, associative, emotionally charged atmospherics. Texture needs logical structure to contain and focus its expansive imprecision; logic needs textural suggestiveness to fill the structures and conventions with emotional resonance and psychological complexity. Analogously, the phonetics of language combines in the one pattern of words both the strict patterns of meter, rhyme, and stanza and the variations which lend the patterns point and nuance and emphasis.

In several later essays, written in the heyday of the New Criticism and reprinted in *Poems and Essays* (1955), Ransom toyed with the notion of a triple, rather than double, function of language resolved in the "three-in-one" or "trinitarian existence" of the words on the page. In a piece on Hardy, Ransom lists without much elaboration "the three dimensions of a poem": the plot or argument, the meters, and something vaguely called "poetic language." An essay about Brooks, entitled "Why Critics Don't Go Mad," restated the categories in the triad of logical form, metaphor, and meter. But "Humanism at Chicago" introduced the fullest version of the poem's triadic ontology portentously:

> I suggest that we think of a poem as constructing and realizing not one poetic object, but three objects at once. . . . But it is necessary in advance to agree not to underestimate the capacity of the poem for embodying three large-scale objects. . . there will also be the grateful sense of the poem as a whole, whose marvellous economy is such that you can take it quite systematically in three different ways and find in it three different things.

Ransom was quick to anticipate the comment that the hard-headed, empirical critic seemed to be declining into mysticism or metaphysics: "Let it be understood, finally, that the three objects do not constitute a Holy Trinity, nor even a Hegelian triad; it is nothing like that!"[85]

But his explanation to the contrary only served to underscore his theological and Hegelian leanings. The first and "most obvious" object is the logical construct: the plot, the argument, the words "in their simple denotative aspect." The second object "is the big formless one which develops irresistibly, though hardly without technical consciousness on the author's part, all the time while the public or logical object is being whipped into shape." It proceeds from "an energy in the words that makes them unwilling to stop with mere denotation, and a kind of lead given them by the poet." All the shadings of overtone and undertone, of connotation and suggestion invest the body of the action or argument from inside with a density of texture that brings it to life and completes it. Nothing new thus far, but Ransom's expatiation on this "community of objects," "this little world of objects," is startling:

> The objects peopling the little world are natural, given, total, and inviolable
> ...the little world [the poem] sets up is a small version of our natural world in
> its original dignity....Indeed, the little world is the imitation of our ancient
> Paradise, when we inhabited it in innocence.

The logical-denotative construct, then, is analogous to our fallen world, "the hustling one we have to live in, and we want it to be handsome as possible," but the textural-connotative construct within the same verbal pattern is analogous to "the one we think we remember to have come from, and we will not let it go."[86] The overlay of texture on logic, the infusion of connotation into denotation, redeems the verbal world and, in a sense, recovers Eden.

A godlike prerogative, and though Ransom's modest demeanor keeps him from saying so, his explanation of the effect of the third construct makes even more astonishing claims. The metrical construct, though "entirely visible and audible," is the most mysterious:

> The rhythm of the meters envelops the two other objects, like an atmosphere;
> it is a constraint and a blessing too. For it is sounding all the time; it is a low-
> grade music making an elemental, cosmic, and eternal object. Very diffidently
> I venture to construe it. I think the meters are an apt imitation of the Platonic
> Ideas, and in permeating our two other worlds permit us to have them *sub
> specie aeternitatis*. For the worst thing about those two worlds is that the
> objects and arrangements we sense so exquisitely and cherish so deeply are
> doomed; they are mortal. That awareness is never withheld from us in the
> poem, but quite the contrary. Nor is there any human equivalent for them,
> really, in a world of Platonic Ideas. But still that world has the distinction of
> being the world of the immortals, and we like to sense it presiding over us.[87]

This could be from Poe's *Eureka* or from one of Hart Crane's headier letters, yet there it is: the poetic world imperfect in its denotation, completed by the connotation but still mortal and doomed, now immortalized in the immutability of a musical form, analogous to, if not continuous with, the harmony of the spheres. The "metaphorical or metaphysical moment" of fusion into the poem's "Concrete Universal" constitutes "that high moment in which we suddenly perceive what we may call the Epiphany of Beauty."[88]

Ransom had come a long way from his feisty insistence to Tate years earlier that art means "our rejection of Third Terms; our denial of Hegel's right to resolve a pair of contradictions with a Triad....Give us a Dualism or we'll give you no art." His development from a dualistic to a triadic ontology of the poem shows how deeply the ironist longed for a resolution. He invoked Christian ("Epiphany") and Romantic ("Beauty," "Concrete Universal") terminology to elevate the Modernist notion that the synthesizing third term is not a metaphysical reality, God or Mind or Oversoul, but the aesthetic medium itself. Hence the elision of "metaphorical or metaphysical," as if to slip in the sly claim that language somehow can reconcile the "two sundered worlds, the free moral world which is wholly inner, and the natural world which is external but determinate and mechanical."[89]

Still, as we have seen, there is in Ransom's own poetry more tension than resolution, more dualism than synthesis; there are few Epiphanies of Beauty, perhaps only the last lines of "Painted Head." But Ransom was the first to confess the limitations of his own poetry in relation to the ideal, and perhaps the elision of "metaphorical or metaphysical" should be seen to run, in his case at least, in the opposite direction. That is to say, what Ransom's poetry really illustrates is rather that in his own words, "the poet's theology is meta-phorical," "something improvised for the literary occasion."[90] For all the hypothesizing about the ontological ideal of the poem – the fallen world rendered in the logical structure, redeemed in the textual structure, and immortalized in the metrical structure – Ransom practiced poetry as an explorer who "does not use nature as a means but as an end," an "inquirer" who submits his mental preconceptions to the text of "nature as nature naturally is."[91] And for all Ransom's gentle and fussy southern manners, he saw as clearly as Frost the violence of our engagement with nature:

> For such moderns as we are the poetry must be modern. It is not as in a state of innocence, to receive the fragrance of the roses on the world's first morning, that our moderns the scarred veterans may enact their poetry, but in the violence of return and regeneration. They re-enter the world, but it is the world which they have marked with their raids, and there is no other world they can enter. It is by its thickness, stubbornness, and power that it must impress them. First must come respect, and then, if then, love.[92]

And like Frost in "The Oven Bird," Ransom answers the question of what to make of a diminished self and a diminished world by making poems of them. He may say that "poetry intends to recover the denser and more refractory original world which we know loosely through our perceptions and memories,"[93] but he knows that his poetry perpetuates an "existence that in actual life is constantly crumbling."[94] The third term is in fact the poem, which must therefore be made "denser and more refractory" than our divided existence. Language holds in tension the "two sundered worlds" of mind and nature and says that they are "so hardly one they terribly are two." The New Criticism refused to idealize nature, but it idealized the poem as perfectly self-contained, lacking and needing nothing, because its statement would only hang together by paradox and irony.

That is why it is not enough to say of Ransom's best poems that they are small in scale and narrow in range. Each element functions in the relations of the whole. The meter contains and yields to shifts of tone and emphasis; the diction is precise enough and resonant enough for its purposes; the metaphor is large enough and small enough to be worked out fully in the limits of the form; there is nothing wanting or in excess. The poem – if not the poet or his world – has reached "best bodiness." In a 1970 sequel to the "Concrete Universal" essay, Ransom spoke his final word on the ontology of the poem. Most of the essay is spent in a discussion of Kant and Hegel, but the last three paragraphs take another turn:

> But the effects of poetry do not necessarily require of the critic a difficult "philosophy" and a very special learning. In recent years I have fancied a version that is simpler, and indeed it is homely, and practical. Let it be said frankly that a poem is an organism in action. But we must figure what the organs are. . . .

Then, reviewing the three aspects of poetry of the world's body, he translated them from elements in a Hegelian triad to anatomical parts: the logic, texture, and meter were, he quipped, the head, the heart, and, yes, the feet of the poem.[95]

2

Wallace Stevens: World as Mundo, Mundo *as World*

Robert Frost liked to tell an anecdote about Wallace Stevens and himself. According to the story, Stevens once remarked to him that the trouble with Frost's poetry was that it was about subjects, in reply to which Frost wisecracked that the trouble with Stevens' poetry was that it was about bric-a-brac. Stevens is made to question Frost's tenacious involvement with external circumstance, which leads him to postulate, at least for the sake of argument, certain scientific, social, and metaphysical hypotheses; Frost's rejoinder is that Stevens' retreat into verbal artifice makes his verse, however glittering and tinselly, detached from reality and so useless except for decorative purposes. Frost's story represents more than a cheap potshot at a fellow poet because it springs from the ingrained Puritan suspicion of art as a lie – and a lie, to boot, which works on and from the bodily senses. Emerson offered a Romantic solution to the problem when he turned the preacher into a poet by making the poet a prophet who sees and says the truth. Frost's modern pragmatism keeps him from following his Emersonian inclinations, and in contrasting his truth telling, albeit skeptical truth telling, with Stevens' fake images, Frost was invoking the old dichotomy to justify his kind of poetry and dismiss Stevens' as frippery.

Needless to say, the complexity of both poets is belied by the joke, though Frost – since it is his joke – comes off better. Still, in its erroneously simple-minded way, it provides a point of departure for two poets who came from different places but from the same time. Frost and Stevens were born in 1874 and 1879, respectively, significantly earlier than Pound and Eliot, Williams and H. D. and even Ransom, decades earlier than Tate and Hart Crane; and they were more thoroughly acculturated by nineteenth-century attitudes than were any of the others except Ransom. Emotionally reticent, personally guarded, they both came to publication comparatively late after careful preparation; in a period of accelerating experimentation, each developed a characteristic manner that avoided autobiographical incident but described and reflected in traditional yet idiosyncratically inflected meters and diction and syntax. Where Frost prided himself on his old-fashioned way of being new,

Stevens insisted that he did not have to be Modernist in technique to be Modernist in viewpoint.

The descriptions and ruminations of both poets provide contrasting glosses on the Romantic dialectic of self and nature, mind and object, in the rapidly shifting circumstances which made Modernism the linear but sometimes parricidal offspring of Romanticism. Frost's and Stevens' distinctive ways of assimilating and construing the terms of the dialectic created the contrast between a poetry of subjects and a poetry of bric-a-brac. Moreover, the particularly American factor behind the choice of divergent courses is a Protestant spirit by their time transcendentalized. The Dutch and German Protestantism of Pennsylvania was different from the Anglo-Saxon strain in New England but equally Protestant, and just as Emerson imbued Frost's religious development, so too Stevens as a young man found his lingering but wavering faith shading off into a vaporous Transcendentalism that demonstrates how Emersonian Protestant sentiment had become by the end of the nineteenth century above the Mason-Dixon line.

Consider these excerpts from a journal Stevens kept between the ages of nineteen and twenty-one: "I wondered why people took books into the woods to read in summertime when there was so much else to be read there that one could not find in books"; "Art must fit with other things; it must be part of the system of the world"; "no one paints Nature's colors as well as Nature's self"; "The first day of one's life in the country is generally a day of wild enthusiasm. Freedom, beauty, sense of power etc. press one from all sides." Here is the youthful Stevens as Thoreauvian naturalist: "This feeling of having exhausted the subject is in turn succeeded by the true and lasting source of country pleasure: the growth of small, specific observation." As Whitmanian camerado: "My feelings to-night vent in this phrase alone: Salut au Monde!" As Emersonian transparent eyeball in Central Park rather than on the Boston Common:

> I hurried through the Mall or Grand Alley or whatever it is; went down those mighty stairs to the fountain; followed a path around the lake, and came to a tower surrounded with a sort of parapet. The park was deserted yet I felt royal in my empty palace. A dozen or more stars were shining. Leaving the tower and parapets I wandered about in a maze of paths some of which led to an invisible cave. By this time it was dark and I stumbled about over little bridges that creaked under my step, up hills, and through trees. An owl hooted. I stopped and suddenly felt the mysterious spirit of nature – the very mysterious spirit, one I thought never to have met with again. I breathed in the air and shook off the lethargy that has controlled me for so long a time. But my Ariel-owl stopped hooting + the spirit slipped away and left me looking with amusement at the extremely unmysterious and not at all spiritual hotels and apartment houses that were lined up like elegant factories on the West side of the Park.

Of course, there is something much more studied and archly gothic about Stevens' account than Emerson's: the king in his empty palace with its tower and parapets, the fountain and lake, the maze of paths and invisible cave, the creaking bridge and hooting winged messenger – all suggest a Poe romance more than a Transcendental gestalt. The climax is a visitation from "the mysterious spirit of nature," which he has met before but "thought never to have met with again." The perfect infinitive "to have met" instead of the more expected "to meet" makes the brief revelation sound already more past than present. And where Emerson's experience generates the ensuing manifesto *Nature*, Stevens' seems a last, waning flicker, almost immediately dissipated by the metropolitan night-glare: the "hotels and apartment houses that were lined up like elegant factories on the West side of the Park." The deflation of the afflatus leaves Stevens with a defensive and self-protective sense of horrified "amusement" that is closer to Frost than it is to Emerson. The journal entry for the New Year which announced the twentieth century reads like an apocalypse: "Horrid din – The Hour strikes – like roar of heavy express – or rolling of great mill – Chimes incoherent, Voices – Mass of sound – like strong wind through telegraph wire...I was trying to say a prayer but could not."[1]

Stevens was later to claim that the "loss of faith is growth," and by the time he reached manhood he had "grown into" disillusionment about metaphysical absolutes: "philosophy, which ought to be pure intellect, has seldom, *if ever*, been so among moderns. We color our language, and Truth being white, becomes blotched in transmission."[2] The "modern" intellect was not pure enough to admit of colorless, immaculate Mind, and the dubious Truth of nature was indecipherably white as well, whether in the monstrous form of Moby-Dick or in the white blur Frost thought he saw once at the bottom of a well. But where Frost's pursuit of subjects kept him asking the unanswered questions ("What was that whiteness? / Truth? A pebble of quartz?"), Stevens, like George Santayana, whom he knew at Harvard, or like Walter Pater, turned to the colors of art as a positive substitute for the blank white of Platonism and naturalism. Aesthetics overtook epistemology: for better or for worse, "we color our language," and that highly colored language began to appear in little magazines some fifteen years before the poems were gathered into *Harmonium* in 1923.

Amid the contrasting colors – the exotic imagery, the rapid shifts of tone and perspective, the playful wit and verbal hijinks – which set the fact of discord against the idea of harmony, "The Snow Man" states early in the volume the dilemma of whiteness: the blank mind confronting and mirroring the colorless void outside. "One must have a mind of winter," the poet says, to acquiesce in a winter world where the observer "nothing himself, beholds / Nothing that is not there and the nothing that is." Toward the end of the volume, "The Man Whose Pharynx Was Bad" finds himself speechless and indifferent in the face of the indifference of the seasonal round and would even prefer the persistence to a final winter death as a quasi-absolute purer than the "malady of the quotidian."

But most of *Harmonium* shows Stevens refusing to persist to the zero point in mind or nature. "Disillusionment of Ten O'Clock"[3] exemplifies Stevens' early manner, with its swaggering and sharp ironic wit:

> The houses are haunted
> By white night-gowns.
> None are green,
> Or purple with green rings,
> Or green with yellow rings,
> Or yellow with blue rings.
> None of them are strange,
> With socks of lace
> And beaded ceintures.
> People are not going
> To dream of baboons and periwinkles.
> Only, here and there, an old sailor,
> Drunk and asleep in his boots,
> Catches tigers
> In red weather.

It is Stevens' droll version of Thoreau's "The mass of men lead lives of quiet desperation." "People" (the collective noun comes two-thirds of the way through the poem) are dehumanized and disembodied into white night-gowns, auto-ghosts with nothing to dream about; their houses are haunted by their own vacuity at bedtime. But a few isolated individuals stand out against such monotonous (one-toned, no-toned) anonymity. The poet's imagination elaborates upon the possibilities of color, each pattern metamorphosing into the next, and finds his unlikely avatar in the old salt, an unwilling house-dweller, ranging a fantastic dreamscape of baboons and periwinkles and tigers in red weather.

But these are dreams and fantasies. Their high spirits mask and compensate not just for the people's lack of illusion but for the poet's disillusionment. Is the schism between mind and world so final that the only way of being in the world is as a snow man in a snow world? Can consciousness never enter its world and find meaning there, find its own meaning through correspondence with, through participation in, something outside itself? A response comes in the poem placed after "Disillusionment of Ten O'Clock" in *Harmonium*. "Sunday Morning"[4] is the major poem of the volume, in the view of many readers Stevens' finest poem, and in the view of Yvor Winters the best poem in English in this century. The first of Stevens' meditative poems in which the mind plays on objective reality, seeking entry and confirmation, "Sunday Morning" begins by describing the vivid colors and pungent smells of a Matisse-like scene and concludes with an ecstatic, if stoic, naturalism.

The poem arrives at its conclusion through the device of an argumentative dialogue between the reflective speaker and a lady still yearning for the religious belief she has come to reject, but it is really a monologue between aspects of the poet's mind as he ponders the terms on which life in the mortal round is possible without despair. In place of the jagged lines and extravagances of "Disillusionment of Ten O'Clock" is sonorous and opulent blank verse worthy of comparison with Milton and Keats:

> Death is the mother of beauty; hence from her,
> Alone, shall come fulfillment to our dreams
> And our desires. Although she strews the leaves
> Of sure obliteration on our paths,
> The path sick sorrow took, the many paths
> Where triumph rang its brassy phrase, or love
> Whispered a little out of tenderness,
> She makes the willow shiver in the sun
> For maidens who were wont to sit and gaze
> Upon the grass, relinquished to their feet.
> She causes boys to pile new plums and pears
> On disregarded plate. The maidens taste
> And stray impassioned in the littering leaves.

The speaker shares the lady's feeling that without religion "we live in an old chaos of the sun, / Or old dependency of day and night, / Or island solitude, unsponsored, free." However, the convolutions of their dialogue bring him to recognize in this frightening and disillusioning freedom a new possibility and a new responsibility: after the death of God, "divinity must live within" ourselves or nowhere. Not, of course, that we can escape mortality, but rather that we can commit ourselves to the round so passionately that our passions mirror its seasons, and vice versa, so unreservedly that we recover on the other side of disillusioned self-consciousness a return to primitive celebration:

> Supple and turbulent, a ring of men
> Shall chant in orgy on a summer morn
> Their boisterous devotion to the sun,
> Not as a god, but as a god might be,
> Naked among them, like a savage source.
> Their chant shall be a chant of paradise....

Paradise regained not by divine intervention but by the transformative power of the human imagination over a fallen world; for the men enter their world in voicing their chant to the sun and "know well the heavenly fellowship / Of men that perish and of summer morn." The resonant cadences and flawless phrasing of the famous last lines convey the exquisitely intensified perception of natural beauty which comes through a resistance to its transience:

> Deer walk upon our mountains, and the quail
> Whistle about us their spontaneous cries;
> Sweet berries ripen in the wilderness;
> And, in the isolation of the sky,
> At evening, casual flocks of pigeons make
> Ambiguous undulations as they sink,
> Downward to darkness, on extended wings.

Some readers have complained that the poem is more rhetorical than argumentative, but this is precisely the point; the problem laid out in the poem is not resolved at the level of argument but at the level of language, and the rhetoric is superbly effective. The disappearance of the speaker's self-reference convinces us for a moment that he is as unconsciously present in the scene as the deer and the quail. But, of course, his words can never be spontaneous like their cries, and the greater achievement of these lines is to convince us of a deeper human experience: the vigilant yet acquiescing attendance of consciousness upon the beauty of the moment despite a fateful awareness that will never afflict the quail or pigeon. "And shall the earth / Seem all of paradise that we shall know?" the speaker asks in mid-poem. By the end, he can answer yes with a feeling of possession as well as dispossession.

It is a long way in American Protestantism from Edward Taylor's *Preparatory Meditations*, written in anticipation of the eucharistic service on Sabbath morning, to Stevens' "Sunday Morning." Between Taylor's Christian incarnationalism and Stevens' secular naturalism stands Emerson's naturalistic Transcendentalism. "Homunculus et La Belle Etoile"[5] from *Harmonium* symbolizes in the evening star the Emersonian premise of a correspondence between spirit and nature and self, and concludes of its radiance:

> It is a good light, then, for those
> That know the ultimate Plato
> Tranquillizing with this jewel [the star]
> The torments of confusion.

In "Sunday Morning" and repeatedly throughout his life, Stevens sought to be unillusioned but not disillusioned so that, without Christian belief or Transcendental mysticism, he experienced moments of participation and transcendence. "The Latest Freed Man"[6] describes "how he was free...how his freedom came" as an Emersonian concentricity of self and nature:

> It was everything being more real, himself
> At the centre of reality, seeing it.
> It was everything bulging and blazing and big in itself,
> The blue of the rug, the portrait of Vidal,
> *Qui fait fi des joliesses banales*, the chairs.

In expansive moments, Stevens could sound like Whitman: "The great poems of heaven and hell have been written and the great poem of the earth remains to be written."[7] And in fact, his conception of his life's oeuvre aimed at something of the large congruity of *Leaves of Grass*. The titles make the point: *Harmonium, Ideas of Order, Parts of a World*. At the beginning of his career, he thought of calling *Harmonium The Grand Poem: Preliminary Minutiae*, and at the end he only reluctantly gave up his intention to call the *Collected Poems The Whole of Harmonium*. At the same time, Stevens was not writing an organically grounded poem like *Leaves of Grass*. Even the titles which allude to nature's round tend to abstraction.[8]

The problem had been momentarily overcome in "Sunday Morning" – hence this poem's special place in Stevens' early work – but had persisted. And it was a problem in epistemology: without God or the Oversoul, how could mind and nature come into relation? What might be the third, mediating, subsuming term? If "divinity must live within" the self as a mental conception, how can the self find freedom "at the centre of reality"? How can the mind's abstraction come to terms with nature's particulars? Stevens' awareness that there was much wish fulfillment in his resort to the oracular tone expressed itself in a calculated and ironic bathos.

In "The Latest Freed Man," the fussy French phrase adds to the reduction of the Whitmanian line "Everything bulging and blazing and big in itself" to the quotidian, if not banal, particulars of the ring, the portrait, the chairs. Just at the point when Stevens might say, with Williams, "No ideas but in things," his tone gives away the mind's uneasy hesitation about material objects. Stevens might even have had Dr. Williams in mind when he described the Freed Man.

In *Harmonium*, "The Comedian as the Letter C" serves as the counterpoint to "Sunday Morning"; Stevens' rueful persona, Crispin, sets out from a "World without Imagination" to discover a world with it, only to encounter instead the ironies inherent in his initial supposition: "Nota: man is the intelligence of his soil, / The sovereign ghost." The enjambment underscores the bathos: without Christian incarnation or the metaphysical correspondences of the "ultimate Plato," it is easy to construe human intelligence as disembodied ghost rather than indwelling spirit.

What was the alternative to being an ox, which lacks language, or a disembodied Platonist, when language fails? The term between the material fact and the mental abstraction is language: the sensuous abstractions and fictions of the verbal imagination. A poem written after "The Comedian as the Letter C" in 1922 argues for this third term with a brio calculated to sweep away moral and religious objections. Like the pseudo-dialogue in "Sunday Morning," this dramatic monologue is really an interior monologue. The lady of "Sunday Morning," melancholy and unable to live in the sensuality of the moment, has stiffened into "A High-toned Old Christian Woman"[9] and is here less interlocutor than adversary. Unlike her predecessor, she is not allowed a presence or voice and remains only dismissively implied by the opening declaration: "Poetry is the supreme fiction, madame." The poet speaker attempts to cajole her by reaching beyond their differences to a shared purpose. "We agree in principle," he says: like her "moral law," hymned from the heaven-pointing cathedrals, his "opposing law," chanted from the horizontal peristyle of his secular temple, also seeks to rise above "the malady of the quotidian," but he does so not by purging but by indulging human sensuality so as to cast its pleasures into imaginative fictions:

> Allow,
> Therefore, that in the planetary scene
> Your disaffected flagellants, well-stuffed,
> Smacking their muzzy bellies in parade,
> Proud of such novelties of the sublime,
> Such tink and tank and tunk-a-tunk-tunk,
> May, merely may, madame, whip from themselves
> A jovial hullabaloo among the spheres.

> This will make widows wince. But fictive things
> Wink as they will. Wink most when widows wince.

The bravado of these lines is again threatened by bathos; the declension from "novelties of the sublime" to "tink and tank and tunk-a-tunk-tunk" almost seems to substantiate Frost's charge of bric-a-brac. But the bravado persists past the bathos to insist that sensual fictions can function as alternatives to truth. To complaints about the absurdity of believing in a fiction, Stevens had a quick reply:

> If there is instinctive in us a will to believe, or if there is a will to believe, whether or not it is instinctive, it seems to me that we can suspend disbelief with reference to a fiction as easily as we can suspend it with reference to anything else. There are fictions that are extensions of reality.[10]

Or again: "The final belief is to believe in a fiction, which you know to be a fiction, there being nothing else. The exquisite truth is to know that it is a fiction and that you believe it willingly."[11]

If the rational intellect "among moderns" was not pure enough for Truth, then the imagination could strive for purity in the exquisite truth of its aesthetic fictions. To one close correspondent he wrote:

> I was on the point of saying that I did not agree with the opinion that my verse is decorative, when I remembered that when HARMONIUM was in the making there was a time when I liked the idea of images and images alone, or images and the music of verse together. I then believed in *pure poetry*, as it was called.
>
> I still have a distinct liking for that sort of thing.[12]

For pure poetry "life is an essential part of literature," and not the reverse. Words hold sway over things; from quotidian discourse they inescapably carry a referentiality to objects and realities outside of consciousness and of language, but that referentiality is only a point of departure for the verbal imagination. Words have connotations as well as denotations; they have sound and rhythm that does not, for the most part, derive from their denotations. Morever, words operate not in isolation but in combination and relation. Words in combination modify and extend and overlay one another, complicate their implications, echo sounds and rhythms. Such interaction and interrelationship create textures of sound and association which do not totally derive from or inhere in the things being described – even in a verbal construct which sets out to describe. The poet's description incorporates verbal elements into sensory and evocative images that take on their own intrinsic character and integrity, independent of the objects to which some of the words in some sense refer and completely dependent on the combination of constitutive verbal elements themselves. The fact that Stevens' attitude anticipates post-structuralism and deconstructive criticism indicates the derivation of contemporary theory from the premises of Modernism.

In Stevens' view, the poet's primary commitment is to the alternate "life" of words in combination. It is the potentialities in such linkages which extend and translate sensed objects into the fictive linguistic world that Stevens came to call the *"mundo* of the imagination." Symbolisme gravitated to the notion of *poésie pure*, especially the Symbolisme of Mallarmé and Valéry. Frost derided *poésie pure* as words "without content," but Eliot grasped the issue more sympathetically and subtly. In "From Poe to Valéry" (1948) he reviewed the evolution of Symbolisme out of Poe's theory and pinpointed the distinctive epistemological and linguistic shift which Symboliste poetics (the pun is apt) constituted in the extreme example of Valéry:

> While the element of *la poésie pure* is necessary to make a poem a poem, no poem can consist of *la poésie pure* solely. But what has happened in the case of Valéry is a change of attitude toward the subject matter. We must be careful to avoid saying that the subject matter becomes "less important." It has rather a different importance: it is important as *means*: the *end* is the poem. The subject exists for the poem, not the poem for the subject. A poem may employ several subjects, combining them in a particular way; and it may be meaningless to ask "What is the subject of the poem?" From the union of several subjects there appears, not another subject, but the poem.[13]

Since poetry consists of words, the more poetry inclines away from descriptive referentiality toward autotelic self-referentiality and hypostasized self-subsistence, the more purely evocative the language.

Temperamentally Eliot was deeply drawn to this position, and his early poetry is strongly Symboliste. But his career traces out his growing resistance to, and finally his rejection of, Symbolisme. As for Stevens, he did not carry the Symboliste inclination as far as Mallarmé or Valéry, and repeatedly made himself return to the inconvertibility of things. But never for long, and increasingly, over his career, as a point of departure for the greater purity of the *mundo*. Eliot's Symbolistes were Baudelaire and Laforgue and Corbière; Stevens' were Valéry and Mallarmé. And with them Stevens assumed the hermeticism of "language as the material of poetry not its mere medium or instrument": "A poet's words are of things that do not exist without the words"; "Poetry is a revelation in words by means of the words"; "Poetry is the subject of the poem."[14]

As Stevens acknowledged in a letter a little earlier, many of the poems in *Harmonium* aim for the kind of purity which ideally would register images in the sounds of words as musical notes in a tonal composition: a synthesis of Mallarmé and Debussy. "The Load of Sugar Cane"[15] is such an exercise:

The going of the glade-boat
Is like water flowing;

Like water flowing
Through the green saw-grass,
Under the rainbows;

Under the rainbows
That are like birds,
Turning, bedizened,

> While the wind still whistles
> As killdeer do,
>
> When they rise
> At the red turban
> Of the boatman.

The poem is all images exfoliating and branching out as a succession of similes. They make for a fantasy of Florida, but as Stevens put it in "Add This to Rhetoric"[16]: "it is posed and it is posed. / But in nature it merely grows"; "Add this. It is to add." The poem begins with the image of a glade-boat, presumably loaded with the sugar cane mentioned in the title, and the short lines, spacing out the phrasal units of the long, seemingly meandering sentence, lead from simile to simile, each generating the next until the last returns to the boat, or rather to the boatman. The progression has not been linear, leading from one place to another, but circular for self-closure.

"Domination of Black," written in 1916, the year after the composition of "Sunday Morning," is a more widely known and more complex example of Stevens' *poésie pure*.[17]

> At night, by the fire,
> The colors of the bushes
> And of the fallen leaves,
> Repeating themselves,
> Turned in the room,
> Like the leaves themselves
> Turning in the wind.
> Yes: but the color of the heavy hemlocks
> Came striding.
> And I remembered the cry of the peacocks.
>
> The colors of their tails
> Were like the leaves themselves
> Turning in the wind,
> In the twilight wind.
> They swept over the room,
> Just as they flew from the boughs of the hemlocks
> Down to the ground.
> I heard them cry – the peacocks.
> Was it a cry against the twilight
> Or against the leaves themselves
> Turning in the wind,
> Turning as the flames
> Turned in the fire,
> Turning as the tails of the peacocks
> Turned in the loud fire,
> Loud as the hemlocks
> Full of the cry of the peacocks?
> Or was it a cry against the hemlocks?
>
> Out of the window,
> I saw how the planets gathered

Like the leaves themselves
Turning in the wind.
I saw how the night came,
Came striding like the color of the heavy hemlocks
I felt afraid.
And I remembered the cry of the peacocks.

As in "The Load of Sugar Cane," *poésie pure* is linked with *vers libre*, in contrast to the blank verse of "Sunday Morning." The poem takes off from night, fire, and leaves, "repeating themselves." But "repeating" is replaced by "turned" and "turning," because the irregular verses enact not simple reiteration but metamorphosis (there are nine repetitions of "turn" in the poem). In fact, as the words and phrases of the poem are repeated, they turn into one another, become figures of speech for one another. The repetition of "like" and "as" throughout the poem – four times each – insists on the ubiquity of the simile's associative and transformative powers. The cumulative indirections of the similes gather the repeated elements of fire, leaves, wind, hemlocks, and peacocks into a revolving pattern that opens out in the last verse paragraph into a trope for the turning of the planets in the night sky.

The ending of "Domination of Black" is apocalyptic, and yet a comparison of Stevens' lines with the concluding lines of Frost's apocalyptic "Once by the Pacific" sums up the differences in the epistemology and so the quality of figuration in the two poets:

You could not tell, and yet it looked as if
The shore was lucky in being backed by cliff,
The cliff in being backed by continent;
It looked as if a night of dark intent
Was coming, and not only a night, an age.
Someone had better be prepared for rage.
There would be more than ocean-water broken
Before God's last *Put out the Light* was spoken.[18]

The principal thrust of Frost's poem is cosmological; of Stevens', psychological. Frost's highly figurative language is nonetheless concerned with the possibility of the end of the world; those "as if's" are mental probes into questions of physics and metaphysics. Stevens' poem implodes the apocalypse into an internal state: the consuming of the mind by a terror which, though stated flatly and almost intrusively in the penultimate line "I felt afraid," has already been successfully conveyed before that "impure" declaration and which only obliquely suggests its cosmological implications.

Poésie pure, then, represents a Platonist gnostic's sensuality. Stevens sounds more like Emerson than like Williams or Frost when he says: "What we see in the mind is as real to us as what we see by the eye." But Emerson resisted his gnostic idealism by a commitment to nature and so to language as the revelation of spirit; he made the poet a sayer because he was antecedently a seer. But Stevens sees the mind and nature as more radically split. Consequently, though "the tongue says less than the mind thinks," "the eye sees less than the tongue says"; in fact, "the tongue is an eye."[19] In the early experiment of "Thirteen Ways of Looking at a Blackbird," the otherwise unengaging datum of a blackbird is reenvisioned into a series of images by the mind's and tongue's eye. The number thirteen is not symbolic but conspicuously arbitrary; the process of metamorphosis could proceed indefinitely.

In "Imagination as Value" Stevens claims that "the Platonic resolution of diversity appears" in the recognition that "the world is no longer an extraneous object, full of other extraneous objects, but an image" and then remarks: "In the last analysis, it is with this image of the world that we are vitally concerned."[20] Or rather with an ongoing series of images, as Stevens proceeds to say, because his rejection of Platonic metaphysics keeps this Platonic resolution from subsuming diversity finally into unity, from subsuming images into an image of unity. One of the defining characteristics even of the supreme fiction is that "It Must Change." "Sea Surface Full of Clouds" is an apt illustration. Its five sections all locate themselves precisely in the same first line "in that November off Tehauntepec," and each section mentions the same scenic features: not just sea and clouds, but night, deck, chocolate, umbrellas, petals, blooms, and so on. But each section then proceeds to describe the scene and its features differently, so that the poem becomes a phantasmagoric kaleidoscope which, like the blackbird poem, need never reach conclusion. Here, for example, is a representative slicing through the poem: the fourth tercet from each of the parallel sections:

> Who, then, evolved the sea-blooms from the clouds
> Diffusing balm in that Pacific calm?
> C'était mon enfant, mon bijou, mon âme.
>
> .   .   .   .
>
> Who saw the mortal massives of the blooms
> Of water moving on the water-floor?
> C'était mon frère, du ciel, ma vie, mon or.
>
> .   .   .   .
>
> Of the milk within the saltiest spurge, heard, then,
> The sea unfolding in the sunken clouds?
> Oh! C'était mon extase et mon amour.
>
> .   .   .   .
>
> Like blooms? Like damasks that were shaken off
> From the loosed girdles in the spangling must.
> C'était ma foi, la nonchalance divine.
>
> .   .   .   .
>
> And the sea as turquoise-turbaned Sambo, neat
> At tossing saucers – cloudy-conjuring sea?
> C'était mon esprit bâtard, l'ignominie.[21]

It is as though Shelley's cloud-and-seascapes devolved to the flamboyant mannerisms of Oscar Wilde or the aestheticism of Walter Pater, who in the conclusion to The Renaissance signaled the disintegration of Romanticism by declaring that we know only our impressions, dreaming our private and separate dreams of the world. In Stevens there is no vision of life as a dome of many-colored glass; instead, in "Esthetique du Mal," "Life is a bitter aspic. We are not / At the centre of a diamond."[22]

The French phrases and the Baudelairean allusion of "Esthetique du Mal" again point to Stevens' indebtedness to French, particularly to Symboliste, poetry and poetics. The French influence on Stevens was immediately recognized by contemporaries, though he tried to play it down even when friends pressed the point. To Hi Simons he admitted to reading "something, more or less," of Baudelaire, Verlaine, Laforgue, Mallarmé, and Valéry, but added, "if I have picked up anything from them, it has been unconsciously." He gave a similarly evasive answer regarding Valéry, and offered no help to Charles Henri Ford with his piece on "Verlaine in Hartford" or to Hi Simons with his essay "Wallace Stevens and Mallarmé."[23] Stevens was understandably touchy about compromising his originality and individuality by admitting predecessors (we shall see Pound's and Williams' early ambivalence about Whitman), and he is right to claim his characteristic language and manner as his own. Nevertheless, readers have not needed Stevens' reticent acknowledgment that "it is always possible that where a man's attitude coincides with your own attitude, or accentuates your own attitude, you get a great deal from him without any effort" or remarks like "the great source of modern poetics is probably France" and "French and English constitute a single language" to feel the profound congruence between the underlying assumptions of Stevens and the Symbolistes.[24]

Poe, the acknowledged American predecessor of the Symbolistes, evolved his theory in reaction against Emersonian Transcendentalism. The scattered references to Poe in Stevens' letters show that he read Poe's work, including the essays, early and appreciatively. In one early letter to his fiancée he views Poe (as Whitman did and Allen Tate would) as a kind of spiritual and moral barometer of the age: "Nowadays, when so many people no longer believe in supernatural things, they find a substitute in the stranger and more freakish phenomena of the mind – hallucinations, mysteries and the like. Hence the revival of Poe." Still, he hears in Poe's neuroses a "cry for life" which "is not to be found in railroading to an office and then railroading back," as Stevens felt he was doing. In the void that yawns between a dead religious ideal and a deadening economic reality, Stevens sympathizes with Poe's escape into an imaginary *mundo*: "it is obviously more exciting to be Poe than to be a lesser 'esquire'."[25]

Stevens' more refined taste restrained him from the melodrama and "tintinabulation" of Poe (though Stevens actually used Poe's coinage in one poem), but much of early Stevens depends, like Poe's verse, on rich effects of sound and rhythm, of rhyme and repetition, as in the last lines of "The Apostrophe to Vincentine":

Monotonous earth I saw become
Illimitable spheres of you,
And that white animal, so lean,
Turned Vincentine,
Turned heavenly Vincentine,
And that white animal, so lean,
Turned heavenly, heavenly Vincentine.[26]

Or in these last lines from "Floral Decorations for Bananas":

> And deck the bananas in leaves
> Plucked from the Carib trees,
> Fibrous and dangling down,
> Oozing cantankerous gum
> Out of their purple maws,
> Darting out of their purple craws
> Their musky and tingling tongues.[27]

The point is not that these are remarkable or memorable lines or that Poe was a direct influence on Stevens, but rather that the tendency toward *poésie pure* from Poe to Mallarmé to Stevens has made for a density of syllabic sound, a hallucinatory repetitiveness of syllable and word and rhythm which is part of what Stevens called "the essential gaudiness of poetry" – at least of that poetry whose "words are of things that do not exist without the words."[28] It is true that Stevens' verse tends to become less chiming and rhyming as it became more meditative after *Harmonium*, but these same verbal characteristics, proceeding from an imaginative inclination he shared with Poe and the Symbolistes, persist in lines and passages to the end. As he put it in "Angel Surrounded by Paysans," the sounds "Rise liquidly in liquid lingerings, / Like watery words awash; like meanings said / By repetitions of half-meanings."[29]

The third section of a poem with the Poe-like title "The Owl in the Sarcophagus" illustrates these verbal characteristics in the later poetry and demonstrates Stevens' uncanny ability to evoke a sense of significant presence that exists only in the spell of the rhetoric:

> There he saw well the foldings in the height
> Of sleep, the whiteness folded into less,
> Like many robings, as moving masses are,
>
> As a moving mountain is, moving through day
> And night, colored from distances, central
> Where luminous agitations come to rest,
>
> In an ever-changing, calmest unity,
> The unique composure, harshest streakings joined
> In a vanishing-vanished violet that wraps round
>
> The giant body the meanings of its folds,
> The weaving and the crinklings and the vex,
> As on water on an afternoon in the wind
>
> After the wind has passed. Sleep realized
> Was the whitness that is the ultimate intellect,
> A diamond jubilance beyond the fire,
>
> That gives its power to the wild-ringed eye.
> Then he breathed deeply the deep atmosphere
> Of sleep, the accomplished, the fulfilling air.[30]

The section is "about" the hero's falling into deep sleep – a sleep, however, which is not oblivion but absorption into that state of "ultimate intellect" where change and rest are reconciled. The metaphorical imagery conjures that internal state as the words mark and erase the line between palpability and impalpability, between unintelligibility and intelligibility. The passage is at once perfectly lucid and perfectly opaque.

The long course of Stevens' career, therefore, charts his hesitation between an inclination toward *poésie pure* and an inclination, as in "Sunday Morning," toward the "poem of the earth." Both inclinations represented two sides of a dilemma. On the one hand, spiritless naturalism devolves into a dispirited materialism – the malady of the quotidian, the white world of the snow man. On the other hand, *poésie pure* expresses itself first in the sensuous colors of the imagination – those nightgowns of purple with green rings, those exotic shimmers on the sea surface full of clouds – but its final tendency, as the preceding passage shows, is to merge those colors into the pure whiteness of the "ultimate intellect" – if not Platonic Mind, then at least the abstracted mind of the dreamer lost to the world. Stevens found himself both a materialist *manqué* and a Platonist *manqué*.

A late letter conceded the poet's divided commitments: "Sometimes I believe most in the imagination for a long time and then, without reasoning about it, turn to reality and believe in that and that alone. But both of these things project themselves endlessly and I want them to do just that."[31] The concession, of course, also made that division the stimulus of the poet's ongoing creativity. At the same time, Stevens' work traces out over the years his growing determination to demonstrate that between the poles of imagination and reality a "universal interdependence exists" which makes them "equal and inseparable."[32]

II

After the publication of *Harmonium* in 1923, there were hardly any poems until the early 1930s. By then Stevens was financially secure as a senior executive of the Hartford Accident and Indemnity Company, free to pursue in the privacy of his mind the endless oscillations between imagination and reality. The poems and the essays, collected in *The Necessary Angel* (1951), are variations on this single theme.

However, the worldwide economic and political crisis of the Depression years sharpened the charges of social irresponsibility against Stevens' poetry just at the point when he was returning to it. Marxists and other leftist critics accused him of bourgeois elitism and escapism; moralists like Winters and Frost spoke of Paterian hedonism and decorative bric-a-brac. One tactical response of Stevens was to concede the point with dismissive but defensive hauteur: "The poetic process is psychologically an escapist process. The chatter about escapism is, to my way of thinking, merely common cant."[33] Stevens' more direct response to the charge of irrelevance came in an exposition of his aesthetic, laid out in poems short and long – "The Idea of Order at Key West" (1934), "The Man with the Blue Guitar" (1937), "Poetry

Is a Destructive Force" (1938), "The Poems of Our Climate" (1938), "Of Modern Poetry" (1940), "Mrs. Alfred Uruguay" (1940), *Notes Toward a Supreme Fiction* (1942), "Esthetique du Mal" (1944) – and in the theoretical essays he began to write in the early 1940s.

In "The Idea of Order at Key West"[34] the poet listens as the voice of a girl singing on the beach transforms "the meaningless plungings of water and the wind" into the beautifully mastered cadences of human speech. As "the single artificer of the world / In which she sang," she is self-absorbed artist, and yet her song is not merely hermetic. Sea and song are, as always, disjunct, yet song affects, or seems to affect, the external circumstances from which and within which the song was abstracted. There was no material change, yet in the ear and mind (or, as he puts it in "Of Modern Poetry," "in the delicatest ear of the mind") of the singer and her audience the meaningless sea assumed "whatever self it had," in fact "became the self / That was her song." "Self" means "identity" here, but Stevens' use of that personifying word in relation to both the sea and the song indicates that it was in art that the subject – first the singer but then, by extension, the hearer – and the object found whatever identity they came to have.

Nor did the effect entirely die with the conclusion of the singing. The poet asks his companion, the aesthetician Ramon Fernandez, why it is that

> The lights in the fishing boats at anchor there,
> As the night descended, tilting in the air,
> Mastered the night and portioned out the sea,
> Fixing emblazoned zones and fiery poles,
> Arranging, deepening, enchanting night.

The active verbs and participles in these famous lines suggest the "blessed rage for order" which impels the human imagination to make a *mundo* as an alternative world. "Rage" is not too strong a word for the passion required to match and overmatch the disorder of nature. Creativity is a "destructive force" yet is "blessed" because its power seems to redound from *mundo* back to world. Metamorphosis occurs not through grace or miracle, but through a psychological effect on the sensibility of the artist and the audience. The world of consciousness is the *mundo*. While in the *mundo*, the perceiver can see the material world for a time as more ordered, or at least more susceptible to order. Does the power of human consciousness, then, extend from *mundo* to world? If "there never was a world for her [the singer] / Except the one she sang and, singing, made," could her *mundo* remake the world? Stevens makes no Shelleyan or Marxist claim for the poet as legislator of humankind or for poetry as a revolutionary force for social change, but he does claim the centrality of the poet to the individual and the communal life of the culture: the poet not as prophet but as enchanter or magician. And in the end, Stevens would argue, this master of illusion is less "sleight-of-hand man" or "connoisseur of chaos"[35] than hero of consciousness.

The artist in "The Idea of Order at Key West" is unusual in being female, and even here she is finally assimilated into the male perspective of the speaker and his companion, "pale Ramon." More characteristically, the women in Stevens' poems serve as foils (as in "Sunday Morning") or contrasts (as in "A High-toned Old Christian Woman") or other versions of anima-muse (as in "The Apostrophe to Vincentine" and "To the One of Fictive Music") to the male poet. In fact, like Poe's, Stevens' poems about women are almost all variations on his relations to the anima. Poe called her" "the One in Paradise"; Stevens, the "One of Fictive Music," acknowledging her various functions for the male poet as "Sister and mother and diviner love."[36] But she was always the object – or subject – of male musing. Wrote Stevens in "The Figure of the Youth as Virile Poet," unmindful of the masculinism of the remark, "the centuries have a way of being male,"[37] and in the later volumes of Stevens career – *Parts of a World* (1942), *Transport to Summer* (1947), *The Auroras of Autumn* (1950), and *The Rock* section of *Collected Poems* (1954) – the hero appears with increasing frequency as the protagonist, assuming his traditional role as archetypal symbol of consciousness in its quest for identity, integration, apotheosis: for "whatever self it had."

"Mrs. Alfred Uruguay" (1940)[38] casts the hero and the lady with the fancy foreign name as polar opposites. She is attired in rich velvet; he is "dressed poorly." She struggles along in the moonlight beloved of Romantics; he clatters by on horseback, seeking the sun's sensuous warmth and intense clarity. The aging lady's neurotic search to arrive at the real in herself traps her in denial of body and self; the "youth, a lover with phosphorescent hair," all will and energy, presses toward "the ultimate elegance: the imagined land." "Her no and no made yes impossible"; he is the "figure of capable imagination," his goal encompassed in his mind. The repetition of the word "capable" four times in the two stanzas describing the hero emphasizes his power to imagine and so attain paradise.

From poem to poem the archetype assumes various names and forms – knight, giant, central man, major man, angel, hero, even antihero – but he is always symbol, both intimation and manifestation, of the self. As youth he is reborn consciousness; as sage he is the summation and culmination of consciousness; as lover he seeks his completion through the anima; as god he rises to a dimension beyond time and space, where he often appears with her in a hierogamy. As a conception of consciousness he is one and diverse, impersonal and personal, unchanging and ever-changing, central and whole in himself but eccentric and partial in individuals, who are nonetheless eccentric parts of the whole.

And as poet he composes the parts into, or toward, the central poem, the supreme fiction. Two essays of these years invoke the poet as hero in their titles: "The Noble Rider and the Sound of Words" and "The Figure of the Youth as Virile Poet." Shortly before the publication of *Parts of a World* (1941), in which "Mrs. Alfred Uruguay" appeared, Stevens wrote to a friend about his gravitation to the center:

> I began to feel that I was on the edge: that I wanted to get to the center: that I
> was isolated, and that I wanted to share the common life. . . . People say that I

live in a world of my own: that sort of thing. Instead of seeking therefore for a "relentless contact," I have been interested in what might be described as an attempt to achieve the normal, the central. So stated, this puts the thing out of all proportion in respect to its relation to the context of life. Of course, I don't agree with the people who say that I live in a world of my own; I think that I am perfectly normal, but I see that there is a center.[39]

Stevens' way of sharing the common life, therefore, was not physical but psychological, not through "relentless contact" with the world around him but through entrance into and participation in the world of archetypes. "I say it," Stevens tells his friend in the letter, "because it may be useful to you in understanding some of the later things." Many of the long and longish poems of the 1940s and 1950s are efforts, necessarily less than final, to comprehend and exemplify the major man, to reach and communicate the central self.

Inescapably the poems extended themselves to accommodate the elusiveness and convolutions of the undertaking, and citation from these poems requires long passages to give any sense of their effect or meaning. The following lines from *Notes Toward a Supreme Fiction* (1942) are the last and summary poem of the first section, "It Must Be Abstract":

> The major abstraction is the idea of man
> And major man is its exponent, abler
> In the abstract than in his singular,
>
> More fecund as principle than particle,
> Happy fecundity, flor-abundant force,
> In being more than an exception, part,
>
> Though an heroic part, of the commonal.
> The major abstraction is the commonal,
> The inanimate, difficult visage. Who is it?
>
> What rabbi, grown furious with human wish,
> What chieftain, walking by himself, crying
> Most miserable, most victorious,
>
> Does not see these separate figures one by one,
> And yet see only one, in his old coat,
> His slouching pantaloons, beyond the town,
>
> Looking for what was, where it used to be?
> Cloudless the morning. It is he. The man
> In that old coat, those sagging pantaloons,
>
> It is of him, ephebe, to make, to confect
> The final elegance, not to console
> Nor sanctify, but plainly to propound.[40]

Here the searching self is a clown – not, however, the pathetic, ironic Pierrot of Laforgue or the back-alley waif of Hart Crane's "Chaplinesque" or even Stevens' "Man on the Dump" but, rather, the disheveled "figure of capable imagination" from "Mrs. Alfred Uruguay" at the end of his gallop about to propound the "imagined land" in its "final elegance." As mediator and expositor, the speaker instructs the fledgling "ephebe" that this hero in mufti is not priest or philosopher, offering neither grace nor consolation, but poet-psychopomp called instead ("it is of him") to compose (a melding of "confect," make with, and "propound" or "propose," put with) from shabby material circumstances his own *mundo* image.

And in assuming full proportions, for example at the conclusion of "A Primitive Like an Orb" (1948), that image sloughs off all extrinsic shabbiness and manifests his strength with a virtuoso's elegant suavity:

> It is a giant, always, that is evolved,
> To be in scale, unless virtue cuts him, snips
> Both size and solitude or thinks it does,
> As in a signed photograph on a mantlepiece.
> But the virtuoso never leaves his shape,
> Still on the horizon elongates his cuts,
> And still angelic and still plenteous,
> Imposes power by the power of his form.
>
> Here, then, is an abstraction given head,
> A giant on the horizon, given arms,
> A massive body and long legs, stretched out,
> A definition with an illustration, not
> Too exactly labelled, a large among the smalls
> Of it, a close, parental magnitude,
> At the centre on the horizon, concentrum, grave
> And prodigious person, patron of origins.
>
> That's it. The lover writes, the believer hears,
> The poet mumbles and the painter sees,
> Each one, his fated eccentricity,
> As a part, but part, but tenacious particle,
> Of the skeleton of the ether, the total
> Of letters, prophecies, perceptions, clods
> Of color, the giant of nothingness, each one
> And the giant ever changing, living in change.[41]

Here again, the verses, enjambed more than is typical of Stevens, move through a hypnotic series of paratactic phrases and clauses to evoke a presence which is meant to seem more compelling and vital and "real" than the objects of material "reality." Is the giant on the horizon, Stevens would ask, any less real for being a conception of the imagination, a matter, if one may so pun, of language? The pattern of repetition with variation suggests the giant's archetypal integrity persisting in and defined by change.

Informed by the indwelling giant, Stevens could at moments imagine, and so feel, a rare correspondence between subject and object. The ground of the sense of correspondence was not God, as Edward Taylor said, or the Oversoul, as Emerson said, but the imagination, but then Stevens echoes Poe's *Eureka* when he says, "God and the imagination are one."[42] "The Latest Freed Man" sees "everything being more real, himself / At the centre of reality, seeing it...everything bulging and blazing and big in itself." "A Rabbit as King of the Ghosts" psychologically occupies his world:

> To be, in the grass, in the peacefullest time,
> Without that monument of cat,
> The cat forgotten in the moon;
> And to feel that the light is a rabbit-light,
> In which everything is meant for you
> And nothing need be explained....
>
> .   .   .   .
>   The grass is full
> And full of yourself. The trees around are for you,
> The whole of the wideness of night is for you,
> A self that touches all edges, . . .
> You become a self that fills the four corners of night.[43]

Such bewitching passages in Stevens echo something of the Romantic synthesis: Keats's "negative capability"; Emerson's "transparent eyeball" and his conviction that if he were to nod to the vegetables they would nod back in reply; Whitman's cosmic identity suggested in the refrain of things "for you" and in the climactic expansiveness of the concluding line. But, as in "The Latest Freed Man," the sly wit of this poem again gives the poet away; the irony, which is at least as strong as the empathy, suggests that Stevens is only watching his mind play rabbit in the rabbit-light in a way that would have broken the spell for Keats or Whitman.

Even in the passage from "A Primitive Like an Orb," the patient construction of the giant's image, phrase by phrase, threatens to deconstruct itself in the penultimate line: "the giant of nothingness, each one." The phrase does not vitiate the image of the giant, but it qualifies it by reminding us that as an *image* it is a fiction. Quite literally a figure of speech; what the Puritans called and even Emerson would still have tended to call a trope so as to distinguish it from a type. A type was an inherently significant and signifying symbol, a manifestation of spiritual truth in material form, to be communicated verbally, whereas a trope was itself figurative language, a metaphorical invention. Coleridge made much the same point in contrasting the imagination with the fancy as faculties of perception. In *The Tenth Muse* I traced the distinction between types and tropes as it shaped American Puritan and Romantic poetry. The blurring of the distinction between these two modes of verbal representation – image as objective symbol extrinsic to language, and image as metaphor invented in language – undermined the authority of the Romantic imagination during the course of the nineteenth century. We find that slippage of signification even in Emerson, and though by Stevens' time type had almost completely disappeared into trope, Stevens' nineteenth-century heritage would not let him forget the distinction. Close to the end of *Notes Toward a Supreme Fiction* the poem turns abruptly on itself and seems to call into question its generating premise:

> But to impose is not
> To discover. To discover an order as of
> A season, to discover summer and know it,
>
> To discover winter and know it well, to find,
> Not to impose, not to have reasoned at all,
> Out of nothing to have come on major weather,
>
> It is possible, possible, possible. It must
> Be possible.[44]

In the lines that follow, "To find the real" elides into its appositive phrase "To be stripped of every fiction except one, / The fiction of an absolute." The verbal maneuver saves the nearly completed poem, but more important, it demonstrates that Stevens began with an acceptance of the difference between tropological fiction and typological truth and that the underlying mission of his poetic career was to try to find in the one a life-enhancing substitute for the other.

As an illustration of how continuous and single-minded these concerns are, consider this passage to his fiancée in 1909 as the germ of "The Noble Rider and the Sound of Words" thirty years later:

> I have lately had a sudden conception of the true nobility of men and women. It is well enough to say that they walk like chickens, or look like monkeys, except when they are fat and look like hippopotamuses. But the zoological point of view is not a happy one; and merely from the desire to think well of men and women I have suddenly seen the very elementary truth (which I had *never* seen before) that their nobility does not lie in what they look like but in what they endure and in the manner in which they endure it. For instance, everybody except a child appreciates that "things are not what they seem"; and the result of disillusion might be fatal to content, if it were not for courage, good will, and the like. The mind is the Arena of Life. Men and women must be judged, to be judged truly, by the valor of their spirits, by their conquest of the natural being, and by their victories in philosophy.[45]

This youthful talk about nobility, farcically reductive about its high-mindedness, only foreshadows the central theme of the essay, and, as for "the sound of words," that later concern arose through Stevens' displacement of noble victories from philosophy to poetry – a clarification of mental inclinations that implied Stevens' resignation to "the Arena of Life" as a "Theatre / Of Trope" (his phrase in *Notes Toward a Supreme Fiction*)[46] rather than as a revelation of types.

At the very least, the "Theatre of Trope" offered distraction and entertainment: "If poetry introduces order, and every competent poem introduces order, and if order means peace, even though that particular peace is an illusion,...[i]sn't a freshening of life a thing of consequence?"[47] But such sentiments smacked too exquisitely of the epicurean, and Stevens also felt impelled to justify the tropological vision on more humane, albeit not political, grounds. As early as "Le Monocle de Mon Oncle," in *Harmonium*, he had intimated that a "trivial trope reveals a way of truth,"[48] without fully knowing how. Later he responded directly to charges like Frost's talk of bric-a-brac and Winters' insinuation of "Paterian hedonism" by asserting the engagement of the tropological imagination: "Certainly the things that I have written recently are intended to express an agreement with reality. I need not say that what is back of hedonism is one thing and what is back of a desire for agreement with reality is a different thing."[49]

"Agreement with reality," "extension of reality" – these key phrases running through the essays suggest some reciprocal accommodation of subject and object in the poetic fiction. Etymologically, "fiction" indicates a made thing: a thing made by the mind out of its impressions of things. Against reason's drive toward abstraction, imagination absorbs "reality as it impinges upon us from outside" and, by translating these impressions of "the individual and the particular" into its own medium – language, for the poet – projects the art object as the mediatory term. From sense impressions to verbal images which convey "the sense that we can touch and feel a solid reality which does not wholly dissolve itself into the conceptions of our own minds";[50] the double, almost punning, association of the word "sense" with mind and object epitomizes the metamorphosis that words enact.

But beyond the capacity of the imagination to make images – which seemed to satisfy the Imagists – lay its greater capacity for the more complex fiction of metaphors. Unlike types, which assume an essential identification between mind and object, object and spirit, spirit and mind, tropes propose areas of resemblance. By Stevens' own testimony, "we are not dealing with identity" or imitation but rather with analogy, for "both in nature and in metaphor identity is the vanishing-point of resemblance."[51] Natural analogies and correspondences are typological, but tropological associations are linguistic: the combination of previously unrelated elements – two images, say, or an image and a mental concept – into a new verbal construct different from what the individual elements had been or would be in their unrelatedness.

Metaphors and the sounds of their words appeal to and satisfy the senses – and so the feelings rather than the reason. Philosophy cannot resolve mind and nature, but within its own terms metaphor can. Consequently, although "we never arrive intellectually," "emotionally we arrive constantly" – so much so that "as soon as I start to rationalize, I lose the poetry of the idea."[52]

The poetry of the idea and the idea of poetry: in metaphorical language the mind not only abstracts nature but concretizes itself; it transcends both matter's particularity and its own abstractness. Citing Baudelaire, Rimbaud, Mallarmé and Valéry as his poetic models, Stevens saw the modern artist as undertaking "a prodigious search of appearance, as if to find a way of saying and of establishing that all things, whether below or above appearance, are one. . . . Under such stress, reality changes from substance to subtlety"[53] – that is, from material object or even pictorial image to metaphor. In the poetry of the idea and the idea of poetry, Stevens postulated the resolution of his naturalism and his Platonism: "it is not too extravagant to think of resemblances and of the repetitions of resemblances as a source of the ideal. In short, metaphor has its aspect of the ideal."[54]

The ideality and hermeticism of *poésie pure*, therefore, remained to the end, but it became less gaudy and nervous, more characteristically a mixture of metaphorical imagery and abstractions, in the later poems. Where poems like "The Load of Sugar Cane" and "Domination of Black," "Thirteen Ways of Looking at a Blackbird" and "Sea Surface Full of Clouds" present their own particular *mundo* constructions, poems like *Notes Toward a Supreme Fiction* and "A Primitive Like an Orb," "The Poem That Took the Place of a Mountain" and "Two Illustrations That the World Is What You Make of It" take a mental step back and describe the very process through which the imagination turns sense impressions into *mundo* metaphors. The tensions in *Harmonium* increasingly give way to a more comfortable acceptance of the oscillations between the mind and reality and to a more assured confidence in the possibilities of their accommodation.

The serenity and confidence of Stevens' later years allowed him to entertain the notion that poetry had, or ought to have, an efficacy in the world that proved rather than compromised its purity:

> There is, in fact, a world of poetry indistinguishable from the world in which we live, or, I ought to say, no doubt, from the world in which we shall come to live, since what makes the poet the potent figure that he is, or was, or ought to be, is that he creates the world to which we turn incessantly and without knowing it and that he gives to life the supreme fictions without which we are unable to conceive of it.[55]

The convolutions and reversals of this passage make it difficult to say whether the "world in which we live" is external reality or the *mundo*, but that strategically guarded ambiguity is the source of the poet's opportunity and potency. The pure poet, Stevens wanted to say to the Marxists and Frost and Winters, need not be a decadent fop; the pure poet can be a hero.

"As You Leave the Room,"[56] completed the year before Stevens' death, is a farewell poem intended to sum up his career and answer his critics:

> *You speak. You say:* Today's character is not
> A skeleton out of its cabinet. Nor am I.
>
> That poem about the pineapple, the one
> About the mind as never satisfied,
>
> The one about the credible hero, the one
> About summer, are not what skeletons think about.
>
> I wonder, have I lived a skeleton's life,
> As a disbeliever in reality,
>
> A countryman of all the bones in the world?
> Now, here, the snow I had forgotten becomes
>
> Part of a major reality, part of
> An appreciation of a reality

> And thus an elevation, as if I left
> With something I could touch, touch every way.
>
> And yet nothing has been changed except what is
> Unreal, as if nothing had been changed at all.

Stevens took a 1947 poem called "First Warmth" and doubled its size by adding three new couplets at the beginning and one at the end of what he had written. What's more, the earlier variants in what are now lines ten and eleven make it clear that "First Warmth" was written as a spring poem: "Now, here, the warmth I had forgotten becomes / Part of the major reality...." The turning of the seasons awakens the poet's imagination to a sense of agreement with an elevated and extended reality.

The three new introductory couplets put the question into the larger context of a lifetime's effort. Like Yeats in "The Circus Animals' Desertion," Stevens summons familiar poems in a last reconfirmation and renewal of purpose. The poems offer evidence that he has not led "a skeleton's life, / As a disbeliever in reality," and the change from "warmth" to "snow" in line ten pointedly includes even the snow man's winter world in the intuition of order, or of an idea of order, which comes in the climactic sixth and seventh couplets. Not just spring but winter too, the polar contradictions, seem "part of a major reality." So far, the revisions make the poem more inclusive and affirmative, but the apparently minor shift from "the major reality" in "First Warmth" to the more qualified and relativized "a major reality" actually anticipates the important qualification of the final added couplet. Everything has been changed, "And yet nothing has been changed except what is / Unreal, as if nothing had been changed at all." The repetitions of "nothing" returns us to the negations at the end of "The Snow Man," as he "beholds / Nothing that is not there and the nothing that is." The "as if" in "as if nothing had been changed at all" reminds us that the elation at the climax of the poem was even at the time modified by another "as if": "as if I left / With something I could touch, touch every way." But if this "as if" suggests that in fact he had not experienced contact with reality, then the second "as if" modifies the statement that "nothing has been changed except what is unreal" by suggesting that a change in the unreal may be a significant and efficacious change after all. The juxtaposition of "The Snow Man" from 1921 and "As You Leave the Room" from 1954 demonstrates that in Stevens' attitudes nothing – and everything – has changed.

"Of Mere Being," written in the last months of Stevens' life, enacts the metamorphosis:

> The palm at the end of the mind,
> Beyond the last thought, rises
> In the bronze decor,
>
> A gold-feathered bird
> Sings in the palm, without human meaning,
> Without human feeling, a foreign song.

You know then that it is not the reason
That makes us happy or unhappy.
The bird sings. Its feathers shine.

The palm stands on the edge of space.
The wind moves slowly in the branches.
The bird's fire-fangled feathers dangle down.[57]

The metamorphosis is delayed until the last line of the poem. The rest of the poem describes the scene outside the mind – the palm, the bird, the sun – "without human meaning, / Without human feeling," and without a suggestion of figurative language except perhaps the odd and Stevensian word "decor." Holly Stevens' note in *The Palm at the End of the Mind* indicates: "As printed in *Opus Posthumous . . .*, the last word of the third line is 'distance.' 'Decor' is the word appearing in the original typescript, and has been restored here." The preceding text follows her emendation, and readers will be divided as to whether "distance" is more suited to the prosaic neutrality of the descriptive language or "decor" is an effective anticipation of the last line. It is there in any case that the imagination humanizes the image of the scene by reconstituting it into poetic language: "The bird's fire-fangled feathers dangle down."

Frost might have mumbled "bric-a-brac," but in that final phrase Stevens' bird becomes a momentary "appreciation of a reality / And thus an elevation, as if I left / With something I could touch, touch every way." Yeats took the goldsmiths' exquisitely wrought bird in "Sailing to Byzantium" as a symbol of the artifice of eternity, but Stevens settled for the fact that the bird his imagination apprehended "at the end of the mind" and wrought into exquisitely decorative words was part of the artifice of time. Nevertheless, even if in that appropriation "nothing has been changed except what is / Unreal," Stevens would not admit that "nothing has been changed at all." His career rests on the opposite proposition.

III

I

Frost and Stevens were among the leading opponents of prosodic experimentation in the Modernist period, and that fact no doubt has something to do with their being elders in the group. And the famous snapshots of the two posed gingerly beside each other by the photographer at a fortuitous meeting on their separate vacations in Florida served to bracket them in the minds of readers, even though there each is doing his best to look oblivious of the other's presence. Not without good reason, as we have seen; Frost, like Ransom and Robinson Jeffers, and like Winters after the 1920s but unlike Stevens, was actually rabidly anti-Modernist. But a reading of Stevens and Williams against one another as Modernists merits careful consideration not only because it engages more searchingly some of the issues that divided Stevens and Frost but also because it carries us into the crucial debates of the Modernist aesthetic.

It is difficult to be precise about the date and circumstances of the meeting between Wallace Stevens and William Carlos Williams, but it occurred late in the decade of the teens, when each was testing his poetic voice and presence while struggling to establish a livelihood in another demanding, time-consuming profession: insurance law for Stevens and medicine for Williams. As poets, both had taken another course from expatriates like Pound and Eliot, already internationally acclaimed by the avant-garde; Stevens and Williams would make their names more slowly in urban, industrial, corporate America, pursuing professional careers on opposite sides of the New York vortex: Stevens in Hartford, Connecticut, and Williams in Rutherford, New Jersey.

There was, then, good reason for them to regard each other with sympathy and respect from the start. The "Prologue" to *Kora in Hell*, dated September 1, 1918, Williams' first polemical contribution to the ferment which was generating a Modernist poetics for the English-speaking world, cited a long letter from Stevens alongside missives from Pound and H. D. in London. Stevens' first volume, *Harmonium* (1923), included a 1918 poem called "Nuances of a Theme by Williams." They saw each other from time to time at gatherings of the New York group which published *Others* late in the 1910–20 decade. Stevens reported that a long-anticipated meeting with Williams in the summer of 1922 was "a blessing...although we were both as nervous as two belles in new dresses."[58] When the Objectivist Press, under Louis Zukovsky's and George Oppen's editorial guidance, offered to reissue Williams' poetry, out of print from small presses, Williams asked not Pound, as one might have expected in those Objectivist circles, but Stevens to supply the "Introduction" to his *Collected Poems 1921–1931*.

What's more, something of the comradely feelings endured to the end. When Williams seemed vulnerable or threatened, Stevens rallied to his side. Trying to coax Williams out of one of his periodic depressions, Stevens congratulated him on an award from the National Institute of Arts and Letters in 1948: "You deserve everything that is coming your way."[59] After Williams' stroke in 1951, Stevens wrote, "You have worked hard all your life and now that you are at the top and need only time and the care of old age and leisure, I hope that what has happened will lead to some resolve (or to the necessity) to be more saving of what you have left."[60] After Williams was deprived of the chair of consultant in poetry at the Library of Congress during the witch hunts of the 1950s because of his leftist affiliations, Stevens' loyalty proved even stronger than his right-wing alarm at a communist conspiracy: "Williams is one of the few people in this country that really has an active and constant interest in writing."[61]

On his side, Williams considered Stevens "his most worthy American contender" and told him (with a Poundian combination of arrogance and condescension) that the two of them constituted "an elder group who are, in fact, in themselves, a critique and a *vade mecum* of an art that is slowly acquiring reality here in our God-forsaken territory."[62] Noting that his haste in having to write the *Autobiography* against a publisher's deadline had resulted in regrettable omissions, Williams wanted it known through the "Preface" that although Stevens was "scarcely mentioned" in the text, "he is constantly in my thoughts."[63] In fact, Williams' 1951 stroke precluded what would have been a major public event in modern poetry: the reunion of the two poets onstage at a Bard College convocation to award Stevens an honorary degree as a sequel to Williams' honorary degree the previous year.[64]

Deeper than the biographical linkages between Williams and Stevens was the fact that they were engaged in parallel ventures of profound importance to literary Modernism: among the major American poets of the High Modernist period, they stood together as the two who most explicitly argued for, and premised their poetry on, the primacy of the imagination. By the early twentieth century the character and efficacy of the imagination were, at the least, very much in doubt. Eighteenth-century Neoclassicism had taken the imagination as the ability to devise effective imagery; it was only one of various mechanically conceived faculties of the mind to be coordinated and regulated by right reason and common sense in the aesthetic contrivance. As a Romantic, Coleridge came to consider this faculty mere fancy, and his postulation of the imagination as the supreme cognitive faculty with mystical and metaphysical intuition gave the new epistemology and aesthetic their most profound, if unsystematic, philosophical exposition in English.

The Romantic imagination, therefore, assumed a crucial unitive function in order to compensate for the accelerating declension of shared philosophical, religious, and moral assumptions in the West since the Renaissance. The individual became the inspired locus for an intuitive perception of the spiritual forms and energies which invested the otherwise fragmented, phenomenal world with an exalted coherence, a significance at once immediate and ultimate. For Wordsworth and Coleridge, Blake and Shelley, Emerson and Whitman, therefore, the imagination was elevated from the image-making talent of the Neoclassicist into the sublime human faculty through which the perceiving subject penetrated to the essential reality and transcendental interrelatedness of the objects of experience.

This Romantic synthesis was an ideal unstable from the outset, precariously conceived and sporadically achieved. Because everything depended on the metamorphic, mutually completing encounter between subject and object, the Romantic ideology made the highest claims for, and put the highest demands upon, individual vision outside the traditional religious and social institutions. When under the stress of such an extreme and ultimate test the individual failed to achieve or to sustain the visionary moment, the basis for meaning in personal and social life was shaken; consciousness felt itself severed from self and world. So Romanticism contained in its vaunting claims of synthesis the seeds of its own dissolution: a drama that raised alarms from the start, accelerated throughout the Victorian period, and seemed to play itself out in *fin de siècle* aestheticism. Consequently, intellectuals and artists of the twentieth century found the efficacy of intuition as well as reason perilously undermined just at the point where they faced a political upheaval so dire and far-reaching that civilization itself seemed threatened. Out of that apocalyptic sense which was to lend Spengler's *Decline of the West* its prophetic aura, Modernism defined itself as the meta-ideology of the twentieth century in response to and against Romanticism. Stevens and Williams believed that the chief challenge to the Modernist poet – and it was of life-or-death urgency – was to redefine the shaky epistemological premises of the imagination so as to reclaim its power in the face of psychological and social circumstances more desperate than those that the Romantics and the Victorians, for all their prescience, had been able to foresee.

Stevens had a contemplative, speculative turn of mind, whereas Williams' scientific empiricism made him genuinely indifferent to, even impatient with, philosophizing. As Modernists, both knew that the argument for the imagination could not rest on metaphysical or mystical claims about the source and ends of its operation; for them and for most of their contemporaries, it could be construed only in human and naturalistic terms. Yet neither Stevens nor Williams was a rationalist; both postulated and strove to substantiate a creative imagination superior to fancy or to the image-making talent of the Neoclassicists, for its discriminations and connections determined the quality of our personal and collective lives.

The Modernist, therefore, assigned to creativity a different origin and end than the Romantic. The twentieth-century poet was less the recipient than the agent of perception: discriminations had to precede connections; only analysis yielded provisional reconstruction. The deformity or formlessness of modern life required decreation as a condition for creation, reduction as the prerequisite for invention. The calculated wildness of Williams' evocation of these dual aspects of the imagination in *Spring and All* (1923) represents his attempt to recapture the dionysian rapture of the Romantics for his own post-Nietzschean, Modernist purposes: "The imagination, intoxicated by prohibitions, rises to drunken heights to destroy the world. Let it rage, let it kill. The imagination is supreme.... Then at last will the world be made anew."[65] The completion of the work, as anticipated in the last sentence, carries Williams past the anarchism of Dada and Futurism into a recreative effort closer to Cubism, an effort to be sustained from moment to moment: "To refine, to clarify, to intensify that eternal moment in which we alone live there is but a single force – the imagination"; "Yes, the imagination, drunk with prohibitions, has destroyed and recreated everything afresh in the likeness of that which it was."[66]

In Williams' view, the imagination which detached things "from ordinary experience" did not forfeit "close identity with life": the circuit completed and objectified itself in the artifact, whose integrity comprised "some approximate co-extension with the universe." The poem, therefore, repudiates "plagiarism after nature" – the futile attempt at realism – to achieve something much more challenging and consequential: a reality not opposed to nature but "apposed to it."[67] In its apposition to nature, the verbal construct serves to mediate the epistemological schism between subject and object:

in great works of the imagination A CREATIVE FORCE IS SHOWN AT
WORK MAKING OBJECTS WHICH ALONE COMPLETE SCIENCE
AND ALLOW INTELLIGENCE TO SURVIVE – his picture lives anew. It
lives as pictures only can: by their power TO ESCAPE ILLUSION and stand
between man and nature as saints once stood between man and the sky – their
reality in such work, say, as that of Juan Gris.[68]

The artist pieces connections from fragments, makes form from chancy
associations, brings consciousness to bear on objects alien to his consciousness, and thereby composes in a lifetime of poetry his relation to the world,
his place in it, his passage through it. As art, his life choices – selections and
rejections – take shape and direction, and the lens of the artist's "personality"
provides the terms and limits within which its "creative force" perceives and
invents.[69]

Wallace Stevens' temper was epicurean where Williams' was dionysian:

> It is the *mundo* of the imagination in which the imaginative man delights and
> not the gaunt world of the reason. The pleasure is the pleasure of powers that
> create a truth that cannot be arrived at by the reason alone, a truth that the
> poet recognizes by sensation. The morality of the poet's radiant and pro-
> ductive atmosphere is the morality of the right sensation.[70]

Nevertheless, for Stevens too, sensation is not just a passively received
impression but an actively and accurately achieved response. Stevens is just as
clear as Williams about the Cubist conviction that "modern reality is a reality
of decreation": "When Braque says 'The senses deform, the mind forms,' he is
speaking to poet, painter, musician and sculptor." And he is just as clear as
Williams that against a "violent" reality the imagination must itself be a
powerful counterforce exerting "a violence from within that protects us from
a violence without."[71]

Consequently, as with Williams, the "truth" of poetry is a function of the
poet's personality: "the imagination of a man disposed to be strongly
influenced by his imagination" abstracts and translates elements from reality
into his chosen medium so that there he can arrange them so as to fashion a
sense, however illusory, of "an agreement with reality, . . . which he believes,
for a time, to be true, expressed in terms of his emotions or, since it is less of a
restriction to say so, in terms of his own personality." The fastidious
convolutions and qualifications of this characteristic statement prepare us for
Stevens' stoic admission that "the difference between philosophical truth and
poetic truth appears to become final." "A High-toned Old Christian
Woman" begins with the famous dictum: "Poetry is the supreme fiction,
madame," and the poem proceeds to dispel the sense of bathetic deflation by
affirming the "supreme fiction" as comparable to the old woman's religious
hypotheses. Stevens' retort to the charges of political irrelevance and decadent
hedonism remained resolute: "the power of the mind over the possibilities of
things," "pressing back against the pressure of reality," provides the means of
"self-preservation" which "enables us to perceive the normal in the abnormal,

the opposite of chaos in chaos"; imaginative fiction, even if illusory, "help[s] people to live their lives" and gives "life whatever savor it possesses."[72]

2

Stevens' and Williams' remarks on the imagination form a concise summary of Modernism as a literary term. For them both, the poet was not the individual locus of vision, the inspired medium who saw into the life of things and tried to find adequate language for this mystical experience, as the Romantics maintained; instead the poet was an individual through whose personality the "constructive faculty" of the imagination strove to compose the fragments of impression and response into an autotelic art object. Anti-idealist and antimystical, the poet did not reveal the divinity of Nature but invented an apposite, aesthetic coherence, necessarily less than absolute in extrinsic terms but, ideally, self-sustained in its own medium. In Stevens' characteristic phrasing, "our revelations are not the revelations of belief, but the precious portents of our own powers"; the repetition of "revelation" subverts religious faith, and the percussive alliteration emphasizes the metamorphic imagination.[73]

Nevertheless, the common allegiance of the two poets to Modernism forced to the surface equally defining tensions between them. Different temperaments and personalities made them testy about, and jealous of, each other; and they maintained a safe distance. Despite the promises and invitations in their correspondence, they saw each other seldom and were not intimate. As early as the "Prologue" to Kora in Hell, Williams lampooned "dear fat Stevens, thawing out so beautifully at forty," "a fine gentleman...who has suddenly become aware of his habits and taken to 'society' in self-defense...immaculately dressed."[74] Each nervously fretted about the other's productivity and reputation. To a publisher Stevens lamented: "Williams, I believe, writes every day or night or both, and his house must be full of manuscript, but it is quite different with me." Complaining directly to Williams in 1925 about the heavy responsibilities of his job and family, Stevens openly expressed envy of Williams, just back from Europe with a lengthening list of published books, but offered Williams a nasty explanation of his prolixity: "But then your imagination has always exploited your fellow-townsmen and the chances are that you don't mind it."[75] Williams' irritation at the Stevens letter quoted in Kora should have warned him against asking Stevens to introduce his Collected Poems a decade later, and the result rankled with him for the rest of his life. More and more, neither read the other's work; Stevens resolutely resisted addressing Paterson, and Williams confessed to Marianne Moore that he was encountering increasing trouble muddling through Stevens' later, longer meditations.[76] At the same time as Stevens was writing to Williams, "You deserve everything that is coming your way" – and in his way he meant it – he was confiding to his friend Barbara Church that Williams seemed "a man somehow disturbed at the core and making all sorts of gestures and using all sorts of figures to conceal it from himself." When Williams' stroke kept him from appearing with Stevens at the Bard convocation, Stevens responded to a standing ovation at the end of the ceremonies with an aside to his host on the platform: "Well, we didn't need the old man after all, did we?" (though he made amends with a tender letter to Williams the next day).[77]

They were right to feel uneasy with each other at a level below that of their real and mutual respect; their differences were matters of substance as well as ego and illustrate an ambiguity within the Modernist aesthetic they both espoused. It was clear from the Stevens letter in the *Kora* "Prologue." Stevens explained in a postscript that he had decided to send Williams the letter reluctantly because "it is quarrelsomely full of my own ideas of discipline." He charged Williams with dissipating his energies and obscuring his voice through his stubborn refusal to develop "a fixed point of view" and "a single manner or mood": "to fidget with points of view leads always to new beginnings and incessant new beginnings lead to sterility."[78] Williams dismissed Stevens' advice with the sneering caricature quoted in the previous paragraph, but he continued from time to time to acknowledge, with a mixture of insecurity and resentment, Stevens' "sophisticated, urbane voice" measuring out its elegant pentameters.[79] For his part, toward the end of his life Stevens hailed the younger Richard Eberhardt as a poet "right in my own way of thinking of things, although I am not too sure that my own way of thinking of things is right, particularly when I come across the universal acceptance of Bill Williams, for instance, who rejects the idea that meaning has the slightest value and describes a poem as a structure of little blocks."[80] In the same year, 1953, he sniffed to Barbara Church: "if the present generation likes the mobile-like arrangements of line to be found in the work of William Carlos Williams or the verbal conglomerates of e. e. cummings, what is the next generation to like? Pretty much the bare page, for that alone would be new."[81]

When Williams called Stevens "his most worthy American contender,"[82] it was obviously a real contention, and though each fretted that the other had met with greater acceptance and so had won the contest, neither wavered in his way of "thinking of things" and giving them utterance. The precise terms of their contention deserve the closest consideration because their efforts to reclaim the imagination from the ruins of Romanticism derived from significantly different literary and epistemological assumptions. Where Williams found himself sharing Pound's Imagist principles, Stevens spoke as a representative of the Symboliste tradition coming into English; as a result, they found themselves at cross-purposes about the functioning of the imagination as it translated experience into language. When Williams chose his stateside compatriot over his transatlantic friend and competitor to attest to his *Collected Poems*, his miscalculation taught him which was his poetic compatriot and which his poetic competitor. The more reserved Stevens told Williams that he was reluctant to write the Introduction, but Williams – unwittingly and to his chagrin – precipitated a long-postponed engagement of their dispute and revealed a schism, or at least an irresolution, at the heart of Modernism.

The adjectives with which Stevens labeled Williams' work caused under-standable offense: "romantic," "sentimental," "anti-poetic," "realist."[83] Stevens suggested a vacillation between Williams' sentimental proclivities (which, for example, exploited his fellow-townsmen) and his antipoetic, realist, "imagist" side. Williams did not balk at the Imagist tag; right off, Pound had recognized Williams and Marianne Moore as the most interesting exemplars of Imagist principles among the poets exiled back in the home country. But Stevens' elision of adjectives seemed to define Imagism as an antipoetic realism – precisely the opposite of Williams' argument in *Spring and All*. Stevens recognized Marianne Moore as antipoetic, realist, and imagist too, but not as baldly so as Williams. The key word was "romantic," and Stevens could not but have known that it was a red flag to a *soi-disant* anti-Romantic like Williams. What could Stevens mean in calling him a twentieth-century romantic? Stevens supplied a curious answer:

> What, then, is a romantic poet now-a-days? He happens to be one who still dwells in an ivory tower, but who insists that life would be intolerable except for the fact that one has, from the top, such an exceptional view of the public dump and the advertising signs of Snider's Catsup, Ivory Soap and Chevrolet Cars; he is the hermit who dwells alone with the sun and moon, but insists on taking a rotten newspaper.[84]

The problem with Stevens' description of the romantic as idealistic solipsist in a shabby, commercialized society is that it fits him more than Williams. It is Stevens who would write "The Man on the Dump" from an ivory tower elevation which permitted the exotic figurations and high-faluting language of that poem; and Williams, never as reclusive as Stevens, would choose to squat on the dump, reading the rotten Paterson or Rutherford paper.

However, Stevens' review of Marianne Moore's *Selected Poems*, written the next year, formulates more coherently what he was fumbling toward in the Williams "Introduction." Commending Moore with the title "A Poet That Really Matters," Stevens distinguished between a good and a bad kind of romanticism. Invoking Irving Babbitt, that rabid anti-Romantic, Stevens associated "romantic in the derogatory sense" with the attempt to treat ordinary objects – "things, like garden furniture or colonial lingerie or, not to burden the imagination, country millinery" – as (in Babbitt's words) "strange, unexpected, intense, probable, superlative, extreme, unique, etc." Stevens' supercilious inventory of objects is calculated to prejudge as palpably silly the imaginative effort to romanticize the world of everyday objects and events, much less to transfigure the Paterson of billboards and urban waste and daily news. Stevens' "Man Whose Pharynx Was Bad" found that "the malady of the quotidian" rendered him voiceless and verseless. On the other hand, Stevens' review goes on to cite A. E. Powell's *Romantic Theory of Poetry*, in defining "romantic in its other sense" – the sense which he wants to praise in Moore – as the poet's ability "to reproduce for us the feeling as it lives within himself."[85]

A reading of the Williams "Introduction" against the Moore review, therefore, pegs Williams as "romantic in the derogatory sense" and Moore as "romantic in its other sense." The Moore whom Stevens praises for rendering internal states of feeling may be hard to reconcile with the poet who insisted on real toads in her imaginary gardens and described things – ostrich, skunk, snail, katydid – with a scrupulously observant eye. Even the poem entitled "The Mind Is an Enchanting Thing" fixes the mind on the minutest discriminations of phenomena. In describing Moore as a reflection of himself, Stevens is trying to reclaim her from Williams' side of the poetic contention.

The underlying issue was Imagism as a mode of poetic perception and expression, and at first Stevens was hesitant to state his discontent with Imagism openly. The following statement about Imagism masks the grounds of Stevens' complaint:

> Imagism . . . is not something superficial. It obeys an instinct. Moreover, [it] is an ancient phase of poetry. It is something permanent. Williams is a writer to whom writing is the grinding of a glass, the polishing of a lens by means of which he hopes to be able to see clearly. His delineations are trials. They are rubbings of reality.[86]

Much less trusting than Williams that rubbings from reality made for clear sight, or for that matter for sight of anything he would take comfort in seeing, Stevens found an alternative for his discomfort in aesthetes like Pater and Santayana and in Symbolistes like Mallarmé and Valéry. Symbolisme and Imagism proved to be the most important and long-lasting influences in modern poetry precisely because they assumed dialectical roles within Modernist poetics. The polarity was recognized from the outset. Pound sometimes gave Imagisme its French spelling in order to designate the new movement as a critique of and an alternative to Symbolisme. Amy Lowell warned the fledgling Poet John Gould Fletcher that he had to choose between her Imagist direction and the mood symphonies of his friend Conrad Aiken.

Lowell's challenge was poetic politics. Symbolisme and Imagism developed as polar aspects of poetic Modernism as a result of the disintegration of the Romantic effort to synthesize subject and object. For this reason, although Modernism constitutes at the first level an overt and programmatic rejection of Romanticism, it also constitutes at a second level an extension of the epistemological issues that the decadence of Romanticism precipitated. In terms of the subject–object split, Imagism represents the attempt to render the objects of experience, whereas Symbolisme represents the attempt to render subjective psychological and affective states. The first mode finds affinities with the visual arts in using language and shaping the poem on the page as ideogram; the second moves toward suggestive imprecision in metaphor and associative language, and relies heavily on auditory and musical effects.

It is true that these two large, diverse movements must not be too dichotomously contrasted. After all, Pound stated as the first and basic premise of

Imagism "the direct presentation of the 'thing,' whether subjective or objective," thus admitting the rendering of a subjective thing as a type of image. And for his part, Stevens kept reminding himself that the imagination must maintain a relation to, and even if possible suggest an agreement with, the world outside the mind; he kept insisting that metaphorical and rhythmic fictions must periodically be dumped on the trash heap of a recalcitrant and unillusioned reality. Faced with a polarity between subject and object, we have to try to accommodate both terms, and under that pressure the terms tend to slip in and out of one another. Nonetheless, the underlying and defining inclination of the "Imagist imagination" – a phrase which in this context is *not* redundant – is to fix the mind and its language on the phenomena of experience, and the corresponding inclination of the Symboliste imagination is to dissolve sense impressions into linguistic evocations of psychic states. Even the converse effort – that is, an Imagist rendering of a psychological state as a subjective thing or a Symboliste evocation of a natural object – underscores, rather than undermines, the distinction made here between Symbolisme and Imagism. For example, a juxtaposition of Pound's "Jewel Stair's Grievance" or Williams' "Flowers by the Sea" with Stevens' "Thirteen Ways of Looking at a Blackbird" or "Sea Surface Full of Clouds" reinforces the impression that Imagism operates by projecting mind and medium to engage things, whereas Symbolisme absorbs things into mind and medium. In the one case, consciousness commits subject to object; in the other, consciousness commits object to subject.

As we have seen, the Modernist in Williams joined Stevens in distinguishing the art object from the objects of nature as autotelic in the words or stone or pigment and canvas that comprises its only existence: "The word must be put down for itself, not as a symbol of nature but a part, cognizant of the whole – aware – civilized."[87] Yet his apposition of the art object to nature is not as extreme as Stevens' notion of a violent opposition of art "against" nature. For Williams, the artwork is not symbolic of nature, as Romantic metaphysics claimed, yet it assumes a place in nature – apart yet a part which as an act of consciousness is, or strives to be, "cognizant of the whole."

In fact, even in the "Preface" to *Spring and All*, perhaps his most combatively Modernist work, Williams saw the imagination working out of "close identity with life" to produce something which is an "approximate co-existence with the universe." The imagination decreates so that "at last the world will be made anew."[88] That prophetic claim could be read to mean that the world is made anew only as the artificial re-creation of the artwork. But Williams anticipated that the artwork could mediate the gap between subject world and object world; in standing "between man and nature as saints once stood between man and the sky," the imaginative work reconstitutes "everything afresh" *not* in its own image but "in the likeness of that which it was." Consciousness makes a difference for the objects of consciousness; it summons them to and invests them with a significance that Williams could at times suggest was their intrinsic significance. The imagination, not God or nature, is the source and agent of meaning, but for that reason it is bent not on transforming but revealing the object:

> Understood in a practical way, without calling upon mystic agencies, of this or that order, it is that life becomes actual only when it is identified with ourselves. When we name it, life exists....My whole life has been spent (so far) in seeking to place a value upon experience and the objects of experience.[89]

Stevens offered his own version of "Imagination as Value," first presented to the English Institute in 1948. It provides a counterstatement not only to such Williams passages as the preceding one but also to his own "Rubbings of Reality" essay (1946) on Williams' Imagism and to his essay, also from 1948, "About One of Marianne Moore's Poems." There Stevens speaks of Moore's imaginative stance and verbal strategies as deriving from "contact with reality as it impinges upon us from outside, the sense that we can touch and feel a solid reality which does not wholly dissolve itself into the conceptions of our own minds."[90] That epistemological conviction is the underlying premise of Imagism, and Stevens' recognition of it in Moore retracts his earlier attempt to claim her as a kind of Symboliste.

It is a conviction, however, that Stevens did not share. In "Imagination as Value" he reiterated his conviction that such an attitude was "romantic" and sentimentally exploitive: "we must somehow cleanse the imagination of the romantic....The romantic belittles it. The imagination is the liberty of the mind. The romantic is a failure to make use of that liberty. It is to the imagination what sentimentality is to feeling."[91] In fact, "Imagination as Value" draws out the consequences of the Symboliste premise that "we live in the mind." For "if we live in the mind, we live with the imagination" – not, admittedly, Coleridge's and Emerson's "imagination as metaphysics" but Mallarmé's and Valéry's "imagination as a power of the mind over external objects, that is to say, reality." Stevens is repeating his earlier distinction between imaginative modes, but without the arguable distinction between good and bad Romanticism. What's more, although an unillusioned, unapologetic acknowledgment of the mind's "power...over the possibilities of things" might seem to make for sentimental exploitation, it can instead be seen to preclude that Imagist weakness because in the Symboliste mode "what is engaging us...has nothing to do with the external world." At that point, the poet becomes an agnostic idealist: "the Platonic resolution of diversity appears. The world is no longer an extraneous object, full of other extraneous objects, but an image. In the last analysis, it is with this image of the world that we are vitally concerned."[92]

But is the vital concern for an "image of the world," or the "world of the image"? The inversion of the grammatical subordination in the phrase makes a subtle but crucial epistemological distinction. Williams or Pound or Moore more characteristically thinks of the poem as offering an "image of the world." But the "world of the image" is a more accurate phrase for Stevens' concern – or, in his own phrase, the *"mundo* of the imagination"; for "a poet's words are of things that do not exist without the words."[93] Stevens would prefer to run the risks of escapism than those of Romantic realism. His Symboliste aestheticism made him, like Santayana, a skeptical Platonist, whereas Williams and Pound, Moore and H. D. believed in their different kinds of empiricism – for Pound and H.D., in fact, an empiricist Platonism.

3

A reading of the poems in which Stevens and Williams engage each other directly substantiates in practice their theoretical differences. "Nuances of a Theme by Williams"[94] appeared in *Harmonium* in 1923 but dates from 1918, the year of Stevens' admonitions about Williams' manner and viewpoint in the *Kora* "Preface." Stevens' "Nuances" reprints Williams' brief, early piece "El Hombre" and rewrites it at greater length so as to reduce the four lines of Williams to a subtext.

"El Hombre" addresses a terse, austere apostrophe to a star, so understated that it uses an exclamation point for concluding emphasis:

> It's a strange courage
> You give me, ancient star:
>
> Shine alone in the sunrise
> toward which you lend no part!

Addressing a star is an instance of the so-called pathetic fallacy, but it is a time-honored convention for expressing intense empathy with the observed object. Except for the underlying association of man and star in the title, Williams employs no figurative language. The colon makes the transition between couplets, so that the second specifies the life-and-death courage which the speaker draws from the star's persistent, solitary shining in and despite the overwhelming light of the rising sun. The irony of the poem lies in the recognition that the cyclic process of nature renewed each dawn dooms star and man.

Stevens fastens on two phrases, "shine alone" and "lend no part," and provides elaborate glosses:

> I
> Shine alone, shine nakedly, shine like bronze,
> that reflects neither my face nor any inner part
> of my being, shine like fire, that mirrors nothing.
>
> II
> Lend no part to any humanity that suffuses
> You in its own light.
> Be not chimera of morning,
> Half-man, half-star.
> Be not an intelligence,
> Like a widow's bird
> Or an old horse.

Stevens rejects the pathetic fallacy as an appropriation of brute nature by human consciousness which denigrates it to the romanticized and sentimental status of kept beast or pet: "Like a widow's bird / Or an old horse." Star is all and only star, not "half-man"; subject and object share no mirroring correspondence, as the Romantics claimed.

On the surface, Stevens' strategy might appear anti-Symboliste, refuting Williams' practice with an Imagistic insistence on the object stripped of human attribution. But whatever the argument of the lines, the quality of the language betrays Stevens' Symboliste allegiances. The incantatory repetitions and rhythms, the proliferation of metaphors and similes create an opaque verbal atmosphere which obscures the central fact which "El Hombre" renders with immediacy: the star's lone shining and waning in the dawn. Williams' language eschews metaphoric indirection to focus consciousness on the object; Stevens' language indulges in metaphor to establish its fictive and self-referential independence of the object.

The last poem in Stevens' *Collected Poems*, "Not Ideas about the Thing but the Thing Itself,"[95] seems, more explicitly than "Nuances," to proclaim, via Williams, an Imagist viewpoint, but again the manner makes the psychological difference between the two poets all the clearer:

> At the earliest ending of winter,
> In March, a scrawny cry from outside
> Seemed like a sound in his mind.
>
> He knew that he heard it,
> A bird's cry, at daylight or before,
> In the early March wind.
>
> The sun was rising at six,
> No longer a battered panache above snow...
> It would have been outside.
>
> It was not from the vast ventriloquism
> Of sleep's faded papier-mâché...
> The sun was coming from outside.
>
> That scrawny cry – it was
> A chorister whose c preceded the choir.
> It was part of the colossal sun,
>
> Surrounded by its choral rings,
> Still far away. It was like
> A new knowledge of reality.

The poem recounts the mind's coming to consciousness of a winter world moving toward spring – a favorite subject of Williams', expressed most famously in "By the road to the contagious hospital." Here Stevens' winter scene is only suggested through two elements, the bird's cry and the sun, drawn into affiliation by the waking mind. The poem follows the process through which the disembodied bird's cry seems to take on increasing objectivity through association with the dawn sun. At first, the cry "seemed like a sound in the mind." But by the third tercet the sun, "rising at six," "would have been outside," and by the end of the next tercet "was coming from outside"; and in the expanded possibilities suggested by the enjambment of the final tercets, the cry "was part of the colossal sun, / Surrounded by its choral rings." The pronoun "it," referring in its recurrence sometimes to the cry and sometimes to the sun, comes in the last sentence to include both and by implication, everything else within the sun's radiant circumambience: "It was like / A new knowledge of reality."

At the same time, however, the sunrise becomes, in the course of the poem, not just the thing observed but a metaphor for the process by which consciousness becomes aware of the thing observed: "He knew that he heard" the bird and saw the sun. The self–circling, self–defining repetition of words and imagery – increasingly characteristic of the late Stevens – enacts the gradual clarification and expansion of the impression in the mind. Objects are absorbed into metaphor, and the metaphor of dawn becomes the verbal construct itself: the words are the dawning.

Williams' famous poem from *Spring and All*[96] makes a revealing comparison with Stevens' rendering of "the earliest ending of winter":

> By the road to the contagious hospital
> under the surge of the blue
> mottled clouds driven from the
> northeast – a cold wind. Beyond, the
> waste of broad, muddy fields
> brown with dried weeds, standing and fallen
>
> patches of standing water
> the scattering of tall trees
>
> All along the road the reddish
> purplish, forked, upstanding, twiggy
> stuff of bushes and small trees
> with dead, brown leaves under them
> leafless vines –
>
> Lifeless in appearance, sluggish
> dazed spring approaches –
>
> They enter the new world naked,
> cold, uncertain of all
> save that they enter. All about them
> the cold familiar wind –
>
> Now the grass, tomorrow
> the stiff curl of wildcarrot leaf
> One by one objects are defined –
> It quickens: clarity, outline of leaf
>
> But now the stark dignity of
> entrance – Still, the profound change
> has come upon them: rooted, they
> grip down and begin to awaken

Like Stevens, Williams traces the mind's awakening to spring's awakening, but in this instance consciousness is almost totally absorbed in the scene – attendant upon, and attentive to the natural process. The meticulous accuracy of the details verifies Williams' negative capability (his early fascination with Keats strengthened his inclination to subject ego to object) and dramatizes the contrast with Stevens' absorption with the lovely tracings of the mind's watching itself watching in words. Williams' poem, rather than Stevens', exemplifies the Imagist dictum "Not Ideas about the Thing but the Thing Itself."

Something different transpires through Stevens' widening verbal sweeps, climaxing in the last two tercets, the only enjambed tercets in the poem. Here, as in other Stevens poems – "Mrs. Alfred Uruguay," for instance – sunrise is the figure for the advent of the imagination to the world: not the false, weak, merely decorative, "romantic" imagination of moonlight or half-light – dismissed in this poem by means of the self-indicting rhetoric of "a battered panache above snow" and "the vast ventriloquism / Of sleep's faded papier-mâché" – but the virile imagination which demonstrates the mind's power over the possibilities of things. Despite the title of the poem, its first and last concern is the mind itself rather than the thing itself.

Consider the difference between "One by one objects are defined – / It quickens" and "It was like / A new knowledge of reality." The Williams poem obliquely acknowledges the lens of consciousness toward the end of the poem through the intrusion of abstract words like "clarity," "the stark dignity of / entrance," "the profound change," but the abstractions feel earned by their grounding in specification. Aside from the personification in "sluggish / dazed spring approaches," there is not a single figure of speech in the poem. By contrast, the Stevens poem begins and ends with a simile; the bird cry which at first only "seemed like a sound in the mind" does become in the course of the poem a sound in the mind: "like / A new knowledge of reality." That "like" at the opening and closing, sealing the poem in simile, is the signature of the Symboliste, as opposed to the Imagist, imagination.

A third pair of poems reverses the roles of the two poets, this time with Williams reacting to and against Stevens. "Description Without Place"[97] might well have been one of those ruminative poems that Williams told Moore he found more and more befuddling. It was included in *Transport to Summer* (1947), the volume which also contained "Esthetique du Mal" and *Notes Toward a Supreme Fiction*, but Williams read "Description" first in its original journal publication and "didn't like [it] at all."[98] What's more, Williams took personal affront at what he took to be a caricature of him in the following lines:

> the hard hidalgo
> Lives in the mountainous character of his speech;
>
> And in that mountainous mirror Spain acquires
> The knowledge of Spain and of the hidalgo's hat –
>
> A seeming of the Spaniard, a style of life,
> The inventor of a nation in a phrase....

Williams did not explain why he considered the hard hidalgo as a portrait of himself (aside, presumably, from the fact of his Spanish blood and his middle name) or why he took offense. But he threw himself into writing "A Place (Any Place) to Transcend All Places" in rebuttal.

It is easy to see why Williams would have rejected Stevens' delicately delineated meditation on the interplay of seeming and being, metaphor and thing, fictions and actualities. But, unlike "Nuances on a Theme by Williams" and "Not Ideas about the Thing but the Thing Itself," "Description Without Place" makes no recognizable nod to Williams, even in the disguise of the "hard hidalgo." The theme and diction are *echt* Stevens, as in the penultimate section:

> Description is revelation. It is not
> The thing described, nor false facsimile.
>
> It is an artificial thing that exists
> In its own seeming, plainly visible,
>
> Yet not too closely the double of our lives,
> Intenser than any actual life could be,
>
> A text we should be born that we might read,
> More explicit than the experience of sun
>
> And moon, the book of reconciliation,
> Book of a concept only possible
>
> In description, canon central in itself,
> The thesis of the plentifullest John.

The poem, then, describes a fictive concept, existent only in the medium in which it is contrived, as superior to any place of reference; this book of revelation, unlike St. John's, does not reconcile us to earth or heaven but draws us into its own ambience. Against such conceptualizing Williams argued furiously that a place (any place, as long as it was the poet's place) is the ground of thought and speech; his title proclaims the particular as transcendent. A catalog of details locates the poet in New York, and although the poem as a whole lacks the shapeliness of Williams' best work, the following lines exemplify in an image from nature his dictum "no ideas but in things":

> leaves filling,
> making, a tree (but
> wait) not just leaves,
> leaves of one design that
> make a certain design,
> no two alike, not like
> the locust either, next in line,
> nor the Rose of Sharon, in
> the pod-stage, near it – a
> tree! Imagine it! Pears
> philosophically hard.

The pear tree – not the adjacent locust or Rose of Sharon – with individual leaves "no two alike," emblemizes a "design" of particulars: the only kind of philosophical knowledge Williams will admit.

As for the Spanish hidalgo, Williams was being unnecessarily defensive; there is no reason to suppose that Stevens had him in mind. In fact, a reading of those lines in the context of the conclusion to "Description Without Place" identifies the hidalgo not as Williams in masquerade but, on the contrary, as the Stevensian hero of capable imagination:

> Thus the theory of description matters most.
> It is the theory of the word for those
>
> For whom the word is the making of the world,
> The buzzing world and lisping firmament.
>
> It is a world of words to the end of it,
> In which nothing solid is its solid self.
>
> As, men make themselves their speech: the hard hidalgo
> Lives in the mountainous character of his speech;
>
> And in that mountainous mirror Spain acquires
> The knowledge of Spain and of the hidalgo's hat –
>
> A seeming of the Spaniard, a style of life,
> The invention of a nation in a phrase,
>
> In a description hollowed out of hollow-bright,
> The artificer of subjects still half night.
>
> It matters, because everything we say
> Of the past is description without place, a cast
>
> Of the imagination, made in sound;
> And because what we say of the future must portend,
>
> Be alive with its own seemings, seeming to be
> Like rubies reddened by rubies reddening.

Nevertheless, Williams' rising to the challenge he thought that Stevens was slyly presenting serves to dramatize again the contrary, in some fundamental ways even contradictory, positions of the Imagist and the Symboliste. The still unsettled dialectic between the two most influential and long-lasting movements in modern poetry has sought to resolve an ambiguity in the philosophical and linguistic assumptions of Modernism itself. The choice between "Pears / philosophically hard" and "rubies reddened by rubies reddening" has again and again been blurred or fuzzed over, sometimes deliberately, but some version of that choice has persistently presented itself whenever fundamental questions have arisen about what the artist sees and says. On the one hand, Williams says "The eyes by this / far quicker than the mind," to which Stevens replies, "Description is/Composed of a sight indifferent to the eye."[99] The elusiveness of the terms – subject and object, mind and nature – makes discriminations about their interaction in the language of the poem all the more difficult and all the more necessary.

To sharpen those discriminations, I have emphasized the differences between the Symboliste and Imagist positions. "A sight indifferent to the eye" may express a purer and more hermetic position than Stevens sometimes took, but "Final Soliloquy of the Interior Paramour" (1950)[100] sums up the archetype of the "figure of capable imagination" as a gnostic Platonist:

> Light the first light of evening, as in a room
> In which we rest and, for small reason, think
> The world imagined is the ultimate good.
>
> This is, therefore, the intensest rendezvous.
> It is in that thought that we collect ourselves,
> Out of all the indifferences, into one thing:
>
> Within a single thing, a single shawl
> Wrapped tightly round us, since we are poor, a warmth,
> A light, a power, the miraculous influence.
>
> Here, now, we forget each other and ourselves.
> We feel the obscurity of an order, a whole,
> A knowledge, that which arranged the rendezvous.
>
> Within its vital boundary, in the mind.
> We say God and the imagination are one...
> How high that highest candle lights the dark.
>
> Out of this same light, out of the central mind,
> We make a dwelling in the evening air,
> In which being there together is enough.

The "of" in the poem's title is deliberately ambiguous; it is difficult to tell whether the interior paramour is speaking to and for and about the virile poet, or vice versa. It is a soliloquy, not a dialogue or even a dramatic monologue. The hero-poet and his anima-muse speak as "we," joined in a hierogamy "in the mind" and "out of the central mind" making the fictive poem in which they dwell, asking no more than to find rest and realization in their words. It is not what they see but what they say; for them, "the tongue is an eye." But almost every phrase, every trope they utter in this "final soliloquy" resumes and resounds with the words of a lifetime: "We say God and the imagination are one...."

3

T. S. Eliot: The Lady Between the Yew Trees

In the imperious humility of his last years, as Ezra Pound ruminated on the indebtedness to Dante which he shared with T. S. Eliot, an American expatriate poet like himself, he wrote of the recently dead friend from his early London years: "His was the true Dantescan voice – not honoured enough, and deserving more than I ever gave him....I can only repeat, but with the urgency of 50 years ago: READ HIM."[1] From their first association, Eliot seemed to Pound the only serious poetic contender in his generation, yet he promoted Eliot's work and plotted to relieve his poverty until their ways diverged, poetically and intellectually as well as geographically, during the 1920s. Their association and their differences will be implicit throughout this discussion because together both the association and the differences, as between Stevens and Williams, offer another way of understanding the dialectic between Symbolisme and Imagism which has produced the range and diversity of American poetry in this century.

They recognized that their differences were as basic as their allegiances. In the divisive "years of *l'entre deux guerres*," Pound was not always deferential to Eliot; he twitted the Christian commitment of the "Rev. Mr. Eliot," and in Canto 46 implied weakness and escapism for "wanting to get through hell in a hurry." Eliot's work refutes the charge, but when Eliot in turn criticized Pound's hell as a place imagined for other people but not for Pound himself, he was suggesting that it was Pound who wanted to get through hell in a hurry, while implicitly acknowledging his own sense of being in hell, or at least in purgatory. Years later he would still say that "here as hereafter the alternative to hell" for fallible human beings "is purgatory," not – or not immediately – heaven.[2] His first volume of poems had an epigraph from the *Purgatorio*, and its title poem, "The Love Song of J. Alfred Prufrock," one from the *Inferno*. The first lines of the poem, "Let us go then, you and I," initiated the account of a lifelong journey in which, as in *The Pisan Cantos* but not as in *The Divine Comedy*, the poet was the sufferer, not a Dantescan observer. Despite Eliot's early impersonal theory of poetry and despite Hugh Kenner's dubbing him the "invisible poet,"[3] Eliot himself came to be annoyed when textual critics took his impersonality as the whole account of his poetry. The theory referred to the effect of the objectified artwork and not to the source and subject matter of the artwork. Eliot shared with Marlowe, Milton, Byron, and Robert Lowell the Puritan-Christian awareness that "I myself am hell." And there can be no question that in some ways Pound benefited from his own more simplistic sense of sin; he attained at least momentary experiences of an earthly paradise earlier and more frequently than Eliot came to his Dantescan vision of Paradise.

Grover Smith remarked that "the tragedy of Eliot's poetry is that, properly speaking, it shows no Beatrice."[4] It was Beatrice, after all, who in Dante's imagination won him access to Paradise. But Smith's remark is somewhat misleading. Eliot came to see human depravity and human loss in an eschatological scheme which is not, in the end, tragic. It is no accident that the plays which occupied much of his last twenty years increasingly revealed their comic bent; for comedy – Chaucer knew it as well as Dante – does not exclude an admission of depravity and even tragedy. Still, Smith's comment hints at a subtler point: that the complications of Eliot's relation to the feminine, and all that implied for him, comprise the crux of his poetry and drama. A reading of Eliot in terms of the feminine brings us to the heart of the work as it developed through a long career of changes and conversions.

"Prufrock," the first poem in the first collection, *Prufrock and Other Observations* (1917), dramatizes the quandary, refracted through or developed in the subsequent poems in the volume. But a reading of the unpublished poems preserved from Eliot's Harvard and early London years provides a fuller, more explicit context for the generally more restrained pieces he selected for publication. Eliot chose the best poems for the *Prufrock* collection and for *Ara Vos Prec* (a volume with a title from the *Purgatorio*, republished minus one poem as *Poems 1920*), but they exist along with many unpublished poems in a notebook and a folder which Eliot sold during the 1920s to John Quinn, the Manhattan banker-patron whom Pound had alerted about Eliot's financial plight.[5] Many of the early poems, published and unpublished, turn on the relationship to women. The woman described in "On a Portrait," which appeared in *The Harvard Advocate* in 1909, looms before the restless, weary speaker as an "immaterial fancy" surrounded by hazy dreams. A longish notebook poem entitled "Convictions" contains a description of a lady with a pen confiding her heartfelt need to her writing pad. Her words are painfully clear: if she could find a man for whom she would be not merely flesh but soul, she would yield herself to him as wife and, with her pen, as muse. But the phrasing confirms her hopelessness; she is trapped in the masculine reduction of woman to body, alien to, indeed corruptive of the pure masculine soul. The dark-eyed woman in "On a Portrait" is seen by the male observer as holding her dark secrets outside the circumference of his mind. The tantalizing, withheld secrets are biological and sexual, the arcana of temporal, material existence, opposed to his aspiration to disembodied affinity with the ideal, eternal absolute.

Sexual distinctions appear categorical: the speaker in "Suite Clownesque" invokes biblical phrasing to call himself the first-born of the absolute; by contrast, the woman in "Conversation Galante" is "the eternal humorist, / The eternal enemy of the absolute."[6] "Humorist" connects her with such noxious corporeal fluids as bile and blood and phlegm. This inflexible polarization issues in a masculine self-consciousness so divided against itself, so disjunct from its material ambience, that his mind is detached not just from the feminine other but also from his own body as his "feminine" aspect. Men become spectral voyeurs, horrified and fascinated – and so obsessed – that their own flesh and blood makes them vulnerable to the snares of the feminine. The speaker in "On a Portrait" identified with the caged parrot spying on his mistress with patient curiosity. The pun in "patience" specifies the passivity of his suffering. The Eliot who conceived the artist as an Eye watching himself[7] called his first volume *Prufrock and Other Observations*.

The dichotomy between mind and body is consistently cast into the conventional stereotypes. In a phantasmagoric notebook poem called "The Little Passion" ("passion" again yokes sexual and religious suffering), one of Eliot's many male nocturnal street wanderers in the urban hell is drawn to a cross on which the nailed soul bleeds. The image anticipates Prufrock "sprawling on a pin," "pinned and wriggling on a wall," but the unpublished poems state even more crudely Eliot's neurotic anxiety about living in a mortal body and his disgust with bodily functions. In "Goldfish (Essence of Summer Magazines)" bodily existence is figured in the Sphinx, the weary but destructive female; in a long poem called "Reflections in a Square: First Debate Between the Body and Soul," composed in January 1910, physical senses are associated with withered leaves, mud, masturbation, defecation; in "Fragment Bacchus and Ariadne: Second Debate Between the Body and Soul," written in 1911, the butterfly-soul is tensed to break free at last from the cell of a chrysalis, a matrix or womb associated with earth and manure.[8] As with the caged parrot earlier, the reference to the cell here makes the body a prison for the winged psyche. It is worth noting that these debates were written during the same years as "Prufrock" and "Portrait of a Lady."

Fear of women as the stimulants of an enslaving, defiling sexual passion is obsessive in these early poems. "Circe's Palace," which appeared in the *Advocate* in 1908, casts it into melodramatic nightmare:

> Around her fountain which flows
> With the voice of men in pain,
> Are flowers that no man knows.
> Their petals are fanged and red
> With hideous streak and stain;
> They sprang from the limbs of the dead. –
> We shall not come here again.[9]

Circe's flowers, fertilized by male corpses, are described not just as sex organs but as toothed vaginas, so that "she" assumes a power of "phallicism" superior to any man's, as the jumbled imagery of the second stanza reveals:

panthers rising from their lairs, a "sluggish python" (capable of suffocating its victim, like the powerful woman, yet immobilized, like the victimized man), peacocks with the eyes of dead men. Eliot views the enchantress's palace neither through Odysseus' eyes nor Elpenor's (as Pound would), but through the adolescent eyes of a youth who dreads venturing into those lurid and alluring precincts.

The "Second Debate between the Body and Soul" is entitled, with self-incriminating bathos, "Bacchus and Ariadne." And "Opera," a notebook poem dated November 1909, mocks Tristan and Isolde as pseudo-tragic, the lovers tormenting themselves into fits of self-indulgence, but Eliot's deflation of their egotism is anything but therapeutic; it merely leaves him feeling like a ghostly young man at the undertakers' ball. By insulating himself from susceptibility to their grand passion, he has anesthetized himself. "Easter: Sensations of April," dated May 1910, anticipates the opening of *The Waste Land*, as the smells of rich earth and spring rain, insinuating themselves into the poet's ordered, sequestered room, flay his nerves and imagination with pleasurable pain. The second stanza of the "Ode," written in 1918 or 1919 and included in *Ara Vos Prec* but suppressed in *Poems 1920* and thereafter, presents the wedding night, several years after Eliot's marriage to Vivienne Haigh-Wood, as a vampires' honeymoon:

> Tortured.
> When the bridegroom smoothed his hair
> There was blood on the bed.
> Morning was already late.
> Children singing in the orchard
> (Io Hymen, Hymenaee)
> Succuba eviscerate.[10]

The lines are a tangle of ambiguous ironies. The Whitman poem "O Hymen! O Hymenee!" aches for the sexual "sting" to be prolonged until the threat comes clear: "Why can you not continue? O why do you now cease? / Is it because if you continued beyond the swift moment you would soon certainly kill me?" And now in Eliot's lines, is it the bride's hymen staining the sheets or the blood of the bridegroom preyed upon by the demon bride? Her metamorphosis into a succuba spells out his emasculation; it "was already late."

Are all women succubae? Only those who are sexual, and those who are not sexual are ethereal and vapid, caught in the same empty social conventions as their male counterparts. A rough draft of a poem tipped into the notebook and called "Paysage Triste" contrasts the sort of girl one might take to the opera with a seasoned tart glimpsed on an omnibus; though Eliot daydreams about her in her bed chamber, hair all unbound, he admits that social intercourse with her is out of the question because she is embarrassingly ignorant of the required forms of dress and etiquette. The torture that fills "Ode" and many of these early poems, therefore, is double-horned: the fear of sexuality and the simultaneous and complementary fear of impotence, each feeding the other and together devouring him like twin succubi. The rejection of a romantic passion like Tristan's dooms him to be a wraith at the dance of death. In a 1909 "Song" he finds his pallid lady with her white flowers insufficient: "Have you no brighter tropic flowers / With scarlet life, for me?";[11] but he cannot blame her for what is basically his own failure. A notebook poem called "Suppressed Complaints" shows a woman alone in bed, clutching the blanket in sexual frustration and breathing hard in her dreams, while the speaker looms in the corner, a shadow spectator at his own nightmare. Another notebook piece, "In the Department Store," says that the consciousness of mortality renders man incapable of making a woman – or himself – happy. These early poems present many images of the failed male lover: in "Goldfish," the Chocolate Soldier (after the popular operetta); in "Nocturne," a pathetic "Romeo, *grand sérieux*,"[12] reaching the "perfect climax all true lovers seek" in Juliet's death "swoon"; in "Bacchus and Ariadne" (in contrast to the myth and to Pound's later version of Dionysus), a poet so shattered by the woman's approach that he imagines himself a bottle broken into scattered bits. "Entretien dans un parc," a notebook poem dated February 1911, depicts the speaker attempting to woo a lady under spring trees; fixated by his own incompetence, he grasps her hand, and when nothing happens, he knows himself, like Prufrock, to be ridiculous. The concluding images are a pot seething on the fire of ridicule, a blind alley, a crumbling wall defaced with tattered posters and graffiti.

The sexual anxiety of these early poems is given its most extreme statement in three violent pieces written during the year before Eliot's surprising marriage to Vivienne Haigh-Wood, in June 1915, within weeks of meeting her.[13] In "The Burnt Dancer" the poet watches a black moth, symbolic of psyche or soul, as he wanders from some purer clime to destroy himself through his heedless fascination with the flame, which consumes desire in pain. The refrain expresses Eliot's empathy with the moth's blind yet willed extinction and joins in the dance of death exultantly. The autoerotic sado-masochism is even more explicit in a dramatic monologue that outdoes Browning's "Porphyria's Lover." The first stanza presents the speaker's fantasy of flogging himself for hours in prayer, rapt by his pain, until his spattered blood glistens in the ring of lamplight and he expires with his head at last cradled between his lady's breasts. The scene overlays a grotesque pieta with a grotesquer madonna with child, but the second stanza switches from masochism to aggression as the speaker now revels in the fantasy of choking his beloved to death. The title – "The Love Song of Saint Sebastian" (which appears above the text not in the notebook but in another manuscript of the poem in the McKeldin Library, University of Maryland)[14] – links the poem to "Prufrock," written several years earlier, and to a poem written soon after "Saint Sebastian," also dealing with autoeroticism, "The Death of Saint Narcissus."[15]

The opening lines of "Saint Narcissus," beginning "Come under the shadow of this gray rock," would be revised for *The Waste Land*. The protagonist is a young man whose enjoyment of his own body ("his limbs smoothly passing each other," "his arms crossed over his breast," the "pointed corners of his eyes," the "pointed tips of his fingers") arouses in him both polymorphously autoerotic pleasure and sadistic attitudes toward other people: "If he walked in city streets, / He seemed to tread on faces, convulsive thighs and knees." The poem presents a sequence of narcissistic images of himself: first as a tree, "twisting its branches among each other, / And tangling its branches among each other"; then as a fish "with slippery white belly held tight in his own fingers, / Writhing in his own clutch, his ancient beauty / Caught fast in the pink tips of his new beauty"; and finally as a young girl "Caught in the woods by a drunken old man," but also as the drunken old man himself, tasting her (his own) luscious whiteness and smoothness. Revulsion from his narcissism compels the young man to go to the desert, where he embraces the arrows that punish his flesh and finds satisfaction at last in martyrdom. For Narcissus, "sainthood" is only sublimated sadomasochism.

The peculiar intensity of Eliot's sexual anxiety stems from the dread force of passion convulsed by an equally fearful compulsion to control the anarchy of the passion which revolts him. Exactly how much of the quandary came from temperament and how much from training is impossible to determine, but there can be no doubt that the Eliots had absorbed New England Puritanism as it evolved from Calvinism through Transcendentalism to Unitarianism. His Massachusetts ancestors had included prominent divines, including John Eliot, the Apostle to the Indians, and though his branch of the family had moved west to St. Louis, it transported the New England spirit to the banks of the Mississippi. His paternal grandfather, William Greenleaf Eliot, a Unitarian minister held in awed reverence for his benevolent but strict piety, was called by Emerson himself the "Saint of the West." His biography, penned by Eliot's mother, Charlotte Champe Eliot, and published in 1904, shortly before Eliot went east to Harvard, was a work of Protestant hagiography. The following observations by Eliot's mother sum up the family temperament, which her son Tom inherited: "Impassioned but never passionate, he appealed to the reason and conscience, and men could not gainsay him. A man of deep and tender affections, whose intensity of feeling was only equaled by his strong power of self-control, Dr. Eliot was reticent in the expression of his own emotions."[16]

Charlotte Eliot, a poetess in her own right, fully imbibed her father-in-law's strongly Emersonian Unitarianism and expressed it in her verses. They were composed mostly for *The Christian Register*, but a thin sheaf was published as *Easter Songs* (1899).[17] Mrs. Eliot was a powerful presence in the family and especially so in the life of her seventh and last child; a congenital double hernia afflicted Eliot from an early age and made him a special object of overweening maternal solicitude. A brother later remarked that of all the children, Tom resembled and took after her most strongly. She acknowledged that he excelled her as a poet even before he went to Harvard, and she wrote him there of her hope that he would achieve the literary recognition she had failed to reach for herself. Later, in 1926, he would find a publisher for her long dramatic poem *Savonarola* and write an introduction to it.[18] The following are representative titles among Charlotte Eliot's *Easter Songs*: "Love Is Eternal," "Saved!," "Force and God," "Not in the Flesh, But the Spirit." The reviewers praised them for their "uplifting influence" and "inspiration to higher thinking and nobler living." Several stanzas from "At Easter-Tide" indicate the tenor of the moral and spiritual influence Charlotte Eliot wielded over her son from childhood:

> The bursting seed and budding stem
> Proclaim the life that lived in them
> > Through Winter's stormy hour,
> While crowded in such tiny space
> Lay hid the beauty and the grace
> > That make the Easter dower.
>
> So, deep within this soul of mine,
> A living principle divine
> > Awaits in day and hour,
> To feel the quickening current flow,
> To feel the heavenly warmth and glow
> > That bursts in bud and flower.
>
> O Spirit, working to create,
> Shall soul alone thy coming wait
> > To vivify anew?
> The undeveloped life complete,
> The marred and blemished make more sweet,
> > And turn the false to true.
>
> Thou who does guard and safely hold
> The life that now begins, unfold
> > The conscious life within!
> There beauty infinite shall bloom,
> Immortal verdure there find room,
> > And endless joys begin.

The father, Henry Ware Eliot, Sr., was a successful St. Louis executive (at the Hydraulic-Press Brick Company) with stern, fixed views on most important subjects, including sex. Biographer Lyndall Gordon writes:

> Another reason for Eliot's inhibition was possibly his father's view of sex as "nastiness." Henry Ware Sr. considered public instruction tantamount to giving children a letter of introduction to the Devil. Syphilis was God's punishment and he hoped a cure would never be found. Otherwise, he said, it might be necessary "to emasculate our children to keep them clean."[19]

No wonder that the young Eliot's combination of impotence and sexual guilt could project itself as a metaphysical nightmare: one manuscript poem ("He said this universe is very clear") envisions the universe as a gigantic spider web in the middle of which the Absolute waits, an explicitly syphilitic (and female) spider, waiting to trap and eat us. Woman, who had elsewhere been despised as the "eternal enemy of the absolute," here triumphs as absolute malevolence.

"Prufrock" was Eliot's first masterpiece; it set the tone for the entire first volume. Eliot's personae in many of the early poems resemble Prufrock, and several passages point specifically to the "Prufrock" poem. "Spleen," published in the *Advocate* early in 1910, when he was working on "Prufrock," concludes its echoing of Baudelaire and Laforgue with:

> And Life, a little bald and gray,
> Languid, fastidious, and bland,
> Waits, hat and gloves in hand,
> Punctilious of tie and suit
> (Somewhat impatient of delay)
>   On the doorstep of the Absolute.[20]

In "Suite Clownesque," another Laforguian piece, the speaker fancies himself a roguish rover walking on the beach in a flannel suit and ogling the bathing girls who are, he notes, beyond his reach. The text breaks off in mid-passage, and "Prufrock" begins immediately below it in the notebook.

In both the published and the unpublished poems, the surroundings of the failed male lover are urban; his is a city world. A series of "Caprices in North Cambridge" anticipate the glimpses of Roxbury gathered together as "Preludes" and epitomize the physical and psychological world of the Eliot persona: dusty rooms and dirty windows, dripping roofs and clogged gutters, muddy streets and alleys, broken bricks and glass, murky evenings and nights, vacant lots littered with ashes and tin cans and debris. The famous opening lines of "The Love Song of J. Alfred Prufrock,"[21] subtitled "Prufrock Among the Women" in the notebook, again present impotence in the urban waste land:

> Let us go then, you and I,
> When the evening is spread out against the sky
> Like a patient etherised upon a table;
> Let us go, through certain half-deserted streets,
> The muttering retreats
> Of restless nights in one-night cheap hotels
> And sawdust restaurants with oyster-shells. . . .

The pretatory lines from the *Inferno* place Prufrock in his own city-hell, split into actor and observer, "you and I." The internal and end rhymes, the alliteration and assonance render his self-consciousness exquisitely and bathetically tying itself into knots:

> Time for you and time for me
> And time yet for a hundred indecisions,
> And for a hundred visions and revisions,
> Before the taking of a toast and tea.

Prufrock never leaves the confinement of his room, but in his mind he imagines the labyrinthine streets under a torpid sky ("patient" again linking suffering with disease) leading literally to entrapment in a room full of women and leading metaphysically to an "overwhelming question" (the first of many questions in the poem). Attention to the seemingly loose and digressive movement of the poem actually reveals a psycho-logic of suppressed, even unconscious, associations. The rhyme of "What is it?" and "make our visit" draws together his metaphysical and sexual insecurities. Prufrock's fantasy of women "talking of Michelangelo" introduces the first of several heroic figures whom he plays ironically off against himself.

When Michelangelo's potency – physical and spiritual, sexual and artistic – induces paralyzed claustrophobia in Prufrock before Michelangelo's female admirers, he projects his state of mind onto the smoky fog muffling the house. He describes the grimy urban fog as feline and female: physical and erotic (e.g., the kinesthetic images of the cat's rubbing its muzzle and licking its tongue into corners), threatening violence ("Slipt by the terrace, made a sudden leap"), and smothering ("Curled once about the house, and fell asleep," in anticipation of the final drowning image of the poem). The line "There will be time to murder and create" encapsulates Eros and Thanatos in the instant of orgasm, and later, though he asks rhetorically, "Should I...have the strength to force the moment to its crisis?" his sense of impotence, even castration, forecloses the possibility. A mere glance from a woman penetrates his carefully groomed persona – morning coat, stiff collar, necktie asserted by a simple pin; a dismissive remark impales him, sprawling on a pin, wriggling on the wall. In contrast to such evidence of physical debility as his spindly limbs, Prufrock is fixated by the women's eyes, which can stare him down, and by their arms enticingly downed with light brown hair. His self-image, depicted in a series of disparate and dismembered parts of the body (think of Ransom's "Captain Carpenter"), shrinks to a "pair of ragged claws / Scuttling across the floors of silent seas." The zodiacal crab of Cancer is a feminine sign linked with sea and moon, but in his evolutionary retrogression Prufrock sees himself lacking a crab's body, reduced to aged claws, retreating across the ocean bottom. Later in the poem the sea is another image of the primordial feminine, and the phrase "the floors of silent seas" recalls the malingering fog which at one point seems to have invaded his flat and lies stretched out on the floor.

Prufrock's sexual defeat exacts its psychological and spiritual punishment. "The hands / That lift and drop a question on your plate" become the hands that carry his head in on a platter like John the Baptist's. He is no prophet, nor has he, like Lazarus, been raised from the dead through spiritual power. In his own estimation, he shrivels from Hamlet through Polonius to the fool. The forceful verbs ("To have bitten off the matter with a smile, / To have squeezed the universe into a ball / To roll it towards some overwhelming question"), already undercut by being cast into the perfect infinitives, trail off into "I grow old...I grow old.../ I shall wear the bottom of my trousers rolled." The specter of the old man stalks Eliot's poetry prematurely from the start – not here the wisdom of age but withered promise prefigured in desiccated youth, like the dry husks of men in Pound's seventh canto. Prufrock's metaphysical questioning ("'Do I dare?' and, 'Do I dare?'") devolves into self-parody: "Do I dare to eat a peach?" In transforming the young girls on the beach in "Suite Clownesque" into mermaids, Eliot made them more archetypal and subjective. Prufrock's erotic fantasy attests, in the musical richness of the language, to the anima's power to arouse and intimidate: "I do not think that they will sing to me." The end is a psychic death:

> We have lingered in the chambers of the sea
> By sea-girls wreathed with seaweed red and brown
> Till human voices wake us, and we drown.

The word "chambers" picks up his isolated room and the room full of women and overlaps with romantic suggestions of French "bedrooms," of hidden caves and recesses, of spiraled sea shells; and the word "lingering" recalls the lingering, malingering fog. The dream is more vital than actual existence, but it is a death dream, and contact with reality precipitates a wakening to extinction. All unfulfilled, "we" – the divided Prufrock – drown in the feminine element: body to rot, consciousness quenched.

"Portrait of a Lady"[22] (Part I before "Suite Clownesque" and "Prufrock" in the notebook, and Parts II and III later and dated February 1910 and November 1911) is a companion piece to "Prufrock" in the 1917 collection. It has an autobiographical basis in Eliot's awkward friendship with Adeleine Moffat, an intense, frustrated Boston lady who held a salon for young Harvard men. The poem alludes to "Prufrock": the gray afternoon, the smoke and fog, the room like Juliet's tomb, the paraphernalia of social gentility, the images of twisting and turning, the questions that unravel themselves, the Laforguian *vers libre* with its "dying fall." The lady seems an embarrassingly pathetic creature, yet the speaker's ego is so weak that she is sufficiently threatening to rout him: "I remain self-possessed except when...My self-possession flares up for a second....My self-possession gutters; we are really in the dark." Although he extricates himself from her importuning presence by escaping abroad (as Eliot would), in his own mind it is still she who vanquishes him. Even should she die in her abandonment, "would she not have the advantage, after all?" The "dying fall" of the music is the aesthetic articulation of impotence and defeat. Something of Adeleine Moffat's mythic power is suggested by Conrad Aiken's droll invocation of her at the teas he attended with Eliot; Aiken recalled "the Jamesian lady of ladies, the enchantress of the Beacon Hill drawingroom – who, like another Circe, had made strange shapes" of various Harvard undergraduates, including Eliot.[23] It is the unstated appeal to his animal nature, even from so circumspect a lady as this, that accounts for the speaker's Circean metamorphoses:

> And I must borrow every changing shape
> ' To find expression...dance, dance
> Like a dancing bear,
> Cry like a parrot, chatter like an ape.

Though she murmurs that he holds her life in his hands, her heedless twisting of the lilacs in her hands signifies her actual, if thwarted, power over him.

"Mr. Apollinax,"[24] written in 1915, the year of Eliot's civil marriage, contrasts with "Prufrock" and "Portrait"; in fact, Mr. Apollinax represents a shadow self, a caricature of the English philosopher Bertrand Russell, whose friendship with Eliot began when Russell taught at Harvard in 1914 and was resumed in the early years of Eliot's marriage. Russell reported that Vivienne Eliot "says she married him to stimulate him, but finds she can't do it. Obviously he married in order to be stimulated." Russell's view of the Eliots may have been distorted: at Russell's suggestion, however, the impoverished couple moved into the second bedroom of his London flat, and in January 1916, Eliot sent his wife off to Torquay for a holiday by the sea with Russell, a well-known womanizer between mistresses at the time. There are no details about their holiday à deux, but Eliot wrote Russell to thank him for possibly saving his wife's life: "I am very sorry you have to come back, and Vivienne says you have been an angel to her....I am sure you have done everything possible, and handled her in the very best way, better than I." Robert Sencourt opined in his memoir of Eliot that the episode "was to alter drastically both her hopes for the future with Tom, and her already fragile grasp on sanity."[25]

At all events, Russell in "Mr. Apollinax" is not an analytic positivist but a satyr, more Dionysus than Apollo, a disturbing, disruptive force among the fragilities of the teacups and drawing room chat. The Prufrockian speaker expects Apollinax to meet the same fate as John the Baptist for violating the social forms and looks for his head "rolling under a chair / Or grinning over a screen / With seaweed in its hair." "Mister" places him in the world of social convention; but his dry social banter betrays its submarine sources, and the speaker is ambivalent toward Apollinax's triumphant primordial energy: "He laughed like an irresponsible foetus." He compares Apollinax to Pan ("his pointed ears") and to a centaur, and it is precisely the abundance of Dionysian energy in the older man that makes him feel that he plays the "shy figure" in the Fragilion painting to Russell's Priapus, or one of the "worried bodies of drowned men" to Russell's "old man of the sea," roistering in the feminine element.

The other poems in *Prufrock and Other Observations* present a gallery of contrasting feminine types. In Eliot's own social class, they all signify sterility and obsolescence: Cousin Harriet, who holds off "the appetites of life" with the *Boston Evening Transcript*; spinster Aunt Helen, whose death allows the housemaid to disport with the footman; the Aunts, who revere "Matthew and Waldo" (Arnold and Emerson) as "guardians" of the Victorian order; Cousin Nancy, whose hollow modern liberation drives her to smoke cigarettes and ride New England hills as barren as herself. But there are other, more disturbing women outside his class: in "Preludes," III, a woman with hair in curlers clasps "the yellow soles of feet / in the palms of both soiled hands";

"Rhapsody on a Windy Night" holds in "lunar synthesis" the prostitute with twisted eye and stained dress, the cat that (like the fog) slips out its tongue to taste and devour, the eyes peering through lighted shutters from secret interiors with "female smells" (Eliot inherited his father's acute sense of smell and often identified women with a smothering and offensive odor); and finally, the pock-faced moon herself, redolent of dust and cologne, twists a paper rose in her hands.[26] The moon image sums up the poet's incipient madness and, as one of his chief symptoms, his neurotic association of women with disease and death.

In the last two poems in the volume the speakers, both poets, contend with the threat of women. "Conversation Galante," a quite early poem dated November 1909 in the notebook, wryly presents the speaker attempting to escape from the woman's presence into romantic conceits, and the woman puncturing his inflated language with pointed questions. In "La Figlia Che Piange," a much subtler poem written in 1911, the year in which Eliot finished "Prufrock" and "Portrait," the artist speaker sacrifices the loving relationship between a man and a woman for the aesthetic pose and gesture which the painful moment of departure provided his imagination and art. Perhaps the artist-speaker observes or imagines another man callously pushing his girl to tears and flight, and preserves the moment in his mind and words; perhaps, split as Prufrock is, the artist observes or imagines himself driving her away and coolly capturing the poignant moment of her farewell. In either case, the shift of verbs from the imperatives of the first stanza (which stage the moment, whether in fact or in fantasy), through the ambiguous subjunctives of the middle stanza, to the mixture of subjunctive possibilities and declarations of separation in the last stanza trace the speaker's emotional retrenchment. The final twist of irony is the observer's recognition that the safe distance of art is achieved only at the cost of life, and that the emotional range of such art is thereby restricted to an ironic view of suffering. For whether the woman is a real person or a figment of the imagination, the volume ends with the poet watching himself mastermind his rejection of her; the poet immortalizes his inspiration in the act of sacrificing her.

The quotations in this chapter illustrate how allusive Eliot's poems are, not merely to works by other authors but, just as important, to one another. Eliot intends that the deliberate reiteration of certain words and a limited range of images fabricate the poem as it coexists with and interacts with the other poems in the corpus. Eliot composes the atmosphere, the texture, the "feeling" of the poem and of the body of work by striving for a Symboliste density of relation and nuance, making the details of a particular poem reverberate with the contexts of other poems. He thought of the literature of Europe or of a nation as comprising a coherence modified and adjusted by each new addition to the organic whole, and he sought to construct his own work as something of a microcosm of that model. In fact, Eliot's description of Ben Jonson's creation of a complete and unique world expressive of his "personal point of view" applies equally to his own achievement:

It is so very conscious and deliberate that we must look with eyes alert to the whole before we apprehend the significance of any part. We cannot call a man's work superficial when it is the creation of a world; a man cannot be accused of dealing superficially with the world which he himself has created; the superficies *is* the world.[27]

The work of art as world is the world as work of art: what Stevens called "the *mundo* of the imagination." That equation subordinates objective fact to aesthetic expression; the object becomes the subject of the poem, and the subject is objectified in the poem.

Even from what has been said so far, it is clear how different in tone and intention Eliot's poetry is from Stevens', but what they shared was a derivation from the French Symbolistes. Eliot learned to divest his verse of the late-Romantic manner still lingering in the *Advocate* poems and to develop his own tone and style by discovering French Symbolisme late in 1908 through Arthur Symons' *The Symbolist Movement in Literature*, which after publication in 1899 became the most important channel for Symbolisme into English-language verse. On several occasions, Eliot said that when he was coming to artistic expression, he could find no models among the poets in English, not even Yeats: "The kind of poetry that I needed, to teach me the use of my own voice, did not exist in English at all; it was only to be found in French" – specifically in the Symboliste example of Baudelaire and Laforgue[28] (while Stevens was learning more from the later Symbolistes Mallarmé and Valéry). Eliot even went so far as to claim that he was more indebted to Laforgue "than to any one poet in any language." From Laforgue he adapted a sinuous, arch *vers libre* for the ironies and self-deflations of the hypersensitive observer, and from Baudelaire as well as Laforgue he

> ...learned that the sort of material that I had, the sort of experience that an adolescent had had, in an industrial city in America, could be the material for poetry; and that the source of new poetry might be found in what had been regarded as the impossible, the sterile, the intractably unpoetic.

The dreamlike urban reality in its dingy sterility became for him the psychological landscape of the modern consciousness. Of Poe's cities Eliot wrote:

> Perhaps all that one can say of Poe is that his was a type of imagination that created its own dream world; that anyone's dream world is conditioned by the world in which he lives; and that the real world behind Poe's fantasy was the world of the Baltimore and Richmond and Philadelphia that he knew.[29]

So, too, Baudelaire's and Laforgue's Paris, Eliot's Boston and London. The "fusion between the sordidly realistic and the phantasmagoric" was bent not on describing a scene but on rendering an emotional, psychological state. It was Eliot's Symboliste rendering the data of experience into mood-play that linked him to Stevens and Hart Crane, with whom he had no personal friendship, and dissociated him from the Imagist Pound even during the years of their closest association.

An examination of "Morning at the Window," one of the less frequently explicated poems in the *Prufrock* volume, demonstrates how carefully threaded the verbal fabric of Eliot's poetry was from the beginning, the contextual complexity of the language transforming a vignette observed near London's Russell Square in 1914 into a hallucinatory psychological state. This is the full text of what seems a slight enough poem:

> They are rattling breakfast plates in basement kitchens,
> And along the trampled edges of the street
> I am aware of the damp souls of housemaids
> Sprouting despondently at area gates.
>
> The brown waves of fog toss up to me
> Twisted faces from the bottom of the street,
> And tear from a passer-by with muddy skirts
> An aimless smile that hovers in the air
> And vanishes along the level of the roofs.[30]

There are only two explicit references to the observing consciousness, but the phrases "I am aware" and "to me" insert the determining angle of vision into each stanza. Presumably the observer is viewing the scene – almost spying on the scene – behind the insulating, distancing panes of glass mentioned in the title. The "window" image brings to mind windows, open and shut, in other poems: "lonely men in shirt sleeves, leaning out of windows" in "Prufrock"; "The showers bent on broken blinds" in "Preludes," I; "eyes in the street / Trying to peer through lighted shutters" and "female smells in shuttered rooms" in "Rhapsody"; "The shutters were drawn and the undertaker wiped his feet" in "Aunt Helen"; and later in *The Waste Land*, "As though a window gave upon the sylvan scene...staring forms / Leaned out, leaning...." The *Prufrock* poems are mostly set in the late afternoon dusk or at night, but "Morning" reminds us of "The morning comes to consciousness / Of faint stale smells of beer..." in "Preludes," II. Almost all of the details that comprise the scene either reinforce or contrast with details from other poems in the *Prufrock* volume. "Breakfast plates" recalls the porcelain crockery in elegant drawing rooms, as well as the plate in "Prufrock" on which the teasing question is dropped and the platter which holds the Baptist's head. The kitchen "housemaids" recall the housemaid in "Aunt Helen" perched on the footman's knees. The "street" figures prominently in "The Boston Evening Transcript" ("If the street were time") and in every vignette of "Preludes," and provides the maze for the perambulations of the neurotic in "Rhapsody on a Windy Night" ("Along the reaches of the street," "The street lamp sputtered... muttered") and in "Prufrock" ("the half-deserted streets of one-night cheap hotels / And sawdust restaurants with oyster shells"). "Tramples" picks up several details from "Preludes": "A lonely cab-horse steams and stamps. / And then the lighting of the lamps"; "the sawdust trampled street / With all its muddy feet that press / to early coffee-stands"; "trampled by insistent feet." "Edges" suggests the borderlines between the psychic states of the observer and the observed, and "the trampled edges of the street" echoes the torn border of the whore's dirty dress and "the last twist of the knife" in

"Rhapsody," even "My self-possession gutters" in "Portrait." The "area gates" which frame the housemaids are a variation of the door which opens on the whore like a grin, and "sprouting" echoes the garden imagery (the hyacinth garden and the lilacs in "Portrait," the rose in "Rhapsody," and the sprouting corpse in *The Waste Land*, all of which anticipate the many gardens in later poems), here undercut immediately by the adverb "despondently."

The muffling fog in "Prufrock" and "Portrait" and the smothering sea in "Prufrock" become the "brown waves of fog" in the second stanza here. "Brown" looks back to the "seaweed red and brown" in "Prufrock" and anticipates the "brown land" of *The Waste Land*. The flotsam which the "waves of fog toss up to me" reiterates the "crowd of twisted things" thrown up "high and dry" by memory in "Rhapsody" and later "the drift of the sea and the drifting wreckage" which "tossed up our losses" in "The Dry Salvages." In this context the "bottom of the street" picks up the "floors of silent seas" and even the restaurants with oyster shells in "Prufrock." "Twisted faces" suggests Prufrock's preparing "a face to meet the faces that you meet," the mirrored face in "Portrait," the leering whore and the pock-faced moon in "Rhapsody." In the same way, the "passer-by with muddy skirts" repeats "the skirts that trail along the floor" in "Prufrock" and the whore's ragged dress "stained with sand." The word "twisted" gathers in many images: from "Prufrock," the fog which "curled once about the house," Purfrock's "wriggling on the wall," the supercilious woman's turning away from Prufrock; in "Portrait," the "windings of the violins," "slowly twisting the lilac stalks," the man "turning" to remark his face in the mirror; in "Preludes," "fancies that are curled / Around these images, and cling"; in "Rhapsody," the whore's eye twisted "like a crooked pin," "a twisted branch upon the beach," "a broken spring in a factory yard, ...curled and ready to snap," "Her hand twists a paper rose," "the last twist of the knife"; in "Conversation Galante," the woman's "giving our vagrant moods the slightest twist"; in "La Figlia," "Fling them to the ground and turn....She turned away"; in several poems the labyrinthine streets of the city. The smile torn from the passer-by is linked to Prufrock biting off the matter "with a smile," the posturing smile of the speaker in "Portrait" ("and do I have the right to smile?"), the whore's leer and the moon's winking grimace in "Rhapsody," Mr. Apollinax's foetal laughter, and "simple and faithless as a smile" in "La Figlia." The phrase "hovers in the air" catches the young man's tendency to imaginary levitation in "Portrait" ("let us take to the air") and recalls the evening "spread out against the sky / Like a patient etherised upon a table" in "Prufrock" and the "soul stretched tight across the skies" in "Preludes," IV. Moreover, the hovering and vanishing repeat the fragile momentariness of states and moods which haunt many of the poems: "I have seen the moment of my greatness flicker" in "Prufrock"; "My self-possession flares up for a second" in "Portrait"; the soul's "thousand sordid images...flickered against the ceiling" in "Preludes," III; the moment of poignant, lost beauty in "La Figlia."

This kind of exegesis would be merely tiresome if it did not demonstrate the extent to which Eliot's linguistic world closes on its own indirections, so that the overtones and nuances accumulate in the repeated words and images themselves. This self-creating, self-sustaining quality of language made Eliot say that poems are "autotelic," that is, are their own subsistent ends. The notion is the opposite of the Romantic conception of language as an expression and extension of nature, and is at odds with the ideogramic conception which Pound learned from Fenollosa and which also roots words in objects; but it is the Symboliste theory which Stevens and Crane and Tate would also, differently, adapt to their own purposes. "Morning at the Window," perhaps the more obviously for its slightness, demonstrates Eliot's characteristic strategy in defining his poetic world through the deepening psychological resonances around recurrent images which turn the sordidly realistic into the phantasmagoric.

All, or virtually all, of the *Prufrock* poems were written before Eliot's marriage in June 1915, and *Ara Vos Prec* in England (1919) and *Poems 1920* in the United States show a new manner in the quatrain poems written after the Prufrock volume. But "Hysteria,"[31] from the first volume, graphically sums up Eliot's neurotic misogynist fears, seeping up from the unconscious, which the quatrain poems sought to suppress with a stronger ironic and prosodic control. In fact, "Hysteria" was written at the same time as the later *Prufrock* poems, just before or after the marriage; in either case, Vivienne's hysteria soon became a disturbing fact of Eliot's life. In this remarkable prose vignette, Eliot's Prufrock persona transforms his laughing woman companion into a nightmare vision of the destructive feminine. The speaker describes his "becoming involved in her laughter and being part of it," while the woman expands monstrously until she looms as large as physical nature. Her teeth are stars and attest to her phallic aggressiveness; her throat gapes dark caverns into which "I was drawn...by short gasps, inhaled at each momentary recovery, lost finally..., bruised by the ripple of unseen muscles." The title of the poem puns etymologically on "womb," and emotional frenzy was thought by the Greeks to be a disease of the womb. The speaker's sense of fascinated helplessness at his own orgasmic, cannibalistic devourment is intruded upon by a waiter trying to seat the couple for tea; the comic anticlimax of the interruption rescues the speaker from the woman – or rather from his hallucination of her: "I decided that if the shaking of her breasts could be stopped, some of the fragments of the afternoon might be collected, and I concentrated my attention with careful subtlety to this end." Male consciousness plots its strategy to bring the predatory feminine and the irrational unconscious again under its control. The final twist of irony, however, is that the reader sees, even if the speaker does not, that whereas the woman is merely laughing, it is he who is hysterical, who suffers womb sickness.

With the exception of "Gerontion," which may be read, as it was once intended, as a blank verse prologue to *The Waste Land*, and of four poems in French, the new pieces in *Poems 1920* were all written in the tightly metered and rhymed quatrains which Pound and Eliot decided upon as a corrective to the opportunity for diffuseness possible in *vers libre*. Pound pressed Théophile Gautier's *Emaux et Camées* on Eliot as the model; the outcome was Pound's *Mauberley* and Eliot's arch, elliptical quatrains of 1917–1919, dealing either with the dislocation between past and present ("Burbank with a Baedeker: Bleistein with a Cigar," "A Cooking Egg") or with the gnostic opposition between matter and spirit ("Sweeney Erect," "The Hippopotamus," "Whispers of Immortality," "Mr. Eliot's Sunday Morning Service," "Sweeney Among the Nightingales"). The "Debate Between the Body and Soul," inaugurated in the unpublished poems, here expresses itself in a pedantic abstraction and compounded allusiveness almost parodic of the disembodied intellect as it contemplates the feline sexuality of Grishkin, the lumpish vulgarity of Bleistein, the pustular progeny of the philistine churchgoers, the sinister bestiality of Sweeney and his associates.

Eliot's ambivalence about physical passion projects itself in a Prufrockian revulsion against the animal, lustful Sweeney, but the disdain is visceral. If Sweeney is Prufrock's shadow, they are both aspects of Eliot, for Eliot is equally fascinated by and fearful of sexuality and impotence. It is Eliot's recognition of Sweeney in himself which forces his Prufrockian fastidiousness to such elliptical and tight-lipped disdain as these quatrains show. When a friend extolled his early poems in 1925, Eliot sent him a clipping from *The Midwives' Gazette* with these words underscored as his own commentary on those poems: "Blood, mucus, shreds of mucus, purulent discharge."[32] Eliot's jesting response betrays a deeper recognition: the poems said that life is a degrading mess – an afterbirth, a festering sexual sore.

Within himself he saw Prufrock and Sweeney impossibly twinned, grotesquely trapped. Eliot said that Sweeney was a composite character based on several sources, and one of them, according to Conrad Aiken, was a Boston Irish prizefighter named Steve O'Donnell.[33] The first long passage excised from *The Waste Land* on Pound's recommendation recounted a bar-crawling expedition from Eliot's Harvard days, and on his first time in London and in Paris he went slumming, drawn to the raw, sordid life of the urban underworld, as though he were seeking out the Sweeney denied in his outward behavior. During the years when he was writing "Prufrock" and "Portrait," he kept concealed in another drawer the bawdy, scatalogical, never-published poems he sometimes shared with his Harvard confreres, among them "Bullshit," "Ballad for Big Louise," and "King Bolo and His Big Black Queen."[34]

But what in particular drove Eliot to project the character of Sweeney during this period? After all, the decision with Pound to write quatrains determined only the form, and Pound's quatrains took a different tack from Eliot's. There can be no doubt that Eliot's marriage was a disaster that overshadowed the rest of his life. He seems to have been bowled over by Vivienne's vivacity, glamour, intelligence, and physical attractiveness. In the first blush of excitement, however adolescent and irrational, he may have hoped that he had found a partner for mind and body. Eliot's father, infuriated at this final insulting evidence of his son's irresponsibility, repudiated him, cut him out of his will, and died in 1919 without seeing him again. Eliot's commitment to Vivienne had the ring of desperate wish fulfillment: "She has everything to give that I want, and she gives it. I owe her everything." They were drawn to one another mentally as well as physically. She was a writer and critic; he published sketches and stories by her in *The Criterion* during the 1920s (even though many were thinly disguised accounts of their marital difficulties), and her hand appears with Pound's in the revision of *The Waste Land*. But strains began to threaten the marriage almost immediately as husband and wife began to drain each other's psychological and physical energy like vampires. Yet even a friend who found Vivienne "terrifying" and sympathized with "poor Tom" still had to conclude: "But she was his muse just the same." After the divorce in 1933 Vivienne still claimed: "As to Tom's *mind*, I am his mind."[35]

This pathetic overstatement nonetheless calls attention to the literary and intellectual dimension of the Eliots' relationship which helped to keep them together, through increasing illnesses and depressions and collapses, for seventeen long years. At the same time, if she aspired to be his mind, he wanted her to give him his body. In 1916, the year after the marriage, Eliot wrote of the arousing of the sexual instinct as perhaps "the only possible escape" from a world rendered "prosaic" by a repressive boyhood and upbringing: Eros could make poetry of life. Perhaps; but soon after the hasty and mismatched marriage, Eliot would be writing poems about his Sweeney shadow, shuddering away from him in disgust: it was "Prufrock" whom Vivienne found for a husband. The strain on them both, mind and body, built to the crackup which found expression in *The Waste Land*. After only six months of marriage, Eliot had written to Aiken, "I have *lived* through material for a score of long poems."[36]

But the long poem would have to wait for the breakdown. The shock and recoil of the first years of marriage made the poems he managed to write so guarded and oblique that the *Prufrock* poems seem confessional by comparison. What the new poems posit with defensively Olympian hauteur is the final incompatibility of mind and matter. A Romantic sense of incarnation led Emerson in *Nature* to posit "the Marriage of Mind and Matter," but Eliot's gnosticism led him to go back to Webster and Donne in "Whispers of Immortality"[37] in order to refute Wordsworth's and Emerson's incarnationalism. In contrast to the Webster and Donne in Eliot's essays, these Jacobeans suffer from a gnostic dissociation of sensibility: "thought clings round dead limbs / Tightening its lusts and luxuries"; "no contact possible to flesh / Allayed the fever of the bone." By contrast, Grishkin's rank, opulent sexuality is impervious to the "Abstract Entities," but the poet finds himself incapacitated by thought for her female and physical comforts: "our lot crawls between dry ribs / To keep our metaphysics warm."

"Mr. Eliot's Sunday Morning Service"[38] is the most outrageous of these quatrain poems. Its manner of expression is as elaborately affected as the hypereducated intellect could contrive in self-parody. The short, rhyming lines – concentrating the wordplay and sound effects and juxtaposing the images without transition or explanation – require, like most of Eliot's poems, the sort of textual explication which was to make him a favored poet of the New Criticism he helped to institutionalize. Moreover, because this poem puts the problem in theological terms, it is especially relevant to Eliot's later development:

> Polyphiloprogenitive
> The sapient sutlers of the Lord
> Drift across the window-panes.
> In the beginning was the Word.
>
> In the beginning was the Word.
> Superfetation of τὸ ἕν,
> And at the mensual turn of time
> Produced enervate Origen.
>
> A painter of the Umbrian school
> Designed upon a gesso ground
> The nimbus of the Baptized God.
> The wilderness is cracked and browned
>
> But through the water pale and thin
> Still shine the unoffending feet
> And there above the painter set
> The Father and the Paraclete.
> .   .   .   .
>
> The sable presbyters approach
> The avenue of penitence;
> The young are red and pustular
> Clutching piaculative pence.
>
> Under the penitential gates
> Sustained by staring Seraphim
> Where the souls of the devout
> Burn invisible and dim.
>
> Along the garden-wall the bees
> With hairy bellies pass between
> The staminate and pistillate,
> Blest office of the epicene.
>
> Sweeney shifts from ham to ham
> Stirring the water in his bath.
> The masters of the subtle schools
> Are controversial, polymath.

The conceit of the bees in the penultimate stanza assimilates the seemingly disparate elements of the foregoing lines and points them toward a conclusion. The image looks back to Origen and to the "sapient sutlers" (who are later the "sable presbyters") and their brood of children, and looks forward to the "subtle schools" and Sweeney (drawn together by the s-sounds) in the last stanza. "Epicene" recalls "enervate Origen," but "hairy bellies" suggests the highly sexed presbyters and Sweeney. Thus the bees are a comic epitome of the contrast in the Church between celibate cleric and procreative layman, between theological speculation and biological fact. Indeed, the fact that the epicene bees pollinate plants by rubbing against their sexual organs provides a ludicrous metaphor for the implication of Spirit in the sexual–material order through the Incarnation.

The doctrine of the Incarnation and its realization in history enter the poem early with the repetition of the opening verse of St. John's Gospel: "In the beginning was the Word," though the Word is then comically paraphrased as "superfetation of τὸ ἕν." (The sense and syntax here are clearer with a comma after the fifth line, as the text did read in its first appearance in *The Little Review*.) The biological meaning of "superfetation" as the fertilization of an already fertilized egg is given a theological sense as well: since God in eternity is already essentially one and complete, the projection of Himself into time in the physical person of Jesus seems an excessive and unnecessary entrance into the order of fertility and propagation. In the history of theological disputation, Origen, who emasculated himself to curb his fleshly nature (hence "epicene"), argued consistently that the Son as Son had to be inferior to the Father. Though Origen's position was later condemned as heretical, it spoke for an ancient and persistent strain of gnosticism in Western religious thought. For God's entrance into the natural order meant implication in the sexual mess. When in the "mensual turn of time" (Eliot wrote "menstrual" and Pound emended it to "mensual") God sent His Spirit into flesh, the One descended into the many; through Jesus descended His Christian offspring: on the one hand, the swarming horde of the Lord's sutlers and, on the other, the schools of subtle theologians.

The poem, therefore, hangs suspended between the "polyphiloprogenitive" sexual drive and the "polymath" theological schools. Can spirit and flesh be reconciled? The last stanza suggests not; it splits into two separate sentences: Sweeney wallowing on his buttocks in his bath, the schoolmasters shifting from one intellectual position to the next. Nevertheless, in the middle of the poem stands the enigmatic figure of Jesus. Is He the living refutation of the paradox or the figment of our unfulfilled wish? The world is a waste land, "cracked and browned," like the flaking paint in which it is depicted. Yet through the waste land flows the baptismal water, and in its midst the "Baptized God" still shines in His sinlessness, joined with the blessing Father and Spirit. On the other hand, the poem moves away from the still synthesis at its center to the harsh oppositions of the final lines and deflates the image of the "Baptized God" into the bathetic image of Sweeney "stirring the water in his bath."

"Sweeney Among the Nightingales,"[39] the next poem and the last in *Poems 1920*, depicts the man we first met in a brothel in "Sweeney Erect," embroiled again with whores and assassins. Is it significant that Sweeney here is the intended victim and that he seems to escape the threat this time? The cry of Agamemnon in the epigraph reminds us that it is our own violence which claims us as victims in the end. The last quatrain leaves little comfort: the death agony echoes through time from Agamemnon till now, and the singing nightingales continue to "stain the stiff dishonoured shroud."

Near the end of the folder of manuscript poems marked in Eliot's hand *Poems 1909–1920*, a single quatrain, entitled from Dante "Su somma sapienza il primo amore" ("On the highest wisdom, the first love"), asks the Lord's patient pardon as the poet resolves to convince (in the double sense of "win over" and "prove guilty") his Romantic inclinations through classical control. Later, writing of Baudelaire words that he could not but have known were applicable to himself, Eliot said:

> Inevitably the offspring of romanticism, and by his nature the first counter-romantic in poetry, he could, like anyone else, only work with the materials which were there. It must not be forgotten that a poet in a romantic age cannot be a "classical" poet except in tendency.[40]

For Eliot, then – as for predecessors like Arnold, contemporaries like T. E. Hulme, and followers like Tate – "classical" became a convenient but none too precisely defined counter in the ideological game by providing a broad term of reference to values not just anti-Romantic but pre-Romantic. Invocation of "classical" norms identifies the backward-looking, often reactionary aspect of Modernism.

The literary reviews and essays that Eliot was beginning to publish after *Prufrock* delineate "classical" principles by which Eliot would convince, again in that double sense, a temperament fully and inevitably as Romantic as Baudelaire's. Because his norms and attitudes assumed magisterial authority for a generation of readers and critics of literature, it is all the more important to recognize the personal basis and function of those judgments and norms. Like his teacher, the Humanist Irving Babbitt (and like Yvor Winters), Eliot came to view Romanticism as the encompassing literary and cultural disease from which his intellectual, psychological, and spiritual afflictions stemmed. Romanticism deluded and infected because it denied our fallen and divided psyches and instead committed the sick and mortal individual to his own muddled subjectivity. The Romantic engagement with nature entailed as well an engagement with the passions and emotions – in short, a dangerous commitment to those areas of experience that men have experienced and objectified as "feminine" and woman-related – and Eliot felt that he had to school himself against the seductions of that Sirens' song. He came to see, more and more clearly, that his own Symboliste inclinations as symptoms of a sick Romanticism, and his expostulations about "classical" and "romantic" were meant to redirect his own psychological disposition – and its Symboliste expression – away from narcissistic subjectivity toward a resolution of the demands of consciousness and the unconscious, intellect and passion, in the authority of an objective reality. Grasped in this personal and psychological framework, the familiar and influential dicta of Eliot's criticism (like Winters') show their limitations and lose some of their unimpeachability – but also take on the vitality of direct reference and relevance.

When Eliot reviewed the second volume of *The Cambridge History of*

American Literature for *The Athenaeum* in 1919, he singled out for special opprobrium the figure who had more than anyone else influenced the moral, religious, and intellectual atmosphere of his youth: "Neither Emerson nor any of the others [i.e., the Unitarians and Transcendentalists] was a real observer of the moral life...the essays of Emerson are already an encumbrance." Against naive Emersonian idealism he commended Hawthorne as a realist whose art mounted a criticism "of the Puritan morality, of the Trans-cendentalist morality."[41]

Eliot testified that in his family the standard for conduct, religious sentiment, and moral judgment was set by his grandfather, a close friend of William Ellery Channing's and Emerson's "Saint of the West." Charlotte Eliot's biography of her father-in-law was dedicated to her children – "Lest They Forget."[42] As the doting mother, she embodied those religious and ethical attitudes for her children and combined them, whatever the poetic results, with an Emersonian sense of the poet as professor of divine truth. William Greenleaf Eliot's sermons (which Emerson praised highly) and her poems preached the Protestant message as it had developed from con-gregational Calvinism to a Unitarianism by then thoroughly imbued with Transcendentalist piety: the inner light shining forth in the work ethic, civic responsibility, and philanthropic service. Transported to the midwestern heartland, it became the Protestantism of Middle America.

Eliot's trumpeting declaration in 1928 that he was "classicist in literature, royalist in politics, and anglo-catholic in religion" can be read as a position taken to controvert Emerson on every point. For although Eliot may not have had Emerson expressly in mind at the time, his adult life assumed its direction in reaction against all that Emerson stood for as a Romantic and as the avatar of his familial religious and cultural values. It is worth noting that Yvor Winters would wage a campaign, from the late 1920s until his death, explicitly against Emerson for giving such a deceptively insouciant appearance to the moral and psychological lunacy that is Romanticism; for Winters, Emerson was the whited sepulcher in which were interred the bones of Poe and Hart Crane.

From the diluted, secularized Protestantism of his family Eliot recoiled – geographically, culturally, literarily, religiously – first back to New England and then back to old England. In the 1920s he wrote a note on the back of an envelope:

> There are only 2 things – Puritanism and Catholicism. You are one or the other. You either believe in the reality of *sin* or you don't – that is the important moral distinction – not whether you are good or bad. Puritanism does not believe in sin: it merely believes that certain things must not be done.

Of course, this dichotomy is an oversimplification. For one thing, Eliot misnamed his antagonist; it was not Puritanism but Transcendentalist Unitarianism. It was, in fact, Eliot's deep-rooted Puritan sense of sin which made him abandon the Unitarianism of his immediate forebears and in time adopt Catholicism. Robert Lowell, a Harvard freshman in 1938, recognized

Eliot as a "Tireless Calvinist"; and his own conversion to Catholicism, like Eliot's, came through a Puritan temperament in recoil from the devolution of the faith of the fathers.[43]

It is difficult to sort out the mixed allegiances of latter-day anti-Emersonian New Englanders like Eliot and Lowell (or, for that matter, Hawthorne and Henry Adams) to Protestantism and Catholicism. Years later, Eliot described himself as combining a "Catholic cast of mind, a Calvinist heritage, and a Puritanical temperament,"[44] and his description applies to New Englanders like Hawthorne, Adams, and Lowell. Granted that, in Eliot's words, "the convert of the intellectual or sensitive type is drawn towards the more Catholic type of worship and doctrine," it is not surprising that Eliot found Pascal a particularly sympathetic figure as a Catholic Jansenist participating in that "Puritan movement within the Church."[45] He came to regard New England as essentially a province of the mother country with distinct local traits,[46] and the momentum of his temperament drew him not just back to New England but right back to the mother country, where the New England spirit had originated and from which it had diverged on its westward course. It is no accident that *Four Quartets* is the finest poem of Christian meditation in American letters since Edward Taylor's *Preparatory Meditations*. From 1914 on, Eliot resided in England, with periodic trips back to the United States, and the conversions of 1927 – baptism and confirmation as an Anglican, adoption of British citizenship – only completed a process begun when he left St. Louis to attend Milton Academy and Harvard College.

Eliot's expatriation, therefore, sprang from American roots. In his old age he pointed out that he remained an American poet ("I'd say that my poetry has obviously more in common with my distinguished contemporaries in America than with anything written in my generation in England. That I'm sure of") and that his poetry was determined by his early American experiences:

> Yes, but I couldn't put it any more definitely than that, you see. It wouldn't be what it is, and I imagine it wouldn't be so good; putting it as modestly as I can, it wouldn't be what it is if I'd been born in England, and it wouldn't be what it is if I'd stayed in America. It's a combination of things. But in its sources, in its emotional springs, it comes from America.[47]

In his opposition to Emerson and the further devolution of liberal Protestantism into the secular Humanism of Babbitt, Eliot would turn to such anti-Emersonian Americans as Hawthorne and Henry James, Adams, and, perhaps most important of all, Poe.

Eliot mentioned Poe more frequently than any other American writer before his own generation. This concern with Poe may seem surprising since Poe exerted no stylistic or thematic influence on Eliot; in fact, he deplored Poe's emotional adolescence and his subversion of language into sound effects. But what drew Eliot to Poe, for all his complaints about Poe's poetic practice, was his sense of sin and the incipient theory of poetry which that sense of sin entailed. Of course, it was Poe's awareness of the fallibility of nature and human nature, of the limits of human perception and articulation, which set him against Emerson's conception of the poet as seer and Emerson's theory of organic form. Art was what the skilled craftsman disciplined himself to make out of the ruins of flawed experience. The conviction that art said what nature did not say, and so could be experienced and grasped only on its own aesthetic terms, made Poe the first New Critic in America. Like Poe and such later expatriates as James, Whistler, and Pound, Eliot deplored the provinciality of American arts and letters and the cultural nationalism of people like Emerson and Whitman or his contemporaries Williams and Sandburg. And so Eliot preferred to commune with Poe through the more sophisticated poetry and poetics of the French Symbolistes – Baudelaire and Mallarmé and Valéry – but he had to acknowledge Poe, almost with embarrassed incredulity, as the antecedent and source for their thinking about art.[48] Poe anticipated his own Symboliste tendencies and illustrated all too clearly the need to resist Symbolisme as the decadence of Romantic subjectivity.

Long before he had a theology, Eliot shared with Poe (and Pascal and Baudelaire) a Calvinistic conviction of original sin. A Puritan did not have to be a theologian or even a firm believer to know that our first conscious reflections disclosed the individual's separateness, incompleteness, failure, need – for which mortality is the sign and seal and the Fall is the myth. Emily Dickinson wrote, "The loss of something ever felt I," and elsewhere: "The Missing All prevented Me / From missing minor Things"; and Poe's poetry – think of "Alone" or "To One in Paradise" – is a sustained outcry against a primordial deprivation. Such self-consciousness disjoins mind from body and projects itself metaphysically as a schism between the orders of nature and grace.

Even Eliot's conversion did not compensate for that sense of dislocation but instead reinforced the distinction between the natural order and the super-natural. In the year after his baptism, he excoriated the secular Humanism of Babbitt that had seemed persuasive during his student days: "There is no avoiding that dilemma: you must be either a naturalist or a supernaturalist." (Eliot was later heartened when Paul Elmer More, the most vocal Humanist after Babbitt, moved, like Eliot, from a Protestant heritage through Humanism to convert to Catholicism.) Thrashing out the idea of a Christian society on the verge of the Second World War, he was equally categorical: "It must be said bluntly that between the Church and the World there is no permanent modus vivendi possible." At the end of the Pascal essay, Eliot singles out as fundamental Pascal's analysis of the discontinuity of "the order of nature, the order of mind, and the order of charity" and concludes that no writer is more enlightening than Pascal to those "who have the mind to conceive, and the sensibility to feel, the disorder, the futility, the meaninglessness, the mystery of life and suffering, and who can only find peace through a satisfaction of the whole being."[49]

In the essays written in the first years after his conversion, Eliot three times cited T. E. Hulme as a modern, non-ecclesiastical philosopher who corroborated his current attitudes. A footnote to the passage on Pascal commends Hulme's *Speculations* for articulating "an important modern theory of discontinuity suggested partly by Pascal." The last words of the Baudelaire essay quote a paragraph positing original sin, the imperfection of human nature, and the consequent necessity for ethical and political discipline and institutions as "not merely negative, but creative and liberating." Eliot concluded his critique of Humanism by recapitulating Hulme's condemnation, lauding Hulme for finding out "for himself that there is an *absolute* to which Man can *never* attain" because of "the radical imperfection" of nature and because of "simple human fallibility." Eliot had met Hulme through Pound soon after arriving in London, and as early as 1916 he had summed up Hulme's philosophy in a lecture: "The classicist's point of view has been defined as essentially a belief in Original Sin – the necessity for austere discipline."[50] Although Hulme was himself not a Christian, his philosophy, laden with theological terms, offered Eliot a literary theory expressive of a conservative, Calvinistic vision.

Eliot's early literary essays repeatedly sound the need for order and tradition because the individual – the writer, the work – is necessarily limited and incomplete: "No poet, no artist of any art, has his complete meaning as one." In lieu of a religious or philosophical absolute, the body of literature itself came to be conceived as a quasi-absolute. In dismissing the metaphysics of Romantic Platonism, Eliot expropriated some of its terms: "the whole of the literature of Europe from Homer and within it the whole of the literature of [one's] own country has a simultaneous existence and composes a simultaneous order" – in fact, "an ideal order" comprised of "organic wholes." Tradition is the ongoing temporal development of the patterns of cultural expression and relationship; consequently any individual who wished to mature must develop a "historical sense," that is, "a perception not only of the pastness of the past, but of its presence."[51] The classicist educated himself into history and tradition, whereas Romantic barbarians like Emerson and Whitman demeaned history to autobiography and subverted the organic wholeness of culture to the organic wholeness of unconscious nature.

"Consciousness of the past" compels the individual to "a continual surrender of himself as he is at the moment to something which is more valuable." The axiom which ties together Eliot's literary, religious, and social pronouncements is the early certainty that "men cannot get on without giving allegiance to something outside themselves," be that something church or state or art, or all three.[52] Returning to St. Louis in his old age, he recalled the grandfather whose liberal Protestant attitudes had formed his point of departure, and for all their differences he expressed gratitude that his grandfather and his family had at least imbued him with reverence for the institutions of church, state, and university and with the duty of subordinating "personal and selfish aims...to the general good which [these institutions] represent."[53] Reflecting during his conversion year, 1927, on F. H. Bradley, the philosopher whom he had studied in his doctoral dissertation, Eliot drew from him the fundamental distinction "between the individual as himself and no more, a mere numbered atom, and the individual in communion with God":[54] the distinction which is the foundation of his declaring himself publicly the next year a classicist, royalist, and Anglo-Catholic.

Eliot's historical sense led him to account for the contemporary crisis. Henry Adams had dated the modern declension from the High Middle Ages of the twelfth century, but in "The Metaphysical Poets" (1921) Eliot dated the decline in English history from the seventeenth century, when "a dissociation of sensibility set in, from which we have never recovered." In the literature of the medieval and early Renaissance periods Eliot saw a consonance of thought and emotion, but the "splitting up of personality" can be seen by the end of the seventeenth century in the polarization of sensibility into Dryden and Milton. The metaphysical poetry of Donne and Herbert, therefore, exemplified the literary sensibility to which we should strive, against the historical current, to return. Among immediate predecessors, the French Symbolistes seemed to Eliot "nearer to the 'school of Donne' than any modern English poet." By the time of his conversion, Eliot came to see the literary achievement of the school of Donne as a manifestation of the strength and vitality of Anglicanism in the early seventeenth century, before the Civil Wars and the Puritan Common-wealth in which Milton was a partisan against king and bishop. Bishops Lancelot Andrewes and John Bramhall joined Donne and Herbert as exemplars of the unified sensibility; in fact, in comparison with Andrewes, Donne could seem almost a Romantic individualist whose need for self-expression already foreshadowed the impending dissociation. Depersonalizing his earlier harsh estimate of Milton in 1947, Eliot saw Milton's failings as manifestations of large cultural forces at work in the West, the underlying causes of which reach "to the depth at which words and concepts fail us."[55] Eliot's historical myth may be as oversimplified as Adams', but he continued to see his own dilemma mirrored and explained in the historical divergence between Puritanism and Anglicanism.

The heated ideological exchange during the 1920s between Eliot and John Middleton Murry as proponents of classicism and Romanticism reiterated these historical and religious associations.[56] Hulme has dubbed Modernism the up-to-date "classicism," and Murry saw Modernist classicism like Hulme's and Eliot's as Catholic in its positing "unquestioned spiritual authority outside the individual." Even as early as 1916, in a lecture on "The Reaction Against Romanticism," Eliot had already declared: "The present-day movement is partly a return to the ideals of the seventeenth century. A classicist in art and literature will therefore be likely to adhere to a monarchial form of government, and to the Catholic Church." In the name of individual responsibility, Murry reiterated the belief of Romantic Idealists that the individual who digs *"deep enough"* in pursuit of self-knowledge "will come upon a self that is universal." The vehemence of Eliot's polemic betrays how fearful he was of the irrational unconscious and of any specious notion of human perfectibility. Addressing through Murry all the would-be and latter-day Romantics of his generation, Eliot asserted that the "inner voice" of "palpitating Narcissi" only "breathes the eternal message of vanity, fear and lust." Desire craves gratification; Murry's psychology comes down to amorality – "doing as one likes": "Why have principles, when one has the inner voice?" Babbitt set up his Humanism against "Rousseau and Romanticism," but Eliot detected its hollowness in the fact that Babbitt could propose no more reliable criterion for mind and will than an "inner check." In 1931 Eliot would even chide the Anglican bishops at the Lambeth Conference for trusting so heavily in the "Individual Conscience" in their pastoral statements on marriage and contraception.[57]

"Tradition and the Individual Talent" established Eliot's critical stance by arguing for an "impersonal theory of poetry," which requires "a continual self-sacrifice, a continual extinction of personality," in order that the individual writer situate himself and his work within the "living whole" of the tradition. In the creative process "the poet has, not a 'personality' to express, but a particular medium, which is only a medium and not a personality...": not the poet-seer as medium but the craftsman's language as medium. The process was not quasi-mystical but quasi-scientific. The poet's mind was a chemist's retort "in which special, or very varied feelings are at liberty to enter into new combinations," or, better yet, a catalytic agent which is necessary for the elements to "unite to form a new compound" but which itself remains "inert, neutral, and unchanged" by the very activity it makes possible. Poetry, therefore, expresses "significant emotion," which has its life in the poem and not in the history of the poet. "The emotion of art is impersonal, and the poet cannot reach this impersonality without surrendering himself wholly to the work to be done." In "The Function of Criticism," written in the midst of the controversy with Middleton Murry, Eliot repeated the same theory in the same stern language of self-sacrifice. In 1940, when a lecture on Yeats provided the chance to review his impersonal theory, he elaborated it without retractions.[58]

In the early essays and most notably in "Tradition and the Individual Talent," Eliot was chastening and subduing the artist's ego not only before the collective tradition but also in relation to his own creative work. The classical, impersonal artist created a self-contained – Eliot's word is "autotelic" – art object. It stands as the "objective correlative" of the emotion it communicates or – better yet – embodies, for the emotion exists only in and as the art-object "which shall be the formula of that *particular* emotion"; "the new object...is no longer purely personal, because it is a work of art itself."

Here is where the aims of Eliot's classicism intersect with the theory and practice of the French Symbolistes, for Symbolisme posited the autotelic work of art both as an expression of and as a counter to its subjectivity. Eliot quoted Baudelaire paraphrasing Poe: "A poem does not say something – it *is* something." In reaction against the Romantic connection between art and personal experience, the classical-Symboliste-Modernist doctrine from Baudelaire and

Rimbaud to Eliot and Stevens, Tate and Crane insisted that "the *end* is the poem," or, as Archibald MacLeish's "Ars Poetica" put it, "a poem should not mean / But be."[59] But Eliot was making the same point when in 1919, the year of "Tradition and the Individual Talent" and the "Hamlet" essay which evoked the phrase "objective correlative," he commended Jonson's plays for creating worlds which can be experienced only on their own terms in the formal integration of their elements and parts. Even if a work of art should come to serve other ends – moral or social – it functions more effectively if it remains unaware of and even indifferent to those ulterior ends.[60]

The classical-Symboliste-Modernist attitude posited a necessary distance not only between the reader and the autotelic work but also between the artist and his work. Thus, "impressions and experiences which are important for the man," Eliot says, "may take no place in the poetry, and those which become important in the poetry may play quite a negligible part in the man, the personality." In fact, an often cited remark pushes the point to an extreme statement: "the more perfect the artist, the more completely separate in him will be the man who suffers and the mind which creates; the more perfectly will the mind digest and transmute the passions which are its material." For the "feminine" emotions rendered in an objective correlative are aesthetic emotions; against and because of the autobiographical impulse behind his poetry, Eliot's early theory presents a defensive and evasive counterthrust: "It is not in his personal emotions, the emotions provoked by particular events in his life, that the poet is in any way remarkable or interesting."[61]

II

Eliot would diverge increasingly from the Symbolistes and Stevens as he came to see the notion of an autotelic artwork as an expression of the "intellectual narcissism" of aesthetes like Poe and Valéry. It is true that even after Eliot's conversion there remains a Pre-Raphaelite and Paterian quality to *Ash-Wednesday*, but after *Four Quartets* he was able to review the development of Symbolisme in "From Poe to Valéry" from a critical distance. In fact, "From Poe to Valéry" is the exorcism of Symbolisme from Eliot's criticism, as the *Quartets* is an exorcism of Symbolisme from his poetry. But even then, compared with the Romantic confusion of art with life, aestheticism still seemed to Eliot valid insofar as it can be taken as an exhortation to the artist to "stick to his job."[62] Joyce's image of the supreme artist paring his nails in masterful detachment expresses the ideal of Hulme's classical Modernism, whereas the "highest point of exaggeration" in the Romantic confusion between the *objet d'art* and the artist's and viewer's life came in "Shelley's famous phrase, 'poets are the unacknowledged legislators of mankind.'" In Eliot's early theory the reader or viewer, like the artist, should "observe always from the outside though with complete understanding."[63]

It is easy to see why Ransom would find Eliot's urbanely authoritative example a major source for the New Criticism. As Eliot admitted from the start, his intention was "to divert interest from the poet to the poetry" so as to "conduce to a juster estimation of actual poetry, good and bad"; "for the poem, in some sense, has its own life...quite different from a body of neatly ordered biographical data; ...the feeling, or emotion, or vision, resulting from the poem is something different from the feeling or emotion or vision in the mind of the poet." Eliot's first and immensely influential collection of essays, *The Sacred Wood* (1920), directed attention to the poetic text, as would Ransom's first collection, *The World's Body*, twenty years later. Since a poem is "excellent words in excellent arrangement and excellent metre," the critic's function is to help the reader attend to the resources and techniques of language so that there can arise a "direct relationship" between the informed and trained reader and the text. Eliot coyly resisted being labeled a New Critic, and in "The Frontiers of Criticism" (1956) he pointed to the limitations of what often devolved into "the lemon-squeezer school of criticism." Nevertheless, that late essay follows Ransom in distinguishing between criticism – a "purely *literary* criticism" – and scholarship: historical studies, biographical studies, psychological studies, source studies, and so on.[64]

Consequently Eliot, like Stevens and Tate, took a classical-Symboliste-Modernist position in informing the Marxist and sociological critics of the 1930s and 1940s that the "social function" of the poet resided in "his direct duty...to his *language*." In the scrutiny of literary means and effects, for which "the *end* is the poem," the poet must be a critic – his own critic. Although criticism can never be autotelic in the sense that art is, it is nevertheless as "inevitable as breathing" for any conscious person, and especially so for the conscious artist bent on mastery of the medium which will change inchoate materials to objectified form. For the ultimate justification of poetry and its criticism, Eliot instructed the unheeding Middleton Murry, is "the possibility of arriving at something outside of ourselves, which may provisionally be called truth."[65]

Eliot remained very much a writer criticizing the writing of others in the tradition, as he interpreted it. The coherence of his critical view, encapsulated in notions like the historical sense, impersonality, objective correlative, dissociation of sensibility, and classicism, had a broad impact on twentieth-century poetry, broader in the first half of the century than that of Imagism. Yet Eliot was honest about the subjective basis for the effort to attain Modernist objectivity. Especially after his admirers elevated his pronouncements to an almost infallible authority, he regularly warned that any artist's criticism should always be read against his creative work, and he admitted that his advocacy of classicism in terms of "a higher and clearer conception of Reason, and a more severe and serene control of emotions by Reason," rested upon the eruptive and irrational chaos of his emotions.[66]

In fact, from the outset the early essays had posited the personal sources of classical impersonality. The comment that "the more perfect the artist, the more completely separate in him will be the man who suffers and the mind which creates" has been detached from the statement in the next clause that the mind requires this distance in order to digest and metamorphose "the passions which are its material." There is never any question in Eliot's mind that "what every poet starts from is his own emotions" and – furthermore – that "it is poetry rather than prose that is concerned with the expression of emotion and feeling." Poetry may contain intellectual content and meaning, but its distinctive materials – contrasted with prose fiction or drama – are the passions and feelings, beginning with the poet's own passions and feelings. Both disciples and detractors of Eliot like to quote such anti-Romantic pronouncements as "Poetry is not a turning loose of emotion, but an escape from emotion; it is not the expression of personality, but an escape from personality." But again, the force of that sentence can only be appreciated in conjunction with the sentence following it: "But of course, only those who have personality and emotions know what it means to want to escape from these things."[67] Art provides escape not through evasion or suppression but through objectification; expression provides catharsis and release from emotions and feelings that would otherwise remain locked in the unconscious, raging in blind darkness.

From the start, Eliot recognized the unconscious sources of conscious expression, and lodged in the largely unconscious sources and materials of art the necessity for the conscious craft to give those materials formal expression. Eliot often used the word "feelings" not as a synonym for "emotions" but in a technical sense adopted from Bradley's philosophy. "Feeling" refers to the complex of associations which surround and inform an object of experience and create its largely unconscious suggestiveness; such feelings invest the particular emotional experience with its distinctive and unique quality. For the writer especially, "particular words or phrases or images" are charged with feelings, for which the expression becomes the symbolic embodiment or objective correlative. In fact, since feelings cannot be apprehended directly or formulated conceptually, they can be brought to consciousness, and so to realization, only through the symbolic enactment of art; art gives form to feelings over which we have "no control" and "which we can only detect, so to speak, out of the corner of the eye and can never completely focus." Eliot was sufficiently Modernist to agree with both the Symbolistes and the Imagists that the poem is the "result of the fusion of feelings so numerous, and ultimately so obscure in their origins, that... the poet may be hardly aware of what he is communicating; and what is there to be communicated was not in existence before the poem was completed."[68]

Frequently, therefore, the poem begins to take shape in what Eliot called the "auditory imagination" – that is, in "the feeling for syllable and rhythm, penetrating far below the conscious levels of thought and feeling,* invigorating every word; sinking to the most primitive and forgotten, returning to the origin and bringing something back, seeking the beginning and the end." In "The Music of Poetry" (1942), written during the composition of

---

*Eliot seems here to be using the word "feeling" in its more customary denotation as "emotion."

Four Quartets, Eliot made the analogy between the two arts not just on the basis of sound effects and the structural recurrence of themes but through the genesis of verse in the auditory imagination: "I know that a poem, or a passage of a poem, may tend to realize itself first as a particular rhythm before it finds expression in words, and that this rhythm may bring to birth the idea and the image."[69]

In "The Three Voices of Poetry" (1953), Eliot takes Gottfried Benn's *Problem der Lyrik* as his point of departure and offers this remarkable reflection on how the archetypal energies assume syllable, rhythm, image:

> There is first, he says, an inert embryo or ('creative germ') [*ein dumpfer schöpferischer Keim*] and, on the other hand, the Language, the resources of the words at the poet's command. He has something germinating in him for which he must find words; but he cannot know what words he wants until he has found the words; he cannot identify this embryo until it has been transformed into an arrangement of the right words in the right order. When you have the words for it, the "thing" for which the words had to be found has disappeared, replaced by a poem. What you start from is nothing so definite as an emotion, in any ordinary sense; it is still more certainly not an idea; it is – to adapt two lines of Beddoes to a different meaning – a
>
> > *bodiless childful of life in the gloom*
> > *Crying with frog voice, "what shall I be?"*
>
> I agree with Gottfried Benn, and I would go a little further. In a poem which is neither didactic nor narrative, and not intimated by any other social purpose, the poet may be concerned solely with expressing in verse – using all his resources of words, with their history, their connotations, their music – this obscure impulse. He does not know what he has to say until he has said it, and in the effort to say it he is not concerned with making other people understand anything. He is not concerned, at this stage, with other people at all: only with finding the right words or, anyhow, the least wrong words. He is not concerned whether anybody else will ever understand them if he does. He is oppressed by a burden which he must bring to birth in order to obtain relief. Or, to change the figure of speech, he is haunted by a demon, a demon against which he feels powerless, because in its first manifestation it has no face, no name, nothing; and the words, the poem he makes, are a kind of form of exorcism of this demon. In other words again, he is going to all that trouble, not in order to communicate with anyone, but to gain relief from acute discomfort; and when the words are finally arranged in the right way – or in what he comes to accept as the best arrangement he can find – he may experience a moment of exhaustion, of appeasement, of absolution, and of something very near annihilation, which is in itself indescribable.[70]

In her letters, Emily Dickinson had several times talked about the poetic process in terms of seeking relief or delivery from an agonizing burden, but Eliot, though a man, goes farther than she did in describing the poet as mother and the inception of the work as a primordial birthing akin to orgasm and death: "a moment of exhaustion, of appeasement, of absolution, and of something very near annihilation." The poem becomes, as he says, at once posses-sion, confession, and exorcism.

This poet, whom Matthiessen called the "most thoroughly conscious" artist in American poetry since Poe, sounds more like the poet of "Song of Myself," when in his "classical" essay "Tradition and the Individual Talent" he deplores a degree of self-consciousness which would "encroach upon [the poet's] necessary receptivity and necessary laziness."[71] By Eliot's own report, he even had moments of seemingly spontaneous composition that he would have considered "automatic writing" but for the fact that the material "has obviously been incubating within the poet":

> It gives me the impression... of having undergone a long incubation, though we do not know until the shell breaks what kind of egg we have been sitting on. To me it seems that at these moments, which are characterized by the sudden lifting of the burden of anxiety and fear which pressed upon our daily life so steadily that we are unaware of it, what happens is something *negative*: that is to say, not "inspiration" as we commonly think of it, but the breaking down of strong habitual barriers – which we tend to re-form very quickly. Some obstruction is temporarily whisked away. The accompanying feeling is less like what we know as positive pleasure, than a sudden relief from an intolerable burden.

Temporary disintegration of the ego's defensive barriers releasing the repressed energies from the unconscious: Eliot identified this gestative phase of the poetic process, as before, with his "feminine" capacities – the hen hatching her nest egg. Eliot footnoted this passage with an observation of A. E. Housman which Eliot said confirmed his own experience: "the production of poetry, in its first stage, is less an active than a passive and involuntary process; ...a secretion; whether a natural secretion, like turpentine in the fir, or a morbid secretion, like the pearl in the oyster."[72] No doubt Eliot agreed with Housman that his poetic secretions tended to be of the morbid variety.

At the same time, Eliot also agreed with Housman that the secretion and gestation of the poetic germ is only the first stage. The poet is not just the birthing mother but the midwife attendant at and facilitating the birth. Delivery and deliverance are the responsibility of a "scrupulous, painstaking and *conscious* practitioner of the *craft*."[73] The conscious and unconscious aspects of the poetic process require each other. The poet occupies the

> ...conscious mind with the craftsman's problems, leaving the deeper meaning to emerge from a lower level. It is a question then of what one chooses to be conscious of, and of how much of the meaning, in a poem, is conveyed direct to the intelligence and how much is conveyed indirectly by the musical impression upon the sensibility.[74]

The good poet realizes both the conscious and unconscious aspects of the creative process; the bad poet exhibits both defective craftsmanship and emotional self-indulgence because he tends to be "unconscious where he ought to be conscious, and conscious where he ought to be unconscious."[75]

In explicating the complementarity of the conscious and unconscious aspects of the creative process, Eliot moved beyond superficial and exclusive notions of personality and impersonality. The paradox is that an objective correlative expresses a personal point of view whose source issues below the intellect; yet the artist expresses his personality – albeit "indirectly through concentrating upon a task which is a task in the same sense as the making of an efficient engine or the turning of a jug or a table-leg."[76] We need not take Eliot's point here any more literally than Poe's when he contended that he wrote "The Raven" as if he were solving a mathematical problem. Although Eliot believed that "what every poet starts from is his own emotions," he also believed that the creative act strives "to transmute his personal and private agonies into... something universal and impersonal." For Eliot both propositions are true: "the great poet, in writing himself, writes his time"; and all verse, even dramatic verse written for fictitious characters, is "one's own voice," "yourself speaking." Lecturing on Yeats in 1940, Eliot refined his earlier theory by distinguishing between "two forms of impersonality." The lesser kind is that of "the mere craftsman" who produces the odd "anthology piece"; the greater impersonality is achieved by the "unique personality which makes one sit up in excitement and eagerness to learn more about the author's mind and personality.... The second impersonality is that of a poet who, out of intense and personal experience, is able to express a general truth."[77]

Allen Tate, profoundly indebted to Eliot as poet and critic, and Robert Lowell, indebted in turn to both, have attested to the fact that in Eliot, the man who suffered and the mind which created were at once separate and the same. Tate on Eliot sounds like Eliot on Yeats: "His poems came out of the fiery crucible of his interior life; yet all of the interior life we know is in the poems; and that is as it should be; for his theory of the impersonality of poetry met no contradiction in the intensely personal origins of the poems."[78]

Now we can see that the Modernist notion of impersonal art as objective correlative, which underlies "Prufrock" and "Rhapsody on a Windy Night," "Mr. Eliot's Sunday Morning Service" and The Waste Land, derives, in ways that parallel the poems, from Eliot's desire to engage, and fear of engaging, the feminine aspects of self and world. Art originates in the subject and issues in the work, submitting feeling and emotion to formal articulation. Eliot became irritated at those admirers who read his impersonal theory too simplistically. Responding to the interpretation of The Waste Land as expressing the mood of the whole Lost Generation after World War I, Eliot took possum pleasure in undermining his impersonal authority:

> Various critics have done me the honour to interpret the poem in terms of criticism of the modern world, have considered it, indeed, as an important bit of social criticism. To me it was only the relief of a personal and wholly insignificant grouse against life; it is just a piece of rhythmical grumbling.[79]

On the other hand, we should not take this self-deprecating remark at face value either. If the impersonal theory of poetry turns out to have personal sources, it is also true – and herein lies Eliot's continuing influence and greatness – that his best poems attain the second level of impersonality he ascribed to Yeats by confabulating a general truth out of the turmoil of private emotions and feelings.

III

By the early 1920s Eliot's basic critical attitudes were established, and he had begun to write a long poem during the years in which Pound was finding his own way into the ideogrammic method of *The Cantos*. Within a year of his marriage, he had said, he had lived through the material for a score of long poems, and most of his mature poetic activity resulted in longish sequences. In 1919 he was writing the last of his quatrains and working on episodes for the poem which became *The Waste Land*: "The Death of the Duchess," for what shaped up as the "Game of Chess" section, and "Gerontion," intended as the introduction to the poem.

Like "Prufrock," "Gerontion" is a dramatic monologue, and indeed the persona is the Prufrock persona grown old. Grown, in fact, from a fastidious Bostonian who was never young into a "little old man" who sounds rather like Henry Adams, whose *Education* Eliot had just reviewed under the title "A Sceptical Patrician."[80] The opening of "Gerontion"[81] plays ironically with the theme of youth and age; the epigraph from *Measure for Measure* ("Thou hast neither youth nor age...") is followed by the old speaker being read to by a boy. Though the literary analogs include Cardinal Newman's "The Dream of Gerontius" and Milton's Samson, this little old man has neither vision nor strength. As in "Prufrock," and later in *Ash-Wednesday* and the *Quartets*, age brings not wisdom but only confirmed decrepitude and impotence. Gerontion points to the Fisher King and Tiresias of *The Waste Land*, and to the associated themes of sexual and spiritual failure. The old man has no prophetic power, nor is the boy a David-like symbol of reborn selfhood. Christ's appearance is anticipated, coming in fearful prophetic power, springing "in the juvescence of the year." But here the Judaic tradition is reduced to the Jewish landlord, and Christian salvation is betrayed ("flowering judas") by the empty rituals of Mr. Silvero, Madame de Tornquist, and the others. Gerontion is only a "dull head," an ego consciousness alienated equally from instinct and passion, on the one hand, and from spiritual vision, on the other. Just as Jesus in "Mr. Eliot's Sunday Morning Service" appeared as the "Baptized God," incarnating the divine commitment to material and sexual life, so here Christ's spiritual power is explicitly erotic and works through the regeneration of nature. But such energy seems only threatening to Waste Landers like Gerontion, dissociated from the feminine in all its aspects: from women, from his own passional nature, from the seasonal round, from Christ as God-in-nature. The only women in the poem are the peevish, sickly old housekeeper and the woman from whose "heart" he feels himself withdrawn (she is "heart" as he is "head"). So the spring rain for which Gerontion waits becomes the symbol, as in *The Waste Land*, for natural and supernatural renewal, and the wind, the manifestation of Spirit in the material order, is desert-dry as it buffets his "dull head."

The following famous passage illustrates Eliot's supple variation of the blank-verse line after the example of the Jacobean dramatists and dramatizes the intellectual and sexual angst reminiscent of Adams:

> After such knowledge, what forgiveness? Think now
> History has many cunning passages, contrived corridors
> And issues, deceives with whispering ambitions,
> Guides us by vanities. Think now
> She gives when our attention is distracted
> And what she gives, gives with such supple confusions
> That the giving famishes the craving. Gives too late
> What's not believed in, or if still believed
> In memory only, reconsidered passion. Gives too soon
> Into weak hands, what's thought can be dispensed with
> Till the refusal propagates a fear. Think
> Neither fear nor courage saves us. Unnatural vices
> Are fathered by our heroism. Virtues
> Are forced upon us by our impudent crimes.
> These tears are shaken from the wrath-bearing tree.

The identification of history as "she" is startling at first, but her "cunning passages, contrived corridors / And issues" indicate Gerontion's fear of the feminine. A little later, he will use words with strong historical associations to the woman from whom he has become disaffected: "to lose beauty in terror, terror in inquisition." History is feminine because she is deceptive, over-powering, unmanning (we have only "reconsidered passion," "weak hands"). Eliot manipulates the line breaks to emphasize and contrast the verbs: Gerontion's reiterated "think now...Think...," punctuating her activity (she "has," "deceives," "guides," repeatedly "gives," finally "defeats through giving"); and his passive verbs expressive of his victimization ("is distracted," "not believed in," "if still believed," "can be dispensed with," "are fathered," "are forced upon," "are shaken from"). Moreover, the erotic implications of "whispering," "supple," "famished," "craving," "passion," and "propagates" build up to the sexual victimization of the three passive verbs, "fathered," "forced," "shaken."

At the same time, Gerontion's clear perception of his plight requires him to link his victimization with his alienation from his senses and his passions:

> I have lost my passion: why should I need to keep it
> Since what is kept must be adulterated?
> I have lost my sight, smell, hearing, taste and touch:
> How should I use them for your closer contact?

The mind to which all passion is adulterated can only perversely stimulate the dead senses with such intellectual contortions as these. By contrast, the images of nature and of Christ suggest an active sexuality: "in the juvescence of the year / Came Christ the tiger / In depraved May..."; "The tiger springs in the new year. Us he devours." The primitive force of the tiger pitches the feline threat of Prufrock's fog and Grishkin's "Brazilian jaguar" and the devouring lady of "Hysteria" into deeper psychological and metaphysical areas through overtones of James's "Beast in the Jungle" and Blake's "Tyger." Since Gerontion cannot experience Christ's passion (in both senses) and resurrection as salvific, he feels them as destructive, and imagines the Spirit-Wind coming not to animate bodies but to splinter them to bits in a final apocalypse: "De Bailhache, Fresca, Mrs. Cammel, whirled / Beyond the circuit of the shuddering Bear / In fractured atoms."

The mythic substructure, the literary allusions, the collagelike juxtapositions of The Waste Land[82] have been explicated skillfully from so many viewpoints that the principal need here is to demonstrate how the spiritual and sexual themes express the relation to the feminine. The epigraph from Petronius presents the Sybil trapped in a living death, and from her image we enter the shadow world of the Waste Land, in which dreams and reality, myth and contemporary vignettes intersect in a rapidly shifting montage suggestive of the splicing and overlay of cinematography. "The Burial of the Dead" takes up again the crucial question of "Gerontion" – the possibility of resurrection: "That corpse you planted last year in your graden, / Has it begun to sprout? Will it bloom this year?" Everything hangs on the answer – both for the poet himself, through his persona, the Fisher King, and for the land and civilization. The invitation to "come in under the shadow of this red rock," where we will be shown a shadow deeper than the one we cast on the ground at sunrise and sunset, confronts us with "fear in a handful of dust."

The fear that reverberates throughout the first section of the poem (Marie's "And I was frightened," Madame Sosostris' "Fear death by water") turns out to be, as in the early poems, a simultaneous dread of sexuality and of impotence, as the very first lines reveal:

> April is the cruelest month, breeding
> Lilacs out of the dead land, mixing
> Memory and desire, stirring
> Dull roots with spring rain.
> Winter kept us warm, covering
> Earth in forgetful snow, feeding
> A little life with dried tubers.

The "dull roots" and "dried tubers" are feebly aroused by the sexual and maternal advance of April, stressed in the active participles hung at the ends of the verses and particularly in the rhyming of "breeding" and "feeding." The coming of spring is a forced seduction and a forced feeding; the protagonist and his fellow Waste Landers feel the terror of the helpless baby or the pubescent son before the advances of the Great Mother. They refuse the birth they desire and dread, choose the death they dread and desire. Alienation from the mother-lover, manifested in the blighted and parched land, curses them all: the Fisher King, the men and women in the Waste Land, patriarchal civilization itself. When Marie cries out in fear of the Alpine sled ride, her cousin the arch-duke, the personification of the old order, is blinder than she about their descent: "Marie, / Marie, hold on tight. And down we went."

"The Burial of the Dead" juxtaposes in alternation episodes of nature and civilization, of sexual and spiritual failure: the April passage; the leisured and aristocratic international set, heedless of their fall; a panorama of the Waste Land, invoking Ezekiel and Ecclesiastes as authentic prophets of doom (unlike the Sybil, Madame Sosostris, and Tiresias); the impotence of the protagonist (here linked with the fertility god Hyacinth) before the girl in the hyacinth garden (reminiscent of the lilac lady in "Portrait" and of the rejected girl in "La Figlia Che Piange") framed by the doomed Wagnerian passion of Tristan and Isolde at sea (remember Eliot's early poem on the opera); Madame Sosostris telling the protagonist's fortune; a prospect of London as a circle of the Inferno; a last scene in which the ritual corpse of the fertility god (Eliot's note refers us to Adonis, Attis, and Osiris) is buried, either to rot away or to rise again. Allusions to Dante, Webster's *The White Devil*, and Baudelaire's "*Au Lecteur*" combine different cultures and epochs in a concentrated apprehension of the Waste Land as contemporary hell. The referentiality of "I" and "you" shifts from episode to episode, ending in the linking of the protagonist ("I") and the reader ("you") in Baudelaire's line: "*mon semblable, mon frère.*" The many voices of the poem tell a single story, ask the same question: will the corpse sprout and bloom this year?

Madame Sosostris, discommoded as she is with a bad cold, is the contemporary Sybil: "the wisest woman in Europe, / With a wicked pack of cards." The fortune she lays before the protagonist from the tarot pack introduces all of the characters – types who through various personifications will play their part in his ambiguous destiny. The protagonist's own card is "the drowned Phoenician sailor," and the line from *The Tempest* ("Those are pearls that were his eyes") indicates a sea change that could mean, as in Shakespeare, either death or rebirth from the maternal deeps. The anima card is Belladonna, whose name, Lovely Lady, is also the name of deadly nightshade; she is "the Lady of the Rocks" (da Vinci's Madonna...or Mona Lisa?) but also "the lady of situations." "The man with three staves" anticipates several characters in the poem, depending on what "staves" means: the impotent King with his fishing pole, Christ hanged in a trinity of crosses, the voice of the Thunder which utters three mysterious staves, or verses, at the conclusion. Is the Wheel the tragic rise and fall of fortune or the mandala which resolves all changes? Is the merchant merely a shadow figure, like the sleazy homosexual Mr. Eugenides, or possibly a secret missionary, like the merchants who carried on their travels the arcana of the mystery religions and later the Christian gospel? The Hanged Man recalls the drowned sailor ("Fear death by water") and the corpse planted in the garden. Is he the sign of the sailor's death, or, as god, of his risen self? From Madame Sosostris as well as from the protagonist at this point, the secret is hidden.

Though the two themes are interrelated throughout, Sections II and III of *The Waste Land* dramatize the sexual theme principally; and Sections IV and V the religious theme principally. "A Game of Chess," from Middelton's *Women Beware Women*, introduces the conceit of sexual play in a pair of episodes involving avatars of Eliot's Prufrock shadow and his Sweeney shadow with two kinds of women. The first title of the section in the manuscript of the poem, "In the Cage," recalls the trapped Sybil; the episodes contrast the neurasthenic sexlessness of a cultured, upper-class couple with the mindless promiscuity of the cockneys in a pub – in both cases, a failure of human love and communication. The first incident is clearly autobiographical, and Vivienne Eliot's markings and emendations in *The Waste Land* manuscript fall in this section. Her comment, written next to the opening description whose rococo opulence ironically compares the neurotic woman to Shakespeare's voluptuous Cleopatra and Vergil's Dido, shows that she missed the point: "Don't see what you had in mind here." However, beside the rest of the passage – the woman's hysterical and ineffectual attempts at communication and the man's unspoken reply – she wrote three times "Wonderful."[83] Though she is no Dido or Cleopatra, even this woman is a threat. The water imagery (her jewels are "poured in rich profusion," her synthetic perfumes "confused / And drowned the sense") recalls "Fear death by water." There are other allusions to the first section, especially in the opening passage: "Stirring dull roots," echoed here by "stirred by the air" and "stirring the pattern on the coffered ceiling"; "feeding / A little life," by "sea-wood fed with copper"; "dried tubers," by "withered stumps." In this sexual game, it is the woman who is again driven to be more active (her hair's "fiery points" "glowed into words"), but the man's silence reduces her to savage stillness. The scene parodies the earlier scene in the hyacinth garden. Where the male protagonist there had admitted, "I could not speak, . . . and my eyes failed, . . . and I knew nothing," the woman spits out at him now, in a staccato of negatives, his inability to see or speak or know. In one draft of the passage the man thinks, "I remember the hyacinth garden," before he repeats the image of the drowned sailor with pearls for eyes. Beside the final lines about the "closed car at four" and the dispirited game of chess, Vivienne wrote "Yes," perhaps because (as Eliot wrote to Russell in 1916) they had once taken an afternoon drive in a hired car after one of her restless nights.[84]

The pub scene is the dramatic monologue of a woman preening herself for having seduced Albert, back from the army, away from his wife Lil, toothless and washed out at thirty-one after the abortion of an unwanted child. Vivienne supplied the cockney speaker with two of her most telling lines: "If you don't like it you can get on with it" and "What you get married for if you don't want children?" Below the modulation of the drunken farewells of the pub-goers into the poignant last words of Ophelia, the wronged virgin, Vivienne wrote, "Splendid last lines."[85] The episodes in "A Game of Chess" illustrate the split consciousness of Eliot's early poetry: the woman confronting the self-conscious speaker renders him impotent by her aggressiveness; the women in the pub compete for Albert's lust. In Prufrock's world, Eliot feels his inferiority; in Sweeney's, he is smugly, snobbishly superior.

Of all the sections, "The Fire Sermon" underwent the most extensive and complicated set of revisions in manuscript. As it finally stands, it opens with the river and the river nymphs. "The nymphs are departed," but they show up at the end of the section as the Thames maidens* to lament their seduction and abandonment in tawdry mimicry of Wagner's ravished Rhine maidens. In between, there is a seamy carnival of Sweeney's London. He is there carousing with Mrs. Porter and her daughter; Mr. Eugenides, the unshaven merchant, mutters his homosexual solicitation (Eliot's note links the seagoing merchant with the sailor protagonist); a floozy named Fresca maneuvers her way through the smart set; the typist and the small house agent's clerk fumble each other like robots as mechanically tooled as the automobiles outside or the phonograph accompanying their coupling. As a result of Pound's prodding, Eliot shortened this last episode (though the quatrains of the longer version are still discernible in the rhyming of the lines) and eliminated entirely the Fresca passage, written in couplets too derivative, Pound felt, from Pope. But the Popean couplets of the longer version display a scatalogical insistence which states more crudely than elsewhere Eliot's misogynist association of women with the oral, anal, and genital functions of the body:[86]

> Leaving the bubbling beverage to cool,
> Fresca slips softly to the needful stool,
> Where the pathetic tale of Richardson
> Eases her labour till the deed is done.
> . . . .
> Odours, confected by the cunning French,
> Disguise the good old hearty female stench.
> . . . .
> (The same eternal and consuming itch
> Can make a martyr, or plain simple bitch);
> Or prudent sly domestic puss cat,
> Or autumn's favourite in a furnished flat,
> Or strolling slattern in a tawdry gown,
> A doorstep dunged by every dog in town.
> For varying forms, one definition's right:
> Unreal emotions, and real appetite.
> Women grown intellectual grow dull,
> And lose the mother wit of natural trull.

Similarly, the fuller version of the seduction scene is cruder than the published revision: the typist and the "young man carbuncular" are compared to "crawling bugs"; she "sprawls / In nerveless torpor on the window seat"; on his departure, he pauses at the corner "to urinate, and spit." Throughout "The Fire Sermon" the gross and sordid amorality of the contemporary scene is played off against the now grimed glory of Spenser's, Shakespeare's, Wren's, Elizabeth and Leicester's London.

The witness to this satyricon identifies himself as Tiresias, another of Eliot's voyeuristic observers, who, Eliot's note indicates, is intended to draw to-

* Vivienne Eliot was known among their Bloomsbury acquaintances as "the river girl" (Stephen Spender, *Eliot* [London Fontana/Collins, 1975, p. 49]).

gether the various male and female characters of the poem into a unifying consciousness: "What Tiresias *sees*, in fact, is the substance of the poem." As wise man and prophet – and androgyne at that – Tiresias ought to serve as an emblem of the total and realized self of the protagonist, as he does throughout Pound's *Cantos*. But in Eliot's psychic world, divided between Prufrock and Sweeney, Tiresias is impotent; "throbbing between two lives," "old man with wrinkled dugs," he is only a suffering spectator. "The Fire Sermon" of the title, Buddha's famous denunciation of lust, returns in the concluding lines, linked with Saint Augustine's plea to God to deliver him from his sinful passions. The jeremiads of these great prophets of East and West anticipate the turning point of the poem and the appearance of Jesus and the Thunder in the closing section, after the death scene in Section IV.

With the transition from a sexual to a religious emphasis, there are almost no references to women in the last two sections of *The Waste Land* (none in Section IV, and in Section V only the "murmur of maternal lamentation," the woman who fiddled music on her hair, and the androgynous stranger on the road). Even in the original manuscript version of Section IV, which before Pound's editing began with a long account of a voyage ending in shipwreck, the female references all connect shore life with women – mothers, girlfriends, whores – whom the sailor has left behind in heading out to sea. Except, of course, that the sea is the primal Mother.

The brief "Death by Water" is the low point of the poem. Phlebas, which means "penis" in Greek, dies into the feminine element. And the hint of the New Testament in "Gentile or Jew" is picked up at the beginning of "What the Thunder Said" in the several images of Jesus, first agonized and betrayed in Gethsemane, then imprisoned and condemned, finally executed, and risen before the disciples on the way to Emmaus. But the poem makes no explicit mention of the resurrection; the disciples to whom Jesus appears on the road do not know Him, and the episode breaks off the Gospel story before the revelation and recognition occur. Instead the poem goes on to present the protagonist as Grail Knight wandering the desert with an unbearable thirst in search of the sacred cup of the Last Supper, which would cure the impotence of the Fisher King and restore the fertility of the Waste Land. At the end of the quest, he finds the chapel which was said to house the Grail ruined, "only the wind's home." All about is evidence of the collapse of civilization, the return of the barbarians, the perversion and pollution of life. Still, their hooded and androgynous God is accompanying the disciples, all unknown, on their journey, and just when the Grail Knight's quest seems to conclude at the empty chapel with the "tumbled graves," the wind springs up, twirling the weathercock: "a damp gust [punning on the wind as Holy Ghost] / Bringing rain."

And the Thunder speaks the words in three staves. In the conjunction of the Thunder from the Hindu Upanishads with the Gospel story of Jesus' passion and resurrection, Eliot again associates Eastern and Western religion. There may also be an American Puritan analogue for the Thunder's voice; in Cotton

Mather's prophetic history of New England, *Magnalia Christi Americana*, Book VI, Chapter III (which Eliot almost surely knew as required reading for Barrett Wendell's course at Harvard), the Voice of God speaks as Thunder to convince New England of its transgression and call it back to repentance and grace.[87] The Thunder is the unseen, awesome Father, but His Word is the New Testament of Love. Unlike Tiresias, the Thunder issues three commands for action – give, sympathize, control – and the Sanskrit is interpreted by the most important lines of the poem:

> DA
> *Datta*: what have we given?
> My friend, blood shaking my heart
> The awful daring of a moment's surrender
> Which an age of prudence can never retract
> By this, and this only, we have existed
> Which is not to be found in our obituaries
> Or in memories draped by the beneficent spider
> Or under seals broken by the lean solicitor
> In our empty rooms
> DA
> *Dayadhvam*: I have heard the key
> Turn in the door once and turn once only
> We think of the key, each in his prison
> Thinking of the key, each confirms a prison
> Only at nightfall, aethereal rumours
> Revive for a moment a broken Coriolanus
> DA
> *Damyata*: The boat responded
> Gaily, to the hand expert with sail and oar
> The sea was calm, your heart would have responded
> Gaily, when invited, beating obedient
> To controlling hands

The Thunder's directives enjoin the ego's submission to the risks of communion: give, give in, give up control, let love shake the heart, dare to surrender, forgo prudent caution, unlock the ego's prison doors, trust yourself to other hands, respond and move when drawn. For Eliot converts the Sanskrit message, "Control youself," into its opposite: "cede control," "respond to the power of the other." The message of complementary submissiveness and responsiveness instructs the protagonist to acknowledge and recover his feminine nature. Only through the anima can ego escape its prison into the possibility of relationship to a knowledge and experience of the other. And is the other human or divine? Both: "she" – dreaded and derided by the masculine ego – holds the liberating key to Eros and Agape, and, as we shall find again in "Marina," "she" moves with wind and water.

In *The Waste Land*, however, the clear call disintegrates into a jumble of fragments in the final lines: a Babel of tongues which seems to announce the imminent end of civilization. As for the protagonist, he answers his own question ambiguously: "Shall I at least set my lands in order?...These fragments I have shored against my ruins." Can he find at least personal coherence and release? The commands are repeated once more, echoed three times by the Sanskrit "Shantih," the "peace which passes all understanding," of which Saint Paul also wrote. Eliot's own gradual realization of the new possibilities of the anima is recounted in *The Hollow Men, Ash-Wednesday*, and the Ariel poems.

The Hollow Men (1925)[88] reworks the theme of *The Waste Land*, but here the short lines chop the syntax into phrases and at the same time weave them together with rhyme and repetition to achieve the incantatory effect of charm and nursery rhyme, rune and litany. The first four sections appeared separately in journals before being gathered together as *The Hollow Men*, with a new and concluding fifth section, in *Poems 1909–1925*. Section V raises the images of the preceding section to conceptual generalization. The hollow men – "we," numbering the speaker and the reader among them – are paralyzed by the shadow tensions that transfix consciousness between idea and physical reality, motion and act, conception and creation, emotion and response, desire and spasm, potency and existence, essence and embodiment. Abstractions define their vacuity by negation: "Shape without form, shade without colour, / Paralyzed force, gesture without motion." The only possibility of reversal comes in a subordinate clause:

> Sightless, unless
> The eyes reappear
> As the perpetual star
> Multifoliate rose
> Of death's twilight kingdom
> The hope only
> Of empty men.

These lines, just before the fifth section, reiterate imagery from the rest of the poem. Moreover, Section III first appeared in 1924, under the title "Doris's Dream Songs," along with two poems not included in *The Hollow Men*. Those poems, "Eyes That Last I Saw in Tears" and "The Wind Sprang Up at Four O'Clock," explicate *The Hollow Men* through the imagery of the eyes and face of a loved one lost now in "death's dream kingdom." The third of "Doris's Dream Songs," now Section III of *The Hollow Men*, repeats the theme of frustrated passion:

> Is it like this
> In death's other kingdom
> Waking alone
> At the hour when we are
> Trembling with tenderness
> Lips that would kiss
> Form prayers to broken stone.

The great tradition of Renaissance and Romantic love poetry – Juliet's eyes to Romeo, the eyes of Elizabethan sonneteers' ladies, Donne's lovers' eyes entwined, Fanny's peerless eyes to Keats – underlies the desperation of the opening lines of Section IV: "The eyes are not here / There are no eyes here / In this valley of dying stars"; lips kissless and eyes "sightless, unless / The eyes reappear." The eyes are his and hers: she has vision, and his sight of her restores his eyes too. But the poem anticipates her reappearance not as wife and not as the decadent Romantics' fleshly dreams of idealized spirit ladies (Poe's necrophilic Lenore and Ligeia or Rossetti's Blessed Damozel warming heaven's bar with her breasts) but as the Virgin: "perpetual star / Multifoliate rose." Two epithets for Mary in the Litany of the Virgin are "Morning Star" and "Mystical Rose."

In the evolution of Eliot's poem, Doris, previously encountered in Sweeney's company in "Sweeney Erect," gives way to the hints of Mary's presence: her "perpetual star" among our "dying stars," her rose among desert cactus. The poem admits that such is "the hope only / Of empty men," but the precariously poised "only" hovers between the suggestion that this hope is only a measure of our desperation and the suggestion that she is the sole hope of empty men. The fragments of the "Lord's Prayer" at the end of *The Hollow Men* stammer to the Father for a vision of the Virgin such as Rossetti's namesake Dante achieved through the lady Beatrice. Either that or death in the desert, and either way a deliverance from fleshly desires.

All of this – the imagery of desert and garden, the Dantescan overtones, the bits of prayers and litany, the incantatory repetition and parallelism – point to *Ash-Wednesday*, three parts of which were published separately in 1927, 1928, and 1929. Speaking with an immediate personal urgency that Eliot had not risked before, *Ash-Wednesday* turns from the waste land he had shared with Vivienne toward the Lady who stands between the yew trees, serving the Virgin and tending the rose garden. When the sequence appeared in 1930, Eliot dedicated it "To My Wife," but he retracted the dedication in subsequent editions after he initiated and obtained a legal separation from Vivienne in 1933. The dedication and the retraction are equally important; *Ash-Wednesday* enacts the repudiation of Eros for Agape intimated in *The Hollow Men.**

Ash-Wednesday[89] turns "the hope only / Of empty men" into a negative affirmation: "Because I do not hope to turn again." But in fact the poem turns again and again on the pivotal moment of conversion as the highly involuted

---

*In one of his Norton Lectures at Harvard during the year of the separation proceedings, Eliot went out of his way to take up I. A. Richards' comment that Eliot displayed a "persistent concern with sex, the problem of our generation, as religion was the problem of the last." Eliot replied that sex and religion were related, not different, problems: "in his [Richards'] contrast of sex and religion he makes a distinction which is too subtle for me to grasp. One might think that sex and religion were 'problems' like Free Trade and Imperial Preference; it seems odd that the human race should have gone on for so many thousands of years before it suddenly realized that religion and sex, one right after the other, presented problems" (*The Use of Poetry and the Use of Criticism*, pp. 126–127).

language – the run-on lines, internal and end rhymes, alliteration and assonance, repeated phrases and images – coils and uncoils itself. The overall direction is marked by a complicated progression from desert to garden and from
the feminine experienced as mediatrix of sexual, natural life (principally in the
first half of the sequence) to the feminine experienced as the virginal mediatrix
of grace.

Thus the first lines invoke a Cavalcanti *ballata*, in which the exiled poet
longs for his lady love, and Shakespeare's twenty-ninth sonnet, in which he
foresakes worldly power for love, but invoke them with a twist; Eliot's words
– the "vanished power of the usual reign," the "infirm glory of the positive
hour," the "one veritable transitory power" – dismiss masculine prerogative
in love as well as in war. Indeed, from Eliot's inverted, converted perspective,
positives appear negative and negation is a positive step. He resolves to "renounce the blessèd face / And renounce the voice" of his beloved, because the
natural order to his time-sick eyes seems a waste land: "I cannot drink / There,
where trees flower, and springs flow, for there is nothing again." The renunciation changes the contorted, self-circling syntax of the opening into
declarations ("I rejoice," "I pray") and supplications ("Teach us," "Pray for
us"). As in *The Hollow Men*, the lover is sublimated into the Virgin; the last
lines of Section I repeat the petition from the Hail Mary: "Pray for us sinners
now and at the hour of our death." In the sonnet, Shakespeare's earthly love
delivers him from his "outcast state" to "heaven's gate," but Eliot finds his
Lady only after acquiescence to death in the desert.

Section II poses the destructive and redemptive aspects of the anima in the
contrast – and link – between the white leopards who have, in a dream fantasy,
devoured Eliot's flesh and scattered his bones, and the white-gowned Lady
who "honours the Virgin in meditation." The leopards complete the work
of the feline fog, which "licked its tongue" and "made a sudden leap" at
Prufrock, and of Grishkin, the "couched Brazilian jaguar," who overcame
"the scampering marmoset / With subtle effluence of cat." At the same time
the Lady's leopards recall Christ the tiger, springing in the new year to devour
us, but where Christ's connection with the feminine in "Gerontion" lay in His
incarnation in the natural order, here the descriptive details of Eliot's symbolic
death – the tree, the skull, the consumption of the broken body – recall that
incarnation led to crucifixion before resurrection. Twice the Old Testament
God of Ezekiel calls the bones to prophesy; but each time they anticipate the
New Testament in hailing the Lady as the psychopomp of regeneration, for
the Virgin she serves was mother of the Savior through birth, death, and
resurrection. The ego's assent to the leopard's jaws and to the desert's oblivion
evokes the Lady in a rose garden and resumes the Litany of the Virgin only
hinted at in *The Hollow Men*:

> Lady of silences
> Calm and distressed
> Torn and most whole
> Rose of memory

Rose of forgetfulness
Exhausted and life-giving
Worried reposeful

As the womb of incarnation, she subsumes the paradoxes of birth and death, death and resurrection, nature and grace. The "single Rose" seeds the entire "multifoliate" Garden where the pangs even of a fouled marriage end (terminate and find their completion).

The single Rose
Is now the Garden
Where all loves end
Terminate torment
Of love unsatisfied
The greater torment
Of love satisfied

This section of *Ash-Wednesday* was published as "Salutation" in 1927, the year of Eliot's conversion. But just as in the Church's calendar Ash-Wednesday is only the first day of the penitential season of Lent, anticipating Easter forty days off, so conversion is no isolated and final moment but an ongoing process of resolution, and Eliot's poem continues to turn on, and return to, its ambiguities. For in Section III the image of the Lady cannot insulate the fancy against recollections or fantasies of earthly love or against the inveterate dream that the Waste Land may be revealed as Arcadia after all. In Section III, published in 1929, no sooner has Eliot, mounting the purgatorial stair (of Dante and Saint John of the Cross), contended, after the initial turning, with the shadow devil of the second stair than that very turning presents a prospect of the sensuous world to tempt him back. Pan is the false and carnal god of the springtime world, his hypnotic, phallic flute conjuring the erotic prize: "Blown hair is sweet, brown hair over the mouth blown, / Lilac and brown hair." The words summon other presences: the women in "Prufrock," arms "downed with light brown hair," the mermaids "wreathed with seaweed red and brown," with the "hair of the waves blown back"; the lady with the lilacs in "Portrait"; "La Figlia," with flowers in her arms and the sun in her hair; the girl in the hyacinth garden with arms full of blooms and hair wet; even the woman in "A Game of Chess," brushing her hair in the firelight. The sexuality of the scene is epitomized by the female conformation of the window framing the pagan pastoral: "a slotted window bellied like the fig's fruit."

Rejection of Arcadia, in turn, allows Section IV to introduce the Lady of the garden. Garbed like the Virgin and taking her place "between the yews [associated with death and mourning], behind the garden god" Pan, she initiates the reclamation of ruined Eden: she "made strong the fountains and made fresh the springs / Made cool the dry rock and made firm the sand." Consequently, Section V reveals her as the second, spiritual Eve, both mother and sister to the "children at the gate," exiled from Eden to the Waste Land, "spitting from the mouth the withered apple-seed." The temptress opened up "the desert in the garden"; the Lady now recovers "the garden in the desert." Vivienne's *Criterion* sketches portrayed the emotional waste land they occupied, but his mother's *Easter Songs* had assured Eliot of a hidden life in the imagery of Paradise regained:

> So, deep within this soul of mine,
> A living principle divine
>   Awaits in day and hour,
> To feel the quickening current flow
> To feel the heavenly warmth and glow
>   That bursts in bud and flower.
>
>   .   .   .   .
>
> Thou who dost guard and safely hold
> The life that now begins, unfold
>   The conscious life within:
> There beauty infinite shall bloom,
> Immortal verdure there find room,
>   And endless joys begin.[90]

But *Ash-Wednesday* is Eliot's long Lenten, not Easter, song. Phrase after phrase in the second half of the poem insists on Eliot's profound sense of personal dilemma, caught "between sleep and waking," "between the profit and the loss," "between dying and birth," "born on the horn between season and season, time and time, between / Hour and hour, word and word, power and power." The vacillation persists even into the final section of the poem. The first lines, "Although I do not hope to turn again / Although I do not hope / Although I do not hope to turn," use the doubleness of Cavalcanti's "perché" ("because" or "although") to make the poem revolve on itself once more. Another pastoral scene gapes through another window on the purgatorial stair:

> And the lost heart stiffens and rejoices
> In the lost lilac and the lost sea voices
> And the weak spirit quickens to rebel
> For the bent golden-rod and the lost sea smell
> Quickens to recover
> The cry of the quail and the whirling plover
> And the blind eye creates
> The empty forms between the ivory gates
> And smell renews the salt savour of the sandy earth

But this marvelous evocation of a polymorphous reveling of all the senses in natural beauty shows a divided consciousness which views physical pleasure as temptation: "lost heart," "weak spirit," "rebel," "blind eye," "empty forms," "the ivory gates" of false dreams in the pagan underworld. On the other hand, compared to the pastoral scene in Section III, the sexuality of this scene is already more diffused; this time, there is no erotic woman with "brown hair over the mouth blown." In Section VI, "tension between dying and birth" reveals the "blessèd face" renounced in Section I, refound now not as desired lover but as "blessèd sister, holy mother" – the feminine principle personified not in Vivienne as the "river girl" or in the ruined Thames maidens but in the "spirit of the fountain, spirit of the garden," "spirit of the river, spirit of the sea." The years in the desert presage not the earthly paradise but the divine garden. The new Eve is the Virgin Mother of the second Adam; through her we find ourselves in Him. The concluding litany to the Lady is, therefore, constellated around Dante's ideal of selfless self-discovery: "Our peace in His will."

Like many religious poems, *Ash-Wednesday* reflects on the relation between God's Word and the poet's language. Eliot enters the penitential season with words – Dante's words, Cavalcanti's and Shakespeare's, the words of Scripture, of liturgical worship and prayer – absorbed into his speech, all turning on themselves to sound the wordless Word. "Let these words answer," Eliot says in Section I, but the optative construction raises the question of human capacity to hear and utter the silent Word. Even if the "blessed face" and "voice" renounced as earthly lover reappear as spiritual sister and mother, she returns as "the lady of silence," her Son the "Word without a word." The litany of Section II identifies the Lady with her Son's mystery: "Speech without word and / Word of no speech."

But later sections admit the possibility of communication and communion. The fragments which end Section IV came from a prayer recited in the Mass just before communion: "Lord, I am not worthy to receive you; but speak the word only, and I shall be healed"; and that prayer paraphrases the Roman soldier's expression of faith in the Gospel story. In Section IV the "silent sister" still "spoke no word," but her spring and yew tree are associated with the bird and wind, both symbolic of the Holy Spirit in the Annunciation of the Word:

> But the fountain sprang up and the bird sang down
> Redeem the time, redeem the dream
> The token of the Word unheard, unspoken
>
> Till the wind shake a thousand whispers from the yew

The concluding fragment of Section IV comes from the "Salve Regina," a prayer to the Virgin which completes the phrase given here, "And after this our exile," with the plea: "Show unto us the blessed fruit of thy womb, Jesus."

Section V recapitulates the theme in a remarkable passage:

> If the lost word is lost, if the spent word is spent
> If the unheard, unspoken
> Word is unspoken, unheard;
> Still is the unspoken word, the Word unheard,
> The Word without a word, the Word within
> The world and for the world;
> And the light shone in darkness and
> Against the Word the unstilled world still whirled
> About the centre of the silent Word.

Eliot is working off of the poetic meditation on the Incarnation which opens Saint John's Gospel:

> In the beginning was the Word, and the Word was with God, and the Word was God. He was with God in the beginning. All things were made through Him, and without Him nothing was made that was made. In Him was life, and that life was the light of men. And the light shines in the darkness, the darkness which could not comprehend it. . . . He was in the world, and the world was made through Him, and the world knew Him not. He came unto His own, and His own received Him not. But those who did receive Him He gave the power to become children of God. And the Word was made flesh, and dwelt among us; and we saw His glory, as of the only-begotten of the Father.

The Gospel text has been subjected to a great deal of exegetical commentary, but its statement of the mystery is direct enough: God expresses Himself to and as creation; the aboriginal Light overcame the original darkness; Word became word. In contrast to John's simple declarative sentences, linked by coordinating conjunctions, Eliot's single complex sentence, with its conditional clauses and ambiguous syntactical relations, suggests (1) the difficulty for human speech even to approximate the Word, (2) the frantic busyness through which human beings drown the Word out, and (3) the persistence of the Word in the midst of the clamor. As Eliot's verses ricochet "word" and "Word" and "world" off one another again and again, the passage seems to emphasize disjunction more than conjunction. Despite the puns and paradoxes suggestive of the difficulty of comprehending (in the sense of "understand" and of "enclose" or "contain") the mystery, finally more is "lost" and "spent" through human perversity than through intrinsic limitation. It is not so much that the Word is unheard because unspoken, but rather that the Word is unspoken because unheard by "those who walk among the noise and deny the voice." The last clause – "unstilled world still whirled," framed by "against the Word" and "about . . . the Word" – insists on the presence of grace despite human sin. "Still" stands at the center, combining the sense of "silent" with "nevertheless" and "always," as the mystery of the unheard Word.

Sin and grace – the character of the individual's Christianity depends on how these two factors of the human situation are related. Eliot's particular psychological and moral disposition determined the way in which he perceived and experienced the Christian mysteries. Eliot was inclined to feel – it was not a matter of doctrine but of temperament – that because the world chooses to oppose the Word about which it turns, he must reject the world in choosing the Word. One Christian attitude sees the Incarnation as signifying a commitment to save the world *in* itself and bring it to divinely immanent completion, but Eliot aligned himself with a gnostic tradition – pre-Christian but strongly influential in Christianity through Saint Augustine – which stated that the world must be saved *from* itself and delivered to the divine other.

This *contemptus mundi* assumed a particularly harsh formulation during the Reformation in the Calvinist sects. It is the ingrained Calvinism in Eliot, and later in Tate and Robert Lowell, that drew them away from the liberal Protestantism of their immediate family and region to Catholicism and that then informed the character of their Catholicism. In Lowell's "Colloquy in Black Rock," Christ breaks into the human dimension as a dive bomber, blasting the soul free from the mire of bodily degradation. In "The Quaker Graveyard in Nantucket," Our Lady has transcended human contradiction, and her face, "expressionless, expresses God." Lowell felt the Apocalypse more violently than Eliot, but for both, as for Tate, awareness of the Incarnation served to define and even heighten their sense of the tension between nature and grace, rather than to resolve it. Nevertheless, *Ash-Wednesday* takes up the human responsibility to hear and utter the silent Word. What's more, Eliot was Catholic, rather than Calvinist, in approaching the Word and the problem of speech through the Virgin Mother. The final litany concludes with the Psalm verse recited as the entrance prayer of the Mass: "And let my cry come unto Thee."

Eliot's "Ariel" poems[91] come from the same years as the sections of *Ash-Wednesday*: "Journey of the Magi," 1927; "A Song for Simeon," 1928; "Animula," 1929; "Marina," 1930; to be followed only much later by "The Cultivation of Christmas Trees" in 1954. Published separately as part of a series of poems issued as Christmas cards by Faber and Faber (the publishing firm for which Eliot was an editor and partner, as well as an author), they can be read as a sequence about the degrees and stages of wisdom granted to age. The Christmas poems develop variously the archetypal association between old man and child, symbolic of the complementarity of ripeness and renewal in the self. The dramatic monologues of the two scriptural wise men recall "Gerontion." Confronted by a birth that spells the death of the old self and the old dispensation, the Magus sees into the Nativity only deeply enough to be unsettled in his former way: "I should be glad of another death." Or does he somehow mean another sort of death, implicit in this new birth? Just before his own death, Simeon sees the Christ child as "the still unspeaking and un-spoken Word" and prophesies the child's crucifixion, the mother's suffering, and the grace of martyrdom for which he is too early. Like Tiresias, these prophets are "throbbing between two lives," but already their vision has progressed beyond his (and Gerontion's) helpless observation of human degradation. In "Animula" the impersonal voice of a believing contemporary Christian, taking off from a verse from the *Purgatorio* ("Issues from the hand of God the simple soul"), rehearses the cycle of life until there "issues from the hand of time the simple soul / Irresolute and selfish, misshapen, lame." Once again, the only hope for this "shadow of his own shadows" is an appeal to the Virgin, here, as in *Ash-Wednesday*, in the words of the Ave Maria. "The Cultivation of Christmas Trees" stands as a coda to the earlier "Ariel" poems, written by a much older and mellower Eliot to mitigate the revulsion from human existence expressed in "Animula." The child's pleasure in the Christmas tree, noted ruefully in the earlier poem, here becomes the anticipated comprehension of the Christmas mystery, so that by the eightieth Christmas

(Simeon had spoken of his eighty years, and Eliot was in his mid-sixties) "the accumulated memories of annual emotion / May be concentrated into a great joy / Which shall be also a great fear."

This stoic resignation to mortal life as a trial and preparation (sickened with "fatigue," "tedium," "death," and "failure") informs the *Quartets* and the plays which Eliot began writing soon after *Ash-Wednesday* and the "Ariel" poems, but "Marina" lifts the "Ariel" sequence to a climax. It is the only ecstatic poem in the Eliot canon. The epigraph from Seneca's *Hercules Furens*, which Eliot's first and last lines adapt, presents the hero at his labors' end, awakening from a lunatic frenzy inflicted by Juno, to discover his children slain by his own hand. But the poem turns this tragic epigraph into an epiphany of the lost offspring. For the title of the poem identifies the actual situation as that of Pericles, not Hercules, awakening in the last act of Shakespeare's play to an unexpected reunion with his daughter Marina, the sea maiden lost and presumed dead. The epiphany transforms Pericles' despair into joy and changes his vision of life and destiny. His sense of bodily existence as debased – the viciousness of dogs, the hummingbird's beauty, pigs' gluttony, animal lust – fades in the miracle of her return: "By this grace dissolved in place." Beholding in Marina a "life / Living to live in a world of time beyond me," Pericles makes a commitment beyond that of Eliot's earlier personae. To begin with, he acquiesces in the cycle of generations: "let me / Resign my life for this life" of his daughter. What's more, he submits even in the knowledge, precipitated by her return, that resignation means his own death, his aged body wrecked and leaking like his ship.

But Pericles' reconciliation to natural process is only part of a larger vision. Unlike Pound's Confucius (and unlike Emerson and, as we shall see, Jeffers), he goes beyond pantheism to perceive a life after death; Marina has her earthly life to live, but her image in his mind suggests to the hero-father a personal survival beyond the cycle of generations. Her appearance is a dissolution: "dissolved in place." The fog, in contrast to the menacing urban fog of the early poems, here manifests the unsubstantiality of material objects, even the shores and gray rocks. The invisible pines are known only by their scent; the woodthrush (cf. the thrush singing in the pine trees in *The Waste Land*, which was a mere desert chimera), by its voice in the fog. Marina is associated with the Spirit ("a wind, / A breath of pine, and the woodsong fog") and with the Christ child (through the allusion, in the phrase "Given or lent," to Alice Meynell's "Unto Us a Son Is Born".)[92] Pericles' response makes it clear that Marina is not just an offspring living "beyond me," but a part of himself. Her pulse beats in his arm; "more distant than stars and nearer than the eye," she becomes his link to immortality. He dies rejoicing in his daughter's life; in her spirit he departs to a new life. A breath from the mother sea, "where all the waters meet," the anima as spirit-maiden assures him of life beyond death; he imagines his daughter as his soul, or his soul as his daughter:

> This form, this face, this life
> Living to live in a world of time beyond me; let me

Resign my life for this life, my speech for that unspoken,
The awakened, lips parted, the hope, the new ships.

The language catches up previous moments. ("the still unspeaking and unspoken Word" of "Gerontion" and *Ash-Wednesday* and "Simeon"; "Is it like this / In death's other kingdom / Waking alone /...Lips that would kiss" from *The Hollow Men*; the burgeoning "hope" of *The Hollow Men* and *Ash-Wednesday*) and pitches them toward a new departure; he sails rapturously toward the foreseen shipwreck and reunion:

> What seas what shores what granite islands towards my timbers
> And woodthrush calling through the fog
> My daughter.

The two sections of the unfinished *Coriolan*,[93] written in 1931 and 1932 soon after *Ash-Wednesday* and "Marina," seem to be moving toward a poetry more concerned with social and political themes, a fact that may explain Eliot's loss of interest in the project. Fascist and Bolshevik totalitarianism was making many intellectuals ponder the interdependence of the strong leader and the malleable masses. Such coherence as *Coriolan* has resides in its double view of the leader: first from the perspective of the feckless mob in "Triumphal March," then in the internal monologue "Difficulties of a Statesman." But the two views create no consistent characterization; Coriolan's self-consciousness incapacitates him as a man of action, as if Prufrock or Gerontion held the reins of government, and he faces calls for his resignation. Still, the drift of his musing provides the transition between the religious poems just discussed and the *Four Quartets*. Alienated from the patriarchal values of his Roman ancestors, he recalls Isaiah's appeal to the Lord: "What shall I cry. All flesh is grass...but the word of our God stands forever." In flight from politics and history, Coriolan fumbles for the still center of the cyclic seasons ("Rising and falling, crowned with dust"), but the God secret remains hidden to him, as to the Magus. His gropings cannot break out of the biological round; his repeated calls return feebly and submissively to the mother: "O mother / What shall I cry?"

Four Quartets (1943)[94] searches out the secret in an extended meditation on the implications of the Annunciation and the Incarnation for the natural round and for linear history. "Burnt Norton" (1935) germinated from passages eliminated from *Murder in the Cathedral* during rehearsal, and the other Quartets date from the war years 1940, 1941, and 1942. The sequence is one of the supreme long poems in English. The broad structural similarity between the *Quartets* and *The Waste Land* – five sections, with the second divided between contrasting developments of the same theme and the fourth a brief elegy – serves to underscore the design of continuities as well as discontinuities. Where *The Waste Land* was a tour de force of many styles and voices and personae, *Four Quartets* is Eliot's own voice, ranging from the discursive and prosaic to the intricately symbolic, but always recognizably his. Where *The Waste Land* was dramatic and used literary allusions and mythic references for compressed ironic contrasts without transitions, the *Quartets* are lyric and meditative, employing admittedly talky passages to interpret and modulate between denser lyrics. In *Four Quartets* personality and impersonality attain equipoise and accommodation. Several of the later essays, for example, "The Music of Poetry," written in the midst of the *Quartets*, stress the musical analogy to the sort of thematic variation and development which Eliot was now attempting and argue for a shift from Modernist experimentation to more formal conventions. Eliot's religious and social conservatism made his earlier Symboliste self-consciousness, soon to be documented and exorcised in "From Poe to Valéry" (1948), seem all the more Romantically narcissistic. In the earlier work, Eliot relied on complex mannerisms and techniques to articulate the quandary of consciousness; in his later verse, he worked hard to speak as plainly as he could about the philosophical and religious paradoxes whose explanation, he now accepted, lay beyond consciousness and so articulation.

The meaning, structure, and sources of the *Quartets* have received excellent commentary. Each Quartet begins with an epiphany, or moment of special understanding, on which the body of the poem attempts to elaborate, and this deepening discernment of the implications of special moments through the passage of time applies as well to the development of the sequence as a whole; Eliot himself thought each Quartet better than the preceding one. Each moment is linked with a location significant in Eliot's own experience, and each poem describes the trek or pilgrimage which brings him in turn to the rose garden at Burnt Norton, an empty manor house in the Cotswolds twice visited with a particular American friend in mid-1930s; to the Somerset village of East Coker, where the Eliot family originated and whence his forebears emigrated to America after the Restoration; to the Mississippi River and the Gloucester coast of his growing up; and to the chapel at Little Gidding, the seventeenth-century Anglican retreat house. The sequence, therefore, begins and ends with Eliot in contemporary England; in between, the poems re-create the westward movement which made his English ancestors Yankees and brought them in time to the mid-continent, from which Eliot returned to New, then old, England. Linear history traces out a circle, and the circular basis for history is established in the association of the Quartets with the four seasons and the four elements, a particular season and element predominant in each Quartet.

This engagement with both history and nature allows the simultaneous linear and circular progression of the sequence. For both of the following propositions are basic to the poem – the first expressing a chronological conception, the second a cyclic conception of experience:

> The knowledge imposes a pattern, and falsifies,
> For the pattern is new in every moment
> And every moment is a new and shocking
> Valuation of all we have been.
>
> ("East Coker," II)

And the end of all our exploring
Will be to arrive where we started
And know the place for the first time.
   ("Little Gidding," V)

Each moment is final yet provisional, to be completed in the total "pattern" (this word recurs throughout the Quartets). Experience is discontinuous, yet cumulative. Its trajectory allows a circling back in the mind, allows the isolated moment to be realized in subsequent experience. Especially with the "sudden illumination," "we had the experience but missed the meaning, / And approach to the meaning restores the experience / In a different form" ("The Dry Salvages," II). Thus time loops back as it advances teleologically, drawing the past toward its end.

Four Quartets elaborates the message grasped in the initial meditation on the rose garden: "Only through time time is conquered." That ambivalent adverb "only" both undermines and underscores the importance of time. On the one hand, the contingencies and discontinuities of time are to be endured "only" for those connective moments that disclose pattern, and particularly for those gracious moments that intimate eternity; and human responsibility enjoins the curbing of natural appetites so that unencumbered spirit might be open to receive and quicken. On the other hand, time is necessary because "only" through its limited and successive forms does eternity gradually manifest itself. Society still seemed a waste land "place of disaffection": "time-ridden faces / Distracted from distraction by distraction," estranged by desires they could neither slake nor slough off, propelled "in appetency, on [the] metalled ways / Of time past and time future," like a subway train rattling to no destination. But Eliot's Christian sense of a spiritual dimension of reality offered alternative and complementary ways of revisioning the Waste Land: either as "plenitude" or as "vacancy" through an enlightened attachment or detachment, associated in "Burnt Norton" with daylight and darkness. In "daylight" the Christian can accept the "transient beauty" of creation because as it turns "with slow rotation," its "plenitude" reveals something of divine "permanence." The descent into "darkness" seeks in "vacancy" "to purify the soul" of the sensual and the temporal in order to be more open to a direct experience of Godhead; it is the "Dark Night of the Senses," which for Saint John of the Cross led to the "Dark Night of the Soul." In either daylight or darkness, a "stillness" beyond the apathetic frenzy of the twilit Waste Land.

Eliot reiterated the notion at the end of the third section of "Little Gidding"; there he associated "attachment to self and to things and to persons" and "detachment / From self and from things and from persons" as alternate but related attitudes, both at odds with the dead "indifference" (like the "disaffection" in "Burnt Norton") of secular society. Eliot's emotional fastidiousness and Calvinist temperament made him suspect that "attachment" would lead to worldliness and that a bright, daylight world of "lucid stillness" might stop short of Christianity and settle for the epicurean naturalism of Stevens' "Sunday Morning" or the pagan "paradiso terrestre" of Pound's

Cantos. Eliot was inclined to trust instead the path of renunciation and negation to find God. Nevertheless, it was the Christian tension between attachment and detachment that produced Eliot's realism and his mysticism, his ability in *Four Quartets* (unlike *Ash-Wednesday*) to respond to the beauty and energy of nature while advocating a strict rule of "Prayer, observance, discipline, thought and action."

There has been nothing like *Four Quartets* in English verse since the work of the metaphysical poets. Eliot's tone is more austere and chaste, his language more abstract and spare, his imagery less sensuous and impassioned, his whole effect more "puritan" than that of the Anglican Donne and Herbert, the Catholic Southwell, and, for that matter, even the American Puritan Edward Taylor. Eliot's Christianity made him value poetry both more and less. The man who in his agnosticism thought poetry autotelic, so that aesthetic order could compensate for natural disorder, came to abandon this basic Modernist attitude and conclude that "the poetry does not matter" ("East Coker," II). Yet, by a further turn of the paradox, the conviction that poetry was not its own end made craftsmanship all the more important as a disciplining means of drawing out and fixing on the secret hidden in the scramble of experience. Form closed on the truth it expressed; making his own measure in verse was the poet's particular way of redeeming the time.

The passages from the middle section of "Burnt Norton" and "Little Gidding" explicate the epigraph from Heraclitus: "The way up and the way down are one and the same," the congruence of divine descent and human resurrection. Through the many particular ascents and descents in *Four Quartets*, the overall progression moves down from the fleeting illumination in the rose garden through the middle Quartets to rise again, in the last movement of "Little Gidding," to reconstitute the rose as the mystical rose, envisioned by Dante at the center of Paradise. Similarly, the progression of elements – air, earth, water, fire – has the lighter elements, associated alchemically with the "masculine" spirit, enclosing and sublimating the heavier elements of "feminine" matter. At the same time, the poem shows that the elements cannot exist in isolation any more than the "masculine" and "feminine"; the Christian finds the Spirit-Father in the incarnated Son, and the Son through the Mother.

Attention to the four revelatory moments delineates even more complexly the archetypal configuration of descent and return. "Burnt Norton" begins with a series of abstract philosophical reflections seeking to resolve the divisions of temporal experience: past and future, potency and act, alternative choices of will – all "point to one end, which is always present." "Point," "end," "always," "present" – these words pace out the sequence as they return in different contexts with new associations. The one "end" (conclusion, result, boundary, aim) which is always present is (1) the immediate moment; (2) eternity, which subsumes chronological discontinuity; and, synthetically, (3) eternity informing the passing moment. But these abstractions need testing and confirmation by personal experience:

Footfalls echo in the memory
Down the passage which we did not take
Towards the door we never opened
Into the rose-garden. My words echo
Thus, in your mind.

"What might have been" but never was in the past becomes present in the rose garden at Burnt Norton – present but ineluctably changed by subsequent acts and choices in the intervening years, the "other echoes" that now inhabit the never-entered garden. "Shall we follow" the thrush (cf. *The Waste Land* and "Marina") into that unknown emptiness full of presences?

As we have seen, women in Eliot's poetry are the agents of change and destiny for the male protagonists: temptress and lover and angel, Grishkin and hyacinth girl and Marina. But increasingly, from *Ash-Wednesday* through the later plays, they become the agents of grace reconciling the male protagonist to the material and spiritual orders. In the preceding lines, the pronouns, the direct personal address, and the intimate tone suggest a direct biographical connection, a woman whose presence in the garden with Eliot mediated the revelation. In fact, as we know from information disclosed after Eliot's death, it was Emily Hale who introduced Eliot to the rose garden at Burnt Norton. Eliot had met her as a lovely, intelligent girl from an old Boston family, perhaps as early as 1908, certainly by 1913. They became friends, apparently fell in love, were parted by Eliot's expatriation, but maintained such close contact that approximately two thousand letters from Eliot to her were deposited at the Princeton library. The course of their friendship remains one of Eliot's secrets (the letters cannot be made public until 2020), but there seems no doubt that it was deep and reciprocal, cooling only after Eliot's second marriage near the end of his life. Emily Hale taught drama at various colleges, and he sent her manuscripts, including that of the next Quartet, "East Coker." Biographers have connected her with the recurrent figure of the lost love ("La Figlia Che Piange," the hyacinth girl), with Agatha in *The Family Reunion*, even with the Lady in *Ash-Wednesday*.[95] Vivienne and Emily and the Lady – that trio creates much of the dramatic poignancy of *Ash-Wednesday*; and in fact the excision of the dedication to Vivienne in *Poems 1909–1935* after the legal separation coincided with the quickening of Eliot's friendship with Emily and the appearance of "Burnt Norton" as the last poem in that volume.

Over the years, Emily Hale and Eliot corresponded and occasionally met in England and America, faithful spinster and married, then separated bachelor, on terms that Thoreau and James and Emily Dickinson would have understood. During Eliot's long alienation from Vivienne, Emily Hale provided the necessary feminine connection under circumstances in which there was no longer a question of romance or marriage, but which precisely allowed her to support and encourage the life of the mind and spirit. Her figure, therefore, came to gather to itself much of the psychological energy of the anima, especially of the anima's spiritual affinities. Renewed acquaintance during Eliot's Harvard year, 1932–1933, led to summer visits in England the following two years. In 1934 and in 1935 they visited Burnt Norton with friends, and in the rose garden of the destroyed manor house, an epiphanic moment seemed to carry them "through the first gate, / Into our first world."

When Eliot read these lines aloud, his voice stressed "first" in both phrases. The description of the events in the garden indicates that "our first world" extends beyond the poignant memory of lost chances with Emily Hale and comes to represent a paradisal harmony, long since lost by volitional choices and errors but beheld again now in our ruins: the man-made landscape garden, the pool empty beside the desolate house, become momentarily "the still point of the turning world." Here, then, is the generative moment of *Four Quartets*:

> There they were dignified, invisible,
> Moving without pressure, over the dead leaves,
> In the autumn heat, through the vibrant air,
> And the bird called, in response to
> The unheard music hidden in the shrubbery,
> And the unseen eyebeam crossed, for the roses
> Had the look of flowers that are looked at.
> There they were as our guests, accepted and accepting.
> So we moved, and they, in a formal pattern,
> Along the empty alley, into the box circle,
> To look down into the drained pool.
> Dry the pool, dry concrete, brown edged,
> And the pool was filled with water out of sunlight,
> And the lotos rose, quietly, quietly,
> The surface glittered out of heart of light,
> And they were behind us, reflected in the pool.

The "heart of light," into which the man in the hyacinth garden stared vacantly, is here the center of vision. The phrase "the lotos rose" links the mystical flowers of East and West. "Unseen eyebeam" suggests the Father's inscrutable providence; and "crossed," the Son's immanent presence. The dry, brown-edged pool recalls landscape details from "Mr. Eliot's Sunday Morning Service," *The Waste Land, The Hollow Men*, and other earlier poems, but now "the pool was filled with water out of sunlight." "Box circle" turns the design of the hedge into a miraculous mandala squaring the circle. "They" – the "Other echoes," shadows and ghosts, of his life – are gathered in, both "accepted and accepting," and, crossed by the eyebeam, are drawn into harmony. Yet – and here is the rub which requires the rest of the Quartets – the vision passes before it can be grasped; the pool, rippling with light and reflecting "them" all together, empties as startlingly as it filled. The music from the shrubbery and the laughing children hidden in the leaves repeat intimations from "Marina," "Difficulties of a Statesman," and "New Hampshire" (1933), and a version of the image recurs in each of the other Quartets. When in dismissal the spirit-bird warns that "human kind cannot bear very much reality," the verb "bear" means at once "endure," "suffer," "carry," and "bring to birth." Therefore, the remainder of "Burnt Norton" and of the sequence substantiates the presences drawn together in the box-circle mandala, and explores the terms of desire and love, so that Eros can be drawn, by line and circle, to Agape. By the "end," which the beginning says is always present, the lost garden will have become paradise regained.

"East Coker" opens with Mary Stuart's motto reversed – "In my beginning is my end" – and concludes with the motto righted in a new departure: "In my end is my beginning." Those framing lines correct the lady's words in "Portrait": "But our beginnings never know our ends." In 1937 Eliot made a pilgrimage to the village of East Coker, the family seat of the Eliots. The photographs he took on that occasion refreshed his memory a few years later when, in the dark early days of the war, he sought to evoke the history of the place. The return of the far-flung son to the point of origin reveals linear history as cyclical: houses, generations, individuals "rise and fall." Life, however cultivated and civilized the human spirit made it, moved through the biological round, and Eliot quotes the measured Renaissance accents of his ancestor Sir Thomas Elyot, the great Christian Humanist, commending marriage as "a dignified and commodious sacrament" and a "necessary coniunction." But the description of the matrimonial dance of peasant pairs about the fire in the village field depicts a spontaneous and instinctual existence amusingly at variance with Elyot's studied decorum:

> Round and round the fire
> Leaping through the flames, or joined in circles,
> Rustically solemn or in rustic laughter
> Lifting heavy feet in clumsy shoes,
> Earth feet, loam feet, lifted in country mirth
> Mirth of those long since under earth
> Nourishing the corn. Keeping time,
> Keeping the rhythm in their dancing
> As in their living in the living seasons
> The time of the seasons and the constellations
> The time of milking and the time of harvest
> The time of the coupling of man and woman
> And that of beasts. Feet rising and falling.
> Eating and drinking. Dung and death.

Eliot's run-on lines, the rhymes and repetitions and alliterations, and the use of present participles re-create the linked circular movement. William Carlos Williams used similar devices to describe Breughel's "The Kermess" in "The Dance," but Williams' zestful enjoyment of the scene, shown in rhythm and in the attention to physical and anatomical details, contrasts with Eliot's sense of remove in spirit as well as time from the earth rhythm of peasants. Eliot's use of repetition and inversion in "Earth feet, loam feet, lifted in country mirth / Mirth of those long since under earth" contrasts with Emerson's use of the same devices in "Hamatreya":

Earth laughs in flowers, to see her boastful boys
Earth-proud, proud of the earth which is not theirs;
Who steer the plough, but cannot steer their feet
Clear of the grave.

Emerson shares Mother Earth's bemusement at the hubris of her "boastful boys," but Eliot observes the childlike behavior of cloddish couples from the perspective of one alienated from earth by consciousness. In the rest of the passage, the Elyot–Eliot voice modulates into the cadences of Ecclesiastes to reduce natural life – "eating and drinking" – to "dung and death." Gravity pulls down "heavy feet in clumsy shoes," lifted however high in dance; "rise and fall" ends in fall: "In my beginning is my end."

Eliot's 1929 essay on Dante explicates the attitude implicit in "East Coker":

> The attitude of Dante to the fundamental experience of the *Vita Nuova* can only be understood by accustoming ourselves to find meaning in *final causes* rather than in origins. It is not, I believe, meant as a description of what he *consciously* felt on his meeting with Beatrice, but rather as a description of what that meant on mature reflection upon it. The final cause is the attraction towards God. A great deal of sentiment has been spilt, especially in the eighteenth and nineteenth centuries, upon idealizing the reciprocal feelings of man and woman towards each other, which various realists have been irritated to denounce: this sentiment ignoring the fact that the love of man and woman (or for that matter of man and man) is only explained and made reasonable by the higher love, or else is simply the coupling of animals.[96]

Dante's "contrast between higher and lower carnal love," "the transition from Beatrice living to Beatrice dead, rising to the cult of the Virgin" Eliot saw as a spiritual ascent rather than as Freudian "sublimation." The crucial lesson of the "antiromantic" Dante was "not to expect more from *life* than it can give or more from *human* beings than they can give; to look to *death* for what life cannot give." Thus the *Vita Nuova* as a work of "vision literature" proceeds from "the Catholic philosophy of disillusion."[97] "East Coker" follows Dante in turning from origins to final causes. In accordance with the "Catholic philosophy of disillusion," the revelation of life as a descent into dung and death inaugurates a further descent, already foreshadowed ("Descend lower ...") in "Burnt Norton," Section III, down to the "internal darkness," which Saint John of the Cross and other mystics pursued to the Beatific Vision.

Thus the lyric opening Section II of "East Coker" inverts the prevailingly upward movement of the parallel lyric in Section II of "Burnt Norton" and plunges toward Apocalypse. Section III accepts the "darkness of God" and restates the *via negativa* from Saint John's *Ascent of Mt. Carmel*. The elegy in Section IV makes the first explicit reference to the Incarnation: the disease of life is cured through death in the crucifixion; God-in-flesh is Himself the "wounded surgeon," attended by a "dying nurse" who admonishes "that, to be restored, our sickness must grow worse." The connection of origin with final causes inverts Mary Stuart's motto: now "In my end is my beginning." But for now, recognition of the end points to an end yet to be reached; the movement "into another intensity / For a further union, a deeper communion" requires a further penetration of nature, in "The Dry Salvages," and of history, in "Little Gidding."

"The Dry Salvages" risks that "backward look behind the assurance / Of recorded history, the backward half-look / Over the shoulder, towards the primitive terror." The power of nature operates so far beyond human regulation and comprehension that nature itself has seemed, to pantheists like Jeffers, divine. So the Mississippi is and remains a "strong brown god," despite our technological ingenuity in crossing and exploiting it. If the river as god is the life course of the individual ("the river is within us"), the sea "all about us" is the womb of Nature into which the river bears the freight and wreckage of material existence. The biological Life Force, for the individual, is the Death Force, as Darwin saw, and in the following lines the pronoun "it" underscores its impersonal brutality:

> The river is within us, the sea is all about us;
> The sea is the land's edge also, the granite
> Into which it reaches, the beaches where it tosses
> Its hints of earlier and other creation:
> The starfish, the horseshoe crab, the whale's backbone;
> The pools where it offers to our curiosity
> The more delicate algae and the sea anemone.
> It tosses up our losses, the torn seine,
> The shattered lobsterpot, the broken oar
> And the gear of foreign dead men. The sea has many voices,
> Many gods and many voices.

The imagery contrasts the survival of the fitter species of lower life with the fragility of human artifacts. The pool in "Burnt Norton" heightened consciousness beyond the usual human limits, but these tide pools offer a retrospective gaze back to evolutionary origins vastly antecedent to East Coker. Yet the consciousness which observes "hints of earlier and other creation" offered "to our curiosity" resists succumbing to the law of nature and aspires to surpass the biological round. Its initial strategy is to comprehend the round, and thereby comprehend its own extinction, as the starfish and hermit crab cannot.

The first section of "The Dry Salvages" makes calculated allusions to Whitman: "nursery bedroom," reminiscent of "Out of the Cradle"; the "April dooryard" of "When Lilacs Last in the Dooryard Bloom'd"; "the menace and caress of the wave," from the Sea-Drift poems; the flotsam of "As I Ebb'd with the Ocean of Life"; the cataloging of imagery; the loose syntax, the repetitive and paratactic phrasing; the long colloquial lines. The lecture on Whitman which Eliot gave at a London club in 1944 (Donald Gallup's notes on the lecture are in the Eliot archive at Harvard) records his interest in Whitman during the war years and his judgment that although Whitman was a great poet, his manner could not be used or imitated because it was inseparable from his message. "The Dry Salvages" invokes Whitman not just because this is the

"American Quartet" but because Eliot is taking up – and rejecting – Whitman's Romantic-pantheistic inclination to accept Mother Nature as the reservoir in which the individual consciousness must submerge itself. It was the message of Emerson's "Hamatreya" and Whitman's sea poems and of Robinson Jeffers' Inhumanism. But Eliot always hoped for another kind of "Death by Water." In "As I Ebb'd with the Ocean of Life," Whitman saw the wreckage in the sea drift as the type and symbol of human life, and the poem is intended to induce consciousness to exult in its own sea death:

> I too but signify at the utmost a little wash'd-up drift,
> A few sands and dead leaves to gather,
> Gather, and merge myself as part of the sands and drift.
>
> . . . .
>
> Ebb, ocean of life, (the flow will return,)
> Cease not your moaning you fierce old mother,
> Endlessly cry for your castaways, but fear not, deny not me...
>
> . . . .
>
> Tufts of straw, sands, fragments,
> Buoy'd hither from many moods, one contradicting another,
> From the storm, the long calm, the darkness, the swell. . . .

The sea as matrix and grave made it for Whitman the "fierce old mother" whose erotic rhythms lulled consciousness back to oblivion. But Eliot's imagination (remember Grishkin, the woman in "Hysteria," Rachel *née* Rabinovitch) turns the sea into the devouring, animalistic female "sea howl," "sea yelp," the "menace and caress of wave that breaks on water," the "granite teeth," the "sea's lips," the "dark throat," and, in "Little Gidding," the "sea jaws" and the "sea's throat."

Consequently, although Section I of "The Dry Salvages" ends with the freest verse in the *Quartets*, the versification and tone of Eliot's lines work at deliberate odds with the characteristically steady, balanced, end-stopped measure with which Whitman re-creates his willed surrender to the mother sea:

> And under the oppression of the silent fog
> The tolling bell
> Measures time not our time, rung by the unhurried
> Ground swell, a time
> Older than the time of chronometers, older
> Than time counted by anxious worried women
> Lying awake, calculating the future,
> Trying to unweave, unwind, unravel
> And piece together the past and the future,
> Between midnight and dawn, when the past is all deception,
> The future futureless, before the morning watch
> When time stops and time is never ending;
> And the ground swell, that is and was from the beginning,
> Clangs
> The bell.

Eliot makes the alternations in line length, the enjambing of most lines, and the counterpointing within the lines suggest the convulsed human response to the sea's upheaval. His empathy is clearly not with the "fierce old mother" but with the women trying to unwind cyclical time into the language of chronometers and linear history. The image recalls a similar one in "Preludes": "The worlds revolve like ancient women / Gathering fuel in vacant lots"; but where earlier the women persist in mute survival, here they bear the burden of consciousness which cannot rest with the cycles of tide and weather. The bell that the sea rocks rings a warning; it is not the message of Whitman the pantheist but of Donne the Dean of St. Paul's, who wrote in Meditation XVII: "therefore never send to know for whom the bell tolls; it tolls for thee....I take mine own death into contemplation and so secure myself by making my recourse to my God, who is our only security."

The Christian perspective is only hinted at in Section I of "The Dry Salvages," to be drawn out in the remainder of the poem. The phrase "ground swell," linking earth and sea, harkens back to "East Coker," and the interplay of endings and beginnings in the last lines of Section I carries over into the superb sestina of Section II. To the question "Where is there an end of it?" – that is, of time as destroyer – the answer comes: "There is no end," but the sestina extends the meaning from the inescapability of temporal suffering to the endlessness of eternity. The pattern delineated by Mircea Eliade, the historian of religions, involves the evolution of consciousness from a more primitive subordination of the individual in the cosmic round to a sense of historical time whose linear course unfolds the end which will deliver historical time from itself.[98] So, whereas the rhyme scheme of Eliot's sestina runs cyclically through each stanza, the transfiguration of time as cycle into teleology is disclosed in the rhyme scheme itself; the rhyming of the last verse of each stanza in the sestina runs as follows: Death's "calamitous annunciation," "Renunciation," "the bell of the last annunciation," "no destination," "does not bear examination," the "sudden illumination," "the one Annunciation." The words "annunciation" and "Annunciation," which conclude the first and last stanzas, are the same and utterly different. The sestina changes "time the destroyer" into "time the preserver."

Section III employs Krishna's instruction to Arjuna in the Bhagavad-Gita as gloss on the emergent Christian "illumination." Because time, destroyer and preserver, is itself "no healer," each person must attend to earthly duty, performing each act as if it were his dying deed, mind intent upon the transcendent end. The reiterated directive "fare forward" (which takes up a phrase from "Animula") enjoins the commitment to time despite its illusoriness and to action despite its inevitable imperfection. For the Christian, the Annunciation inaugurates God's historical Incarnation in the person of Jesus through the motherhood of Mary. Dante's epithet – *Figlia del tuo figlio* ("Daughter of your son") – sums up Mary's mediatory role in the Annunciation and Incarnation. Section IV utters the "hardly, barely prayable / Prayer of the one Annunciation" mentioned in Section II; it asks the Lady to rescue humankind from the devouring sea. The final image transforms the sea bell into "perpetual angelus." "Angelus" means "angel" or "messenger," and refers as well to the prayer to the Virgin which begins with the angel's words of Annunciation and to which the Christian is called each day by the church bell tolled at morning, noon, and sunset.

Section V explicitly sets the Incarnation above the "daemonic, chthonic / Powers" of earth and sea:

> The hint half guessed, the gift half understood, is
>   Incarnation.
> Here the impossible union
> Of spheres of existence is actual,
> Here the past and future
> Are conquered, and reconciled....

The passage explicates the "hints" in "Burnt Norton" when the poet guesses that "only through time time is conquered" and feels that the relentless pursuit of boar and boarhound is somehow "reconciled among the stars."

Eliot's Calvinist sense of the dislocation between nature and grace allowed no easy presumption that the "impossible union" would illuminate existence in anything but broken refractions. Nevertheless, the belief in that union, however imperfectly manifest in nature and history, differentiated Eliot's attitude from the Romantic egoism of Middleton Murry, on the one hand, and from the secular Humanism of Irving Babbitt, on the other. The immanence of grace in flawed nature permitted the fallible self (in the last words of "The Dry Salvages") to "nourish / (Not too far from the yew-tree) / The life of significant soil." The adjective denotes not just "meaningful" but "symbolic of a further meaning," and this incarnational conviction carries Eliot past Whitman's naturalistic pantheism and past Arjuna's Hindu sense of matter as illusion to the Christian sacramentality which Thomas Elyot proclaimed in "East Coker." Those rare moments both "in and out of time" – in the rose garden at Burnt Norton, in the field at East Coker – reveal the subtending significance of the Incarnation.

And the most important "point of intersection of the timeless / With time" came to Eliot during World War II at Little Gidding, carrying him past the cyclic movement of nature and embroiling him in the lesson of patriarchal history. The "midwinter spring" with which the poem opens, the unbudding and unfading snow blossoms on the shrubbery, places the epiphany outside the natural cycle. The lyric in Section II rehearses the death of the physical elements. But how does this moment "not in the scheme of generation" judge history? For England during the blitz, national survival seemed in doubt. Was this the last act in the tragic decline begun by the English Civil War of the seventeenth century, in which the royalist Anglican community at Little Gidding played an important part on the losing side? History charted war rather than peace, yet the prayerful meditation in the chapel at Little Gidding, which had survived many battles, even survived the destruction of the retreat house, revealed to Eliot church and country "renewed, transfigured, in another pattern." History, which otherwise would spell "servitude" to striving factions, offers the "freedom" to discern the field of action from the end of action. Not that our involvement in history is less; like Arjuna, we battle on the messy field, but now with the recognition that opposing forces both are only "perfected in death," "folded in a single party." Eliot at Little Gidding thinks of Charles I and of Milton who came there separately, "united in the strife which divided them." As before, mediation comes through a "lady," here the medieval English mystic Dame Julian of Norwich, whose visions of an androgynous Christ changed patriarchal history from a record of fall to a record of faltering ascent. "Sin is behovely [is useful, plays its part in the pattern], but / All shall be well, and / All manner of thing shall be well." Only through history, scarred by human pride and error, history is conquered:

> A people without history,
> Is not redeemed from time, for history is a pattern
> Of timeless moments. So, while the light fails
> On a winter's afternoon, in a secluded chapel
> History is now and England.

Teleological history anticipated an apocalypse. With fire bombs bringing down London and other cities, just as "What the Thunder Said" had foreseen, the Apocalypse seemed at hand. In some sermons the Apocalypse comes by fire; and in others, by ice – as Frost observed stoically in "Fire and Ice." The elegy in "East Coker" spoke of "frigid purgatorial fires / Of which the flame is roses, and the smoke is briars." But in "Little Gidding" the Luftwaffe fire bombers are startlingly transformed into the Holy Spirit descending in fire: not so much Apocalypse as the first Pentecost, which in Christian history established the Church and inaugurated the conversion of the world. Details scattered through Sections I and II ("pentecostal fire," "tongued with fire," the bombers as the "dark drove with flickering tongue," "dawn wind") climax in Section IV:

> The dove descending breaks the air
> With flame of incandescent terror
> Of which the tongues declare
> The one discharge from sin and error.
> The only hope, or else despair
>   Lies in the choice of pyre or pyre –
>   To be redeemed from fire by fire.

The hope, only of empty men, has become the only hope. Writing "Colloquy at Black Rock" near the end of the war, Lowell would also depict an apocalyptic Christ as a bomber plane bringing redemption despite and through human violence: "my heart, / The blue kingfisher dives on you in fire."[99]

The conjunction of Purgatory and Pentecost is dramatized in "Little Gidding," II, the famous Dantescan canto written in unrhymed *terza rima*. Eliot said that he worked harder on it than on anything else he wrote. Eliot served as a fire watcher at Faber and Faber during the blitz, and the episode presents him standing on a street "between three districts whence the smoke arose [a rose]" after the departure of the bomber dove "with flickering tongue," and encountering on the "dawn wind" "a familiar compound ghost." The apparition, who has associations with Dante, Arnaut Daniel, Mallarmé, Yeats, and other poets, is a projection of an aspect of Eliot himself. Assuming a "double part," he enters into dialogue with his self-image. The apparition's words bring to a conclusion the theme of wisdom and age which extended from "Gerontion" through Ash-Wednesday and the "Ariel" poems to the Quartets. "East Coker," II, scorned the egoistic folly of old men and urged humility as the only wisdom, but the conclusion affirmed that "old men ought to be explorers" moving into "a deeper communion." Now, however, the spirit exposes again the impotence and guilty shame of age, "unless restored by that refining fire / Where you must move in measure, like a dancer." The phrasing recalls the pivotal "unless" in The Hollow Men, and "refining fire" relates "The Fire Sermon" and the Spirit's "pentecostal fire" to the Arnaut Daniel episode of the Purgatorio alluded to in the jumbled ending of The Waste Land.

"Little Gidding" brings to a culmination the theme of art and language which runs through the Quartets. "Burnt Norton," V, assigns to art the difficult, perhaps impossible, certainly paradoxical task of fixing in time the timeless moment which is "the still point of the turning world," even though the artist's imperfect medium and faulty control fail under the concentrated pressure of articulation:

> Words strain,
> Crack and sometimes break, under the burden,
> Under the tension, slip, slide, perish,
> Decay with imprecision, will not stay in place,
> Will not stay still.

Temporal arts like poetry and music must approach the stillness of spatial form, in which beginning and end coexist; for

> Only by the form, the pattern,
> Can words and music reach
> The stillness, as a Chinese jar still
> Moves perpetually in its stillness.

The possibility of attaining such dynamic fixity recedes further in the gloom of "East Coker"; where "the intolerable wrestle / With words and meanings" (Section II) botches each attempt "because one has only learnt to get the better of words / For the thing one no longer has to say, or the way in which / One is no longer disposed to say it" (Section V). "The Dry Salvages" does not even take up the theme, and the archetypal poet of "Little Gidding" accepts the relativity of any poet's "thought and theory" in the effort (in Mallarmé's phrase) "to purify the dialect of the tribe": "For last year's words belong to last year's language / And next year's words await another's voice."

Nevertheless, *Four Quartets* represents a prodigious attempt on Eliot's part to discern, through the act of language, the pattern intuited in nature's upheavals and history's battles; to shape fractious, intractable words so that the convergences of form resonate the speechless Word. The ranges of tone and tempo, of diction, of versification both formal and free constellate around that soundless pitch. The last section of "Little Gidding" restates the aesthetic idea more specifically than "Burnt Norton" could, because it is now more fully realized:

> And every phrase
> And sentence that is right (where every word is at home,
> Taking its place to support the others,
> The word neither diffident nor ostentatious,
> An easy commerce of the old and the new,
> The common word exact without vulgarity,
> The formal word precise but not pedantic,
> The complete consort dancing together)
> Every phrase and every sentence is an end and a beginning,
> Every poem an epitaph.

The concluding statement of *Four Quartets* weaves all that has gone before into a climactic integration of phrase and image:

> At the source of the longest river
> The voice of the hidden waterfall
> And the children in the apple-tree
> Not known, because not looked for
> But heard, half-heard, in the stillness
> Between two waves of the sea.
> Quick now, here, now, always –
> A condition of complete simplicity
> (Costing not less than everything)
> And all shall be well and
> All manner of thing shall be well
> When the tongues of flame are in-folded
> Into the crowned knot of fire
> And the fire and the rose are one.

The truncated revelation in the rose garden has survived the abyss of nature and the trial of history ("The moment of the rose and the moment of the yew-tree / Are of equal duration") to anticipate the paradisal rose. The sexual dance in "East Coker" has become "the complete consort dancing together" through Eliot's masterful integration of Julian and Dante into his own cadences.

IV

Discussing Yeats's development in 1940, shortly after his death, Eliot admitted, "It is my experience that towards middle age a man has three choices: to stop writing altogether, to repeat himself with perhaps an increasing skill of virtuosity, or by taking thought to adapt himself to middle age and find a different way of working."[100] By that time, Eliot had made the third choice and was well launched on the new development of his later career: the writing of the most distinguished twentieth-century verse dramas in English (with the possible exception of those of Yeats). Eliot had always been interested in verse drama, and many of his early poems are monologues. Moreover, cultural elitist and political reactionary though he was, Eliot worried, as did his contemporaries, about the restricted audience for Modernist poetry. They could fault Poe and Longfellow and Tennyson on many intellectual, emotional, and aesthetic grounds, but those poets had, and continued to have, a larger audience than Mallarmé and Pound and Eliot.

One could argue for a pure, autotelic art in which communication was a secondary, perhaps even a peripheral, aim; one could even argue, as Eliot did in "The Three Voices of Poetry," that the poem arose out of the poet's need to articulate something to himself, something even he might still not understand. But as the essay goes on to indicate, the poet then wants to be overheard by others, and the need to communicate with an audience took on more urgency after Eliot's conversion. Winding up his Harvard lectures in the early 1930s, Eliot declared, with an Arnoldian mixture of social responsibility and distaste for the philistine bourgeoisie:

> After admitting the possible existence of minor "difficult" poets whose public must always be small, I believe that the poet naturally prefers to write for as large and miscellaneous an audience as possible, and that it is the half-educated and ill-educated, rather than the uneducated, who stand in his way: I myself should like an audience which could neither read nor write. The most useful poetry, socially, would be one which could cut across all the present stratifications of public taste – stratifications which are perhaps a sign of social disintegration.[101]

After his return to England from Harvard, Eliot became increasingly involved during the 1930s in writing for public theatrical performance. "Burnt Norton," the only poem of the decade, took shape from passages excised from *Murder in the Cathedral*, and Eliot felt that his theatrical experience benefited the *Quartets* through "a greater simplification of language" and through "speaking in a way which is more like conversing with your reader."[102]

Eliot reviewed his search for the proper form and verse line for contemporary plays in the essay "Poetry and Drama," and his director, E. Martin Browne, wrote an account of their collaboration for the stage.[103] The problematics of language and communication lay at the heart of Eliot's first fragmentary experiment with the theater: two scenes, published separately in 1926 and 1927 and together in 1932 as *Sweeney Agonistes*.[104] Eliot described the strategy of the play:

> My intention was to have one character whose sensibility and intelligence should be on the plane of the most sensitive and intelligent members of the audience; his speeches should be addressed to them as much as to the other personages in the play – or rather, should be addressed to the latter, who were to be material, literal-minded and visionless, with the consciousness of being

overheard by the former. There was to be an understanding between this protagonist and a small number of the audience, while the rest of the audience would share the responses of the other characters in the play.[105]

Eliot would become less condescending to the mass audience as he wrestled with the problem of writing for the commercial stage, but the problem remained: was it possible to entertain an audience and at the same time challenge and change its perceptions and values? From *Sweeney Agonistes* on, the drama of all the plays, in fact, turns on differing levels of awareness and the possibility of changing levels of awareness. Here Eliot introduces a more discerning perspective on Sweeney's underworld, not by introducing a Prufrockian character into it but, rather (and the device corroborates how much Prufrock and Sweeney are related aspects of Eliot), by investing this Sweeney with a Prufrockian comprehension and irony quite inconsistent with his character and slangy diction.

Before Sweeney's appearance, the prologue – mostly a stylized, syncopated dialogue between Doris (from "Sweeney Erect") and Dusty, another "lady of situations" – establishes the lower level of awareness in a materialistic existence based on money and sex. Doris' fortune telling builds up a suspenseful atmosphere of impending doom as the cards foretell violence and death. In "Fragment of an Agon," a bizarre mélange of Greek and expressionist drama, jazz and music hall, Sweeney serves as the choral commentator who cannot communicate his boredom and horror to his vulgar companions. Sweeney's crude misogyny stems from his identification of women with the sexual, biological round ("Birth and copulation and death"), and since it spells death ("Death is life and life is death"), Sweeney understands the male urge to violence against the object of his sexual attraction:

> I knew a man once did a girl in
> Any man might do a girl in
> Any man has to, needs to, wants to
> Once in a lifetime, do a girl in.

"Do a girl in" turns the male libido into a lust to kill. When Sweeney tells of a friend who murdered a girl and kept her body "with a gallon of lysol in a bath," the spooked Doris complains bathetically: "A woman runs a terrible risk." Whether Sweeney is reporting or fantasizing, whether he is speaking of someone else or himself, the result is psychosis:

> He didn't know if he was alive
>   and the girl was dead
> He didn't know if the girl was alive
>   and he was dead
> He didn't know if they both were alive
>   or both were dead.

At the end, Sweeney is left waiting helplessly for the hangman to knock at the door. The play breaks off because it has nowhere to go.

Sweeney Agonistes came at the turning point in Eliot's career, and all of his subsequent plays deal with the theme of salvation. The allegorical pageant drama *The Rock* (1943)[106] demonstrated that Eliot could write effective choruses in public performance, with a long, flexible line, but the real challenge lay in embodying his Christian themes in character and situation. *Murder in the Cathedral* (1935),[107] first performed in Canterbury Cathedral, integrated the choral device into a symmetrically designed presentation of Saint Thomas Becket's final days and martyrdom. The dramatic style deftly mixed elements of Greek drama, medieval morality play, and saint's life with expressionist experimentation. The conflict in Part I between Thomas and his four shadow tempters and in Part II between Thomas and the four knightly assassins is played off against the growing comprehension of the mystery of salvation on the part of the Chorus of the "poor women of Canterbury." At the beginning they speak for the round of nature, and the priests and assassins for the ecclesiastical and secular institutions of patriarchal history. The women see themselves as "living and partly living" from season to season, but resist the new kind of "death" and "doom" which Thomas' impending martyrdom intrudes upon the natural cycle. Thomas' outfacing of the shadow tempters brings Part I to a climax in a powerful colloquy concerning perfection of the will in accord with a higher law than the biological. By the final chorus of Part II, the women's wills have been raised and directed, through their witness of Thomas' sacrifice, to accept the need to submit, however painfully, fallen nature to redemptive grace.

As Eliot observed in "Poetry and Drama," *The Family Reunion* (1939)[108] represents his first attempt to address the problems involved in writing successful verse drama for the commercial theater. He had to find an effective vehicle and conventions for treating religious and psychological themes in modern situations on the secular stage, and he had to develop out of his previous practice an idiom and meter which the contemporary playgoers could hear without being too conscious of it as verse, stripped of the rhetoric of Shakespeare and of Yeats yet somewhat elevated from colloquial conversation. In *The Family Reunion* he devised the overall solutions he would employ in all of his subsequent plays: a modern plot with a Greek play – in this case *The Eumenides* – as the mythic and dramatic point of reference; and a line of varying length and number of syllables, usually with three major stresses and a caesura falling somewhere among the stresses.

In Eliot's hands, *The Eumenides* becomes a psychodrama of conversion with strong autobiographical overtones. The protagonist, Harry, is a modern Orestes, and in the course of the play his flight from sin – his own, his family's – is transformed into a pilgrimage toward his true and redeemed self. Wishwood, the country house and family seat to which Harry returns for his ailing mother's birthday, is the place of illusion, and the Furies are the reality which pursue him even there. Initially, no one sees the Furies except Harry and his chauffeur, Downing, who turns out to be a guardian spirit. Harry echoes Thomas' "Human kind cannot bear too much reality" and the related passage in "Burnt Norton," I, when he blurts out to his family: "You have gone through life in sleep, / Never woken to the nightmare. I tell you, life would be unendurable / If you were wide awake." The waste land imagery ("the sudden solitude in a crowded desert") in Harry's speeches expresses his obsession with the "noxious smell" of original sin, the "slow stain" of mortality, "the cancer / That eats away the self."

Harry's particular sense of guilt derives from his relation with women: his mother and his wife. As goddesses of the feminine underworld, the Furies demand retribution. Like his father, Harry feels himself trapped by dominating women; and just as his father plotted to kill his mother, so he admits to pushing his wife overboard to her death, and on the day of his return, he drives his mother to a fatal heart attack. In the iconography of the play, Amy, the possessive wife and castrating mother, is played off against her sister, Agatha; and Harry's wife is played off against Mary, whom Amy had used unsuccessfully as a pawn in the hope of keeping control of Harry through "a tame daughter-in-law" and whom Harry encounters again now as a middle-aged spinster.

Emily Hale, with whom Eliot had visited Burnt Norton and its rose garden about two years earlier, stands behind the two redemptive female characters, Agatha and Mary. They are connected throughout the play, and together they deliver the incantation at the close; moreover, it is to Mary that Agatha describes Harry's marriage and his dead wife in terms that recall Eliot's years with Vivienne:

> I was sorry for her;
> I could see that she distrusted me – she was frightened of the family,
> She wanted to fight them – with the weapons of the weak,
> Which are too violent. And it could not have been easy,
> Living with Harry. It's not what she did to Harry,
> That's important, I think, but what he did to himself.

Harry's renewed acquaintance with Mary in Part I and with Agatha in Part II, during which each comes to glimpse Harry's Furies, changes the Furies into "bright angels" who set him off at the end of the play on a lonely pilgrimage of self-discovery. Mary becomes the spiritual anima for Harry, telling him about "your real self," "the real you"; she even sacrifices her reawakened friendship with him by denying that she has seen the Furies, thereby impelling him on his separate way. Later, Agatha, whose love for his father had freed him from Amy's domination for a time, becomes the liberating mother to Harry. Just as she had prevented his father's murder of the pregnant Amy, and thereby allowed Harry to be born, she now assists, a wiser woman herself, at his spiritual rebirth. Agatha wonders whether Harry may be "the consciousness of your unhappy family, / Its bird sent flying through the purgatorial flame" to atone for the family curse. Reaching a hallucinated state in the intensity of their communion, Harry and Agatha chant a vision of human love emblemized in the rose garden, the loss of which allows no alternatives but a living death or an expiatory trek toward a selfhood more capable of love. Immediately thereafter, Agatha pronounces an exorcism and dispatches Harry on his quest.

The echoes of "Burnt Norton" are obvious, and the theme is by now a familiar one in Eliot: that Eros must give way, through penitential suffering, to Agape; or, in the vocabulary of *Four Quartets*, that human desire must lose (and find) itself in transcendent love. As in *Ash-Wednesday* and the *Quartets*, the poignant but somewhat chilling message of *The Family Reunion* is that the burden of consciousness and conscience condemns the person to ascetic, penitential solitude. Harry makes what may be a radical conversion to the saint's path; Mary and Agatha prepare to live out their lonely lives in the light of their wisdom. As for the others, Amy dies and the aunts and uncles live, all unenlightened by Harry's visit and departure.

A later remark acknowledges Eliot's dissatisfaction with the outcome and offers a response to the play which runs counter to its intended meaning. By the time he had written *The Cocktail Party*, after the war and the *Quartets*, Eliot said that he was unsure whether *The Family Reunion* concerned "the tragedy of the mother or the salvation of the son": "My sympathies now have come to be all with the mother, who seems to me, except perhaps for the chauffeur, the only complete human being in the play," whereas "my hero now strikes me as an insufferable prig." Though Eliot laid the blame on a "failure of adjustment between the Greek story and the modern situation," the cause lay deeper than theatrical mechanics: his spiritually enlightened character seemed to him less believable and sympathetic than the supposed antagonist.[109]

The Cocktail Party (1950) and *The Confidential Clerk* (1954) set out to dramatize some of these same themes more effectively by reducing the poetic symbolism and trying to achieve a more realistic comic treatment. Eliot adopted the tight plot construction of social comedy and settled for a plainer verse that could rise on occasion from clear exposition to a tempered eloquence and from witty repartee to psychological and moral aperçus. The plays explicate the alternative paths to salvation which in the intervening years had been given explicit formulation in "The Dry Salvages," V: either the saint's lifetime of "ardour and selflessness and self-surrender" in contemplating the "intersection of the timeless / With time" or, "for most of us," "only the unattended / Moment, the moment in and out of time, / The distraction fit, lost in a shaft of sunlight."

The Cocktail Party[110] employs a Noel Coward triangle to subvert the worldly sophistication of a Coward play. Act I follows the conventions of drawing-room farce to introduce the characters: a husband, his wife and his mistress, and the guardian figures who work with a psychiatrist-confessor-guru named Reilly to guide the trio to Reilly's care. Act II takes place in Reilly's office: first with Edward and his estranged wife Lavinia, and then with Celia. Reilly, who hints at his divine connections by bawling out a song about "One-Eyed-Riley," leads Edward and Lavinia to see that they are bound together by their symbiotic neuroses, his inability to love and her unlovableness, and leads them further to admit that this mutual need provides a basis for a life together. When Edward observes that this would only be making the best of a bad job, Reilly pulls him up short:

> When you find, Mr. Chamberlayne,
> The best of a bad job is all any of us make of it –
> Except of course, the saint – such as those who go
> To the sanatorium – you will forget this phrase,
> And in forgetting it will alter the situation.

Because Celia is "more conscious than the rest of us," her deeper sense of solitude and of sin – like Harry's in *The Family Reunion* – does send her, through Reilly's connections, to the saints' "sanatorium" and eventually to martyrdom, but unlike Harry she *is* the strongest and most interesting character in the play. She rejects the course of reconciliation to the human condition which Reilly has offered the Chamberlaynes and chooses instead the way of renunciation which will lead, Reilly assures her, "towards possession / Of what you have sought for in the wrong place" as sexual love. When Celia asks which course of commitment is preferable, Reilly declares: "Neither way is better. / Both ways are necessary. It is also necessary / To make a choice between them." Reilly pronounces the same words of benediction on Edward and Lavinia and on Celia – "Go in peace. And work out your salvation with diligence" – and leads the other guardians in a ritual libation both for those who "build the hearth" and for "those who go upon a journey." For Eliot could empathize with both life choices: he operated in the social world, like Edward and Lavinia, but with a sense of sin akin to Celia's alienation from it. As dramatist and moralist he wanted to maintain the viability of both options, but he had trouble again with his last act, though for the opposite reason from that affecting *The Family Reunion*. Here the pilgrim character is so strong and compelling and so dominates the first two acts that her absence gives the brief third act the feeling of anticlimax, and the announcement of Celia's crucifixion on an ant hill jars with the cocktail party badinage exemplary of the Chamberlaynes' life choice.

Where *The Cocktail Party* employed a plot situation reminiscent of Euripides' *Alcestis*, *The Confidential Clerk*[111] took off from Euripides' *Ion* in an intricate drawing-room farce that surpasses even Wilde's *The Importance of Being Earnest* in the dizzy revelations of the last act. Moreover, because the life choices are less extreme than those in *The Cocktail Party*, the comic conventions are able to assimilate the religious themes with less sense of strain. The climax of Act I comes at an interchange between Sir Claude Mulhammer and his illegitimate son Colby, who is now employed as his recently hired confidential clerk. Each has disclosed to the other his deep dissatisfaction with the gap between subjective ideals and objective limitations: Sir Claude became a public servant when he failed to prove a first-rate potter, and Colby is a musician frustrated and disappointed by his own limitations. Sir Claude tries to comfort Colby with the worldly wisdom of practical compromise:

> I dare say truly religious people –
> I've never known any – can find some unity.
> Then there are also men of genius.
> There are others, it seems to me, who have at best to live

> In two worlds – each a kind of make-believe.
> That's you and me.

But practical compromise masks bitter resignation to the diminished terms life imposes.

The climax of Act II is a conversation between Colby and Lucasta Angel, Sir Claude's lovely but supposedly silly ward. Uncharacteristically, each risks communication with the other: he as her animus and she as his anima, each sharing a secret with the other and drawing the other out. Colby describes his inner world metaphorically as a secret garden which his music allows him to enter but in which he remains alone, without God or companion – unlike Eggerson, the former, now retired confidential clerk, who husbands a real garden for his wife. Lucasta, in turn, confesses to Colby that she is Sir Claude's illegitimate daughter, but their moment of communion is abruptly broken off when, ignorant of Colby's own parentage, she misunderstands his distress at her unwitting revelation that she is his half-sister. Nevertheless, the conversation has disclosed the asceticism of Colby's religious temperament for which, as Lucasta observes, his music is only a symbol and vehicle. Later she tells Sir Claude:

> Colby doesn't need me.
> He doesn't need anyone. He's fascinating,
> But he's undependable. He has his own world,
> And he might vanish into it at any moment –
> At just the moment when you needed him most!

Lucasta, living in the palpable world, depends on human contact and sees Colby as another sort of person:

> But you're terribly cold. Or else you've some fire
> To warm you, that isn't the same kind of fire
> That warms other people. You're either an egoist
> Or something so different from the rest of us
> That we can't judge you. That's you, Colby.

On the rebound, Lucasta becomes sensibly engaged to a successful, intelligent, loving businessman named B. Kaghan, who turns out, to everyone's surprise, to be Lady Elizabeth Mulhammer's illegitimate child. Kaghan sums up Colby shrewdly: "He's the sort of fellow who might chuck it all / And go to live on a desert island." In the scramble of discoveries in Act III, Colby hears that his father is not Sir Claude after all, but an obscure and disappointed musician. When Colby learns of his real father, he is freed from Sir Claude and his broken compromises: free to follow his father and find himself, acknowledging his limits without relinquishing his aspirations, dedicated to realizing his ideal within the possibilities of his ability. Like Harry with Downing, Colby has Eggerson as his attendant spirit; he sets off, under Eggerson's sponsorship, to live with him and Mrs. Eggerson, serve as organist in his little country church, and eventually, Eggerson foretells, to study for the priesthood and use his music in worship. The ordinary couples are left together at the end: Sir Claude and Lady Elizabeth and their now betrothed children, Lucasta and Kaghan. Their task, like that of Edward and Lavinia, is to learn to know and love one another, and their mutual recognition allows more scope for growth than the vapid social round of the Chamberlaynes.

Eliot rightly judged *The Confidential Clerk* to be his most perfectly constructed play since *Murder in the Cathedral*. The hard-earned theatrical craftsmanship and the serviceable verse line, capable of a range of effects without extraneous poeticizing, prepared the way for *The Elder Statesman* (1959).[112] Eliot's last play took *Oedipus at Colonus* as its mythic base, and according to E. Martin Browne, Eliot's close collaborator in the theater, Eliot thought of it as a final statement.[113] In any case, the play marks a thematic culmination and a new departure. Undertaken shortly after his marriage to Valerie Fletcher,[114] his secretary for a number of years at Faber and Faber, the play radiates the changed perspective with which the happy marriage invested his final years.

As in the other plays, the plot has a divided focus: the elder statesman Lord Claverton, retired and closer to death than he knows, and his daughter Monica, who loves and is loved by a young M.P. named Charles Hemington. The play opens with their confession of love and then presents Claverton contemplating the nothingness his life has become. As a public man, like Sir Claude, he has grown into the facade of his social persona. At the sanatorium to which he goes with Monica, his past catches up with him and shatters the persona; unexpectedly, he is confronted by two people who had been involved, years before, in dishonorable and shameful episodes in his life. Fred Culverwell, alias Federico Gomez, who knew Claverton as Dick Ferry, recalls Ferry's flight in drunken terror from the scene of a fatal accident. Mrs. Carghill, born Maisie Batterson and formerly Maisie Montjoy of the musical stage, reminds the man she knew as Richard Claverton-Ferry of their passion for each other at an early stage of his political career and of his breaking his promise of marriage under family pressure to make a more useful though loveless match. The various names for the same character make farcical fun of the roles people play in society, but as the voice of his shadow and his betrayed anima, Gomez and Maisie pitilessly force "Lord Claverton" to acknowledge his buried life. Mrs. Carghill is a marvelous comic creation (her hit song was "It's Never Too Late for You to Love Me"); however, details like the family opposition to Maisie, her threat of a breach of action suit, and her image of the two of them together in hell suggest that Eliot was still atoning for his painful entanglement with and separation from Vivienne.

In Act II, Claverton is brought face to face with his younger self in his difficult younger son, Michael. Michael is a slightly wild youth, irresponsible with money and girls, as his father had been, in flight from the social image of himself as Lord Claverton's scion. When Michael wants to embark to some far-off place "to lead a life of my own," his father preaches the lesson that he must himself learn; and by the last lines of the act he sees the link between Michael and himself:

> What I want to escape from
> Is myself, is the past. But what a coward I am,
> To talk of escaping! And what a hypocrite!
> A few minutes ago I was pleading with Michael
> Not to try to escape from his own past failures;
> I said I knew from experience. Do I understand the meaning
> Of the lesson I would teach? Come, I'll start to learn again.
> Michael and I shall go to school together.
> We'll sit side by side, at little desks
> And suffer the same humiliations
> At the hands of the same master. But have I still time?
> There is time for Michael. Is it too late for me, Monica?

Claverton addresses the question to Monica because she loves them all – him and Michael and Charles. Daughter and sister and beloved in one, she expresses the capacity for love.

The third act turns on words like "sin," "contrition," "confession," "absolution." Claverton tells the young lovers:

> If a man has one person, just one in his life,
> To whom he is willing to confess everything –
> And that includes, mind you, not only things criminal,
> Not only turpitude, meanness and cowardice,
> But also situations which are simply ridiculous,
> When he has played the fool (as who has not?) –
> Then he loves that person, and his love will save him.
> I'm afraid that I've never loved anyone, really.
> No, I do love my Monica. . . .

When Monica says that there is nothing she is afraid to learn about him or Charles, Claverton confesses and arrives at peace. Before going off to die, he confers his benediction upon all:

> It is worth while dying, to find out what life is.
> And I love you, my daughter, the more truly for knowing
> That there is someone you love more than your father –
> That you love and are loved. And now that I love Michael,
> I think, for the first time--remember, my dear,
> I am only a beginner in the practice of loving –
> Well, that is something.

It is Claverton's – and Eliot's – valedictory statement. It is no accident that Maisie and Monica share the same initial, as did Vivienne and Valerie.

The important development in this play lies in the fact that Monica embodies both filial and romantic affection. She is the first woman in Eliot's writings to offer and awaken both physical and spiritual love; she encompasses Eros and Agape. Claverton loves Monica the more, she loves him the more, for the love she shares with Charles. Desire and love can coexist because their source and end are limitless and eternal. To Charles, Monica speaks in phrases that link her with the feminine figure of Wisdom in the Bible: "I've loved you from the beginning of the world. / Before you and I were born, the love was always there / That brought us together." In their complementary relation to Monica, both Claverton and Charles represent aspects of Eliot himself: Claverton, the old Eliot, confessing guilt in the failure of an earlier marriage, but dying with a wisdom that embraces human love; Charles, Eliot reborn in a passionate devotion such as he had never known in youth.

The connection between Monica and Valerie Eliot is the wellspring of the play. The conversations between Charles and Monica are the only love scenes ever attempted by Eliot, and Charles's words in the last scene "I love you to the limits of speech and beyond. / It's strange that words are so inadequate" echo the closing lines of Eliot's poem dedicating the play to his young wife:

> To you I dedicate this book, to return as best I can
> With words a little part of what you have given me.
> The words mean what they say, but some have further meaning
>   For you and me only.

This last turning in Eliot's life issued in a last poem, "A Dedication to My Wife." The full and revised text stands at the end of the *Collected Poems*,[115] modifying the design and outcome of his life's work:

> To whom I owe the leaping delight
> That quickens my senses in our wakingtime
> And the rhythm that governs the repose of our sleepingtime,
>   The breathing in unison
>
> Of lovers whose bodies smell of each other
> Who think the same thoughts without need of speech
> And babble the same speech without need of meaning.
>
> No peevish winter wind shall chill
> No sullen tropic sun shall wither
> The roses in the rose-garden which is ours and ours only
>
> But this dedication is for others to read:
> These are private words addressed to you in public.

The loathsome bodily odors which filled the earlier poems become here the aura of a love which embraces mind and body. There is no mention of the Incarnation, but the poem betokens Eliot's most personal and intimate experience of that mystery. The unspoken Word stands behind the lovers' speechless thoughts and babbled speech; the rose has bedded in the garden which is theirs only in season and beyond seasons.

Some commentators, trained to the mask of the impersonal poet, blushed at what seemed the slight awkwardness of the love scenes of *The Elder Statesman* and the intimacy of its dedicatory poem, embarrassed that the dignified Mr. Eliot, who acted old so young, should now act the lover at his advanced age. But his angst, even his misogyny, was, from the outset, a measure of his capacity for passion. C. Day-Lewis' elegy for Eliot took all this in:

> We rejoice for one
> Whose heart a midsummer's long winter,
> Though ashen-skied and droughtful, could not harden

Against the melting of midwinter spring,
When the gate into the rose garden
Opening at last permitted him to enter
Where wise man becomes child, child plays at king.[116]

Though Eliot's plays were successfully produced and generally well reviewed, and drew larger audiences than might have been expected, and though some of them were sufficient hits to become part of the drama repertory, they did little to enhance Eliot's standing as a Modernist. *Sweeney Agonistes* was experimental with its odd leaps and gaps, its syncopations and discontinuities, its accumulation of ironically charged and stylized fragments, but it was an unfinished closet drama, performed rarely to small houses of avant-garde afficionados. The plays, after the special case of *Murder in the Cathedral*, deliberately sought dramatic continuity and well-made construction in increasingly prosaic verse to reach the theatergoers of Edinburgh and London and New York. Among those who had admired *The Waste Land* and even *Four Quartets*, Pound stood out for his interest as well in Eliot's experiment in popular writing.

But in fact, the high point of Modernism had come during the years just before and after World War I – say, from 1908 to 1925 – and dates in painting from the impact of Fauvism, Cubism and Futurism and in English poetry from the impact of Symbolisme and Imagism. Hart Crane's death coincided with the turning point for American Modernism during the Depression years. In the 1930s Modernism, though still the dominant mode, began to wane under virulent attack from Marxist and other leftist critics for being an elitist, haut-bourgeois, reactionary ideology, as in many respects it was. Moreover, and equally importantly, many of the great Modernists were by that time themselves modifying or moving away from the earlier, more programmatic positions through which they had defined Modernism out of and against a vestigial Romanticism and established its hegemony. In pursuing their individual courses, they came to accommodate what they had learned into stances and modes of expression which sometimes departed from, sometimes even contradicted, the essential tenets of Modernism.

After publication of her *Collected Poems* in 1925, H. D. found her lingering reputation as the perfect Imagist an increasingly misleading distraction, particularly from the import of her late, long sequences about the occult secret of the universe. Pound's cantos came to articulate a natural supernaturalism that masked its Romantic Platonism as Oriental wisdom. Stevens and Williams remained more characteristically Modernist in viewpoint; even so, the flashy and eccentric panoply of the *poésie pure* of *Harmonium* settled into the richly brocaded sonorities of the later meditations, and the Cubistic angularities of *Spring and All* and the collage constructions of *Paterson* gave way to the ruminative and measured discursiveness of the verse triads of Williams' last years. Winters had become expressly anti-Modernist by the end of the 1920s, but he remained enough of a Modernist to prefer the early Stevens and Williams to the later.

Eliot said that the modern artist, like Baudelaire, had to be anti-Romantic because his dilemma was inescapably Romantic. Eliot's Modernism served as the ideology for his agnostic years, positing an objective aesthetic absolute to counter a narcissistic consciousness alienated from nature and adrift without metaphysical absolutes. But Eliot's anti-Romanticism carried him past the persistent Romanticism, disguised or reconstituted, of his contemporaries – the differing Platonisms of Stevens and Pound and H. D., the naturalistic organicism of Williams, the Blakean optimism of Middleton Murry, the secular Humanism of Babbitt – to a Christian and classical position which rendered obsolete and false the impersonal manner necessitated by his Symboliste subjectivity.

The divergence between Pound and Eliot after *The Waste Land* was more than a matter of geographical distance. Modernism had brought them together, but after 1922 they went their separate ways. *The Hollow Men* and *Sweeney Agonistes* were Eliot's last unquestionably Modernist works. Notions of the artwork as objective correlative, "meaning" coexistent with statement, provided the theory for Eliot's earlier work, but as the influence of Pound and Hulme, Baudelaire and Laforgue receded, the influence of the Catholic Dante and the Anglican Andrewes became stronger. Modernism had not resolved the Romantic dilemma for Eliot, and he sought to identify himself instead with the unified sensibility and holistic sense of reality he saw in the Middle Ages in Europe, saw even for a last tense period in seventeenth-century England. Dante's Christian vision had earlier been invoked as ironic counterpoint to the secular purgatory of Prufrock, the secular inferno of Waste Land London, but in *Ash-Wednesday* and *Four Quartets* the invocation of Dante has moved beyond irony. It is integral to their meaning, and what those works are trying to express is a vision of reality extrinsic to the works themselves. Far from an autotelic embodiment of its own truth, the closest approach that Modernism made to the absolute, "the poetry does not matter" as poetry, only as the human effort to comprehend objective truth.

Pound too had spent a lifetime invoking and responding to Dante, but in fact he was closer in spirit to the Neoplatonist Cavalcanti and to his Platonized image of Confucius. So Pound was right when in a posthumous tribute he pronounced Eliot and not himself the "true Dantescan voice."[117] What Eliot heard in Dante's voice, and tried to express in his own, was not just a religious vision but a religious vision enacted and realized through the poet's engagement with the feminine. Eliot described the "system of Dante's organization of sensibility" as "the contrast between higher and lower carnal love, the transition from Beatrice living to Beatrice dead, rising to the cult of the Virgin."[118] *Ash-Wednesday* and the *Quartets* trace that pattern.

It is not necessary to claim that the plays have the same depth and intensity as the later poems to see the plays as consistent with this last assumption in their effort to communicate the wisdom of a lifetime to as large an audience as possible. The major poems, early and late, had come out of major crises and transitions in Eliot's life and perspective, and such was not the case with the plays, with the exception of *The Elder Statesman*. But unexpectedly for Eliot, life took a final turn – back to Beatrice living. Just at the end, the Lady between the yew trees assumed present, palpable, human form, reconciling heaven and earth, reconciling him *in extremis* to earth as well as heaven. During the closing moments of *The Elder Statesman*, Charles says to Monica of her father, "The dead has poured a blessing on the living."

Written thirty years after "A Song for Simeon," the line represents Eliot's own *nunc dimittis*, a quieter, more serene conclusion than Pound's "what / SPLENDOUR / IT ALL COHERES" in *Women of Trachis*. There are interesting parallels between these late adaptations of Sophocles, both in the 1950s, by the two old friends. But where Pound's adaptation arrives at stoic comprehension of tragic destiny, Eliot's domesticated version of *Oedipus at Colonus* dramatizes the acknowledgment of past sins "in the certainty of love unchanging."

4

Ezra Pound: Between Kung and Eleusis

I

Just after the advent of the new century, Ezra Pound, an only child born in 1885 in the pioneer mining town of Hailey, Idaho, and reared by adoring parents in suburban Philadelphia, was pondering his calling as a poet. Moreover, like Homer (we can presume), like Vergil (quite clearly), like Dante and Spenser and Milton (we know), he was thinking how to be a great poet. By about 1904, not yet twenty and still an undergraduate at Hamilton College, he had conceived the ambition of writing an epic, as his worthy predecessors had.[1] Furthermore, since he recognized the national character of the epic poets, he had to ask himself how to be the great American poet. Finally, steeped in, but (he hoped) emerging from, the cloyed atmosphere of *fin de siècle* Romanticism, he determined to make himself the great *modern* American poet.

From what he knew about American poetry before him, Pound could take only Walt Whitman seriously enough to grumble about: it was against Whitman that he had to define himself. Whitman had been naive in his optimistic celebration of American urban and technological culture, he had been shaggy and rough-hewn in his expression; but for the youthful Pound, brash but unproved, he was the magnetic but intimidating literary father. It is a decisive fact for twentieth-century American poetry that Pound chose not to reject Whitman's bardic energy but to sophisticate it for his own purposes. Instead of Oedipal patricide, Pound chose to make "A Pact" with his "pig-headed father," and the strutting condescension of the son unwittingly acknowledged Whitman's awesome potency:

> I make a pact with you, Walt Whitman –
> I have detested you long enough.
> I come to you as a grown child
> Who has had a pig-headed father;
> I am old enough now to make friends.
> It was you that broke the new wood,
> Now is a time for carving.
> We have one sap and one root –
> Let there be commerce between us.[2]

By the time Pound wrote this poem, he was well along in his apprenticeship. At the University of Pennsylvania, across the river from Camden, where Whitman had spent his late years, he had had William Carlos Williams and Hilda Doolittle as friends and fellow poets, but Europe, whose monuments and ruins he had relished on a grand tour with a wealthy aunt some years before, lured him from the immediate environs of Whitman. By the time of "A Pact" he was already in his Imagist phase, publishing poems with Provençal, Latin, and Greek titles and imitating something of these poets' manner.

An earlier prose note, written about 1909, the year of his expatriation to Europe, bristles with his grudging acknowledgment of, and combative resistance to, Whitman:

> From this side of the Atlantic I am for the first time able to read Whitman, and from the vantage of my education and – if it be permitted a man of my scant years – my world citizenship: I see him America's poet. . . .
>
> He is America. His crudity is an exceeding great stench, but it *is* America. He is the hollow place in the rock that echoes with his time. He *does* "chant the crucial stage" and he is the "voice triumphant." He is disgusting. He is an exceedingly nauseating pill, but he accomplishes his mission. . . .
>
> I honour him for he prophesied me while I can only recognise him as a forebear of whom I ought to be proud. . . .
>
> And yet I am but one of his "ages and ages' encrustations" or to be exact an encrustation of the next age. The vital part of my message, taken from the sap and fibre of America, is the same as his.
>
> Mentally I am a Walt Whitman who has learned to wear a collar and a dress shirt (although at times inimical to both). Personally I might be very glad to conceal my relationship to my spiritual father and brag about my more congenial ancestry – Dante, Shakespeare, Theocritus, Villon, but the descent is a bit difficult to establish. And, to be frank, Whitman is to my fatherland (*Patriam quam odi et amo* for no uncertain reasons) what Dante is to Italy and I at my best can only be a strife for a renaissance in America of all the lost or temporarily mislaid beauty, truth, valour, glory of Greece, Italy, England and all the rest of it. . . .
>
> It seems to me I should like to drive Whitman into the old world. I sledge, he drill – and to scourge America with all the old beauty. (For Beauty *is* an accusation) and with a thousand thongs from Homer to Yeats, from Theocritus to Marcel Schwob. This desire is because I am young and impatient, were I old and wise I should content myself in seeing and saying that these things will come. But now, since I am by no means sure it would be true prophecy, I am fain set my own hand to the labour.
>
> It is a great thing, reading a man to know, not "His Tricks are not as yet my Tricks, but I can easily make them mine" but "His message is my message. We will see that men hear it."[3]

This statement, like Emerson's 1855 letter to Whitman (and like Charles Olson's 1950 essay on "Projective Verse"), is one of the connective documents establishing the transmission of the American poetic tradition from one period to the next. In the space of a mere page or two, the crude denunciation of

Whitman's own crudity resolves itself in a filial handclasp as the son sets out to journey abroad through the Old World, but with the same New World message as the father.

But, in order to be authentic, the message and the voice would have to find their own more complex and cultivated forms. Addressing himself for once to urban America, Pound in 1913 sent *Smart Set* the following apostrophe to "N.Y." (to which "Madison Avenue, 1910" was later appended as subtitle):

> My City, my beloved, my white! Ah, slender,
> Listen! Listen to me, and I will breathe into thee a soul.
> Delicately upon the reed, attend me!
>
> Now do I know that I am mad,
> For here are a million people surly with traffic;
> This is no maid.
> Neither could I play upon any reed if I had one.
>
> My City, my beloved,
> Thou art a maid with no breasts,
> Thou art slender as a silver reed.
> Listen to me, attend me!
> And I will breathe into thee a soul,
> And thou shalt live for ever.[4]

The tone is comically (and deliberately) unconvincing, as though Whitman were lisping the stale conceits of *fin de siècle* decadence. An italicized middle section undercuts both the Whitmanian pose and the fake pastoral manner. Williams might find his voice and measure in urban America, but Pound would have to find his message to his country abroad.

Thus the early poem "From Chebar" links the poet with the prophet Ezekiel among the exiles on the foreign river Chebar, but the poet's exile is chosen. The voice of civilization speaks for Pound in hurling this jeremiad scornfully back home across the Atlantic:

> Before you were, America!
> I did not begin with you,
> I do not end with you, America.
> . . . .
> I have seen the dawn mist
> Move in the yellow grain,
> I have seen the daubed purple sunset;
> You may kill me, but I do not accede,
> You may ignore me, you may keep me in exile,
> You may assail me with negations, or you may keep me, a while, well hidden,
> But I am after you and before you,
> And above all, I do not accede.

Later the poem sees Whitman as *passé* and identifies Old World culture with the emergent spirit of the modern age: "There is no use your quoting Whitman against me, / His time is not our time, his day and hour were different."[5] As late as 1917, Pound addressed an American city in the role of

Whitman-with-a-difference; entering a competition sponsored by the city of Newark to honor the 250th anniversary of its founding, Pound was splenetic on a theme that would become most familiar in the Usury Canto:

> You, with your promises,
>   You, with your claims to life,
> Will you see fine things perish?
> Will you always take sides with the heavy;
> Will you, having got the songs you ask for,
>   Choose only the worst, the coarsest?
> Will you choose flattering tongues?
>   .   .   .   .
> Will you let quiet men
>   live and continue among you,
>   Making, this one, a fane,
>   This one, a building;
> Or this bedevilled, casual, sluggish fellow
> Do, once in a life, the single perfect poem,
>   And let him go unstoned?[6]

The poem moved one of the judges to toss it into the wastebasket, but it appeared in the volume of *Newark Anniversary Poems*, quite improbably and incongruously, not as one of the three prizewinners ("Will you choose flattering tongues?") but among the ten fifty-dollar runners-up.

Pound learned early that in order to develop a different sensibility and voice, he would have to find other models. In England he encountered two fellow countrymen who had chosen expatriation for cultural reasons much like his own and who were now honored equally at home and abroad. Their finesse manifested what an international American could accomplish. Pound left warm testimony in conversation, letters, and essays to his admiration for Henry James, and the image of James in Canto 7 presents the aesthete as mage:

> And the great domed head, *con gli occhi honesti e tardi*
> Moves before me, phantom with weighted motion,
> *Grave incessu*, drinking the tone of things,
> And the old voice lifts itself
>   weaving an endless sentence.[7]

In 1912 Pound sent Harriet Monroe's *Poetry* (Chicago), for which he had become foreign editor, his address to the other expatriate whose example countered Whitman's. "To Whistler, American" acclaims him as model with a presumptuousness that would have galled the prickly painter:

> You also, our first great,
> Had tried all ways;
> Tested and pried and worked in many fashions,
> And this much gives me heart to play the game.
>
> Here is a part that's slight, and part gone wrong,
> And much of little moment, and some few
> Perfect as Durer!

"In the Studio" and these two portraits, if I had my choice!
And then these sketches in the mood of Greece?

You had your searches, your uncertainties,
And this is good to know – for us, I mean,
Who bear the brunt of our America
And try to wrench her impulse into art.

You were not always sure, not always set
To hiding night or tuning "symphonies";
Had not one style from birth, but tried and pried
And stretched and tampered with the media.

You and Abe Lincoln from that mass of dolts
Show us there's chance at least of winning through.[8]

The final lines, with their startling linkage of Lincoln and Whistler, fastened on the point at issue: the chance of winning through to genuine greatness. Lincoln had done so by committing himself to the struggle here, as his friend Williams was choosing to do, but Pound found himself drawn, like Whistler and James and soon his friend Eliot, to the history and tradition of the Old World. In *Ripostes* (1912), as he was acquiring a voice that sounded more and more like his own, this boast appears only a few poems after "A Pact" under the dismissive title "The Rest":

O helpless few in my country,
O remnant enslaved!

Artists broken against her,
A-stray, lost in the villages,
Mistrusted, spoken-against,

Lovers of beauty, starved,
Thwarted with systems,
Helpless against the control;

You who can not wear yourselves out
By persisting to successes,
You who can only speak,
Who can not steel yourselves into reiteration;

You of the finer sense,
Broken against false knowledge,
You who can know at first hand,
Hated, shut in, mistrusted:

Take thought:
I have weathered the storm,
I have beaten out my exile.[9]

This strenuous and supercilious posturing would appear merely bombastic if Pound had failed to achieve so much of his large ambition. Edwin Fussell is surely correct in *Lucifer in Harness* that the Whitman–Pound axis establishes the major link between the beginnings of American poetry in the nineteenth century and its renaissance in the early twentieth century. If, as "A Pact" acknowledges, Whitman made American poetry possible, Pound, more than any other individual, extended and internationalized its possibilities. Where *Leaves of Grass* stands as the epic of nineteenth-century American poetry, *The Cantos* stands as the epic of twentieth-century American poetry. So, for all the vehemence and petulance of his harangue against Whitman, Pound was right to feel an avatar.

For, like Whitman, Pound had known instinctively from the outset that his epic could not be an objective, historical narrative about a legendary hero whose battles and destiny enacted his nation's character and values: the model which Homer, Vergil, and Spenser had followed and which Milton had adapted to his own theological purposes. In Whitman and Pound the poet himself personified and enacted the cultural drama. For by the nineteenth, not to say the twentieth, century, the modern sensibility was not just too complicated and fragmented but also too self-conscious and idiosyncratic to accept the conventions of the classical epic. Just as in *Leaves of Grass* the poet became a symbolic American of his time, so *The Cantos* would render Pound – all he knew and felt and read. And if an epic was (in Pound's phrase) "a poem including history," his scope as internationalized American meant incorporating a longer, fuller historical awareness than Whitman had wanted for his New World chants.

What, then, could provide the structural conventions for this modern epic of consciousness? The epics of the English Renaissance had harkened back to classical antecedents, but in a 1905 letter to his mother, the twenty-year-old Pound speculated that he would find in Dante's personalizing and interiorizing of the epic something closer to his own needs – namely, an epic which incorporated its multitude of characters into the poet's personal quest and which for all its history and philosophy and theology, dramatized a consciousness, at once central and inclusive, all-seeing and all-saying, in the process of self-definition and integration. In this respect *The Divine Comedy* can be seen to adumbrate such modern epics of consciousness as *The Prelude* and *Leaves of Grass*.

The Cantos belongs generically with those two Romantic poems more than with *The Divine Comedy*, but Pound preferred to call upon Dante rather than Wordsworth or Whitman because he hoped to avoid their autobiographical subjectivity. Could a poem be truly epic if it merely delineated "The Growth of a Poet's Mind," if it intended merely to "celebrate myself" and "sing myself"? Of the poets of the preceding century, perhaps only Browning, in a poem like *Sordello*, demonstrated how to amalgamate narrative, monologue, history, psychology, even direct intrusions of the poet's voice. But beyond that, Pound wanted the images, myths, and historical figures constellated in his psyche and in his poem to register as objective correlatives with the seeming impersonality which Modernist rebels against Romanticism came to think of as classical. Yet, confronted by doubts about *The Cantos* even from friends like Yeats and Williams, Pound could only contrast his poem with Dante's: his epic had no Aquinas map, no established direction or structured symmetry, but ventured a "sailing after knowledge," an existential searching out of what it needed and found. Like other Romantic voyagers – the Ancient Mariner, Childe Harold, Ishmael, Huck Finn – he would find his own way by setting out. The poem would plot his periplum and map his chart; he could name his cantos only when they had completed their design: the subject objectified.

But in 1905 and 1910 this was still some way off; Pound had to train himself for the verse voyage. Rereading *A Lume Spento* and *A Quinzane for This Yule*, his first two published books, Pound knew that he had to rid himself (and the poetic scene) of the residue of the nineteenth century: the languidly mechanical meters, the tired metaphors, the diction blurred out of mental and emotional focus. Pound's early poetry is an echo chamber of late Romantic decadence, and a decade or more later, *Hugh Selwyn Mauberley* was still trying to exorcise the *fin de siècle* with a wistfulness that betrayed how much Pound himself had ingested it. In *A Lume Spento*[10] we meet again and again the shade of Rossetti:

> Surely a bolder maid art thou
> Than one in tearful, fearful longing
> That should wait
> Lily-cinctured at the gate
> Of high heaven, star-diadem'd,
> Crying that I should come to thee.
> > ("Donzella Beata")

And of Wilde and Johnson:

> Ye blood-red spears-men of the dawn's array
> That drive my dusk-clad knights of dream away,
> Hold! For I will not yield.
>
> My moated soul shall dream in your despite
> A refuge for the vanquished hosts of night
> That *can* not yield.
> > ("To the Dawn: Defiance")

And of Swinburne:

> O High Priest of Iacchus,
> Being now near to the border of the sands
> Where the sapphire girdle of the sea
> Encinctureth the maiden
> Prosephone, released for the spring.
> > ("Salve O Pontifex!")

"The Decadence" begins:

> Tarnished we! Tarnished! Wastrels all!
> And yet the art goes on, goes on.
> Broken our strength, yea as crushed reeds we fall,
> And yet the art, the *art* goes on.

But decadence bespeaks impotence, and Pound trained himself with the discipline of an American athlete not just to go on but to set new records. He had to make the tradition his own. Greek and Latin he had, and all but a Ph.D. at Pennsylvania in the romance languages. He had specialized in the Provençal poets and had done research on a dissertation topic which later helped him to write *The Spirit of Romance* about the troubadours and their cultural milieu. He was learning about Italian poetry, especially about Dante and Cavalcanti. And the discovery of Japanese haiku offered a new and fascinating kind of imaginative perception and expression.

Pound's early poems are finger exercises in the poetic styles he wanted to make his own, but his goal was not academic imitation but Modernist experimentation. An early critic observed that Pound sought "to give people new eyes, not to make them see some particular new thing."[11] To the very end, even when he feared that his verse voyage had ended in shipwreck, he reiterated his purpose: "to 'see again,' / the verb is 'see.'" And so, between 1910 and 1920, Pound's virtuoso finger exercises were paralleled and motivated by the effort – through correspondences and manifestos and cafe conversations – to formulate the distinctive Modernist way of seeing which would revitalize the tradition. Imagism was its first tentative formulation, and it launched Modernist poetry in English. Pound frequently gave it a French spelling – *Imagisme* – to designate it as an alternative way of seeing and saying to Symbolisme, but the point of connection and contrast attests, as this book has consistently argued, to the continuities that underpin the contentions between Romanticism and Modernism.

Consider the tenets of Imagism. Drawn up by Pound with Hilda Doolittle and Richard Aldington, the three axioms, though they have become almost clichés, deserve a summation here as the redefinition of Emerson's organic form for the Modernist period:

1. Direct treatment of the "thing," whether subjective or objective.
2. To use absolutely no word that does not contribute to the presentation.
3. As regarding rhythm: to compose in the sequence of the musical phrase, not in sequence of a metronome.[12]

Pound would have snorted at the Emersonian connection; in his mind, these axioms rejected the gushing subjectivity, the effusive rhetoric, the mechanical musicality of the nineteenth-century heritage. But it was Emerson who most forcefully postulated for American poets the notion of poetic form as organic to the verbal experience. Pound would boast: "To break the pentameter, that was the first heave"; but some of Emerson's best poems, not to mention Whitman's, had broken it long before.

Moreover, Pound's influential definition of the image – "an intellectual and emotional complex in an instant of time"[13] – also reveals its source in Romantic impressionism all the way from Wordsworth's "spots of time" to Pater's "moments." The Modernist would not want to invest the "instant" with the metaphysical significance that Wordsworth and Emerson would, but the substitution of an aesthetic validation for a metaphysical one only highlighted the static limitations of an art of epiphany, such as both Romanticism and Modernism espoused. Keats's odes formulated the dilemma, and his long poems, even the aborted "Hyperion" poems, were his attempts to resolve it, just as Wordsworth's short lyrics sought resolution in *The Prelude*. The problem for the Modernists was more perplexing because they did not have recourse to straightforward narrative continuity, but the fragmented structure of "spatial" poems like *The Cantos, Paterson*, and *Helen in Egypt*, as we shall see, represents an effort to galvanize space into motion and thus locate the Imagist moment again in the temporal continuum.

"In the Station of the Metro," a paradigmatic Imagist poem, illustrates the problem:

> The apparition of these faces in the crowd:
> Petals on a wet, black bough.[14]

The poem, Pound has told us, records the "precise instant when a thing outward and objective transforms itself, or darts into a thing inward and subjective."[15] But the "organic" verbalization of that instant required a reduction of an initial thirty-line version through various revisions to the haiku-like pair whose juxtaposition turns the image of the first line on the pivotal colon into a visual equivalent in the second. Imagist principles predicate ideally what Pound terms the "single-image poem," and the challenge for Pound, as well as for H. D. and Williams, was to accommodate what they learned about concision and precision and concentration in the image into the variety and developmental complexity of the long poem.

Pound's epic ambitions, therefore, made his Imagist period – 1912 to 1914 – predictably brief. In *The ABC of Reading* he would claim that Imagism, at least as he conceived it, had sought from the outset the "moving image,"[16] and soon after sending the three principles of Imagism off to *Poetry* as directives to the American poetry scene, Pound had moved on to the next effort to define the aesthetic of the image. Even before Amy Lowell mobilized her wealth and connections to popularize Imagism, and thereby, in Pound's mind, to subvert it to her lax standards, Pound was involved with new friends, among them the writer-artist Wyndham Lewis and the sculptor Henri Gaudier-Brzeska. Pound dubbed their movement "Vorticism"; its heyday came in the years just before World War I, and the two issues of *Blast* (one in June 1914 and a War Issue in July 1915) and Pound's memoir for Gaudier-Brzeska after his death in the trenches stand as its manifestos and epitaphs.

Energy is the keynote to Vorticism – the energy of the dynamo or engine. In contrast to the Imagist concentration of energies into a static center, the English Vorticists, like the Italian Futurists, depicted the clashing forces and exploding vectors of the Machine Age. Moreover, the artwork as vortex, its design radiating power lines in and out, mirrored the cultural life of the nation magnetized in a major city like London or Rome. We shall be noting the theme of cities in *The Cantos*; in 1913, at the heart of the London vortex, Pound began *Patria Mia* with a lament that sounds like Whitman without Manhattan:

"America, my country, is almost a continent and hardly yet a nation, for no nation can be considered historically as such until it has achieved within itself a city to which all roads lead, and from which there goes out an authority."[17] Such cultural energy would draw all the arts together in dynamic interaction, as seemed to be happening in Pound's and Lewis' little group. Jacob Epstein's sculpture *Rock Drill* showed a powerful bronze man, face ominously masked in a jutting metal visor, straddling his phallic jackhammer, the embryo of the new epoch self-engendered and enwombed in his rib cage. Pound's sentence "I should like to drive Whitman into the old world, I sledge, he drill" expresses the Vorticist spirit.

The philosopher-critic T. E. Hulme, who died in France like Gaudier, summed up the new aesthetic in pointed opposition to the Romantic aesthetic. In the 1914 lecture "Modern Art" Hulme distinguished categorically between "vital" art and "geometric" art. The first is naturalistic and organic, claiming to follow "the forms and movements to be found in nature" out of "a happy pantheistic relation between man and the outside world." In geometric art the artist imposes a form of his own creation on his materials to compensate for "the messiness, the confusion, and the accidental details of all existing things; this kind of art tends to abstraction out of the artist's alienation from nature and society." Geometric art and vital art parallel the distinction Hulme also drew between the "classical," which was "dry" and "hard" in its intellectual clarity and precision, and the "romantic," which gushed from "soft," "wet" feelings and intuitions. Hulme's philosophical exposition confirmed for the English Modernists the superiority of geometric, classical art both in conception and in technical demands.[18]

In his own 1914 essay on Vorticism, incorporated in *Gaudier-Brzeska*, Pound made a similar distinction between the perceptual artist and the conceptual artist:

> Firstly, you may think of him [i.e., man in general, but particularly the artist] as that toward which perception moves, as the toy of circumstance, as the plastic substance *receiving* impressions; secondly, you may think of him as directing a certain fluid force against circumstance, as *conceiving* instead of merely reflecting and observing....In the eighties there were symbolists opposed to impressionists, now you have vorticism, which is, roughly speaking, expressionism, neo-cubism, and imagism gathered together in one camp and futurism in the other. Futurism is descended from impressionism. It is, in so far as it is an art movement, a kind of accelerated impressionism. It is a spreading, or surface, art, as opposed to vorticism, which is intensive.[19]

Despite the blur of "isms," Pound's oppositions are revealing. He lumps Futurism with Impressionism as vital, organic, Romantic, perceptual art, and he associates Vorticism, Expressionism, Cubism, and Imagism with classical, geometric, conceptual art. Elsewhere in *Gaudier-Brzeska*, Pound explains the same distinction by pointing out that for the perceptual Romantic the artist is himself the medium through whom impulses move to articulation, whereas for the conceptual Modernist the work itself is the medium – that is, the means are the meaning. Throughout the memoir, Pound the Vorticist presents his most combatively Modernist persona, advocating the impress of conception over mere receptivity to the swarm of circumstantial impressions.

Nevertheless, Pound's Vorticist period, like his Imagist period, was brief – and for good reason. Advocacy of hard, dry, conceptual art could not solve the psychological and aesthetic problem of releasing the moment back into the temporal continuum. Vorticist energy did not produce the "moving image," as Pound had hoped, but instead locked itself in spatial tensions. In contrast with Picasso's and Braque's Cubist experiments or Boccioni's and Balla's Futurist paintings, Lewis' Vorticist canvases and drawings are crammed and cramped with lines, planes, angles, the rectangles and trapezoids and triangles tightly braced and fitted, even jammed against one another, and held thereby in place: movement deadlocked in hermetic space. At first, contemporary commentators equated Vorticism and Futurism, and the Englishmen and the Italians were initially curious about each other. But Lewis and company increasingly insisted on differentiating themselves from the Futurists. Where the Italians strained to explode the enclosed rectangle of the canvas with vectors and spirals of violent color in order to render speed of movement (for example, in the juggernaut power of the racing car or airplane), Vorticism followed Cubism in subduing movement and even color by recomposing geometrical fragments into flat, taut patterns within the confines of the picture space. Futurism gave primacy to time and Vorticism to space; in Pound's terms, Futurism was extensive and Vorticism intensive. Hence Vorticism links Futurism to Impressionism as perceptual-Romantic, still "merely reflecting and observing" external circumstance (now cityscapes instead of landscapes), whereas Vorticism, Modernist-Cubist in purpose, exerted mind and will on, even "against," external circumstance to define an artificial space through internal countertensions.

The Romantic tended to see the creative process in archetypally feminine terms; the artist was the awakening vessel within which the creation gestates, quickened by forces beyond the control of the artist's mind and will. The Modernist tended to see himself in an aggressively masculine posture: Epstein's *Rock Drill* man, whose offspring in the sculpture seemed self-spawned from its sheer, shattering phallic impact on inert material circumstance. Reflecting on Remy de Gourmont's philosophy of sex, the Modernist in Pound seemed to accept the "integration of the male in the male organ," which was intent on "charging, head-on, the female chaos." Pound could fantasize about generating the new cultural Vortex in terms of "driving any new idea into the great passive vulva of London,"[20] and the sexual stereotypes, as we shall see, underlie much of *The Cantos*.

The hard, tensed Vorticist scorned the unstable organicism of the Romantic. *Blast* had dismissed the temporal philosophy of Henri Bergson in favor of the more spatially oriented philosophy of F. H. Bradley (who was the subject of Eliot's doctoral dissertation). Lewis' *Time and Western Man* (1927) would attack the fixation with time as the besetting problem of Western history and would call for a spatial conception of relationships, denouncing Pound in the process for his interest in music, especially in its connection with poetry. The force of Lewis' precept was so strong that the first published version of Canto 1 (in the June 1917 issue of *Poetry*) cites Picasso and Lewis in corroboration of Pound's intention "to write to paint, and not to music."

Hugh Kenner has argued in *The Pound Era* that Vorticism was a casualty of World War I, but the movement would probably have been short-lived anyway because it was a rigidly dogmatic and coldly cerebral version of Modernism. Its shrill opposition to temporality suited painters and sculptors, not writers or musicians. Lewis' and Gaudier's productivity during these years was not matched by that of Pound, who wrote little verse, and most of that a brittle *vers de société*. Even at that time, Pound's description of the vortex revealed how far he was from Lewis. Lewis advocated "machine-forms" as representing "the hard, the cold, the mechanical, and the static," but Pound spoke of the "fluid force" of the vortex as "a radiant node or cluster..., from which and through which, and into which ideas are constantly rushing." The language suggests not a generator or dynamo but moving images of natural processes such as a whirlwind or waterspout (and Donald Davie would discuss the method of *The Cantos* as a complicated pattern of waterspouts). Consequently, even if the war had not dispersed the London Vortex, Pound would still have had to find a way to break out of the gridlock of Vorticist space and gain effective access back to organic time.[21]

As it turned out, Pound's reentry into nature and time and history, and his consequent discovery of an adequate conception of the moving image, came roundabout by way of the Orient. In 1913, even before the first issue of *Blast*, Ernest Fenollosa's widow had turned over to Pound all of her husband's notebooks and papers. After receiving his Ph.D. degree in philosophy from Harvard, Fenollosa had spent most of his life teaching in Japan, where he became totally absorbed in Oriental culture, especially the language and literature of Japan and China. In his notebooks, Pound found transliterations, ideogram by ideogram, of Chinese poems which Pound would re-create as English poems in *Cathay* (1915). More important in the long run, the notebooks contained in draft form a philosophical essay on the Chinese language which Pound edited into *The Chinese Written Character as a Medium for Poetry*, first published in *Instigations* (1920). Through Fenollosa, Pound recovered a sense of the vital relation of language to organic process. Over the decades Pound continued to try to gain for Fenollosa's essay a wider and more serious reading; issued jointly as it is under their two names, it is the most instructive introduction to the method and the religious and philosophical assumptions of *The Cantos*.

Fenollosa described the Chinese ideogram as a "thought-picture," an "alive" and "continuous moving picture," a *"verbal idea of action,"* "shorthand pictures of actions and processes" – in short, a "vivid shorthand picture of the operations of nature." Because in the experience of nature "the eye sees noun and verb as one," "the Chinese conception tends to represent them" as ideograms. The nature of the ideogram as noun-verb, a pictograph of the thing enacting itself, subverts logical Western distinctions between parts of speech and categories of grammatical function. According to Fenollosa, the sequence of noun-verbs in Chinese sentence has no analytic syntax with phrasal and clausal elements in modification or coordination or subordination. It presents rather a series of "moving images" whose sequentiality implies "the natural order – that is, the order of cause and effect." Reading the sentence requires the imaginative participation of the reader in intuiting the relationships among the ideogramic elements as aspects and manifestations of the order subtending the cosmos. The ideogram is a dynamism, not a dynamo; its transformative energy stems from the depiction of the object with a "concrete *verb* quality" and, as an aspect of nature, proceeds from the "fundamental reality of *time*." The inferiority of the English sentence to the Chinese is that the former organizes temporal experience into the artificial spatial structure of diagrammable syntax, whereas the latter "has the unique advantage" of rendering spatial images pictographically in their temporal sequence.[22]

Imagism, as Pound implemented it, sought to break the discursiveness of the grammatical sentence and present the image as an immediate experience, but the absence of a verb in "In a Station of the Metro" epitomized the static fixity of the isolated Imagist moment. Pound via Fenollosa seized upon a notion of the ideogramic character of language not just as a way to put the verb back in but as a way to organize a sequence of "moving images" into longer, more complex verbal structures – into a poem with a temporal factor, into an epic "poem including history."

In other words, through Fenollosa, Pound recovered the Romantic connection between linguistic and organic processes:

> One of the most interesting things about the Chinese language is that in it we can see, not only the forms of sentences, but literally the parts of speech growing up, budding forth one from another. Like nature, the Chinese words are alive and plastic, because *thing* and *action* are not formally separated. The Chinese language naturally knows no grammar.

The word "naturally" here is a pun. Fenollosa postulated the essentially symbolic nature of all words, a notion which Emerson declared in the "Language" chapter of *Nature* and Whitman echoed in "Slang in America": "The whole delicate substance of speech is built upon the substrata of metaphor. Abstract terms, pressed by etymology, reveal their ancient roots still embedded in direct action." Uncannily, many of the examples of this etymological symbolism which Whitman repeated from Emerson recur in Fenollosa's examples from the Chinese. Moreover, this symbolic language is not limited to mere descriptive statements of sense impressions but rises to "lofty thoughts, spiritual suggestions and obscure relations" through the "use of material images to suggest immaterial relations." Such images, in the old Puritan distinction, are types and not tropes, symbols and not mere figures of speech.[23]

Thus, just as Emerson saw a continuum between language and nature and the Oversoul, in fact rooted the connection between language and nature in the Oversoul, so now Fenollosa revealed the metaphysical basis of his linguistic theory:

> The primitive metaphors do not spring from arbitrary *subjective* processes. They are possible only because they follow objective lines of relation in nature herself. Relations are more real and more important than the things which they relate....This is more than analogy, it is identity of structure. Nature furnishes her own clues. Had not the world been full of homologies, sympathies, and identities, thought would have been starved and language chained to the obvious. There would have been no bridge whereby to cross from the minor truth of the seen to the major truth of the unseen.[24]

Pound wanted to see no contradiction between Fenollosa's theory of the ideogram and his own Modernist pronouncements, in fact wanted to see in Fenollosa the reconciliation of Modernist precision with its organic base. So, hailing Fenollosa as a "forerunner" of modern Western art, Pound listed Fenollosa with his Vorticist friends in *Gaudier-Brzeska* and cited Vorticism in several footnotes to the Fenollosa text; with Fenollosa, Pound "looked to an American renaissance" based on Eastern "motives and principles" largely "unrecognized in the West."[25]

In this way, Pound was attempting to disprove or, at any rate, to fuzz over Hulme's distinction between the "general attitude towards the world" behind organic, vital art and that behind geometric, abstract art. *Pace* Pound, Fenollosa was no Vorticist; after all, the philosophy Fenollosa had brought with him from Harvard to Japan was a version of Romantic Idealism heavily infused with Emersonian Transcendentalism.[26]

Nevertheless, Fenollosa's ideogramic method allowed Pound to end his long apprenticeship and launch his life's voyage of *The Cantos*. Linguists have disputed and disproved Fenollosa's theory of the Chinese character and sentence, but it reconnected Pound to his Romantic roots without requiring him to acknowledge the nineteenth-century culture he found prudish and provincial. This is not to deny Pound's claim as a pioneering Modernist, but it does complicate the picture of him presented by Kenner in *The Pound Era* and by Marjorie Perloff in *The Poetics of Indeterminacy* and *The Dance of the Intellect* by making the point that his Modernism is in part modified by, in part undermined by, his deep-seated Romanticism. As we shall see, that tension constitutes one level of the dualisms that *The Cantos* were written to resolve.

Pound's Romanticism antedated his Modernism and persisted through it, gathering force and conviction in the course of his career. Even before Imagism, in "I Gather the Limbs of Osiris," a long essay published in twelve parts in *The New Age* during 1911 and 1912, Pound casts himself not as the phallic *Rock Drill* man but as the progenetrix Isis, and insists that the cultivation of technical expertise must not keep the artist from participating in the mysteries of nature; "our life is, in so far as it is worth living, made up in great part of things indefinite, impalpable," rendered into myth.[27] Even earlier, *The*

Spirit of Romance (1910) had distinguished between "works of art which are beautiful objects" – for example, the autotelic art of Symbolisme and the Modernism just then defining itself – and other "works of art which are keys or passwords admitting one to a deeper knowledge, to a finer perception of beauty." As instances of this more esoteric strain, Pound cites the troubadours in terms that recall Emerson and Whitman and anticipate what he would find soon in Fenollosa and much later in Jung:

> We have about us the universe of fluid force, and below us the germinal universe of wood alive, of stone alive....[For those whose minds are as fluid and germinal as nature] their thoughts are in them as the thought of the tree is in the seed, or in the grass, or the grain, or the blossom. And these minds are the more poetic, and they affect mind about them, and transmute it as the seed the earth.[28]

Even at the peak of Imagism in 1913, Pound described the genesis of art in almost Transcendentalist terms that substantiate inspiration in the correspondence between the unconscious and natural processes:

> We might come to believe that the thing that matters in art is a sort of energy, something more or less like electricity or radio-activity, a force transfusing, welding, and unifying. A force rather like water when it spurts up through very bright sand and sets it in swift motion. You may make what image you like.[29]

Pound regarded nineteenth-century Romanticism as a decadent devolution from an enervated Christianity, and when Eliot found his way out of his Romantic dilemma back to Christianity, Pound turned nasty and intolerant. In 1930, the year of Eliot's conversion poem *Ash-Wednesday*, Pound published his own "Credo," in which he made a point of dismissing Eliot's choice: "Mr. Eliot...is at times an excellent poet...who has arrived at the supreme Eminence among English critics largely through disguising himself as a corpse."[30] His reading from his graduate student days had convinced him of an alternative to Christianity in a natural polytheism persisting in the West from ancient paganism and gnosticism into the Christian era in hermetic and heretic sects – notably in the courtly love tradition and in occult Platonism. Though he had no ready-made and orthodox Aquinas map for *The Cantos*, he told his old professor Felix Schelling that modern intellectuals and artists were adrift without a theology, and now he had found in Fenollosa a Confucian and Taoist analogue to the hermetic tradition that he traced back to the roots of Western civilization. The Greeks and the Chinese shared the same natural religion, and Pound's "Credo" substituted the Confucian texts and Ovid's *Metamorphoses* for the biblical Testaments as his sacred scriptures. Pound was sure that Confucius would have understood his pantheistic piety:

> Given the material means I would replace the statue of Venus on the cliffs of Terracina. I would erect a temple to Artemis in Park Lane. I believe that a light from Eleusis persisted throughout the middle ages and set beauty in the song of Provence and of Italy.[31]

Moreover, Fenollosa's connection between theological attitude and linguistic form provided Pound with the literary method to release his Modernism. Those generative impulses from nature and the unconscious took form in the medium: "The best work does pour forth, but it does so AFTER the use of the medium has become 'second nature.'"[32] There need be no contradiction between inspiration and achievement; the medium was "second nature" to nature. He could see now that all along he had been looking for an equivalent in English, with its parts of speech and syntax, to the Chinese "pictorial method." Imagism and Vorticism had helped him to fashion the "luminous details" of special moments into poems with something of the concision and elusiveness of haiku and of Chinese poetry, but the final note to the "Vorticism" essay worried "whether there can be a long imagiste or vorticist poem." "A firm hold on major form" ought to make for "freedom of detail," but the countertendency also holds: "a pedantic insistence on detail tends to drive out 'major form.'"[33] But now he hoped that the ideogramic method would reconcile the spatial and temporal aspects of form so that he could gather those hard-edged, clean-faceted, luminous details, which satisfied Hulme's criteria for Modernist, classical art, into his life's epic.

The method provided no Aquinas map but a means of exploratory inquiry. Design is a processive function of content and arises from the relationship implicit in the juxtaposition of imagistic elements on the page. There images, hard-edged as ever, gather into clusters, clusters into the more complicated configurations of passages, passages into cantos, cantos into groups of cantos, and so on. Whereas Marjorie Perloff would emphasize the collagelike character of The Cantos and argue that the discontinuity between the bits and fragments produces indeterminacy of meaning, I emphasize the intentional continuity between bits and fragments to create a meaningful gestalt, much like what occurs in reading a Chinese sentence. Meaning comes from the mind's encompassing of sequence, but the sequence is not arbitrary or inconsequential. Pound describes the process with these words: "The ideogramic method consists of presenting one facet and then another until at some point one gets off the dead and desensitized surface of the reader's mind, onto a part that will register."[34] Again, as in defining the Image as a complex in an instant of time, he states that language registers psychological processes, but now the ideogramic method orders those images into a purposeful sequence.

The first mention of Pound's taking up his long-anticipated epic came in September 1915, just after the successful experimentation with the short lyrics in Cathay: "I am also at work on a cryselephantine poem of immeasurable length which will occupy me for the next four decades."[35] He was beginning with little settled except a notion of method and its underlying religious, psychological, and linguistic philosophy. But in an enormous act of faith in his own powers and training and in the implications of the ideogramic method, Pound undertook the life poem toward which he had been moving through a decade of preparation.

II

Though there is little published information about the conception and gestation of *The Cantos*, we know that there were false and halting starts – not surprisingly, given the scope of Pound's ambitions and the uncertainty of his intentions and strategies. Drafts of three cantos appeared in *Poetry* magazine in 1917. But they were loose and undirected, and sounded too much of Browning's timbre and cadence. So, after taking time to work on two longish sequences, *Homage to Sextus Propertius* (1919) and *Hugh Selwyn Mauberley* (1920), Pound scrapped those 1917 cantos and incorporated only occasional passages and images into the new cantos he began to write.

Most of what had appeared as Canto 3 in 1917 became in the early 1920s the opening passage of *The Cantos*. And a stunning opening it is: a single dramatic episode adapted from Book XI of The Odyssey, which Pound took to be the oldest episode in the poem, the famous *nekuia* or descent into the underworld. The narrative is maintained through almost seventy lines, broken off by the poet's own voice delineating the "descent" of his translation and then concluding with an evocation of Aphrodite from the *Homeric Hymns*. From the outset, therefore, Pound establishes the two major and controlling tones of voice which will run with many modulations through the entire sequence of *The Cantos*: the prophetic and mythic voice, intoning in strong bardic rhythms and charged imagery, is briefly interrupted by the voice of the pedagogue, direct and even prosaic, didactic and slightly testy. As we shall see, these two voices correspond to polar aspects of Pound's personality which the poem is straining to express and accommodate.

The first words come from Odysseus, the archetypal voyager-adventurer, in mid-sentence, already in motion, with the subject of those verbs ("went down," "set keel") undesignated, so that the reader is included in the headlong action, and by line 3 "we set up mast and sail on that swart ship." His blood offering will give the many shades of the poem voice. The directions to the underworld had come from Circe, and progress moves with a mysterious fatefulness: with "winds from sternward," we navigate "onward" to the horizon, where the ocean flows "backward," and then we go down to the underworld, only to emerge "thence outward and away" into the extended and devious periplum of the poem. The abrupt ending of the canto does not break off; it opens out.

To the ends of the known world – and down. What is that descent? First of all, it is a descent into the past: not personal history only, but the collective memory of the West. Pound's pedagogical voice intrudes to inform us that one of the shades he has come to know in his cultural *nekuia* is Andreas Divus; Pound's twentieth-century English rendition of the episode comes from Divus' Renaissance Latin version of the original Homeric Greek, just as the adaptation of the Homeric hymn to Aphrodite in the concluding lines is mediated through the Latin translation of Georgius Dartona the Cretan. From these Latin cribs, purchased at a bookstall in Paris, Pound ingested this much of the literary tradition and made it his own in modern English verses that suggest the Germanic roots of our language (to complement the Mediterranean materials) and imitate the stressed, alliterative verses of the Anglo-Saxon epics *Beowulf* and *The Seafarer*.

But the excursus to recover and recapitulate literary and cultural sources also inaugurates engagement with psychological sources. This *nekuia* carries Pound-Odysseus (and us, if we go along) beneath the public and social persona, down into the psyche: both into the collective consciousness, whose record is history and philosophy, and into the collective unconscious, whose record is myth and legend and certain ranges of art. Specifically, Canto I presents proleptically the primary and governing archetypes with which Pound-Odysseus (and, by implication, the reader) will have to contend in his psychological journey. The shifting of the *nekuia* passage from the 1917 Canto 3 to serve as the way into *The Cantos* was an intuitive stroke of genius. Quite uncannily, in ways that Pound could not have planned or foreknown in the early 1920s, the *nekuia* passage put him in contact with the archetypes for virtually the entire cast of mythic and historical characters in the rest of the poem and brought into play those psychic factors which the undertaking of the poem was meant to bring to resolution in its course. In this way, Canto I can be seen retrospectively not just as the point of departure but also as the matrix for everything that followed. An archetypal reading of the whole poem would elucidate what is prefigured in Canto I, following out the loci of conflict, the nodes of connection, the lines of development and regression as the metamorphosis of archetypal images unfolds the pattern of the poem.

Pound did not read Jung until the 1960s, after he had stopped working on *The Cantos*, but when he did, his response was enthusiastic and positive. Reviewing his life poem to choose the passages for a *Selected Cantos*, he cited Jung in the "Foreword" (1966), stating that the artist had done "the best that is in him by giving [the artwork] form and...must leave interpretation to others and to the future." Pound could not have been aware of all the motives which drew him to choose the *nekuia* as the entry into *The Cantos*, but that fact would serve to corroborate rather than disprove the intrinsic efficacy of the archetypes. In any case, as we have seen, fifty years before Pound read Jung, he was already convinced that the originating "impulse" comes not from consciousness but from a connection with nature and the unconscious. It was this conviction that prompted Pound to counter Lewis' image of the vortex as dynamo with the image of the vortex as "fluid force" – "a force rather like water when it spurts up through very bright sand and sets it in swift motion. You may make what image you like."[36] It is Pound's version of Emerson's dictum: "It is not metres, but a metre-making argument that makes a poem.... The thought and the form are equal in the order of time, but in the order of genesis the thought is prior to the form." Or his version of Whitman's characterization of the prophet: "one whose mind bubbles up and pours forth as a fountain, from inner, divine spontaneities revealing God."[37] Pound was

less overtly Transcendental, but for him, too, expression began with transpersonal energy welling up from unsuspected depths in response to the
stimulus of an experience or impression and embodying itself in an image
which fuses stimulus and response. Through such an advent of archetypal
energy "you may make what image you like."

It is revealing of the differences between them that Pound spoke of the
"image" whereas Emerson used the more abstract and cerebral words
"thought" and "argument." Nevertheless, Pound also clearly distinguished
between the made poem, which permitted him to bring to bear on matters of
craft and technique everything Modernism had taught him, and the genesis of
the poem as a psychological impulse responding to an external stimulus. With
regard to the artifact itself Pound was a Modernist, but with regard to the
artistic process he was a Romantic. The Imagist poem arises from a gestalt and
is the expression of that gestalt. The restless succession of movements and
manifestos records Pound's effort to define a technique adequate to his
empowering intuition that the image's "luminous detail" provides the
"permanent basis of psychology and metaphysics,"[38] and he found it in
Fenollosa's essay, in which the theory of language as the transference of energy
enacting the speaker's participation in, and response to, natural process reads
like a gloss on the "Language" chapter of Emerson's Nature and anticipates
Olson's "Projective Verse."

So the periplum of The Cantos takes off from a necessary retrogression not
only into the literary and historical past, which is the sum of collective
consciousness, but also into the archetypal matrix from which this epic of
consciousness will evolve its ideogramic shape and direction. To the horizons
of the known world – "day's end" at the "bounds of deepest water" – and then
down: the journey back to the point of origin begins on the final shore.

As Homer recorded it, Odysseus could not get final instructions for the
voyage home from Circe, his sorceress consort, but she did give him directions to the underworld, where Tiresias, if anyone, would prophesy the way
back. Androgynous wise man, beyond the polarities of time and space,
Tiresias is the image here and in later cantos of the protagonist's ideal and
achieved self. Up to this point the hero has fought to manhood in order to
establish a name and identity: Odysseus in the battles of the Trojan War,
Pound in the literary apprenticeship extending through World War I. But
now, in the second phase of life, after the achievement of manhood's initial
goals (Jung said that it usually began in one's thirties; in 1920 Pound was
thirty-five), ego consciousness has to risk itself again to the unconscious in
order to break through the established patterns which make up the social
persona and open the ego to the deeper potentialities of the emergent self.
Through Circe, Odysseus descends to make the necessary contact with
Tiresias so that Tiresias can point him on the course which will return him,
sadder but wiser, to his position as Penelope's husband, Telemachus' father,
Ithaca's king.

But in 1920 Ithaca was far away and the protagonist's end uncertain, whether homecoming or shipwreck. Though it begins in mid-sentence and epically *in medias res*, Canto I also provides the schema for the entire sequence by moving the protagonist's questing ego into engagement with the archetypes which will govern the course of his individuation – the shadow, the anima, the self. The shadow confronts the individual with his or her negative capacity – evil deeds or potentialities, acts of or impulses toward violence and self-destruction. The anima confronts the man with his susceptibility to his own feminine aspect, with those capacities and responses within himself which he has been acculturated to regard as feminine, and so as antithetical or other. (Similarly, the woman's animus confronts her with her own masculine aspects.) Individuation, therefore, is a dialectical process of assimilating oppositions into a more comprehensive psychological realization and requires the ego to accommodate the "other" into an evolving self – or to be destroyed by the other. Thus the ego consciousness must recognize and take into account the shadow in order to avoid arousing and falling prey to that latent destructiveness, and the man must find in his anima, as the woman must in her animus, the key to his sexual and spiritual identity, the clue to the integration (or disintegration) of the personality into a realized self. It is indicative of Pound's psychological bent that his important chapter on "Psychology and the Troubadors" in *The Spirit of Romance* posits years before *The Cantos* germinal notions of the shadow (as a "dark night of the soul," which here he dismisses all too naively as morbid), of the anima (as the woman who serves as inspiration and revelation), and of the self (as the androgynous reconciliation of polarities). The fourfold configuration of ego, shadow, anima, and self provides a typology for the dramatis personae of *The Cantos* and supplies the coordinates for plotting the succession of ideogramic images and episodes which constitute the evolutionary (i.e., temporal) continuity and coherence of the periplum.

And so, in Canto I, Odysseus-Pound's descent is crossed by a couple of disturbing confrontations before he makes any contact with Tiresias. "First Elpenor came, our friend Elpenor." The shadow figure blocks the way, pleading for recognition and deliverance. Like many of Odysseus' men, Elpenor had succumbed to the temptations of Circe's island, eating and swilling and whoring, and for their carnality Circe had turned them into swine. Through the power of the moly presented to him as talisman by his patron Hermes, Odysseus resisted the domination of Circe and found the strength to draw her to his side as his consort. Through a year's dalliance he had not surrendered his will to her. For that reason, he was able to secure release for himself and his men and to compel Circe to provide them with a ship to sail and with directions to the underworld. Odysseus' superiority to Circe's wiles transformed the temptress into a positive feminine force who directs him to Tiresias as prophet of the essential self. Elpenor is Odysseus' opposite, the image of his weaker self. He broke his neck in a drunken fall, and his besotted corpse has been left behind on Circe's island. Odysseus, facing Elpenor now among the "sunless dead" of the "joyless region" of Hades, stands agape yet comprehending, seeing in Elpenor the fate he had himself avoided.

The negative attributes of Elpenor emphasize his shadow character: "ill fate," "unguarded," "unwept," "unburied," "no fortune," no grave or marker, no name. Or rather "with a name to come." Pound's translation here accentuates the salvific effect of Odysseus' decision to acknowledge Elpenor and go back to bury him and mark his grave. The line which Pound gives as "A man of no fortune, and with a name to come" Robert Fitzgerald renders more bleakly in his version as "an unknown sailor's mark for men to come."[39] Odysseus' fate might have been Elpenor's, and in future adventures might still turn out to be so should he weaken. But now, through the recognition of his friend as his shadow, Odysseus earns for Elpenor rest and the restoration of his name, and earns for himself access to Tiresias.

Not, however, without another interference – this time from his mother Anticlea, through whom he first came in touch with the feminine. Her shade presses forward, and he has to fend off her overweening maternal solicitude to reach Tiresias: "And Anticlea came, whom I beat off, and then Tiresias Theban." The aged prophet, immediately identifying Odysseus, addresses him as "man of ill star" (the phrase echoing the "ill fate" of Elpenor and underscoring Odysseus' affinity with Elpenor) and foretells his return, in the course of which "spiteful" and "dark" tribulations will cost him all his companions. Pound had no way of anticipating at the time the cage at Pisa and the years in the asylum, but Tiresias' words emphasize at the start the solitary character of the voyage and its tragic consequences, especially for those closest to the protagonist. Pound breaks off Tiresias' speech with a bare assurance of return and omits the detailed instructions and forewarnings that Homer gives to Tiresias. Pound had good reason for the omission; his Tiresias map could not supply the defining details to be discovered only en route. Nonetheless, Tiresias' unequivocal prediction propels Odysseus' mind and will into forward motion with a rapid sequence of archetypal feminine images: Anticlea, admitted now, and then the Sirens, Circe once more, and Aphrodite.

Pound's handling of these feminine figures deserves close attention. He eliminates the long exchange between mother and son (in Homer, longer than the dialogue with Tiresias), as though his Odysseus did not have or need much business with the mother. Instead, after the intrusion of the poet's pedagogical voice to lay the shade of Divus to rest (as Odysseus had laid Elpenor's), Pound goes down again to conclude with an accelerated sequence of anima figures. In *The Barb of Time*,[40] Daniel Pearlman has pointed out Pound's inversion of the order of the episodes in Homer by placing the return to Circe after the meeting with the Sirens. Pearlman argues convincingly that Pound has deliberately reversed the order of these episodes so as to arrange the women in ascending order: the destructive Sirens, the ambiguous and pivotal Circe (whose power, as we have seen, spells destruction to the weak, as with Elpenor, but works for the strong, as with Odysseus), the goddess Aphrodite in radiant splendor.

Interpreted archetypally, these feminine images delineate the spectrum of possibilities which the anima can hold for the protagonist in his quest for identity. Moreover, as with all things psychological, categorical oppositions prove illusory. Polarities are not contradictions but complements which relate to and penetrate each other. Each element contains its opposite and reveals its capacity for joining with, or metamorphosing into, its opposite. So here the seeming polarity between the Sirens and Aphrodite rests on and pivots on Circe. Things turn into what was taken to be their opposite. The night sea journey of Canto 1 – described in terms of "dark coast," "dark seas," "dark blood," the black sacrificial sheep for Tiresias – ends with the vision of the goddess, all light and gold. And, just as Tiresias amid the shades held a "golden wand," so the goddess holds an element of shadow: the "dark eyelids" prominently noted in the penultimate line.

In the final opposition-conjunction of the canto, Pound associates Aphrodite with Hermes, Odysseus' patron, and this golden pair match, here overmatch "Pluto the strong" and Proserpine, the king and queen of the shades, mentioned just before the series of transformative encounters begins. In the Homeric text it is clear that Hermes, not Aphrodite, is "bearing the golden wand," but Pound depicts Aphrodite with the phallic bough of her consort, Hermes the slayer of Argus. This divine syzygy recalls the hermaphroditic character of the self, just as in Pound's text the phrase "bearing the golden bough" links the conjunction of Hermes and Aphrodite with Tiresias.

In Jungian theory the self is the supreme and subsuming archetype, the source and ground of all the archetypes, and provides the motivating impulse for the process of its own realization. Tiresias, the intimation of Odysseus' self, assures him of the successful conclusion of the voyage and sends him on his way. No more: the particulars remain to be disclosed. Pound could only tell friends who were confounded by his opening cantos that his epic would take perhaps forty years and run to 100 or 120 cantos. Already, however, better than he was able then to know, he held the map for the periplum in his hands in rough but bold outline: Canto 1 laid out the types for the dramatis personae of his psychodrama. And Pound's vague prognostications proved canny enough. Forty-odd years later the poem had run its course in 120 cantos, and Pound *had* come to a sense of himself, though to some extent on terms he could not have foreseen and would not have elected. But all that hangs from the final, projective "So that:."

III

Canto 2 is Pound's first attempt to apply the ideogramic method[41] throughout a canto. Canto 1 consists almost completely of a single, densely significant passage, but the next canto in the first collection of cantos in 1925 draws images and episodes into an intricate design introducing some of the principles and motifs of the entire sequence.

The first four lines bid a respectful farewell to Browning's discursive manner as Pound embarks on his own technique for bringing together historical persons (Sordello) as personal archetypes (my sordello) in a literary work

("Sordello"). The second four lines illustrate Pound's new ideogramic method with "So-shu churned in the sea." So-shu functions as the conscious, almost godlike artist, churning in the primordial waters of the unconscious matrix; the ensuing episodes are what he churns up. He is mentioned again toward the end of the canto: "And So-shu churned in the sea, So-shu also, / using the long moon for a churn-stick." So-shu "also" – like Homer, Ovid, and the other poets alluded to in the course of the canto; and he plies the moon, pared to a phallic instrument, to plumb the womb-sea. The alliterative ono-matopoeia throughout the passage is the first of Pound's attempts to match Homer's Greek rendering of the ceaseless slosh of the sea. The word "sea" puns with "see" and elides into the first word of the next image: "Seal sports in the spray-whited circles of cliff-wash." Then the seal's head becomes, alliteratively, the "sleek head" of the "daughter of Lir," a Celtic sea god (hence "lithe daughter of Ocean"), and her eyes "under black fur-hood" become the "eyes of Picasso" – not just the staring, almond-eyed women in Picasso's portraits but also the artist's own wide, unblinking eyes.

Pound signals the transition between ideogramic episodes with the co-ordinating conjunction: "And the wave runs in the beach-groove." The Homeric image recurs frequently in *The Cantos*. Here it works off of the earlier "cliff-wash" to introduce Homer, old and blind and wise, like Tiresias. In place of Picasso's eyes, he has "ear for the sea-surge," and recounts the fear in which the old Trojans hold Helen as destroyer of ships and cities. She looks like a goddess, but her sexuality pits men against one another to destroy patriarchal civilization. Is their dread of the woman a sign of the old men's wisdom or, instead, of their weakness? There can, in any case, be no doubt about Helen's transfixing, destructive power. The next episode follows from a repetition of the wave imagery ("And by the beach-run..."), and the reader begins to see that the image depicts reiterated flux within channels, each impulsion following yet reshaping the beach-groove. In contrast to the preceding lines, this episode, drawn from the eleventh book of Ovid's *Metamorphoses* and the eleventh book (the *nekuia*) of *The Odyssey*, tells of old Poseidon aroused by the beautiful Tyro, as the sea god's rippling sinews fold her in a momentary but climactic embrace:

> Twisted arms of the sea-god,
> Lithe sinews of water, gripping her, cross-hold,
> And the blue-gray glass of the wave tents them,
> Glare azure of water, cold-welter, close cover.

What do such metamorphic moments – on a single page we have already encountered several – signify in *The Cantos*? In denominating *The Metamorphoses* as one of his sacred texts, Pound was making a religious as well as a literary judgment. Ovid's retold legends mythicize a world of materialized energies whose sole unwavering principle is ceaseless evolution. Joseph Campbell has observed that mythology characteristically "focuses on the growing-point. Transformation, fluidity, not stubborn ponderosity, is the characteristic of the living God." The gods (Campbell, like Pound, speaks polytheistically) are the transpersonal, cosmic powers operating in and through nature, or, in Campbell's words, "symbolic personifications of the laws governing this flow." In Fenollosa, Pound found that "Nature furnishes her own clues. . . . The known interprets the obscure, the universe is alive with myth." But even before that, Pound had experienced such a natural vitalism. In 1908, after an overwhelmingly beautiful dawn, his impressions took poetic form only after "the beauty of the morning. . . took unto itself a personality": "Of such perceptions rise the ancient myths of the origin of demi-gods. Even as the ancient myths of metamorphosis rise out of flashes of cosmic consciousness." And Pound cited his poem "The Tree" (from *A Lume Spento*) as one attempt "to express a sensation or perception which revealed to me the inner matter of the Dafne story."[42]

This early notebook sketch expresses Pound's Transcendentalist affinities long before he reencountered them in Fenollosa. The phrase "cosmic consciousness" recalls the title of R. M. Bucke's book written to disseminate the religious philosophy of his friend Whitman. Emerson too had spoken of "the endless passing of one element into new forms, the incessant metamorphosis," so that "Beauty is the moment of transition, as if the form were just ready to flow into other forms." "This," observed Emerson, "is the charm of running water, sea-waves, the flight of birds and the locomotion of animals" (which are, not at all fortuitously, the dominant images of Canto 2). Even Pound's rendering of the dawn as a mythic personification has a direct parallel in Emerson. In "The Poet" Emerson tells of a sculptor friend who communicated by "wonderful indirections":

> He rose one day, according to his habit, before the dawn, and saw the morning break, grand as the eternity out of which it came, and for many days after, he strove to express this tranquility, and lo! his chisel had fashioned out of marble the form of a beautiful youth, Phosphorus, whose aspect is such that it is said all persons who look on it become silent.[43]

Both Emerson's and Pound's descriptions call attention to the function of the imagination in the mythicizing process. For Emerson, "the nature of things is flowing, a metamorphosis," but "the imagination is the reader of these forms." The imagination can interpret because the gods and demi-gods are personifications of energies operative in nature and in human beings as psychological states – for example, Phosphorus or Dafne. Pound made this very point in a remarkable 1918 piece called "Religio": "A god," he wrote, "is an eternal state of mind" – or what Jung would call an archetype. When a person enters that psychic state, when the archetype arises in the person, the epiphany of god or goddess appears not just to the mind's eye but even sometimes to the visual sense as well. Legends and myths contain the "tradition of the gods," and although immediate experiential knowledge obviously takes precedence over ex post facto literary hearsay, the tradition does help us name our gods and sort out our archetypal experience.[44]

The mythicizing mind, therefore, correlates the god as archetype and the god as natural force. In Campbell's words:

> As the consciousness of the individual rests on a sea of night into which it descends in slumber and out of which it mysteriously wakes, so, in the imagery of myth, the universe is precipitated out of, and reposes upon, a timelessness back into which it again dissolves.[45]

The correspondence between psyche and nature rests upon a cosmological schema, and within the psyche that cosmology leads the perceiving ego to see a correspondence between what lies above and below ego consciousness. Consequently, Campbell writes:

> The key to the modern systems of psychological interpretation...is this: the metaphysical realm = the unconscious. Correspondingly, the key to open the door the other way is the same equation in reverse: the unconscious = the metaphysical realm.[46]

As a psychologist, Jung made the same correlations between inner and outer, upper and lower realms:

> [The archetypes] are the ruling powers, the gods, images of the dominant laws and principles, and of typical, regularly occurring events in the soul's cycle of experience. In so far as these images are more or less faithful replicas of psychic events, their archetypes, that is, their general characteristics which have been emphasized through the accumulation of similar experiences, also correspond to certain general characteristics of the physical world. Archetypal images can therefore be taken metaphorically, as intuitive concepts for physical phenomena.[47]

Now we can see how profoundly significant, in fact how central to the religious philosophy of *The Cantos*, the conjunction of Tyro and Poseidon is. It is only the first of a multitude of such episodes in the poem. At these metamorphic moments the various but interconnected polarities of nature (Emerson's law of "compensation") seem to be resolved or transcended: male and female, matter and spirit, soma and psyche, human and divine. Process seems to encircle itself for a flicker of time before dissolving back into motion. Thus, in *Guide to Kulchur*, Pound invoked the imagery of the Tyro-Poseidon episode to describe the activity of the life force and the transformative "enthusiasm" which Plato and his followers have aroused down the centuries:

> [They] have caused man after man to be suddenly conscious of the reality of the *nous*, of mind, apart from any man's individual mind, of the sea crystalline and enduring, of the bright as it were molten glass that envelops us, full of light.

For Pound, the danger of Platonism is that it becomes too transcendental (Emerson is a notable instance) and betrays the palpable sensory world into an idealistic void. Hence, in the "Cavalcanti" essay (written off and on between 1910 and 1930), Pound contrasts the "Mediterranean sanity" of the Greeks and Italians to what he takes to be the disembodying tendencies of the "Hebrew disease" (the Judeo-Christian tradition) and the "Hindoo disease" (extended to include Taoism and Buddhism). Here the imagery of the sane and holistic Mediterranean world again recalls the lines about Tyro and Poseidon: "the radiant world, where one thought cuts through another with a clean edge, a world of moving energies..., magnetisms that take form, that are seen or that border the visible, the matter of Dante's *paradiso*, the glass under water, the form that seems a form seen in a mirror, these realities perceptible to the sense."[48] Again and again, the imagery in Canto 2 evokes the radiance that held Tyro and Poseidon: "blue-gray glass of the wave," "glare azure of water," "tin flash in the sun-dazzle." Even the beasts appear "like shadows in glass."

The canto's long central episode concerning Dionysus is framed on one side by the accounts of Helen and Tyro and on the other by the description of Ileuthyeria and a reprise of Tyro. It is appropriate that Dionysus' first appearance should receive such fully developed treatment, for he represents one pole of identity which *The Cantos* from beginning to end will strive to integrate with its opposite. Dionysus is flanked by women because he symbolizes to Pound the masculine capacity for affinity with and responsiveness to his anima, that is, to the feminine principle within himself. In fact, so feminine is Dionysus that he is often presented in legend and art as an androgyne with the soft curves of a woman's body. In turn, women respond to him and are drawn to follow and worship him, because in him feminine power attains masculine direction and drive. Dionysus is associated, therefore, with the dark mysteries of earth, with nature and fertility, with the body and sexuality. The anecdote which Pound adapts (from Book III of the *Metamorphoses* and from the Homeric Hymn to Dionysus) recounts the epiphany of Dionysus to the crew of the ship which tried to capture him and sell him into slavery. Pound merely notes the economic motive here and concentrates instead – through the hallucinatory rhythms and suspended phrases, all nouns and participles – on the revelation of the "young boy loggy with wine-must" as a god. The ship stands stock still in the waves; vines and vegetation entwine it; the great cats of Dionysus pad the deck; the sailors become dolphins and fish.

All except Acoetes, who recognized the god and survived to tell the tale to King Pentheus of Thebes. The account is cast as a dramatic monologue, with Acoetes forewarning Pentheus of the futility of opposing Dionysus: "I have seen what I have seen." Dionysus has disrupted the civic and social order of Thebes with his cult of women and their dark mysteries, and Pentheus, as fearful of passion as the old Trojans, has determined to pit his reason against their irreason, his patriarchal authority against what he takes to be their anarchic profligacy. Tiresias and Cadmus, two wise old men, have recognized Dionysus' power and joined his followers, but the threatening subversion of masculine rationality and control stiffen King Pentheus all the more adamantly in categorical opposition. As we read Canto 2, we know (from *The Bacchae*, for example) that Pentheus will not heed Acoetes' admonitions any more than Tiresias' and that he will be dismembered by Dionysus' enraged women, led by his own mother. Pound presents Dionysus and Pentheus as shadow figures for each other, and the episode admonishes rational consciousness of the violent consequences of suppressing the unconscious. Later cantos (beginning with Canto 13) will present Confucius as the complementary figure to

Dionysus, and so as the opposite sort of political figure to Pentheus. In Pound's pantheon, Confucius personifies a consciousness responsive to the unconscious and to nature, drawing them to realization under its guidance. The Confucian accommodation of the natural order and economic order, of intuition and ethics, generates poetry and art. But here Acoetes' words anticipate violence breeding violence, Dionysus' triumph in Pentheus' downfall.

The images of Ileuthyeria, the sea Dafne fleeing the Tritons, and of Tyro and Poseidon, twisting in the enveloping wave, repeat the paradoxical interdependence of "unstillness" and "stillness," of time and the moment, of process and fulfillment. The interplay of different shades and colors, of different textures and species in the final images of the canto suggests complementarity, not conflict, in the diversity of nature as Poseidon is replaced by Proteus, the sea deity of many shapes. The phrases "half seen," "half-dune," "half-light" emphasize, after the glare and dazzle of the metamorphic epiphanies, the necessary coexistence of opposites in natural process. The world is divided between dune and wave; the visible world is only half of what is to be seen; the mysteries of light and the mysteries of darkness presuppose one another. The final "And..." reminds us that there is no conclusion to the dialectic governing natural and psychological process.

The first two cantos break off rather abruptly to dramatize their fragmentary nature and their open-ended anticipation of further cantos. But the "So that:" of Canto 1 and the "And..." of Canto 2 are clues to the different but complementary kinds of open-endedness that proceed from Pound's attempt to reconcile Modernist space with Romantic time. Where the "And..." of Canto 2 suggests the paratactic and metanymic accretion of ideogramic elements which leads Marjorie Perloff to emphasize the collage-like discontinuity of the spatial organization of The Cantos, the "So that:" of Canto 1 points to the other principle of structure – namely, the consequential continuity of the parts which gives The Cantos a coherence more akin to the direction and temporal development of a psychological narrative.

The brief Canto 3 lays out the problem for this epic of consciousness in three cleanly juxtaposed ideogramic segments. It introduces for the first time the autobiographical Pound, young, poor, struck by the weight of history and the beauty of its ruins, trying to define himself (his self) in relation to nature and to history. The second ideogramic element is another of those glorious moments in The Cantos when earth reveals itself as paradise and natural phenomena unveil their animating spirits as gods and nymphs. The light-drenched epiphany includes recognition of the dark mysteries as well; the scene is framed by references to the peacocks in the house where Kore reigns as Proserpine and to the gray steps leading up to and from her underworld. Though the moment is thus related to process, it seems complete and so timeless: floating, like the gods on the azure air, in "the first light" before the fall into time ("back before dew was shed...was fallen"). Taking off from this last word, the third ideogramic element indicates the tragic burden of historical time through two doomed figures, one male and the other female: Ruy Diaz (el Cid), heroically resisting his adversaries, and Ignez da Castro, the innocent victim of male pride and greed.

The contrast between two modes of apprehending temporal experience is the subject of Mircea Eliade's *Cosmos and History*.[49] As a historian of religions, Eliade has observed two ways in which people have, over the centuries, lived in time and space. In earlier cultures, where people felt themselves more immediately a part of their world, they lived acceptingly in nature's cycles, so that individual lives were subordinated to collective tribal existence in the "eternity" of process. The evolution of self-awareness made the participation in natural process increasingly strained and shattered the tribal community into the crossfire of individualism and nationalism. Living in cosmos, people experienced time as circular and nature as self-completing; living in (fallen into) history, people came to experience time as linear and so requiring a teleological completion such as Nirvana or the Christian heaven.

The psychologist Erich Neumann saw what Eliade described in terms of a sense of cosmos and history as expressive of contrasting kinds of consciousness: the latter, a "masculine" or patriarchal consciousness, so called because the conscious and deliberate supplanting of nature by culture has corresponded historically with patriarchal hegemony; the former, a "feminine" or matriarchal consciousness more submissive to unconscious instincts and natural rhythms, which, some have even speculated, indicates a matriarchal period antedating patriarchal history.[50] Even if there is no philogenetic or autogenetic basis for matriarchy – indeed, though these categories perpetuate acculturated stereotypes about gender – they nonetheless present the dominant images by which women as well as men have historically symbolized the dilemma of personal integration with nature and society.

So the "I" of Canto 3 confronts all that is implied in the dislocation between cosmos and history and by the fall of paradisal moments into historical time. The scene, like many of Pound's cosmic moments, depicts a remembered experience of an actual place – in this case, Sirmione on the Lago di Garda. The indented line "As Poggio has remarked" relates the timeless moment to linear history; Poggio was a fifteenth-century papal secretary who was struck, as Pound was, but in a different time and place, by bathers in a pool.[51]

Daniel Pearlman's *Barb of Time* takes its title from Canto 5, which explores the difficulty of maintaining the visionary moment on the "barb of time," which splinters the light into the hues of the spectrum. Pound consistently associates the visionary moment with nature and historical time with cities. So, in Canto 3, he observes his youthful self on the steps of the old treasury house, a latecomer to a long-decadent Venice, confronting in the fall from nature into history the cyclic fate of heroes and dynasties. The canto ends with images of gathering doom. The Cid, the legendary but historical hero of the Spanish epic, rides boldly to victory at Valencia, but the child who greets him at Burgos warns him of the irresistible forces which will soon bring his downfall and death. Another historical tragedy (this time from the Portuguese epic the *Lusiads*) shows us Ignez da Castro murdered at the behest of Alphonso IV for her love for his son and heir. The fate of individuals, no matter how strong, and of families and cultures, no matter how noble, is emblemized in the stripped wall, the tattered silk, the flaking pigment and plaster.

Dionysus represented to Pound the man with a matriarchal consciousness, whose trust in instinct opened the passage into nature and into his own psyche. But who could provide the image for the man of history and patriarchal culture? As questing ego, Odysseus had much to learn, but at this point Pound could not go much farther than the stoic resolution embroidered on the tattered silk banner: *Nec Spe Nec Metu* ("Neither in Hope nor in Fear").

Canto 4 recapitulates Canto 3 in its opening lines by contrasting the ruins of Troy and Thebes with another Dionysian dawn scene in which the sexual dance of animal and deity, of male and female, moves in perfect measure ("Choros nympharum, goat-foot with the pale foot alternate") and climaxes in the conception of Aphrodite in the sea foam. But the dance rhythm ("Beat, beat, whirr, thud, in the soft turf") fades into sexual discord, image overlaid with image of passion's destructiveness: Itys, fed to his father, Tereus, by his mother, Procne, to avenge Tereus' seduction and mutilation of her sister, Philomela (the accusative form of his name, Ityn, punning gruesomely with "eaten"); Marguerite, driven to suicide after being fed the heart of her troubadour lover, Cabistan, by her cuckolded husband; Actaeon (like Pentheus and unlike the grandfather Cadmus), contemptuous of feminine power and "eaten" by his own hounds at Diana's command after he saw her and her nymphs bathing; the troubadour Pierre Vidal, driven mad by his passion for Loba de Penautier, roaming the woods in wolf skins and attacked by hounds. The overlaying of mythic and actual persons makes the point that the myths merely describe what happens in life. The "old man seated" and weaving the tales together collapses the image of the poet on the Dogana's steps with that of Homer telling of the old men's fears of Helen, and finally becomes old Vidal, "stumbling along in the wood, / Muttering, muttering Ovid." Poets and bards have sung of the havoc woman's power over man has wreaked throughout history – jealousy, obsession, betrayal. Adultery and war leave behind the "palace in smoky light," "a heap of smouldering boundary stones."

In these early cantos, women are destroyers of cities and men are city builders, like "Cadmus of Golden Prows," invoked in the opening of Canto 4 as the counterpoint to pillaged Troy. But Pound's city builders, precisely like the founder of Thebes, are men who acknowledge and respond to the power of the feminine. "Golden Prows" links Cadmus back to Hermes' "golden bough" and Tiresias' "golden wand," and we know that, with Tiresias, the grandfather of Pentheus and Actaeon joined the Bacchae in worshiping Dionysus. Futile attempts by masculine rationality to subjugate sexuality and nature precipitate greater devastation. Even Zeus, the king of the gods, lusts – and he seizes Danaë, despite her royal father's attempt to sequester her in a tower. In a parallel incident, the Chinese emperor must learn, like Pentheus,

that the wind is not the "wind of the palace, / Shaking imperial water-jets."
Beyond patriarchal authority, the life force blows through men and women
for good and ill, destroying and inspiring. "No wind is the king's wind"
(pp. 15–16).

Despite the male threat of violation, the female reigns inviolate: Diana, as
Actaeon saw her, bathed in the sunlight in the "liquid and rushing crystal" of
the "black soft water"; the Virgin Mary, still hailed as Queen in procession
and still enshrined as "Madonna in the Garden" in the miracle-working
painting which Cavalcanti had described. Virginity and sexuality, purity and
possession – the dilemma constitutes no simple contradiction. The sexual
tragedies which fill Canto 4 are bracketed between Catullus' marriage song for
Aurunculeia and the satyr's dance at the beginning and end of the hymn to the
Virgin accompanying the unceasing sexual dance ("The Centaur's heel plants
in the earth loam"). As attentive spectators, we readers sit "in the arena" of the
poet's consciousness at the crosspoint of the conundrum – both "here" and
"there," in the present and the past, in China and Provence and Greece, in
nature and history, with the city builders and the city destroyers. Pound's
gamble is that the point of contradiction is the point of resolution.

These early cantos turn on the interplay between men and women, sexuality
and politics. The ideogramic evidence, presented in what Pound took to be
"luminous details," comes from the late Middle Ages and the Renaissance, the
periods of his graduate research. These historical figures take on archetypal
significance in Pound's consciousness, and the archetypes are characteristically
Janus-faced. The double aspect of women in the intersection of sex and politics
is epitomized in Canto 6 in the contrast between Eleanor of Aquitaine and
Cunizza da Romano, whose attractiveness and wealth made them pawns in the
patriarchy but whose intelligence and will preserved their independence.
Fearful men turn their susceptibility into domination of women: bound by
law, bartered as dowry, charged with bearing male heirs. Eleanor was a
medieval Helen, trapped in marriage, first with the French king, then with the
English king, but she made her court a center for extramarital love and
troubadour song. Whereas Eleanor was the captive of kings, Cunizza was the
liberator of slaves. Her life of passion (the troubadour Sordello was one of her
lovers) led to the great act of her old age – the manumission of her slaves into
manhood, "'free of person, free of will / free to buy, witness, sell, testate'"
(p. 23).

The double aspect on the masculine side is epitomized in the pairs of blood
relatives in Canto 5: Giovanni Borgia, drowned in the Tiber, presumably at
the command of his brother Cesare, and Alessandro de Medici, butchered at
the command of his cousin Lorenzino. Elsewhere Pound presents alternatives
to a patriarchy of combating ambitions and competing greeds, but here his
practical point is that within such a system only the tough individual can
survive; the passive man will fall victim to the man of action. Alessandro's
"abuleia," or lack of willpower, renders him helpless before Lorenzino's
aggressiveness. Moralizers have found Odysseus ruthless to men and women

alike, but at the opening of Canto 6, Pound steps back from his persona long enough to commend him as a man of action: "Odysseus, / We know what you have done." For Pound morality was a function of "directio voluntatis," direction of the will, and a messy, ruthless system makes for messy choices.

The troubadours were Pound's heroes in that world because they engaged the feminine; they were lovers and poets as well as adventurers. He was aware of their seductions and treacheries and recounted them in *The Spirit of Romance*, which is a useful source book for these cantos. They exercised their sexual and artistic and survival skills without pity or self-pity; their virtue – or, rather, their virtu – was as hard as their vices. In Pound's version at least, they sang their lady's praises, took their chances with her and her husband, submitted their fate to her, determined not to live except empowered by love of her. Canto 6 ends with Sordello's apostrophizing Cunizza as a liberating force.

Canto 7 makes the autobiographical connection by carrying these themes forward into the London of the abortive Vortex, the London that Eliot and Pound knew. Written in 1920, Canto 7 is related to the *Mauberley* sequence, published that same year. It invokes Helen/Eleanor again as "destroyer of ships, of men, of cities," but Homer and Ovid and Sordello are displaced by Henry James in that world of phantoms and men as unsexed as the old Trojans in Canto 2. Pound speaks in his own voice: "Thin husks I had known as men, / Dry casques of departed locusts / speaking a shell of speech" (p. 26). Women languish, weep, age, die; language shrivels: "the words rattle: shells given out by shells." Though deep in himself "the passion endures," the young man finds only stale "aromas" and "rooms" in the place of past "action" and "chronicles" of action. Lines parodic of "Prufrock" depict Pound and Eliot searching for the lost anima: "We also made ghostly visits, and the stair / That knew us, found us again on the turn of it, / Knocking at empty rooms, seeking for buried beauty..." (p. 25). The figure of Alessandro de Medici as a "dry phantom" returns from Canto 5: "thrice warned, watcher, / Eternal watcher of things, / Of things, of men, of passions" with his "stiff, still features" (p. 27).

When several cantos appeared in Eliot's periodical *The Criterion* in July 1923, under the title "Malatesta Cantos," Pound was signaling the different route he was taking by proposing the figure of Sigismundo Malatesta as an antithesis to Eliot's Jamesian world. In Cantos 8–11 Pound invents a new kind of verbal collage, stitching together passages from letters and documents into a fragmented chronicle and portrait of Malatesta as "live man" and therefore as another image of the protagonist's adventuring ego. Many readers of *The Cantos* have been pained by Pound's admiration for so hard-driving and bloody-handed an egoist. In the brawls of Renaissance Italy, from which Pound's Europe devolved, Malatesta had made implacable enemies, and Pound included some evidence of his amoral ruthlessness. But Pound preferred to emphasize what Malatesta had made of himself in an amoral society: "In a Europe not YET rotten by usury, but outside the then system, and pretty much against the power that was, and in any case without great material resources, Sigismundo cut his notch. He registered a state of mind, of sensibility, of all-roundness and awareness."[52] Hence the Malatesta Cantos, he said, are "openly volitionist, establishing, I think clearly, the effect of the factive personality": "Sigismundo, an entire man," a Vorticist in Renaissance doublet, a swaggering, flamboyant fantasy of Pound's own attitudes.

As (admittedly unconvincing) evidence of Malatesta's "high sense of justice," for all his faults, Pound pointed out that "Gemisto wd. be even more forgotten without Sigismundo's piety" toward him.[53] Gemisthus Plethon is one of the Neoplatonist philosophers (Canto 5 had already cited Iamblicus and Porphyry) whom Pound saw as carrying forward the tradition of the pagan mysteries through the Christian Middle Ages into the Renaissance. Gemisthus attended the Council of Ferrara, at which Malatesta was also present, and Canto 8 presents him, in the midst of the war councils, holding forth on philosophy and religion – specifically, on Poseidon as the mythic representation of the cosmic spirit or *"concret Allgemeine."* (In Canto 83 Pound will repeat: "Gemisto stemmed all from Neptune" as the mythological personification of the *nous*, or mind emanating into the material order.)[54] Pound gives "concrete universal" in German from Fritz Schultze's description of Plethon (in his 1874 *Study of the Philosophy of the Renaissance*) as Pound's sort of Platonist:

> Plethon is a complete Platonic realist in the Medieval sense. The universal is for him the final reality. But this universal is not abstractly general, as the Nominalists consider it, but the *concrete universal*, which includes in itself all particulars; it is not a mere abstract of all particulars, but the full totality of all particulars.[55]

In Pound's portrait, Malatesta's Platonist realism generated sound attitudes and effective measures in the areas of economics and the arts. Though Malatesta had to struggle to get enough money from the princes who used his military services, he distributed it, with a sense of the just price and the needs of his dependents, in a manner that reflected Pound's growing interest in the Social Credit economics of Major C. H. Douglas, whom Pound had met in 1918: "And Vanni must give that peasant a decent price for his horses, / Say that I will refund" (p. 50). (Remember the Cid's insistence on getting "pay for his menie," even by tricking the Jewish pawnbrokers.) Moreover, Sigismundo became a generous patron of artists, concerned less with their volume of production than with creating the freedom in which their imagination might flourish. His greatest artistic achievement was the building of the Tempio Malatestiana, for which he employed architects, artists, and craftsmen of all kinds. They remade an old gothic church into a temple decorated with pagan myths in limestone bas reliefs and with one exterior wall lined with sarcophagi honoring great men. (Sigismundo transported Gemisthus' ashes from Greece for deposit in one of the sarcophagi.) Pius II charged that the Tempio was "so full of pagan works of art that it seemed less a Christian sanctuary than a temple of heathen devil worshippers," but Pound professed to see in its combination of Christian, mythological, and astrological elements the possibility of a "clean and beneficent Christianity."[56]

Like Pound laboring over the years on his *Cantos*, "he, Sigismundo, *templum aedificavit*" (p. 32) and left it at his death uncompleted yet still standing: an unimpeachable monument of and to himself – or, rather, to himself and Isotta. He could subject women to his own brutal uses, like "that German-Burgundian female" mentioned in Canto 9, but his love for Isotta disclosed his highest and noblest self. The Latin inscription at the end of Canto 9 reads: "And he loved Isotta degli Acti to distraction, and she was worthy of him. Constant in purpose, she delighted the prince's eyes – beautiful to look at and pleasing to the people and to the honor of Italy." In Isotta's combination of physical and moral beauty his anima found its validation: "She was worthy of him," and together they formed – at least in Sigismundo's eyes – the perfect pair. Immortalizing their union in his temple of love, Sigismundo had their intertwined initials inscribed everywhere as a testimonial to their syzygy.

In love and war, in philosophy and religion, in economics and art, Malatesta was – in Pound's minority view – a constructive and self-constructive force: "All that a single man could, Malatesta managed *against* the current of power." In much the same way, Pound saw Odysseus transcending the realpolitik of his situation: "HOMER: Odyssey: intelligence set above brute force."[57] In Canto 9 Pound links Odysseus and Sigismundo to indicate that the hero is not just "Polumetis," the Homeric epithet for Odysseus as "man of many counsels, many-minded man," but "Poliocetes," Pisanello's name for Malatesta as "taker of cities." Such myopic tolerance toward the unbridled exertion of will and power by the superior few in the name of higher values lay Pound open to a romanticizing of fascism during the next decade. This streak of brutality had been part of the Vorticist and Futurist exaltation of energy and force, epitomized in the brass knuckles which Gaudier had made for Hulme and which became Hulme's prize possession. Marinetti hailed "War – The World's Only Hygiene," and both Hulme and Gaudier wrote similarly in the grip of the war which would claim them. Pound mourned them and the waste of war for the rest of his life, but by the mid-1930s his use of the word "totalitarian" in *Guide to Kulchur* with a completely positive connotation indicated his judgment about the intractable social deadlock against which the "live man" must force his way. The personae for Pound's questing ego – Odysseus, the Cid, the Provençal troubadours, Sigismundo – anticipate his later admiration of Mussolini. Such insensitivity and coarseness of judgment bespeak a serious distortion in Pound's moral vision, but in the first decade or so of the cantos, the most serious fault is Alessandro's *abuleia*.

But in fact, Pound's moral vision extended beyond Sigismundo as Dionysian Vorticist. Canto 13 introduces Confucius to *The Cantos* (though he had already been mentioned in the 1917 version of what was then Canto 1). He and his philosophy are meant to complement Dionysus and to temper the Dionysian perspective celebrated in Canto 2. Pound saw that the complete man would have to accommodate both Dionysus and Confucius, as

Sigismundo did not. Where Dionysus represents the aspect of the protagonist responsive to emotion and instinct, Confucius represents the polar aspect responsible to reason and will; where Dionysus is the man of nature, Confucius is the man of cities; where Dionysus foments an anarchic and amoral individualism, Confucius cultivates the individual's ethical commitment to the social order; where Dionysus expresses matriarchal consciousness, Confucius expresses patriarchal consciousness; where Dionysus stands for the generative impulse of artistic expression, Confucius stands for crafted artwork.

Pound would say that these poles are universal and fundamental, as is the necessity of constraining them to creative interaction, all the more so in a time of violent extremities like ours. Robert Duncan has acclaimed Pound as the great poet of the century for living out in his life and art our violent contradictions. Archetypally, *The Cantos* expresses the schism between Dionysus and Confucius that afflicts the protagonist and his world as well as the protagonist's heroic, if often wrong-headed, effort to bring them into accord in himself and his world. The kaleidoscope of ideogramic episodes records the Hegelian process of trying to synthesize nature and culture, individual intuition and collective ethics. At this point in his life and in his poem, Pound could only veer between Dionysus and Confucius, but he thought he was beginning to see Dionysian instinct as not necessarily inimical to social order, as indeed the basis of a good economy, and to see the possibility that Confucian ethics was a humanizing of natural rhythms into the economic and social spheres. The main thrust of Pound's life poem is to assert that Dionysus and Confucius do not cancel but complete each other and (the more difficult task for someone as divided as Pound) to search out the terms on which that complementarity can be achieved.

So the limpid directness and dignified pace of Canto 13 are calculated to contrast initially with the rhythmic and verbal energy of Canto 2. Where Dionysus was surrounded by women and by episodes of sexual passion, the sage and his male disciples are engaged in commodious rational discourse. Canto 13 is a dialogue in which Kung (Kung-fu-tsu, anglicized into Confucius) instructs his pupils in the root ideas of his social philosophy. The word "order" recurs like a refrain, especially in the summary of Confucian ethics adapted from *The Great Digest* (which Pound would translate in the years to come):

> If a man have not order within him
> He can not spread order about him;
> And if a man have not order within him
> His family will not act with due order;
>   And if the prince have not order within him
> He cannot put order in his dominions.
> And Kung gave the words "order"
> and "brotherly deference"
> And said nothing of the "life after death."
>   (p. 59)

The good society is, then, patriarchal and hierarchical, predicated not on rewards in an afterlife but on a good earthly existence for its citizens. The only mention of women in the canto comes when the master holds up as moral examples two patriarchs who selflessly gave their daughters in marriage to husbands who could bring no social or political advancement to the family. At the same time, the rigid verticality of the social order rests on a certain concept of individualism. Each man who has authority and responsibility (whether in a larger or smaller sphere, a higher or lower position) creates order within himself by bringing mind and heart, intellect and will into accord, so that each can act "in his nature," or, as Pound would say in *The Pisan Cantos*, "each in the name of his god." The integration of the individual makes him into what Pound would later call the "Unwobbling Pivot," from the ideogram *chung*: "Anyone can run to excesses, / It is easy to shoot past the mark, / It is hard to stand firm in the middle" (p. 59). Self-rootedness allows the man to impose order on the world of his activity and influence: the husband on his family, the prince on his dominion. Moreover self-rootedness frees each person to contribute to the diversity of society by assuming the role and function – prince or monk or laborer, soldier or poet – dictated by his "nature."

Canto 13 is unabashedly didactic and axiomatic, presented mostly in end-stopped lines strung together unobtrusively by a litany of "ands," and it adumbrates the social philosophy on which subsequent cantos will expatiate. In theory at least, each person fulfills himself and helps to sustain the total scheme by active participation in his proper place. The only person rebuked is Yuan Jang, who though Kung's elder, had not attained the wisdom commensurate with his years but instead only "sat by the roadside pretending to / be receiving wisdom." The sage's injunction to the old "fool" to "get up and do something useful" (p. 59) is an early formulation of Pound's maxim of translating "ideas into action."

Confucius thus speaks for the side of Pound which is conservative, traditional, sexist, mandarin, rationalist; in a Confucian utopia Sigismundo's volitionist egotism would be subjected to the discipline of an organic society. Pound's identification with the power elite allowed him to think that he could advocate both individualism and hierarchical structure, and the notion of the strong individual directing the inchoate mass of his subordinates left him vulnerable to Mussolini's fascism in the years ahead. Nevertheless, Confucianism enunciates an ethics and a politics which shaped Chinese history for centuries and which are superior to any ethics or politics that Sigismundo knew or conceived, and it is important to note that Confucius is a much more important figure in *The Cantos* than Malatesta.

Moreover, from Canto 13 on, the Confucian society is presented as being open to, and dependent on, the Dionysian world of natural process. In our first glimpse of Kung, he is walking "by the dynastic temple" (markedly different from the monument to himself which Sigismundo erected amid the political chaos), but then *past* the temple "into the cedar grove, / and then out by the lower river" (p. 58), there to initiate his disciples into their natures in the temple of nature herself. And at the end, Confucius is left musing on the book of Odes, which expresses cyclic flux by attempting to fix its passing seasons in poems: "The blossoms of the apricot / blow from the east to the west. / And I have tried to keep them from falling" (p. 60). The poem is not a violation of natural process but a conscious acknowledgment of the passing moment in the art's futile resistance to its passing. Confucius is presented as the urbane man of rational consciousness who has kept alive within himself the Dionysian access to nature and the creative unconscious.

But such consonance can come, if at all, only after the voyaging ego admits to dissonance and faces the shadow. The Confucian evocation of order is followed by the Hell Cantos, 14 and 15. For if Elpenor represents the shadow of the protagonist's Dionysian aspect, the usurer becomes identified as the shadow of his Confucian aspect. So Cantos 14 and 15 enact another *nekuia*, and the first line of Canto 14 – "I came into a place devoid of any light" – identifies as the literary and moral antecedent of this shadow world not Homer's Elysium, where Odysseus encountered Elpenor, but Dante's Inferno, in one circle of which the usurers and sodomites are damned together. Pound told Wyndham Lewis that his Hell was "a portrait of contemporary England,"[58] and it is peopled with betrayers, exploiters, obstructors in the institutionalized professions administering the corrupt patriarchy. Such everyday locutions as "money-lust," "filthy lucre," and "dirty cash" testify to the deep-seated psychological association of money with sexual corruption, particularly with anal perversity, and a major section of Norman O. Brown's *Life Against Death: The Psychoanalytic Meaning of History*[59] deals extensively with the identification of money with feces. If, as Pound contends, "Dante's hell reeks with money," his own economic hell is a fetid, cloacal nightmare of oozing mud, pus, and excrement. The cantos parade in scatalogical caricature a menagerie of prelates, politicians, professors, journalists, and businessmen, many identified by names inked out on the page against libel suits, all in Pound's eyes "obstructors of distribution" (p. 63) in their particular professions.

"Obstructors of distribution": this last and summary phrase of Canto 14 provides the link between the Confucian world of social structure and the Dionysian world of natural process – that is to say, between Pound's economics and his religious philosophy. From nature, conceived as eternally abundant, renewing itself in the cyclic activity of a life force immanent in the material universe and anthropomorphosed into gods and goddesses, all good flows. And so all goods flow, even if the raw materials are subsequently modified by human labor and manufacture. Money has no intrinsic value; it is – or ought to be – a convenient and stable medium of exchange to facilitate and regulate the conversion of human labor into the wide range of goods and services needed for a humane and cultivated existence.

In other words, economics is – or, again, ought to be – the extension of the laws of natural process into the human and social sphere, with that sphere regulated by the laws of nature: Confucius and Dionysus in consonance. Only when money comes to assume an artificial value in itself, only when people conspire to attribute an intrinsic worth to those small discs of stamped silver and gold or to the paper slips said to represent silver and gold, does the possession of money become an end in itself; only then can control of the distribution of money become a pernicious power, restricting the amount and flow of money and using limited currency to make more money out of what is already possessed. Money then breeds, perversely, not out of nature's fertility but out of its own misvalued nullity; in Canto 46, "the bank makes it *ex nihil*" (p. 233).

Divorced from the ground of nature, money can be lent and borrowed, and the interest charged for the use of the original sum increases the borrower's indebtedness to the lender. Whoever has money makes more; whoever needs to borrow finds himself the poorer – unless he can, in turn, manipulate his own finances so as to make even more than he borrowed. And so it goes, binding more and more people more and more inextricably into an economic system opposed to "natural increase." Money should be linked with the production of goods by human labor, and usury (in Pound's definition appended to Canto 45, the Usury Canto) is "a charge for the use of purchasing power, levied without regard to production; often without regard to the possibilities of production" (p. 230). "By great wisdom," therefore, "sodomy and usury are seen coupled together...the great sin *contra naturam*,...the prime sin against natural increase." The medieval Church condemned usury; usurers and sodomites occupied the same circle in the *Inferno*, and in *The Merchant of Venice* Shylock "wants no mere shinbone or elbow, but wants to end Antonio's natural increase."[60]

Pound denounced the greed and materialism of bourgeois capitalism as subversive of Jeffersonian agrarianism and thought he had found in Major Douglas' Social Credit and in Mussolini's fascism adaptations of the Jeffersonian ideal to an urban, industrial society. Hence his 1935 polemic called, bizarrely, *Jefferson and / or Mussolini*. During the 1930s his tone would become shriller and his diatribes more virulently anti-Semitic as he increasingly identified the diabolical cabal of bankers and capitalists and munitions makers with the Jews. Pound's anti-Semitism indicates how distorted and deluded his attitudes became as war clouds closed over the world. And his obsessiveness stemmed in part from his Whitmanian insistence that art not be marginalized and that the prophetic poet be responsible to the crises of his time. If some were already calling him crazy, he knew that prophets had been called that before, usually by those most responsible for the crisis.

From that perspective, the course of the particular vices of journalists, politicians, and businessmen is "USURIA," obstructing the distribution of goods, obstructing the interchange of ideas and understanding and love, perverting language and communication and relationships. In the 1972 "Foreword" to his *Selected Prose* Pound would write: "re USURY: I was out of focus, taking a symptom for a cause. The cause is AVARICE." But Pound had always conceived usury less in terms of the specific economic practices than in terms of the moral and psychological state which generates corrupt practices: a sterile, self-circling, avaricious ego which reduces people to objects and nature to cash and then feeds on its debased possessions, breeding them monstrously in its swollen but barren womb. With this deeper root sense of usury, Pound wrote that the "power of hell" is "usura."[61]

Pound's allegorical excursion through this exclusively male hell finds its exit in Canto 16 through the confederated agency of the philosophers Plotinus, Iamblicus, and Porphyry and of the feminine archetype, symbolized in the Medusa head on Athene's shield. Iamblicus and Porphyry were, like Gemisthus Plethon later, Plotinean Neoplatonists. Iamblicus wrote a fourth-century treatise on light as the manifestation of the divine life energy as it animates material nature. In Canto 16 Plotinus overcomes the protagonist's *abuleia*, using the Medusa's visage on the shield to harden the excremental muck into stone providing passage for their steps; he guides the exhausted protagonist, now "blind with the sunlight," to the shores of the purgatorial lake, where he sinks into the "darkness unconscious" of sleep.

The dream in Canto 16 presents the lake as an image of incessant ferment between infernal descent and paradisal ascent:

> Palux Laerna,
> the lake of bodies, aqua morta,
> of limbs fluid, and mingled, like fish heaped in a bin,
> and here an arm upward, clutching a fragment of marble,
> And the embryos, in flux,
>   new inflow, submerging,
> Here an arm upward, trout, submerged by the eels;
>   and from the bank, the stiff herbage
> the dry nobbled path, saw many known, and unknown,
> for an instant;
>   submerging,
> The face gone, generation.
>
>   (p. 69)

Other versions of this description will recur in the next ten cantos or so. But the "aqua morta" where all living things sink into oblivion reveals itself as also the sea of "generation." "Submergence" is matched by the thrust "upward" into new creation, and "flux" clarifies itself as patterned process.

That revelation opens the way to a fuller vision of Plotinean light and air suffusing the sea of generation and the transfigured earth:

> Then light air, under saplings,
> the blue banded lake under aether,
>   an oasis, the stones, the calm field,
> the grass quiet,
>   and passing the tree of the bough
> The grey stone posts,
>   and the stair of gray stone,
> the passage clean-squared in granite:
>   descending,

and I through this, and into the earth,
    patet terra,
entered the quiet air
    the new sky, ·
the light as after a sun-set,
    and by their fountains, the heroes,
Sigismundo, and Malatesta Novello,
    and founders, gazing at the mounts of their cities.

                 (p. 69)

The correspondence of the upper and lower realms in serene stillness does not replace the cycle of generation but rather comprehends it as a temporal paradise, imaged as the gardened city. Stone imagery, reminiscent of the petrifaction of the infernal ooze in the previous canto, runs through the passage: the "fragment of marble" clutched by the arm emerging from the aqua morta, the stones near the lake in the "calm field," again the "grey stone posts" and "clean-squared" staircase to Persephone's underworld, the fountains, and finally the cities erected by the heroic founders. Taken together, the details establish the archetypal connection of stone with both personal and cultural identity. The fragment of marble testifies that cities fall and are subsequently built again, and the cities are a monument to their founders. The earthly city replaces the City of God as the paradisal image: "Augustine, gazing toward the invisible" becomes the "founders, gazing at the mounts of their cities."

In earlier cantos Cadmus and Sigismundo were city builders, and now in the dream "one man rose from his fountain / and went off into the plain," and his journey comprises one of the great visionary passages, Canto 17, the Venice Canto. With Cantos 13 and 17 the Confucian and Dionysian ideals frame the Hell Cantos. The life force of the first lines of Canto 17 is Dionysian: "So that the vines burst from my fingers / And the bees weighted with pollen / Move heavily in the vine shoots." The opening "So that" not only harkens back to the conclusion of Canto 1, which announced the first epiphany of Dionysus, it also announces the present epiphany as erupting from the confusion of war and revolution at the end of the previous canto. For, refusing the tragic disillusionment of American writers like Cooper and Faulkner and Frost, Pound joined Emerson and Whitman in insisting on the compatibility of the natural and social orders, or at least of the good society with nature. So, just as Canto 13 linked Confucian society to natural process, Canto 17 shows natural process building the city as cultural vortex. Dionysian energy hurls up, in a sublime ejaculation, the palazzi of Venice as earthly paradise. Cosmos and history intersect and, for the visionary moment at least, coexist.

The imagery of Canto 17 extends from previous cantos the interconnections between light, air, water, stone, and crystal. Natural process (wind and water) and Neoplatonic *nous* ("the light, now, not of the sun") take form in the walls and columns of stonework: "trees growing in the water, / Marble trunks out of stillness." Or, to put it another way, the stones of Venice are petrified light, like the light-filled crystal which symbolized to Coleridge the interpenetration of matter and spirit in sensible form. Donald Davie has directed our attention to Adrian Stokes' *Stones of Rimini*, in which the art historian, very much under Pound's influence, describes Venice and the Tempio Malatestiana in terms of the affinity of limestone (and marble) for water and light.[62] For Pound such architecture symbolized the "Mediterranean sanity" which synthesized matter and spirit. Canto 17 follows (is it several voyages or a montage of the same voyage?) the Odysseus-like sailor through hallucinated mythological landscapes and amatory dalliances to a vision of the city of water and stone trees:

> There, in the forest of marble,
> the stone trees – out of water –
> the arbours of stone –
> marble leaf, over leaf,
> silver, steel over steel,
> silver beaks rising and crossing,
> prow set against prow,
> stone, ply over ply,
> the gilt beams flare of an evening
>   (p. 78)

The "stone trees" recall Ileuthyeria, the sea Dafne turned to coral in Canto 2, and the phrase "ply over ply" refers back to the Diana episodes in Canto 4, written with the same rhythmically hypnotic repetitions.

In Venice the dream entered history and underwent the hard test of realization. "Thither, at one time, time after time," others have come under the same compulsion as our voyaging protagonist: "Borso, Carmagnola, the men of craft, i vitrei [the glassblowers]." The phrase "the men of craft" yokes Venetian artisans to the schemers who have made its history a record of money lust and power struggles. And so the dream, splintered on the barb of time, must be pursued again and again. Cavalcanti may exemplify "Mediterranean sanity," but Pound knew that Machiavelli and Malatesta were Italian too. Canto 17 moves from the erection of the city to the fall of three who came "thither": Borso, shot with a barbed arrow; Carmagnola, executed "between the two columns" in the Piazza; Sigismundo, shipwrecked. The "light, now, not of the sun" becomes, in the haiku-like conclusion, "Sunset like the grasshopper flying" (p. 79).

What makes the world a purgatory is that paradise and hell interpenetrate one another, metamorphosing into one another from one moment to the next, and the eccentricity of the structure of *The Cantos* – individually, in sections, and as a whole – renders the volatile dialectic of temporal experience, whether that be perceived as cosmic process or dialectical history. Canto 17 is, therefore, characteristic in *not* closing with the paradisal vision of Venice; instead, in collapsing the vision back into tragic historical reality, it returns the poem to the dialectical quest in the next canto. The frequent recurrence of the word "between" in the poem states its sense of division and the burden of resolution. The cantos of the 1920s and 1930s, up to Canto 51, shunt back and forth – sometimes from canto to canto, sometimes within a canto – between the basic poles of experience: the acculturatedly masculine world of politics, which needs feminine creativity, and the acculturatedly feminine world of nature, which needs masculine direction of will. The lapse into history from the vision of Venice in Canto 17 continues, in the ensuing cantos, to portray history as decline or, from another perspective, as the ascendancy of usurious "men of craft," resisted here and there by heroic craftsmen. It is a long way down from the medieval Florentines, who "rushed out and built the duomo, / Went as one man without leaders / And the perfect measure took form" (p. 130), to the Renaissance strongman Sigismundo constructing a temple to himself and Isotta, to the Bolshevik tovarish whose lament is "I neither build nor reap" (p. 132). In this age of revolutions, "Can you tell the down from the up?"

Pound once summed up the universal concerns as "Money and sex and tomorrow."[63] The fact that the economic passages in *The Cantos* are flatter and less engaging than those dealing with women and nature is a function partly of the subject matter but also of Pound's more problematic and so more engaging relation with the feminine. His unwavering interpretation of Confucianism sorted out economic history; he had the rule of thumb to identify the enlightened leaders and to castigate the usurious oppressors. He thought that he had identified the shadow and cast him out – too quickly and too smugly, it will turn out. The projection of evil is often the avoidance rather than the recognition of the shadow, and that fatal error in self-knowledge will in time undermine the psychological process and the historical construct of *The Cantos*. But throughout the 1930s, Pound's Confucian side found it easy to condemn with a categorical and self-satisfied sense of righteousness.

Some of his Confucian heroes were American: among the Founding Fathers, Jefferson and Adams (Cantos 31 and 32), followed by John Quincy Adams (Canto 34), then Jackson and Van Buren (Canto 37), who preserved the independence of the banks – but then no president, not even Lincoln, much less the hated Wilson and Roosevelt. Canto after canto documents the spreading corruption of usury. The great Usury Canto, 45, is flanked by accounts of a good bank, the Monte dei Paschi (Cantos 42 and 43) and of the benevolent Duke of Tuscany on one side, and on the other by an account of the Bank of England as the chief of the "hell banks." In a characteristic polarization of complex issues into simple dichotomies for simple answers, Pound declared: "Two kinds of banks have existed: the MONTE DEI PASCHI and the devils. Banks built for beneficence, for reconstruction; and banks created to prey on the people." In contrast to the Bank of England, which "'hath benefit of interest on all / the moneys which it, the bank, creates out of nothing'" (p. 233), the Monte dei Paschi's "CREDIT rests *in ultimate* on the ABUNDANCE OF NATURE, on the grazing grass that can nourish the living sheep [i.e., on the grazing lands offered by Siena to the Medici as security for underwriting the new bank]...to restart the life and productivity of Siena." With natural process as the source and basis of economic activity and with interest charged for the use of money only at a rate to cover overhead expenses, the "mount of pastures" proved its worth in history: it is "the *only* bank that has stood from 1600 till our time. . . .It outlasted Napoleon. You can open an account there tomorrow."[64]

The prophetic persuasiveness of Canto 45 is diminished when it is read out of the context of the surrounding ideogramic configuration; its effect depends on the accumulation of evidence to give resonance to Pound's sustained outrage that usury has corrupted both economic and natural process, both Confucian order and Dionysian creativity. The chant of bluntly reiterative assertions in mostly end-stopped lines climaxes in these images of sexuality perverted by money:

> Usura slayeth the child in the womb
> It stayeth the young man's courting
> It hath brought palsy to bed, lyeth
> They have brought whores for Eleusis
> Corpses are set to banquet
> At behest of usura
>
> (p. 230)

At the same time, threaded through the black-and-white assertions about the public world are turbid and exotic passages on the sexual theme, for Pound's vexed and ambivalent relation to his anima had to be clarified before his Dionysian aspect could attain enough assurance to be reconciled with his Confucian aspect. Back in Canto 16, after the Hell Cantos but before the vision of Venice in Canto 17, the lake of death and generation presented the confused purgatorial state between the inferno and paradise. The image recurs a number of times in subsequent cantos, as here in Canto 20:

> Jungle:
> Glaze green and red feathers, jungle,
> Basis of renewal, renewals;
> Rising over the soul, green virid, of the jungle,
> Lozenge of the pavement, clear shapes,
> Broken, disrupted, body eternal,
> Wilderness of renewals, confusion
> Basis of renewals, subsistence,
> Glazed green of the jungle;
> Zoe, Marozia, Zothar,
>   loud over the banners,
> Glazed grape, and the crimson,
> HO BIOS [LIFE]
>
> (pp. 91–92)

The passage is echoed in Canto 21: "Moon on the palm-leaf, / / confusion; / Confusion, source of renewals" (p. 100); and by Canto 29, biological process is explicitly personified in the generative female as a threat to male consciousness:

> ...the female
> Is an element, the female
> Is a chaos,
> An octopus
> A biological process
> . . . .
>
> She is submarine, she is an octopus, she is
> A biological process....

(pp. 144–145)

Canto 29 pits the sexes in crudest opposition: "'Nel ventro tuo, o nella mente mia [in your belly or in my mind], / Yes, Milady, precisely, if you wd. / have anything properly made'" (p. 144). The refrain "TAN AOIDAN" seems here to label all women as "Sirens." Under the pressure of mortal transience ("Time is the evil. Evil."), Canto 30 chooses Artemis over Pound's usual favorite, Aphrodite, because Artemis rejects soft virtues like pity ("Pity spareth so many an evil thing. Pity befouleth April"), whereas through pity Aphrodite spurns "young Mars" for the "doddering fool" Hephaestus (p. 147). Constructing something – a temple, a city, a poem, an identity – in time and against time requires Vorticist, Modernist, Mars-like ruthlessness that Aphrodite is taken here to lack.

But Pound's misogyny is balanced by a satirical portrait of the "menta mia" in the figure of the abstracted Juventus:

> By the lawn of the senior elder
> He continued his ambulation:
> "Matter is the lightest of all things
> "Chaff, rolled into balls, tossed, whirled in the aether,
> "Undoubtedly crushed by the weight,
> "Light also proceeds from the eye:
> "In the globe over my head
> "Twenty feet in diameter, thirty feet in diameter
> "Glassy, the glaring surface –
> "There are many reflections
> "So that one may watch them turning and moving
> "With heads down now, and now up.

(p. 145)

Punning on "light" here as "having little weight," the passage wittily calls into question the "light" philosophy of Iamblicus and Porphyry unless it is grounded in a realist's sense of material objects as physical emanations of Gemisthus' "concrete universal." Pound's point is that if in the earlier passage Milady is "seeking a guide, a mentor" for proper creation, then Juventus equally needs a biological chaos to quicken his mental sterility. This sexist formula provided Pound with a way to correlate Confucius and Dionysus: the philosopher has to commit himself to matter in order to comprehend natural "chaos" as patterned cycles and to extend that comprehension to the making of a civilized economy.

The jungle is the "source of renewals" and the matrix of forms, but it is the mind that grasps the forms with the precision prescribed by Confucianism and Modernism: "the water there in the cut / Between the two lower meadows" (p. 90), "in the sunlight, gate cut by the shadow; And then faceted air" (p. 92) and "aerial, cut in the aether" (p. 93) from Canto 20; "the boughs cut on the air, / The leaves cut on the air" (p. 99) from Canto 21; "The cut cool of the air, / Blossom cut on the wind, by Helios / Lord of the Light's edge" (p. 145) from Canto 29. The recurrent word "cut" suggests the facets of gems or, more commonly in these cantos, the sharp edges and planed surfaces of stone or marble in nature and architecture: "The road cut in under the rock / Square groove in the cliff's face, as chiostro [cloisters]" (p. 95) from Canto 20; "steps, cut in the basalt" (p. 100) from Canto 21; "the wave pattern cut in the stone / Spire-top alevel the well-curb / And the tower with cut stone" and "the tower, ivory, the clear sky / Ivory rigid in sunlight" (p. 145) from Canto 29. The wave incised into the stone at Excedeuil, like the marble trees of Venice, exemplifies the conjunction of mind and matter, nature and culture. The phrase "Lord of the Light" personifies the activity of *nous* in matter in a divinized male agent: "the fire of the gods, *tou ton theon pyros*, . . .comes down into a man and produces superior ecstacies"[65] in which incarnation ("the air burst into leaf," Canto 27) and sublimation ("the trees melted in air," Canto 29) are in ceaseless metamorphosis:

> Form, forms and renewal, gods held in the air,
> Forms seen, and then clearness,
> Bright void, without image, Napishtim,
> Casting the gods back into the *nous* [Mind]
>
> (p. 119)

Moreover, Pound traced the metaphysics of light not just to Greece, informing the nature mysteries of Dionysus and of Persephone at Eleusis, but also to China, standing behind the social ethics of Confucius. To his translation of *The Unwobbling Pivot* Pound added the following Neoplatonist statement:

> The *unmixed* functions [in time and space] without bourne.
> This unmixed is the tensile light, the
> Immaculata. There is no end
> to its action.[66]

Canto 40 will trace the action back to its source through ascending levels of experience: from the quotidian flux (here, economic disorder) through cyclic pattern (here, a variation on Odysseus' periplum in the translated account of the Carthaginian Hanno's circumnavigation of the Mediterranean) to intimations of phenomena returning "to the high air, to the stratosphere, to the imperial calm, to the empyrean, to the baily of the four towers / the NOUS, the ineffable crystal" (p. 201). The image of the celestial city reinforces the pun on "imperial," "empyrean" in associating the Confucian and economic episodes in *The Cantos* with the *nous*, and the image of the "ineffable crystal" connects the episodes of Dionysian ecstacy with the *nous*.

The artist, then, is a visionary, like Emerson's "transparent eyeball":

> "as the sculptor sees the form in the air
>   before he sets hand to mallet,
> "and as he sees the in, and the through,
>   the four-sides
> "not the one face to the painter

(p. 117)

The words are in quotation marks because they come to the artist from the anima-muse figure of Sulpicia, just as later, in Canto 23, immediately after the previously quoted lines about forms being renewed and passing back into the *nous*, the similar words of Aphrodite arouse an epiphany in the poet in which time and space, form and flux, mind and matter, nature and art co-exist:

> "as the sculptor sees the form in the air...
> "as glass seen under water,
> "King Otreus, my father...
> and saw the waves taking form as crystal,
> notes as facets of air,
> and the mind there, before them, moving,
> so that notes need not move.

(p. 119)

This moment repeats an Aphroditean moment at the end of Canto 23, in which wave and crystal are again interchangeable:

> "King Otreus, of Phrygia,
> "That king is my father."
>   and saw then, as of waves taking form,
> As the sea, hard, a glitter of crystal.
> And the waves rising but formed, holding their form.
> No light reaching through them.

(p. 109)

The alchemical and occult suggestions in all of these passages invoke the *conjunctio oppositorum* of "Mediterranean sanity," and these last lines conclude a canto which begins with the Neoplatonist Psellos' maxim "Every mind is omniform"; "'Et omniformis,' Psellos, 'omnis / Intellectus est.' God's fire" (p. 107).

The mystical dimension of the sexual theme receives its most extended expression in Canto 36, the Cavalcanti Canto, most of which is a line-by-line translation of the "Canzone d'Amore." Also called "the philosophical canzone," the "Donna mi priegha" must be read as a complement to the Confucian social philosophy of Canto 13, as a corrective to Juventus' dis-embodied Platonism, and as a sublimation of the Dionysian sexuality of Canto 2. Just as Canto 13 states axiomatic principles for all of the Confucian materials and references in subsequent cantos, so Canto 36 catches up all of the previous and subsequent references to Neoplatonism and gives "Mediter-ranean sanity" its fullest philosophical statement. The "Donna mi priegha" associates Love with light and celebrates Love light as the life energy, undivided and timeless, animating all temporal, corporeal phenomena. The reciprocity of light and Love indicates the linkage between Neoplatonist occultism and the courtly love tradition of the troubadours. There are detailed explications of this canto, and Pound has provided his own extended commentary on the canzone, along with a variant translation, in his essay on Cavalcanti, completed shortly before the writing of Canto 36 (cf. *Literary Essays*, pp. 149–200).

Pound's interest in the canzone lay in the fact that it gave lyric voice to an alternative philosophy to the medieval Christian scholasticism that informed Dante's epic. Pound was convinced that Cavalcanti had not "swallowed Aquinas," as Dante had, but instead, without challenging accepted orthodoxies, drew on the age-old yet (for Pound) "more 'modern'" tradition of occult mysticism which the scholastic hegemony had driven underground but which still found expression in Christian theology through Platonists like Saint Albertus Magnus, Scotus Erigena, Richard of Saint Victor, and Robert Grosseteste, Bishop of Lincoln. Albertus' "proof by experience" (or "natural demonstration," as Pound calls it in Canto 36) stands "against the tyranny of the syllogism, blinding and obscurantist," and attests to an intuitive experience of spirit subsuming all physical objects.[67] According to Pound, it was Aquinas who "lacked faith" by needing the confirmation of fallible reason.[68] After the Cavalcanti translation in Canto 36, Pound derides the condemnation of Erigena by Church authorities and scoffs at "Aquinas head down in a vacuum, / Aristotle which way in a vacuum?" In the Cavalcanti essay, Pound glosses the canzone as "a sort of metaphor on the generation of light" and cites the following summary of Grosseteste's philosophy:

> Light is a very subtle corporeal substance, moving again into the incorporeal. Its characteristic properties are the perpetual engendering of itself and the instantaneous diffusing of itself around a point. Given a point of light, it instantly engenders around this point as center an immense luminous sphere. The diffusion of light can be controverted only for two reasons: either it encounters an obscurity which stops it, or it ends by reaching the extreme limit of its rarefaction and the propagation of light ends thereby. This extremely fine substance is also the stuff of which all things are made; it is the first corporeal form, and what certain people designate as corporeality.

Pound admits that "Grosseteste on Light may or may not be scientific but at least his mind gives us a structure."[69] His great insight ascertains the spirituality of matter and the corporeality of spirit.

Or, in Cavalcanti's metaphor, Light is love and Eros is light. The mysteries of light and of darkness interpenetrate each other: light in shade, shade in light. That supreme paradox makes for the quality of the poem. Pound wrote that "if ever poem seemed to me a struggle for clear definition, that poem is the *Donna mi Prega*," and yet inescapably "THE POEM IS VERY OBSCURE." Accordingly, George Dekker concludes, "Pound has quite consciously written a 'translation' which, while developing and emphasizing certain ideas quite clearly, succeeds in communicating one primary quality of the original – its impenetrability."[70] The structure of the canzone is delineated in the last five lines of the first stanza, which isolate aspects of light-Love which the next five stanzas will ponder, summed up in the envoi. But the compounded convolutions and archaisms of the language, the imprecision of reference and connective and syntax, the inadequate punctuation, the invocation of words like "intellect possible," "intention," and "emanation" in abstruse senses which were obscure even to Cavalcanti's readers – all bespeak the arcane, even occult mystery. Its meaning is not open to analysis but can only be experienced, as Albertus Magnus said; and so it can be known only by initiates ("present knowers" and "understanders"). "With others [i.e., the rationalists] hast thou [the canzone] no will to make company."

Read psychologically, the canzone assumes archetypal significance. "A lady asks me / I speak in season / She seeks reason for an affect" – namely, Love. The rhyme of "season" and "reason" establishes the conventional feminine-masculine polarity, but the poem operates to transform and reconcile the polarity. The man supplies his lady with reason for the passion she has made him experience, and both thereby come to reason and passion. The unconscious anima–muse moves the "I" or ego to articulation. Aphrodite's overcoming of her false pity for Hephaesthus (a "doddering fool" in Canto 30, like the dry husks in Canto 7 and the old fool in Canto 13) now allows a fruitful union with "young Mars." The conception of Eros ("Formed like a diaphan from light on shade / Which shadow cometh of Mars and remaineth," p. 177) inverts the usual patriarchal associations of feminine and masculine by linking Aphrodite with light and Mars with darkness. In Eros the father's darkness is made diaphanous through the mother's light.

The canzone celebrates the fact that as a god Eros is timeless but is born again and again in a series of temporal loci. These partial and imperfect manifestations are refracted shades and colored emanations of "the white light that is allness" (p. 179). So in the sequence of stanzas Love draws time and space to the *nous*, works our weakness into strength, moves us toward stillness, enfolds falsifying divisions into unity. For the undivided light becomes divided only as it is refracted in the "shades" of sense experience; in itself it is divided only in the sense of being "divided from all falsity," "set out [distinguished] from colour." Therefore, Eros, the child of Aphrodite and Mars, is an intimation of the self: imperfect and weak in all its human efforts but strong in the underlying urge which in time draws these imperfections to a realization that the individual is one with the Spirit of the cosmos. Again, both personally and transcendentally, Eros is light: "Sacrum, sacrum, inluminatio coitu [Holy, holy, illumination in coition]" (p. 180).

In an essay written during the early 1930s, Pound cited the following passage as "fact not in the least well *known*":

> Paganism, which at the base of its cosmogonic philosophy set the sexual phenomena whereby Life perpetuates itself mysteriously throughout the universe, not only did not disdain the erotic factor in its religious institutions but celebrated and exalted it, precisely because it encountered in it

the marvelous vital principle infused by invisible Divinity into manifest nature.[71]

Such a religious sensibility found its ritual observance in the seasonal mysteries and fertility cults of paganism: "Paganism included a certain attitude toward, a certain understanding of, coitus, which is the mysterium. The other rites are the festivals of fecundity of the grain and the sun festivals, without revival of which religion can not return to the hearts of the people."[72]

Canto 36 is typically asymmetrical and eccentric in not residing in sexual mysticism but instead returning it to the contradictions and conflicts of history. The reader may wonder what Cavalcanti's hermetic canzone has to do with the jumbled conclusion about the ecclesiastical persecution of the Manicheans and the travails of Sordello. The question is worth pursuing because it lays bare the psychology underlying the poem: throughout the ongoing contention between Dionysus and Confucius, a radical dualism driving his perception of issues and answers in both the Dionysian and the Confucian realms. In the present instance, what lies behind the confusion at the end of Canto 36 is Pound's conviction that the "Mediterranean sanity" of "inluminatio coitu" links Eleusinian mystery cults and gnostic sects like Manicheism and Albigensianism in holistic opposition to the "Hebrew disease" of Christian spirituality perceived (on the basis of his early experience of Victorian bourgeois Protestantism) as pitched toward a bodiless "life after death." Hence, in Pound's version of things, the Church's condemnation of Manicheism and persecution of the Albigensians.

In point of historical fact, the various gnostic sects shared an inflexible light – dark dualism that condemned material existence as the corrupt creation of the devil and looked teleologically to the destruction of currupt matter for the deliverance of the spirit from its bondage. It is true that gnostic Neoplatonism had considerable influence on early Christianity; but it stood in contradiction of the incarnational spirit of the Gospels, and in the end the Church rejected Manicheism and Albigensianism as heresies precisely for denying the Incarnation. Pound misread and distorted the record to suit his predilections, and he made a similar mistake in dismissing Buddhism and Taoism as instances of the "Hindoo disease," while ignoring the Buddhist impact on Chinese culture and the Taoist influence on Confucianism. Pound's errors are symptomatic of a habit of mind which stubbornly reduced complicated matters to good and evil polarities; as pedagogue and moralist he championed the one and excoriated the other, but his schematism dictated a projection of the shadow that would skew his perceptions, sometimes with disastrous results, both in the Dionysian realm of personal ecstacy and in the Confucian realm of public order.

In any case, Canto 36 linked Cavalcanti and the Manicheans in the effort, however historically confused, to affirm Platonist realism and rescue Platonism from idealistic disembodiment. It was an old problem for American poets. Whitman, long before Pound, had faced the dilemma of American idealism and had sought to resolve it by polarizing the viewpoint of Leaves of Grass against Emerson's Transcendentalism: "L. of G.'s word is *the body, including all*, including the intellect and soul; E.'s word is mind (or intellect or soul)."[73] But that distinction did not settle the matter for Whitman, and his later work vacillated even more than the earlier work between pantheism and idealism. Pound set about balancing the idealism inherent in Canto 36 with the graphic sexuality of Canto 39, as philosophic statement gives way to mythic enactment. The two cantos present the paradox of Pound's Platonist *inluminatio coitu* in complementary images of light and shadow: in Canto 36, the light-irradiating bodies; in Canto 39, bodies kindling themselves into light. Together they present complementary images of light and shadow.

Canto 39 brings the reader back with Odysseus and his companions to Circe's island, in Book X of the Odyssey, before the *nekuia* (Book XI) of Canto 1. Circe appears as the feminine in both her destructive and creative capacities; as anima she merely reflects the character of the individual. Her affinity with unconscious nature and instinctual drives challenges the mind and will of Odysseus and his men. The Lady of the Beasts[74] is destructive to those who surrender abjectly to instinct and thus turn themselves into animals, but to those who submit instinct to controlling will, she yields access to her secret powers – mind and will. As in Canto 1, Elpenor and his fellows represent Odysseus' shadow, but here the contrast is fully developed and marks an important point in the moral and psychological development of Odysseus as the poet's persona.

The first half of the canto renders in the heavy, thick sounds, strong stresses, and hypnotic alliteration (introduced by the "Thgk, thkk" of Circe's loom) the animality of the men metamorphosed into beasts by food and drugs and sex. Elpenor is not mentioned by name, but we recognize from Canto 1 his shadow relationship with Odysseus in these words: "When I lay in the ingle of Circe / I heard a song of that kind." Homer's description of the Sirens' song in Canto 20 – "Ligur' aoide" or "sharp song" – returns now as "the sharp sound of a song / under olives" and "Song sharp at the edge." For Elpenor, Circe's song was as deadly as the Sirens'.

But unlike his shadow companions, Odysseus "did not go to the pig-sty," as he tells us several times – despite Circe's importuning. No Pentheus, he submits himself to the feminine archetype, enters Circe's chamber, and, with the power of the herb which his divine patron Hermes gave him, maintains mind and will against the undertow of passion and instinctual drive. Erich Neumann wrote of the ambivalent nature of the anima for the male psyche: "The ambivalent female mana figure may guide the male or beguile him. Side by side with sublimation stands abasement, as, for example, where man is transformed into an animal, where the human is lost to a superior bestial power." Nevertheless,

> Even when the anima is seemingly negative and "intends," for example, to poison the male consciousness, to endanger it by intoxication, and so on – even then a positive reversal is possible, for the anima figure is always subject to defeat. When Circe, the enchantress who turns men into beasts, meets the

superior figure of Odysseus, she does not kill herself like the Sphinx, whose riddle Oedipus has solved, but invites him to share her bed.[75]

For, paradoxically, his defeat of her autonomy allows him to put himself in her power. Because Odysseus does not capitulate to the unconscious, he is able to integrate the anima as a mediatrix of the unconscious; he can respond to her urgings and promptings precisely because she functions as the creative force of his self-clarifying identity. The Circe who was for Elpenor "Venter venustus, cunni cultrix" and to whom the crew proclaimed "Whether goddess or woman...let us raise our voices without delay" is transfigured into an unquestionably beneficent goddess to whom Pound applies the line from the Paradiso in which the angels sing to the Virgin Mary as Queen of Heaven so joyously "that the delight never leaves me." In fragments of English and Latin and in five lines of the original Greek, Pound presents the turning point in Odysseus' fortunes. Circe turns him from what he had lost toward what he would yet find ("Always with your mind on the past.... Been to hell in a boat yet?") as she directs him to Persephone's underworld to seek out Tiresias. Tiresias as an image of the self is here related to Glaucus, who plunged into the sea under the influence of a magic herb and was metamorphosed into a sea god with the gift of prophecy.

The "submarine" realm of the feminine (here Hathor as well as Persephone) is transformed into the womb in which the hierogamy transpires and from which the self will in time be born. The coupling of Circe and Odysseus, rhapsodically hymned in snatches of pastoral Latin and Greek and Chaucerian English, foreshadows the reunion with Penelope (who, like Circe, worked the loom), for in this canto Circe embraces not only the mysteries of Persephone, as celebrated at Eleusis, but also those of Aphrodite, whose statue stood looking toward the sea from her shrine at Terracina. Erich Neumann refers to the "Aphroditelike Circe of the Odyssey,"[76] and in Canto 39 the "Venus" hidden in "venter venustus [beautiful belly]" reveals herself to Hermes' surrogate as the conjunction proceeds to Dionysian rhythms:

> To the beat of the measure
> From star up to half-dark
> From half-dark to half-dark
> > Unceasing the measure
> > (p. 195)

"Half-dark" is "half-light," as at the end of Canto 2. In the union of dark and light—"'Fac deum!' 'Est factus!' ['Make the god!' 'He is made.']"—"Fac" and "factus" pick up and sublimate the crude Anglo-Saxon "fucking" and "fucked" from the Elpenor half of the canto to proclaim the conception of a god. In fact, "est factus" echoes the verse in the Creed which affirms the Incarnation: "Et Verbum caro factum est [And the Word was made flesh]." The conflicted sexuality of Canto 29 ("'Nel ventre tuo, o nella mente mia'"), where nothing is "properly made," becomes in Canto 39 "his rod hath made god in my belly" (p. 196).

The hierogamy is both personal and cosmic: it symbolizes what Whitman in

"Song of Myself" called the "knit of identity," and at the same time it symbolizes the coherence of the whole pattern in which the individual is a participant. The conception of the god, therefore, marks both the renewal of the seasonal cycle ("Ver novum! [new spring]") and the birth of the androgynous, embryonic self (suggestive of Hermaphroditus, the offspring of Aphrodite and Hermes). The concluding epithalamion hails the orgiastic mystery in which darkness rouses the lightning into inseminating the darkness. Where in Canto 36 Aphrodite is light and Mars is shadow, here Circe is darkness to Odysseus' flame. "Beaten from flesh into light / Hath swallowed the fire-ball / . . . I have eaten the flame" (p. 196). For in this syzygy each becomes, both become, "half-dark" and "half-light."

From the beginning of his career, even before he had begun *The Cantos*, Pound had acknowledged the psychological and religious nature of the sexual drive. In a 1912 piece called "Psychology and Troubadours," later interpolated into *The Spirit of Romance*, Pound speculated about two paths to androgynous wholeness: "the one ascetic, the other for want of a better term 'chivalric.'" The ascetic, monk or otherwise, develops both sexual poles within himself, so that in his contemplative life he is masculine and feminine, yin and yang, "both 'sun' and 'moon.'" In the more usual life pattern, the *conjunctio oppositorum* occurs "between the predominant natural poles of two human mechanisms." In either case, the process ends in a religious participation in the life of the cosmos, since each microcosm "'corresponds'" to the macrocosm. Consequently, sex has a function beyond reproduction ("HO BIOS"). The sexual act takes on "mediumistic properties" which are "interpretive of the divine order" of "the cosmos by feeling." Just as mystics and ascetics describe their enlightened moments in sexual terms, so at certain times and moments in erotic experience "a man feels his immortality upon him." Such is the secret celebrated in the Dionysian and other pagan mysteries and in the cult of chivalric love. In fact, Pound contends, all "forms of ecstatic religion" (and here he links Christianity with pagan cults, as distinguished from the "Hebrew disease" of Judaism) are concerned less with dogma or ethics than with the epiphany and ecstasy which awaken "a sort of confidence in the life-force."[77] This is a different conception of Christianity, to say the least, from that to which Eliot committed himself, but it is characteristic that Pound's construction of Christianity is Dionysian.

Daniel Pearlman has referred to Cantos 47 and 49 as twin cantos,[78] and they can best be read in relation to the previously twinned Cantos 36 and 39. Canto 47 takes off immediately from Canto 39; the first line translates one of the Greek lines spoken by Circe in Canto 39. Pearlman divides the canto into three sections. The first has Circe addressing Odysseus; the second, Tiresias addressing Odysseus; the third, Odysseus himself speaking. The configuration is of great archetypal significance. Guided by the anima and the self, Odysseus attains new self-articulation. Circe's reference to the psychological wholeness of Tiresias in the first line posits from the start the affinity between the anima and the self as psychopomps: "Who even dead, yet hath his mind entire"

(p. 236). Thus the canto reiterates the generative point of *The Cantos*: Circe's directive "to the bower of Ceres' daughter Proserpine" and the *nekuia* to the underworld where Tiresias awaits Odysseus "with his mind entire." As in Canto 39, Circe stands between Persephone and Aphrodite in a trinity of goddesses. Odysseus' descent is overlaid with a folk ritual commemorating the death and rebirth of Adonis. In one version of the myth, Aphrodite and Persephone quarrel over the beautiful young mortal, and Zeus has to decree that Adonis will spend half the year in the underworld with Persephone and the other half above ground with Aphrodite. In the rite described lyrically in Canto 47 the peasants, addressing Adonis as Tamuz, reenact his death by floating lighted lamps out to sea and streaking the waves with red, until the "sea's claw" drags the lamps down, so that his blood can seed the new year. His fate symbolizes the fact that man is son-lover of the Great Mother, dark in the aspect of Persephone, glorious in the aspect of Aphrodite. The mothers may weep for the victim, as the refrain tells us, but they know that the sacrifice is necessary: from the archetypally feminine perspective, man lives and dies within the cycle that causes his rebirth; Tamuz the shepherd becomes immortalized as Adonis in the round of the Great Mother.

So the second section begins with Tiresias drawing a distinction between feminine "intention" and masculine "intention." Hers is nature's round, governed by biological instinct, and all unconscious creatures move helplessly to her rhythm, like the bull who "runs blind on the sword, *naturans*." However, says Tiresias, Odysseus has another intention indicative of his complementary calling. Consciousness enlightens blind instinct and allows for a range of discrimination and choice which transforms the possibilities of biological process: "The stars are not in her counting, / To her they are but wandering holes" (p. 237). And yet ego consciousness foresees in the cycles, as the blind bull cannot, its own extinction and pronounces its own end: "Thus was it in time." So the light of consciousness casts its own darkness, as Tiresias' lament insists:

> And the small stars now fall from the olive branch,
> Forked shadow falls dark on the terrace
> More black than the floating martin
>   that has no care for your presence,
> His wing-print is black on the roof tiles
> And the print is gone with his cry.
> So light is thy weight on Tellus
> Thy notch no deeper indented
> Thy weight less than the shadow
>
> (pp. 237–238)

Nevertheless, Tiresias, now a shade himself more fully conscious than "beefy men," instructs Odysseus that he must yield to the feminine round: "Begin thy plowing." The essential paradox is that acceptance of mortality empowers generation; agriculture is no bucolic metaphor but the economics of a basic truth: the man who plants his field digs his grave, and vice versa. The

preceding lines about the ephemerality of individual existence lead immediately to paradoxical lines about power over nature: "Yet hast thou gnawed
through the mountain, / Scylla's white teeth less sharp." The pun on
"gnawed" and "teeth" with "indented" in the preceding passage tells us that
Odysseus can notch Tellus deeply enough. Tiresias' parting words instruct
him that his potency depends on his death in earth: "Hast thou a deeper
planting, doth thy death year / Bring swifter shoot? / Hast thou entered more
deeply the mountain?" (p. 238).

And in fact Odysseus' descent in the third section is triumphant and
provides one of the great visionary moments of *The Cantos*.

> The light has entered the cave. Io! Io!
> The light has gone down into the cave,
> Splendour on splendour.
> By prong have I entered these hills:
> That the grass grow from my body,
> That I hear the roots speaking together....
>   (p. 238)

"By this gate art thou measured," repeated in each of the previous sections,
becomes here a conjunction of opposites: "By this door have I entered the
hill." The self has led the ego to submit to the unconscious and illumine its
darkness with consciousness. Odysseus the "many-minded" takes on Circe's
powers as the Lady of the Beasts in an assumption of the androgynous
selfhood which Tiresias foreshadowed: now he "hath the gift of healing, hath
the power over wild beasts" (p. 239). Fallen like Adonis and sprung up again
as wheat shoots, Odysseus names himself son of the Great Mother and father
of himself, like Whitman at the end of "Song of Myself": "I bequeath myself
to the dirt to grow from the grass I love, / If you want me again look for me
under your boot-soles."

The repetition of the phrase "And hath power over wild beasts" as the last
line of Canto 49 makes explicit the connection with Canto 47. But where the
Dionysian energy of Canto 47 presents agriculture as psychological process,
the Confucian calm of Canto 49 presents personal and imperial fulfillment in
terms of natural process. Daniel Pearlman has described the manuscript source
for the "Seven Lakes Canto": a small book of Chinese and Japanese poems
with paintings, given to Pound in the mid-1930s. After the intensive activity
of the Greek Cantos, 39 and 47, the subdued tone, the gentle rhythms, the
precise images economically rendered, as in the clean lines of a Chinese
painting, attain the effect of a preternatural and supernal calm:

> Broad water; geese line out with the autumn
> Rooks clatter over the fishermen's lanthorns,
> A light moves on the north sky line;
> Where the young boys prod stones for shrimp.
>   (pp. 244–245)

The voyage has, for the moment at least, risen to the fourth dimension: the "dimension of stillness." It is as if the seasons coexist, as if the sun and moon shine together, as in the ideogram for the "total light process." The ideogram comes to stand for the "intelligence,"[79] and here the intelligence apprehends natural process (the *tao*) encompassed by the timeless *nous*, recapitulated in the opening lines of Canto 51:

> Shines
> in the mind of heaven God
> who made it
> more than the sun
> in our eye.
>
> (p. 250)

Here Pound reaches what Eliot called the "still point of the turning world," not in the philosophic abstractions of "Burnt Norton" but in a pure visual lyricism.

The first fifty cantos, then, constitute a titanic effort to reconcile, on both the personal and societal levels, Dionysus and Confucius. As Canto 52 sums it up, the poem hangs suspended "Between KUNG and ELEUSIS" (p. 258). At about this time, Pound described "my Cantos" in *Guide to Kulchur* as the "record of a personal struggle," a "record of struggle."[80] With Cantos 36, 39, 47, and 49, the centering of the Dionysian in the feminine archetype had come to rest in the round of nature. The two explicitly sexual cantos (39 and 47) are flanked by a Mediterranean (36) and an Oriental (49) evocation of the light process: inluminatio coitu. As for Confucius, these twinned cantos have been interspersed with economic cantos; then Canto 50 returns to the isolated efforts of Adams and Ferdinand of Tuscany to establish civic order, and Canto 51 repeats the Usury Canto after the Neoplatonist-Confucian opening, previously quoted, about the sun shining in the mind of God.

Ironically, however, Pound seemed to have attained something of "the dimension of stillness" within his psyche just as war was preparing to break over the world. *The Fifth Decad of Cantos* was published in 1937, and with Kung and Eleusis apparently in better balance within himself, Pound felt driven to stave off war by providing evidence that the ideals of Confucius and of the American Revolution could be extended to inform a whole society for a significant period of time. During the next three years, amid fevered economic and political activity, Pound hastily got together and published in 1940 as *Cantos LI–LXXI* ten new cantos on Chinese history and ten on John Adams. These cantos might take their place beside *Jefferson and/or Mussolini* under the title *Confucius and/or Adams*.

In Canto 52 the Confucian Book of Rites brings together Kung and Eleusis, social man and natural cycle, in the prescribed ceremonial rituals governed by the signs of the zodiac. Cantos 53 through 61, outlined by Pound in a table of contents, propel us rapidly from legendary prehistory to the mid–eighteenth century. There is one main source for Pound's redaction of Chinese history, the twelve-volume *Histoire Générale de la Chine* by the Jesuit missionary Joseph-Anne Marie Moyriac de Mailla, published between 1777 and 1785.

And there is a simple, single theme pursued relentlessly and rehearsed in the prose with the ideologue's clarity: "Whenever and wherever order has been set up in China; whenever there has been a notable reform or constructive national action, you find a group of Confucians 'behind it,' or at the centre"; "The dynasties of Han, Tang, Sung, Ming rose on the Confucian idea; it is inscribed in the lives of the great emperors.... When the idea was not held to, decadence supervened."[81] Or, as Pound puts it in Canto 54, "KUNG sank in abuleia. TANG rising," the moral of which, at once homespun and Transcendental, is "Kung is to China as water is to fishes" (p. 285). The forces opposing the Confucian emperors and ministers are by now familiar: militarists, merchants, taxmen, eunuchs, Buddhists, Taoists, Christian missionaries (religion linked again with otherworldliness, on the one hand, and with materialism, on the other: the split in Mediterranean and Confucian sanity). Pound moved through the volumes of de Mailla's history briskly to illustrate his thesis in a journalistic and often slangy style, only here and there departing from his source to add ideogramic touches: a couple of lines in Canto 55 from Grosseteste's *De Luce*, some Latin and a phrase from "Donna mi priegha" in Canto 59, a reference to the American Revolution and John Adams in the last Chinese History Canto, 61. The long historical survey ends with the pointed moral: three emperors, Kang Hi, Yong Tching, and Kien Long, though Manchu and "foreign," adopted the traditional Confucian values to become good emperors.

De Mailla's account concludes at about the time of Adams' birth, and the example of the last three emperors establishes the exportability of Confucianism and anticipates "the rise of the Adamses" (Canto 61, p. 339). Pound explained why Adams came to interest him more than Jefferson: "John Adams believed in heredity. Jefferson left no sons. Adams left the only line of descendants who have steadily and without a break felt their responsibility and persistently participated in American government throughout its 160 years."[82] In other words, Adams instituted the closest thing to an American dynasty. And again, as with de Mailla, Pound proceeds through the volumes of Adams' *Works*, filling ten long cantos with often confusing and disjointed detail to illustrate the translation of Confucian principles to modern republican America, with only occasional interpolations from other sources.

However understandable, the neglect of the Chinese History Cantos and the Adams Cantos distorts our sense of the proportions of *The Cantos* as a whole. Pound devotes more pages of *The Cantos* to John Adams than to anyone else – more than to Malatesta and far more than to Mussolini. Mary de Rachewiltz has correctly pointed out that the man in the middle of *The Cantos* as its unwobbling pivot is John Adams, standing by the Constitution, the American version of Pound's Confucian self.[83] At the end of the Adams Cantos the verses from Cleanthes' "Hymn to Zeus" once again locate in "the mind of God" (Zeus) the correspondence of natural and civic law, of Dionysus and Confucius. Pound's translation from the Greek runs: "Glorious, deathless of many names, Zeus aye ruling all things, founder of the inborn qualities of nature, by law piloting all things." The poem had reached – or seemed to have reached – an integration of process and law, nature and economy, cosmos and history.

By 1940, therefore, Pound in his mid-fifties expressed satisfaction in seeing his monumental "record of struggle" almost finished. In a letter he claimed that the poem was "complete as it stands, tho' there's a final volume to be done." After all, in 1906 he had anticipated a "40-year epic." Now that he had investigated the relation of nature to economics, the final matters to be integrated turned on religious belief. To George Santayana he wrote that with the issue of "money in history" now sorted out, he would now have to define his "philosophy or my 'paradise.'" At the same time, he admitted to having nagging questions about the poem: "As to the *form* of *The Cantos*: All I can say or pray is: *wait* till it's there. I mean wait till I get 'em written and then if it don't show, I will start exegesis."[84]

The old protest about his not having a preconceived Aquinas map like Dante's had a hollower ring this late in the poem. For all his inveighing against theology, Pound had remarked to Felix Schelling in the early 1920s that contemporary confusion stemmed from the lack of "any theology to fall back on." The 1930s and early 1940s deepened his conviction that the answers to the immediate problems rested on the answers to ultimate questions. Consequently, he airily informed his American editor, James Laughlin: "From 72 on we will enter the empyrean, philosophy, Geo. Santayana etc." Santayana was an important presence for Pound during these years, not merely as another American expatriate in Mussolini's Italy but as a philosopher who sought to define a Platonic materialism mediated by the aesthetic consciousness. Pound recommended his Cavalcanti essay to Santayana for its intimations of his philosophical tendencies and referred Santayana as well to several Chinese texts. Pound cautioned Santayana that his "ideogramic method" arrived at definitions not through systematic or "abstract thought" but through associational leaps connecting discrete particulars. It was not reassuring that Santayana's reply fretted that such an irrational procedure might end in the "utter miscellaneousness" of "a mental grab-bag." On another occasion he admonished Pound to derive his philosophy from his own experience, not Santayana's, because each person's "questions are apt to imply a philosophy and don't admit of answers in terms of any other."[85]

Santayana was voicing Pound's own worst fear: that his insistence on "method" (Pound invoked the word constantly) only disclosed his need for a method. The boasts that the Chinese History and Adams Cantos had established the historical ground for his paradisal conclusion have an eerie air of self-deception about them. By the time of their publication, World War II had begun. In 1939 Pound had sailed back to the United States for the first time in almost three decades, convinced that the rights and wrongs were so clear that with his exposition of basic economics he could singlehandedly persuade the politicians in Washington, even Roosevelt, of the lunacy of being drawn into a war of capitalist usurers against Mussolini's new economic order. The prophet seemed a crank, if not a dupe, if not a crackpot. Still, Pound was desperately planning another manic trip in 1940 before circumstances intervened. The schematization of history in Cantos 52–71 is just one indication of how much the pressures of the realpolitik had forced Pound to retreat into a fantasy of a social order which rejected the destroyers of culture and enforced the principles of the enlightened few on the masses. In his quirky way, Pound courageously persisted in being responsible for the world he lived in, but his old habit of opposing his circle of economic, philosophic, and artistic heroes to the benighted enemies outside made him blind to the shadow in which he stood. The almost reflex reaction that evil was external and other objectified the threatening shadow as something or someone – a nameable, blamable individual or, better yet, a class or group or institution – outside himself and inimical to his primary felt values. This act of displacement located the shadow as the enemy to be opposed pitilessly (remember Artemis' complaint in Canto 30). Such an objectification of evil prevents one from being able to say, as Prospero said to Caliban, "This thing of darkness I acknowledge mine." Instead, projection exonerates the self and brands the other, exalts the self and degrades the other into abjection: women, capitalists, Jews. That psychological disposition in Pound made for an arrogant self-righteousness, even with friends, and for the nascent paranoia that the psychiatrists at Saint Elizabeth's Hospital found full-blown in 1945.

It was all too clear to him. There were the embattled forces of good and the relentless forces of evil. Earlier in the poem, Pound had played down Malatesta's cruelty and opportunism and imputed those vices to others, because they were Sigismundo's adversaries; such a distortion led Pound to accept Malatesta's depiction of Pope Pius II as a vindictive and venal monster, with no hint that he was one of the great humanists of Renaissance Italy. Similarly, Pound attributed to the opponents of Albigensians the very gnosticism which was the Albigensian heresy, and derided the Taoists as enemies of the Confucians, blind to the influence of Taoism on Confucian thought. As the 1930s careened from political crisis to crisis, his desperation led Pound to identify fascism with Jeffersonian democracy, and so convinced him that his opposition to Roosevelt's America and his support for Mussolini's Italy stemmed from his American adherence to the Constitution and the principles of the Founding Fathers. Isolated in Rapallo, outraged at the American declaration of war against the Axis powers, Pound took to Rome Radio to vent his fury and disgust.

Pound was sincere in thinking that he was a patriot rather than a traitor in making these broadcasts, but Eliot's early objection to the Hell Cantos pinpoints his tragic flaw: his displacement of the shadow allows him to create "a Hell for the *other people*, the people we read about in newspapers, not for oneself and one's friends."[86] The "good guys" – whether Dionysus or Confucius, Mani or Mussolini – needed defending from the "bad guys," and *The Pisan Cantos* begins with the double crucifixion of Mani and Mussolini. This wrongheaded projection of the shadow rendered Pound, inevitably, vulnerable and defenseless before the violence he had rendered himself incapable of comprehending.

IV

By the end of the Adams segment, therefore, *The Cantos*, bent as it is on the *conjunctio oppositorum*, has instead reached the breaking point, is actually broken in two there. The missing cantos, 72 and 73 (written in Italian during the war but never published), dramatize the fracture. The Allied victory in Europe found Pound in the spring of 1945 caught in the tragic aftermath of war. It is all implied in the first long line of Canto 74: "The enormous tragedy of the dream in the peasant's bent shoulders" (p. 425). The collision of historical forces had shattered his imaginary world, and his life lay in ruins amid the battlefields and bombed cities. He had survived, only to be caged by the American military in a detention camp near Pisa; there for six months he awaited his fate. In the fall he was brought back to Washington, accused of treason for broadcasting against his country. Only a psychiatric declaration of his mental unfitness to stand trial saved him from that ignominy, but this turn of events ironically condemned him to the ignominy of thirteen years of confinement in an insane asylum without the opportunity to answer or refute the charge of treason.

There were many tragic ironies in Pound's situation. To begin with, Pound clearly felt that he had been exercising his constitutional rights as an American in the broadcasts ("Free speech without free radio speech is as zero," p. 426) and had insisted on a declaration to that effect at the beginning and end of each session on Rome Radio. In her memoir *Discretions*, Mary de Rachewiltz described her father's frustrated outrage during the war years, a fury so ferocious that he used the medium of language irresponsibly and thus betrayed the standard of precision to which he had devoted his artistic life. The broadcasts ranged from remarks on contemporary poetry and culture to readings from *The Cantos* and the work of other American poets to vicious attacks on bankers, militarists, and Jews, and on the American and British leaders for sacrificing thousands of lives to Usura. As for the American authorities, there can be no doubt about the special cruelty of their treatment of Pound. Kept in a small caged cell open to the extremes of rain and sun in the Pisan spring and summer (his cage specially reinforced with double wire to forestall any fascist attempt to rescue him), Pound was the only prisoner in this camp for the army's most dangerous criminals to be held in utter isolation: meals alone in his cage, no recreation outside of his cage, not even the guards permitted to speak to him, at night only blankets on the cement floor of the open cage under an electric light. After three weeks the sixty-year-old Pound broke down physically and psychologically. Thereafter, he was allowed a small tent for his isolation, and was eventually granted the use of the infirmary typewriter after hours to recopy some new cantos and a translation of Confucius that he had somehow produced in his infernal solitude.

For the almost incredible fact is that under stresses which put his mind and body to excruciating trial, Pound refused to capitulate. Amid the rubble of war, against the inhumanity of his American captors, his life in jeopardy, he directed his will to salvage his sanity and dignity – and his ideal of personal and civic order. With no books except the Confucius and the Chinese dictionary that had been in his pockets at his arrest, with nothing except his memory and his senses, he began to sift through the fragments and rebuild his mind, his poem, his dream. "Nor shall diamond die in the avalanche," he wrote in Canto 74, "be it torn from its setting" (p. 430) – not, that is, if it withstands the test as the hardest and most translucent of crystals. *The Pisan Cantos* (1948) is one of the great heroic poems in all literature. After years of masking as various archetypal adventurers from history and literature, Pound became himself the indisputable hero during the six months recorded in the Pisan sequence, and for that effort he required all the wiles of the many-minded Odysseus, all the volitional force of Malatesta, all the inner resources of Confucius.

The heroism is achieved through another *nekuia* – not an imagined one now but an actual dark night of soul. Just when he thought he had earned paradise, he found himself again in hell. This time, unlike the long venture initiated in Canto I, the descent forced an engagement with himself profounder than he had ever had to experience. The shadow of the gibbet allows no literary posing or psychological projection. He had to choose whether to acquiesce in disintegration or gather his scattered experience and test it all again on exacerbated nerve ends, convulsed emotions, senses concentrated on immediate details by the imminence of death. Thrown back on himself, he made the poem his lifeline. The rapid shifts of focus, the splintered phrases and clauses, the cross-current of rhythms render the effort of consciousness to master the welter of impressions that threaten to overwhelm it. These cantos must be read differently from the previous ones. The ideogramic elements are fragments, often only a single line, yet the bits and pieces of these eleven cantos comprise a sustained dramatic experience recorded even as it was transpiring. The poem becomes more collagelike from this point on; or at any rate, the fragments become smaller and briefer, the movement from point to point more rapid, the conceptualizing into spatial configurations more complex. And yet, for many readers, the *Pisans* are more immediate than the earlier cantos, not only because most of the materials rehearsed here are by now familiar and need less expatiation but also because the autobiographical constellation of the fragments in Pound's psychomachia is more the explicit subject of these cantos.

In the descent into the unconscious which *The Pisan Cantos* enacts, the fragments of autobiographical reminiscence, remembered reading, and observed details in the detention camp take on an almost hallucinogenic urgency and immediacy. Under circumstances that should have made for the "utter miscellaneousness" that Santayana feared in the ideogramic method, *The Pisan Cantos* is, on the contrary, a feat of self-integration, the psyche recomposing itself, humbly, stubbornly, even with ironic humor.

Canto 74, the longest of the *Pisans* and the epitome of the sequence, inaugurates the long-delayed and now enforced engagement of the shadow which Pound had consistently projected onto functionaries, usurers, bankers, Jews. Now he is surrounded and besieged by shadow figures of himself; the *Pisans* chronicle a catalogue of shadow identifications. On the first page of Canto 74, Lucifer, the angelic light bearer, falls to hell because of his demonic pride, and Odysseus, the light bearer to the dark cave in Canto 47, calls himself Ou Tis, No Man, in the cave of the Cyclops monster ("I am no man, my name is no man," p. 426). Later, in Canto 80, Ou Tis will be described as "akronos," "timeless," not because he has attained immortality but because he faces death: "now there are no more days." Three times Pound identifies himself as a "man on whom the sun has gone down," once placing the line with the Chinese ideogram for negation (p. 430). Odysseus as Ou Tis now sees himself as Elpenor, still unburied long after his spectral apparition in Canto 1. Elpenor's epithet refrain is repeated: "of no fortune and with a name to come"; there are references to Circe's sty, but now Odysseus wallows there with the rest. In Canto 39 he boasted, "I did not go to the pig-sty," but in Pisa he is forced to confess: "so lay men in Circe's swine-sty; ivi in harum *ego* ac vidi cadaveres animae [*I* went to the sty and saw the soul's cadavers]" (Canto 74, p. 436). From his cage Pound sees the nearby "Tower of Ugolino," who was imprisoned there for treason and starved to death, and placed by Dante in the infernal circle of traitors. A little later Pound sees himself as Guido de Montefeltro in hell, telling Dante that if he thought that he was speaking to someone who could return to earth, his flame would fall silent and shake no more.

Early in the canto Ou Tis becomes Wanjina, who in the Australian myth got into trouble, like Pound, for speaking too much and creating havoc with his words: "Ouan Jin spoke and thereby created the named / thereby making clutter / the bane of men moving / and so his mouth was removed" (p. 427). Pound sees Wanjina as Ouan Jin, "the man with an education" and for that reason an outcast, and connects him with Villon, the poet-criminal, whose "Epitaph" reads in part: "Under the six gallows absolve, may you absolve us all." Immediately Villon becomes Barabbas, the criminal freed so that Jesus might be executed. The second line of Canto 74 had introduced the theme of crucifixion: Manes, the Persian sage who founded Manicheism, flayed and crucified at Ecbatan; Mussolini, shot and hung from a lamppost in Milan with his mistress; both "twice crucified." In Canto 80, "this calvario 'we will not descend from,' sd / the *prete* [priest]"; and the canto goes on to tell a story in Italian about a boy nailed to the ground in the form of a cross. In Canto 74 Pound speaks Christ's dying words: "est consummatum." There is, of course, a defiant self-aggrandizement in the association of Christ's crucifixion with the fate of Manes, Mussolini, and himself. But just as real, in fact more insistent, is Pound's identification in his "crucifixion" with the criminal shadow Barabbas: "lay there Barabbas and two thieves beside him"; and later in the canto, "with Barabbas and two thieves beside me."

Like Villon's gallows, Pound's were not metaphors and allowed no appeal:

"Till was hung yesterday / for murder and rape with trimmings" (Canto 74, p. 430); "Bright dawn on the sht house / next day / with the shadow of the gibbets attendant" (Canto 77, p. 466). Till makes Pound see himself in the spider dangling above his head: "Arachne, che mi porta fortuna [who brings me fortune], go spin on that tent rope" (Canto 76, p. 461). And in Canto 77 the "gibbetiform posts supporting barbed wire" make Pound think again of Till and canonize him wryly with his nickname: "'St. Louis Till' as Green called him" (p. 473). These moments, along with the references to Ugolino's tower and to the "Rupe Tarpeia" (the Tarpeian Rock in Rome, from which traitors were hurled to their death), implicitly acknowledge the charge against him, and at the end of Canto 82 the prospect of his execution suddenly devastates him: "the loneliness of death came upon me / (at 3 P.M., for an instant)" (p. 527).

Isolated from the other prisoners, he nonetheless felt one of them; he picked up their names, along with vivid snatches of conversation, amused that so many bore the names of American presidents and heroes. When he calls them "comites miseriae [comrades of misery]," he not altogether mockingly invokes the fellowship of Anglo-Saxon warriors for their wretched and fallen state. He is "amid the slaves learning slavery" (Canto 74, p. 431); they are all "po'eri di'aoli [poor devils] sent to the slaughter" (Canto 76, p. 462). The slave references recur: in Canto 74, "black that die in captivity" (p. 432), "the wards like a slave ship," "of the slaver as seen between decks" (p. 436); in Canto 77, "in limbo no victories, there, are no victories – / that is limbo; between decks of the slaver / 10 years, 5 years" (p. 470). The large number of blacks in the detention camp as guards and prisoners only confirms his rueful identification with the shadow: "I like a certain number of shades in my landscape" (Canto 79, p. 484). Hermes is Odysseus' patron, but now as the "god of thieves" in sadly compromised circumstances: "your caduceus / is now used by the American Army / as witness this packing case" (Canto 77, p. 471).

Pound's identification with slaves and criminals is an act of humility and self-recognition unknown in his previous experience. He was hectoring and vitriolic to enemies, loyal and generous, though difficult, to friends, but no one called him humble. Now his enforced humility lets him laugh and cry at his abject situation. The man who in Canto 30 scorned pity's weak tears now finds himself weeping in the rain ditch because he "had been a hard man in some ways." With neither shame nor self-pity, the tears that begin in Canto 74 well up again and again: in Cantos 76 and 82 the refrain of the Greek for "weeping"; in Canto 76, "lisciate con lagrime / politis lachrymis [smoothed with tears / polished tears]"; in Canto 80, a paraphrase of Dumas *fils*' remark "I weep because I have tears," and "Les larmes qui j'ai creées m'inondent [the tears I have created drown me]"; in Canto 84, the Provençal line "Si tuit li dohl el plor [If all the griefs and tears]."

Canto 74 admits the need for confession (in the reference to the Catholic chaplain's manual for confession) and absolution (in Villon's prayer for absolution before the gallows), and in Canto 79 the prayer from the Catholic

Mass that Pound must have been able to witness from the cage begs mercy: "Kyrie eleison." Back to the wall, Pound summons the honesty to see in himself the common curse, the root of usury: an egotism that uses others for its own purposes. Not that usurers and warmongers were less reprehensible; he found texts in the Army-issue Bible, from both the Old and the New Testaments, condemning usurious practices. But, in however good a cause, his own heart, the source of Confucian ethics, had been toughened by an aggressive and ruthless self-centeredness that violated and exploited even those nearest to him and most vulnerable to his egotism. Among his chief victims were his daughter, Mary; her mother, Olga; and his wife, Dorothy. In fighting the shadow without recognizing it in himself, he had fallen prey to it.

It is his failure to love over which he weeps in deepening contrition: in Canto 76, "J'ai eu pitié des autres / probablement pas assez [I have had pity on others, probably not enough], and at moments that suited my own convenience"; in Canto 80, "Tard, très tard je t'ai connu, la Tristesse [Late, too late, I've known you, Sadness], I have been hard as youth sixty years." In his dark night of the soul, he tries to fend off madness with an ironic deflation of Saint John of the Cross:

> is it blacker? was it blacker? Nux animae [Night of the soul]?
> is there a blacker or was it merely San Juan with a belly ache writing ad
> posteros [to those after him]
> in short shall we look for a deeper or is this the bottom?
>
> (p. 438)

In extremis his will never succumbed to the *abuleia* which would have left him, like Alessandro di Medici in Cantos 5 and 7, helpless before fate. Adopting the unbending words of Bianca Capello, he resolves in Canto 74 that if he must fall, it won't be on his knees before his would-be superiors, for whom, he reports, the guards had a regard even "lower than that of the prisoners." Pound relishes the scatalogical GI slang he heard outside his tent expressing the underdog's humorous contempt for his oppressors. To the impending charge of defection to the fascist enemy, Pound holds up the American Constitution and the guard's words that actually the generals are "all of 'em fascists."

In his landscape of shades, Pound learns discernment: "whereas the sight of a good nigger is cheering, the bad 'uns wont look you straight" (p. 485). The racial slurs (which he must have heard as well from the blacks at the detention camp) betray a prejudice that continued to want to project the shadow as other. Nevertheless, his enforced identification with his fellow outcasts began to change the way in which Pound saw others as well as himself. In the last *Pisan*, he gives a final roll call of prisoners and calls them "benedicti [blessed]." In Canto 74, the black guard who, breaking a strict prohibition that could have brought him punishment, makes Pound a writing table out of a packing box appears unexpectedly as a dark angel, a "jacent benignity," an agent of "charity," whose act of civilized grace Pound remembers in Canto 81:

> What counts is the cultural level,
>> thank Benin for this table expacking box
>>> "doan yu tell no one I made it"
>>>> from a mask as fine as any in Frankfurt
>> "It'll get you off'n th' groun"
>>> Light as the branch of Kuanon
>>>> (pp. 518–519)

From this face, black as the African masks he saw in Frobenius' anthropological institute in Frankfurt, shines the mercy of the Chinese goddess.

For the recognition of the shadow is literally eye-opening: the dark night is, repeatedly and without warning, shot through with paradisal light. In a remarkable passage in the middle of Canto 74, Pound re-creates such a moment, drawing together allusions to Dionysus and Aphrodite, to Christ's dying words of salvation ("It is consummated," overheard perhaps at an open-air Mass in the camp, along with the dismissal prayer, "Ite, missa est [Go forth]"), and to the Chinese sacred mountain Taishan, the name he gave a nearby Italian peak that often lifted his spirits out of the prison world:

> black that die in captivity
>> night green of his pupil, as grape flesh and sea wave
> undying luminous and translucent
>
>> Est consummatum, Ite:
>
> surrounded by nerds and by cohorts looked on Mt. Taishan
>> (p. 432)

Tl e paradisal moments are generally associated with nature or women or both, because, as before, the anima is the tranformative agent in Pound's psyche and effects the metamorphosis. The "sauve eyes" of Aphrodite appear on the first page of Canto 74, as well as "sorella la luna [sister moon]." Soon "Mt. Taishan Pisa" recalls a scene of supernal stillness at Lago di Garda and a friend chanting "La donna, la donna, la donna!" Later in the canto "Mr. Bullington," either prisoner or guard, "lay on his back like an ape," invoking the beneficent anima by singing "o Lady be good." The remembered women of *The Cantos* comfort and strengthen Pound: Isotta, Cunizza, Tyro, Bianca Capello. But most prominent are the goddesses: Kuanon, Aphrodite, Artemis, Demeter, Persephone, Kore. Occasionally the feminine appears in her destructive aspect: "femina, femina, that wd / not be dragged into paradise by the hair"; glimpses of Circe as sorceress; a reference to the Sirens. But the Sirens here are immediately metamorphosed into the Graces, for in Pound's psychic life the anima had come to prevail as a beneficent agent, initiating him into the dark mysteries of earth as Persephone or Gea and into the mysteries of light and air as Aphrodite or Kuanon.

Moreover, the goddess reveals herself as triune: one in three, three in one. The feminine figures, evoked at first individually, begin to triangulate: in Canto 74 alone, the references to the three Charites (Graces), to "La donna, la donna, la donna," and to "three ladies" call attention to the repeated triadic configurations: Cythera (Aphrodite), Isotta, and Santa Maria dei Miracoli; Kuanon, Mother Earth, and Aphrodite; Persephone, Sirens/Charites, Aphrodite. These trinities are, for Pound, not metaphors or imaginative fictions but visionary visitors. At the beginning of Canto 76:

> Dirce et Ixotta e che fu chiamata Primavera
> [she who is called Spring]
> in the timeless air
>
> that they suddenly stand in my room here
> between me and the olive tree
> or nel clivo ed al triedro [in the slope and at the corner]?
>
> (p. 452)

And at the end of Canto 78:

> eyes of Doña Juana la loca,
> Cunizza's shade al triedro and that presage
> in the air
> which means that nothing will happen that will
> be visible to the sargeants
> Tre donne intorno alla mia mente [Three ladies inside my mind]
>
> (p. 483)

The two sustained climaxes of the *Pisans* substantiate further the trinity of the feminine archetype. The first epiphany comes at the conclusion of the magnificent lynx song ending Canto 79, which Dorothy Pound and H. D. each took as addressed to her. As the archetypal image of the anima-related man since Canto 2, Dionysus appears frequently through the *Pisan* sequence. In the first lines of Canto 74 he is the life force: the twice-born as opposed to the twice-crucified Mani and Mussolini. The lynxes suggest Circe as well as Dionysus, but the lynx song addresses Aphrodite as Cythera and in one passage specifically chooses Cythera's roses over the acorns and thorns that Circe fed her beasts: "Will you trade roses for acorns / Will lynxes eat thorn leaves?" (p. 491). A series of triadic images introduce the lynx song, and the mention of "three nights amid lynxes" twice and the line "The Graces have brought [Aphrodite]" initiate the conclusion, punctuated by ecstatic invocation of the goddess' names: "This goddess was born of sea-foam / She is lighter than air under Hesperus." Her aspect is double: "terrible in resistance" yet "a petal lighter than sea-foam." And her manifestation is triune: Kore and Delia and Maia, "trine as praeludio" (p. 492). Kore is Demeter's daughter, who took the name of Persephone during her months as queen of the underworld; Delia is another name for Artemis, virgin goddess of the woods; Maia is the mother of Hermes. The "trine" configuration of daughter-virgin-mother presents the feminine as it moves through and transcends biological process: the three aspects of the one cycle. Canto 79 also mentions the Sirens and Circe in conjunction with Aphrodite: a reprise of the trinity of anima figures in Canto 1. Similarly, in Canto 80, three female saints invoked together in the Mass – Perpetua, Agatha, Anastasia – are subsumed into Immaculata

Regina, the Virgin Mary as Immaculate Queen. So here at the climax of the lynx song the trine of women is prelude to the revelation of the Great Goddess: Aphrodite, born of sea-foam, all light and air, sexuality shining as spirit. In her, man (remember Anchises) meets his soul and glimpses godhood.

The revelation of Aphrodite as the unity of the feminine trinity anticipates the appearance of the goddesses in Pound's tent in Canto 81, which is, in Daniel Pearlman's words, "the visionary climax of *The Pisan Cantos*" and perhaps of the entire poem.[87] The passage is so redolent of key passages cited earlier that it should be quoted at length:

> Ed ascoltando al leggier mormorio [And listening to the light murmur]
>   there came new subtlety of eyes into my tent,
> whether of spirit or hypostasis,
>   but what the blindfold hides
> or at carneval
>
>   nor any pair showed anger
>   Saw but the eyes and stance between the eyes,
> colour, diastasis,
>   careless or unaware it had not the
>   whole tent's room
> nor was place for the full Εἰδὼς [Knowing]
> interpass, penetrate
>   casting but shade beyond the other lights
>   sky's clear
>   night's sea
>   green of the mountain pool
>   shone from the unmasked eyes in half-mask's space.
>
>   (p. 520)

This is the fullest revelation of divinity granted to Pound. The divine eyes have regularly been associated with Aphrodite: absolute transparency manifest in the opacities of physical possibility, "the unmasked eyes in half-mask's space." As in the "Donna mi priegha," light casts shade on poor human eyes, but in this world of betweens and halves that shade shines "beyond the other lights." The paradox is caught in the rhyming of "hypostasis" and "diastasis." In Greek the first means "essence" or "substantial nature" and the second, "separation." In theology "hypostasis" refers to the union of three divine persons in the Trinity and to the person of Jesus Christ as the incarnated Second Person of the Trinity, in whom human and divine natures coexist. "Diastasis" complements that union without contradicting it, suggesting the separation of transcendent unity into successive aspects, like light splintered into the color spectrum.

Thus the full Knowing manifests itself in time and space as process, the Chinese *tao*: "sky's clear / night's sea / green of the mountain pool." The sun's incandescence is reflected in the moon's phases, which our human sight can gaze upon and comprehend, as in the epiphany at the end of Canto 83, which complements the epiphany of Canto 81:

> clouds lift their small mountains
>   before the elder hills
>
> A fat moon rises lop-sided over the mountain
> The eyes, this time my world,
>   But pass and look *from* mine
>   between my lids
>   sea, sky, and pool
>   alternate
>   pool, sky, sea,
>
>   morning moon against sunrise
>   (p. 535)

These superb passages bear out Confucius' sense (on the first page of Canto 74) that everything "is of the process," that "What you depart from is not the way" (p. 425).

As Canto 81 goes on to say, "First came the seen, then thus the palpable / Elysium, though it were in the halls of hell" (p. 521). The eyes in the tent open up a new vision of the world, and that vision completes the moral and emotional metamorphosis which the recognition of the shadow began. The most famous passage in the *Pisans* comes immediately after "the unmasked eyes in half-mask's space":

> What thou lovest well remains,
>   the rest is dross
> What thou lov'st well shall not be reft from thee
> What thou lov'st well is thy true heritage
>
> .   .   .   .
>
> The ant's a centaur in his dragon world.
> Pull down thy vanity, it is not man
> Made courage, or made order, or made grace,
>   Pull down thy vanity, I say pull down.
> Learn of the green world what can be thy place
> In scaled invention or true artistry,
> Pull down thy vanity,
>   Paquin pull down.
>   (pp. 520–521)

Love and ego are antitheses; the "hard" man must be broken open and exposed to the elements:

> Thou art a beaten dog beneath the hail,
> A swollen magpie in a fitful sun,
> Half black, half white...
>   How mean thy hates
> Fostered in vanity,
>   Pull down thy vanity,
> Rathe to destroy, niggard in charity....
>   (p. 521)

This central insight into the shadow truth is surrounded by personal expressions of charity: the loving recollections of Joyce and Ford and Yeats and of the fellowship of Parisian restaurants; the exclamation to Olga Rudge: "O white-chested martin, God damn it, / as no one else will carry a message, / say to La Cara, amo" (Canto 76, p. 459); "O lynx, my love, my lovely lynx" (Canto 79); "Amo ergo sum [I love, therefore I am], and in just that proportion" (Canto 80, p. 493). Moreover, this inversion of Cartesian rationalism is the source not merely of private passion but of civic grace and decorum, as each person assumes a place in the economy and ecology of the "green world." John Adams' dictum in Canto 70 "DUM SPIRO AMO [WHILE I BREATHE, I LOVE]" had already stated the compatibility of Confucius with Dionysus in their affinity with the feminine. For it is the goddess who in Canto 74 stands behind the "filial, fraternal affection" which Confucius names "the root of the process" and who makes possible the "charity" which Saint Paul names the "greatest" Christian virtue.

At her most sublime, the anima is linked with the emergent self. Hence Canto 74 begins to wed the masculine and feminine archetypes: "Sponsa Christi [Bride of Christ]" on the first page; a little later, "Light tensile immaculata," the adjective transforming the masculine *nous* into the feminine *lux* (just as Whitman addressed the Holy Spirit in "Chanting the Square Deific" as "Santa Spirita"); near the end of the canto, the phrase " 'Spiritus veni' " from the Catholic hymn supplies the syllable "ven" to link the coming of Aphrodite with the blowing of the Spirit: "Venere, Cytherea 'aut Rhodon' / vento ligure, vendi [in a sharp wind, come]." Images of archetypal union are reiterated throughout the later *Pisans*. The tally – a Confucian image, but also one of Whitman's favorite words for the conjunction of seeming polarities – occurs in Canto 77: "Very potent, can they again put one together / as the two halves of a seal, or a tally stick?" (p. 467). The lynx song in Canto 79 hails the syzygy of Dionysus and Aphrodite, which conceived Priapus, and at the end also links Aphrodite to both Hermes and Helios. Canto 81 begins with the syzygy of Zeus and Ceres (Demeter) which conceived Kore. In Canto 82 Pound alludes to Whitman's great elegies to celebrate the masculine marriage with Gea Terra: "man, earth: two halves of the tally" (p. 526). Near the end of Canto 84, the last of the *Pisans*, stand *ming*, the Chinese ideogram which depicts the sun and the moon together as the total light process, and *chung*, the unwobbling pivot (pp. 539, 540).

As in the Eleusinian mysteries, the syzygy heralds the birth of the new self: in the refrain that runs through the *Pisans*, "each one in the name of his god." Lines from Canto 74 use the opening of Saint John's Gospel (from the Bible issued to all the prisoners in the camp) to identify "in principio verbum [in the beginning was the Word]" with the "paraclete [the Holy Spirit as advocate] or the verbum perfectum [the Word perfected]: sinceritas" (p. 427). That is to say, the name of each person's god is immanent from birth, to be brought to definition ("perfectum") through the activity of spirit. The perfection is "sinceritas," which means not merely "sincerity" but, in Pound's exposition of the Chinese ideogram, "the precise definition of the word, pictorially the sun's lance coming to rest on the precise spot verbally. The right-hand half of this compound [ideogram] means: to perfect, bring to focus."[88] One could not name his god at the beginning, but one's life is the process of learning his name.

Pound had named Dionysus / Kung as the Janus-face of his unitary self: the instinctuality of the sexual young man perfected in the wise old philosopher. But now he felt nameless, No Man, or at most, like Elpenor (and like his poem) with "a name to come." Caged like one of Dionysus' panthers, weeping like a woman and fearful of his sanity, Pound pondered. Was he, like the "Old fool" in Canto 13, like the old Trojans in Canto 2 before Helen, like the dry husks in Canto 7, worthy only of Confucius' scorn: comical "Old Ez"? And yet...why yearn for youth? His own now seemed a futile exercise in "hard" and driven egotism. In German, Pound quotes Anacreon to say: "The ladies say to me, you are an old man." "Philosophy is not for young men," but need the old men be impotent? The aged Tiresias proclaimed the Dionysian mysteries to Pentheus and now is twice associated with the Eleusinian mysteries (Cantos 74 and 80). Might it be true that even in the Pisan hell he "still hath his mind entire"? On the strength of the Dionysian lynx song in Canto 79, Pound begins Canto 80 by asserting the potency of age: "Amo ergo sum" becomes "senesco sed amo [I am old but I love]" (p. 493). Canto 77 ends with a conjunction of pairs: ch'êng, the Chinese ideogram for "to complete," inscribed twice with the Confucian "bringest to focus" placed between and above Zagreus (Dionysus), also repeated twice (p. 475).

Intimations of paradisal completion, both personal and societal, are also represented in the circle and square imagery of the mandala, which Jung saw as symbolizing the resolution of the opposition in totality: circularity, reiterated throughout the *Pisans*, particularly in the refrain of "periplum"; and quarternity, which completes trinity, in the four-sided Ecbatan ("the city of Dioce"), the four-gated village of Wagadu (rebuilt four times), even the square prison camp with its guard towers at the corners. In Canto 76, Pound asks ruefully: "In heaven have I to make?" On the previous page he had posed the counterquestion: "Why not rebuild it?" And that affirmative spirit grows: replace the altar in the grove, erect Aphrodite's statue at Terracina, raise high "the city of Dioce whose terraces are the colour of stars." Already in Canto 74 the lute of Gassir arouses the chant for the reconstruction of Wagadu, as of old:

> 4 times was the city rebuilded, Hooo Fasa
>   Gassir, Hooo Fasa dell' Italia tradita [of Italy betrayed]
> now in the mind indestructible, Gassir, Hooo Fasa,
> With the four giants at the four corners
> and four gates mid-wall Hooo Fasa
> and a terrace the colour of stars

(p. 430)

Canto 77 repeats the chant with the phrase "now in the heart indestructible" (p. 476). But is the vision of the paradisal city indestructible only there? Only to be ravaged by war and avarice in purgatorial history? "These fragments I have shored against the ruins"; Eliot's words, mocked by a more arrogant Pound in Canto 8, must have besieged his memories, along with the apocalyptic lines echoed in Canto 74 from *The Hollow Men*.

But something in Pound – was it newly earned humility and faith or still stubborn ego? – resisted as *abuleia* both tragic resignation and a passive, decadent Platonism. These lines, bracketing the statement "that the drama is wholly subjective," undermine that notion:

> Sunt lumina [They are lights]
>   that the drama is wholly subjective
>   stone knowing the form which the carver imparts it
>   the stone knows the form

(p. 430)

If the drama were wholly subjective – as the *fin de siècle* believed, following Pater's "Conclusion" to *The Renaissance* – then the individual did only "dream his own dream of a world." But Pound rejected alienated, antisocial solipsism. Like the carver or city builder, the poet did not impose form on inchoate nature by dint of will and ego but imparted the form inherent in things themselves. Matter enlightens mind because, as in Scotus Erigena's maxim "all things that are are lights," things take their form from informing essence. The natural object "knows" the inhering form which the carver intuits and imparts. Amid the rubble of Europe, Pound clung to the possibility of organic construction: if in a sculpture, then in a city; if in an artwork, then in a civilization.

So, at the beginning of Canto 74, Pound declares flatly, "Le Paradis n'est pas artificiel," and he repeats the statement throughout the Pisan sequence. Inverting *Les Paradis Artificiels*, Baudelaire's book of narcotic hallucinations, he unequivocally rejected the Symboliste tradition that extended from Baudelaire and Poe to Pater and Mallarmé to Yeats and Stevens. In the hell pit of the Pisan prison, with more reason than ever to doubt nature as well as history, Pound proclaimed himself once and for all a perceptual rather than conceptual artist. The concluding lines of Canto 74 illustrate how the work of art evokes a natural paradise:

> Serenely in the crystal jet
>   as the bright ball that the fountain tosses
> (Verlaine) as diamond clearness
>   How soft the wind under Taishan
>   where the sea is remembered
>   out of hell, the pit
>   out of the dust and glare evil
>   Zephyrus/Apeliota
> This liquid is certainly a
>   property of the mind
> nec accidens est but an element
>   in the mind's make-up
> est agens and functions dust to a fountain pan otherwise

> Hast 'ou seen the rose in the steel dust
>   (or swansdown ever?)
> so light is the urging, so ordered the dark petals of iron
> we who have passed over Lethe.

(p. 449)

This is one of the great summary passages in *The Cantos*, and virtually every phrase and image resonates with previous passages. In such concentrated nodal passages (we have examined others) *The Cantos* gathers its particulars into clarification for a new departure,[89] as here at the close of the opening poem of the Pisan sequence.

The activity of mind which creates the poem raises the poet "out of hell, the pit / out of the dust and glare evil" toward a vision of terrestrial paradise. The streaming life of the natural scene ("wind," "sea," "Taishan") becomes a "property of the mind," an aspect of its essence (not an accident: "nec accidens est") only when the mind channels the flow through its narrow conduit to make the "crystal jet" and "bright ball" of the fountain: the issuing of natural forces in aesthetic form. (Recall Whitman's description of the prophet's mind as it "bubbles and pours forth as a fountain, from inner, divine spontaneities revealing God.") In another famous image, the mind magnetizes the scattered iron filings into a rose. The reciprocal attraction between magnet and filings creates form and thereby shows both mind and nature as elements in a larger field of energies: "so light is the urging, so ordered the dark petals of iron." "The rose in the steel dust" recalls the passage from the Cavalcanti essay about the "radiant world" of the medieval Platonist lost to the modern empiricist. Psychologically and philosophically the medievalist lives in

> ...the radiant world where one thought cuts through another with clean edge, a world of moving energies "*mezzo oscuro rade*," "*risplende in sè per-petuale effecto*," magnetisms that take form, that are seen, or that border the visible, the matter of Dante's *paradiso*, the glass under water, the form that seems a form seen in a mirror, these realities perceptible to the sense, interact-ing, "*a lui so tiri*."[90]

The forces at the disposal of the modern scientist, unsuspected by the medievalist, do not, in Pound's view, lead the scientist to see those forces as convergent in a coherent and organic natural process. However:

> A medieval "natural philosopher" would find this modern world full of enchantments, not only the light in the electric bulb, but the thought of the current hidden in air and in wire would give him a mind full of forms, "*Fuor di color*" or having their hyper-colours. The medieval philosopher would probably have been unable to think the electric world, and *not* think of it as a world of forms.

Mind conforms to nature, and only in a world whose energies converge will the rose appear in the iron filings. Otherwise, in a phrase that links the rose image to the fountain image, the filings would fall as "dust to a fountain pan."

It is the experience of the possibilities of form, even on the brink of madness and death, the renewed conviction, even in his Pisan extremities, of subject and object linked by convergent energies, that allows Pound to recover his memory and reestablish his mind and his world in organic relation. The exploitiveness of ego and the destruction of war are madness and death, are accidental aberrations from the perfection of form. Nature is paradise if the human mind can but perceive the inherent organic character of its process. But if the mind can enter and participate in natural process, it can humanize the process by extending those ordering tendencies into what it makes of the natural order. The *nous* emanates the *tao* of nature, and the human creator is faced with making an aesthetic and political order either in accordance with or in violation of the *tao*. The havoc of World War II does not disprove the paradisal vision but validates it with a new urgency for the enlightened elite. "We who have passed over Lethe" (p. 449), beyond the hell of the warlords, hold "indestructible" the secret of art and civilization. Even in abjection Pound clung defiantly to his basic principles. The great litany of "Pull down thy vanity" concludes:

> But to have done instead of not doing
> this is not vanity.
> . . . .
> Here error is all in the not done,
> all in the diffidence that faltered. . .
>
> (pp. 521–522)

Canto 75 begins with the thrice-repeated invocation "out of Phlegethon," another underworld river that surrounded Tartarus, the walled prison of hell. After twenty-five pages of Canto 74 there are only seven lines in Canto 75, a concerted upward thrust. And then the sheet music for Gerhart Münch's modern transcription for violin of Janequin's Renaissance lute setting of the original music for a canzone in which Arnaut Daniel "made the birds sing IN HIS WORDS."[91] Pound conflates his memory of his friend Münch's performance of the bird music with the birds singing on the barbed wire of the detention camp. Pictographically the birds are the notes on the musical staff (an image repeated throughout the *Pisans*) as the remembered music rises through the death camp. Before the war, in *Guide to Kulchur*, Pound had associated the indestructibility of the musical form with the image of "the rose in the steel dust":

> The *forma*, the immortal *concetto*, the concept, the dynamic form which is like the rose pattern driven into the dead iron-filings by the magnet...the dust and filings rise and spring into order. Thus the *forma*, the concept rises from death....Janequin's concept takes a third life in our time.[92]

And now a fourth life: out of Tartarus rises Elysian song.

The song could not, of course, deliver him from Tartarus, even imaginatively, for long. "Le Paradis n'est pas artificiel," but our actual experience of "paradiso terrestre" is "spezzato apparently / it exists only in fragments" (p. 438). The subsequent *Pisans* record the shifting interplay between hell, purgatory, and heaven, between shadow, anima, and self. "By no means an orderly Dantescan rising" (p. 443): the sequence has no grand climax; the epiphanies had arrived earlier. Through all its vagaries and relapses, the sequence verifies the ascension, nonetheless, toward the integration and transcendence which Cantos 74 and 75 inaugurate.

V

Committed indefinitely to St. Elizabeth's, a federal psychiatric hospital in Washington, D.C., after being declared mentally unfit to stand trial for treason,[93] Pound was still the "caged panther" (p. 530); but he had survived the prisons, and he would survive the asylum. He soon had his books, a growing number of visitors, even a coterie of young admirers who sat at his feet during daily visiting hours; and he was tirelessly at work on cantos, translations, and polemical prose. The next two segments of cantos, *Section: Rock-Drill* (1955) and *Thrones* (1959), written in a madhouse, represent the attempt to project the personal experience of a paradisal nature into the erection of a sane society.

Inescapably, *Rock-Drill* and *Thrones* are bookish, at times claustrophobically so, often derived from unfamiliar and obscure sources. *Rock-Drill* is, of course, the Epstein Vorticist sculpture. Pound was reminded of it when Wyndham Lewis applied the image to Pound himself in a review of his *Letters*: "his rock-drill action is impressive; he blasts away tirelessly."[94] Thomas Grieve has described the structure of *Rock-Drill* as "two distinct movements: Cantos 85 through 89 present historical foundation; Cantos 90 through 95 visionary extension. Seen in this way, *Section: Rock-Drill* is a consolidation of the corresponding division between the two preceeding [sic] groups of Cantos, that is *The China Cantos* and *The Pisan Cantos*."[95] This ideogramic structure

> . . . informs the articulation of a Paradiso in the later Cantos of the poem. . . .
> What Pound presents here is a mode of social order against which the chaos of usury, and its progeny *bellum perenne* [perennial war], is defined. But equally present, revealed through the signs that are selected, is a semiology that adumbrates a visionary order of fruition, renewal, and plenitude.

The reader may question how effectively Pound has reconciled the personal and political dimensions, but the intention – and the tension – of these cantos are clear.

Moreover, the shadow, the anima, and the self remain the structuring archetypes. Near the beginning of Canto 85, Elizabeth and Cleopatra stand as two strong and complementary women rulers: one translating Ovid's metamorphic vision into her native tongue, the other enunciating sound fiscal policy. But they are virtually the only women mentioned in Cantos 85 through 89. The first half of *Rock-Drill* attends to patriarchal rule (even Elizabeth and Cleopatra rule in a patriarchal system) with familiar juxtapositions: Confucians versus Buddhists and Taoists, American constitutionalists versus American capitalists, patricians versus nouveaux riches, rulers of the people. ("he, Andy Jackson / POPULUM AEDIFICAVIT [BUILT

THE PEOPLE]," Canto 89, p. 596) versus oppressors of the people, distributors of currency versus usurers. On the first page of Canto 85 the mention of a "gnomon" – an astronomical instrument for measuring the height of the sun by its shadow at noon and, more popularly, the indicator on a sundial – is explained by the observation: "Our science is from the watching of shadows..." (p. 543). That is to say, we define things by their shadows in order to affirm the light represented in the often enlarged Chinese ideograms: *ling*, or sensibility ("Our dynasty came in because of a great sensibility," Canto 85); virtue; education; the four *tuan* or foundations of Confucianism (love, duty, propriety, wisdom); *chung*, the unwobbling pivot, rendered in Latin as "medium [the middle]" and "centrum circuli [the center of the circle]" (Canto 87). Pound the rock-drill was pressing his hierarchical Confucianism "tirelessly" (in Lewis' phrase) on a cold war world which seemed to have learned appallingly little from the debacle it had barely survived.

The last five *Rock-Drill* cantos rise up again from the shadow world into light and air:

> out of Erebus, the delivered,
>> Tyro, Alcmene, free now, ascending
> e i cavalieri [and the cavaliers],
>> ascending,
> no shades more,
>> lights among them, enkindled....
>>> (p. 608)

Instead of the gnomon, "the room in Poitiers where one can stand / casting no shadow" (p. 605). On the next page, the Muses' fountain of Castalia on Parnassus echoes the fountain image at the end of Canto 74 to specify the feminine inspiration for ascent:

> out of Erebus, the deep-lying
>> from the wind under the earth,
>>> m'elevasti [You have lifted me up, (from Dante's
>>>> *Paradiso*)]
>> from the dulled air and the dust,
>>> m'elevasti
> by the great flight,
>> m'elevasti,
>>> Isis Kuanon
>>>> (p. 606)

The realm of light is, as before, filled with transformative feminine presences, with Aphrodite as supreme goddess. Her motto – "UBI AMOR IBI OCULUS EST [WHERE LOVE IS, THERE THE EYE IS]" (p. 609) – identifies love and vision. The anima is the volatile and subtlizing element distilling matter into spirit; in fact, "Deus est anima [rather than the masculine animus] mundi" (p. 643). In a reiteration of Pound's earlier sexual mysticism, Canto 91 casts the invocation of the anima (associated here with the painter

Sheri Martinelli, one of Pound's inner circle at St. Elizabeth's) in alchemical terms:

> that the body of light come forth
>   from the body of fire
> And that your eyes come to the surface
>   from the deep wherein they were sunken,
> Reina [Queen] – for 300 years,
>   and now sunken
> That your eyes come forth from their caves
> (p. 610)

The Queen is Elizabeth, who moved her men under Drake to victorious action against the Spanish Armada:

> Miss Tudor moved them with galleons
> from deep eye, versus armada
> from the green deep
>   he saw it,
> in the green deep of an eye:
>   Crystal waves weaving together the gt/healing
> (p. 611)

The anima as queen links psychological process with imperial rule, and again the four-square stone city is the emblem of both personal identity and social structure: "Then knelt with the sphere of crystal / That she should touch with her hands, / Coeli Regina, / The four altars at the four coigns of that place..." (p. 619). In her hands the circle is squared into a mandala. In the same vein, the miraculous rescue of the shipwrecked Odysseus by Leucothea – the most recurrent motif in *Rock-Drill* – not only saves the hero from drowning but also sends him home to resume rule in his kingdom.

The selfhood which makes Odysseus king is personified in Apollonius of Tyana. Commenting on Canto 94, James Neault wrote: "Odysseus is subsumed into the identity of Apollonius"; and James Wilhelm contended that Apollonius was a "Neoplatonic saint of the first century" who represented "to the European world what Confucius is to the Oriental: a sensible sage who acknowledged a cosmos of ideals, but who also stressed the relevance of the here and now."[96] Pound's re-creation in bits and pieces from Philostratus' *Life*, interspersed with Chinese ideograms, shows Apollonius moving with authority in court circles, counseling emperors, teaching purity and nobility by example as well as precept. At the same time, Pound underplays the asceticism in Philostratus' *Life* in order to invest Apollonius with something of a Dionysian character. For example, Pound omits his attack on myth as lying fictions which subvert morals by extolling promiscuity, but has Apollonius restore a "shrine that will hold ten people drinking"; the presence of the great cats in Canto 94 ("Apollonius made his peace with the animals," Canto 93, p. 623) – leopards, tigers, lions – underscores the Dionysian basis for his Confucian wisdom. So "by the nymphs" Apollonius has "ecstasy, sober," knowing "that the universe is alive." Pound sums up Apollonius' preaching, prophesying, cures, and miracles in the concluding phrase "To build light," which casts the temple building of Sigismundo and the people building of Jackson into the mystical dimension. Pound places the phrase with the Confucian maxim "Make it new" and attributes both phrases to the Neoplatonist Ocellus, whose name picks up "oculus" and all of the eye imagery of the previous Canto 93.

Thrones (Cantos 96–109) strives to extend the integration adumbrated in Apollonius farther into the social and political order. Pound was unusually explicit about his didactic intention:

> The thrones in Dante's *Paradiso* are for the spirits of the people who have been responsible for good government. The thrones in *The Cantos* are an attempt to move out from egoism and to establish some definition of an order possible or at any rate conceivable on earth.... *Thrones* concerns the states of mind of people responsible for something more than their personal conduct.[97]

The image of thrones occurred as far back as Canto 36; the first line after the translation of "Donna mi priegha" comes from Dante: "Called thrones, balascio or topaze." It returns in Canto 88: "Belascio or Topaze, and not have it sqush, / a 'throne', something God can sit on / without having it sqush." And at the end of the sketch of Apollonius, "That it is of thrones, / and above them: Justice."

But Pound the mandarin remained at odds with Pound the educator; he was preaching to the converted clique of Poundians. The controlling ideas are clear enough, though wearying in the repetition, but the pertinence and the ideogramic interconnections of the evidentiary details are often simply not presented in the assembly of fragments from quite arcane sources: in Canto 96, Paul the Deacon's eighth-century *History of the Lombards* and the ninth-century *Eparch's Book* of the Byzantine emperor Leo the Wise; in Canto 97, American historian Alexander del Mar's *History of Monetary Systems* (1898); in Cantos 98 and 99 (Pound's most comprehensive redaction of Confucian norms), the seventeenth-century *Sacred Edict of Emperor K'ang Hsi*; in Canto 101, the *Memoires de Mme. de Ramuset 1802–1808*, about the Napoleonic era; also in Canto 101 and in subsequent cantos, Joseph Rock's *The Ancient Na Khi Kingdom of Southwest China* (1947), about the recently discovered Tibetan tribe whose culture, extending from pre-Confucian times to the present, Pound took as exemplifying the persistence of the "paradiso terrestre"; in Canto 105, the *Vita, Monologion*, and *Prologion* of Saint Anselm of Canterbury; in Cantos 107, 108, and 109, the triumph of English common law and constitutional government, culminating in the American Constitution, for which Sir Edward Coke's *Institutes* and Catherine Drinker Bowen's history *The Lion and the Throne* were Pound's chief sources.

However, threaded through this relentless survey of patriarchal rule down the many centuries of various Eastern and Western cultures is the reminder that law springs from and rests on feminine and Dionysian creativity. Pound commends Saint Anselm for associating the Trinity with the feminine principle through the grammatical gender of "essence" in Latin:

```
                        ...had a clear line on the Trinity, and
          By sheer grammar: Essentia
                              feminine
                                    Immaculata

          Immaculabile        [unspottable]
                                          (p. 750)
```

The passage echoes "Light tensile immaculata" and "Deus est anima" to insist again that man is saved by his anima. In the lovely invocation of goddesses in Canto 106, process blossoms: "So slow is the rose to open"; "trees open, their minds stand before them" (p. 752); "Trees open in Paros, / ...The sky is leaded with elm boughs" (p. 754); "that great acorn of light bulging outward" (p. 755).

Moreover, interspersed with the excerpts from Coke's *Institutes* is the vision of Elizabeth as "Angliae Amor," Britain's Aphrodite terrestre. In Canto 107: "her mind / like the underwave," "the crystal body of air / deep green over azure," "god's antennae" (pp. 761–762); and in Canto 108:

```
          Enrolled in the ball of fire
                              as brightness
                                    clear emerald
          for the kindness,
                        infinite,
                        of her hands....
                                    (p. 764)
```

Nevertheless, for the most part, there is the same kind of stifling claustrophobia in *Rock-Drill* and most of *Thrones* that also sealed even well-disposed readers out of the Chinese History Cantos and the Adams Cantos. As in the 1930s, so now during the St. Elizabeth years, when Pound intended to "move out from egoism to establish some definition of an order possible or at any rate conceivable on earth," he was – ironically – most cloistered in the labyrinth of his own mind. And, as before, that solipsism caused a dramatic break in his life and in his poem. For the second time, the structures on which he had staked his life and his poem tottered, and he had to begin again to reformulate them. The final segment of *The Cantos* is called *Drafts and Fragments*. Whereas the previous fracture is manifest in the missing cantos, 72 and 73, before the *Pisans*, the fissures run throughout the last decade of cantos. Only five are final and complete texts; the rest are notes, or pieces, or entirely missing.

Canto 110 enacts the overshadowing of paradise. The earthly paradise is presented in the rhythms of natural process (symbolized in the "gaiety" and "exultance" of the cresting wave pattern), in the invocation of Artemis and Kuanon, and in glimpses of the Na-Khi Kingdom and its rites (with the juniper "in the center" of the altar, a Tree of Life rooting heaven in earth). But in Canto 110 death and ruin darken the paradisal light. Again and again, the feminine is betrayed by the masculine: the young girl Ka in the Na-Khi legend; Eurydice and Daphne; Awoi and Komachi, tragic heroines of Noh plays.

"That love be the cause of hate, / something is twisted...." And thoughts of war close in on him: the "hell of a row" in the U.S. Senate on the issue of war and the League of Nations, recollections of World War II (with an echo of *The Waste Land*: "From time's wreckage shored, / these fragments shored against ruin"), the prospect of apocalypse in the atomic age:

> Falling spiders and scorpions,
> Give light against falling poison,
> A wind of darkness hurls against forest
> > the candle flickers
> > > is faint
> Lux enim –
> > versus this tempest.

> (p. 781)

It seems difficult at first to account for Pound's sudden gloom. In 1958 he was at last released from the asylum, in Dorothy Pound's custody, on the ground that he would never be psychologically fit to stand trial. With Dorothy he returned to Italy, where Olga Rudge, their daughter Mary, and Mary's husband and children waited to welcome him. As World War II and the scandal of the treason charge receded, many Americans were prepared to honor Pound and tolerate his persistent criticism. *The Cantos* were beginning to be taught in some college courses and studied by a generation of critics after the New Critics. Some members of the younger generation saw in his denunciations of usury and banks and the military-industrial complex a prophetic insight into the system which had spawned the Vietnam War and American imperialism. Moreover, during the 1950s and 1960s the American poetry scene changed radically. Eliot's reigning preeminence began to wane, along with the influence of the New Critics, under the impact of a new wave of experimentation with open form. The Beats – Allen Ginsberg, Lawrence Ferlinghetti, Gregory Corso – derived their sense of line and form not just from Whitman but also, to some extent, from Pound and Williams; and the Projectivists – Charles Olson, Robert Duncan, Denise Levertov – proceeded explicitly from Pound and Williams. In 1969 Richard Howard dedicated *Alone with America*, his ground-breaking book on postwar poetry, to Pound.

Nevertheless, when asked by an interviewer in 1960 if his return to Italy had been a disappointment, Pound left no doubt about it:

> Undoubtedly. Europe was a shock. The shock of no longer feeling oneself in the center of something is probably part of it. Then there is the incomprehension, Europe's incomprehension, of organic America. There are so many things which I, as an American, cannot say to a European with any hope of being understood. Somebody said that I am the last American living the tragedy of Europe.[98]

St. Elizabeth's had been a cloister, but it had, oddly enough, been a haven too. The coterie of disciples had given him a sense of being at the center of a mini-vortex, and to his surprise he suddenly felt an exile back in Italy. Moreover, return to his loved ones placed him in the cross-tension between Dorothy and

Olga and Mary: "When one's friends hate each other / how can there be peace in the world?" (p. 794); "If love be not in the house there is nothing" (p. 796). At the same time, his strong physical constitution began to give way when he no longer had to maintain his survival. Suddenly he felt old, afflicted with illnesses and operations, uprooted and uncentered, wondering if his life and work had come to anything.

Nor could he honestly project the blame or the strain on others anymore. In Canto 113 he comments wryly, "As to sin, they invented it – eh? / to implement domination / eh? largely" (p. 789). Largely, but not entirely. In freedom Pound found himself confronted by the shadow more threateningly even than at Pisa. These last cantos have an autobiographical immediacy that links them with the *Pisans*, and now Pound includes himself in the circle of destructive ego in lines of Learlike simplicity and candor:

> That love be the cause of hate,
> something is twisted....
> (Canto 110, p. 780)

> Until the mind jumps without building
> *chih* [the position one is in and works from]
> and there is no *chih* and no root.
> (Canto 110, pp. 780-781)

> The hells move in cycles,
> No man can see his own end.
> The Gods have not returned. "They have never left us."
> They have not returned....
> Pride, jealousy, possessiveness
> 3 pains of hell
> (Canto 113, p. 787)

> And of man seeking good,
> doing evil.
> (Canto 115, p. 794)

> ...my errors and wrecks lie about me.
> And I am not a demigod,
> I cannot make it cohere.
> If love be not in the house there is nothing.
> (Canto 116, p. 796)

> M'amour, m'amour
> what do I love and
> where are you?
> That I lost my center
> fighting the world.
> The dreams clash
> and are shattered –
> and that I tried to make a paradiso
> terrestre.
> (Canto 117, p. 802)

So heavy is the shadow's pall that for the first time Pound questions the integrity of his life's project. Each in the name of his god, he had said, and his name would come with the title which would subsume his long cantos. Through all the twists and turns of his life the thread of the poem spun out, reknotted when broken, to lead him out of the maze; no wonder that in his despair he calls on Ariadne in Canto 116. At the beginning of *Rock-Drill*, even after the Pisan death camp, indeed on the basis of the reconsolidation of *The Pisan Cantos*, he could still say in Canto 85, "But if you will follow this process," followed by the ideogram for the "acquisition of truth":

> not a lot of signs, but the one sign
> > etcetera
> > plus always [Τέχνη] ["skill in art, in making things,"
> > > *Guide to Kulchur*, p. 327]
> and from [Τέχνη] back to [σεαυτόν] [self-knowledge]
> > > > (p. 546)

In Canto 93, when Mussolini inquires how or why Pound wants to put his ideas in order, Pound snaps back: "Pel mio poema [through or for mv poem]" (p. 626). When Pound is asked in Canto 104: "What part ob yu iz deh poEM??" the response is roundabout but clear: "The production IS the beloved" (pp. 741, 742). Now the whole production seemed rocking on unsteady foundations. Was it only a Modernist ruin to an ego whose vaunting selfishness had erected the illusion that he was a "demigod"? If so, *The Cantos* disintegrated of its own insubstantiality: "I am not a demigod, I cannot make it cohere" (p. 796). And again:

> Many errors,
> > a little rightness,
> to excuse his hell
> > > and my paradiso.
> And as to why they go wrong,
> > > thinking of rightness
> And as to who will copy this palimpsest?
> > al poco giorno [in little light]
> > > ed al gran cerchio d'ombra
> > > [and in the great circle of shadow]
> > > > (p. 797)

Was it only vanity that "I tried to make a paradiso / terrestre" (p. 802)? To his old beloved H. D. he wrote plaintively, "What have I done with my life?"[99]

The *Drafts and Fragments* were written between *Thrones* in 1958 and about 1960. In the early 1960s, Pound began to tell friends and interviewers that he had botched the poem. He lapsed more and more into silence, refraining from further pronouncements, he said, because he had done too much harm already by saying foolish and wrongheaded things. In the 1972 "Foreword" to the *Selected Prose*, ostentatiously dated July 4, just months before his death, he warned against the projection of the shadow which had vitiated his opinions and pointed to the egotism which divides groups and races into "we" who are right and "they" who are wrong. In a momentous meeting in 1967 with Allen Ginsberg, Pound lamented that the poem was a "mess," filled with "stupidity and ignorance all the way through," and seized the occasion to confess to the Jewish Ginsberg that his "greatest stupidity was stupid suburban anti-Semitic prejudice."[100]

Those who had long been hostile to Pound on political or literary grounds gloated over these self-recriminations. Nevertheless, however chagrined Pound felt about *The Cantos*, he did not abandon the poem. On the contrary, he personally chose the contents for a *Selected Cantos* (1967), read excerpts, including some of the last cantos, at the Spoleto Festival in 1966, made a long-playing record from *The Cantos* for commercial release, and agreed to the publication of *Drafts and Fragments* in 1969.

An attentive reading of these last poetic statements reveals that this recognition of the shadow eventuated not in acceptance of disaster but in a vista beyond. In Canto 110 the "falling spiders and scorpions" and the flickering candle amid "a wind of darkness" are met by "light against falling poison," "Lux enim – / versus this tempest," and the canto ends by affirming the forms and signatures in nature and the "power" of prayer (p. 781). Consistently in these cantos darkness passes into light, hell yawns on paradise:

> The eyes holding trouble –
>   no light
>   ex profundis –
> naught from feigning.
> Soul melts into air,
>   anima into aura,
>   Serenitas.
>   (Canto 111, p. 783)

> And who no longer make gods out of beauty
>   [θρῆνος] this is a dying.

> Yet to walk with Mozart, Agassiz and Linnaeus
>   'neath overhanging air under sun-beat
>   Here take thy mind's space
>   And to this garden, Marcella, ever seeking by petal, by leaf-vein
>   out of dark, and toward half-light
>   (Canto 113, p. 786)

> Pride, jealousy and possessiveness
>   3 pains of hell
> and a clear wind over garofani [carnations]
>   over Portofino 3 lights in triangulation
>   (Canto 113, p. 787)

> A blown husk that is finished
>   but the light sings eternal
>   (Canto 115, p. 794)

Nekuia again moves toward ascension and transfiguration. Where there had been hate, he comes to be able to say with Voltaire: "I hate no one, not even Fréron" (p. 791). In place of eyes clouded by possessiveness, the hypostasis of love beyond contention:

ubi amor, ibi oculus. [Where love is, there is the eye]
But these had thrones,
  and in my mind were still, uncontending –
not to possession, in hypostasis

(p. 793)

Despite jealousies and betrayals and treason, the Dionysian-Confucian possibility of a new birth, a new building:

Under the Rupe Tarpeia
  weep out your jealousies –
To make a church
  or an altar to Zagreus Ζαγρεύσ
Son of Semele Σεμελη
Without jealousy

(p. 801)

The key to the redemption from the shadow is "pity / *compassione* / Amor," and the process is expressed in the transformation of the anima from Siren through Circe to Aphrodite, as in Canto 1: "Amor, / cold mermaid up from the black water" (p. 783). "Winnowed in fate's tray / neath / luna" (p. 785). Canto 30 had concluded the first large segment of the poem by commending Artemis for lack of pity and condemning Aphrodite for her pity. Now the two goddesses are linked in the equivalence of *compassione* and Amor: "And in every woman, somewhere in the snarl is a tenderness" (p. 789); "Justification is from kindness of heart / and from her hands floweth mercy" (p. 788); "God's eye art 'ou, do not surrender perception. / And in thy mind beauty, O Artemis" (p. 790); "The kindness, infinite, of her hands" (p. 793). Centered on her, Pound moves beyond the "demigod" of ego to intimations of the "God of all men, none excluded," even the shadowiest – the god of the feminine round. Canto 113 opens:

Thru the 12 Houses of Heaven
  seeing the just and the unjust,
  tasting the sweet and the sorry,
Pater Helios turning.

(p. 786)

And later: "Out of dark, thou, Father Helios, leadest, /, but the mind as Ixion, unstill, ever turning" (p. 790). The whole human travail is retrieved from failure and oblivion in the totality and continuity of the *tao*: "and to know beauty and death and despair / and to think that what has been shall be, / flowing, ever unstill" (p. 787). History turns cyclic, capable of renewal, redeemed from tragedy; it records not just the death of beauty and the defeat of values but their survival beyond "death and despair." Dying into Father Helios' light, the individual can exclaim with Pound's Herakles after his Ixion-like labors: "what / SPLENDOUR, / IT ALL COHERES." Out of such a conviction the self – and the poem – survive the self-doubts and recriminations. Canto 116 mounts to a great summation in which personal tragedy is encompassed by a stubborn aspiration toward transcendence:

> I have brought the great ball of crystal;
>   who can lift it?
> Can you enter the great acorn of light?
>   But the beauty is not the madness
> Tho' my errors and wrecks lie about me.
> .   .   .   .
> To confess wrong without losing rightness:
> Charity I have had sometimes,
>   I cannot make it flow thru.
> A little light like a rush light
>   to lead back to splendour.
>   (795–796, 797)

In the end, like Dante in the first canto of the *Purgatorio*, Pound gathers a rush to illuminate the ascent up Mount Purgatory to Paradise. His error lay not in the effort to "build light" but in the possessive egotism of the effort.

Pound's Modernist sense of encroaching chaos steeled him to build light in making the poem; he would will a verbal paradise at least. But experience had taught him that Baudelaire was wrong: "le Paradis n'est pas artificiel." This profound insight, at once humbling and exalting, came to him in Pisa, and after the delusive hubris of the St. Elizabeth years came to him again in the final cantos. The Modernist made the whole venture of coherence ride on the medium and the mastery of technique, but at the end Pound concluded that paradise was not a condition of saying but of seeing, albeit spezzato seeing, as here in the summation of Canto 116:

> but about that terzo
>   third heaven,
>   that Venere,
>   again is all "paradiso"
>   a nice quiet paradise
>   over the shambles,
>   and some climbing
>   before the take-off,
>   to "see again,"
>   the verb is "see," not "walk on"
>   i.e. it coheres all right
>   even if my notes do not cohere.
>   (pp. 796–797)

It was Pound's way of saying, as Eliot did in "East Coker," "The poetry does not matter." Pound came to see how right his instinct was from the start to pit his notion of the image and the vortex and the ideogram against the Symboliste notion of the "supreme fiction." Poetry was validated by its fidelity, or approximation, to a reality antecedent to and independent of the poem: "i.e. it coheres all right / even if my notes do not cohere." Pound is punning on the fact that the process is "all right" (could he have had in mind Eliot's "all shall be well and / All manner of thing shall be well"?), and the word "notes" combines at least four senses: (1) the fragmentariness of (2) the data recorded in (3) the music of (4) *The Cantos*. Symbolisme assumes that the art work *is* the objective correlative, but Imagism is based on the assumption, sometimes unacknowledged, sometimes even contested, that aesthetic coherence depends on rather than supersedes objective reality. *Guide to Kulchur* provides the best gloss on Canto 116: "I mean or imply that certain truth exists. Certain colours exist in nature though great painters have striven vainly, and though the colour film is not yet perfected. Truth is not untrue'd by reason of our failing to fix it on paper."[101]

Pound allowed the poem to stand in its incompleteness not just as a Modernist ruin but, more importantly, as an affirmation of its struggle for coherence within the larger coherence. Curiously, the acknowledgment of relative failure at the aesthetic level validates the imperfect poem at a higher level, and the further paradox is that these last cantos radiate a lucidity, a lyricism, an earned serenity that bring *The Cantos* to an unexpected yet convincing point of rest. The poem has found not its name but its conclusion in Canto 120, the last and briefest of the entire sequence:

> I have tried to write Paradise
>
> Do not move
>> Let the wind speak
>> that is paradise.
>
> Let the Gods forgive what I
>> have made
> Let those I love try to forgive
>> what I have made.
>> (p. 803)

With that Pound was satisfied to lapse into a silence as prophetic as his speech.

In *Patria Mia* (1913), Pound took Whitman as striking "our American keynote": "a certain generosity; a certain carelessness, or looseness, if you will; a hatred of the sordid, an ability to forget the part for the sake of the whole, a desire for largeness, a willingness to stand exposed." "The artist is ready to endure personally a strain which his craftsmanship would scarcely endure," yet he "will undertake nothing in his art for which [he] will not be in person responsible."[102] There is no more telling description of Pound's commitment to poetry. With a more ostentatiously internationalist view of culture than Whitman's, with the Modernist's sophistication about formal experimentation, Pound put on paper a twentieth-century American, as Whitman had prided himself on doing in the previous century.

Besides, when read in terms of psychological process, as it asks to be read, this teeming poem, crisscrossed by contradictions bent on locating the unwobbling pivot, assumes a kind of coherence that Pound seemed able to discern at the end, though he had been too vocal a Modernist earlier to rest as easily as Whitman in achieving a great, incomplete process poem. *The Cantos* were, he said, the record of a personal struggle, and in any such record, human and artistic, the flaws are inseparable from the excellences; what was not done is inseparable from what was done. The aged Pound found much that he regretted saying, but by then he had outgrown the poem's limits morally as well as aesthetically. The last fragment before Canto 120 speaks of "moving" toward a "bridge over worlds...to enter arcanum" (p. 802).

5

H. D.: Helen in Bethlehem, Hilda in Egypt

I

For women like Hilda Doolittle, Marianne Moore, and Amy Lowell, trying to define themselves as poets between 1910 and 1920, there seemed no available female predecessors – only their struggling selves. Even Emily Dickinson was not available; the posthumous interest Dickinson received in the 1890s had passed, and it was not until the 1920s that rediscovery would bring out new poems and renewed attention. Even then, when she was taken up as a proto-Modernist in technique, her sensibility seemed too cloistered and renunciatory for the liberated 1920s, too bourgeois and self-involved for the Marxist 1930s.

Amy Lowell, shortly before her death in 1925, began "The Sisters," a monologue about the melancholy and loneliness of female poets, with these lines:

> Taking us by and large, we're a queer lot
> We women who write poetry. And when you think
> How few of us there've been, it's queerer still.
> I wonder what it is that makes us do it,
> Singles us out to scribble down, man-wise,
> The fragments of ourselves. Why are we
> Already mother-creatures, double bearing,
> With matrices in body and in brain?[1]

Although the question is left hanging in the air, the suggestion is that the woman poet ought ideally to be a double mother "with matrices in body and in brain." But if the challenge or the circumstances of patriarchy proved too daunting, can she still be mother in brain, if not in body? Can her poems become the parthenogenetic offspring of her "man-wise" powers, which proclaim her at once mother and daughter and virgin?

These remained rueful questions for Amy Lowell. She had not herself been "double bearing"; like Dickinson and Moore, she died childless and un-married. And the poem complains bitterly of the psychological distance that keeps Lowell from communing even with the sisters whose response she wanted and needed most: Sappho, Elizabeth Barrett Browning, Emily

Dickinson. Contemporary feminists like Adrienne Rich have echoed Lowell's observation of the inhibiting effects of the male literary and critical establishment on female artists. To Wallace Stevens' pronouncement that "the centuries have a way of being male,"[2] Rich at mid-century could only add the irony absent in Stevens: "Time is male / and in his cups her drinks to the fair."[3] But the irony does not resolve the question: How is the poet to be mother and the mother to be poet?

Though not without some irony of her own, Anne Bradstreet settled into her frontier situation sufficiently to accommodate biological and poetic motherhood, writing for and about her children and treating her verses as threadbare progeny, while at the same time chiding the Puritan patriarchs for consigning women to inferior roles. Bradstreet was much loved and admired by her male contemporaries for her long historical and philosophical poems, but her continuing fame rests on her private and domestic poems. And in her singularity she was an anomaly, though a less threatening one than her contemporary Anne Hutchinson, who was driven into the wilderness to perish for her heresy.

By the nineteenth century, there were many female poets popular enough to support themselves on their sales, but Lowell spoke of "how few of us there've been" because those nineteenth-century women, insofar as they were considered at all, were dismissed as poetesses rather than real poets. They earned and kept their large audiences by restricting themselves to the domestic arena and glorying in the sufferings of motherhood on earth for the ultimately triumphant reunion with husband and offspring in heaven. Lydia Sigourney, the "Sweet Singer of Hartford," was the type, repeating the enormous success of Mrs. Felicia Hemans in England; what Mrs. Sigourney (the designation was delimiting as well as honorific) represented was not the poet as mother but the mother as poetess.

Mrs. Sigourney began her *Letters to Mothers on their various important duties and privileges* by identifying herself (and the female reader) completely with the maternal role: "You are sitting with your child in your arms. So am I. And I have never been as happy before.... What a loss, had we passed through the world without tasting this purest, most exquisite fount of love." She revels in her humility, for on earth no role is "more fearfully important than that of the Mother," whose charge it is to convey "this beautiful and mysterious creature to the light of knowledge, the perfect bliss of immortality." Neither temporal power nor laurels can approach her apotheosis; "in point of precedence, she is next to the Creator."[4] Anticipating the censure of male critics (as well as the complaints of women writers, then and later, about the broken schedules and distractions of the household routine), Mrs. Sigourney admitted that her poems "reveal by their brevity, the short periods of time allotted to their construction" – especially "amid domestic and maternal chores."[5] Nevertheless, this restriction was more than compensated for, admirers kept assuring her, by her inspired responsiveness to her special theme.

A selection of titles in a single volume of hers, *Pocahontas and Other Poems*

(1841), enshrines the mother in her travail of birth and death: "Widow at Her Daughter's Funeral," "Death of an Infant in Its Mother's Arms," "The Widow's Prayer," "Hymn in Sickness," "Request of the Dying Child," "Wife of a Missionary at Her Husband's Grave," "The Dying Mother," "The Mother Summoned," "Babe Dying in Its Mother's Absence," "The Young Mother." In her all-encompassing functions – the mother birthing and burying, the mother healing and solacing, the mother suffering and dying and surviving – she approaches godhead. No deprivation can be more injurious, therefore, especially for a girl, than the loss of a mother. "Baptism of an Infant at Its Mother's Funeral" lingers lovingly over the loss:

> – Tears were thy baptism, thou unconscious one,
> And Sorrow took thee at the gate of life,
> Into her cradle. Thou may'st never know
> The welcome of a nursing mother's kiss,
> When lost in wondering ecstasy, she marks
> A thrilling growth of new affections spread
> Fresh greenness o'er her soul.
> Thou may'st never share
> Her hallowed teachings, nor suffuse her eye
> With joy, as the first gleams of infant thought
> Unfold, in lisping sound.[6]

Mrs. Sigourney wrung every shuddering tremor from her theme by identifying with both the mother and the child at the cross-point of life and death.

Though Emily Dickinson read such sentimental women's poetry avidly, and at times displayed a necrophilic streak akin to Mrs. Sigourney's, she herself refused to be mother or daughter – or poet – on those terms. In her letters she remarked on her mother's intellectual and literary deficiencies, which she felt so deeply that she once confessed that she never had a mother. Imaginatively, she grew up under the level gaze of the God whom she loved and feared and of the lawyer father whom she had to appease and resist for her own psychological survival. The male presences in her poems, human and divine, are sons of this father–Father. As I have argued elsewhere,[7] the abiding drama of her poetry lies in her long psychological contention with the masculine principle: the figure of the man-God within her mind who constituted at one and the same time a threat to her womanhood and a potentiality within herself for the full realization of her womanhood. Her personal conclusion was that she could achieve personal wholeness only by avoiding entangling masculine relationships for the sake of the sacred marriage to the man within; the inner life seemed to exact the sacrifice of her biological womanhood. As a poet, Dickinson strategically adopted the role of the saucy, disobedient daughter, but never the mother's role; there was no contradiction between her brother Austin's underscoring of the words "never married" on her death certificate and the "wife" and "marriage" poems. As a poem written about 1860 indicates, she strove to become her own "Czar" in order to become "Wife" and "Woman" within herself.[8] Her sense of the jeopardy of her situation made her dissociate the functions of poet and mother and determined the life choices that confirmed her a spinster under her father's roof.

In the next half-century, Marianne Moore and Hilda Doolittle are paired by their differences as well as their connections. Briefly undergraduates together at Bryn Mawr in 1904, they are by consensus the two most important women poets of their time, and both achieved the public notice that Dickinson had to wait for, too late, posthumously. Both were associated with the new experimentation spearheaded by Imagism – Moore in New York, H. D. abroad – and both earned early the respect of their male colleagues. H. D.'s 1916 remark about Moore sounds, not surprisingly, like Ezra Pound on William Carlos Williams: "She is fighting in her country a battle against squalor and commercialism. We are all fighting the same battle. And we must strengthen each other in this one absolute bond – our devotion to the beautiful English language."[9] Moore's first volume of poems was a slim selection made by H. D. (with Bryher and Robert McAlmon) for publication in England in 1921. But the two were actually very different women – and poets. In the literary New York of Williams and Hart Crane and Waldo Frank, Marianne Moore played the keen-eyed, exacting, but somewhat fey and eccentric spinster, withdrawing to Brooklyn where she lived with her mother and was a pillar of the local Presbyterian church. H. D.'s connection with Pound and Richard Aldington at the inception of Imagism was romantic as well as literary: she and Pound had been engaged to be married; she followed Pound to England and defied parental wishes by deciding to stay when Pound took her writing seriously; when she married Aldington in 1913, at the height of the Imagist association, Pound stood as witness.

In fact, in their differences, Moore's and H. D.'s public careers dramatize the still-unresolved dilemma at the heart of Dickinson's situation as a female poet. Like Dickinson in her white dress and snood, Miss Moore, as she came to be (and wanted to be) called, dressed to a calculated self-image: prim braids tight-coiled around her head, odd tricornered hat, proper gloves, old-fashioned cape. In her wry meditation on "Marriage"[10] she wondered:

> what Adam and Eve
> think of it by this time,
> this fire-gilt steel
> alive with goldenness;
> how bright it shows –
> "of circular traditions and impostures,
> committing many spoils,"
> requiring all one's criminal ingenuity
> to avoid!

But in contrast to the reclusive "Miss Emily," "Miss Moore" ventured from her Brooklyn retreat to the male literary world of Manhattan and became a redoubtable presence, expert in wielding her shy reserve as a defensive weapon. Eventually she even became a popular figure on campuses and on television, chatting with winning modesty while giving nothing away.

By nature and choice she was an oddity among the Modernists, but a much admired oddity. The distinctive quality of her diction and metaphors and the inventiveness of her irregular syllabic stanzas drew praise from Symboliste and Imagist alike – Stevens and Williams, Eliot and Pound. But the eccentric mannerisms of her poetry expressed a religious orthodoxy of a straight-laced and fundamental kind. The blending of exact descriptive detail and aphorisms exhibited a religious sensibility that was allegorical and emblematic and moralistic rather than mystical, like H. D.'s religious sensibility. The direct presentation of Moore's often surprising observations and associations and the commonsensical prosiness of her wonder at flora and fauna reflect her plain conviction that the world requires the most scrupulous inspection because in its myriad complexity are refracted the truths and lessons essential to human wisdom and conduct. The poem which begins "The mind is an enchanting thing" immediately amends the statement to "The mind is an enchanted thing." The enchantment is struck reciprocally in the interchange between subject and object. Marianne Moore's central premise is that the bedazzlement of mind by sense is "trued by regnant certainty."[11]

At the same time, the terms on which Moore negotiated her life and art precluded large areas of experience and of personal expression. Describing the dancer Arthur Mitchell, she said that the function of art was at once to reveal and veil.[12] She dissected the interpenetration of mind and eye, but her heart and psyche she reserved as matters not open for inspection. The harshest statement of Moore's limitations – overstatement really – is in Gilbert Sorrentino's review of her *Complete Poems*: "As Miss Moore continually faced a world that frightened her, except in its more eccentric delights, mostly bookish, she falsified her language.... The poet failed as her language failed, and her language failed because she shut out the real."[13] In his advocacy of a Williamsesque engagement with the uglier, grittier aspects of contemporaneity, Sorrentino will not grant the terms within which Moore's poems work successfully. Williams would not let what he regarded as her fastidiousness undermine his respect for the precision and sheen of her poetry despite his more empirical, less didactic form of Imagism. When Moore berated Williams for the pastoral in *Paterson IV*, which recounts the lesbian lust of Corydon and the heterosexual lust of Dr. P. for Phyllis the city nymph, he did not protest; he must have expected it.

We do not know what H. D. thought of Williams' pastoral, but her objections would have been different from Moore's. She might well have considered it crude and banal, but in contrast to Moore, she excluded no area of her experience from consideration. In fact, she so exclusively made her consciousness the matrix of her art, as did Dickinson, that her poetry and fiction cannot be understood in their sources and impulse unless they are read autobiographically and psychologically. If Marianne Moore recalls the maidenly Dickinson, whose senses attended on natural curiosities as clues to further mysteries, H. D. harks back, by contrast, to the Dickinson of the love poems and the wife poems – but with a distinguishing difference. H. D.

was willing to risk herself, more personally than Dickinson chose, to that contention with the masculine other in love and death which Dickinson confined to her own psyche. As a result, H. D. celebrated, more flamboyantly and heterodoxly than Dickinson, the status she attained thereby as priestess and oracle and goddess.

The difference between Moore and H. D. as artists corresponds, in part, to a distinction Adrienne Rich made between the "feminine" and the "female": the feminine settling for the "secondary role" assigned to women artists and confining herself to expressing "amenity," "elegance," and a "genius for decoration"; and the female, by contrast, exhibiting a "form of potency" commensurate with that of the male artist. Rich cites Moore and Edith Sitwell as instances of the feminine; Sappho and Louise Labé as instances of the female.[14] Robert Duncan contrasted Moore and H. D. on much the same grounds and explained the willingness of the male establishment to tender Moore readier acknowledgment than H. D. by the fact that Moore's poetry did not conjure the "specter of the female will to trouble [the male] idea of woman's genius": "So, Marianne Moore in her modestly claiming no more than an honest craft was commended and even admired, but H. D. or Dame Edith Sitwell, writing in the personae of the inspired seer, pretenders to the throne of Poetry that gives voice to divine will in an age which mistrusts even the metaphor, excited contempt" from academic poet-critics like Randall Jarrell, Richard Wilbur, and Dudley Fitts.[15]

The fact that Rich and Duncan associate Sitwell with opposite poles of the dichotomy remind us how subjective and selective the basis of particular critical estimates can be. Nevertheless, the terms serve to make a clarifying distinction which helps to define H. D.'s special achievement among women poets – a distinction not just between conceptions of the poet's function but also between the precedent notions of moral stance and the consequent notions of the function of form and language. Thus, for Duncan, "Marianne Moore is a master of poetry that is periodic in its concept – as if art were a convention – which has its counterpart in her concern for social conformities, in her admiration for rigor, for the survival of vitality where character-armor takes over to resist areas of experience that cannot be included in the imagined social contract of poetry." A structure of periodic stanzas is, in Duncan's view, "inorganic":

> Once the stanza is set, there is no further form, no further "experience," realized in its extension. The number of stanzas is arbitrary. The poem presents examples of itself. . . . The form of the whole, in conventional verse, does not rest in the fulfillment of or growth of its parts toward the revelation of their "life" but in the illustration of the taste and arbitration of the poet. . . . The very crux of the poem is its mechanical expertness.

Duncan's own inclinations lean so much the other way that although he genuinely admires Moore's accomplishment, especially in the earlier verse, he finds it "not creative but exemplary in form" (as it was emblematic in content). By contrast, he links H. D. with his other great masters, Pound and

Williams, as poets whose vital, organic conception of poetry directed them to "move in their work through phases of growth," so that the work came to enact a "process of rebirth, of an evolving apprehension of form in [the] work." The profound development which the late *Cantos*, *Paterson* and *Pictures from Brueghel*, the *Trilogy* and *Helen in Egypt* constitute was possible, Duncan argues, only for someone "whose poetry had come to be a 'life' work,"[16] whose work, in other words, was not illustrative like Moore's but constitutive of its own moral and psychological exploration.

In various ways, therefore, Moore and H. D. posed alternative choices for American women poets after Emily Dickinson – alternatives that, in broad terms, obtained until the feminism of the 1970s. Thus, for instance, Elizabeth Bishop and Jean Garrigue followed Marianne Moore in skirting or masking autobiography to record observations with a fine discrimination of eye and word, but their observations lacked the moral and religious vision which enlarged and enlivened Moore's play with the intricacies of form and language. On the other side, what distinguished H. D. from such other chroniclers of the heart as Edna St. Vincent Millay and Elinor Wylie is the rapt assurance of her self-concern, which invested her lines with the translucent energy of "the inspired seer."

And that culmination was made possible, as we shall see, by the painful process of assimilating the father and the lover within the rediscovery of the poet as mother.

II

As Pound and H. D. conceived Imagism, verbal precision was the consequence and expression of a more incisive and dynamic way of seeing; the psyche of the poet was the matrix of the Image. In defining the Image in terms of an "intellectual and emotional complex in an instant of time," Pound explicitly indicated that he was employing "complex" in the new usage of the psychologists, and later he explained that "In a Station of the Metro" recorded "the precise instant when a thing outward and objective transforms itself, or darts into a thing inward and subjective."[17] It may be true that there is very little Imagist verse in this strict sense, even by Pound and H. D., but Pound did invoke the epithet "Imagiste" to designate to Harriet Monroe and the readers of *Poetry* what was revolutionary and distinctive about H. D.'s quality of Image, and in the subsequent scuffling with Amy Lowell over the direction of the Imagist movement, Pound was attempting, in part, to preserve this special sense of the Image as psychological gestalt or epiphany from the usual sense of image as sense impression or vivid metaphor. Something of the difference between Imagism and what Pound dubbed "Amygism" can be seen in the juxtaposition of one of Lowell's "imagistic" poems with H. D.'s much anthologized "Oread." First, Lowell's "Wind and Silver":

> Greatly shining,
> The Autumn moon floats in the thin sky;
> And the fish-ponds shake their backs and flash their dragon scales
> As she passes over them.[18]

The metaphor which associates the moonlit pond with the scaly back of a dragon is dramatic and effective, but it does not achieve the transfusion of elements which makes "Oread" remarkable:

> Whirl up, sea –
> whirl your pointed pines,
> splash your great pines
> on our rocks,
> hurl your green over us,
> cover us with your pools of fir.[19]

The poem makes us see sea as forest, forest as sea; the association between forest and sea is so complete that the poem does not so much develop a metaphor or even a metaphysical conceit as present a new world charged with the energy of its metamorphic manifestation. It is not a matter of figurative description but of a transfigurative act of seeing. Williams' "The Red Wheelbarrow," for all its precise observation, would not be an Imagist poem by this narrowly defined criterion, but "Flowers by the Sea" would be:

> When over the flowery, sharp pasture's
> edge, unseen, the salt ocean
>
> lifts its form – chicory and daisies
> tied, released, seem hardly flowers alone
>
> but color and the movement – or the shape
> perhaps – of restlessness, whereas
>
> the sea is circled and sways
> peacefully upon its plantlike stem.[20]

Even when Imagist poems did not really conform to this particular kind of synthesis or synesthesia, they were striving for a penetrating kind of seeing which made sight insight. Robert Duncan is maintaining the Pound–Williams heritage when he contends that the image is not a sensation or impression but an "evocation of depth,...partly conscious and partly unconscious," which does not merely illustrate the appearances of objects but constitutes an experience conveying the "reciprocity of inner and outer realities."[21] Joseph Riddel correctly perceives H. D.'s "Greek" poems as psychological landscapes expressive of emotional states.[22] She did not visit Greece or the Mediterranean until 1920, and the details of the early poetry are, in part, recollections of the Atlantic shoreline she had known in summers as a girl.[23]

The point about the nature of the Image may seem to blur the working distinction in these chapters between Symbolisme and Imagism, but in fact it reinforces the distinction. How, then, is the Image's expression of the "reciprocity of inner and outer realities" different from the tendency of Symbolisme, as Stevens acknowledged and as Eliot came to admit in "From Poe to Valéry," to subvert the integrity of objects and reduce them to mental impressions capable of ever more subtle and invented combinations? But in fact, the historical argument of this book rests on the significant difference – and the significance of the difference – between, say, H. D.'s dream world and

Stevens'. The Imagist does not blindly overlook the dynamic, even determining function of the psyche in the act of perception; no aware person after
Kant could. But the Imagist was much closer to the Romantic than to the
Symboliste in assuming a creative interdependence and interchange between
subject and object as the essential act of perception. The spiraling subjectivity
of Symbolisme represented the implosion of Romantic epistemology. But
whereas Imagism adopted a Modernist stance to clear away Romantic
metaphysics which seemed to make for egoism and for an increasingly soft
clutter of self-indulgent rhetoric, its epistemological aim was more Romantic
than its founders, in the midst of their anti-idealist polemics, could recognize.
The Imagist instinctively resists the surrender of objects to the inventions and
impositions of the disintegrative, reintegrative mind because, in Duncan's
words again, Imagism is grounded in "the belief that meaning is not given to
the world about us but derived from the world about us." For Imagists like
Pound and H. D. (herein, too, lay Lawrence's connections with Imagism) the
psychological "complex" which the Image registers remains a genuine
"sign," which carries "into human language a word or phrase (in Pound's later
poetics, the ideogram; in H. D.'s the hieroglyph) of the great language in
which the universe itself is written."[24]

A naturalist like Williams (or Lawrence) tended to shy away from and even
deny the metaphysical implications of the Imagist epistemology, but Duncan
rightly argues that for H. D. and Pound the psychological "nexus" of the
Image was "not unrelated to the neo-Platonic Images, to idea and eidolon."
Thus poems like Pound's "The Tree" and "A Virginal" and H. D.'s "Oread"
and "Garden" are "addressed to a natural force in a world in which inner and
outer nature were one." The poems in H. D.'s first three books – *Sea Garden*
(1915), *Hymen* (1921), and *Heliodora* (1924), gathered into the 1925 *Collected
Poems* –

> ...gave presence to, and were aroused by a presence in, rocks and sea,
> thunderous surfs, gardens and orchards exposed or sheltered....The line of
> her verse grew taut,...tensed to provide a mode in which reverberations of
> these presences might be heard. The image and the voice or dramatic persona
> provided a nexus in poetry corresponding to the outer and inner worlds in
> which she worked towards higher and finer modes.[25]

From the beginning, then, when all three were together in Philadelphia,
H. D. shared more with Pound than with Williams; they aspired to a poetry in
which "cosmic powers appear as presences and even as persons in inner being
to the imagination." Such a poetry is avowedly phenomenological and
archetypal, and its expressive form is evolutionary and organic: what Denise
Levertov described in H. D. as "the music of word-sounds and the rhythmic
structure built of them."[26] Those qualities of language which earned H. D. the
reputation of being the most consistent, the purest, the most crystalline of the
Imagists were linked, therefore, to a cosmology that looked back through the
Romantics to Plato, and her sense of nature and of the psyche was, like

Pound's, polytheistic. In some of her early poems the gods do not even have to be named because they are the speakers; "Pursuit" might be the words of Apollo on the trail of Daphne, and "Huntress" might be Diana's challenge to Actaeon.

Platonists resort to the polyglot of language because they know the silent One only in the clamor of the many; their polytheistic myths confabulate their experience of difference and so of conflict in nature and the psyche. Consequently the archetypal "Greece" of the *Sea Garden* is no harmonious Arcadia but a world of violent extremes, all the more painful to nerve ends, like H. D.'s, so tinglingly acute that her skin winced at the sting of sand grains in the sea breeze. The poems in that first book present a landscape divided into lush orchard and harsh sea, noon heat and biting wind, soft loam and bruising stone; the individual is caught in the contending elements, and in the strife of love and war for which the elemental strife serves as image.

The connection between love and war constitutes a sexual politics which draws these seemingly objective and descriptive lyrics into a psychological sequence. Thomas Swann has pointed to the tension between H. D.'s pagan and "classical" indulgence in sensual pleasure and her "Puritan" fear of physical passion.[27] The erotic details of "Orchard" present a world humming with a sexual force from which the poet seeks protection ("spare us from loveliness") because its seductions betray and overwhelm her: leave her "prostrate" before the depradations of the sexual male, personified in the "rough-hewn god of the orchard" (the poem was originally entitled "Priapus"):

> I saw the first pear
> as it fell –
> the honey-seeking, golden-banded,
> the yellow swarm
> was not more fleet than I,
> (spare us from loveliness)
> and I fell prostrate
> crying:
> you have flayed us
> with your blossoms,
> spare us the beauty
> of fruit-trees.
>
> The honey-seeking
> paused not,
> the air thundered their song,
> and I alone was prostrate.
>
> O rough-hewn
> god of the orchard,
> I bring you an offering –
> do you, alone unbeautiful,
> son of the god,
> spare us from loveliness:

these fallen hazel-nuts,
stripped late of their green sheaths,
grapes, red-purple,
their berries
dripping with wine,
pomegranates already broken,
and shrunken figs
and quinces untouched,
I bring you as offering.[28]

Her susceptibility to sensual pleasure has precipitated her downfall, and the irony of the final lines is that the only offering she has with which to placate her ravisher – the split, female fruits of the earth – merely concedes her ravishment. As sacrificial victim she is her own offering: stripped and fallen hazel-nuts, bleeding grapes, pomegranates crushed and gaping, at once virgin quince and wrinkled fig.

"Sheltered Garden" begins: "I have had enough. / I gasp for breath." The garden's excessive and smothering sweetness drives her to long for the sting of pain and danger:

O for some sharp swish of a branch –
. . . .
O to blot out this garden
to forget, to find a new beauty
in some terrible
wind-tortured place.

Her "torn, twisted" condition would at least testify that "the fight was valiant." In "Mid-Day" she feels beaten, startled, anguished, defeated, spent, torn, scattered, shriveled, split, and aspires to the deep-rootedness of the heroic poplar erect atop the hill.[29]

No wonder that in other poems her imagination shrinks away from the orchard to the sea:

another life holds what this lacks
a sea, unmoving, quiet –
not forcing our strength
to rise to it, beat on beat –
a stretch of sand,
no garden beyond, strangling
with its myrrh-lilies –
a hill, not set with black violets
but stones, stones, bare rocks,
dwarf-trees, twisted, no beauty
to distract – to crowd
madness upon madness.[30]

Both the garden and the sea are feminine worlds, but in the *hortus inclosus* the feminine flowers are open to violation by the superior priapic power. The sea, by contrast, however, represents a feminine force superior to the garden's soft

allure, superior even to the strength of mortal men. Still, when H. D. spurns
the predatory male's enclosed garden for the open water, it is not in identification but in contention with the mother sea. So stormy is that anonymous
expanse that she takes ship not as daughter but as seaman testing fate with his
fellows.

> Though oak-beams split,
> though boats and sea-men flounder,
> and the strait grind sand with sand
> and cut boulders to sand and drift –

she takes her place with the men aboard ship, and as "The Helmsman" she sets
out on the waves whose rhythms suggest sexuality and death as the double-
challenge and double-doom:

> We were enchanted with the fields,
> the tufts of coarse grass
> in the shorter grass –
> we loved all this.
>
> But now, our boat climbs – hesitates – drops –
> climbs – hesitates – crawls back –
> climbs – hesitates –
> O be swift –
> we have always known you wanted us.[31]

But better still than the ships is the shoreline between garden and sea. In
"The Shrine" H. D. chooses as her goddess the one who "watches over the
sea," the "spirit between the headlands / and the further rocks." On the
wavering line where land meets sea, if anywhere, beauty and strength can
meet. "Beauty without strength chokes out life," but the "new beauty" of the
"wind-tortured place" would be sinewy, tensed and tempered by adversity.[32]
In other poems, too, the "new beauty" takes on masculine associations; for
survival, the woman too required the endurance of the helmsman, the athlete,
the warrior. Her friend Bryher described H. D. as "the most beautiful figure
that I have ever seen in my life, with a face that came directly from a Greek
statue and, almost to the end, the body of an athlete," and H. D. gave as an
ideal of beauty the "male torso" described in "The Contest":

> Your stature is modelled
> with straight tool-edge:
> you are chiselled like rocks
> that are eaten into by the sea.
>
> With the turn and grasp of your wrist
> and the chords' stretch,
> there is a glint like worn brass.
>
> The ridge of your breast is taut,
> and under each the shadow is sharp,
> and between the clenched muscles
> of your slender hips.

From the circle of your cropped hair
there is light,
and about your male torso
and the foot-arch and the straight ankle.[33]

A hard-chiseled beauty is less susceptible to being cut and torn. In fact, its clean lines and planes, even amid garden lushness, display the sharp edge of stone and metal. The complementary parts of the much anthologized poem "Garden" first give the rose the invulnerability of rock and then invoke the wind to cut through the erotic heat spell:

I
You are clear
O rose, cut in rock,
hard as the descent of hail.

I could scrape the colour
from the petals
like spilt dye from a rock.

If I could break you
I could break a tree.

If I could stir
I could break a tree –
I could break you.

II
O wind, rend open the heat,
cut apart the heat,
rend it to tatters.

Fruit cannot drop
through this thick air –
fruit cannot fall into heat
that presses up and blunts
the points of pears
and rounds the grapes.

Cut the heat –
plough through it,
turning it on either side
of your path.[34]

Throughout these early poems the word "cut" recurs again and again: the survival of a strong beauty requires the capacity both for cutting and for sustaining cuts.

So, when she is not at sea with the sailors, the stony ridges of the windswept coast become her place, and her woman's emblem is not the sheltered flower but the "Sea Rose," "Sea Lily," "Sea Poppies," "Sea Iris."[35] Their scarred tenacity is "more precious" than the dewy, spicy fragility of the cultivated bloom. They make the coast a *Sea Garden*:

Rose, harsh rose,
marred and with stint of petals,

> meagre flower, thin,
> sparse of leaf,
>
> more precious
> than a wet rose
> single on a stem –
> you are caught in the drift.
>
> Stunted, with small leaf,
> you are flung on the sand,
> you are lifted
> in the crisp sand
> that drives in the wind.
>
> Can the spice-rose
> drip such acrid fragrance
> hardened in a leaf?

The violence endured by the sea lily is overmatched by her own endurance and ensures her triumph:

> though the whole wind
> slash at your bark,
> you are lifted up,
> aye–though it hiss
> to cover you with froth.

III

The descriptive lyrics of *Sea Garden*, then, present psychologically charged landscapes. The thrill and threat of sexuality inform most of the poems in the next two volumes, *Hymen* and *Heliodora*, as well. Several poems celebrate sexual love as harmonious and ecstatic union: "Hymen," "Leda," "Evadne," "Song," "Holy Satyr"; but a larger number portray the woe of the woman in love – dependent, cast off, wracked with longing: "Demeter," "Circe," "Cuckoo Song," "The Islands," "At Baia," "Phaedra," and numbers 40, 41, and 68 of the re-created Sapphic fragments. Again and again, susceptibility to sexual love is weighed against the vulnerability of virgin chastity: "Hippolytus Temporizes," the Phaedra poems "She Contrasts Herself with Hippolyta" and "She Rebukes Hippolyta," "Cassandra," "Wash of Cold River" (placed next to "Holy Satyr" for contrast). In "Telesila" Aphrodite is in conflict first with the chaste Athene and then with Ares, the martial aggressor, and in "Fragment 68" the lover is again cast as a soldier.

Even the aesthetic sphere demonstrates woman's subordination: "Heliodora" is only the muse memorialized in the poetry of competing men, and "Pygmalion" is the sculptor of his Galatea. But even oppressed women have their own resources. In "Eurydice" (which is placed just after "Pygmalion"), the wife of the singing Orpheus turns her tragedy into triumph: lost to the world of light and consigned to Hades through her husband's "arrogance" and "ruthlessness," Eurydice becomes a type of the woman artist, finding in her deprivation transformative powers superior to his:

Against the black
I have more fervour
than you in all the splendour of that place,
against the blackness
and the stark grey
I have more light;

. . . . .

I have the fervour of myself for a presence
and my own spirit for light;

and my spirit with its loss
knows this;
though small against the black
small against the formless rocks,
hell must break before I am lost;

before I am lost,
hell must open like a red rose
for the dead to pass.[36]

These lines lack the verbal concision of H. D.'s best early verses, but they are forceful because in them the autobiographical basis for all of these poems presses close to the surface. *Sea Garden* was published in the midst of World War I, two years after H. D.'s marriage to Richard Aldington, and all three early volumes, gathered together under the premature title *Collected Poems* in the mid-1920s, proceeded directly from a steady succession of shocks and defeats: love and marriage threatened by war far from family and country; Aldington's service as an army officer in France; his anxiety, his possible shell shock in the trenches, and his compulsive sexual infidelities, which kept the marriage in constant strain during his brief leaves from the front; H. D.'s miscarriage in 1915, which botched her first attempt at biological motherhood; the death of her favorite brother at the front in 1918; after hesitations and reunions, the final, agonized break with Aldington late in 1918 or in 1919, which left her exhausted and pregnant with another man's child; the 1918 epidemic, which infected her with pneumonia during her solitary last weeks of pregnancy and threatened the life of mother and child; the survival of both, against doctors' prognostications, after the birth of Frances Perdita in March 1919; her father's fatal stroke the same year out of grief for his son; through it all, physical separation from the mother from whom she had felt psychologically alienated since childhood. And, amid the gathering doom, as late in 1918 she awaited birth and death, the unexpected advent of a determined and devoted young English woman named Winifred Ellerman, who renamed herself Bryher after one of the wind-swept Scilly Islands and wanted to be a poet like her idol, H. D. Bryher unhesitatingly rescued and cared for mother and then daughter, and the wealth of her tycoon father provided the means for Bryher to carry them off at last to Greece in the spring of 1920.

Such a barrage of traumatic experiences might have shattered the most phlegmatic of people, let alone someone of H. D.'s sensitivity, always on the verge of splintering under the intensity of stress. It is no exaggeration that H. D. spent her imaginative life living over and living through those familial and marital crises, untangling the snarled skein again and again to weave fictional and mythological patterns in which she might wring from the convulsions of her experience some integration of herself as a woman, poet, and mother. The story needs to be told fully to supplement the versions H. D. gave in her fiction. When she later told Sigmund Freud about it in analysis, however, the professor was confident that he was identifying the central clue to her life when he told her that Greece represented for her the lost and longed-for mother upon whose recovery depended the daughter's identity and destiny as a woman. Hilda's mother's name was Helen, like Poe's famous Helen as well as Homer's, a Greco-American hybrid, as H. D. herself admitted: "I was physically in Greece, in Hellas (Helen). I had come home to the glory that was Greece."[37]

Bryher provided the entrée to Dr. Freud in Vienna through her own analyst, Hans Sacks, one of the doctor's disciples. H. D. had already consulted other analysts, including Havelock Ellis and Sacks himself. But in her account of the sessions with Freud, she said that she needed to seek him out in order "to sort out, relive, and reassemble the singular series of events and dreams that belonged in historical time to the 1914–1919 period" – the years she called "my actual personal war-shock."[38] The resolution of "my own problems" lay, she already felt, in "my own intense, dynamic interest in the unfolding of the unconscious or the subconscious pattern," and she conceived the unconscious in terms so far beyond Freud's that her words about Freud might better apply to Jung's notion of the concentricity of the personal and collective unconscious. (She would say much later that she saw no conflict between Freud and Jung, her near neighbor during her last years in Küsnacht, Switzerland.) Here are H. D.'s words from *Tribute to Freud*:

> He had dared to say that the dream came from an unexplored depth in man's consciousness and that this unexplored depth ran like a great stream or ocean underground, and the vast depth of that ocean was the same vast depth that to-day, as in Joseph's day, overflowing in man's small consciousness, produced inspiration, madness, creative idea or the dregs of the dreariest symptoms of mental unrest and disease. He had dared to say that it was the same ocean of universal consciousness, and even if not stated in so many words, he had dared to imply that this consciousness proclaimed all men one; all nations and races met in the universal world of the dream; and he had dared to say that the dream-symbol could be interpreted; its language, its imagery were common to the whole race, not only of the living but of those ten thousand years dead. The picture-writing, the hieroglyph of the dream, was the common property of the whole race.[39]

H. D. spent about three or four months in analysis with Freud, five days a week, beginning in March 1933, and about five more weeks beginning in December 1934. She regretted that before she could delve farther into the traumas of the Great War years, her sessions with Freud were interrupted by the Nazi activity in Austria, foreshadowing another world war. According to the account in *Tribute to Freud*, written in 1944 as that war turned at last toward defeat for the Nazis, she talked to Freud principally about her early years in America and about certain crucial dream and visionary experiences, but the major fictions published during her lifetime – *Palimpsest* (1926), *Hedylus* (1928), *Bid Me to Live (A Madrigal)* (1960, but written just before and after World War II in 1939 and 1948) – deal with the marital and emotional crises of the war years. H. D.'s fiction, therefore, provides an unparalleled context for a psychological and archetypal account of her poetry.

Palimpsest introduced the technique that H. D. would employ in her subsequent fiction: an extreme impressionism which explores point of view, with virtually no plot or action and only a very few closely related characters. The overriding concern is the sensibility of the protagonist, invariably a persona for H. D., and the nuances of the prose hover and shimmer about certain decisive yet indecipherable words, gestures, perceptions. Impressionism was, of course, the mode of experimental fiction in the literary London of James and Conrad, Pound and Ford, and it was in fact to H. D., along with Aldington and Brigid Patmore, that Ford Madox Ford dictated the text of *The Good Soldier*. H. D. acknowledged that her stories all concerned the same woman – herself – and a letter of 1922 noted that her impressionistic technique had been compared to the late manner of Henry James.[40]

The three novellas in *Palimpsest*,[41] set in different times and places, illustrate H. D.'s abiding conviction, implied in the title, that all experience, personal and historical, is a record of overlaid levels and layers – the present inscribed on the past, the past visible in the latest script. The consciousnesses of the three female protagonists compose H. D.'s palimpsest. *Hipparchia*, the first novella, uses what will become a repeated strategy of linking the heroine to the author through the initial letter of her name. A Greek woman carried off to Rome by the conquering legions, she has survived in exile by surrendering herself as mistress to a blunt, physical, sexual officer named Marius Decius, a thinly disguised version of Aldington posturing in Roman garb. Hipparchia establishes the type of later H. D. personae: tall, handsome, angular, somewhat careless about fashion and dress, exquisitely sensitive, and perceived as frigid by the predatory and aggressive male. The Greek homeland is the lost ideal by which the modernity of Rome is measured and found to be tawdry and materialistic. In her economic and sexual bondage to Decius, Hipparchia harkens back obsessively to the "family problem" which afflicted her even before exile.

The autobiographical parallels are unmistakable. Hipparchia's "dour" father, Crates, is a "professional pedagogue" (69). Charles Doolittle had been a professor of mathematics and astronomy at Lehigh University in Bethlehem, Pennsylvania, where Hilda had been born, and later at the University of Pennsylvania in Philadelphia. His profession had been consonant with his rationalist philosophy of life; his intellectual and academic career had taken precedence over all else at home – not just the children's lives but also the talents of his wife, Helen, as an artist and musician. Indeed, it had been her role to make the domestic routine conform smoothly to his professional regimen. The fictional mother, also named Hipparchia (the *H*s of their names also linked Hilda to Helen, for all of the psychological distance between daughter and mother), disappointed the daughter by subjecting herself to patriarchal demands and withholding herself from her children. Consequently, the young Hipparchia's emotional life came to center on her foster uncle, Philip, who was like an adored older brother (reminiscent of Hilda's brother Gilbert). Caught now in the toils of Marius' sexuality, she regresses to the virginal love she shared with him; their "intimacy without intercourse" (74) offered spiritual union without physical violation.

Marius turns from Hipparchia's neurasthenia to the ready pleasures of Olivia's bed. (*Bid Me to Live* would give a more direct rendering of Aldington's crass rejection of H. D. for Dorothy Yorke, with whom he had an affair under their very roof.) Hipparchia retaliates by going to live with Verrus beside the sea in Capua (as Julia in *Bid Me to Live* would leave the Aldington character to live in Cornwall with a man called Vane, Cecil Gray in real life). At first, Hipparchia is happy because Verrus makes no demands on her; she is free to haunt the coast and allow the sea and air to soothe her anguished spirit. But before long his effete passivity comes to seem like weakness, and the ideal Philip, slain by the Romans (recalling Gilbert's war death), eclipses the two live men in her fevered imagination. Consequently, Hipparchia leaves Verrus and settles in a place near Rome, where, "wedded" (74) in her mind to Philip's memory and inspired by his animus presence, she throws herself with feverish abandon into completing his book on Greece. She hopes thereby to find herself by synthesizing, through Philip, religion, poetry, and ethics, but the mental strain of her compulsion, complicated by a fever, brings Hipparchia close to madness and death. A rich young woman named Julia Augusta Cornelia, who is an ardent admirer of Hipparchia's poetry about Greece, finds her in this desperate state (much as Bryher found H. D. in the Ealing boardinghouse in 1918) and dedicates her will and her father's funds to the rescue of her idol.

Hipparchia has expected redemption from her god, Helios (because of the opening *H*, H. D. almost always referred to Apollo as Helios). She discovered that Helios was not to be found in either Marius or Verrus (they "had cut her doubly from herself," p. 92) or in the ghost of the slain Philip. Instead, "Helios, god of colonists" (93), sent Julia Augusta as his emissary to save Hipparchia's life and deliver her back to Greece. Bryher's memoir recorded that when H. D., strangling with pneumonia in Ealing, said fiercely, "If I could walk to Delphi, I should be healed," her spontaneous response was: "I will take you to Greece as soon as you are well";[42] and that act sealed their lifelong association. In the final words of the story, Hipparchia admits to her benefactress that Greece is not so much a place as a psychological state: "*Greece is a spirit. Greece is not lost. I will come with you*" (94). There she might recover herself as she re-created Greece in her poems.

"Murex," the second novella in *Palimpsest*, takes place in a single long afternoon and evening in London in 1926 during which Raymonde Ransome is made to relive the crisis that ended her marriage in London almost a decade before. Raymonde is an expatriate American poet whose *nom de plume* is abbreviated to Ray Bart. The name establishes the animus basis for her sense of genius; she associates the part of her that is Ray Bart with a "sword of pure steel," and especially with a visionary "helmet" (148) that descends upon her head when she is inspired to write. (In *Notes on Thought and Vision*, a notebook kept in 1919 and published in 1983, H. D. describes the experience of special states of elevated consciousness as a cap that comes down over her head and forehead, affecting her vision so that she sees things clearly but as if under water.) During the war, Raymonde lost her soldier husband Freddie to Mavis Landour (Brigit Patmore, with whom Aldington had an extended affair) while she lay in the hospital, weak and distraught after the miscarriage of the baby Freddie never wanted.

Raymonde has carefully repressed her recollection of this betrayal until she receives an unwanted visit from a young woman named Ermentrude Solomon, whose husband was killed during the war and whose lover, Martin, has recently been seduced and won away by this same Mavis ten years after Raymonde's grievance. Just as Freddie and Martin represent different aspects of H. D.'s complaints against Aldington, so Ermentrude represents to Raymonde/H. D. her own shadow. The long Jamesian conversation between the two women ends with Ermy's plea that Raymonde avenge them both by seducing Martin away from Mavis. Shaken by Ermy's directness, Raymonde refuses; but in her solitary reverie in the London dusk, she faces the episode at last and reconciles herself to Freddie, Mavis, and her former self. Raymonde demonstrates her resolve by declining a telephone invitation from Mavis to the country place which Mavis is sharing with Martin.

Raymonde's new psychological control issues cathartically in a series of poems, and the process of their emergence under Ray Bart's helmet is rendered in compelling detail. The episode deliberately recalls Stephen Dedalus' coming to poetic expression at the end of *Portrait of the Artist as a Young Man*. Joyce was right, Raymonde thinks, in trying to recover the magic lost to art in modern times. Magic permitted the artist to see through the so-called real world into the reality of the eternal values for which antiquity is a symbol, to see through the turbulent surface, through the distorting opacity of the "jellyfish" of modernity, to the abiding presences of antiquity (158). Thereby pain and hurt are healed to peace and love. To her own repeated question, "Who fished the murex up?" comes the recognition that her "verses were the murex," "her own treasure" (160) brought to consciousness from forgotten or denied deeps.

Under "Helios the god of necromancy" (162) the words verified the old moral values: not just the negative prohibitions of the Ten Commandments but also Jesus' affirmative injunction to love even your enemies, which tallied with Helios' law of hospitality and taste, incised on the temple at Delphi. So in

Raymonde's imagination the Jewish Ermy is transformed into an Egyptian priestess, her futile vengefulness into "depths of Asiatic wisdom" (162). In the words of her poems Raymonde effects the conversion of her Old Testament and Puritan self, objectified in Ermy, into a hieratic figure at once Greek and Egyptian and Christian, capable of accepting, forgiving, even loving them all – her enemies and her old self. The last lines of her poems and of the novella link the three women together: "I love her [Mavis] / who has sent you [Ermy] to my door" (172).

The third and shortest of the novellas, "Secret Name," is situated in "Excavator's Egypt" around 1925. H. D. had traveled to Egypt with her mother and Bryher in 1923, fortuitously in time for the opening of Tutankhamun's tomb, and had visited the archeological site at Karnak. Her persona here is named Helen, an American classicist passionately committed to the "avid intellectuality" of Greek thought, who is touring Karnak with a young girl named Mary and Mary's mother. Helen, uneasy and unfulfilled, feels the need to balance "the self of intellect" with "the self of the drift and dream of anodyne" (209). Whereas Greece represents the aspiration of rational consciousness to godhead, the atmosphere of Egypt, mysterious and erotic, subverts selfhood and consciousness to the mysteries of darkness. (Much the same complementary contrast between Greece and Egypt would inform *Helen in Egypt*.)

The psychological issues are brought to a head by Helen's immediate infatuation with ex-captain Rafton, another Aldington character (compare Rafton to Rafe in *Bid Me to Live*). The question for Helen the Greek, now in Egypt, is whether Rafton is "just the most ordinary of ex-army captains" (cf. p. 224), just "some incredibly carnal Roman" (179; remember Marius Decius), or the man of her dreams, the manifestation of "the massive beautiful Theseus male form" (210), even of Zeus himself (219). "She wanted to dive deep, deep, courageously into some unexploited region of the consciousness, into some common deep sea of unrecorded knowledge and bring, triumphant, to the surface some treasure buried, lost, forgotten" (179): a murex like Raymonde's. Perhaps, as Rafton insisted, Greece must yield to Egypt. Under the magical moonlight of the temple at Karnak, Helen and Rafton find, almost miraculously, a little Greek-looking Nike shrine among the Egyptian ruins: a "tiny temple or tomb or birth-house" (214). Helen sinks so deeply into the maternal life rhythm below or above rational consciousness, in any case beyond it, that her woman's response to Rafton's male plea for care and nourishment – "you will look after me, won't you?" (218) – is acquiescence, a surrender that seems to enfold them together in the security of the Great Mother, "as if they in some strange exact and precious period of pre-birth, twins, lovers, were held, sheltered beneath some throbbing heart" (220).

In *Helen in Egypt*, Helen and Achilles would come to the point of resolution, but here the rational light of a fresh day convinces this Helen that the revelation had been a delusion, that she cannot surrender herself to Rafton. Returning to Karnak in sunlight, she cannot even find the little temple and feels only irritated condescension toward Mary's girlish flirtation with a callow young man named Jerry: "O Mary, do be practical. If you want Jerry, take him, and God-be-with-you, but don't go on linking superstitiously the idea of marriage with any chance intuition you may have had last night. Jerry caught you" (237). Ruefully, Helen resolves to remain uncaught and elects Greece over Egypt, even if the choice consigns her to her unsatisfied and divided self.

In the course of his discussion of H. D.'s writing as "the monologue of a self-occupied, high-strung woman," Vincent Quinn commends *Hedylus*[43] for at least freeing itself from the claustrophobia of the single point of view and attempting the counterpoint of two characters.[44] However, he fails to see that *Hedylus* is as autobiographical a book as *Palimpsest* because both Hedylus and his mother, Hedyle, represent aspects of H. D. herself; the consonantal sequence of *H* and *D* in their names is their signature. The novel opens and closes with the mother; the first sentence reads: "Hedyle of Athens let go the polished mirror." She is an aging beauty, "self-preoccupied" because of the loss of her father and mother, her exploitation by several men, and exile from her beloved Athens. A benumbed alienation makes her emotionally unresponsive to Douris, the tyrant of Samos, to whom she is hetaira, and even to Hedylus, the son who, beneath her undemonstrative manner, is the consuming focus of her life.

Her father is another version of Dr. Doolittle, whom H. D. recalled in *Tribute to Freud* poring over his "rows and rows of numbers," "columns and columns of numbers."[45] Hedyle aches for vision beyond his "arid pragmatism" (26). As a girl she wanted to believe in the gods, especially in Helios, as the manifestation of a supernal beauty and a transcendental reality. However, her father's remote but powerful presence and the death of her mother operated to seal her off and seal her in, so that now she is a coolly possessive and demanding mother of her own namesake, who is himself even more exiled from Athens and alienated from self than she, brooding on his lack of identity: "My mother is a goddess, she had me with a god. I am nameless, bearing her name" (33). Hedyle had a father and no mother; Hedylus has no father and a mother whose presence creates a vacuum. His problem is his lack of identity through his identification with the mother; hers is the reconciliation of her identity with her motherhood.

H. D. knew both dilemmas: both her father and her mother were, in different and unsettling ways, too present and too absent, dominating and disabling. Her father's study was the intellectual sanctum where she, as favorite daughter and so "in some way privileged" oedipally, was permitted to read silently while he sorted scholarly data at his desk. When she saw Freud's study in Vienna, it reminded her of her father's, even to the couch, even to the same Rembrandt engraving of a medical dissection on the walls of the two studies. She confessed to Freud a traumatic episode which involved her in a guilty association with her brother, in violation of her father's rules and of the sanctum of the study. Despite a prohibition against ever touching or disturbing anything on the desk, her brother had taken a magnifying glass to kindle, Prometheus-like, illicit fire; Hilda stood by as spectator until they were caught red-handed. The paternal rebuke vented itself not in anger but in "an icy chill" that froze the incident in her memory, even though she was herself only circumstantially "implicated, though in no way blamed."[46]

In fact, the authority and favor of the rationalist doctor father failed her deepest needs, for which her mother was the source and tally. Helen Wolle's family belonged to the Moravian Brotherhood, the inner-light Protestant sect which had migrated to America and founded Bethlehem, Hilda's birthplace. (She was to write a "Hymn" to Count Zinzendorf, patriarch of the Moravians, and leave an account of her Moravian roots in an autobiographical prose work called *The Gift*, published in abbreviated form in 1982.) Her father's rationalism was all he had left of his family's New England Puritanism, and though Freud was born in Moravia, his Judaism had given way to atheism. H. D.'s religious temperament came from her Moravian mother – and her aesthetic temperament as well: "I derive my imaginative faculties through my musician-artist mother."[47]

Helen, however, seemed to withhold herself from the daughter, who needed access to those sources. The wife's capitulation to the husband's scientific career, and her social circle in suburban academe, came between Helen and Hilda. H. D. remembers thinking, "The trouble is, she knows so many people and they come and interrupt. And besides that, she likes my brother better. If I stay with my brother, become part almost of my brother, perhaps I can get nearer to *her*." Through him, perhaps, she might win maternal blessing and favor, and yet she told Freud of a childhood incident in which her identification with the brother earned Helen's derisive amusement. He had snubbed his mother on the street and refused to come home, threatening instead to run away with his sister. When Hilda joined him in sitting defiantly on the curbstone, the mother laughed at them both. In H. D.'s memory, "she obtains supporters; strangers and near-strangers repeat her words like a Greek chorus, following the promptings of their leader." H. D. describes the different reactions of the children when Helen walked away from them seemingly abandoning them in disgrace:

> *He* knows that she will come back because he is older and is admittedly his mother's favorite. But *she* does not know this. But though her brain is in a turmoil of anxiety and pride and terror, it has not even occurred to her that she might throw her small weight into the balance of conventional behavior by following her mother and leaving her brother to his fate.[48]

H. D.'s deep ambivalence damned her either way. She needed Helen's nurturing: "*If* one could stay near her always, there would be no break in consciousness." But just as the girl chose defiance over the "conventional behavior" her mother seemed to expect, so the young woman made the break and chose independence over conformity. She loved Pound and his poetry, planned to marry him, followed him to London; she joined the expatriate poets, settled in literary London, and married Aldington, with Pound's blessing. But the rebel paid bitterly for her willfulness. By the end of the decade, everything had gone smash except the poetry. The family problems were snarled in the marital and sexual problems, as "Hipparchia" and *Hedylus* indicate. When H. D. sought Freud in Vienna in the 1930s, she wanted him to unravel this snarl by playing mother as well as father. It was his combination of aesthetic taste and scientific analysis that made her consider the professor "midwife to the soul." To her relief, upon arrival, his house and study felt like home: "The house in some indescribable way depends on father-mother. At the point of integration or regeneration, there is no conflict over rival loyalties."[49]

Tribute to Freud underscores the doubleness that ran through her sense of relationships: "There were two's and two's and two's in my life" – parents, brothers, half brothers, America and England, "two distinct racial or biological or psychological entities."[50] That sense of doubleness is written into Hedyle and Hedylus. They are a pair, motherless daughter of an authoritarian father who becomes possessive mother to her fatherless son: the parental and sexual dilemma compounded again. So locked are they in their unaddressed need that they seem less mother and son than "twins, lovers" (like Helen and Rafton in "Secret Name"). Hedyle will come to realize by the end that "we were too close, a single sort of being" (p. 136), and the paradox of the resolution is that only in separation can each approach integration and regeneration. Hedyle's bracelet of the snake biting its tail symbolizes the cyclic round of the uroboros, but it is only through dislocation that mother is fulfilled in son, that son lives out her dreams. Hedyle – hard mother and cold mistress, torn between head and heart, Athens and Aphrodite – has striven to bind her son to her will, reminding him of his "fall" years before, in which his head and, by implication, his identity had split open. The injury, she keeps telling him, has doomed him as a poet, and so his sudden plan to leave her and find his personal and poetic destiny with the young Irene is a ruinous decision. The novel, however, is written to bring them each separately to acknowledge that the child must break with the mother in an act of "primitive disobedience" (20) for the sake of both.

On one level, the enactment of this further "fall" of Hedylus is H. D.'s attempt to resolve the crucial issue of the relationship or opposition between motherhood and artistic vocation. Must the mother – Helen in relation to Hilda, but also Hilda in relation to H. D. – foresake the artist in herself and her offspring, and vice versa? *Hedylus*, published the year after Helen's death in 1927, moves to a break based on a mutual release and recognition. At their parting, Hedyle and Hedylus acknowledge and bless each other. The future lies open, but the doctrine of the fortunate fall predicates "primitive disobedience" as the sacrificial condition for a higher reunion.

The personal and sexual destiny of both characters depends on the blessing of the parent. Hedyle must find the mother in herself so that in freeing her poet son she can discover her own identity. Hedylus, then, must find the father whose confirmation will strengthen him to free himself from the mother so that he can find his destiny in Alexandria with Irene. In fictional fantasy, H. D. takes the male child's role to resist the biological mother in order to become the artist her mother never fought to be, and at the same time she takes the role of the woman who learns to express her repressed sensibility by finding her independence from the male, whether son or lover. By the late 1920s, this double story allowed H. D. to look back on her departure from her family in 1911 and her departure from Aldington and England in 1920. In the story, the agent of realization for Hedylus and Hedyle is the same mysterious male character: Demion, whose name conjures up both Demon and Daemon. To son and mother he appears separately as a preternatural presence, as much divine as human, perhaps the embodiment of Helios. As archetypal psychopomp he comes and goes, but his apparition makes a decisive difference in the lives of son and mother.

H. D. found the name Hedylus mentioned, along with those of other Alexandrian poets, in the "Garland" of Meleager. The fictional Hedylus, a fashionable wit who pens merely clever *vers de société* at Douris' court, lives with his mother on Samos. Alone on a beach one night, he unburdens himself by declaiming an impassioned hymn to Helios and a lyric about his divided love for Hedyle and the boyish Irene. He is on the point of committing suicide when a figure comes out of the night. Man? God? Unknown father? Helios himself? In the long, roundabout dialogue that ensues, Demion confirms Hedylus' vocation as a serious poet and guides him to a sense of identity, first by exposing Hedyle's tyranny and then by exemplifying in himself a masculinity at once nobler and more compassionate than that of the court poetasters or the men in his mother's life. Demion offers an ideal in stark contrast to the crudely priapic Demetrius and the kindly but dull Douris (fictional versions of Aldington and Cecil Gray, which parallel Decius and Verrus in "Hipparchia" and Rafe and Vane in *Bid Me to Live*, as well as Clarix and the unnamed lover in Hedyle's life, as will be explained). Now, almost by revelation, Hedylus knows that "the old cleft" that split his identity the day he split his brow is "healed and each self satisfied" (85). Viewing his mother dispassionately awakens a new compassion for her as a sad, aging, lonely woman.

Demion even suggests that Hedylus win the laconic Irene by admitting his dependence on her. Bryher was not laconic; however, Irene's small stature, boyish manner, and independence recall Bryher; and like Irene, Bryher even confessed in her memoirs to wanting to run off to sea. Moreover, in the spirit of Bryher's pledge to H. D. at Ealing, Irene agrees to accompany Hedylus on his life's venture: "I'm coming...staying with you. Tell me about your work and...Helios" (116). The moment recalls Hipparchia's departure to a new life with Julia Augusta – but with a notable difference. The narrative shift here from Hipparchia's abject submission to Julia to Hedylus' superiority over Irene as helpmate in the service of the god reflects H. D.'s lifelong struggle to balance her affection for, and gratitude to, Bryher with her resistance to the possessive domination of Bryher's personality and financial status.

As for Hedyle, she tearfully comforts herself after Hedylus' departure with the assurance that her reserve really trained him "so that when·necessary he could fight me" (118). In the rest of the novel Hedyle rehearses her life to Demion, whom, it turns out, she had loved at first sight at their only meeting years before. His importance to her, then and now, lies in the place he assumed in her difficult relationship with the masculine. Recoil from the rational empiricism of her father threw her into the arms of Clarix; betrayal by Clarix led her to an unnamed lover. Pregnant and desperate, but still defiant of her father's skepticism, she prayed for a divine sign, which she perceived as coming not from Aphrodite, as expected, but from Helios. She resolved to bear the child as Helios' godchild. After her father's death, Demetrius the Dionysian took her as his mistress and sheltered her child until she became so revolted by the gross sensuality of decadent Athens that she took refuge at Samos as Douris' mistress. The initial encounter with Demion had taken place at Demetrius' house; spontaneously, he approached her neither as an intellectual nor as an object of his lust but – for the first time in her experience – as a loving woman and mother. "You saw the thing in me," Hedyle confesses to him now, "that had been nearly blighted"; because "you saw me as a lover" and "asked tenderly of my child," "I made a god of you" (131). For that very reason, however, she refused his offer to go off with him; she needed him not as lover or husband but as godlike animus figure: "the so perfect materialization of...just what I wanted" (129). Demion represented, to her and in her, a pure passion of spirit.

Hedylus, therefore, seemed as much the offspring of her spirit as of her body; in any case, he was living evidence of her dilemma. And so she accepted Douris as the compromise between Demion and Demetrius – a succession of characters whose *D* names match the *H* characters to complete the H. D. anagram. Douris' position and wealth provided security for her and an education for Hedylus (Bryher's wealth provided similarly for H. D. and Perdita in the 1920s and 1930s) but could not touch her inner life. In their daily relations, Demion would have dominated her spirit as Demetrius had her flesh, but "Douris allowed me my soul's integrity" (140). Alone in that integrity, she has waited until now for the manifestation of Helios, which comes at last in this second visitation from Demion.

When Demion asks at the end if she is happy, Hedyle reveals her capacity for moments of ecstatic harmony with the natural world through her spiritual union with Helios-Demion (H. D.):

> Life is climax, anticlimax. I am happy in moments when the sun sets and lies across my lilies, like authentic touch of Demion. I am happy when the stars rise and again when the stars go and dawn says "Demion is behind the mountains waiting." My love for you is linked with an absolute illiterate faith in the materialization, in the reality of beauty. It exists for me in Demion, in the sunlight. I catch Demion in a bird-wing, and sometimes in a dream, he finds me. When Douris embraces me, it is Demion. When my child becomes stern and aloof and secretive, it is his father in him. That is Demion. Demion was the sun and the sun and the sun. (140)

In the place of the lover who would bind her to earthly servitude, Demion is the partner in a syzygy that divinizes her.

The following sentence from *Hedylus* provides a gloss not only on Hedyle's and Hedylus' obsession with verbalizing themselves but also on H. D.'s use of fiction and poetry as psychodrama: "Thinking self-consciously was art, a subtle projection really, almost visible, of one's being" (33). Such art served as a projection and objectification of a self-consciousness seeking deliverance from its divisions and finding it – characteristically in H. D. – not in others but through participation in an organic harmony at once natural and cosmic, personal and transpersonal. No wonder, then, that this kind of art satisfied the artist as a lover might, or a father, or a mother. Without quite knowing what he meant, Hedylus "supposed, facing it frankly, his work was his secret mother, the mother that answered when he claimed her, that gave him return for caresses" (43).

The impressionist monologues of *Palimpsest* and *Hedylus* anticipate the sessions with Freud in the early 1930s, and by the time *Bid Me to Live (A Madrigal)*[51] was completed at the end of H. D.'s extraordinary period of creativity during the war years, she could be candid about the sources of her fiction. Though *Bid Me to Live* covers much of the same ground as the previous fiction, H. D. pointedly (if needlessly) called it a *roman à clef*. The H. D. character here is named Julia (no *H* name this time, curiously), a handsome, intense, frigid poet who looks like a figure on the Parthenon frieze; the Aldington character is Rafe Ashton (cf. Rafton in "Secret Name"), an egoistic, oversexed officer described as a Roman (like Marius and Rafton); Verrus (Cecil Gray) in "Hipparchia" is here Vane, an effete, languid musician; the sexual Olivia is now Bella (Dorothy Yorke), an American woman who lived upstairs from the Aldingtons/Ashtons. The significant new character is Frederick – D. H. Lawrence – who displaces the Bryher character and fleshes out Demion as the redemptive figure for Julia/H. D. Lawrence and Frieda were already acquaintances of the Aldingtons before coming to share their flat in Mecklenburgh Square from October to December 1917, after they had been expelled by the authorities from the Cornish coast because of suspicion of Frieda's German blood. During these tense weeks, when Aldington was either with his combat unit or carrying on an affair openly with Dorothy Yorke, the curious affinity between Lawrence and H. D. came to a kind of climax. Though they never saw each other again afterward, H. D. wondered later whether she did not adopt the name Julia because she subconsciously remembered that Julia was the name Lawrence had given the H. D. character in *Aaron's Rod*.[52]

As always, fictionalizing is the strategy for self-creation: "The story must write *me*, the story must create *me*" (181); and it turns here again on the relation to the mother, the sexual betrayal by Aldington, and the relation to her own body and sexuality. The second paragraph introduces the archetypal feminine, polarized into the familiar virgin–whore dichotomy: Bella as harlot, Julia as nun. Rafe protests defensively to Julia: "I love you, but I desire *l'autre*"; "I would give her a mind, I would give you a body" (70, 78). As presented in the novel, Julia's frigidity is associated with the 1915 miscarriage and with the stern admonition of the nurse not to have another child until after the war. (The child had been conceived at the outbreak of the conflict and was linked in H. D.'s mind with the larger tragedy that engulfed their lives.) Julia understands Rafe's horror at the trench warfare but is repelled by the mechanical translation of his death fears into crude phallic aggression. H. D.'s correspondence with John Cournos (an American writer and close associate of the Aldingtons', who left Dorothy Yorke in his room upstairs from their flat when he was transferred out of London) throughout these years shows sympathetic concern about Aldington's psychological state, which she described to another friend as "frightfully uneven and sort of half shell-shocked."[53]

Whereas Julia saw Rafe as a coarse Dionysus, she saw Frederick, nicknamed Rico (Lawrence was called Lorenzo by friends), as Apollo. Rico's intense but mental passion drew her to him and away from the sexual Rafe: "It was Frederick who had taken her away (cerebrally), it was Bella who had broken across (physically)" (57). When Rico had hailed her poetry at their first meeting a few years earlier, she had almost thought of him as the father of her recently conceived child, and she wrote an Orpheus sequence for him. Now he seems again to be summoning her to full womanhood, mocking her "frozen altars," urging her to "kick over" her dream life and fly with him "where the angels come down to earth" (57). Despite his sexism ("man-is-man, woman-is-woman," p. 62), it seems to Julia, paradoxically, that Rico has disclosed the possibility of a new way of being, beyond parental and sexual neuroses: "This mood, this realm of consciousness was sexless, or all sex, it was child-consciousness, it was heaven. In heaven, there is neither marriage nor giving in marriage" (62). Yet when Julia, enraptured by seeing Rico writing in the sunlight like some radiant apparition, approaches and tremblingly touches his sleeve, he shudders away, offended and annoyed. This aborted moment is their closest contact, calling into question the nature and purpose of Rico's verbal intimacies; yet he is shocked and disapproving when Julia, distraught at his rebuff and disgusted at finding Rafe and Bella in her own conjugal bed, accepts Vane's invitation to share his cottage in Cornwall.

There Julia feels "very cold, very old," as though "already she was out of her body" (127, 119), and the friendship which the pallid Vane, with his bad heart, offers only adds to her dejection. As in her previous fiction, however, painful human failure and betrayal are subsumed into the total transhuman pattern of existence. Like Raymonde and Hedyle, Julia receives her moment through the agency of a male animus figure, in this case Rico, but apart from and in some ways despite the actual men in her life, including Rico. The epiphany arrives in an unexpected psychic form. Critics have complained about H. D.'s reliance on the *deus ex machina* to rescue her heroines from their misery, but for her the sudden reversal represents life's rhythm as she experienced it. Emily Dickinson would have known exactly what Hedyle meant by "Life is climax, anticlimax." Dickinson too was convinced that "the

Soul's Superior instants/Occur to her – alone" and that she earns them by coming "to learn the Transport by the Pain." One poem delineates the fateful sequence from the soul's "Bandaged moments" to the "moments of Escape" to "the Soul's retaken moments."[54] H. D.'s fiction characteristically builds to a "moment of Escape." Julia's "Superior instant" comes to her on a foggy cliffside walk along the paths to which Rico had (symbolically) directed her. Dissolution of ego boundaries suddenly frees in her a sense of participation in a fluid existence governed, for all life's pangs and death's certitude, by a benevolent Spirit. The Cornish landscape suggests both Greece (162) and the "hieratic writing" of Egyptian hieroglyphs (146); the misty air seems a "divine Spirit" animating her body (147). "If the sex-union they so vaunted was important, it was important to them. To her? But in another direction or another mode, or another element" (148–149).

The experience enables Julia to return to London and take up her life, but on other terms. In the final section, which H. D. wrote after World War II, Julia writes to Rico, whom she will never see again, a notebook entry that she will never send to him. She affirms their relationship – but in that other mode or element she came to understand in Cornwall. Rico's "love-cry, death-cry" that "man-is-man, woman-is-woman" is not true, at least not for the artist: Just as in that dimension "the man was woman-man" (witness Lawrence himself), so equally "the woman was man-woman...the woman gifted as a man, with the same, with other problems. Each two people, making four people. As she and Rafe had been in the beginning" (136). The perfect square of double androgyny was difficult to attain, much less maintain, as Julia learned with Rafe and now with Rico.

Writing to Rico, Julia recognizes that even for the individual, attainment of this psychic state beyond sexual polarities is in some ways like a return to the mother, like a recovery of the womb state before gender makes a difference. Rico had reached it at times, for example in his poem about the *gloire-de-Dijon* roses, neither red nor white but miraculous gold. The artist begins like the child in nature's womb, latent, expectant, undifferentiated from his circumambience, waiting to enter and become his world. So, Julia muses, "The child is the *gloire* before it is born...the story isn't born yet. While I live in the unborn story, I am in the *gloire*. I must keep it alive, myself living with it" (177, 181). Rico's empathy with his *gloire* rose makes Julia think of another artist whom Rico resembles in physique as well as in this negative capability: Vincent van Gogh "would get into the cypress tree, through his genius, through his daemon...alive in the cypress tree, alive in his mother" (181). But the gestative process is completed only when the artist is transformed from child to mother – that is, only when negative capability issues in the artwork.

So the artist is always "going back" and "going forward," "not yet born" and projecting himself into the work (183). Julia had intuited earlier that the dimension she shared with Rico was not so much preconscious as postconscious, not really "sexless" but "all sex," not regressive "child-consciousness" but arrival at "heaven" on "earth" (62). At first, the male artist as "woman-man" tends to conceive through the agency of the anima as a return to the unconscious matrix which makes him a child of nature, and the female artist as "man-woman" tends to conceive creativity through the agency of the animus as the articulation of shape and form which makes her a mother, by tradition a son-bearing mother. But actually, the creative process requires both phases of both male and female artists. Perhaps this conjunction of aspects, linked by acculturation to gender roles, is what still links Julia and Rico, as it once linked Julia and Rafe. *Bid Me to Live* ends with Julia alone, communing with her animus imaged in Rico, like Raymonde with Ray Bart and Hedyle with Demion.

Years later, dreaming in the blackout of the London blitz, H. D. saw Lawrence as a "fiery golden presence," bringing her prophetic assurance from the grave with the words: "Hilda, you are the only one of the whole crowd, who can really write."[55] And she knew that she had been a figure in his dreams too. In the final words of *Bid Me to Live*, Julia recalls that on the morning after he had shrunk from her touch, Rico had said to her: "You were singing in a dream. I woke and found my face wet with tears" (184). In their separate ways they shared a great deal; their birthdays were so close that, as she put it, "for one day in the year H. D. and D. H. Lawrence were twins." During the sessions with Freud, Lawrence, dead only a couple of years, haunted her thoughts. When a friend presented her with his last fiction, *The Man Who Died*, and told her that she was the model for the priestess of Isis who tends and revives Jesus after the crucifixion, she recalled the fact that she had written a novel, *Pilate's Wife*, still unpublished, about "the wounded but still living Christ, waking up in the rock-tomb." Her first reaction was annoyance at Lawrence for stealing her fictional ploy, but her deeper response was acceptance: "Whether or not he meant me as the priestess of Isis in that book does not alter the fact that his last book reconciled me to him." She wanted to rest in that reconciliation, for "Isis is incomplete without Osiris."[56] But – again in ways that Emily Dickinson would have understood – her temperament and experience taught her that psychological union sometimes required physical separation. In her imagination she could not be his, but he could remain hers.

IV

H. D.'s early adaptations of Greek choruses led to the original verse drama *Hippolytus Temporizes* (1927),[57] published between *Palimpsest* and *Hedylus*. Prosodically and thematically, the play is more closely related to the lyrics of the later 1920s collected in *Red Roses for Bronze* (1931).[58] The play and the poems both employ a looser, flatter verse than the Imagist lyrics; the short, often choppy and breathless lines, sometimes consisting of just one word, rely on repetition and parataxis for emphasis and declare themselves with nervous intensity. Moreover, both the play and the poems place the conflict between the virginal Artemis and the passionate Aphrodite at the heart of the human dilemma. There will be no easy answer to the prayer (uttered near the end of *Red Roses for Bronze* in "Triplex") that the aspects of the feminine personified in the triad of Athene, Artemis, and Aphrodite may come to harmonious resolution in the poet herself.

The play developed from the poem "Hippolytus Temporizes" in *Hymen*, in which the son of King Theseus and the Amazon Hippolyta is torn between his consciously chaste allegiance to his dead mother's friend Artemis and the ferment of passions which Aphrodite has aroused in him for his stepmother, Phaedra. The single location of the play is a sandy beach beneath a wild gorge sacred to Artemis and consequently the haunt of Hippolytus (like Hedylus, his mother's namesake). The entire drama centers on Hippolytus, caught between contending female forces; Theseus does not even appear. The first act belongs to Artemis. Out of love for his dead mother, the youth proclaims his repudiation of the new "queen / of spice and perfume" from Crete to worship the "sister of ice and wind, queen only of the soul, white Artemis" (32). But a boy, later revealed as Eros, son of Aphrodite, appears shipwrecked from his mother's sea, recognizes the unacknowledged "passion" in Hippolytus' eyes, and in an interchange concludes: "It seems his lady is like mine / at home – ...Yes, she is much, is very much / like mine –" (41). The first act ends with the audience aware that Hippolytus temporizes because his own feelings are divided and compromised in ways of which he is yet unaware.

In the second act Aphrodite prevails. Phaedra longs for the tropical heat and colors of her homeland, far removed from the icy rocks of Greece, sacrilegiously invokes Aphrodite at Artemis' very shrine, and desecrates the place by conspiring with wily Eros to trick Hippolytus into sleeping with Phaedra under the delusion that she is Artemis and demands his capitulation. Their deception works because it plays on his self-deception. Hippolytus tries to protest his chastity, even after the seduction, because love with a goddess elevates him above the "stale and perilous lust" of "vile humanity" (76). But in vain: Phaedra's perfidy and Hippolytus' fall drive her to suicide and him to his fatal chariot ride, to be wrecked in Aphrodite's sea.

The third act begins with a dialogue between Artemis and her brother Helios (H. D. added her favorite deity to this version of the legend), debating the issues over Hippolytus' broken body to determine whether he should be allowed to die or be restored to life. Hippolytus awakens, still asking for Artemis' kiss and celebrating in Artemis' love their ecstatic union of body and spirit. In lines that alternate with Artemis' outrage, Hippolytus cries out:

> – and all my spirit
> and my soul were joined –
>   . . . .
> – forever and forever
> with my veins –
>   . . . . . .
> – my flesh, my hands, my feet –
> all, all was spirit.
>
> (109–110)

Helios supports Eros' claim that Hippolytus "shows more holy for the stain of love," asks compassion for the youth's "exquisite consummation / and sheer bliss," and confronts his sister with: "You are less strong, O Delian, / than love —" (113). To maintain her inviolate purity, Artemis wants Hippolytus dead, his flesh dissolved into nature or into spirit; such would be their union:

> Chill against my heart,
> I, I, would cherish,
> I would shelter him
> turned to a spirit....
> (128)

When Helios rouses the dying youth in a final effort to placate Artemis, Hippolytus seals his fate by praising her for her sensual warmth and imagining himself transported to Aphrodite's Cyprus. Artemis orders his demise. In a surprising change from the Helios of *Palimpsest* and *Hedylus*, the god here departs mourning his failure once again "to prove / my absolute, / my passionate love" for Aphrodite (136–137). Artemis is left on stage, alone and "implacable" in her determination to efface from her sanctuary every defiling vestige of the human taint. H. D. called *Hippolytus Temporizes* a tragedy[59] not merely because the characters die but because the radical conflict at the heart of the human condition, as presented here, remains unresolved. Fire and ice — neither offers hope for survival; the love of Aphrodite and of Artemis both spell death. Does Hippolytus in fact "show more holy" or more corrupt for falling into passion? For a single moment, body and spirit seemed one. Was that moment a doomed self-delusion or a climax too intense to last?

Hippolytus is, of course, another persona for H. D., and the sequences in *Red Roses for Bronze* pose the same dilemma for the woman caught between Aphrodite and Artemis as she contends with men as factors in her emotional life and with the animus as a factor in her psychological and creative life. "In the Rain" narrates the dissolution of a love relationship. The speaker, for whom "love is a trap, / a snare," projects her rejuvenation in separation:

> I am young,
> I am young,
> I am young
> whom Love
> had made old.
> (217)

She will be free in a world "devoid of your touch," "devoid of your kiss" (221), and so open now to paradisal realization:

> then,
> the air
> will be full of multiple wings;
> the fountain-basin, bare
> of ripple and circlet, will spring
> into life,
> with duplicate ring

on translucent ring
of amethyst water...
(218)

Yet the sequence reverses itself and reaches the conclusion that without him there will be no life:

I was dead
and you woke me,
now you are gone,
I am dead.

(222)

The title poem of the volume pushes this ambivalence to violent confrontation and artistic sublimation. The male figure in *Red Roses for Bronze* is an image of Paul Robeson, the Afro-American singer-actor, with whom H. D. starred in Kenneth MacPherson's experimental film *Borderline*, but the figure is also, as usual, representative and archetypal. Is the man a god like Mars, or merely the intruder "Actaeon / the Huntress Artemis / bids her hounds / to leap upon" (214)? The speaker's first response to his duplicitous, condescending manipulation is to "force you to grasp my soul's sincerity,"

and single out
me,
me,
something to challenge,
handle differently.
(213)

But instead she converts her anger and aggression into creation, carving his head for a monumental bronze, decapitating him into art. The sequence which begins

if I might take dark bronze
and hammer in
the line beneath your underlip
(the slightly mocking,
slightly cynical smile
you choose to wear)
if I might ease my fingers and my brain
with stroke,
stroke,
stroke,
stroke,
stroke at – something
(211)

concludes with the finished bronze sculpture of his head, set about with her red roses, beside which the tributes of her competitors for his favor blanch into incomparable paleness. It is a tribute, and yet a triumph as well. She had constrained the threatening man to her own ends, turned anger into animus energy, and made "him" an image indisputably hers. With less display of anger and more show of submissiveness, Emily Dickinson's love poems come to a similarly contorted and curiously inverted triumph.

HERmione (written in 1927 and published in 1982) reveals in her courtship with Pound, as *Bid Me to Live* did in her marriage to Aldington, how physically and psychically attractive and threatening she found male aggressiveness; the response in both cases was to seek solace and confirmation in women. From Pound she turned to Frances Gregg, from Aldington and Lawrence and Cecil Gray to Bryher. Emily Dickinson's poems and letters indicate that for her too, intense love and friendship with women provided a sheltered security and emotional satisfaction unknown in contention with the masculine other. And yet for H. D., as for Dickinson, that contention remained necessary, even primary, whatever the hazards, because the masculine other, rather than the feminine alter ego, aroused the most complex creative responses. In greater risk lay deeper challenge.

"Let Zeus Record" is one of the few instances in H. D.'s published verse which describe her relation with Bryher. There is no question about her profound and abiding gratitude to Bryher for saving her from death and from Aldington and for providing the financial means for the cosmopolitan life they were privileged to enjoy. In the poetic sequence she is committed to Bryher by "Love's authority" and wants these verses to set her "on a height" so that "all men" might "see the grace of you" (282). At the same time, the sequence describes Bryher's "innate strength" in quite forbidding terms: "your calm inveterate chill smile," "keen and chiselled and frigid lips" (281); "stark autocracy" (282); "disenchanted, cold, imperious face," "lone and frigid tryst" (284). The last two phrases come from poem VI in the sequence, which H. D. used separately to dedicate *Palimpsest* to Bryher. Nevertheless, the astronomical conceit of the poem leaves no doubt that Bryher's star, though "steel-set" for the guidance of such storm-tossed people as H. D., is not as "rare," "great," "bright," "gracious," or "luminous" as the great untrustworthy male stars – Hesperus, Aldebaran, Sirius, even Mars.

When H. D. showed Freud snapshots of Bryher, Freud described her appearance as male: "a boy" or "page in an Italian fresco" in one photo, and in another "an Arctic explorer." Freud found Bryher's letters to him surprisingly "kind" and "pliable" after her "so decisive, so unyielding" appearance. H. D. informed him how "staunch" and "loyal" Bryher had been,[60] for she found in her friend and companion the austere and flinty strength, Artemis-like, that she had seen in the seacoasts of her Imagist poems – a strength that, she hoped, would shield her against harm.

The narrative situation of "Halcyon," in which an older woman finds herself dependent on a young woman who has come to her rescue, sums up H. D.'s ambivalence toward Bryher: on the one hand the comfort she offers, on the other hand the demands she makes. Like Bryher, the young woman resembles "an Elf, no Grace, / an odd little castaway" (273). The accumulation of adjectives like "impatient, unkind," "invariably blind," "bitter and crude," "cruel, whimsical" ("lovers aren't that, / so it can't be love," pp. 273–274) lends some credence to the nasty accounts of Bryher given by William Carlos Williams and by his friend Robert McAlmon, who for some years during the 1920s was Bryher's husband in an arranged marriage of convenience. The shrill quarrel over a dress recounted in Sections VI and VII of "Halcyon" recalls Williams' report, from McAlmon, of "long train trips about the continent" with "the two women quarreling in the compartment driving him insane." McAlmon described Bryher's "idea of a loving relationship" in vicious terms: "The beloved was to be reduced to a state of shrieking, trembling hysteria, and then she [Bryher] would be conciliatory and say, 'There, there, calm, calm. It's a nice kitten.'" According to McAlmon, Bryher's ruthless reduction of the other person to helpless dependence extended even to H. D. "By merely mentioning experiences of the war years or an unhappy episode in Hilda's past, and dwelling on it long enough, she soon had the highstrung Hilda acting much like a candidate for the strait jacket."[61]

Neither Williams nor McAlmon was a sympathetic observer. Williams had played second fiddle to Pound in courting H. D. back in Philadelphia, and his aggrieved resentment influenced his conviction that H. D. had promoted the marriage between the homosexual McAlmon and the lesbian Bryher as a respectable front, giving the two women freedom to travel as they wished. But other testimony, including that of Perdita Aldington Shaffner in her introductions to *Hedylus* and *HERmione*, confirms the strains between the two women in the odd *ménage à trois*. Soon after her divorce from McAlmon in 1927, Bryher married Kenneth MacPherson, the avant-grade film buff who had been H. D.'s lover briefly and whose bisexuality offended H. D. when, a few years later, he took a male Italian lover. In "Narthex" H. D. recounted the honeymoon trip she made with Bryher and MacPherson, and her portrayal of Bryher as Gareth made friends wonder what Bryher thought of the unflattering presentation. Her unpublished journals and notebooks, as well as "Narthex" and the other short fictions about this second trio, indicate that the relationship with Bryher was anything but easy and settled and often approached the breaking point.

The fact that it did not break off despite all the strains confirms Bryher's importance to H. D. Her love had saved H. D. from despair and death, and their reciprocated feelings survived the intensity of their first months on the Scilly Islands and the isles of Greece and lasted through all the years of flaring tempers and smarting nerves until H. D.'s death. H. D. came to depend on the constancy of devoted concern and the privileges of affluence which Bryher offered, but Bryher never became the wellspring of her creativity.

Though unpublished manuscripts, particularly the correspondence between H. D. and Bryher, will shed needed light on their relationship, it is clear that Bryher did not share H. D.'s lifelong fascination and involvement with the masculine. H. D. accepted Freud's description of her as bisexual, but her session with him also helped her to realize how different her sexual orientation was from that of Bryher, who felt that it was a tragic biological accident that she had not been born male.[62] H. D.'s creative energy originated in her sense of her womanhood in vexed relation with the masculine. Bryher never held that central role, during all of the time they spent together, off and on, increasingly more off than on, over the years. Even during World War II, when the two women shared a small apartment throughout the London blitz, Bryher remained outside the closed door behind which H. D. was writing *Trilogy*, *Tribute to Freud*, and the novels about her infatuation with Lord Dowding. The first part of *Trilogy* is dedicated to her, but she told Osbert Sitwell that H. D. "seldom shows me anything before it is printed."[63]

"Triplex" offers a prayer that a triune configuration of archetypal goddesses – Athene, Artemis, Aphrodite – may make peace in her, but she envisions that process as instituted by the masculine muse. In *The Pisan Cantos* the recurrent configuration of three women or goddesses operates for Pound, as I argued earlier, in an opposite but complementary way, as feminine muses make possible the integration of his male psyche. For H. D. too, that integration is the work of the late, long sequences. *Red Roses for Bronze* concludes with "The Mysteries," in which a masculine voice addresses the poet from the gathering apocalypse and promises peace and holy renewal out of the holocaust. The subtitle, "Renaissance Choros," indicates that the title refers not just to the Christian mysteries but also to the ancient mysteries of Greece, which she and Pound believed had persisted underground through the Middle Ages, to re-emerge openly in Renaissance paganism. Consequently, the voice in "The Mysteries" is identified early as "rare / enchanter / and magician / and arch-mage" (p. 301), and since the occult tradition is assimilated into the Christian, the Gospel imagery throughout the poem identifies the arch-mage as Jesus: the sparrow on which the father's eye rests, the wheat grain that falls to earth to rise again ("the mysteries / are in the grass / and rain," p. 304), the sacramental bread and wine persist throughout history to the present:

> I keep the law,
> I hold the mysteries true,
> I am the vine,
> the branches, you
> and you.
>
> (305)

"The Mysteries," therefore, anticipates the poems that would go into *Trilogy* to constitute H. D.'s next major development more than a decade later.

V

H. D.'s prematurely titled *Collected Poems* (1925) summed up her Imagist phase, in which Pound, Aldington, and Lawrence were powerful but threatening presences. *Red Roses for Bronze* (1931) gathered together the poems of the previous six years but showed the poet in an agitated and uncertain state about herself and her work. Then no volumes of poems were produced until *The Walls Do Not Fall* (1944), followed by *Tribute to the Angels* (1945) and *The Flowering of the Rod* (1946), the first written in 1942 and the other two in separate fortnights in May and December 1944. The sequences were obviously closely related to one another but were first published together as *Trilogy* only posthumously in 1973.[64] Nonetheless, *Trilogy* opens the late, great phase of H. D.'s poetry and must be ranked with *Four Quartets* and *The Pisan Cantos* as the major poems in English to come out of the war.

There had been less writing during the 1930s than in previous and subsequent decades; the war clouds that hung over H. D.'s sessions with Freud broke, as feared, and drove her and Freud separately to London for shelter. Freud died – fortunately, H. D. came to feel – before the blitz, which at times rained daily terror but which she refused to escape by seeking asylum in America. As in World War I, when she had refused Aldington's suggestion that she return to her family in Pennsylvania, she resolved to stick it out. The political upheaval of the twentieth century had again put her sense of self and cosmos to the incendiary test, and she knew instinctively that she had somehow to meet the challenge.

Robert Duncan charted H. D.'s development from her early Greek Imagism as a deepening engagement with the metaphysics of the Image, which connected the riddle of the psyche with the mystery of the universe:

> H. D. had come to be concerned...with finding out the gods in levels of many meanings, as personae of states of mind, but also as guides in reading the message of the universe. Here, the Image is also a Sign.... Image and Fact are now Logos, revelations that we must receive. The Universe is a book of what we are and asks us to put it all together, to learn to read.

Early on, "the Image was the nexus of the individual consciousness and the Presence," and "the *sense* (awareness as feeling) of Presence was all." But "now [in the 1940s] H. D. must search out the sense anew in the meaning *sense* has of import (awareness as knowledge of meaning); she must read the message the Presence presents."[65]

Like Pound, H. D. saw the mystery cults which interpreted that message as running from Greece to Provence, and then from "a branch of the dispersed or 'lost' church of Provence, the Church of Love that we touch on in *By Avon River*,"[66] to the Moravian Brotherhood which established her hometown of Bethlehem, Pennsylvania. When in old age she revisited her mother's family's church, where as a girl she had attended the love feasts, she certified her continuing identification by signing the register "Baptized Moravian."[67]

Simultaneously, her growing interest in the Egyptian mysteries drew her by the 1940s to their formulation in Rosicrucianism. Again as with Pound, various elements – Greek and Egyptian, Jewish and Christian – intermingled in her mind as they had for centuries in the ancient world. In the process, as her close friend Norman Holmes Pearson put it, "like many Freudians, she became quasi-Jungian and could bring the cabala, astrology, magic, Christianity, classical and Egyptian mythology, and personal experience into a joint sense of Ancient Wisdom." In World War II London, she and Bryher held seances at H. D.'s insistence regularly, often daily, with Arthur Bhaduri, a

Eurasian medium, and his mother. They soon found a tripod in H. D.'s possession, which had once belonged to William Morris, more effective than a table for receiving the messages tapped out from the other world. An unpublished manuscript entitled *Majic Ring* gives an account of the messages she received from slain Royal Air Force pilots. When in October 1943 she heard Lord Hugh Dowding – the retired air marshal who during the Battle of Britain had been responsible for the heroic defense of the homeland – lecture about his own spirit messages from some of his dead airmen, H. D. took the coincidence of their initials as a sign of their deep personal affinity. To Dowding's bafflement, she sought him out as her soul mate and fictionalized him as Lord Howell in *Majic Ring*.[68] By the time of the writing of *Trilogy*, therefore, H. D. was thoroughly steeped in the occult: a fact which produced the eclectic theology but also the compelling religious and imaginative vision of the poems.

Like the other two poems in *Trilogy*, *The Walls Do Not Fall* consists of forty-three sections of various lengths, written in pairs of free verse lines which accommodate language ranging from the colloquially discursive to the intricately rhythmic and densely associative. *Walls* is dedicated to Bryher, who spent the war years with H. D. in London. The opening section overlays the the bombed-out city with the ruined temple at Karnak, which the two women had visited in 1923; now night fires lit the sky outside their windows, and day broke on ruins which seemed to announce apocalypse. Bryher's memoirs of these years would come later in *The Days of Mars* (1972), but H. D.'s were recorded on the spot in *Trilogy*, the unpublished autobiographical fictions, and *Tribute to Freud*.

H. D.'s initial reaction to the explosion of war was to withdraw into the psyche as protective shell. In a poem early in *The Walls* she becomes a shellfish, not now a rare murex but a lowly oyster or other mollusk, whose cunning contrives survival in the jaws of Leviathan:

> I sense my own limit,
> my shell-jaws snap shut
>
> . . . .
>
> so I in my own way know
> that the whale
>
> can not digest me:
> be firm in your own small, static, limited
>
> orbit and the shark-jaws
> of outer circumstance
>
> will spit you forth:
> be indigestible, hard, ungiving.
>
> (9)

It was a strategy she had learned during World War I, yet she had learned too that "there is a spell...in every sea-shell" which allows "that flabby, amorphous hermit" to quicken and flourish (8). So the shellfish becomes an "egg in egg-shell" (9), and the imagery of female gestation in *The Walls Do Not Fall* goes on to include the cocoon (anticipating *Tribute to the Angels*) and the myrrh jar (anticipating *The Flowering of the Rod*). The enclosure is hermetic in a double sense: sealed and magical. The shell becomes an alchemical crucible within which "you beget, self-out-of-self, / selfless, / that pearl-of-great-price" (9). So in the course of the poem the hermetic crucible splits in birth, as "my heart-shell / breaks open" (35) to deliver the pearl, the precious oils, the bird, the butterfly – all images of the parthenogenetic self.

Trilogy enacts the phases of that parthenogenesis: in *The Walls Do Not Fall*, through H. D.'s "man-wise" identification with the male scribes of antiquity; in *Tribute to the Angels*, through her self-identification as Virgin Scribe (her astrological sign was Virgo); in *The Flowering of the Rod*, through her self-identification as Virgin Mother. So this account of self-mothering begins – not so paradoxically – with her masculine initiators, paternal and sibling, auto-biographical and mythic. In the paternal line, Professor Freud, the "blameless physician," had succeeded Professor Doolittle; among her siblings, Pound and Aldington and Lawrence would give way to Lord Dowding. But collectively they served to define for H. D. her "man-wise" powers, personified in her animus. His scepter, the flowering "rod of power" (cf. "A sceptre / and a flower-shaft" in "The Mysteries," p. 141), is the caduceus of Hermes the Greek healer, of his Egyptian counterpart Thoth, and of the Roman Aesculapius. She had told Freud of a girlhood dream wherein she saw a stone divided into halves into which were incised a coiled, erect serpent and a thistle; in *Tribute to Freud* she associated the glyphs with Moses' staff, Aaron's rod, and Aesculapius' caduceus, and associated the serpent's S with Sigmund and with the tau cross of Thoth. Years later she found that precise image on a Greco-Roman signet ring in the Louvre and, still later, in writing the Freud book, finally associated it with "H. D."[69] Those male symbols and hieroglyphs inscribed her own hermetic signet.

There were many reasons why Hermes came to stand with Helios in H. D.'s pantheon. In addition to healing, Hermes was a heroic explorer – again like Freud and like her father, whom she also acclaimed as "a pathfinder, an explorer."[70] The key to Hermes' multiple powers is that he acts as an agent of change. True to his Roman avatar, his nature is mercurial, and H. D. was struck by the astrological fact that her sun sign, Virgo, was ruled by Mercury. Moreover, Hermes was a messenger of the other gods, and the Greek root of "angel" as "messenger" allowed H. D. to link Hermes with the archangel Michael, "Captain or Centurion of the hosts of heaven." And finally, the hermetic messenger becomes a word mage in his communication with humans, in various guises: Thoth, the inventor of hieroglyphs; Hermes Trismegistus, the alchemical scribe; Amenhotep, the pharoah scribe; Christos, the divine Logos; Saint John, the author of Revelations.[71]

Healer, pathfinder, messenger, mystic, scribe: such were the male gods and demigods. But in her own life, Doctors Doolittle and Freud, awesome as their power might be, restricted their area of exploration and refused to submit human reason to the realm of mystery. Her father was a professor of astronomy, not an astrologer; it was her mother who as Moravian, musician, and artist was the daughter's covert link with the world of mystery. In the first "happiness of the quest" on which Freud set her, she wanted to believe that his psychology was a "philosophy" which could reconcile "my father's science and my mother's art." Unlike Professor Doolittle, the surrogate father seemed to have an aesthetic sense, and might admit the woman's powers to the family group and encourage them. But further experience forced her to recognize that Freud's aesthetic sense – unlike her mother's – did not extend to the religious: "About the greater transcendental issues, we never argued. But there was an argument implicit in our very bones."[72] The difference never came to argument because Freud refused to theorize about such matters; he "shut the door on transcendental speculations" and limited his study to the "personal reactions, dreams, thought associations or thought 'transferences' of the individual human mind. It was the human individual that concerned him." Freud's denial of "this dream of heaven, this hope of eternal life," H. D. came sadly to believe, doomed him to a "courageous pessimism," and it pained her that his agnostic disbelief in personal immortality afforded him "little hope for the world."[73]

No more than her father, then, could Freud be hermetic; there were some messages that neither could deliver or decipher. One of the principal matters she had come to Freud to discuss was what she called "the writing on the wall" – not writing really, but an astonishing succession of images of light, which she had seen on the wall of a hotel room on Corfu in spring 1920 with Bryher. The series of archetypal images began with the head and shoulders of a soldier or airman, unrecognized but suggestive of Aldington and her brother ("dead brother?" H. D. mused; maybe, but also "lost friend"). He was followed on the wall by light images of a goblet or mystic chalice, a tripos like the one used by Apollo's priestess at Delphi (and later by H. D. in her seances), a ladder spanning heaven and earth, and a figure like Nike, Athene triumphant. The intensity of the experience overwhelmed H. D. at this point, and she averted her eyes. But Bryher, who though present had until then seen nothing, now began to see the double image which completed the vision: Helios in his sun disk "reaching out to draw the image of a woman (my Nike) into the sun beside him." She did not insist that it had been a supernatural revelation and entertained the possibility that the vision was "merely an extension of the artist's mind, a *picture* or an illustrated poem." But she knew that the apparition was in any case of enormous symbolic significance, and she was disappointed and dismayed when Freud warned that such an experience was a "dangerous" symptom, perhaps her only dangerous symptom.[74]

So Freud could not heal her wholly. The antique figures on Freud's desk and in his glass cases he loved not as gods but as artifacts. Though she did not argue with the professor at the time, H. D. insisted that the art of healing went beyond the terms he set. After all, Hermes was called "Psychopompos," mediator of the underworld, where psyche and spirit meet, where human shades mingle with deities. As psychopomp Hermes was affiliated with the artist; by devising the lyre he made possible Apollo's song. His Egyptian predecessor, Thoth, was also the god of learning, who invented all the arts and sciences – not only doctor and healer, mathematician and astronomer, but musician and writer – and was specifically the creator of the hieroglyphs and the scribe of the gods. Long before her sessions with Freud, Pound and Aldington and Lawrence, sibling poets, had introduced her to the hermetic world, but in breaking the parental bonds they had separated her from mother as well as father. The assimilation of the animus-scribe's hermeticism in *The Walls Do Not Fall* permits the rediscovery of the scribe's feminine and then maternal character in the other two sequences. Such is the subtending impulse and secret meaning of *Trilogy*.

But first, physical survival requires the invocation of Hermes and Thoth against the fiery rain of the blitz:

> Thoth, Hermes, the stylus,
> the palette, the pen, the quill endure,
>
> though our books are a floor
> of smouldering ash under our feet....
>
> (16)

H. D. wrote to Norman Holmes Pearson that she had been stung into writing *The Walls Do Not Fall* as a "vindication of the writer, or the 'scribe,'" in response to letters from an acquaintance who doubted the efficacy of literature in crises of war and survival.[75] H. D.'s response to the damning question was unequivocal:

> so what good are your scribblings?
> this – we take them with us
>
> beyond death; Mercury, Hermes, Thoth
> invented the script, letters, palette;
>
> the indicated flute or lyre-notes
> on papyrus or parchment
>
> are magic, indelibly stamped
> on the atmosphere somewhere,
>
> forever....
>
> (17)

The "smouldering ash" of burned books requires the reinscription for which she assumes responsibility in the present crisis; she will stand among the remaining walls against the war. Her correspondent's word "scribblings" demeans the power of the word, but the pun which makes the "word" mightier than the "sword" is meant to assert the power of language over physical force. For that reason, the Egyptian scribe "takes precedence of the priest, / stands second only to the Pharoah" (15) – that is, she told Pearson, "stands second only to God."[76]

Saint John and Christos the Word, the scribe and his God. The sections of

The Walls Do Not Fall interweave the Christian references with invocations of ancient male scribes and deities, with the "Amen" of Amenhotep's name as the punning link. In the remarkable dream of Section 16, "Ra, Osiris, *Amen* appeared" in the "spacious, bare meeting-house" where, as a girl, H. D. had worshiped with her mother's Moravian family. The god is first identified as "the world-father, / father of past aeons / present and future equally," but then is surprisingly described as "beardless, not at all like Jehovah." The unapproachable Father – Ra, Jehovah – manifests Himself as the Son, Christos, Osiris, Amen: "upright, slender, / impressive as the Memnon monolith" (25).

Moreover, in Section 21, the transformation of the Father into the Son is effected through the connection of the masculine with the feminine:

> Splintered the crystal of identity,
> shattered the vessel of integrity,
>
> till the Lord *Amen*,
> paw-er of the ground,
>
> bearer of the curled horns,
> bellows from the horizon:
>
> here am I, Amen-Ra,
> *Amen*, Aries, the Ram;
>
> time, time for you to begin a new spiral,
> see – I toss you into the star-whirlpool;
>
> till pitying, pitying,
> snuffing the ground,
>
> here am I, Amen-Ra whispers,
> *Amen*, Aries, the Ram
>
> be cocoon, smothered in wool,
> be Lamb, mothered again.
>
> (30)

"Amen-Ra" is the archetypal father; the pun on "paw-er" as "father" links Ra with the Ram, the "bearer of the curled horns." But "a new spiral" brings metamorphosis, summed up in the pun on "smothered/mothered": the Ram becomes mother ("cocoon, smothered in wool") and so Son ("Lamb, mothered again"). In the next section, the alchemical word play ("worm/warm," "fleece/grass," "sun/son") runs through H. D.'s prayer that the father bear her as Hermes, Helios/Christos:

> Now my right hand,
> now my left hand
>
> clutch your curled fleece;
> take me home, take me home,
>
> my voice wails from the ground;
> take me home, Father:

pale as the worm in the grass,
yet I am a spark

struck by your hoof from a rock:
Amen, you are so warm,

hide me in your fleece,
crop me up with the new-grass;

let your teeth devour me,
let me be warm in your belly,

the sun-disk,
the re-born Sun.

(31)

The refrain "take me home, Father" means "take me home to Mother."
H. D. had hoped her visits to Freud, whose office felt like "home," would
effect a reconciliation with her lost father and mother, so that she might come
to a sense of her own identity. The late poetry voices the effort to return home
as the place of rebirth; in her beginning would be her end. "Take me home,
Father"; let me be smothered/mothered in the father's fleece, "let me be warm
in your belly" and in the name of the Sun/Son let the daughter be born again
to the mother who in life had favored her sons over her daughter. As sibling
poet, Pound had rescued the daughter from that bruising domestic situation
and initiated her into womanhood in the Sunship/Sonship of the scribes. But
some essential connection had been obscured, and now the alchemy of the
word seeks to restore her psychologically to the mother she missed in life.

As we can already see, the punning throughout *Trilogy* is no mere trick or
game. It creates a language appropriate to a world in which there are meanings
within meanings, meanings beyond meanings. In the concluding sections of
The Walls Do Not Fall the personal and psychological synthesis is characteristically merged into the cosmic design. The play on "O-sir-is or O-Sire-is" fuses
the names of Osiris and his sister-wife, Isis, in a cyclic pattern of death and
rebirth which constitutes the recurrent manifestation of "the One in the
beginning": "Fosterer, Begetter, the Same-forever / in the papyrus-swamp /
in the Judean meadow" (54–55). Perhaps intentionally, H. D. indicated the
American source of the Neoplatonism she shared with Pound in her use of
Emerson's epithet "the over-soul" (42), whose immanence confers on
everyday objects a sacramental significance:

grape, knife, cup, wheat

are symbols in eternity,
and every concrete object

has abstract value, is timeless
in the dream parallel

whose relative sigil has not changed
since Nineveh and Babel.

(24)

The play on the names of Osiris and Isis points to their ultimate union: "O,

Sire, is this the path?...drawn to the temple-gate, O, Sire, / is this union at last?" (p. 57). Since the ruins of London still stand like the remnants of the temple at Karnak, *"possibly we will reach haven, / heaven"* (59). These last words of the poem conjoin the maternal haven with the paternal heaven, but the prospect still lies in the future. In the second poem of *Trilogy* the question will recur for further resolution:

> what is this mother-father
> to tear at our entrails?
>
> what is this unsatisfied duality
> which you can not satisfy?
>
> (72)

Tribute to the Angels was written in a fortnight during a "wonderful pause just before D-Day" as a "sort of premature peace poem."[77] The unexpected epiphany which generated this Easter-spring poem occurred on a London bus when H. D. glimpsed a charred apple tree flowering again amid the rubble of a burned-out square. Hermes Trismegistus (Thoth) and Saint John are still present at the beginning of the sequence. Hermes, however, leads to Aphrodite; Christos, to Mary. Their animus inspiration directs the poem through the divination of the angels to an astonishing manifestation of the feminine.

The angels of Saint John's Revelation who attend the divine throne appear as emissaries, and four of the seven have been named and addressed – Raphael (Birth), Gabriel (Change), Azrael (Death), and Uriel (the fire of God's judgment and will) – before the first premonition of the archetypal feminine, whose appearance is rendered as alchemical "Transubstantiation" (87):

> Now polish the crucible
> and in the bowl distill
>
> a word most bitter, *marah*,
> a word bitterer still, *mar*,
>
> sea, brine, breaker, seducer,
> giver of life, giver of tears;
>
> Now polish the crucible
> and set the jet of flame
>
> under, till *marah-mar*
> are melted, fuse and join
>
> and change and alter,
> mer, mere, mère, mater, Maia, Mary,
> Star of the Sea,
> Mother.
>
> (71)

The bitter and destructive sea, nature's womb and tomb, becomes the virgin-mother goddess. "Star of the Sea," an epithet from the Litany of the Blessed Virgin, precipitates the association of Mary with "Venus, Aphrodite, Astarte," who appears in double aspect as a star, "Phosphorus / at sun rise, /

Hesperus at sun-set" (73). This evocation of the feminine calls forth the fifth angel, Annael, the peace of God, designated by H. D. as the Mohammedan Venus, and linked in turn with the Hebrew Anna, Hannah or Grace.[78] Moreover, she appears in a syzygy with Uriel, the angel of God's fiery breath; the pair intimates the Sancta Spiritus: "So we hail them together, / one to contrast the other" (80). After this annunciation, God's bride blooms in war-torn London: "We see her visible and actual, / beauty incarnate" in the miraculous spring flowering of the scorched tree in a garden square behind a demolished house (82–83).

Then, unexpectedly, the apparition of the Lady appears in a dream to H. D. and two female friends. Remembering perhaps the triune goddesses in "Triplex," the poet wonders whether "we three together" could summon the supernatural, "yet it was all natural enough, we agreed" (90). For when the poet wakens from the dream, the Presence is "there more than ever, / as if she had miraculously / related herself to time here" (91). Who is this Lady? Earlier in the poem, when

> my patron [Freud or Bryher or both] said, "name it";
>
> I said, I can not name it,
> there is no name;
>
> he said,
> "invent it."
>
> (76)

So here the patron's voice in her head tells her that if she cannot define the Lady by name, she can at least invent images. Though the Lady be a Presence and "no rune nor riddle" (84), the scribe suggests her mysterious charisma in rich details from Renaissance painters and their Pre-Raphaelite imitators:

> Our Lady of the Goldfinch,
> Our Lady of the Candelabra,
>
> Our Lady of the Pomegranate,
> Our Lady of the Chair;
>
> we have seen her, an empress,
> magnificent in pomp and grace,
>
> and we have seen her
> with a single flower
>
> or a cluster of garden-pinks
> in a glass beside her;
>
> we have seen her snood
> drawn over her hair,
>
> or her face set in profile
> with the blue hood and stars;
>
> we have seen her head bowed down
> with the weight of a domed crown,

or we have seen her, a wisp of a girl
trapped in a golden halo....

(93)

H. D. goes on to designate the voice which delineates these images, gorgeous though they are, as "you" – not her truest voice but Bryher's or Freud's voice in her mind, turning her to aesthetic inventions for the Lady. Without taking back any of the gorgeous images, the voice of "I," H. D. speaking for herself, insists that the Lady, far from being "a hieratic figure, the veiled Goddess" (as "you would have her"), is more human and approachable: a Vestal, perhaps, of the *Bona Dea* but in any case a living reality, no mere art image. In fact, as it turns out, "she is psyche, the butterfly, / out of the cocoon" at last (103).

The Lady is, then, the apotheosized self. Her specific character, as she manifested herself at H. D.'s bedside that night in 1944, is disclosed when she is paired with the sixth angel, Michael, earlier linked to Thoth and Hermes and here "regent of the planet Mercury" (99). H. D. suggested to Pearson that "she is the Troubadour or Poet's Lady,"[79] but in fact she is something more than muse. She is H. D.'s archetype: the troubadour as woman, the woman as troubadour, the woman troubadour herself. In her arms the Lady bears no Son ("the Child was not with her," p. 97; "the Lamb was not with her," p. 104) but instead her writings: "she looked so kindly at us / under her drift of veils, / and she carried a book" (100). The Madonna anticipated earlier ("Star of the Sea / Mother") turns out to be the Virgin Scribe. What's more, "her book is our book" (105), is in fact H. D.'s poem in the reader's hand:

She carried a book, either to imply
she was one of us with us,

or to suggest she was satisfied
with our purpose, a tribute to the Angels....

(107)

Just as the revelation of the masculine as scribe and psychopomp in *The Walls Do Not Fall* opened the way to the revelation of the Virgin Scribe in *Tribute to the Angels*, so the Virgin Scribe makes possible a fuller exfoliation of the feminine archetype in *The Flowering of the Rod*, and preparation for that further exfoliation summons the masculine once more. The seventh and last angel is Zadkiel:

regent of Jupiter,
or Zeus-pater or Theus-pater,

Theus, God; God-the-father, father-god
or the Angel god-father,

himself, heaven yet at home in a star....

(108)

Such is the scribe's witness: "I John saw. I testify" (109). The final address to Zadkiel specifically foreshadows the third poem in the image of the Lady's "face like a Christmas-rose" (110). So the Easter-spring poem of the angels and the Lady grows into a Christmas poem, *The Flowering of the Rod*, dated December 18–31, 1944. It is the book the Lady holds. Though the Lady's book is blank when she appears in *Tribute to the Angels*, it is announced as "a tale of a Fisherman / a tale of a jar or jars" (105), the third sequence of *Trilogy*.

The tale of the Fisherman and the two jars of Kaspar – the jar the Wise Man presented to Mary and the Christ child at His birth and the twin jar he provided to Mary Magdalene to anoint the Christ man at His death – is both traditional and heterodox. Jesus and the two Marys – but the episodes are here told in reverse order. The poem first presents the episode of Mary Magdalene, the reformed courtesan, attending upon Jesus at the end of His life and moves on to conclude with Mary the Virgin Mother with the baby Jesus in the stable at Bethlehem: a chronological inversion if this were a narrative of Jesus' life, but a psychological progression in H. D.'s deepening engagement with the mother archetype. The alienation from the mother with whom she felt deep religious and artistic affinity had thwarted Hilda's psychological realization of herself as woman and mother. She brooded over her miscarriage of Aldington's baby during World War I; when she bore Cecil Gray's child in 1919, she called her Perdita, the lost one, and had difficulty in assuming and fulfilling the mothering role. On Corfu the year after Perdita's birth she took Athene Nike, the motherless maiden daughter of Zeus, as "my own especial sign or part of my hieroglyph."[80]

In *Hippolytus Temporizes* and *Red Roses for Bronze* the Artemis and Athene in H. D. had contended with the Aphrodite. The Lady in *Tribute to the Angels* is explicitly the Virgin but not the lover or mother; though she is "innocent / and immaculate...like the Lamb's Bride," "the Lamb is not with her either as Bridegroom or Child" (104). Now *The Flowering of the Rod* presents the two Marys as versions of Aphrodite and Artemis – but with paradoxical complications: Magdalene's passion is purified, and the Virgin bears a child. Mary the courtesan, redeemed of sexual sin and preparing the Redeemer for His death, is succeeded by and assimilated into the Mary whose immaculate flesh incarnates God. Because the burgeoning of the blasted tree images not death from life but rebirth from death, in this telling crucifixion precedes nativity. The Old English "rood" links the Cross with the Tree of Life. The Easter mystery, alluded to in the references to Jesus' transfiguration, crucifixion, and resurrection, is subsumed in the Christmas mystery. The flowering of the rood is a Christmas rose: Deus manifest in Mater, material spirit.

H. D. recalled, in the Freud memoir written in the same year as this poem, that "the Professor translated the pictures on the wall, or the picture-writing on the wall...in Corfu...as a desire for union with my mother."[81] The Mediterranean world H. D. sought was a substitute homeland; Hellas, she came to see, stood for Helen, and Helen had accompanied her to the Mediterranean in 1923. Now we can see why the surrogate father's acknowledgment of the primacy of the mother seemed to H. D. a "coming home" and why Freud's office felt like a "home" she associated with "father-mother."[82] The plea "Take me home, Father" opened the way for the advent of the Lady, and the psychological breakthrough from her visitation carried H. D. past Greece all the way back to Bethlehem and mother. For just as the Greece of *Sea Garden* was the lost America of her childhood memories, so now Bethlehem is as much in Pennsylvania as in Palestine. In one session, when H. D. was reminiscing about her hometown, Freud made the connection: "Bethlehem is the town of Mary"[83] – yes, and the town where Helen bore Hilda.

The mystery of Mary, then, is the culmination of the poem, and her metamorphosis is reflected in the puns on her name. The playing upon "Marah" (bitter), "mar" (sea), and "mère" (mother) in *Tribute to the Angels* is extended by the linking of "myrrh" and "Mary" as H. D. articulates her parthenogenesis: "through my will and my power, /Mary shall be myrrh," "(though I am Mara, bitter) I shall be Mary-myrrh" (135); "*I am Mary, the incense-flower of the incense-tree, / myself worshipping, weeping, shall be changed to myrrh*" (138). The blasted tree blossoming amid the blitz yields the woman-flower, "face like a Christmas rose" (110). Her burgeoning, like that of Yeats' "great-rooted blossomer," enfolds the cycle of birth, death, and resurrection. Her precious oils are bitter to the tongue but incomparably sweet in the nostrils; the myrrh vessels are crucibles in an alchemical sublimation, for alchemy was, as Jung demonstrated, the science – or art – of psychological and spiritual transformation.

Kaspar, with his two fabled jars of myrrh, provides H. D.'s fictional link between the two Marys; one he gives to Mary Magdalene and the other he had presented years before in Bethlehem. In *The Walls Do Not Fall*, Love was identified as a "Mage, / bringing myrrh" (10). In H. D.'s version, the Mage is the man with woman-wisdom, the woman-wise man who matches and mirrors the man-wise woman. Kaspar understands the old goddesses as "unalterably part" of Mary: "Isis, Astarte, Cyprus," "Gemeter, De-Meter, earth-mother," "Venus / in a star" (145). For him the "Star of the Sea" is one with the star of Bethlehem. In his encounter with Mary Magdalene, Kaspar is granted a vision of the three primordial mothers: Eve, and before her Lilith, and even before her a nameless mother from the lost paradise of Atlantis. The feminine is symbolized as a flower opening, petal on petal, circle on circle, both backward and forward through time to infinity (cf. pp. 153–157). Her full revelation includes origin and fall and redemption: Paradise, Paradise lost, Paradise regained.

Kaspar gives Magdalene the jar to anoint the Christ for His death because in her he recalls the other Mary, the second Eve at the nativity. For what he had knelt to in the stable at Bethlehem was not the Spirit-Father, the I-Am or Jehovah, but instead God as Son of Mary: the "Holy-Presence-Manifest," the "Great Word" (170). Kaspar wordlessly offers Mary myrrh, but she speaks:

> she said, Sir, it is a most beautiful fragrance,
> as of all flowering things together;
>
> but Kaspar knew the seal of the jar was unbroken.
> he did not know whether she knew

the fragrance came from the bundle of myrrh
she held in her arms.

(172)

In personal terms, Hilda has found herself as Helen in Bethlehem, and the bittersweet discovery of Mary-myrrh has profound and far-reaching implications for herself and for her readers. The poems of *Trilogy* have led to the widening and cumulative revelation of the Scribe, the Virgin with Book, and the Madonna with Child. In the sequence of things, the Madonna with Child subsumes the Virgin with Book. Or rather, the Virgin Scribe writes the book of the Virgin Mother. The "bundle of myrrh / she held in her arms" is the Child and the poem, the Child in the poem, the poem as Child. The poet-mother cradles the essence of flowers and the leaves of *Trilogy*, and as readers we kneel with Kaspar at the Epiphany: "Her book is our book" (105). In our patriarchal society, this is perhaps the closest a female poet has come to claiming the prophetic representativeness which Whitman claimed for the male bard in *Leaves of Grass*.

Two contemporary poets – a man and a woman – offer separate glosses on the poet as mother. Robert Duncan describes the irresistible pull of Poetry – backward and forward at once – as a need to "re-member" the Mother:

> Back of the Muses, so the old teaching goes, is Mnemosyne, Mother of the Muses. Freud, too, teaches that the Art has something to do with restoring, re-membering, the Mother. Poetry itself may then be the Mother of those who have destroyed their mothers. But no. The image Freud projects of dismembering and remembering is the image of his own creative process in Psychoanalysis which he reads into all Arts. Mnemosyne, the Mother-Memory of Poetry, is our made-up life, the matrix of fictions. Poetry is the Mother of those who have created their own mothers.[84]

In Duncan's convolutions mother and child are almost indistinguishable; the poet and the poem are each both mother and child of the other. Marilyn Farwell has found the basis for an organic feminist criticism in Adrienne Rich's growing concern with motherhood and in her consequent emphasis on the "relational" aspect of art.[85] Farwell argues that Rich has rejected the notion of art as a depersonalized "creation," projected spermatically by the "creative" artist (as male criticism tends to conceive it), because such an attitude regards the artwork as an object existing in and of itself, beyond change and outside the flux of experience. However, for Rich or Duncan or anyone else who views art organically as inseparable from the flux of experience, the art object or the text of the poem has no significance or meaning except in its relational function, as the artist or reader engages and experiences it. "Creation," from this point of view, is not a completed act but an ongoing process of gestation which extends even to the reader Duncan's notion of the poet's being his or her own mother and child. Poetry is not only parthenogenetic but matrogenetic simultaneously. Moreover, such a conception of art determines form as well as substance. Rich has observed of her own development:

Today, I have to say that what I know I know through making poems. Like the novelist who finds that his characters begin to have a life of their own and to demand certain experiences, I find that I can no longer go to write a poem with a neat handful of materials and express those materials according to a prior plan: the poem itself engenders new sensations, new awareness in me as it progresses. Without for one moment turning my back on conscious choice and selection, I have been increasingly willing to let the unconscious offer its materials, to listen to more than the one voice of a single idea. Perhaps a simple way of putting it would be to say that instead of poems *about* experiences I am getting poems that *are* experiences, that contribute to my knowledge and my emotional life even while they reflect and assimilate it. In my earlier poems I told you, as precisely and eloquently as I knew how, about something; in the more recent poems something is happening, something has happened to me and, if I have been a good parent to the poem, something will happen to you who read it.[86]

In the early 1960s, when Rich wrote this, she used the neutral term "parent," but there is no question that today she would seek to be a good "mother" to the poem and in a certain sense expect the reader, male as well as female, to be so too.

Certainly for H. D., the re-membering of the Mother required a new kind of poetry. Those who prefer the Imagist poems find the long later sequences looser, more associative, more opaque. But Denise Levertov is correct in seeing the continuity of the work in its differences. For her, "the icily passionate precision of the earlier work, the 'Greek' vision, had not been an *end*, a closed statement, but a preparation" for the long works of the later years. As a matter of fact, a rereading of the 1925 *Collected Poems* convinced Levertov that even "the poems I had thought of as shadowless were full of shadows, planes, movement; correspondences of what was to come."[87] H. D. herself resented the critical view, reflected in anthology selections, that treated her as though she had ceased writing or developing in 1925. She pointedly and proudly proclaimed *Trilogy* "runic, divinatory" – "not the 'crystalline' poetry that my early critics would insist on."[88] For H. D. the stylistic differences beneath the thematic continuities running through her work were important because the difference in language and stance indicated a deepening of the psychological and spiritual comprehension of those thematic materials. The later work – not just the work centered on World War II (*Trilogy, Tribute to Freud, Bid Me to Live, By Avon River*) but also the long poems of her last decade – is unashamedly more personal and religious, more autobiographical and mystical, than the more Modernist manner of her Imagist phase.

To return to Duncan's distinction, which introduced this discussion of *Trilogy*, H. D.'s early Images were "personae of states of mind," and the personae in that psychodrama were either hetairas subject to male power or male heroes and poets. But the Images which served as "guides in reading the message of the universe" tended more and more to constellate themselves around the figure of the mother, especially the virgin mother, whose word was not spermatic but parthenogenetic and matrogenetic. It was a long way from the lean, hard-torsoed athlete of *Sea Garden* to the Madonna of *The Flowering of the Rod*, but it was the way she had been seeking from the beginning.

VI

H. D. always wrote about her personal psychological dilemma against and within the political turmoil of the twentieth century, the toils of love enmeshed in the convulsions of war. Her marriage to and separation from Richard Aldington turn on World War I, and that concatenation of private and public trauma stands behind the Imagist poems of her first creative phase, summed up in the *Collected Poems* of 1925. The sequences of *Trilogy*, written during the London blitz of World War II, usher in the longer, multivalent, and more associative poems of her later years. But her last years were to bring a third great burst of creativity. The travail of aging and illness did not issue in the stoic silence which made Pound leave incomplete his life's work in *The Cantos*, but instead, as with William Carlos Williams, produced a climactic efflorescence of poetic expression. The results of this third phase were *Helen in Egypt*,[89] published in 1961, almost concurrently with her death, and *Hermetic Definition*, published posthumously in 1972.

Even the reviewers who shied away from dealing with *Helen in Egypt* as a poem by detaching particular lyrics for dutiful praise (as though they were still Imagist pieces) recognized dimly that *Helen* was the culmination of a life in poetry. But it is an event even more culturally signal than that: it is the most ambitious and successful long poem ever written by a woman poet, certainly in English. It is so often observed as to take on a kind of fatality that no woman has ever written an epic, that women poets seem constrained to the minor note and the confabulations of the heart. H. D. confounds that complacent dictum by assuming and redefining the grounds of the epic. Early on the poem asks:

> Is Fate inexorable?
> does Zeus decree that, forever,
> Love should be born of War?
> (32)

The Iliad showed War born of Love, but H. D. repossessed the Trojan materials that have inspired the Western epic from Homer to Pound and converted them into an anti-epic centered not on heroes like Achilles and Hector but on a heroine, none other than the fabulous woman who, male poets have told us, roused men to Love, and so to War.

Many of the masterworks of American writing – *Walden* and *Moby-Dick* and *Absolom, Absalom!*, *Leaves of Grass* and *The Cantos*, *Four Quartets* and *Paterson* – are *sui generis*. They make their idiosyncratic statement in their own unique form. So *Helen in Egypt* draws Greek and Egyptian myths, epic and psychoanalysis and occult gnosticism into an "odyssey" of consciousness played out as a series of lyrics written in irregular free verse tercets of varying length, linked by prose commentaries sometimes longer than the lyrics. The poem is divided into books, eight lyrics to a book, seven books to Part I, "Pallinode," and to Part II, "Leuké," and six to the concluding part, "Eidolon." "Pallinode" was written at Lugano in the summer of 1952; "Leuké," the next year at the Küsnacht Klinik near Zurich, H. D.'s base of residence after 1953; and "Eidolon," again at Lugano during the summer of 1954. H. D. came to think of the poem as another "Trilogy," and the narrative too is laid out in a number of interrelated triangles. The speakers in "Pallinode," which takes place in an Egyptian temple near the coast after the war, are Helen, who was rumored to have spent the war there rather than at Troy, and Achilles, the nemesis of Troy, lost at sea and shipwrecked on the coast of Egypt; the speakers in Part II are Helen and her old lover Paris on Leuké, *l'isle blanche*, and then Helen and Theseus, her old benefactor and counselor, in Athens; the triad of voices in "Eidolon" comprises Helen, Paris, and Achilles. Helen is, of course, H. D.'s persona as she writes her epic of consciousness, as the groundswell of the three male voices is integrated into the piont of view of the subsuming consciousness. The action transpires in no time and no place, and so in any time and place: in Helen's psyche, where the dead are quick and where the past is present, pregnant with fatality.

A notebook entry in 1955 observed: "I had found myself, I had found my alter-ego or my double – and that my mother's name was Helen had no doubt something to do with it." And the configuration of male characters around Helen re-creates fantasized versions of her governing relationships with men as she strove, now on an epic scale, to lift "the tragic events and sordid realities of *my* life" into myth.[90]

Theseus is the easiest to designate. Most readers have recognized in him an image of Sigmund Freud. He served H. D. during the 1930s and after as wise old man, surrounded in his study by ancient Greek figurines, as he applied reason to help her sort out the confusion of her life and feelings. Like Freud for H. D., Theseus is for Helen the paternal authority who offers his couch to her for rest and an analytic rehearsal of her amatory embroilments.

The associations with Paris and with Achilles are more elusive and inclusive; they span all H. D.'s adult life up to the time of her writing of the poem. As for Paris, her involvement with Dr. Eric Heydt, her doctor and analyst at Küsnacht Klinik, had almost immediately passed from the professional to the personal and romantic despite the fact that she was decades older than he, and in a notebook she confessed that the complications of that relationship extended the poem into its second part and specifically led to the introduction of Paris. But behind Heydt stood Pound; in *HERmione* she saw the young Pound as "Paris with the apple," saw his luxuriant red hair as "the Phrygian cap of Paris." He called her his "Dryad," and she signed her letters to him with that name for the rest of her life. He wrote his famous invocation "The Tree" for her in the "Hilda Book" during their courtship, and *HERmione* echoes her acceptance: "I am a tree. TREE is my new name out of the Revelations."[91] And now, years later, her Paris calls his Helen "Dendritis,...Helena of the trees" (141).

In the "Compassionate Friendship" notebook (which also dates from the mid-1950s), H. D. mused over "the sequence of my initiators" throughout her life: Pound; Aldington; from the London days of World War I John Cournos and D. H. Lawrence and Cecil Gray ("Lawrence in the middle"); Bryher's second husband, Kenneth MacPherson (who had been H. D.'s lover and served "as a later double, as it were, of Gray"); Walter Schmideberg, her analyst and close friend during the time of the final divorce decree from Aldington in 1938; and now Eric Heydt as the "inheritor" of the long male line of initiators.[92] In much the same way, the figure of Paris summed up all the men in her life, from Pound to Heydt, including Aldington.

Moreover, she associated Heydt particularly with Pound. When Heydt gave her an injection at perhaps their initial encounter at the Klinik, he transfixed her with the question "You know Ezra Pound, don't you?" "This was a shock coming from a stranger," she told her journal. "Perhaps he injected me or re-injected me with Ezra." The sexual image is appropriate enough; Heydt persisted in pressing her about her relationship with her first lover, and once even asked her – to her distaste – whether the relationship had been sexual. The Pound memoir *End to Torment* H. D. wrote in 1958 after repeated urging from Heydt that she recover her memories of the young man who had loved her and confirmed her a poet. Testimony that Pound was a living presence in her mind extends beyond *End to Torment* to the separate Helen sequence "Winter Love," written in 1959 and published in *Hermetic Definition*, in which Helen/Hilda relives her early love for Odysseus/Pound. So she incorporated into the Paris of her *Helen*, she said, an imaginative presence or medium who stood behind Heydt and was associated with "the history of poor Ezra and my connection with him."[93]

The figure of Achilles is a composite in much the same way as that of Paris is. Notebook entries specifically connect him with Lord Hugh Dowding, the air marshal of the Battle of Britain, with whom H. D. shared spiritualist experiences and for whom she served briefly as medium. Though she saw Dowding only at two lectures about his communications with lost Royal Air Force pilots and at seven meetings (with others present at four of those sessions), she felt an affinity with him that was like an "engagement." She was shattered when he broke off their acquaintance, and "in 1952, after I knew of the Air Marshall's [sic] marriage (Sept. 1951), I wrote the first section of the *Helen* sequence." The rupture released creative energy to cope with the situation, as had the separation from Aldington earlier:

> We had come together through and for the messages. There was a feeling of exaltation in my later discovery, it was not I, personally, who was repudiated. An "engagement" was broken, but broken on a new level....My life was enriched, my creative energy was almost abnormal. I wrote the *Avon*, I wrote three "works" (unpublished) on my unparalleled experiences. I wrote the long *Helen* sequence.[94]

But Achilles was associated with other figures as well. Dowding reminded her of her father in some ways: "I know *ad astra*, my father's profession, the iridescent moons he shows us. I know *ad astra*, the Air Marshall's profession. I know the wide-faring, hypnotic, rather mad grey eyes of both of them." In another notebook she recounts a dream in which her older brother Gilbert (for whom she felt such love and such competition for her mother's love) is strangling her, and she associates the dream with the episode in which Achilles tries to strangle Helen.[95] But more importantly, just as Pound stands behind Heydt in Paris, so Aldington stands behind Dowding in Achilles. Paris' and Achilles' initials are as autobiographically important as Helen's. And where Paris represents the line of those initiators in H. D.'s life who in one way or another carried her away, Achilles represents the rough and devastating threat of the masculine, not unrelated to the romantic Paris aspect but specifically that aspect of the masculine which cast her off and cast her down. The poem enacts Helen's apotheosis as she transcends Paris' power over her and transforms Achilles' rejection into a divine marriage, a *conjunctio oppositorum* ordained by the gods.

"Is Fate inexorable? / does Zeus decree that, forever, / Love should be born of War?" (32). The poem finally answers *yes*: divine decree requires that we submit ourselves to Life, for all the war wounds and mortal blows, so that, providentially, in comprehending the train of temporal events which enact our violation, we can accept and transcend them; participation in the temporal design decreed for mortality at last earns identity. *Helen in Egypt* is H. D.'s death song, which is at once a capitulation to and a reconstitution of life.

Helen's union with Achilles is posited from the start. She tells his lost companions:

> ...God for his own purpose
> wills it so, that I
>
> stricken, forsaken draw to me,
> through magic greater than the trial of arms,
> your own invincible, unchallenged Sire....
>
> (5)

Paris and Theseus play their parts; but everything contributes, however unwittingly, to the foreordained syzygy of Helen and Achilles, and God's emissary and instigator is Thetis, mother goddess of the sea. Thetis it was who had unintentionally precipitated the war by failing to invite Eris (Strife), along with the other gods, to the banquet for her marriage to Peleus. Excluded from the celebration of Eros, Eris sowed the discord which after ten years killed Achilles, son of Thetis and Peleus. Eris was devious in her revenge; she tossed a golden apple marked "for the fairest" into the banquet hall, and when Hera, Athene, and Aphrodite began to wrangle for it, Zeus ordered that the quarrel be settled by the judgment of Paris, the youthful shepherd son of the Trojan king. Aphrodite won the apple by promising Paris the most beautiful woman in the world, who turned out to be Helen, Menelaus' queen. Thetis had counterschemes to thwart Eris' vengeance and save her son: she sought immortality for her son by dipping him into the river Styx; she charged Chiron with tutoring him in peaceful pursuits; she settled him into a safe, remote marriage with the daughter of the king of Scyros. All in vain: with Patroclus he left that safe haven to enter the deadly game of love and war, to take various women as his prizes of conquest, and in the end to meet his death; with Greek victory at hand under Achilles' command, the vengeful Paris slew his arch foe with Apollo's arrow, shooting it into the heel which Thetis had held when the waters of the Styx rendered Achilles otherwise invulnerable.

All this background is sketched through flashbacks and memories, but the poem begins with the dramatic encounter between Helen and Achilles. In death beyond the "fire of battle" and the "fire of desire" (285), he is ferried to Egypt, an alien shore where he does not recognize the dread Helen brooding on the hieroglyphs in the temple of Amen. From the time when Helen's glance from the Trojan ramparts locked with his below on the plains, his fate was set. They have moved, all unknowing, to this meeting, and Thetis is the catalyst: "How did we know each other? / was it the sea-enchantment in his eyes of Thetis his sea-mother?" (7). When Achilles grieves with a boy's petulant outrage at suffering the mortal fate of a mere man, Helen prays to comfort him like a mother:

> let me love him, as Thetis, his mother,
> for I knew him, I saw in his eyes
> the sea-enchantment, but he
>
> knew not yet, Helen of Sparta,
> knew not Helen of Troy,
> knew not Helen, hated of Greece.
>
> (14)

When he does recognize her, he clutches "my throat / with his fingers' remorseless steel," but Helen's plea to Thetis relaxes his grip (17). The last book of "Pallinode" presents Thetis speaking now "in complete harmony with Helen" (93). For Thetis becomes Helen's mother too – her surrogate mother, adopted by the mutually consenting love of "mother" and "daughter". Thetis is Helen, and Helen is Hilda.

From her mother Helen, Hilda felt that she drew her poetic and religious capabilities, her affinity with the power of the word and the Word. But that Helen seemed to withhold maternal instruction or blessing, seemed instead to prefer Gilbert to Hilda. Even before H. D. brought the problem to Freud in the 1930s, she had stated her disappointment in *HERmione*. There the daughter resents her mother, a failed artist conforming to patriarchal norms, because she has "no midwife power," "can't lift me out of" thwarted inarticulateness; and yet "one should sing hymns of worship to her, powerful, powerless, all-powerful" (80–81). *The Flowering of the Rod* and, more explicitly, *Helen* are the hymns she could not sing before in *HERmione*. For in the *Helen* poem Hilda assumes her mother's name at last and speaks.

And it is the mother name of Thetis which Helen gasps to the murderous Achilles. With that word, aggressor becomes brother, hetaira becomes sister, mother embraces daughter with son; with that name Helen and Achilles are reconciled as lovers and siblings. So complete is the mother's harmony with the filial Helen at the climax of "Pallinode" that she acts as psychopomp adumbrating Helen's selfhood, to be achieved under her aegis. Thetis' lyric rune inaugurates Helen's initiation into arcane female mysteries, drawn from the deeps of nature and of the psyche:

> A woman's wiles are a net;
> they would take the stars
> or a grasshopper in its mesh;
>
> they would sweep the sea
> for a bubble's iridescence
> or a flying-fish;
>
> they would plunge beneath the surface,
> without fear of the treacherous deep
> or a monstrous octopus;
>
> what unexpected treasure,
> what talisman or magic ring
> may the net find?
>
> frailer than spider spins,
> or a worm for its bier,
> deep as a lion or a fox
>
> or a panther's lair,
> leaf upon leaf, hair upon hair
> as a bird's nest,
>
> Phoenix
> has vanquished
> that ancient enemy, Sphinx.

(93–94)

Thetis' unriddling of the temple hieroglyphs reveals Helen's name rising from the rubble of war:

> The Lords have passed a decree,
> the Lords of the Hierarchy,
> that Helen be worshipped,
>
> be offered incense
> upon the altars of Greece,
> with her brothers, the Dioscuri;
>
> from Argos, from distant Scythia,
> from Delos, from Arcady,
> the harp-strings will answer
>
> the chant, the rhythm, the metre,
> the syllables H-E-L-E-N-A;
> Helena, reads the decree,
>
> shall be shrined forever;
> in Melos, in Thessaly,
> they shall honour the name of Love,

begot of the Ships and of War;
one indestructible name,
to inspire the Scribe and refute

the doubts of the dissolute;
this is the Law,
this, the Mandate:

let no man strive against Fate,
Helena has withstood
the rancour of time and of hate.

(95)

Thetis goes on to distinguish Helen's fate from that of her twin sister Clytemnestra, for Clytemnestra's relation to the masculine has been destructive and self-destructive. As Helen's "shadow" (2, 68), Clytemnestra has obscured her sister's self-perception, but now Thetis directs Helen to self-discovery through a creative connection with the masculine. Helen shall be immortalized with her twin brothers, the Dioscuri. The decree of Amen-Thoth, "Nameless-of-many-Names," is

that *Helena* shall remain
one name, inseparable
from the names of the Dioscuri,

who are not two but many,
as you read the writing, the script,
the thousand-petalled lily.

(104)

And the union with the brothers is concurrent with, or consequent to, the divine decree that "Helena / be joined to Achilles" (102). The hieroglyphs have sealed Helen's destiny, but the periplum to Achilles is a circumnavigation, first to Paris on the white isle of Leuké and then to Theseus in Athens to find the future by sorting out the past.

Why Leuké, *l'isle blanche*? "Because," the prose commentary says, "here, Achilles is said to have married Helen who bore him a son, Euphorion" (109). The import of this remark will become clearer later, but at the present it seems misleading since the first three books of "Leuké" narrate the reencountering of Paris and his "*Dendritis*,...Helena of the trees" (141). Paris mythicizes them as "Adonis and Cytheraea" (140), associating Helen with his goddess, Aphrodite, and seeks to rouse her from Egyptian divination and Greek intellection to rekindled sexual passion: "O Helena, tangled in thought, / be Rhodes' Helena, *Dendritis*, / why remember Achilles?" (142); "I say he never loved you" (144). Paris harkens back to a life of passion on the old terms, now to Helen past feeling and past recall. *End to Torment* recounts an ecstatic moment of passion shared by Pound and his dryad in a tree in the Doolittles' back yard; in 1958 H. D. still harkens back to that poignant moment: "Why had I ever come down out of that tree?" Out of that paradisal garden-love into a world torn by Love and War, Eros and Thanatos. The love poems of "Hilda's Book," inscribed and bound for her by Pound and only recently reprinted with *End to Torment*, celebrate her as Hilda of the trees: "My Lady is tall and fair to see / She swayeth as a poplar tree"; "Thou that art sweeter than all orchard's breath"; "She hath some tree-born spirit of the wood / About her"; and, most glowingly, "The Tree," which survived the juvenilia of "Hilda's Book" in *A Lume Spento* and *Personae*: "I stood still and was a tree amid the wood / Knowing the truth of things unseen before / Of Daphne and the laurel brow."[96] From his prison camp at Pisa, Pound had called out to his Dryas in Canto 83 and again in the famous lynx song of Canto 79. Now, after years of separation, they were again in touch. After his return to Italy he invited her to Venice (Venus' city), but her identification with Helen-Thetis kept her from going back to old loves and old lovers.

Helen flees Paris' importuning for the counsel of the aged Theseus, who wraps her in the security of warm blankets on his couch, like a swaddled baby or cocooned butterfly. At first, Theseus counters her recoil from "Paris as Eros-Adonis" (160) with Athenian reasonableness, urging happiness with Paris and denouncing Achilles as Thanatos: "even a Spirit loves laughter, / did you laugh with Achilles? No" (161); "you found life here with Paris" (173). Why should she choose to "flame out, incandescent" in death (187) with Achilles, who has exploited women all his life? Gradually in the course of their conversation, Theseus reluctantly recognizes that Helen is no longer Paris' Dendritis and that Achilles may not be his old self either.

Paris now seems to Helen too fevered and puerile to be the one she seeks. Theseus comes to see that she longs for a new and perfect Lover "beyond Trojan and Greek" (165); she is the Phoenix tensed to rise from the ashes, the butterfly cracking the chrysalis and "wavering / like a Psyche / with half-dried wings" (166). Though Theseus acknowledges Helen's development and stops pleading Paris' case, he turns to importuning for himself because he has been smitten by Helen since she was a girl. H. D. probably had in mind Freud's angry complaint during a therapeutic session that his pupil found him too old to love. Theseus' suggestion that she view him for the nonce as someone "half-way" to her ideal lover is tender and poignant – but out of the question. As with Freud and H. D., Theseus has become Helen's "god-father" by pointing her to a wisdom radically different from his own. His awkward offer of himself requires her to clarify her own goal and prepares her to relinquish him as well as Paris in order to seek out Achilles once and for all. As for old transgressions, Achilles and she are "past caring" (177); the future need not be blocked by the past; life can only lead to afterlife.

Paris' adolescent eroticism makes him seem her own child, perhaps even Achilles' son – yes, "incarnate / Helen-Achilles" – so that her life has come round to a perfect circle like the snake with its tail in its mouth: "He, my first lover, was created by my last" (185). On one level, this line may recall again the special connection between Pound and Heydt in the sequence of male initiators, and the reemergence of Pound as a potent psychological presence during H. D.'s late years, largely through the agency of Heydt. But another reading of the line would see Helen as setting aside as outdated and outgrown all the lovers and initiators of her previous life for a new kind of love to be found with Achilles. When the prose commentary at the beginning of Part II said that on Leuké "Achilles is said to have married Helen who bore him a son" (109), the statement seemed mistaken or misleading, for Helen met not Achilles but Paris on Leuké. But as it turns out, her refusal to turn back the life cycle makes Paris seem, regressively, a child to her. Through Theseus her heightened consciousness reconstitutes her by reclaiming her past with a new maturity. And so, by a kind of hindsight discovery, the recognition of Paris as child confirms Achilles as husband-father.

For in this poem, Achilles and Paris matter only in relation to and in definition of Helen. The central insight which opens the resolution of the poem is the realization that she is the Phoenix, the Psyche self-born:

> beyond all other, the Child,
> the child in the father,
> the child in the mother,
>
> the child-mother, yourself. . . .
> (187)

Helen enwombs the entire process; the "child-mother" bears herself. When Helen asks Theseus how the masculine dualities – her twin brothers Castor and Pollux, Achilles and Theseus – can be reconciled, he answers that all polarities meet in herself. His insight unexpectedly and uncharacteristically carries him past Greek rationality to ecstatic vision, the verbal echoes and rhythms rocking the lines to a hallucinated resolution beyond words. His incantation, at once limpid and opaque, veiling the revelation in the act of revealing the veiled secret, brings "Leuké" to a climax:

> Thus, thus, thus,
> as day, night,
> as wrong, right,
>
> as dark, light,
> as water, fire,
> as earth, air,
>
> as storm, calm,
> as fruit, flower,
> as life, death,
>
> as death, life;
> the rose deflowered,
> the rose re-born;
>
> Helen in Egypt,
> Helen at home,
> Helen in Hellas forever.
> (190)

The prose commentary informs us that "Helen understands, though we do not know exactly what it is that she understands" (191), but the interplay of compensatory opposites in a transcendent pattern (Emerson called the cosmic law "Compensation") now appears to her "very simple" (192). Reconciled "to Hellas forever," she sets out to return to Achilles in Egypt for the long-appointed union; Theseus has no choice but to bless her voyage to "Dis, Hades, Achilles" (199). Her fate is not her dead life with Paris, but renewal with the dead Achilles; her myth is not Venus and Adonis, as Paris urged, but Persephone and Hades. And the hierogamy will be personal and psychological: "I will encompass the infinite / in time, in the crystal, / in my thought here" (201).

Early in Part III, "Eidolon," Paris abandons his recriminations against Pluto-Achilles ("his is a death-cult," p. 216) and accepts him as father, with Helen replacing Hecuba as mother. Now the poem circles back with deeper comprehension to the meeting with which it began, when Achilles, raging against his mortality, attacks Helen, until his mother's – Helen's godmother's – intervention relaxes his death grip into an embrace. Achilles had forsaken his mother when he went to war; only after ten years on the Trojan plain did he promise to return to her if she helped him seize victory. But with victory in his grasp, he suffered his human destiny. Paris' arrow found Achilles' heel, and he returned to his mother in a strange land, finding her in the eyes and person of Helen. With Paris reclaimed as son, Helen reaches her apotheosis as mother. The single word "Thetis," gasped from Achilles' strangle grasp, metamorphoses Helen in his eyes into a sea goddess. For that mother-name

> would weld him to her
> who spoke it, who thought it,
>
> who stared through the fire,
> who stood as if to withstand
> the onslaught of fury and battle,
>
> who stood unwavering but made
> as if to dive down, unbroken,
> undefeated in the tempest roar
>
> and thunder, inviting mountains
> of snow-clad foam-tipped
> green walls of sea-water
>
> to rise like ramparts about her,
> walls to protect yet walls to dive under,
> dive through and dive over....
>
> (278)

The two "will always" for that "eternal moment" comprise a syzygy of L'Amour, La Mort (271, 277): "this is Love, this is Death, / this is my last Lover" (268). Paris, discarded as lover, is reborn as their child, and the offspring of their syzygy is not just Paris but themselves restored: Achilles the "child in Chiron's cave," Helen the maid at Theseus' knee (289–290). The mythic psychological status which Helen attains in the poem encompasses mother and wife and restored daughter: Demeter-Persephone-Kore in one. In writing her own Helen text, H. D. arrived at a reading of identity which resumed and surpassed the past. That moment – between time and eternity and participating in both – is the "final illumination" of the poem (271), and it is the moment of death. Through the mother-goddess she has conceived and come full term, dying and rising to herself. That metamorphosis, spelled out in the poem, has sealed her life cycle in the eternal pattern. "Sealed" in several senses: it brings her life to fulfillment and conclusion, it impresses on that life its distinctive sign or hieroglyph, and it affirms that life with irrevocable authority. Helen had said: "to me, the wheel is a seal.../ the wheel is still" (203). Under the name of Helen, H. D. spelled out her hermetic definition. Though *Helen in Egypt* is a death hymn, H. D. told her notebook: "I am alive in the *Helen* sequence" because "there I had found myself"; those poems "give me everything."[97]

Early in the poem Helen asks: "is it only the true immortals / who partake of mortality?" (28). The poem's response inverts the proposition: true partakers of mortality achieve immortality. The moment of death is the moment of gnosis, in which life and consciousness conclude and transcend themselves; Helen becomes, with Achilles, a "New Mortal" (10, 263, 300) – L'Amour/La Mort in a higher configuration. This is what the last lyric of Book III postulates in lines whose declarative simplicity does not designate the mystery they bespeak:

> Paris before Egypt, Paris after,
> is Eros, even as Thetis,
> the sea-mother, is Paphos;
>
> so the dart of Love
> is the dart of Death,
> and the secret is no secret;
>
> the simple path
> refutes at last
> the threat of the Labyrinth,
>
> the Sphinx is seen,
> the Beast is slain
> and the Phoenix-nest
>
> reveals the innermost
> key or the clue to the rest
> of the mystery;
>
> there is no before and no after,
> there is one finite moment
> that no infinite joy can disperse
>
> or thought of past happiness
> tempt from or dissipate;
> now I know the best and the worst;
>
> the seasons revolve around
> a pause in the infinite rhythm
> of the heart and of heaven.
>
> (303–304)

To some readers the "final illumination" to which *Helen in Egypt* builds will seem gnomic, perhaps nonsensical. But the vision of the eternal moment, with time concentered individually and cosmically in eternity, is H. D.'s occult version of Eliot's Christian "still point of the turning world." In fact, the conclusion of *Helen in Egypt*[98] deserves to be set beside such exalted moments in poems of old age as Eliot's in the *Quartets*, when "the fire and the rose are one." Or Frost's arrival, in "Directive," back at the spring source which is his watering place ("Drink and be whole again"). Or Williams' declaration through his dead "Sparrow": "This was I, / a sparrow. I did my best; / farewell." Or Pound's conclusion to *The Cantos*: "Do not move. / Let the wind speak. / That is Paradise"; or his version of Herakles' expiring words:

what

SPLENDOUR,

IT ALL COHERES.

Different in tone and perspective as these moments are, the reader either is or is not already there with the poet. By this point, in the particular poem and in the evolution of the poet's life's work, evocation has become invocation; image and symbol, bare statement. Further demonstration is out of the question.

Whereas Frost's final sense of things remained skeptical and Williams' naturalistic, H. D.'s like Eliot's, was religious and, like Pound's, heterodoxly so. No resume or excerpting of passages can indicate how subtly the images and leitmotifs of *Helen in Egypt* are woven into the design. Some reviewers found the prose passages distracting intrusions among the lyrics, but H. D. wanted, like the other poets cited in their poetic summations, a counterpoint of lyric expression and reflective commentary. In identification with the mother-goddess, assimilating Greek and Egyptian, Christian and gnostic wisdom, H. D. came to read the scribble of her life as hieroglyph. Nothing need be forgotten; nothing could be denied; everything was caught up in the resolution.

The summons of the sea-mother which closes Part I, "Helen – come home" (p. 108), and initiates a refrain that echoes throughout the poem, receives a gloss in a notebook entry: "We say (old-fashioned people used to say) when someone dies, he or she has *gone home*. I was looking for home, I think. But a sort of heaven-is-my-home."[99] The recovery of the mother as self, the discovery of the mother in herself and herself in the mother, constituted "heaven-is-my-home," and allowed, in the concluding lyric, a return of the lover twins to the mother-sea:

> But what could Paris know of the sea,
> its beat and long reverberation,
> its booming and delicate echo,
>
> its ripple that spells a charm
> on the sand, the rock-lichen,
> the sea-moss, the sand,
>
> and again and again, the sand;
> what does Paris know of the hill and hollow
> of billows, the sea-road?

> *what could he know of the ships*
> *from his Idaean home,*
> *the crash and spray of the foam,*
>
> *the wind, the shoal, the broken shale,*
> *the infinite loneliness*
> *when one is never alone?*
>
> *only Achilles could break his heart*
> *and the world for a token,*
> *a memory forgotten.*
>
> (304)

As the poem indicates, Helen's recovery of the mother coincides with a shift in her relation to the masculine, away from the dominating Paris, who used to have power over her, to a chastened Achilles, and the shift signals a reimagining of the central theme of H. D.'s fiction and verse.

The biographical sources of the sexual anxiety are clear: the broken engagement to Pound, the broken marriage to Aldington in the years during and immediately after World War I, the rejections by Lawrence, Dowding, and Heydt. But she continued to seek the reconciliation that would heal the psychic wounds. Her correspondence with John Cournos, a member of their London circle, shows her intense concern about Aldington before, during, even after the separation. As late as February 1929, she wanted to scotch any rumor Cournos had heard of a "final quarrel" with Aldington, and in July she sent Cournos this excited word:

> ...without any intervention R. wrote me and I have been in close touch with him ever since....We saw one another much in Paris and write constantly. We are very, very close to one another intellectually and spiritually. There may be some definite separation later, but if there is, it will be because of FRIENDLINESS and nothing else. There is no question of R. and self ever becoming in any way "intimate" again and that is why this other relationship is so exquisite and sustaining.[100]

In fact, as she might well have suspected, she was never to reach "this other relationship" – intellectual and spiritual without the compulsions and vulnerabilities of the physical – with Aldington, but even their divorce in 1938 did not break off communications between them. They went their separate, and often stormy, ways; but during the years at Küsnacht Klinik they were still corresponding, and Dr. Heydt was as curious about Aldington as he was about Pound. A journal from those late years, dealing often with her relation to Heydt, is called "Compassionate Friendship."

It is clear that after she fell from the innocence of that first love with Pound in the tree into the betrayals and counterbetrayals of sexual relationships, she often asked herself, "Why had I ever come down out of that tree?" By the time Achilles succeeds Paris at the end of *Helen*, those male characters have achieved archetypal functions within the design of female consciousness. H. D. saw the whole succession of initiators, including Heydt, in Pound, and she also saw in Achilles, as she told her notebook, the "heros fatale" who had failed her repeatedly – Pound and Aldington, "Lord Howell" (Dowding) of the unpublished World War II novels, and now Heydt at the Klinik. Yet since the "heros fatale" held the key to her self-fulfillment, she must imagine the terms on which Helen would marry Achilles: a sea-changed Achilles, Aldington re-possessed once and for all in the consanguinity of the mother. The mother gave her the word, and the word was her own name – and Hilda's Helen poem. There, in the imagined possibilities of the word, she attained at last, at great cost, the "exquisite and sustaining" relationship she could never establish in life.

More especially so since the union resolved the parental as well as the sexual crisis. In a notebook passage, previously quoted, which mentions the asso-ciation of her astronomer father with the airman Dowding in the figure of Achilles, H. D. notes again the association of Helen with her mother. The passage then continues: "in the sequence, Helen is ideally or poetically or epi-cally 'married' to Achilles. . . .I know the father, the mother, and the third of the trio or trilogy, the poem, the creation, the thing they begot or conceived between them. It is all perfect." The creation of the poem has reached perfec-tion; Helen is mother-daughter-wife: the completed feminine archetype. In the ideal-poetic-epic marriage of Helen to Achilles, H. D. attains "the final and complete solution of the life-long search for the answer – the companion in-time and out-of-time together."[101] In the poem Achilles is Helen's "Achilles" now, father-husband-son, and together they consign themselves to the sea.

The perfect union of Helen and Achilles is therefore a death marriage, as in the "marriage" poems of Emily Dickinson, realized in the imaginative crea-tion. If Dickinson's "love" poetry remains more indirect and inhibited than Helen in Egypt, the cause may lie in part in Dickinson's attachment to her stern father: a bonding so strong that it kept her from the experience of the wife and the mother and allowed her to experience the masculine principally as the virgin daughter, at the furthest extreme as the virgin bride: Kore rather than Persephone or Demeter. H. D.'s Helen would not be daughter to Theseus or hetaira to Paris; through Thetis she made Achilles her own, husband and father and son, as she was wife and mother and daughter. Helen Doolittle was the source of Hilda's visionary and artistic power, and in her Helen poem Hilda formulated her most complete hermetic definition.

The scope of that vision also made for another notable difference between Helen in Egypt and Dickinson's love poems. Wrenching and exhilarating as they are, Dickinson's love poems remain a collection of individual pieces at cross-purposes, recording ambivalences that kept her the father's virgin daughter. In the long, tortuous, fragmented history of women writing about their womanhood, the supreme distinction of Helen in Egypt, with all its idio-syncrasies, is that it transforms the man's war epic into the woman's love lyric sustained at a peak of intensity for an epic's length, and its myth posits the supremacy of the mother: Helen self-born in Thetis, Hilda self-born in Helen.

VII

When Bid Me to Live was released in 1960 – H. D.'s first published novel in over thirty years, and an enticing roman à clef at that – Newsweek magazine assigned correspondent Lionel Durand, a Haitian who served then as chief of its Paris bureau, to interview the author at the Küsnacht Klinik for a "Talk with the Author" to accompany its review of the novel. The review, captioned "Life in a Hothouse," noted "the quivering impressionist prose" which caught the "peculiar and sometimes silly intensity" of the characters and concluded coolly, "This is the way they lived and thought and felt then, and it was in this manner of being that they made their special contributions to the world of letters. It is interesting as history, and if you can stand its preciousness, it has its fascinations as a novel." "Talk with the Author" on the same page described, in tones of breezy, journalistic condescension, "the tall, gaunt woman of 73," ailing and getting about the clinic on metal canes, whose mind was "still aflame with provocative thoughts, strong opinions, and the literary temper."[102]

Durand had no inkling how "aflame" H. D. could "still" be, or that in becoming her last "Paris" he provoked a remarkable last utterance, her most openly confessional poem, in the final months of her life. Written from the late summer 1960 into the winter of the next year, "Hermetic Definition"[103] begins with abrupt and bold directness:

> Why did you come
> to trouble my decline?
> I am old (I was old till you came);
>
> the reddest rose unfolds....
>
> (3)

The interview had taken place in April 1960; she would see Durand only once more, at a crowded cocktail party during her trip to New York the next month. But these two brief, superficial encounters had thrown H. D. into a young girl's romantic passion for a man little more than half her age. As in the case of Dickinson's love poems, the romance transpires entirely in the poet's own psyche, where the image of the man functions as a charismatic projection of her animus, the male figure in her psychological life who seemed to hold the key to the secret of her identity, body and soul.

All unwittingly, therefore, Durand came to represent to H. D. "religion or majic...together, matched, / mated, exactly the same, / equal in power, together yet separate, / your eyes' amber" (4). As with previous initiators, personifying in her imagination erotic and spiritual fulfillment, he was the new avatar of Paris:

> Isis, Iris,
> fleur de lis,
> Bar-Isis is son of Isis,
>
> (bar ou ber ou ben, significant fils).
> so Bar-Isis is Par-isis?
> Paris, anyway....
>
> (5)

She had been reading Robert Ambelain's *Dans l'ombre des cathedrals* (1939), and she was transfixed by his account of the assimilation of elements from the Greek and Egyptian hermetic mysteries into Christianity. Just as Pound saw the Albigensians and the Provençal poets as descendants of the "Mediterranean sanity" of classical mystery cults, so H. D. took her mother's Moravian sect as the Christian extension of the love religion of Provence. Now, through Ambelain, she considered calling the new sequence *Notre Dame d'Amour*.

Durand was the emissary from Paris, the city of Notre Dame, and from Ambelain the first part of the poem develops the occult symbolism in the imagery and inscriptions of the cathedral's three doors, associated in this version with astrology, alchemy, and magic. The poet's archetype is Isis, become Mary, now become Venus: Notre Dame d'Amour. So her imagination speeds Paris to Venice, Venus' city of love: "now I walk into you, / Doge – Venice – / you are my whole estate" (6). The poem resumes the rose symbolism of *Red Roses for Bronze*, but here the rose takes on the visionary eroticism of Georgia O'Keeffe's paintings of flowers. The earlier poem had come out of her frustrated infatuation with Paul Robeson, with whom she had played in the experimental film *Borderline*, and she thought of it again in 1960 when another black man entered her life, as before not to fulfill but again merely to vex her frustrated passion.

For the red promise of the unfolding rose is thwarted by Durand/Paris' indifference to her as a woman and an artist ("you brushed aside / my verse"). She waits in vain for an answer to her letter. She is insulted by his apparent aloofness at the New York party; his refusal of the wine and salted nuts seems to her a calculated ritual of rejection, passed off with the rumor of a weak heart. Why does she write? he asked her; and, as in *The Walls Do Not Fall*, the hostile or uncomprehending questioning of the scribe's vocation triggers an oracular self-exoneration: "She," her divine self-image, "commands, / write, write or die" (7).

At the same time, so vulnerable and fragile was her assurance before the dismissive male judge, even after *Trilogy* and *Helen in Egypt*, that Durand's coolness seemed to call her life's work into question. When Pound, her old Paris, wrote from Italy that he feared he could not pull off his *Cantos*, his doubts reinforced her own; echoing Pound, she asked of herself: "What have I done with my life?" (17). In Canto 106 Pound had written of her, "so slow is the rose to open," but now it seemed that once again, with Durand, she had opened herself to the wrong man at great risk. Nevertheless, for all her equivocation, "Red Rose and a Beggar," the first section of "Hermetic Definition," ends, characteristically, not in resigned defeat but in a resumption of the quest:

> I must keep my identity,
> walk unfalteringly toward a Lover,
> the *hachish supérieur* of dream.
>
> (21)

In Norman Holmes Pearson's words, H. D.'s "way of symbolizing what she was searching for was through males." His comment distinguishes and associates the several levels on which the animus functions: "H. D. was after a thing that might be called in the broadest sense the lover. This could be a physical lover; or could be God the Father as lover, or Father the God as lover within her own family, or even Freud the lover – the almost Neoplatonic sense of love." In H. D.'s words, "Isis takes many forms, as does Osiris. . . . women are individually seeking, as one woman, fragments of the Eternal Lover. As the Eternal Lover has been scattered or dissociated, so she in her search for him." At the beginning of his career, Pound, identifying himself as poet with Isis, named the archetypal source of his poetry in the title "I Gather the Limbs of Osiris." "Hermetic Definition" recounts a similar quest for Durand as Osiris, Bar-Isis, Paris.

Pearson's remarks – and H. D.'s – remind us again of the surprising affinity between H. D. and Emily Dickinson in fundamental ways. The "He" in Dickinson's poems is at once man and God, lover and Jesus. While Marianne Moore, a half century after Dickinson, would avoid acknowledgment of her animus, H. D.'s writing traces out an odyssey of engagements and separations which falls short, one way or another, of the animus ideal. What links her with Dickinson, rather than with her contemporary Moore, is the animus engagement; that is to say, as Pearson observed, she "endowed" certain men "in a poetic way" with the powers and qualities she desired. For – again as with Dickinson – it was "not the man or the flesh" she sought but "the principle of malehood and womanhood combined into a wholeness" within herself.[104] "The *Helen* always satisfies me," she had written, because there under the empowerment of the mother name she imagined Achilles as "the companion in-time and out-of-time together."[105] And even after *Helen*, "Hermetic Definition" reaffirms the interdependence of "my identity" and the "Lover": both the dependence of her identity upon the Lover and, correspondingly, the function of the Lover within her identity.

In "Grove of Academe," Part 2 of "Hermetic Definition," Durand is replaced and countered by the figure of St. John Perse, the French poet whom H. D. met for the first and only time on the 1960 trip to New York. Just a month after her interview with Durand, she had come to New York to be the first woman recipient of the American Academy's Gold Medal for poetry. As she made her way from her seat on the platform to the podium to receive the acclaim of the distinguished company, her crippled leg gave way, and she was saved from a humiliating and dangerous fall by Perse's hand at her elbow, as he reached out from his seat behind her to support and steady her. After Durand had spurned her, Perse rescued her. That simple act at their single meeting becomes in the poem a prefigurative gesture of redemption. During the ensuing autumn of waiting for a communication from Durand, H. D. immersed herself in Perse's verse, and it becomes, in her metaphor, the rock on which she relocates herself as poet. Not only did his presence at the New York ceremony indicate that he honored her just as she honored him, poet to poet, but his poetry reconfirmed for her a vision of the cosmos gloriously alive and harmoniously sustained in its transcendent mystery. Counter-animus to Durand, "you draw me out to compete with your frenzy"; "your words free me / I am alive in your recognition" (33). Freud would call it sublimation, but the visionary "frenzy" he offers lifts her out of the erotic susceptibility which has exposed her again to male betrayal. (In *Bid Me to Live*, Lawrence performed a similar function in releasing her from Aldington's domination.) Again in her life "Athene stands guardian" safely against Venus, "and there is ecstasy and healing / in her acceptance of [the poet's] fantasy" (33). For, of course, the rock is not just Perse's poetry but her own; to the woman's flaming rose he proffers the silver-green olive of salvation and the poet's cool laurel.

The final irony, however, is that H. D. is called upon to lay Durand to rest in a way she had never anticipated. "Star of Day," Part 3 of the sequence, is its abbreviated conclusion. "Red Rose and a Beggar" and "Grove of Academe" each consisted of eighteen lyrics; "Star of Day" has but eight. Dated January 24 – February 19, 1961, they were composed in the weeks immediately following the word in January 1961 that Durand had died suddenly of the heart trouble she refused to credit as his excuse for unsociability in New York. H. D. would die less than two months later. The poem ends with the shaken poet resigned to

> draw my nun-grey about me
> and know adequately,
>
> *the reddest rose,*
> *the unalterable law* . . .
> Night brings the Day.
>
>   (55)

And yet the unalterable law requires the grey nun not to deny but to acknowledge the reddest rose. In a characteristic reversal, grief and shock are themselves caught up and resolved in a sense of the cosmic cycle that Perse's words had restored to her. The winter solstice is both the dark of the year and the turn toward light. Durand had died around Christmas, the birthday at the year's end. As in "Little Gidding," where the fire and the rose become one, so now

> just as my Christmas candles
> had burnt out,
>
> that you were born,
> (you had died, they said),
> integrated with the Star of Day.
>   (48)

As in H. D.'s other poems and fiction, victimization issues in triumph; vulnerability seals inviolability. Just before her own death, the nun-mother, chaste but not barren, had given birth to a final poem, in which broken passion yields the secret of immortality:

I wrote furiously,
I was in a fever, you were lost,
just as I had found you,

but I went on, I had to go on,
the writing was the un-born,
the conception.

(54)

It is, she notes, "a little over nine months to the day" since the meeting with Durand. His life for her, his life within her, has come to term *as the poem*, where Mary supplants or subsumes Venus after all as the poet's archetype: not the Notre Dame d'Amour now but Isis gathering the limbs of Bar-Isis or, better still, the Magdalen-Mary of the Pieta. Like Helen, Hilda divines the lost lover as the poem-son. Loved, he must be relinquished; relinquished, he must be held as an image of immortality, must die into art. When she had called him "*significant fils*" in Part 1, she had not known that he would signify as poem. It is not just "nuns and mothers" who "worship images," as Yeats wrote, but poets too.[106] Here the poet arrives at the meaning of "H. D.," her "Hermetic Definition," by understanding the poet-lover as nun-mother.

Those paradoxical pairings suggest both the tensions and the resolution of H. D.'s life and art. In *The Great Mother*[107] Erich Neumann studied the triune configuration of the feminine archetype: virgin, mother, daughter. The names might be Persephone, Demeter, Kore or Artemis, Aphrodite, Athene. Virgin and daughter are the beginning and the end of the cycle, but mother is the still and turning pivot. Among the virgin-daughter-scribes, H. D. conceived herself – unlike Emily Dickinson and Marianne Moore – as mother. Not the mother as artist: not Anne Bradstreet, much less Mrs. Sigourney. Perdita did not occupy H. D.'s imaginative attention except for the single fairy tale of *The Hedgehog*. No, not the mother as artist, but the artist as mother, resuming her lover-sons into a parthenogenetic self-renewal. And so the artist-mother of the poem-son is virgin-daughter. The animus strength she learned, and earned, from Professors Doolittle and Freud, from Pound and Aldington and Lawrence, from Dowding and Heydt, and, at the last, from Perse and Durand made the virgin-mother-poet, Persephone-Demeter-Kore, Artemis-Aphrodite-Athene, violate and ever inviolate.

6

William Carlos Williams: Mother-Son and Paterson

I

As Pound's irrepressible arrogance seemed, in the eyes of most of the American literary public, to veer dangerously toward insane or criminal behavior – the poet as crank, the prophet as crackpot and bigot – Pound's life-long friend, fellow student, and brother poet at the University of Pennsylvania took on something of the venerable, lovable aura of Whitman: the American bard as doctor and healer, as cultural wound dresser. There are many connections between Whitman and William Carlos Williams. They were both volatile, contradictory, calculatedly outgoing personalities with a dark under-streak of depression and self-doubt. Toward the end of his life, Wallace Stevens spoke of Williams as a "man somehow disturbed at the core and making all sorts of gestures...to conceal it from himself," just as earlier, in the 1920s, he had warned Williams, to Williams' annoyance, that his inconsistent shifting of perspective consigned him to "incessant new beginnings," which would end in "sterility."[1] Although it is true of all poets that their poetry serves to express the discordant aspects of their psyches, it is truest, most urgent, and most difficult for poets like Whitman and Dickinson, Pound and Williams, who, unlike Stevens or Frost, take the risk of entrusting more of their personal contradictions to the alembic of poetry in the hope of transmutation and resolution.

"Incessant new beginnings," instead of elaboration and development. Whitman said that each poem was a new venture, but over the years he came to operate from an increasingly explicit philosophical position. Williams did not have Whitman's metaphysics (in fact, scorned it) or the philosophic turn of mind which steadied Stevens' and Frost's composure from an aesthetic distance. The "supreme fiction" had to change, but not the underlying temperament, tone of voice, angle of vision. Williams, *faute de mieux* from Stevens' point of view, had to pursue the course of new beginnings – not without uncertainties and depressions at times, but overall with infectious gusto.

Mike Weaver closes his study of Williams with a passage from an unpublished letter of 1926 which indicates the poet's ambivalence about seeking and finding a pattern in his life and in his art:

> I must look and digest, swallow and break up a situation in myself before it can get to me. It is due to my wanting to encircle too much. It is due to my lack of pattern. For if I were working inside a pattern, everyone working in other patterns beside me... would be understood by me at once – and they are not so understood by me. As I exist, omnivorous, everything I touch seems incomplete until I can swallow, digest and make it a part of myself.
>
> But my failure to work inside a pattern – a positive sin – is the cause of my virtues. I cannot work inside a pattern because I can't find a pattern that will have me. My whole effort... is to find a pattern, large enough, modern enough, flexible enough to include my desires. And if I should find it I'd wither and die.[2]

Life's venture was to press toward coherence, but for the unphilosophic Williams, that coherence could only be provisional and aesthetic, because the poet who had written his final poem was dead. The paradox for the Modernist was that in a world without absolutes the work of art had to be provisional – and absolute, or at least quasi-absolute.

In the passage, the feminine imagery of encirclement, ingestion, and gestation, which reflects Williams' experience as an obstetrician and his naturalistic view of life as a biological process, recalls Whitman as well; but as a Modernist, Williams had to feel more acutely than Whitman the tension between an insatiable susceptibility to experience, on the one hand, and the exactitudes of form, on the other. How to turn "lack of pattern" and "incessant new beginnings" to advantage? How to draw inchoate materials into coherent form? As much as Williams honored Whitman throughout his life and admitted his influence from the time of his earliest writings, he just as regularly rejected the expansive formlessness of free verse and attributed it to the Romantic passivity of Whitman's temperament and the flaccidity of his metaphysics.

For Williams, as much as for Whitman, the creative power which issued in language was explicitly identified with sexuality: "Pan," wrote Williams, "is the artist's patron." To Robert McAlmon, who had spent many years as an expatriate like Pound, he described the "innate" authority in which they all participated as artists as "a sexual component in the Freudian sense" and endorsed McAlmon's extension of it over language: "Your definition of it as an evocative power over the word is good.... It's the authority behind it that gives the word power. Something that is in the man himself, really great – and unaccountable."[3] It is not surprising that Williams sent D. H. Lawrence a spontaneous fan letter and, even though sorely disappointed at receiving no acknowledgment, composed an elegy to salute Lawrence after his death. Although Williams would have scoffed at spelling the sexual life force with capital letters and thus attributing to it a transcendent dimension beyond the workings of nature, the erotic seemed to him the closest experience he knew of the divine: "love of God and love of women – almost indistinguishable to the poet though he made ample gestures both ways." In the Freudian sense again, poetry is the sublimation of the sexual drive through which the power of Pan and Dionysus is brought to fruition up and down the whole scale of human experience. Williams' *Autobiography* makes the point at the beginning of the "Foreword": "What relations I have had with men and women, such encounters as have interested me most profoundly, have not occurred in bed. I am extremely sexual in my desires; I carry them everywhere and at all times. I think that from that arises the drive which empowers us all. Given that drive, a man does with it what his mind directs. In the manner in which he directs that power lies his secret."[4] The poet's ego draws upon the id and lifts its largely unconscious materials into expressive direction and containment. But the source is sexual: Williams pointedly called attention to Stuart Davis' design for the cover of *Kora in Hell* as a symbol of the imaginative act: "an ovum surrounded by a horde of spermatozoa about it, a dark one being accepted." He meant his "burning with the lust to write" less as a metaphor than as a descriptive fact.[5]

Because both Whitman and Williams felt their poetic power as sexual and their sexual power as poetic, the differences in their sexual orientation and development created the definitive differences in their poetic theory and practice. Whitman's father, a stern and ignorant man whose shiftlessness left the family poor and psychologically scarred, played no conscious part in Whitman's mental, emotional, and imaginative life; but his equally uneducated mother's emotional domination and capacity for suffering, endurance, and acceptance became overwhelming factors in his psychological development, as critics and biographers have repeatedly observed. The feminine archetype was so totally fixed in the image of the mother that Whitman was incapacitated for heterosexual relationships, and apparently for overtly sexual relationships of any kind. Instead, he submitted his manhood to the mother flux of experience as son-lover, lulled by her waves and currents and tides, translating her rhythms into his long but self-circling verses. The Whitman poem hankered to be all-inclusive in its relationships, the poet's ego submerged in the myriad particulars of the sea drift and the particular statements of inclusiveness accumulated into his ongoing life poem.

But Williams saw that unchecked undertow of the mother as drawing those verses to dissolution rather than definition. He wanted the interplay of the masculine with the feminine which would give form to his intuitive openness to experience. Williams conceived the masculine and feminine principles in clear terms, ideally complementary but in fact often at variance with each other: "Men have given the direction to my life and women have always supplied the energy."[6] The masculine represented the inclination toward clarity, definition, unity; the feminine, the inclination toward instinct, indeterminacy, multiplicity. (H. D., by contrast, would associate her poetic definition as a woman with submitting masculine clarity to maternal mystery.)

Williams' poems proclaimed his heterosexuality as insistently as they proclaimed their drive toward form. (Though he would contribute the "Introduction" to Allen Ginsberg's *Howl*, he was disturbed by, and disapproving of, the strong homosexual strain in Beat writers.) Williams' poetic power is associated with his heterosexuality: "Paterson, / keep your pecker up," he joshingly admonishes himself still at the end of the life and of the poem. (Even Whitman maintained a public stance of heterosexuality.) So the psychological and aesthetic drama of resolving empathy and form, energy and direction, was thrown back on the paternal and maternal archetypes and was played out explicitly in terms of Williams' complicated relationships with his father and mother.

Williams' assertive Americanness was in part a negative response to the proper and intransigently English father whose first name he bore. William Williams was an émigré who worked hard all through his married life as a salesman traveling through the Americas for the Florida Water Company in New York, with his family based in the nearby industrialized town of Rutherford, New Jersey. The tension between father and son remained to the end. The elder Williams' death on Christmas Day of 1918 came when his son was thirty-five, struggling to support his family as a general practitioner while attempting to prove to himself, as much as to anyone, that he could be a poet even under such inauspicious circumstances (while his old friends Pound and H. D. created a stir in the London poetry world). The son was temperamentally so different from his punctilious father that they came to bitter clashes. Yet Williams could later refer in his *Autobiography* to "my blessed father" not wholly ironically, and the old Chinese philosopher on the bell which was the elder Williams' Christmas present for his son on the day he died seemed to Williams to represent his lost father, or at least the authority of his father's image in his mind.

Williams associated his father with economic necessity and his mother with art, but his father played a crucial negative role in his sense of himself as poet. For Williams' respect for paternal authority invested his father with the authoritative and unsettling judgment of the critic. The son felt obliged to submit the manuscript of his first volume, *Poems* (1909), to his father's unsmiling scrutiny, and he made "corrections and suggestions all over it – changes most of which I adopted. Poor Pop, how he must have suffered."[7] Williams is obviously retaliating by projecting his own suffering onto the cause of his suffering. Nevertheless, he grudgingly came to agree with Pound that "I never laid proper stress in my life upon the part played in it by my father rather than my mother. Oh, the woman of it is important, he [Pound] would acknowledge, but the form of it, if not the drive, came unacknowledged by me from the old man, the Englishman."[8] Williams' linking Pound and his father as critics with a sense of poetic form indicates his ambivalence about the critical authority of father and fraternal rival. The elder Williams liked Pound and, in contrast to his treatment of his son's poetry, liked to discuss Pound's poems with him. Williams frequently told the anecdote in which his father challenged Pound about the function and meaning of a metaphor in one of Pound's poems. His father criticized merely decorative figures of speech and plumped for direct statement, and "Ezra," Williams mused, "appears never to have forgotten the lesson."[9] Nor did he. The oedipal conflict pitted father-critic against poet-son on the precise point of his identity and adequacy as a poet. Even after the paternally corrected *Poems* was published, his father's only response to his presentation copy was a take out his pencil and silently mark more errors.

But the persistent, if not rebellious, son wanted to make his own errors, if need be. Having collected his critical pieces for his *Selected Essays* in 1954, Williams admitted in the "Preface": "My father warned me to give poetry a wide berth. But I knew best what was good for me."[10] The old man's death in 1918, at the crux of Williams' struggle for poetic identity and just before the dramatic breakthrough of *Kora in Hell* (1920) and *Spring and All* (1923), brought their contention to a terrible and liberating climax. The episode is its own Freudian commentary. In *The Autobiography* Williams had to admit that the fatal stroke on Christmas Day probably resulted from his own efforts to give the old man relief by forcing an enema tube into his "emaciated body." Williams tried to understate the trauma: "I'll never forget Pop's death." But even on his deathbed the old man made the final dismissive gesture to prove the son wrong: "'He's gone,' I said. But he shook his head slowly from side to side. It was the last thing I could ever say in my father's presence and it was disastrous." He was called away to the hospital to deliver a baby, and when he got back his father "was gone" Physically, but not psychologically: he "killed" his father, only to see him rise again in dream:

> I'll never forget the dream I had a few days after he died, after a wasting illness, on Christmas Day, 1918. I saw him coming down a peculiar flight of exposed steps, steps I have since identified as those before the dais of Pontius Pilate in some well-known painting. But this was in a New York office building, Pop's office. He was bareheaded and had some business letters in his hand on which he was concentrating as he descended. I noticed him and with joy cried out, "Pop! So, you're not dead!" But he only looked up at me over his right shoulder and commented severely, "You know all that poetry you're writing. Well, it's no good." I was left speechless and woke trembling. I have never dreamed of him since.

The son's need for the paternal benediction is met by the father's withering denial. His Pilate-like judgment "killed" the son as a poet, rendering him "speechless." Nevertheless, in the son's mind his haughty father wrote only business letters, and his vindication would come when he became a poet over his father's buried body: "I have never dreamed of him since."[11]

His surrogate father-critic was "Uncle Billy" Abbott of Horace Mann High School in Manhattan, who gave him his first "A" in English. Williams paid Abbott frequent and elaborate filial honor because his encouragement provided the blessing he felt his father had withheld. His "tutelage" marked the "beginning" of his engagement with writing – that "A" "was my first literary success" – and in return he dedicated the criticism gathered in *Selected Essays* to Abbott. But Uncle Billy was only the alter ego for father William, who could not be banished from memory or the unconscious. Years later, but only after he had proved himself against his father's judgment, Williams commented that whatever capacity for "critical judgment" he had attained had developed in large part from the "attacks and defences" in those long arguments with his father over the dining room table.[12]

At the same time, there was something fortuitously symbolic about his leaving his father's deathbed to attend upon "a maternity case." Pound was correct in detecting Williams' primary affinity with the feminine, personified less in his wife Floss than in his paternal English grandmother and his Latin mother. He recalled his father's frequent absence on business trips and added, "I hope I take after my female ancestors." In *The Autobiography* Williams called his identification with women "the best part of me," even though it put him at odds with the patriarchy, personified in this passage by Edmund Gosse (the literary establishment), Stanley Baldwin (the political establishment), and his father, "all defendants of a society which refuses me, would jail me if it would, any of them, right down to my nearest friends." Williams contrasted his father's guilty verdict with "Mother's saving way of facing the world." The fact that she had studied painting in Paris established her as an artist, in contrast to the paternal function as hard-working businessman or hard-nosed critic.[13] In retrospect, he could see that "somehow poetry and the female sex were allied in my mind. The beauty of girls seemed the same to me as the beauty of a poem. I knew nothing at all about the sexual approach but I had to do something about it. I did it in the only terms I knew, through poetry."[14]

But even as poet he seemed less deeply moved by the "beauty of girls" than by the inspiration of the mother. His father's English mother lived nearby and was a powerful presence throughout his childhood and youth. In "The Wanderer," his long early poem about the Passaic River as the source of his poetic vocation, she was mythologized as the "spirit of the river" and so his muse: "I identified my grandmother with my poetic unconscious. She was the personification of poetry."[15] His own mother, Heléne, a Puerto Rican with Basque and Jewish blood uprooted to New Jersey by marriage, had been an aspiring artist before sacrificing her career to her husband and sons. But she had given him his Spanish middle name to balance his father's name, and after the elder Williams' death in 1918, Heléne moved in with her son and his new wife and reigned there as matriarch, threatening at times to take over the house and her son from Floss. Williams marveled at her combination of powers as a spiritualist medium with earthy, often racy, language energized by idiosyncratic rhythms and phrases. She became in his imagination "a mythical figure," "a heroic figure, a poetic ideal." At his instigation, they collaborated in translating Phillipe Soupault's *Last Nights of Paris* and Don Francisco Quevedo's *The Dog and the Fever*. For years, despite her sharp-tongued protestations, he intended to write a full-length biography of his mother, and although he became too badly crippled in his last years to realize all of his ambition, he did manage a belated tribute by stringing together excerpts from her conversation for his last prose book, *Yes, Mrs. Williams*.

At the same time, Williams had Whitman as a warning that too long or too abject surrender to the nurturing female could retard or endanger male growth and potency. Williams remembered the shame that he felt at still sucking a bottle at the age of nearly six, and in *The Autobiography* he worried about being "unmanned by the older woman." "What do I look for in a woman? Death, I suppose, since it's all I see anyhow in those various perfections [i.e., in various perfections of women to whom he was been drawn]. I want them all in lesser or greater degree. Most men make me laugh, especially when they most 'possess' a woman."[16] Possession by the muse might be a kind of unmanning as well; after all, he had come to literature by a physical failure. A collapse after a track meet, diagnosed as a heart murmur, ended male competition in athletic strength and endurance and handed him over to the woman-anima-muse: "I was forced back on myself. I had to think about myself, look into myself. And I began to read."[17]

Measured against his brother Edgar, William seemed a relative failure, both professionally and romantically. They "grew up together to become as one person" in "passionate identification" and competition.[18] Edgar, the younger but physically larger brother, seemed to put his elder sibling to shame. Edgar won the prestigious Prix de Rome to study architecture abroad, whereas William banged out his little poems on a typewriter, hurried and tired, between patients or after long hours in his office and at the hospital. Earlier, when Edgar had been at MIT, he had arranged for William to bring some manuscripts for evaluation by Arlo Bates, but the vulnerable young poet felt damned with the faintest of praise by the professor-critic. The two Williams boys were simultaneously smitten by the dramatic beauty Charlotte Herman (who did become an actress), but when they agreed to let Edgar present both their suits to Charlotte and allow her to choose, she chose Edgar. William recoiled from this ignominious rebuff by proposing marriage almost immediately to Charlotte's plainer, steadier sister, Florence, confessing his present lack of passion but prepared to build his domestic security around her.

Williams' competition with his poetic sibling Pound had fared little better in the early years. More flamboyant and better educated, Pound overshadowed him from the start as lover, poet, and critic. Both fell in love with Hilda Doolittle at the University of Pennsylvania, but she favored Ezra and kept Williams on a longer string. Pound's talk was dazzling, and he spoke as though he knew what he was doing in his poems. Soon his bohemian life amid the artists of London and Paris brought him acclaim, notoriety, and influence over writers and publishers. Williams' remarks about Pound over the years exhibit the ambivalence that held them together and at odds throughout their long friendship and rivalry. Williams was to recall that the chief topic of discussion between them was how to shape into line and poem the materials gestated by "the females of our souls."[19]

Psychologically and aesthetically, then, Williams' relation to the feminine comprised a central commitment and challenge of his life. He was struck by Otto Weininger's loudly acclaimed psychological study *Sex and Character*, translated from the German in 1906. Despite Weininger's suicide in his early twenties after completing the manuscript, the book was taken at the time as a scientific treatise on sexual character, but its impact stemmed from Weininger's ability to dramatize the sexual stereotypes of his cultural biases through the exaggerating lenses of his own neuroses. Williams never succumbed to Weininger's blatant misogyny, but he accepted the notion of polarized genders, which, in Weininger's version, reduced women's nature to the material and sexual and but took men's nature (and dilemma) as both spiritual and sexual. Hence men's physical attraction to and dependence on the women to whom they are superior; hence, too, women's threat to the men to whom they are mentally and spiritually inferior.

Williams instinctively sought to overcome this crude and demeaning dichotomy by mythologizing his grandmother as "spirit of the river" and by elevating his mother to a "poetic ideal," but these psychological stereotypes continued to inform his view of himself and of the imaginative process. The man's connection with women and with nature becomes the mechanism by which he grounds his genius and substantiates his spirit. The following sentences weave together Williams' words, not Weininger's. Because of the "universal lack of attachment between the male and an objective world," "male psychology is characterized by an inability to concede reality to fact... the male, aside from his extremely simple sex function, is wholly unnecessary to objective life: the only life which his sense perceives." Since "man is the vague generalizer, woman the concrete thinker," so man localizes himself by repeatedly committing himself to his feminine ambience. Male friends are few and individual, but the individual male must know many women, can never know enough women: "Men know it [sexual passion] as babies know the mother – as a place.... It is a force which can be felt, it is multiform – I have felt it to command me in opposite ways."[20] Consequently, although "Flossie, my wife,... is the rock on which I have built," "as far as my wish is concerned, I could not be satisfied by five hundred women." Stung by Stevens' criticism that he lacked a consistent poetic viewpoint and a "single manner," Williams turned the creative process into sexual strategy and proclaimed his polygamy: *What would you have me do with my Circe, Stevens, now that I have double-crossed her game, marry her? It is not what Odysseus did.*[21]

So the multiform feminine – not just women themselves but the whole world of sensory, objective fact – performs a complex biological and imaginative function for the male psyche. The connection between the sexual and the imaginative act allowed Williams to speak of "the whole body of the management of words to the formal purposes of expression." Men needed women for embodiment, and poetry was an extended manifestation and function of that need. But fulfillment was not easy or guaranteed; the disembodied male psyche had to "manage" an engagement with matter which was never final and often seemed specious: "We express ourselves there (men) as we might on the whole body of the various female could we ever gain access to her (which we cannot and never shall)." Wanting "only to clarify" the "parts of the great body," the man must experiment again and again. "She" awaits his spermatic word: "Woman is honored and fertilized as a creature of the imagination."[22]

"She" is, therefore, a "creature of the imagination" in a double sense: subject and object, source and repository, inspiration and incarnation. The early poem "Transitional" says that "it is the woman in us / That makes us write" and makes the male artist a psychological androgyne "conscious / (of the two sides),"[23] but it is "mastery" of the woman that makes him a successful writer. Williams had read his Weininger closely enough to know that he ought never succumb to "her." Since matter breeds indiscriminately, the nurturer can turn devourer; if she gives him form, it is the form he gives her. Citing Pygmalion's statue of Galatea, Williams argued that the statue "becomes something a woman never was, something a woman at her best may imitate – a work of art. . . . It is what the imagination *adds* to the woman that makes the statue great." The "work of man" "enlarges" and elevates nature. Consequently, the man who serves as "mother to woman" will degenerate into passive effeminacy because he has relinquished his ordained yet "revolutionary character" – namely, "touching woman and going on from there" to father another poem in his next imaginative copulation.[24]

Williams could not learn much from Stevens' poet as virile youth – he was too Platonic – or from Pound's friend Eliot: "You don't get far with women by quoting Eliot to them." He did learn a lot from Pound, but he could not let Pound dominate him either: "I liked him but I didn't want to be like him."[25] The artistic virility of the Modernist required experimentation free even of the influence of compatriots: "the deeper at moments of penetration is his mastery of their work, the more vigorously at other moments must he fling himself off from them to remain himself and man." Williams' self-conscious oedipal task was "to establish his own mastery"[26] in response to the living mother but to the satisfaction of the dead father.

II

Williams' attempts at painting, following his mother's unfulfilled example, led him to the awesome example of male painters like Picasso and Kandinsky (whom Pound's "Vortex" had called the father and mother of Modernism) and to the immediate example of contemporaries in New York like Charles Sheeler and Stuart Davis and Charles Demuth. In fact, Williams' theory and practice of Imagism can be seen to have developed as an accommodation of his mother's inspiration and his father's critical judgment, her spatial sensuality and his sense of formal decorum. It was the "woman in us that made us write," but the man in us made us write art (think of Williams' patronizing of H. D. in *The Autobiography* and of Paterson's condescension to Cress).

"Transitional," the poem which uses that phrase, appeared in *The Tempers* (1913), which followed the privately printed and derivative *Poems* (1909). *The Tempers* is a book to and about women. Several of the poems in it ("Postlude,"

"First Praise," "Homage," "Crude Lament," "The Ordeal," "Appeal," "Portrait of a Lady") are addressed to women, and several others ("Song from 'The Birth of Venus,'" "To Mark Anthony in Heaven," "Transitional," "The Revelation") depict woman as muse or anima. In contrast, two poems, working off of Pound imitating Browning, explicitly invoke sexual and artistic heroism: Lancelot as lover and warrior ("Con Brio"), Franco and Beethoven as musical geniuses ("The Death of Franco of Cologne: His Prophecy of Beethoven"). Despite its literary echoes, *The Tempers* already shows Williams' characteristic colloquial directness, and his subsequent books continue to sort out the distinctive style for his materials: *Al Que Quiere* (1917), *Kora in Hell* (1920), and *Sour Grapes* (1921), climaxing in *Spring and All* (1923).

The title *Kora in Hell* (provided by Pound) identified the muse with the murky unconscious beneath the "claptrap of the conscious mind." Williams frequently spoke of the unconscious as the source of imaginative expression: "everyone writes to reveal his soul," "to strike straight to the core of his inner self, by words." In an unpublished note to himself Williams declared: "Over all the imagination, the dream. I accept implicitly that the subconscious is the whole substance of poetry, that the revelation is its purpose." So he could speak of "the 'dream' of the poem."[27] The prose "improvisations" of *Kora in Hell* come as close to dream writing as anything Williams ever did. Williams derived his notion of improvisation from Wassily Kandinsky's *On the Spiritual in Art*, one of the seminal documents of early Modernism: "a largely unconscious, spontaneous expression of inner character, nonmaterial in nature."[28]

The "broken style" of the prose, dashed off and unrevised, attempted to register the mind's rapid associations and leaps, and sometimes even the supposedly explanatory paragraphs added later are not of much help in construing the verbal surrealism. However, once the improvisations had performed the therapeutic function of opening access to the unconscious, Williams did not dally long with Kora in that murky underworld. After all, Kora emerged again in springtime, and the object of penetrating to the unconscious was to allow its energies to rise to the light of conscious awareness. Dada and surrealism were the *jeux d'esprit* of Modernism but peripheral, even antithetical, to its defining values and purposes. Williams made the point repeatedly: "It's alright to give the subconscious play but not *carte blanche* to spill everything that comes out of it. We let it go to see what it will turn up, but everything it turns up isn't equally valuable and significant. That's why we have developed a conscious brain"; "I'm afraid that Freud's influence has been the trigger to all this. The Surrealists followed him. Everything must be tapped into the subconscious, the unconscious − as if poetry had ever been different. But poetry has also been a construction in the words"; "I wanted always to be conscious."[29]

Kora's ascent from the depths issued in *Spring and All*, in which the jagged angularity of the poems emerges from a running prose commentary which is less rational discourse than wild Dionysian assertion of the imagination's primacy. The prose is not as surreal as the *Kora* improvisations but is still "broken" into telegraphic utterances, capital letters, irregularities in numbering and typography. But the poems, intended to illustrate the aesthetic thrashed out in the prose, "were kept pure – no typographical tricks when they appear – set off from the prose." Although Williams later described the prose as a "mixture of philosophy and nonsense"[30] symptomatic of "my disturbed mind" at the time, the book constitutes his High Modernist manifesto and contains some of his best poems.

Curiously enough, though Pound had Williams simmering, simmering, simmering, it was Eliot who brought him to the boil. Boiling mad – and one result was *Spring and All*. For the rest of his life, Williams testified obsessively to the traumatic effect of the publication of *The Waste Land* in 1922. The poem epitomized for Williams Eliot's reneging on the challenge to devise a modern American speech and his capitulation to a moribund tradition. Ransom told Allen Tate that *The Waste Land* was dangerously iconoclastic, but Williams saw it as reactionary. The disillusioned impotence expressed in the poem was, for Williams, the price of expatriation, but, paradoxically, its masterful expression of impotence in a parody of the dead tradition gave it all the more enervating an influence on the upcoming generation of poets. Hart Crane's Symboliste response to *The Waste Land* would appear almost a decade later in *The Bridge*, but Williams' riposte the next year, *Spring and All*, paraded the potency of the Imagist imagination.

The first prose section proclaims, with exclamations, rhetorical questions, and oracular pronouncements, that this poetry will concentrate on the immediate instant, always fleeting and always present, "that eternal moment in which alone we live." (The difference between Williams' completely naturalistic "eternal moment" and Eliot's mystical one reveals much about the contrast between the two poets.) "To refine, to clarify, to intensify" the moment "there is but a single force – the imagination." But its ability to fix on the moment is dependent on its ability to destroy the immediately previous moment; the world is each instant to be annihilated and "made anew": "The imagination, intoxicated by prohibitions, rises to drunken heights to destroy the world. Let it rage, let it kill. The imagination is supreme." Consequently, "the meaning of 'art'" is that, before our astonished eyes, the imagination "has destroyed and recreated everything afresh in the likeness of that which it was." The quickening rhetoric at the approach of SPRING reaches the peremptory announcement that "THE WORLD IS NEW,"[31] and the first two poems follow – "By the road to the contagious hospital" and "Pink confused with white" – which we will examine in some detail later as examples of the imagination's supreme power.

The rhetorical high jinks of the commentary, however, is calculated to distract attention from the mixture of Romantic and Modernist assumptions which lie at the heart of Williams' Imagism. Although Williams took pride in being hailed as an American Modernist, Keats and Whitman dominated his first efforts at writing, and he would later link Shakespeare's greatness with a quality that Keats and Whitman shared: the "negative capability" to subordinate the subjective, personal concerns of the writer's ego to an empathetic identification with the object of attention. Williams' phrasing combines echoes of both Keats and Whitman: "To be nothing and unaffected by the results, to unlock and flow, uncolored, smooth, carelessly – not cling to the unsolvable lumps of personality (yourself and your concessions, poems) concretions –."[32] The obsession with maintaining contact with the local environment (Eliot seemed to him the arch-exile from the local) represented his effort to identify the poet-subject with the objects of his consciousness.

Williams cited as the philosophic source for his notion of the "local" John Dewey's "Americanism and Localism," published in *The Dial* in 1920,[33] and during the years 1920–1923, when he was working toward *Spring and All*, he edited the magazine *Contact* with Robert McAlmon. In one of the magazine's manifestos, Williams specified "contact with an immediate objective world of actual experience" as "the essential quality in literature." The local is the episte-mological key, and that act of perception generates "the poetic line, the way the image was to lie on the page." Because the local poet "does not translate the sensuality of his materials into symbols but deals with them directly," he "shows the world at one with itself." "The bastardy of the simile" and of other figures of speech, the principal devices of Symboliste subjectivity, are illegitimate because they are the offspring of the mind and interdict participa-tion in a palpable world in a way that localized Imagism does not.[34]

It is precisely the fundamental split between Imagist and Symboliste tendencies that separates Pound and Williams from Eliot, Stevens, and Crane. The difference made Williams' write to Horace Gregory of Crane that "I like the man but I stick on his verse": "I suppose the thing was that he was searching for something inside, while I was all for a sharp use of the materials." "Use your imagination" meant, or ought to mean, "realistic observation related into an equally real schematic whole," and this governing principle extended Imagism through the 1920s to the Objectivism of the 1930s. It is this facet of Williams which made him seem like Whitman in twentieth-century (instead of nineteenth-century) New Jersey. A few years after *Spring and All* he would maintain: "The only human value of anything, writing included, is the intense vision of the facts," and he would assess his friend, the painter Charles Sheeler, in terms of the "bewildering directness of his vision."[35]

But how to reconcile the alienated artist's mastery and the empathetic artist's negative capability, the Modernist assumption of a separation between art and life and the Romantic assumption of a "residual contact between life and imagination which is essential to freedom"? Imagism provided Williams' response. It offered "an escape from crude symbolism, the annihilation of strained associations, complicated ritualistic forms designed to separate the work from 'reality' – such as rhyme, meter as meter and not as the essential of the work, one of its words." The word properly used serves "not as a symbol of nature" but rather as a "part" of nature, "cognizant of the whole – aware – civilized."[36] Sounding more like Emerson and Fenollosa than like Hulme or Wyndham Lewis, Williams claimed, even in *Spring and All*, that the connective experience between subject and object supplied "the external as well as internal means of expression" and raised the observing subject to "some approximate co-extension with the universe":

> In the composition, the artist does exactly what every eye must do with life, fix the particular with the universality of his own personality – Taught by the largeness of his imagination to feel every form which he sees moving within himself, he must prove the truth of this by expression.[37]

However, at the same time that the precept "no ideas but in things" argued against a solipsistic Symbolisme that the source of meaning lay "not in our imaginations" but "there, there in the fact," Williams' same empiricism also rejected not just Emerson's and Whitman's Romantic Idealism and Eliot's Christianity but also the Platonism behind Pound's ideogram and H. D.'s hieroglyph. Williams' Imagism, therefore, must not just be defined against the Symbolisme of Stevens, Tate, and Crane but must also be distinguished from the Imagism of H. D. and Pound. Williams took a more purely Modernist position than any of those others in insisting that "art has nothing to do with metaphysics." It is true that "the discovery of the new in art forms" does represent "some sort of honest answer"; nevertheless, "to mix that up with metaphysics is the prime intellectual offense of my day."[38] As a Modernist, Williams, like Stevens, adhered to the notion which Pound and Eliot came to recant: namely, that meaning arises only from the aesthetic construction of the work itself.

Objectivists like Louis Zukofsky and George Oppen revered Pound, and he noisily encouraged them. But by the 1930s Pound had modified his Modernism more even than he said, and the Objectivists were closer to Williams in their insistence that the object of the poem was not just the phenomenon observed but – perhaps more importantly – the poem itself as object. In *The Autobiography* Williams summed up Objectivism: "The poem being an object (like a symphony or cubist painting) it must be the purpose of the poet to make of his words a new form: to invent, that is, an object consonant with his day." Cubism had constituted the Modernist point of departure, asserting the formal arrangement of the artistic medium over the depiction of objective reality, but from the outset Modernism rejected traditional formal conventions for experimentation no less strictly formalist in its intent. The medium made the meaning, or, in Williams' words, the poem "in itself formally presents its case and its meaning by the very form it assumes."[39]

Oddly enough, therefore, in Pound's distinction between the perceptual and the conceptual artist, Williams remained, for all his naturalism, more conceptual – and so in this respect more Modernist – than Pound. To the end, Williams could not say with Pound in his old age: "it [the cosmos] coheres all right / even if my notes [my poems] do not cohere." From the conceptual-Modernist point of view, "the real purpose" of art is "to lift the world of the senses to the level of the imagination and so give it new currency." Then the artwork is its own unimpeachable "evidence, in its structure, of a new world which it has been created to affirm." Williams would even come to describe poetry, in the oft-quoted "Introduction" to his volume *The Wedge* (1944), as "a small (or large) machine made of words," and the technological model led to the further assertion that "it isn't what [the poet] *says* that counts as a work of art, it's what he makes, with such intensity of perception that it lives with an intrinsic movement of its own to verify its authenticity.... What does it matter what the line 'says'?"[40]

Williams learned from the contemporaries he most admired – Gertrude Stein, Joyce, Stevens, Pound, Marianne Moore – the Modernist lesson that "technique is itself substance." Thus Marianne Moore "undertakes in her work to separate the poetry from the subject entirely – like all the moderns." Writers used words as painters use pigments: not as symbols of nature (as Emerson had said) but as a medium for invention. Romantics called the work of art organic because it derived from and stood witness to an order extrinsic to itself, but Modernism redefined organicism as intrinsic rather than extrinsic to the artistic "organism" or "machine." The work was not organic to a larger world; it was its own microcosm. In Williams' words, "art is a transference – for psychic reasons – from the actual to the formal."[41] Despite the opposition of Imagism to Symbolisme, Williams echoed Stevens and Poe, whom he admired (rather than Emerson) as our first great poet and critic, in declaring the poem autotelic: "the end of poetry is a poem."[42]

Thus, although the prose commentary in *Spring and All* speaks of the "residual contact between life and the imagination" and of the artist's "approximate co-extension with the universe,"[43] a radically different, even contradictory, attitude appears – often on the same page or the next: a Modernist attitude that Williams absorbed largely from visual artists, as Pound did from the Vorticist painters and sculptors. The Romantic in Williams made the obstetrician associate the creative process with birthing: "I would be like a woman at term; no matter what else was up, that demand had to be met.... something growing inside me demanded reaping. It had to be attended to."[44] But the Modernist in Williams led him to the masculinism which made him expostulate to the bewildered female students at Bennington: "If you want to write poetry, you've got to be men! You've got to be men!"[45]

Fortunately, his mother mediated the aesthetic world of men for him; in drawing him to the visual arena, she provided the master he needed. As Mike Weaver and Bram Djikstra, among others, have demonstrated,[46] Williams' encounters with Dada and, especially, with Cubism, as well as his sustained association with the American Modernist painters in Alfred Stieglitz's stable after the Armory Show of 1913, were decisive in his technical development. He would say that "music doesn't mean much to me" and would even trace Imagism to his interest in painting:

> Because of my interest in painting, the Imagists appealed to me. It was an image that I was seeking.... If an image were set down on canvas, it was both a poem and a picture at the same time, and it was a very fertile thing to me to

> deal with....When I found Pound talking of the image I accepted it as a
> poem....The design of the painting and of the poem I've attempted to fuse.

In a poem, as on a canvas, the "relation of the parts to themselves" achieved a form that is "all surface, believe it or not. We think it is depth, but it is not. It is surface. But that surface must bespeak depth. It is words Gertrude Stein kept insisting."[47]

To begin with, then, painting offered a model, or at least an analogy, for an attempt at a spatial mode of poetry. M. M. Bakhtin has demonstrated at length that every artwork arises from and expresses a distinctive chronotope or time – space interrelationship, and that genres like poetry and fiction ought to be seen in terms of the broader and defining generic chronotopes of which the individual works offer various expressions.[48] The Romantic emphasis on temporal process soon aroused a complementary desire for spatial stasis: the "Grecian Urn" to balance the "Melancholy" of transient experience. And the Modernist found it all the more urgent that if experience was all flux and cycle, the art object be self-contained: whether Stevens' sealed Mason jar in the Tennessee wilderness or his crystal mundo revolving in its orbit. There is, of course, a spatial aspect to literature, as there is a temporal aspect to painting, but the Modernist inclination to spatial structure generated a special challenge for predominantly temporal arts like literature and music. Pound's and Williams' breaking of the pentameter signaled a shattering of metrical form, with its musical analogy, that impelled verse, against the nature of the medium, away from affinity with music in the direction of affinity with painting and sculpture. Modern poets and even novelists (dependent on plot, as lyric poets were not) experimented with the spatializing of temporal materials, and Williams' biographical associations of his mother with the visual arts and of his father with poetry and criticism gave his own early experiments with form a special emphasis: mother-space over father-time.

Moreover, in matters of technique and form, Williams was less deeply influenced by Dadaist and Surrealist efforts to release unconscious associations and impulses than by the Cubist restructuring of natural phenomena into conceptual designs. It was Picasso and Gris, not Miró, whom Williams cited in *Spring and All*. There he cited his favorite Cubist, Gris, for refusing a false "plagiarism after nature" in favor of the "modern" effort "to separate things of the imagination from life." Unlike photographers or realists like Goya and Velázquez or Impressionists like Monet, painters like Cézanne and Gris and Williams' American friends Marsden Hartley and Charles Demuth (to whom *Spring and All* is dedicated) labored to "detach" objects "from ordinary experience" so that the artistic image may "ESCAPE ILLUSION and stand between man and nature" as a third term. "The hint to composition" which nature offers lies specifically in its "quality of independent existence": "it [nature] is not opposed to art but apposed to it"; thus nature and art coexist, but as separate and related entities. Without a "resort to mysticism," modern art exalts the imagination as the highest human faculty and demands "the transposition of the faculties to the only world of reality that men know: the world of the imagination, wholly our own."[49] Oddly enough, it is the would-be representational work which presents a false and falsifying illusion; the Modernist goal is "not 'realism' but reality itself," and it is an aesthetic reality, a "new form dealt with as a reality in itself."[50]

But mother-space was not just the surface of the canvas and the volume of the sculpture but also the body of the material world. If she taught Williams to use a temporal medium spatially, as though what appeared on the rectangular page were "both a poem and a picture at the same time," she also drew him as poet-painter to the objects of experience and kept him from the abstracting tendencies of Picasso and Miró, Kandinsky and Mondrian. Barbara Novak and John Wilmerding have called attention to American artists' commitment to the phenomena of experience – not just of Romantic landscape painters but also of the American Modernists, who turned the structural techniques and compositional effects of their European models away from abstraction toward presenting objects, often graphically detailed, in three-dimensional space. It is no accident, therefore, that Gris, the most representational of the Cubists, became Williams' favorite, but he was conceptually and technically even closer to the Cubist Realism of Demuth and the Precisionism of Sheeler. Stevens would argue that the supreme fiction must be abstract, but Imagism and Objectivism represented an alternative, antiabstractionist Modernism.

As we have seen, Williams held the art object as not opposed to nature but apposed to it. The art object was a reality different in kind and form from nature, and dynamized with feeling and significance by the act of human apprehension and expression as nature in itself could not be. The breach between subject and object charged the subject with de-creating the sense impression of the object and re-creating it as words. The words invent and impose a pattern not present or at least not so manifest in the objects of experience, and thus the new verbal construct becomes itself an object of experience. Paradoxically, therefore, its apartness from nature makes the art object a part of nature; as an act of articulated and objectified awareness, it locates artist and reader / viewer in, mediates vital contact with, the world from which we are alienated.

This resolution of the opposition and apposition between nature and art is what Williams meant when he wrote in *Spring and All* that "the imagination...had destroyed and recreated everything afresh in the likeness of that which it was"[51] – not an exact copy but a composed image. For all his admiration of Picasso and Gris, he dedicated *Spring and All* to Demuth, the Cubist Realist, and maintained to the end that "I always wanted to write a poem celebrating the local material...to have no connection with the European world, but to be purely American, to celebrate it as an American."[52] A Whitmanian hyperbole: sometimes the local material seemed to him, as to Stevens, the "malady of the quotidian," and sometimes he envied Pound his Old World cosmopolitanism. But the truth in the statement is deeper than the oversimplification, and Williams' glory is that he succeeded Whitman in rising to the challenge that neither Stevens nor Pound met: he invented a Modernist line and structure to celebrate the local materials.

III

The other leading poetic nationalists celebrating local materials – Robert Frost and Carl Sandburg – offered no useful clues, in fact exemplified opposite mistakes. Of Frost's metered vignettes of New England, Williams could only say, "The bucolic simplicity of Robert Frost seems to me a halt."[53] Sandburg's long-lined free verse went to the other extreme from Frost's intricate closed forms and showed the devolution of Whitman's prolixity and inclusiveness. When Sandburg's *Complete Poems* was published in 1948, Williams, in the midst of writing *Paterson*, asked to review it for *Poetry* magazine and made it an occasion to denounce the bad effects of Whitman's influence. When Sandburg followed Whitman in surrendering himself to "the sheer mass" of impressions, "the facts were too overpowering, he himself was swept off his feet by their flood." Adrift in "the whole body of the various female," with no measure for selectivity or concentration, the lines simply swelled with accumulated and unassimilated data. There could be no "structural interest" because there was "nothing to inform it, nothing to drive it forward" into new perceptions and inventions, not even Whitman's now outmoded Romantic Transcendentalism. The distance between Sandburg and Williams had widened with the years and with Sandburg's popularity, and Williams took venomous pleasure in concluding of Sandburg's life's work that "the very formlessness of the material, its failure to affirm anything formal," merely recorded "the drift of aimless life through the six hundred and seventy-six pages that is the form."[54]

Frost's closed forms were the result of his nostalgia for, and skepticism about, Romantic Transcendentalism; Sandburg's Whitmanian formlessness indicated its collapse. It was easy, in any case, for Williams to reject Frost's meters and rhymes as vestiges of the devitalized and superseded European tradition; the challenge was to avoid the passivity and diffuseness of Whitmanian free verse and devise an American open form capable of registering its recalcitrant materials analytically and empirically without resort to metaphysics. Birthing the poem required not submission but control; the poet was not just mother but master, and his mastery lay in disciplined use of the expressive medium. The deployment of language in functional line units makes the decisive difference between Sandburg's dead and inert "realism" and a verbal apprehension of "reality."

In the slim volumes after the 1909 *Poems* – which his father had riddled with corrections – Williams set about developing suppler lines, more precise diction, more colloquial rhythms. Then the poems in *Spring and All* displayed the verbal Cubist Realism which is the distinctive manner of his short lyric poems. The force of spring in nature has been associated with the force of the imagination in the mind, and the first poem about the approach of spring to a dead landscape lineates itself coolly and cleanly out of the frenetic prose commentary proclaiming the de-creative–re-creative power of the imagination:

> By the road to the contagious hospital
> under the surge of the blue

mottled clouds driven from the
northeast – a cold wind. Beyond, the
waste of broad, muddy fields
brown with dried weeds, standing and fallen

patches of standing water
the scattering of tall trees

All along the road the reddish
purplish, forked, upstanding, twiggy
stuff of bushes and small trees
with dead, brown leaves under them
leafless vines –

Lifeless in appearance, sluggish
dazed spring approaches –

They enter the new world naked,
cold, uncertain of all
save that they enter. All about them
the cold, familiar wind –

Now the grass, tomorrow
the stiff curl of wildcarrot leaf
One by one objects are defined –
It quickens: clarity, outline of leaf

But now the stark dignity of
entrance – Still, the profound change
has come upon them: rooted, they
grip down and begin to awaken[55]

The poem is a fine example of Williams' verbal Cubist Realism. The
descriptiveness of the verses seems straightforward but is actually a carefully
contrived verbal effect. The first line brings Whitman to Eliot's ailing world;
the open road has led to the contagious hospital at the bleak end of winter. The
first group of irregular, unrhymed lines seems to gloss *The Waste Land*,
published the year before. "The wind / Crosses the brown land, unheard,"
Eliot wrote, and Williams' redaction also uses the reiterated dental consonants
– *d*'s and *t*'s – especially at the end of words and syllables, to suggest the balked
stasis of the scene: "road," "clouds," "cold," "wind," "mottled," "northeast,"
"cold wind," "beyond," "waste," "broad," "muddy," "fields," "dried
weeds," "standing," and so on. In addition, the alliteration, assonance, and
internal near rhymes further link the details in a pervasive sterility: "road,"
"cold"; "driven," "wind"; "northeast," "waste"; "broad," "brown"; "fields,"
"weeds"; "dried weeds." Though there is no human person present, the
implications of the scene for human life are intimated not just by the hospital
but by the anthropomorphic associations of words like "standing and fallen,"
"upstanding," "forked," and "naked" (the last two perhaps echoes of Lear's
unillusioned description of man). So, from the very beginning, the word play
and sound play insist to the reader on the character of the medium as medium
and thus on the verbal composition of the scene.

The dropping of the expected capital letter at the beginning of each line insists on the interplay between lines, as does the heavy enjambment. But paradoxically, the enjambment also emphasizes the fact that each line is an individual structural unit shaped to reinforce the dynamic process of sensory and intellective apprehension rather than the syntactic organization of the sentence. The Whitmanian free verse line, capitalized and end-stopped, stretches itself out to be as long and inclusive as possible, gathering in detail after detail, phrasal group after phrasal group, concluding only when the breath has run out, to begin again with the next breath to sum up the interrelatedness of all things; the lines accumulate paratactically as repeated efforts to submerge the particulars in the cosmic design. Williams' line is shorter, tenser, more nervous; the enjambment cuts and splices the grammatical elements of the sentence, using the highlighting at the beginning and end of the verse to focus on the discrete but related elements of the re-created scene. The line units work against, rather than with, the sentence; and the resulting line fragments remake the sentence – and the scene – into a unique pattern.

Thus the suspension between "blue" and "mottled" emphasizes both adjectival qualities, individually and in contrast, before substantiating them in "clouds." The next two lines end, startlingly, in the unspecified article "the," emphasizing even more the nouns at the beginning of the following lines. The effect of such Cubistic rearrangement can be easily grasped if the same words are lineated to observe grammatical groupings:

> under the surge
> of the blue mottled clouds
> driven from the northeast –
> a cold wind.
> Beyond, the waste of broad muddy fields

Or, in longer lines:

> under the surge of the blue mottled clouds
> driven from the northeast – a cold wind.
> Beyond, the waste of broad muddy fields.

The vivid particularity of details is muted without the hang and turn and shift of Williams' jagged enjambment, maintained throughout the poem.

The second and third verse paragraphs extend the description. The "standing and fallen" weeds in the fields give way to "standing water" and "tall trees," and the off-rhyming of "patch" and "scat" at the beginning of the lines further blocks out the verbalization of the landscape. The next group of lines begins "All along the road," echoing and extending the opening "By the road" and picking up the "all" of the title *Spring and All*. "All" recurs four times in the poem, as spring takes the world over, and it rhymes internally with "fallen, tall, small." The network of verbal echoes and sound play continues to integrate the individual details into the "picture": "wind," "waste," "weeds," "water"; "dried," "dead"; "standing," "upstanding"; "fallen," "tall," "small"; "road," "reddish," "dead"; "reddish," "purplish," "sluggish," "bushes"; "trees," "leaves," "leafless," "lifeless"; and so on.

The turn in the poem takes place between the third and fourth verse paragraphs. The first-word rhyming of "leafless" and "lifeless" signals the association between "leaf" and "life." "Lifeless" repeats "leafless," just as "sluggish" picks up on "reddish, purplish...stuff." But in the second half of the poem the association between "leaf" and "life" turns from negation to renewal: "wildcarrot leaf," "outline of leaf." Even from the start, the poem has given clues that spring will arrive to break winter's deadlock. The word "surge" is the first premonition (recall "Urge and urge and urge, / Always the procreant urge of the world" from the third section of "Song of Myself"), and the wind as the breath of spring, though "cold" in the first paragraph, becomes "familiar" as it blows life in, the process punctuated by temporal markers: "Now," "tomorrow," "One by one," "But now," "Still." The last "all" finds the transformative wind "all about them," and the waste land is a "new world."

The somewhat unusual use of "save" as a preposition (the French "sauf") puns on "save" as "redeem," with mingled suggestions of birth and resurrection ("enter," "entrance," "quicken," "grip," "awaken") in the final lines. The Latinate source of "save" as "sauf" calls attention to the sudden proliferation of multisyllabic, Latinate words in the second half of the poem, which also serve to elevate the elemental character of the birth process: "appearance," "approaches," "enter," "familiar," "objects," "defined," "clarity," "dignity," "profound," "change." At the same time, elemental Germanic words remain to the end contrasting and blended with the Latinate diction: for example, in the juxtaposition of the "stiff curl of wildcarrot leaf" with "objects are defined"; in "rooted, they / grip down" flanked by "profound change" and "awaken"; in "stark" modifying "dignity of / entrance." The omission of the period at the end signifies that the remaking of the world has not reached its conclusion. Although Williams was even farther beyond the pale of the New Criticism than Pound, a textual explication like this one demonstrates that the New Criticism has taught us to scrutinize analytically poems very different in structure and technique from those the New Critics themselves analyzed and promoted.

"The Pot of Flowers," the second poem of Spring and All, creates a microcosm in its verbal "painting," and in fact was written as the verbal rendering of a Demuth watercolor of tuberoses:

Pink confused with white
flowers and flowers reversed
take and spill the shaded flame
darting it back into the lamp's horn

petals aslant darkened with mauve

red where in whorls
petal lays its glow upon petal
round flamegreen throats

> petals radiant with transpiercing light
> contending
> > above
>
> the leaves
> reaching up their modest green
> from the pot's rim
>
> and there, wholly dark, the pot
> gay with rough moss.[56]

The breaking of the long single sentence into jagged verses also functions to compose the details for the eye somewhat as though the eye were "reading" a watercolor. The image presents the interpenetration of light and dark in the spectrum of shades in between. The details create the effect of circularity ("flowers and flowers reversed," "darting it back," "whorls," "rim," "reaching up") and of totality (pink – white – mauve – red – "transpiercing light," and also "shaded flame," "flamegreen," "modest green," "wholly dark"). The *yang* of the masculine, "transpiercing light" from the "lamp's horn" and the *yin* of the dark matrix of the feminine pot comprise the *tao* of the aesthetic microcosm.

The third poem in *Spring and All* introduces a human agent – a farmer – into the winter landscape of the first poem. Williams' farmer, however, is no Emersonian or even Frostian figure but is explicitly the conceptual Modernist artist whose relation to the land in some sense is that of the "antagonist." Before spring even comes, as in the first poem, "in his head the harvest is already planted."[57] His concept encloses planting and harvest and spatializes temporal process, and his harvest is not grass and wildcarrot but man-made produce.

The distinction between the natural phenomenon and the artistic image is the theme of Poem VII, a verbal adaptation of a 1914 Gris collage of a rose in which the "geometry" of the versification displaces the actual rose as "obsolete" and achieves absolute existence in its own aesthetically defined space:

> From the petal's edge a line starts
> that being of steel
> infinitely fine, infinitely
> rigid penetrates
> the Milky Way
> without contact – lifting
> from it – neither hanging
> nor pushing –
>
> The fragility of the flower
> unbruised
> penetrates space.[58]

The reassembling of fractured forms into a clean-faceted aesthetic geometry finds verbal exemplification in the incomplete or truncated phrases and the splintered, refitted syntax of the enjambed lines.

Nevertheless, it is by now abundantly clear that although Williams stoutly maintained the integrity of the verbal object, he also maintained an unshakable respect, even at the height of his Modernism in *Spring and All*, for the integrity of the object being rendered into words. Demuth's watercolor was no more that pot of flowers than his poem was, but both presented images of it; and Williams wanted to maintain both the opposition and the apposition. For Williams, unlike many deconstructed Postmodernists, the signifier still *does* signify. In his famous poem about the red wheelbarrow, the opening couplet, "so much depends / upon," immediately posits the mind as the source of connections and signification, and the mental act of signification depends on an actual configuration of barrow, rain, and chickens. The poem assumes an independent existence but acknowledges a dependence on natural phenomena as the point of origin and relevance.

On the other hand, Williams subscribes not to Romantic organicism but to Modernist apposition. Words are not things; things are de-created/re-created into words:

> so much depends
> upon
>
> a red wheel
> barrow
>
> glazed by rain
> water
>
> beside the white
> chickens.[59]

These verses seem almost baldly plain, but the more attentively we experience the words as words, the more deliberately patterned the verbal arrangement proves to be. The four two-line groupings are set out in a symmetrical syllabic arrangement: 4–2, 3–2, 3–2, 4–2. The movement of the reader's eye on the page determines the mind's movement in assimilating the details of the impression. The form establishes visually and spatially the dependence (Latin root: hang from) and interdependence of details: "red wheel" and "barrow," "rain" and "water," and "white" and "chickens" separately, as well as "red wheelbarrow" and "rain water" and "white chickens" together.

Any least change in the words or even the verbal arrangement constitutes a different verbal experience. So much depends on the spatial disposition that any other pattern becomes a substantively different experience of words, and so a different poem. Take, for example, the presentation of the same words in the single, all-inclusive Whitmanian line:

> so much depends upon a red wheelbarrow glazed by rain water
> beside the white chickens.

Or the couplet:

> so much depends upon a red wheelbarrow
> glazed by rain water beside the white chickens.

Or the quatrain:

so much depends upon
a red wheelbarrow
glazed by rain water
beside the white chickens.

Or the inversion of the published two-line arrangement with the single word
on top:

so
much depends upon

a
red wheelbarrow

glazed
by rain water

beside
the white chickens.

The visual and spatial form of the poem makes us see the details individually
and interrelatedly in a particular way before the period definitively concludes
the composition. We know these "objects" only in the poem-object.

There is, therefore, no redundancy in the following quatrain from a poem
addressed "To a Poor Old Woman," which repeats the same simple sentence
three times:[60]

They taste good to her.
They taste good
to her. They taste
good to her.

Williams is giving the woman words she never had for the deep and sustained
pleasure of munching a plum, and so much of the pleasure depends, we know
from the title, upon the fact that she is "poor" and "old." The reiteration of
the five bare words not only prolongs the delicious sensation, but the line units
remake it to discover subtle nuances of emphasis and relation in the pleasure.
By the time the statement is repeated a fourth time as the concluding line of the
poem, the reader has received the human significance of savoring that plum.

In a similar way, the juxtaposition of two published versions of "The Locust
Tree in Flower" demonstrates how defining the verbal form is:

Among	Among
the leaves	of
bright	green
green	stiff
of wrist-thick	old
tree	bright
and old	broken
stiff broken	branch
branch	come
ferncool	white

```
swaying           sweet
loosely strung –  May

come May          again[61]
again
white blossom

clusters
hide
to spill

their sweets
almost
unnoticed

down
and quickly
fall
```

Notice the differences between the texts: the words of the shorter version can be found in the longer one, but reading the two is a significantly different experience. In both instances, the normal rules governing parts of speech and sentence structure are violated or ignored so that the words can function outside of the expected grammatical organization of the sentence. Williams would like the words to function as objects in themselves, independent of imposed syntactic logic, word by word, like strokes and smears and globs of paint. The clipped lines of the longer version become the discrete words of the shorter, each word an object occupying its own space.

The shorter version is more effective in its extreme economy. It discards some details of the longer one and does not even mention the tree, concentrating instead on a synecdochic branch and implying the larger organism through the double preposition at the beginning: "among / of." The succession of isolated words complicates the interplay "of" and "among" them. For example, "stiff" – with age? with new sap? – is suspended between "green" and "old." The same paradox is repeated in the alliterated "bright / broken / branch" immediately afterward. The spacing between the three-word clusters intensifies the play between the sides of the paradox: this old tree with broken branches is also stiff with sap and bright with blossoms. The verb "come," its implications of sexual potency picking up those in "stiff," has no particular tense or subject and encompasses all the elements of the poem. The capital *M* elevates Maytime without transcendentalizing it. "Again" (pun on "a gain"?) stands alone with a final emphasis that is conclusive – and inconclusive.

Careful attention to the lineation and language gives even anecdotal poems a self-consciousness about craftsmanship. "The Young Housewife," an early poem, turns out to be about the distance between art and life:

> At ten a.m. the young housewife
> moves about in negligee behind
> the wooden walls of her husband's house.
> I pass solitary in my car.

Then again she comes to the curb
to call the ice-man, fish-man, and stands
shy, uncorseted, tucking in
stray ends of hair, and I compare her
to a fallen leaf.

The noiseless wheels of my car
rush with a crackling sound over
dried leaves as I bow and pass smiling.[62]

The first phrase fixes the moment in time, and the line breaks and line groupings serve to establish the connection and separation between the woman and the observer. The inverted word order of "housewife" and "her husband's house" at the ends of lines 1 and 3 states her physical and psychological emprisonment by the patriarchy, especially when the end of the intervening line places her "behind" the walls of the house. More subtly, the parallelism of "her husband's house" and "my car" implies not only the poet's isolation from the woman but his male conspiratorial complicity with the husband. The second group of lines also moves from the woman to the poet in the last clause. The details substantiate her frustrated misery: she escapes the house but only as far as "the curb," where she calls out futilely to any man who enters her domestic neighborhood. The poet reads her psychological desperation in her slovenliness ("negligee," "uncorseted," "tucking in / stray ends") and makes it into a figure of speech: "and I compare her / to a fallen leaf." The last sentence of the poem stands apart to draw out the irony of the poet's self-perception. The clichéd metaphor of the fallen leaf indicts the superficial stock response in the poet's seeming compassion, but becomes chilling fact when the poet observes the dried leaves (and, by extension of the metaphor, the momentarily escaped housewife) crushed under the wheels of his machine (Williams would call the poem a "verbal machine"). The poet remains insulated in his mechanical contrivance as he passes her by with a self-protective, patronizing smile.

But such wry self-parody was not Williams' characteristic stance – and for good reason: he tried not to falsify his subject through figurative ornament. Stevens accused Williams of sentimental exploitation of his neighbors, but Thom Gunn understood the ethical purpose behind Williams' acts of attention: "It is a humane action to attempt the rendering of a thing, person, or experience in the exact terms of its existence."[63] What saves Williams from sentimentality is the keenly observed, unmetaphorical language and the analytic lineation. So much, including the exact terms of presentation, depends on control and disposition of the medium.

For "when we let go we get a loose nothing, a rhythmic blur, a formlessness which is abhorrent," but "when we close down on the line we get classic imitation or tightness."[64] Adequate form resolves the seeming disjunction between the perceptual and conceptual modes of imaginative activity – that is, between a passive surrender to impressions from outside and a solipsistic imposition of artificial pattern. Language, then, could be both autotelic *and* referential; form could be presentational without forgoing the representational. It locates the poet in his world by its internal aesthetic coherence. In "Poetry" Marianne Moore spoke of putting "real toads in imaginary gardens."

Obviously, what Williams meant by "classic" was not what Eliot meant, but it was what Hulme meant by "classic" Modernism: a commitment to invention that rejects realistic representation for the presentation of an aesthetic reality. But for Williams that aesthetic reality could be a "classic imitation": the presentation of an aesthetic reality apposite to the physical reality. Like his friend Sheeler, Williams intended a greater recognizable referentiality than did abstract artists such as the Vorticists, with whom Hulme and Pound were associated. Nevertheless, even for Williams and Sheeler at their most "realistic" and apparently representational, presentation required de-creation – detachment and abstraction, selectivity and composition – as in "Classic Landscape," based on Sheeler's painting *Classic Scene*:

> A power-house
> in the shape of
> a red brick chair
> 90 feet high
>
> on the seat of which
> sit the figures
> of two metal
> stacks – aluminum –
>
> commanding an area
> of squalid shacks
> side by side –
> from one of which
>
> buff smoke
> streams while under
> a grey sky
> the other remains
>
> passive today –[65]

Williams' involvement with the visual arts lasted all his life, and his writings on the arts are reprinted in the *Selected Essays* and in the posthumous *A Recognizable Image*. His spatial deployment of a temporal medium dislocated and reformulated language to invent the verbal equivalent of Cubist Realism, and that invention influenced the succeeding generations of poets: Zukofsky and Oppen and Carl Rakosi, Denise Levertov and Robert Creeley and Robert Duncan, Ed Dorn and Gary Snyder and Ron Loewinsohn.

IV

But it was not enough for Williams: he could not be satisfied with his accomplishment in the short poems. He had come to terms with the mother's responsibility – the fixing of natural flux in spatial composition – but not yet the father's – the rendering of temporal duration and succession into transcendent measure. He was writing fewer poems (though some of his best) during the 1930s and more often approached temporal experience through fiction that reflected the social realism of the Depression – two collections of stories, *The Knife of the Times* (1932) and *Life Along the Passaic River* (1938), and the first two novels of the Stecher family trilogy, *White Mule* (1937) and *In the Money* (1940).

His letters indicate how deeply he felt the limits of his poetic achievement, felt the Imagist's need, as Pound and H. D. did in their development, to stretch the poem of the moment and write a long poem. Robert Lowell expressed the surprise of many of Williams' admirers when *Paterson* began to appear: "If the short poems show Williams as an excellent stylist, there is nothing in them to indicate that their thematic structure could be extended to a long poem." In 1943, writing to his publisher, James Laughlin, Williams was uncomfortably aware of *The Waste Land* and *Four Quartets* and of the seventy-odd *Cantos* already in print, and wanted to establish the incipient *Paterson* as a "keg-cracking assault upon the cults and the kind of thought that destroyed Pound and made what it has made of Eliot."[66] Lowell was one of the first to note the connection with (and difference from) *Leaves of Grass*, describing *Paterson* as "Whitman's America, grown pathetic and tragic, brutalized by inequality, disorganized by industrial chaos, and faced with annihilation."[67]

In 1914 he had written a ten-page poem, "The Wanderer,"[68] in which, as the nascent poet, he is guided through urban life along the Passaic River by a mythological witch-muse, modeled after his English grandmother. The climax is a baptismal rite in which she immerses him in the "filthy Passaic,"

> Till I felt the utter depth of its rottenness
> The vile breath of its degradation
> And dropped down knowing this was me now.

The poem was a first, awkward response to the question she posed for him: "How shall I be a mirror to this modernity?" According to Williams, "The Wanderer" was a "reconstruction from memory of my early Keatsian *Endymion* imitation that I destroyed,"[69] still informed by the old-fashioned notion of art as "mirror" to the river flow of time.

"The Wanderer" was, in fact, the "genesis of *Paterson*," but that poem was long in coming. Although the material (mater-ial) was obviously there from the start, Williams did not know, nor did Imagism teach him, how to shift from the short lyric to the epic or meditative mode – in other words, how to incorporate time into the method of the poem and history into its content. Bakhtin spoke of "the problem of assimilating real time, that is, the problem of assimilating historical reality into the poetic image,"[70] and the problem was the more acute for the Imagists because their poetics advocated the freezing of time in the static spatiality of condensed visual composition.

As it turned out, the crucial identification of the protagonist, Paterson, with the city led Williams to engage the problem of time and history. That identification with place came as early as an 85 line "Paterson" in 1928 (which helped win Williams the Dial Award) and recurred in a short piece in *The Broken Span* (1941), later incorporated into the first book of *Paterson*:

> For the Poem
> Paterson
> A man like a city and a woman like a flower –
> who are in love. Two women. Three women.
> Innumerable women, each like a flower. But only
> one man – like a city.

The maternal mage-muse of "The Wanderer," which the poet associated both with his "poetic unconscious" and with "the spirit of the river," rooted the poet in material place.[71] But as *Paterson* emerged, book by book, it became increasingly clear that the poem represented Williams' attempt to strengthen and deepen his association with the masculine principle as progenitor of the temporal cycle without losing contact with the feminine principle as muse and matrix.

By the late 1930s and early 1940s, Williams could no longer play down the father in favor of the mother, nor could he, as the lyrics succeeded in doing, merely approach the father through the mother, on her terms, treating his temporal medium as though it were spatial. It was no longer sufficient to treat time spatially; he had to learn to approach the mother as a man, on the father's terms, and treat space – his own local place – temporally. In short, he had to face, more fully than he had found possible until now, time as a basic and essential factor of space and of the dynamics of the poem. Williams' association of Pound and Eliot and of his own father with critical authority made *Paterson* not just an attempt to vie with and surpass his more famous brother poets in the critic father's judgment, but an attempt to discover and justify his own conditions of sonship. In 1929 he wrote to his own sons: "After a lifetime batting the air it is time now for me to get to work on the construction that will unite those parts in a whole." *The Autobiography* recollected *Paterson* as the search for the means of articulating "an image large enough to embody the whole knowable world about me," and the key to it, he came to see, lay in the symbol that "The Wanderer" had fastened on from the start: the river flowing through the city.[72] In fact, what drew him to neighboring Paterson as the locale for the poem instead of his native Rutherford was the fact that Paterson also bordered the Passaic but, unlike Rutherford, had a long and significant history. Mike Weaver has pointed out that there was even "a tradition of poems on the Passaic region," especially the falls, including Washington Irving's "On Passaic Falls" (1806), and has demonstrated that Williams almost certainly knew of the existence of the 150-page *Passaic, a Group of Poems Touching That River* (1842) by a doctor-poet from Newark named Thomas Ward.[73] Williams' poem, long in gestation, represented his need to be Paterson as well as mother-son, living out time and history in his place. He began to speak of a sequence of books which as it traced the river's run through the city to the sea, resumed a day's course, the seasons' cycle, the protagonist's life, the city's history within the nation's history.

This "thread"[74] announced a wholly new chronotope which required a new prosody and structure. A 1936 letter to Pound made the first mention of *Paterson*, and Williams pointedly contrasted "seven new short poems – two of them as good as anything I've ever done, maybe the best" – with "that magnum opus I've always wanted to do" and its demands for a radically different form. Writing to Stevens in 1944, he called *Paterson* an "impossible poem." The next year he told Horace Gregory, "The old approach is outdated, and I shall have to work like a fiend to make myself new again. But there is no escape. Either I remake myself or I am done."[75] By the time he began to take notes and write passages for *Paterson* in the late 1930s, he had come to view the spatialized construction he had passed on to his Objectivist colleague Zukofsky as a dead end:

> I admire Louis but his work is either the end, the collapse or the final justification of the objective method. . . .He is placing sentences, paragraphs, slices of speech in a line...by that to build...a monument, a literary creation. . . .But is it literature? I dunno. I don't know. I do not know. It seems an impossible method, without sequence, without "swing," without consecutiveness [76]

Breaking the pentameter was only the first heave; spatializing verse was a limited solution to the problem of form because it ignored, or at least heeded insufficiently, the temporal character of experience and of the verbal medium. The long poem, composed over a number of years, required the assimilation of many Imagist moments into an effective sequence, propelled into consecutiveness by the "swing" of the measure. Up to now, Williams had claimed a deeper affinity with painting than with music, but the long poem forced a confrontation with poetry's affiliation with music as another primarily temporal art. So Williams was almost inordinately gratified when the reviews of *Paterson I* by Lowell and Randall Jarrell, two brilliant younger poet disciples of the academically established New Critics, both hailed the poem as a landmark in American letters and both singled out for particular praise its structural coherence, which was, in Jarrell's phrase, "musical to an almost unprecedented degree." By 1947, with the first book published and acclaimed, Williams could boast: "I reject almost all poetry as at present written, including my own. . . .I am trying in *Paterson* to work out the problems of a new prosody."[77]

Any poem of Paterson's length had to evolve through time, and time, in the double sense of history and poetic measure, is also the explicit and obsessive concern of the poem. The several full-dress explications[78] of *Paterson*[79] allow this discussion to concentrate on the archetypal structure underlying Williams' effort to place himself in time – his own life span and local history – in his own prosodic invention.

Joel Conarroe has set out the various literary analogues and generic antecedents for *Paterson*: autobiographical explorations of native locale such as *Walden* or Joyce's *Ulysses* and *Finnegans Wake*; epics from Homer to Whitman to Pound; picaresque adventures, such as Huck Finn's journey downriver; quest and pilgrimage literature, especially such Romantic instances as *Endymion, Alastor* and *The Prelude*; long American verse sequences like *Leaves of Grass, The Waste Land, Four Quartets, The Bridge*, and especially *The Cantos*.[80] Time is a crucial factor in the theme and structure of these works, and the Whitmanian, Joycean catalogue just before the opening of the poem acknowledges some of its precedents: Thoreau and Joyce ("a local pride"); Whitman ("a celebration"); Homer, Virgil, Pound ("a reply to Greek and Latin with bare hands"); Romantic autobiography ("a confession"); Romantic process ("by multiplication a reduction to one;...an identification"); tragedy ("daring; a fall"); masculine and feminine archetypes ("a basket; a column"). And throughout the catalogue, the ubiquity of process: "spring, summer, fall and the sea"; "the clouds resolved into a sandy sluice"; "a plan for action to supplant a plan for action"; "a gathering up;...taking up of slack; a dispersal and a metamorphosis" (2).

The masculine and feminine archetypes are also implicit in the opening words of the "Preface," which stands in place of the conventional invocation to the muse: "Rigor of beauty is the quest. But how will you find beauty when it is locked in the mind past all remonstrance?" (3). Mental beauty remains uncreative, unsubstantiated anima; the quest is to unlock the mind to the flux of material particulars in order to reduce flux to mental – that is to say, aesthetic – design:

> To make a start,
> out of particulars
> and make them general, rolling
> up the sum, by defective means –
>
> (3)

This abstract statement about the poet as maker concludes in the comic, anti-heroic image of the poet as three-legged dog "sniffing the trees." But since "the rest have run out" – expatriates like Pound and Eliot – it's up to the lame dog to begin. And he begins with a parody of Eliotic paradoxes:

> For the beginning is assuredly
> the end – since we know nothing, pure
> and simple, beyond
> our own complexities.
>
> (3)

The goal is simplicity: "by multiplication a reduction to one." In the "interpenetration, both ways," lies the resolution of the paradoxes which run through the "Preface": simplicity and complexity, ignorance and knowledge, unity and multiplicity, dispersion and integration, design and detail, generality and particularity, order and chaos. In the individual the two become one; as would-be protagonist, Paterson describes himself as androgyne (like Tiresias in *The Waste Land*): the pregnant man, the father-mother-son, "heavy" (4) with the gestation of himself in his poem.

Williams' easy identification with the mother came from his strongly feminine nature (so strong that he felt compelled to flaunt his masculinity and his poetic mastery of the materials). The training of his mother, Heléne, as a painter and the vernacular tang of her speech gave her son his entrée into the world of painting. As we have already seen, "Transitional" declared: "It is the woman in us / That makes us write," and through "her" he learned to present physical phenomena verbally in a visually and spatially oriented Imagism/Objectivism. But his mother was a talker, not a poet, and his father had scoffed at his poems and left him with a lifelong worry: "You know all that poetry you're writing. Well, it's no good." He had learned to write the visual-spatial mother-poem; but now he had to come to terms with his father's dismissive criticism, and he could only lay that ghost by writing the father-poem. So the obsession of his last twenty-five years, when he was a man past randiness, and the aging father of two grown sons, was to complete his sense of self and his poetic achievement through an attempted identification with his long-buried father. Imagism had served its purpose, but the father-poem posed the greater challenge of finding the verbal means and form to set space in motion and integrate place with time. Not so much, then, the father-poem as the marriage poem of father and mother in which movement in time was in the fourth dimension of space and movement in space was the measure of time. That union engenders the poet and the poem, the poet in the poem.

But what would be the strategy and the form of such a poem? It would be his big poem. He had Pound's experiment as example – and warning. It is difficult to consider *Paterson* without the precedent of *The Cantos*, but Williams' own struggles with *The Cantos* made him all the more determined at least to set out a clearer focus and an overall structure. To begin with, his long poem, unlike Pound's, would be American in speech and rhythm and local in subject matter. Moreover, it would have four books consisting of three sections each, and there was a purpose to the numerical organization: "Many years ago I was impressed with the four-sided parallelogram, in short with the cube...the trinity always seemed unstable. It lacked a fourth member, the devil. I found myself always conceiving my abstract designs as possessing four sides." For all its craftsmanship, Williams found that the "triple unity" of *The Divine Comedy*, carried out even in the meter, gave the effect of being "unfinished."[81] Whitman the pantheist had earlier written "Chanting the Square Deific" to include the contradictory element of the devil. Now Williams planned that the oppositions which generated the poem would test their turns and counterturns in the instabilities of the triadic sections so as to arrive at resolution in the quaternity of books: twos move through threes to four (two twos). If *Spring and All* represented Williams' response to *The Waste Land*, *Paterson* is his response to *Four Quartets* as well as *The Cantos*.

The chronotope of *Paterson* was plotted in terms of the Passaic River as it emerged from its sources (Book I) to spill in a great falls from Garrett Mountain above the city (Book II), thence to run through the city (Book III) and finally expend itself into the Atlantic (Book IV). An "Author's Note" before the poem relates the account of the city to the phases of the protagonist's life cycle:

> *Paterson* is a long poem in four parts – that a man in himself is a city, beginning, seeking, achieving, and concluding his life in ways which the various aspects of the city may embody – if imaginatively conceived – any city, all the details of which may be made to voice his most intimate convictions. Part One introduces the elemental character of the place. The Second Part comprises the modern replicas. Three will seek a language to make them vocal, and Four, the river below the falls, will be reminiscent of episodes – all that one man may achieve in a lifetime.

Drawing on Joyce's *Finnegans Wake* and a 1940 painting by his friend Pavel Tchelitchew, *Paterson I* (1946), entitled "The Delineaments of the Giants," describes the "elemental character of the place" in terms of the topographical opposition and complementarity between the archetypal mother and father: Garrett Mountain and Garrett Park beside the giant Paterson "rousing" from his sleep. The poem presents Paterson's arousal (simultaneously and interrelatedly a sexual arousal and an arousal to consciousness and speech) and his wedding of his place; or rather, the poem presents Paterson's efforts at arousal and speech to wed his place. As a number of commentators have observed, the marriage theme is linked from the outset to the language theme, so that Paterson's potency is a function and test of his adequacy as a poet.

The mythology of the poem, which treats its seemingly unheroic materials with a Rabelaisian earthiness and Joycean irony, associates the giant Paterson, from whom the Passaic Falls spurted ("PISS-AGH! The giant lets fly!"), with the dwarf Pieter van Winkle. His name continues the mictatory punning, and as the "genius of the falls" yet a "monster in human form," van Winkle is Paterson's homunculus and shadow.[82] The falls themselves present Paterson's dilemma: can he drench himself in the cataract he spouted without being swept away and lost? If the people of Paterson are his thoughts, the falls seem the roar of their inarticulateness: can he still summon the old bardic power in this city of factories and slums and become the *vox populi* by mastering the swirling currents of thwarted speech and translating them into "straight lines" of verse?

> (What common language to unravel?
> ...combed into straight lines
> from that rafter of a rock's
> lip.)
>
>   (7)

People live and die "incommunicado" without articulate communication; in the following lines, "fails" puns on "falls":

The language, the language
            fails them
They do not know the words

. . . . . .

They may look at the torrent in
            their minds
and it is foreign to them   .

. . . .

            – the language
is divorced from their minds....
            (11–12)

Paterson sees and hears the falls at the outset and knows his task: "Say it! No ideas but in things. Mr. / Paterson has gone away / to rest and write" (9). But does the ensuing poem announce a semiotics of divorce and alienation or of marriage and increase? Is the poem an epithalamion or an elegy?

A passage describing the happy (and unquestioningly masculinist) polygamy of an African chief and his nine wives lined up in a *National Geographic* photograph on a single phallic log) is juxtaposed to a prose account of the unexpected "divorce" of the Reverend Mr. Cumming of Newark and his wife, Sarah. They came to the falls as newlyweds, but she either fell or threw herself over the brink without a word:

A false language pouring – a
language (misunderstood) pouring (misinterpreted) without
dignity, without minister, crashing upon a stone ear. At least
it settled it for her. Patch too, as a matter of fact.
            (15)

Sam Patch had become a popular hero by diving into the falls and surviving. In Paterson's telling, his survival was a function of his power of speech: "These were the words that Sam Patch said.... As he spoke he jumped," and later he fell to his death from the falls because "speech had failed him. He was confused. The word had been drained of its meaning" (17). Is Paterson more like the potent African chief or the wifeless minister, absurdly named Cumming? Is he, like Patch, a daring high-wire artist or an egoistic charlatan? Will he turn out to be the master or the victim of the falls?

The poem offers no quick assurances or answers. Beneath the symmetry of sections and books projected in the "Author's Note," *Paterson* plunges the reader into a disorienting rush of fragments and episodes, lyric and descriptive and narrative, often in prose, the versification various; as they follow one another, page after page, the lines do not seem straight, at least in their sequentiality and direction, and their apparent rambling raises the question of consequentiality and coherence. Stevens would shake his head, believing that Williams' "incessant new beginnings" did dissipate his energies in the end, as he had warned.

But readers immersed in the cataract of words begin to sense that though Paterson encounters in his odyssey many women, the marriage toward which the poem is pressing is never a consummated and perfected fact but remains an anxious striving to formulate, to communicate, to connect – a striving often thwarted, sometimes despaired of, but doggedly resumed in a subsequent episode. Section ii begins with the dreaded conclusion that "Divorce is / the sign of knowledge in our time, / divorce! divorce!" (18) but then proceeds to attempt to disprove it. Roused to speech, Paterson is moved to copulate with the female world, personified here by an anonymous woman, through language ("as if the bed were the bed of a stream") (24). "Events dancing two / and two with language" generates the single plural pronoun "we": "we two, isolated in the stream, / we also: three alike – " (23, 24): he and she and the word, he and she in the word. But they are not able to "seize the moment" and their talk ends in "silence and / unacknowledged desire" (24, 25). But the silence requires further talk.

Adequate or not, obsessively self-questioning, the words do not falter. And as readers move more easily into the words and with the words, they realize that *Paterson* is a poem of process which answers the question about whether it is a poem only by posing the problem again and again as the poem-in-process. The question is its own response, and the response is the reiterated question. Not the dynamic stasis of the Grecian urn or Stevens' revolving crystal at the end of *Notes Toward a Supreme Fiction*, but, rather, in this temporal poem, the gritty, flawed drive toward articulation and response.

The question of whether Paterson will be master or victim of the falls can only be answered by the poem. But the process poem is a Romantic notion and challenges the basic assumptions and techniques of Williams' Modernist aesthetic. Pound is quoted late in Book I admonishing Williams: "Your interest is in the bloody loam but what / I'm after is the finished product" (37). Elsewhere Williams recalled that during their discussions of poetry at the University of Pennsylvania, "I'd say 'bread' and he'd say 'caviar.' It was a sort of simplification of our positions."[83] It was more of a simplification than Williams let on. Williams' tastes were not as recherché and continental as Pound's, but Canto 45 reminds us of Pound's passionate taste for good wheat bread and Williams' pronouncements remind us of his Modernist concern for the finished work of art. In fact, Williams is invoking Pound here to excoriate his own Modernism in order to valorize the process poem he was engaged in writing. A letter from Williams' friend, Edward Dahlberg, at the end of Section ii contrasts Williams' Modernist detachment with his own Romantic identification of art with life: "With you the book is one thing, and the man who wrote it another" (29), and the letters from Cress (Marcia Nardi) interpolated into *Paterson* indict Paterson/Williams' silent aloofness from her as a woman and as a poet.

But Section iii gives us on its second page a lyric, entitled "The Sycamore" in a draft manuscript, which in contrast to the fixing and spatializing of temporal process in poems like "The Pot of Flowers" and "The Locust Tree in Flower," offers a different chronotope by imagining the process of growth as expanding rings of organic self-encirclement:

I enclose it and
  persist, go on.
. . . . . .

My surface is myself.
  Under which
to witness, youth is
  buried. Roots?
Everybody has roots.
                (32)

And the poem proceeds: "We go on living, we permit ourselves / to continue
–" (32). In fact, Book I closes with the powerful image of "snail-like" thought,
clambering up the wet rocks beside the falls to a cave amid the roaring waters.
Thought "has its birth and death there," for "that moist chamber" enwombs
Nature's paternal poet: "Earth, the chatterer, father of all / speech" (39).
Mother earth's inarticulate chatter, like the indiscriminate, preverbal roar of
the falls, necessitates the insemination of paternal thought and the birth of the
poem. Even as we read, the sequence of words down the page enacts "the
myth / that holds up the rock, / that holds up the water"; thought takes form
as the poem-offspring, Pater-son.

After this archetypal moment, the opening lines of *Paterson II*, "Sunday in
the Park" (1948), initiate a substantiation of the myth as Paterson moves out
among the people of his city:

    Outside
              outside myself
                    there is a world,
    he rumbled, subject to my incursions
                (43)

The "Author's Note" indicated that Book II would show Paterson "seeking"
identification with the "modern replicas" of the archetypes carousing on a
sunny summer afternoon in Garrett Park all about the falls in what seems
to Paterson a "ceremonial of love" (48). Several times the poem quotes
Alexander Hamilton's elitist denigration of the common people as the "great
beast," but the episodes from the city's early history and contemporary
situation, included in Books I and II, indict Hamilton himself as the
mastermind behind the exploitive scheme of capitalist development which
harnessed the power of the falls to profitable industry and in short order
produced from the wondrous beauty of the locale the squalid city of factories
and slums where the people work and live in economic oppression. Paterson
confronts their brutalization and "deformity" (61) on his "incursion" into
their proletarian bacchanal. But Williams eliminated Eliotic allusions to
Pervigilium Veneris from an early draft to make the scene less ironic and more
compassionate. For Paterson rises to a Whitmanian and Breughelesque identification with his folk, which shows them, despite their ugly vulgarity, as
somehow remarkable in their raw energy and even "not undignified" (52) in
their tragicomic debauche.

Nonetheless, Paterson is not a participant in the saturnalia; he passes among the lovers in the elderly Whitmanian figure of the beneficent father-poet. Years later, Williams admitted that although "I was impassioned when I wrote Part II," its success was prosodic and depended on his finding the "measure" to "lift to distinction" the wordless unconsciousness of his revelers: "It is a contrast between the vulgarity of the lovers in the park and the fineness, the aristocracy of the metrical arrangement of the verse."[84] In the midst of the description of the scene the great hymn to invention arises (its paratactic reiterativeness reminiscent of the litany against Usura in Canto 45):

> Without invention nothing is well spaced,
> unless the mind change, unless
> the stars are new measured, according
> to their relative positions, the
> line will not change, the necessity
> will not matriculate: unless there is
> a new mind there cannot be a new
> line. . . .

(50)

But Section ii of "Sunday in the Park" begins: "Blocked. / (Make a song out of that: concretely)" (62) and concludes with a verse passage, labeled "Address to the Deity" in a draft, which ends in "despair." The address (it could hardly by called a prayer) apostrophizes a naturalistic life force ("the eternal bride / and father") who reigns in "the multiplicity of your debacle" (75). The draft had read "the multiplicity of your universe," but the substitution of "debacle"[85] prepares for the perpetual round of "composition and decomposition" – a phrase which links the poetic process with natural process in a final "despair." Section iii anticipates "a reversal of despair" but consists of a frustrated encounter between "He" and "She" – mostly She's desperate expostulations: "Marry us! Marry us! / Or! be dragged down, dragged / under and lost" (83). (The verse passage is followed by Cress' six-plus closely packed pages of bitter denunciation of Paterson, which conclude Book II.) But as anima She reminds him of the dwarf of the waterfall, his homunculus, and urges him to "compose" again:

> Go home. Write. Compose.
>
> Ha!
>
> Be reconciled, poet, with your world, it is
> the only truth!
>
> Ha!
> – the language is worn out.

(84)

And again: "You have abandoned me! / . . . / Invent (if you can) discover or / nothing is clear" (84).

Instead of going home to write, he goes to "The Library" in Paterson III (1949), the "Author's Note" tells us, to seek and achieve from the record of the city's past a language to make it vocal in the present. Now he is midcity, with the river below the falls flowing past, and the three sections of Book III dramatize the natural disasters which made 1902 the city's *annus mirabilis*: a tornado, a fire, and a flood. The Library seems at first the airless repository of dead books about a dead history. Paterson imagines the ghosts of the books clamoring at the windows for fresh air; their cries seem to "castrate" and "execrate the imagination," and he is tempted to heed their siren call:

> Give up
> the poem. Give up the shilly-
> shally of art.
>
>   What can you, what
> can YOU hope to conclude –
> on a heap of dirty linen?
>
>   (108)

But the Library plays a paradoxical role, for the winds are already blowing there, from the printed account of the tornado through the poet's mind to generate a tornado in his poem. In each successive section of Book III the wind, the flames, the floodwaters of 1902 rouse the imagination rather than castrating it; the city's history reconciles the poet to its present deformed state and commits the imagination to its material base: "The province of the poem is the world" (99), "Embrace the / foulness" (103). So each section chants the imagination's participation in the destructive/re-creative force of nature, epitomized, for example, in the old bottle charred to a thing of beauty in the 1902 conflagration: "deflowered, reflowered there by the flame" (118). The refrain "So be it," recalling Pound's great litany to humility ("Pull down thy vanity") in Canto 81, tolls through "The Library" with gathering strength as the imagination makes the poem of its conscious acquiescence in natural and historical process.

For the phrase "Embrace the / foulness" offers the solution to the "marriage riddle" of the poem (105), "the riddle of a man and a woman" (106, 107). Acquiescence more and more reveals what the foulness hides – the "Beautiful Thing," the indestructible generative energy of the feminine, manifest in "a dark flame, / a wind, a flood – counter to all staleness" (100). Marie Curie seems the type of the artist, persisting in her experiments with the foul "pitch-blend" until the "radiant gist" glowed in the bottom of her retort. In a note, Williams referred to "the image of our age: boiling down the pitch-blend for that strain of radiance."[86] The invocation of "Beautiful Thing" leads up to a double apparition in Section ii: a woman of dubious virtue on a damp bed in a basement "under the mudplashed windows among the scabrous / dirt of the holy sheets" (125); another in a white lace dress and high heels, her nose broken in a street-gang fight. Like *The Cantos, Paterson* had been weaving the theme of economic exploitation along with its other themes, but just as Williams' anticapitalism took a leftist-populist turn, whereas Pound's turned rightist-elitist, so now without Pound's Ovidian mythology or Neoplatonism, the Paterson poet encounters the goddess not as Aphrodite (as in Canto 81, for example) but in a battered woman in the Paterson slums. Still, there is no mistaking the encounter:

> attendant upon you, shaken by your beauty
>
> Shaken by your beauty   .
>
> > > Shaken.
> > >   (125)

Section iii reflects again on the linguistic style and form appropriate to embracing the foulness and bends Modernist prescriptions for conscious control to suggest, for the moment, that the best way to catch the flash of essential vitality is for language to try to move with something of the unchecked propulsion of floodwaters: "Only one answer: write carelessly so that nothing that is not green will survive" (129) – that is, so that all that is green will. And yet, to make an effective replica of the flood or the falls, the poet must "find a place / apart from it," or become "its slave, / its sleeper." And so he circles back by the end of the section to his characteristic position:

> I must
> find my meaning and lay it, white,
> beside the white water: myself –
> comb out the language – or succumb
> > (145)

Again, the apposition between art and nature; the artwork as the third and mediating term, the marriage term, which presents her in terms of "myself," "myself" in terms of her. With that confirmation he can leave the Library for "The Run to the Sea," the final phase of his life and poem: "Let / me out! (Well, go!) this rhetoric / is real!" (145).

In *Paterson IV* (1951), the aging protagonist facing the end is explicitly presented in the paternal role he began to assume on his excursion through the park. But Section i begins Book IV with a comic parody of a pastoral idyl and presents Paterson as the fumbling would-be father-lover of the modern unlettered nymph Phyllis, who has left her drunken Pappy at home to seek her fortune in Manhattan. She finds herself in an odd triangle, shuttling between the lesbian poet Corydon and the paternal doctor-poet. Neither proves to be an adequate mate for Phyllis; nor an adequate poet: Paterson sounds like a Symboliste pastiche of Eliot ("he is the city of cheap hotels and private / entrances . of taxis at the door, the car / standing in the rain hour after hour" [154]) and Corydon like a Symboliste pastiche of Crane ("a whirring pterodactyl / of a contrivance, to remind one of Da Vinci, / searches the Hellgate current for some corpse" [161]). Paterson is ineffectual and inarticulate in his role as protector/seducer, and Phyllis is left to her own very practical devices, determined that "I can talk my own language" (168).

She is no more the Beautiful Thing than Paterson is her poet. The dust jacket of Book III had foretold the theme of its successor: "Book IV shows the perverse confusions that come of a failure to untangle the language and make it our own as both man and woman are carried helplessly toward the sea (of blood) which, by their failure of speech, awaits them. The poet alone in this world holds the key to their final rescue." After the "perverse confusions" in the language of all three characters in the first section, Section ii begins to demonstrate the poet's ability to suffer and survive. The protagonist is specifically the father: first to his own son, as he recalls to him their attendance at a lecture explaining the mystery of atomic fission and recounts to him Marie Curie's discovery of radium; and then to young Allen Ginsberg of Paterson, whose letters proclaim his sonship to the older poet: "I know you will be pleased to realize that at least one actual citizen of your community has inherited your experience in his struggle to love and know his world-city, through your work, which is an accomplishment you almost cannot have hoped to achieve" (174). Marie Curie is depicted as the poet-physician's alter ego: a self-begetter, pregnant with genius (gender in a genius, Williams says, is "of no importance") and producing thereby the "radiant gist." In a note for the poem, Williams sums up the aesthetic and economic implications of modern scientific discoveries which Section ii explores:

> The lecture on uranium (Curie), the splitting of the atom (first time explained to *me*) has a literary meaning... in the splitting of the foot... (sprung meter of Hopkins) and consequently is connected to human life or death.... Three discoveries here: 1. radium. 2. poet's discovery of modern idiom. 3. political scientist's discovery of a cure for economic ills.[87]

Williams' involvement with Social Credit economics antedated Pound's advocating Major Douglas to him, and in 1935 he contributed to the American Social Credit journal *New Democracy* a piece called "A Social Diagnosis for Surgery: A Poet-Physician on the Money-Cancer."[88] But Pound would, of course, have understood Williams' conviction that the sickness or cure for all aspects of culture is inseparable.

But having instructed his sons about "'the radiant gist' against all that / scants our lives" (186), the "Poet-Physician" Pater-son faces marriage-death-rebirth in the mother-sea: "The ocean yawns! / It is almost the hour" (187). The "radiant gist" holds the secret of death as well as life: the discovery of radium ended in Marie Curie's death, and now the poem carries Paterson to his end. Section iii mingles attention to offspring – a snatch of lullaby, a salute to the new Williams grandchild – with episodes telling of the violent deaths of fathers, including a murder by John Johnson (John's son). We know from *The Autobiography*, published the same year, that Williams' father had died as a result of the physical ministrations of his doctor-son, and earlier in Book IV, Williams had told his son that "the best thing a man can do for his son, when he is born, is to die," because "I give you another, bigger than yourself, to contend with" (171). Paterson suffers no violence, but he consigns himself to extinction, with the motto of his old-age effort inscribed on a sea-shell:

> porcelain inscribed
> with the legend, *La Vertue*

> *est toute dans l'effort*
baked into the material,
> > maroon on white, a glazed
> Venerian scallop
>
> > > (189)

It is significant of the final marriage that this wisdom about virtue, in the sense of manliness or virtu, comes from Venus the Great Mother, and the next verse passage associates Venus and her wisdom with recollections of his own mother, who taught him the same lesson. Moreover, the son–now–father has come to realize that virtu "takes connivance, / takes convoluted forms, takes / time!" (189). Both the hang of the line and the exclamation point emphasize the commitment to time. It is Williams' secular, naturalistic version of Eliot's "Only through time time is conquered."

The refrain wells up: "The sea is our home," and the capitulation to the sea recalls Whitman's great "Sea-Drift" elegies:

> Thalassa
> immaculata: our home, our nostalgic
> mother in whom the dead, enwombed again
> cry out to us to return   .
> > the blood dark sea!
>
> > > (202)

But in this poem, unlike the elegies, capitulation engenders counterpoint, even resistance; finally, "The sea is not our home / . . . / . . not our home! It is NOT / our home" (201, 202). At the last moment comes the reversal: "Turn back I warn you," and Williams dates it "(October 10, 1950)" (200). Pater rises from the sea as son:

> Seed
> of Venus, you will return . to
> a girl standing upon a tilted shell, rose
> pink   .
>
> > (202)

Spitting out the seed from the plum he is eating, Paterson, accompanied by his dog, heads inland, like other archetypal American heroes: Leatherstocking, Thoreau, Huck Finn, and particularly Whitman – overalls, rolled sleeves, hat, and all.

Williams was explicit about his archetypal intentions: "Paterson IV ends with the protagonist breaking through the bushes, identifying himself with the land, with America. He will finally die but it can't be categorically stated that death ends *anything.* . . . Art . . . will go beyond him into the lives of young people."[89] And again:

> I had to think hard as to how I was going to end the poem. It wouldn't do to
> have a grand and soul-satisfying conclusion, because I didn't see any in my
> subject. Nor was I going to be confused or depressed or evangelical about it. It
> didn't belong to my subject. It would have been easy to make a great smash-

up with a "beautiful" sunset at sea, or a flight of pigeons, love's end and the welter of man's fate. Instead...Odysseus swims in as man must do, he doesn't drown, he is too able, but, accompanied by his dog, strikes inland (toward Camden) to begin again.[90]

There are glancing allusions to Stevens with the "flight of pigeons" and to Pound with the swimming Odysseus, but Camden was, of course, Whitman's Paterson: the other Jersey city, Williams reminds us in *The Autobiography*, where Whitman, "much traduced, lived the latter years of his life and died."[91] And one manuscript version of the conclusion cites Whitman as Paterson's poetic father:

> The greatest moment in the history
> of the American poem was when
> Walt Whitman stood looking to sea
> from the shelving sands
> and the waves
> called to him and
> he answered drilling his voice to
> their advance
> driving his voice above
> the returning clatter of stone.
> With courage, labor and abandon
> the word, the word, the word.[92]

But in fact, Williams' word is significantly different from Whitman's. The "word from the sea" in "Out of the Cradle Endlessly Rocking" was "death, death, death, death, death," and it called forth the poems to reconcile Whitman to the sea. But in Williams' case "the word, the word, the word" is precisely the word itself, or rather the poem which delivers him from the sea and turns him inland again. He averted a tragic ending not just for the extraneous (and temporary) reason that he was still physically alive and active, but because of his reliance on the poetic word to survive him in time by its own measure. Without resorting to a "grand and soul-satisfying conclusion" that appeared false to him, Williams sired himself as *Paterson*, for "art...will be beyond him into the lives of young people," father to son.

Moreover, Williams could not end his poem there, with the quaternity of books he had planned. It was not just a matter of his physical survival, even survival of the strokes which afflicted him soon after the publication of *The Autobiography* and *Paterson IV*; the survival of the poem to the next generation was in question. Despite the praise of *Paterson I* by Lowell and Jarrell, the reviews had become increasingly dubious and even downright hostile as succeeding books appeared. Reviewers and even some admirers could not grasp the method and musical structure, and complained of increasing prolixity and prosaic flatness. By Book IV, Williams was incorporating criticism into the poem from Floss ("What I miss, said your mother, is the poetry, the pure poem of the first parts" [171]), even from Ginsberg ("I seldom dig exactly what you are doing with cadences, line length, sometimes syntax, etc. . . . I don't understand the measure" [174–175]). Such doubts made Williams defensive: "The poem to me (until I go broke) is an attempt, an experiment, a failing experiment, toward assertion with broken means but an assertion, always, of a new and total culture."[93] Commenting on Book IV, Jarrell retracted his earlier enthusiasm: "*Paterson* has been getting rather steadily worse. . . . Book IV is so disappointing that I do not want to write about it at any length: it would not satisfactorily conclude even a quite mediocre poem." And then the *coup de grace*: "In his long one-sided war with Eliot Dr. Williams seems to be coming off badly – particularly so when we compare the whole of *Paterson* with *Four Quartets*."[94]

Williams might have expected Jarrell to meet *Paterson* with distaste and incomprehension; his New Critical training directed him to other poetic assumptions, procedures, values. Moreover, with the decline of the New Criticism and the revival of open form poetry during the 1950s, *Paterson* began to fare very differently with poets and critics. At the same time that the influences of *Four Quartets* and *Notes Toward a Supreme Fiction* were receding, *Paterson* (like *The Cantos*) was coming to exert a wide and powerful influence on poetry of the 1950s and after: Olson's *Maximus Poems*, Duncan's *Passages*, Levertov's *To Stay Alive*, Dorn's *Slinger*, Ginsberg's "Howl," even Lowell's "Life Studies." Nevertheless, the loudly expressed doubts about *Paterson* disturbed Williams, and his self-searching about the project required the poem's extension beyond the planned quaternity into a fifth book. *Paterson V* (1958) was delayed by the strokes and by the depression which illness, age, and self-doubt inflicted, but the gap before its appearance is in its way fitting. *Paterson V* provides a coda for the four previous books, but in a voice and style that belong to Williams' last, post-*Paterson* phase. Sherman Paul has argued that the apparent inability of *Paterson* to vindicate the poet as the savior of culture caused a decisive shift in Williams' subsequent poetry: "From this time forward – and chiefly by means of the transition provided by 'The Desert Music' – he turned from the cultural to the personal aspects of his myth of America."[95]

Not that *Paterson V* silenced criticism. There were new complaints about the blurring of the Objectivist precision and concision of the shorter poems, and also now about the disappearance of the dramatic and narrative episodes of the earlier books into the univocality of the poet. Even Olson missed the more impersonal "distance" of the earlier books in the autobiographical meditativeness of *Paterson V*.[96] But Paul's formulation of the undoubted change in Williams' perspective and style is too simplistic; if worries about the alleged failure of *Paterson* generated the last book, the result stands as a validation of the artistic process, and specifically of art as process. A poem which develops through time instead of fixing the isolated moment spatially is necessarily incomplete and imperfectly realized; virtue is all in the effort rather than in the finished product, in cultivating the bloody loam rather than in glazing the Grecian urn.

Book IV had arrived at a sense of the poet surviving the temporal cycle as his life poem. But how can the poem participate in time and not be subject to it? The individual consciousness, no matter how naturalistically time bound and earth bound, dreads its own extinction. Thoreau's *Journals*, chronicling the seasons year after year, necessitated *Walden* as a cunningly contrived strategy of consciousness to ensure the "immortality" of the cyclic pattern as a work of art. The single, personal voice of the poet allows a sustained development that makes *Paterson V* in many ways the culmination of the poem, and the theme which holds the book together and rounds the entire poem out is the individual's relation to time – in fact, the poet's discernment of different temporal modalities. Williams implied as much when he observed of Book V: "When the river ended in the sea I had no place to go but back in life. I had to take the spirit of the River up in the air."[97] The poet wanted not merely to repeat the cycle, to go round and round, but instead to project the natural cycle itself into a different dimension: water and earth sublimated into spirit and air. Williams, like Thoreau but without his Transcendentalism, craved a transcendence which secured the self in time; he wanted to find in art a temporal mode which contained cyclic time and thus made movement into pattern.

The cyclic round Williams associates, stereotypically, with the phases of the feminine: "the whore and the virgin, an identity" (210). And quickly the duality of the feminine sorts out into a cycle of three – virgin-wife-daughter – or, most fully, into a quaternity of virgin-wife-mother-daughter, the completed square as magic circle in the image of the Uroboros: "a sphere, a snake with its tail in its mouth" (214). (The whore in the prose passage Williams quotes in Section i from Gilbert Sorrentino insists on "FOUR no three" as their price.)

The symbiosis between virgin and whore requires virginity to sacrifice its stainlessness to the life process. Early in Section i the poet urges the virgin not to cheapen her maidenhead by bartering it (like Phyllis) but instead to "throw it away! (as she [the whore] did)" (208). Rather than "putrefy / or petrify / for fear of venereal disease," "'Loose your love to flow' / while you are yet young / male and female" (216). Though these admonitions raise ideological and ethical questions of masculinist aggression against the female, Williams develops the theme less crudely in the Unicorn, the central and unifying image of *Paterson V*. In many places the Unicorn is identified with the feminine round. Immediately after the call for the virgin to throw away her maidenhead, the Unicorn is introduced and described as thrashing about, "calling / for its own murder" (208) – that is, for its own violation and death in the life process. Near the end of the book the Unicorn is referred to as "my beloved." But then "she" is associated with "the god of love / of virgin birth" (208): not Mary and Venus now, therefore, but their sons, Jesus and Eros. For as unifying image the Unicorn presents – and reconciles – both the submissive feminine and the potent male; from its first appearance it is the "white one-horned beast" (208) that while calling for its own murder, nonetheless resists its attackers. It is the androgynous character of the Unicorn, at once victim and victor in the sequence of tapestries, that makes him-her Paterson/Williams' totem animal.

A passage near the end of Book V completes the cycle of life, struggle, and death by casting it into another dimension with the apotheosis of the Unicorn: the "dead beast," sacrificed in the hunt, becomes first the merely "wounded" beast and then the "survivor of the chase," who "lies down to rest a while, / his regal neck / fast in a jewelled collar" (234–235). The collar symbolizes the round within which "she" is bound but within which "he" nonetheless rears his head and horn triumphant.

Moreover, on one of the occasions in which the Unicorn is explicitly called by the masculine pronoun, he is linked with the artist:

> The Unicorn
> has no match
> or mate . the artist
> has no peer .
> (211)

Although there is mention of a number of female artists – Gertrude Stein, Josephine Herbst, Sappho, and Bessie Smith – the entire book is studded with references to male artists: Toulouse-Lautrec (to whose memory Book V is dedicated), Soupault, Sorrentino, Audubon, Whitman, Ginsberg, Pollock, Gauguin, Pound, Klee, Dürer, Leonardo, Freud, Picasso, Gris, Beethoven, Cummings, Breughel, Matisse. So, in fabricating the Unicorn sequentially, like the tapestry makers, Williams as artist follows the natural round to its tragic conclusion – and survives in his comprehension of it! He is contained within the round and yet contains it. For, unlike most visual representations, the cycle of tapestries does not merely spatialize the temporal moment but renders the temporal round into aesthetic time: transcendence not into a superior order of existence but into a conscious enactment of the moving pattern of experience.

Williams' image was of taking "the spirit of the River up in the air." The first lines of *Paterson V* are:

> In old age
> the mind
> casts off
> rebelliously
> an eagle
> from its crag
> (207)

And a little later: "Paterson, from the air / . . .has returned to the old scenes / to witness" (209). The high-wire act of the poem witnesses the tragedy of the falls. But, given Sam Patch's ending, the witness' performance makes the lasting difference; centuries after the weavers have crumbled to dust, the tapestries of the Unicorn hunt constitute "A WORLD OF ART / THAT THROUGH THE YEARS HAS // SURVIVED!" (209). The artist's potency ("Paterson, / keep your pecker up" [235]) is proved in his imaginative ability to conceive himself (again Pater-son) in a "living fiction" (234) which suffers time but "escapes intact" (212) and ever virgin. Through the Unicorn tapestries the old man imagines "Paterson, the King-self" (234) as

> a young man
> sharing the female world
> in Hell's despight, graciously
>   – once on a time   .
>   on a time: (238)

So the poem lives in time by finding its own special poetic time:

> The measure intervenes, to measure is all we know,
>
>   a choice among the measure .
>
>   the measured dance
>
> .   .   .   .
>
> We know nothing and can know nothing   .
>   but
> the dance, to dance to a measure
> contrapuntally,
>   Satyrically, the tragic foot.
>   (239)

Not, it turns out, the measure of music so much as the measure of the dance: the dance – not music – reconciles space with time. An Imagist poem like "By the road to the contagious hospital" implied process by submitting time to space, fixing a transitional moment in a visual-verbal structure, but suspicion of that strategy as resistance to the reality of time had precipitated the further experiment in *Paterson*. Williams would never renounce the image (how could he?), and visual artists alternate with writers in *Paterson V*. However, the Unicorn tapestries come to supplant the Cubist painting as the visual analogue for the poem as a whole because *Paterson* found its form not by submitting time to space, as in the earlier work, but by submitting space to time as measure. The poem measures out its tragic destiny not for the musical ear alone but for the eye and ear at once, like the bodily rhythms of the dance.

The mention of the "scent of a rose" and "a / chess game" in the lines omitted here from the previously cited passage recall Eliot for counterpoint in these final paradoxical pronouncements, as the allusions to the dance recall "Burnt Norton": "Except for the point, the still point, / there would be no dance, and there is only the dance." But the satyr dance compounds these Eliotic allusions (the word "compounded" occurs as a pun in the intervening lines as well) with Pound's "Beat, beat, whirr, thud, in the soft turf / under the apple trees, / Choros nympharum, goat-foot with the pale foot alternate." Of course, the allusions are deliberately invoked in order to establish Williams' difference: his wisdom is neither Christian nor Platonist: "Not prophecy! NOT prophecy! / but the thing itself!" (208). For him there is no still point, only the aesthetic dance of our mortal destiny. He would have rewritten Eliot's "Only through time time is conquered" and "The poetry does not matter" to read "Only through the poetic dance is time conquered." And he would have rewritten Pound's "it [nature] coheres all right / even if my notes do not cohere" to read "it cannot cohere *unless* the notes of the dance do."[98] The dance celebrates the mortal marriage of space to time, through which the poet comes to his measure as "I, Paterson, the King-self."

V

Music and measure became insistent topics in the letters and essays starting in the late 1930s, as painting had been in the 1920s. Already in 1931, reviewing Pound's first thirty cantos, Williams noted the "measure" and "movement" of Pound's distinctive line as the "evidence of invention." In 1939, moving toward the *Paterson* experiment, he insisted to James Laughlin that "an auditory quality, a NEW auditory quality, underlies and determines the visual quality" of verse and dismissed any who would say "that you can't mix auditory and visual standards in poetry." His important 1948 essay "The Poem as a Field of Action," written in the midst of *Paterson*, comprehended the field – a spatial conception – in temporal terms: "The only reality that we can know is MEASURE."[99] Olson saw Pound's perceptual and structural achievement in *The Cantos* as a successful attempt to translate time into space, to reconstruct history into a Modernist spatial design. But for the poets themselves, the challenge came more and more to be rather the accounting for and accommodating of history and prosodic time and sequential design into a Modernist spatial methodology. By 1954, with the first four books of *Paterson* out and with Book V under way, Williams told Richard Eberhardt: "By its *music* shall the best of modern verse be known and the *resources* of the music."[100]

In "The Desert Music,"[101] read as the Phi Beta Kappa poem at Harvard in 1951, Williams celebrates his ability to translate unconscious, unspoken experience into the dance of language: "the counted poem, to an exact measure." The almost unbelieving proclamation "I *am* a poet! I / am. I am. I am a poet" near the end of "The Desert Music" indicates his childlike exultance in old age at this rediscovery. A 1954 letter recalled early intimations that "I had in the compass of my head a great discovery" concerning the measurement of verse, which "would not only settle my own internal conflicts but be of transcendent [N.B. the word] use to the men and women around me,"[102] but he was having more trouble than he wanted to admit in conceptualizing its specifications. He regularly associated the new measure with Einstein's theory of relativity,[103] which discovered a "relative order" on all levels of experience, and so redefined the "structure of our lives all along the line." "Line" here puns: our confused lives would take on relative order in the irregular prosodic structure of the verse line. Williams wanted the variability and particularity of a relative prosody brought to conscious and deliberate realization as a "discipline" and "rule" so as to regulate the line beyond anything Whitman or Sandburg even understood. The individual line's rhythm should be "exact" in its particularity, but as late as his 1953 statement

"On Measure" for the new generation of poets in Cid Corman's *Origin* magazine, he could speak no more descriptively than of "a *relatively* stable foot, not a rigid one," as in metered verse.[104]

How to indicate on the page, as on a musical score, the underlying unit of time that infuses a consistency of what we could convincingly call measure into the variety of rhythms, numbers of stresses and syllables, lengths and phrasal subdivisions of lines? That unit of measure was what Williams referred to in the essays and correspondence of his last years as "the variable foot," and the letter to Eberhardt the year after "On Measure" is much more explicit about how and why the variable foot measures. Williams quotes passages from recent poems and instructs Eberhart to count a "single beat" for each line, no matter how many words or syllables or stresses the line contains.[105] The lines he cited were arranged in triads, spaced with indentations down the page, and the visual grace and consistency of the poem on the page call attention to the integrity and individuality of the lines as temporal as well as spatial units. Lines are like bars of music, all roughly equal in time but each capable of infinite variation in the number and duration of syllables, like the notes comprising the bars. The simplicity of the insight Williams took to be a gauge of its fundamental rightness.

Williams seemed to take a long and halting time to formulate this basic principle, but there is an early typescript on "Speech Rhythm," reprinted by Mike Weaver, which anticipates the notion of the variable foot. It was probably written in 1913 for *Poetry* magazine and then forgotten after it was rejected, especially after Williams became engaged in developing the visual-spatial analogues for poetic form which Modernist painting offered. Nevertheless, the early distinction Williams made between what he here calls the old-fashioned "poetic foot" and the "rhythmic unit" anticipated the distinction between meter and the variable foot that would occupy his last decade:

> The one thing essential to rhythm is not sound but motion, of the two kinds: forward and up and down, rapidity of motion and quality of motion.
> Thus the number of sounds in the rhythm unit do not because of their number give the unit any quality but only as they give motion in one of the two directions.
> For this reason the poetic foot – dependent on the number of sounds composing it – cannot, except by chance, embody the rhythm unit. The motion might be given by either a greater or less number of sounds in the same unit.
> By seeing the rhythm apart from the sounds clustering about it the old meter forms are enlarged into a unit more flexible and accurate.[106]

Williams had often enough organized his lines in triads or tercets, usually lined up at the left-hand margin. However, it was only in the stepped triads of a passage in *Paterson II*, published separately as "The Descent," that he felt he had found an adequate way of marking the new measure, and it was only "several years" after writing "The Descent" that he came to perceive his almost unwitting discovery.[107] A number of commentators have charged that the variable foot was no more a new device than it was an exact measure, and even so sympathetic a critic as Hugh Kenner suggested that the triadic spacing was a spatial device to help Williams read and write on a typewriter after the strokes of the early 1950s had damaged his brain and paralyzed his arm.[108] In any case, Williams' conviction that the variable foot constituted "my final conception of what my own poetry should be" propelled him, against the ravages of the strokes, into a last decade of prodigious accomplishment: *The Desert Music* (1954) and *Journey to Love* (1955), then *Pictures from Brueghel and Other Poems* (1962) in the year of his death, with *Paterson V* (1958) at its midpoint.

Much of this work, including *Paterson V*, was written in spaced tercets or triads. The sense of confident achievement, combined with the inherent instability of the triadic configuration, made for longish poems, not book-length as *Paterson* is but longer than the typical early lyrics. Even when they turn, as did the early lyrics, on a moment of perception, the moment is grasped now more palpably in terms of temporal process, and the poem, more loosely associative in structure, more discursive in development, needs time to let its implications unfold. As the poet acknowledges his presence and his active participation in the process of exfoliation, the pronoun "I" threads through the poem in a way that Imagism and Objectivism, reacting against Romantic personalism, tried to eschew. The tension between the impersonal Objectivist observer and his world recedes; language is used with a more relaxed sense of its relational and connective potentialities rather than its disjunctiveness as a third term. As a result, these ruminative poems are more oral; even the reader experiences them as a speaking voice. In Thom Gunn's words, "Statement emerges from Williams as both subject and author of the poem, not from him merely as author." And Gunn is correct in observing (whatever Williams might have thought) that the "new ease in his relationship with the external world" permitted a concourse of the personal and impersonal, the particular and the general, which, Gunn observes, "bears an astonishing – though we may hardly assume derivative – resemblance to some of the best passages in *Four Quartets*."[109]

At last, in "Asphodel, That Greeny Flower," the thirty-page centerpiece of the *Journey to Love* volume dedicated "To My Wife," Williams wrote his own marriage poem, a sustained celebration of the love which he and Floss consummated painfully, despite his betrayals, over a lifetime. These final poems to friends and family are all love poems. "For Eleanor and Bill Monahan" is Williams' most religious poem; it assumes his friends' Catholicism to pray "Mother of God! Our Lady!," asking forgiveness in the words of the "Hail Mary," seeking submission "to Your rule" so that she may "make us / humble and obedient to His rule," and apotheosizing the maternal archetype with a Latin verse from the "Salve Regina":

> The female principle of the world
> 　　is my appeal
> 　　　　in the extremity

to which I have come.
           O clemens! O pia! O dolcis!
                    Maria![110]

And at last, too, after many poems to the mother, he was able to write his
father poem. Here is the full text of "The Sparrow: For My Father":

    This sparrow
            who comes to sit at my window
                    is a poetic truth
    more than a natural one.
            His voice,
                    his movements,
    his habits —
            how he loves to
                    flutter his wings
    in the dust —
            all attest it;
                    granted, he does it
    to rid himself of lice
            but the relief he feels
                    makes him
    cry out lustily —
            which is a trait
                    more related to music
    than otherwise.
            Wherever he finds himself
                    in early spring,
    on back streets
            or beside palaces,
                    he carries on
    unaffectedly
            his amours.
                    It begins in the egg,
    his sex genders it:
            What is more pretentiously
                    useless
    or about which
            we more pride ourselves?
                    It leads as often as not
    to our undoing.
            The cockerel, the crow
                    with their challenging voices
    cannot surpass
            the insistence
                    of his cheep!
    Once
            at El Paso

                    toward evening,
I saw – and heard! –
            ten thousand sparrows
                    who had come in from
the desert
            to roost. They filled the trees
                    of a small park. Men fled
(with ears ringing!)
            from their droppings,
                    leaving the premises
to the alligators
            who inhabit
                    the fountain. His image
is familiar
            as that of the aristocratic
                    unicorn, a pity
there are not more oats eaten
            nowadays
                    to make living easier
for him.
            At that,
                    his small size,
keen eyes,
            serviceable beak
                    and general truculence
assure his survival –
            to say nothing
                    of his innumerable
brood.
            Even the Japanese
                    know him
and have painted him
            sympathetically,
                    with profound insight
into his minor
            characteristics.
                    Nothing even remotely
subtle
            about his lovemaking.
                    He crouches
before the female,
            drags his wings,
                    waltzing,
throws back his head
            and simply –
                    yells! The din
is terrific.
            The way he swipes his bill
                    across a plank

to clean it,
        is decisive.
                So with everything
he does. His coppery
        eyebrows
                give him the air
of being always
        a winner – and yet
                I saw once,
the female of his species
        clinging determinedly
                to the edge of
a water pipe,
        catch him
                by his crown-feathers
to hold him
        silent,
                subdued,
hanging above the city streets
        until
                she was through with him.
What was the use
        of that?
                She hung there
herself,
        puzzled at her success.
                I laughed heartily.
Practical to the end,
        it is the poem
                of his existence
that triumphed
        finally;
                a wisp of feathers
flattened to the pavement,
        wings spread symmetrically
                as if in flight,
the head gone,
        the black escutcheon of the breast
                undecipherable,
an effigy of a sparrow,
        a dried wafer only,
                left to say
and it says it
        without offense,
                beautifully;
This was I,
        a sparrow.
                I did my best;
farewell.[111]

The appearance of a sparrow at the poet's window – an event remarkable only for its everyday familiarity – triggers recollections which sum up a lifetime of sparrows. The sparrow becomes a kaleidoscopic image of the poet himself: the pluck and endurance, the swaggering sexuality, the vulnerability to the female, the self-assertion, the lack of either apology or self-pity. In the sparrow's erratic progression from egg to mating to roost to brood to crushed remains, this street bird with his lice-filled plumage and gutter manners becomes Everyman, a totem of the self risen through its humble circumstances to sufficiently heroic stature to withstand the ironic allusions to "the aristocratic / unicorn," Japanese paintings, and the chivalric escutcheon – and to invert the irony to acclamation.

In speaking of the sparrow itself as "poetic truth," in speaking of "the poem / of his existence," Williams sounds like Whitman and comes close to dissolving his earlier Modernist disjunction between life and art. And yet it is "The Sparrow" *as poem* which expresses his existence as a truth; it is Williams, not the sparrow, who can come to say "without offense, / beautifully":

> This was I,
>   a sparrow.
>   I did my best;
>   farewell.

Williams' sense of mastering the measure eased the tension between his Modernist and Romantic allegiances, reconciled him to time, and in his extremity permitted him, more autobiographically even than in *Paterson*, to merge with the father for once. And for all.

7

Allen Tate and Hart Crane: Diptych with Angels and Demons

I

John Crowe Ransom characterized his most brilliant student and lifelong friend in terms of coherence and consistency: "Allen Tate's mind is exceptional in its harmony. . . . His personality is as whole and undivided, and it is as steady, as it is vivid. Allen would readily have found his role in the Golden Age of Hellenism, or in classical Rome or the Elizabethan Renaissance."[1] Since Tate's poems and essays depict no Golden Age but a world of almost insupportable tension and anguish, Ransom's words may sound like an affectionate but deceptive extravagance. But although Tate's vision voiced the tormented divisions of the modern spirit, his angle of vision was steady, and from the outset his entire purpose was to find a basis for harmony. Tate's dilemma, like Eliot's, was precisely that of the would-be Christian classicist with the Romantic's psychological and spiritual problems.

As the first undergraduate invited to join the Vanderbilt professors who formed the Fugitive Group around Ransom, Tate was even then exceptional for the intellectual energy that restlessly pursued related lines of inquiry – literary, philosophic, social – to locate his psychological malaise in the larger cultural crisis. Already Tate aspired to be (in the title of an important essay of 1952) "The Man of Letters in the Modern World." If he throve on his elders' company and attention, he also set about shaking them wide awake. Ransom remembered his earnestness and remembered too that praise from this relative youth was the most satisfying to the senior members of the group because it was the hardest earned.

Tate was a Kentuckian by birth, with the story of the Tidewater plantation, razed by the Yankees, scored into his consciousness, and he became for a while passionately involved in the ideas of the Vanderbilt Agrarians. Yet all the time his mind resisted regional provinciality. He tried to introduce his confreres to the French Symbolistes and to such Anglo-American followers in their generation as Eliot. When Ransom attacked the pessimism and the collagelike technique of *The Waste Land*, Tate wrote such a strong rejoinder that Ransom remembered it as their sharpest disagreement. Despite his Confederate sympathies (he wrote biographies of Stonewall Jackson and Jefferson Davis), Tate knew that the historical burden could cripple the postbellum southerner, whether he be Faulkner's Quentin Compson or Ransom's "Man Without Sense of Direction" or the speaker in his own "Ode to the Confederate Dead." Moreover, as a writer, he knew that the literary soil of the South, especially outside Vanderbilt, was thin and uncultivated: besides the many volumes of forensic oratory and political debate, only the histrionics of Poe and the folk comedy of Clemens. So he moved to New York, and for several edgy months Hart Crane, an exile from the Midwest, shared a house with him and his wife, Carolyn Gordon; better still, he went to Europe twice on Guggenheim Fellowships and mingled for a while with the expatriate set.

But neither Manhattan nor Paris allayed his restlessness. His roots were southern, and their grip, like that of Poe's, exiled him elsewhere as they throttled him at home. For him the southern dilemma is linked to the general modern crisis precisely by being its shadow obverse, as the country is related to the city and paralysis to rootless mobility. Tate the southerner *is* Tate the critic of contemporary society. Faulkner and most of the Vanderbilt colleagues chose to remain close to native soil, but Tate felt trapped there. On the one hand, the southerner must not become "merely a 'modern' writer," alienated and unable to go home again, and "the Southern writer should if possible be a Southerner in the South"; on the other hand, Tate noted, no uprooted modern but Milton the classicist allowed that "wherever we do well is home: wherever we are allowed best to realize our natures – a realization that, for an artist, presupposes permission to follow his craft."[2] Even though the verse often ties itself willfully into kinks and knots, even though the tone of the social or literary commentary crusts over with self-righteous condescension, even though we may not associate Tate with classical Greece or Elizabethan England, the range and quality of his writing from the outset – the slim body of poems whose concentration affected younger poets like Robert Lowell and John Berryman, the biographies, the superb novel *The Fathers*, the densely intelligent and sometimes abrasively challenging essays – made Tate a southern man of letters in the modern world. His no-man's-land on the Mason-Dixon line was his problem – and his inspiration.

For Tate, then, what is the responsibility of the man of letters? Certainly not direct political action and social engineering, as liberals like Archibald MacLeish and Van Wyck Brooks urged. (He answered them in the essay "To Whom Is the Poet Responsible?" and in the "Ode to Our Pro-Consuls of the Air.") But Tate found Eliot's prose as early as his poetry, and found there the poet's and critic's personal responsibility to scrutinize and discriminate the literary means for the articulation of a large moral and social vision. When Tate followed Eliot in calling for "the rediscovery of the human condition in the living arts," Marxists sniffed out in such Humanism a conservative and elitist politics; and it was Eliot's affinity for the traditional South which prompted him to give the (even, later, to him) unfortunate lectures published as *After Strange Gods*. Tate met the Marxists head-on as the enemy; he endorsed Agrarian economics, denounced the threat of collectivism, and labeled one collection *Reactionary Essays*. Crossing Eliot's Arnoldian classicism with Ransom's New Criticism, Tate determined "to preserve the integrity, the purity, and the reality of language" in order to "recreate for his age the image of man."[3]

The poem is, therefore, a "configuration of meaning which it is the duty of the critic to examine and evaluate." In "Tension in Poetry," which appeared in 1938, the year of Ransom's *World's Body*, Tate wrote, "The meaning of poetry is its 'tension,' the full organized body of all the extension and intension that we can find in it." Its extension is more or less what Ransom called the "structure" of syntax, argument, and plot, which comprise the denotation of the poem; the intension resides in the "peripheral connections" of words in syntagmatic relation to one another, more or less the connotative dimension that Ransom called "texture."

Roman Jacobson would make a similar contrast in his influential distinction between metonymic and metaphorical modes of expression, but the New Critic distinguished between extension and intension in order to postulate an aesthetic resolution. The successful poem exhibits the poet's effort to push language against the proclivity of his personality and culture in the direction of the opposite pole, so that in the language itself "intension and extension are...one, and...enrich each other." Thus, "the metaphysical poet as a rationalist begins at or near the extensive or denoting end of the line; the romantic or Symbolist poet at the other, intensive end; and each by a straining feat of the imagination tries to push his meanings as far as he can towards the opposite end, so as to occupy the entire scale."[4] A poet like Dryden, for example, had to charge his ideas with affective energy, whereas a poet like Rimbaud had to give his formal coherence.

In our era of Romantic-Modernist poetry, therefore, when, for complicated reasons, poets are driven to seek the suggestiveness of intension, the supreme challenge is to achieve the structure of extension, and Tate's essays sort out his contemporaries by that criterion. Consequently, Pound is admired for his revitalization of poetic language but is found sadly deficient in "coherent form," whereas Tate's fellow southerner John Peale Bishop is commended for striving, against the tendency of the age, for formal structures. Thus "the statement is form, the fixed point of reference; 'all that we have gained since Rimbaud' is the enrichment of language that we have gained to offset our weakness in form." In seeking to inculcate greater extension of verbal organization against the prevailingly intensive inclination of modern poetry, the New Criticism adopted a paradoxical but commendable position, for "in ages weak in form, such as our own age, theory will concentrate upon form, but practice upon the ultimate possibilities of language."

For Tate, as for Ransom, the lack of coherent literary forms manifests the religious, moral, and psychological confusion of the age. For intellectual and emotional was well as aesthetic reasons Tate declared: "I assume that a poet is a man eager to come under the bondage of limitations if he can find them."[5] Yeats and Eliot were the great modern poets in English because Yeats found the effective forms for his rich emotional life and, even more remarkably, Eliot learned to join the extension of the metaphysicals with the intension of the Symbolistes.

Tate's own poetry aims at maximum concentration of extension and intension, and therein lies the cause of the characteristic difficulties of his verse: the rigidity of form, on the one hand; the privacy of reference, on the other. The lines are sometimes too packed with meaning and sound, like coils twisted to the snapping point; they cannot bear, or can scarcely bear, the pressures they are made to bear. Robert Lowell remembered that Tate taught him that the words must be "tinkered with and recast until one's eyes pop out of one's head" because "a good poem had nothing to do with exalted feelings of being moved by the spirit. It was simply a piece of craftsmanship, an intelligible or *cognitive* object." Few of Tate's poems are *simply* a piece of craftsmanship, but Tate had made Lowell's point in "Tension in Poetry": poetry is more interested "in bringing to formal order what is sometimes called 'the affective state' than arousing that state" in the reader.[6] Words and images should not be crude electrical stimuli shocking the reader into a commotion, cheap and unenlightening because unfocused. As with the prying open of Pandora's box, language can force the release of pent-up pressures, but without a point of reference and control such release is only therapeutic, like blowing off steam, if not destructive, like detonating a bomb – in any case, not clarification but dissipation, emotional entropy.

However, when volatile and unstable emotions are confined and defined in the poem, language establishes the terms and limits so that we are made to respond to the poem itself as cognitive object. So, said Tate, "we know the particular poem, not what it says that we can restate." In fact, Tate formulated the most extreme statement of the notion – shared by the New Critics and the young Eliot and, as we shall see, Hart Crane – of the verbal construct as autotelic: "In a manner of speaking, the poem is its own knower, neither poet nor reader knowing anything that the poem says apart from the words of the poem."[7] Here Eliot's impersonal poetry fuses with the Symboliste creation of states of mind and feeling in the structured nuances or nuanced structure of words; the image is of a sealed chemical, or alchemical, retort: a pseudo-scientific development of Keats' Grecian urn or Stevens' jar in Tennessee. And indeed, perhaps no poetry in English, including Eliot's and Stevens' – except for Hart Crane's – exists with such hermetic exclusiveness in the language itself as does Tate's.

For example, in "Seasons of the Soul," which some critics have called his masterpiece, Tate set himself the task of writing ten-line stanzas with lines of only three beats each, rhyming in the pattern: a-b-a-c-b-d-e-c-d-e. These stanzas are then blocked out into four sections of six stanzas, each of which represents a season of the year and one of the four elements. At the same time, within this tight structure of verbal conventions, the language is not permitted explicit statement; so the effect registers itself almost exclusively through the sound and the elliptical imagery. The tension of the poem is a fusion of maximum extension and intension, a definition of suggestiveness, a directing of indirection. Here are two characteristically pressurized stanzas from "Seasons of the Soul":

> And now the winter sea:
> Within her hollow rind
> What sleek facility
> Of sea-conceited scop
> To plumb the nether mind!
> Eternal winters blow
> Shivering flakes, and shove
> Bodies that wheel and drop –
> Cold soot upon the snow
> Their livid wound of love.
>
> Beyond the undertow
> The gray sea-foliage
> Transpires a phosphor glow
> Into the circular miles:
> In the centre of his cage
> The pacing animal
> Surveys the jungle cove
> And slicks his slithering wiles
> To turn the venereal awl
> In the livid wound of love.
>
> $(119)^8$

A poem of more manageable length for inclusion here would be "The Wolves" or "The Ancestors" or "The Subway," the last quoted below:

> Dark accurate plunger down the successive knell
> Of arch on arch, where ogives burst a red
> Reverberance of hail upon the dead
> Thunder like an exploding crucible!
> Harshly articulate, musical steel shell
> Of angry worship, hurled religiously
> Upon your business of humility
> Into the iron forestries of hell:
>
> Till broken in the shift of quieter
> Dense altitudes tangential of your steel,
> I am become geometries, and glut
> Expansions like a blind astronomer
> Dazed, while the worldless heavens bulge and reel
> In the cold revery of an idiot.
>
> (19)

The poem is virtually contemporaneous with "The Tunnel," Hart Crane's re-creation of the subway as an urban inferno. But Tate compresses the already compacted associations and synesthesia of his imagery ("plunger down the successive knell / Of arch on arch," "ogives burst a red / Reverberance of hail," "musical steel shell / Of angry worship") into the metered and rhymed octave of a Petrarchan sonnet. The denotative title is necessary because the language is almost completely metaphorical and because the sonnet does not complete the sentence. The quatrains of the octave each build up an elaborate apostrophe to the subway (as "Dark accurate plunger" and "musical steel shell"), in which the bizarre juxtaposition of sexual and religious overtones makes the experience into a demonic rite; then the sextet shifts abruptly to a mazelike subordinate clause, whose many qualifying elements spin out and dissipate the violences of the octave. The parts of the incomplete sentence make a truncated and fractured and bifurcated whole. The sonnet breaks at the volta, where the subway, overlaid with accelerating psychological associations, turns inward, implodes, and becomes the poet's labyrinthine psyche, which in turn yawns, mindlessly and blindly, on the blank infinity of an entropic universe. The noise and heat and violence of the train ride end in the dazed inertia of an idiot's "cold revery." Locked into place by the meter, rhyme, and structure of the sonnet, the words cohere in the "logic" of metaphor.

2

In his essays, Tate analyzed the sources of his angst and traced his poetic ancestry. In the spasmodic and eccentric development of American poetry, several figures came to typify the worsening situation of the modern artist from the nineteenth to the twentieth century. Tate's essay "Emily Dickinson" is one of his best known, and his reading of Dickinson has broad implications. Hers was, he claims, in an odd way "the perfect literary situation." From New England Puritanism she had inherited, without even having to think about it, "a body of ideas" which "dramatized the human soul" and "gave an heroic proportion and a tragic mode to the experience of the individual." That intellectual-religious-moral system was coherent enough to inform even the strongest and acutest individuals within it, but not without the friction of putting the tradition "to the test of experience." Tate goes on:

> A culture cannot be consciously created. It is an available source of ideas that are imbedded in a complete and homogeneous society. The poet finds himself balanced upon the moment when such a world is about to fall, when it threatens to run out into looser and less self-sufficient impulses. This world order is assimilated, in Miss Dickinson, as medievalism was in Shakespeare, to the poetic vision; it is brought down from abstraction to personal sensibility.

Thus the values and forms of the past become "the lens through which [the artist] brings nature to focus and control – the clarifying medium that concentrates his personal feeling." The balance makes for "a special and perhaps the most distinguished kind of poet" because subject and object, ideas and sensation, extension and intension articulate themselves as one – that is, as the cognitive object which is the poem.[9]

The Dickinson essay is dated 1932, and a couple of years later, Tate interpreted the southern literary renaissance in much the same terms:

From the peculiarly historical consciousness of the Southern writer has come good work of a special order; but the focus of this consciousness is quite temporary. It has made possible the curious burst of intelligence that we get at a crossing of the ways, not unlike, on an infinitesimal scale, the outburst of poetic genius at the end of the sixteenth century when commercial England had already begun to crush feudal England.

Or, as he said later, "With the war of 1914–1918, the South reentered the world – but gave a backward glance as it stepped over the border: that backward glance gave us the Southern renaissance, a literature conscious of the past in the present." So "the very backwardness of Mississippi, and of the South as a whole, might partially explain the rise of a new literature which has won the attention not only of Americans but of the western world." But the other part of the explanation lies in the fact that "the great writer, the spokesman of a culture, carries in himself the fundamental dialectic of that culture: the deeper conflicts of which his contemporaries are perhaps only dimly aware," so that "the inner strains, stresses, tensions, the shocked self-consciousness of a highly differentiated and complex society, issue in the dialectic of the high arts." Because the Old South was "remarkably free of this self-consciousness," "the strains that it felt were external," and its literary expression was, with the single exception of Poe, highfalutin talk: political rhetoric, tall tales, romantic fiction. But as soon as the southern consciousness was compelled to look critically at itself, to put inherited and felt values to the trial of experience, serious literature was possible, and Tate sees *Huckleberry Finn*, written after the Civil War about the antebellum period, as the breakthrough that foreshadowed the southern renaissance of the 1920s.[10] The southern writer after World War I found himself in another version of "the perfect literary situation," in any case in a much better situation than that of his contemporaries except perhaps for Eliot and Yeats.

But "perfect" only in the limited literary sense that the cultural tensions demanded and stimulated individual expression and creativity. Tate saw it all adumbrated early in the nineteenth century in Edgar Allan Poe, the only southern literateur of significance before Mark Twain. This domed and doomed figure became Tate's shadow image; he called one essay "Our Cousin, Mr. Poe," and the name recurs throughout his prose as a motif and emblem. Poe was doomed, North and South, and Tate came to see in his spiritual cousin not just the tragedy which would befall his region before the materialistic and mechanized forces of the industrial North but also the plight of the modern consciousness bereft of a native and organic culture.

In two important essays of the early 1950s, "The Symbolic Imagination: The Mirrors of Dante" and "The Angelic Imagination: Poe as God," Tate tried to gives a condensed statement of why the "Christian civilization" of the West had disintegrated into the secular materialism of the industrial mass state, whether that be Soviet Russia, Nazi Germany, or the American welfare state. Tate insisted that he was not indulging in myopic nostalgia about the Middle Ages any more than he had been about the Old South during the 1930s. The traditional society, he said, "has never existed, can never exist, and is a delusion. But the perfect traditional society as an imperative of reference – not as an absolute lump to be measured and weighted – has always existed and will continue to haunt the moral imagination of men." Therefore, "we are wasting our time if we suppose that St. Thomas, religious authority, the Catholic church, were more than approximations of a moral ideal by certain men under certain conditions."[11] Nonetheless, that ideal, when operative, has transformed, however imperfectly, individuals and societies in the West, and Tate commended the landed oligarchy of the antebellum South as having made a last, flawed gesture toward the ideal. (Tate was so much more concerned with the threat to the ideal from the Industrial Revolution than with the flaws in its manifestation that his essay "Remarks on Southern Religion" in *I'll Take My Stand* regrets slavery as a fatal interposition of a foreign race between the gentry and their native soil, which obviated the rooting of an organic society.)

Eliot's attack on the disintegration of religious and cultural values anticipated his conversion to Catholicism in the late 1920s. During the 1930s, Tate opposed an already defeated Agrarianism to the rise of socialism and communism, contributed to the Agrarian manifesto *I'll Take My Stand* (1930), and wrote such essays as "Religion and the Old South" (1930), "The Profession of Letters in the South" (1935), and "What Is a Traditional Society?" (this last delivered in 1936 at the University of Virginia, where Eliot had delivered *After Strange Gods* several years earlier). In 1945 Tate summed up his ideal as "Christian civilization" and remarked in "The New Provincialism" that "the kind of unity prevailing in the West until the nineteenth century has been well described by Christopher Dawson as a peculiar balance of Greek culture and Christian other-worldliness."[12] By the time Tate gave "The Symbolic Imagination" and "The Angelic Imagination" as the Candlemas Lectures at the Jesuit Boston College in 1951, he himself had become a convert to Roman Catholicism.

Henry Adams had contrasted the Virgin and the Dynamo, the era of *Mont St. Michel and Chartres* and the time of his own *Education*. Eliot took the seventeenth century as the turning point for English religion and culture, with Donne as the wobbling pivot between the medieval Dante and the dissociated modern sensibilities of Dryden and Milton. Similarly, Tate's argument presents Dante and Poe as exemplars of what he dubs the "symbolic imagination" and the "angelic imagination." "The symbolic imagination conducts an action through analogy, of the human to the divine, of the natural to the supernatural, of the low to the high, of time to eternity." Not only does natural process transpire within an absolute order but – just as important – the absolute expresses itself within temporal and spatial terms, within limited manifestations and historical contingencies. Therefore, "the symbolic imagination takes rise from a definite limitation of human rationality which was recognized in the West until the seventeenth century; in this view the intellect cannot have direct knowledge of essences" but can only come to perceive essences in objects, the essences of phenomena. Consequently, the symbolic imagination commits itself "to the order of temporal sequence – to action," or, to recall Ransom's phrase, to "the body of this world." Paradoxically, religious conviction leads the believer to commit himself to the "concrete experience" of "the physical world." So Dante's "vision is imagined, it is *imaged*; its essence is not possessed." The symbolic imagination takes as its central mystery the Incarnation, as a result of which all things and events take their being in a spiritual relation. In this realization the symbolic imagination does not aspire to the abstract purity of Platonism or to the tropes of the private imagination but to the type or symbol, "compounded of spiritual insight and physical perception."[13]

By contrast, Tate argues,

> Imagination in an angel is thus inconceivable, for the angelic mind transcends the mediation of both image and discourse. I call that human imagination angelic which tries to disintegrate or to circumvent the image in the illusory pursuit of essence.

It is precisely Poe's angelic imagination which makes him fascinating and symptomatic, and accounts for "an engagement with him that men on both sides of the Atlantic have acknowledged for more than a century" out of all proportion to his intrinsic literary merit. In Tate's historical sequence of emblematic figures, Descartes intervened between Dante and Poe. The Cartesian axiom "I think; therefore, I am" analyzed the organicism of the person into mind and body and gave primacy to the perceiving mind; the Cartesian method turned the individual in on himself, so that consciousness became aware of and fixated on its reflexiveness, dissecting thought from feeling, feeling from will. The result is, in a phrase deliberately reminiscent of Eliot, "the disintegration of the modern personality," of which Poe was a chilling instance early in American, and southern, culture. The questioning of the functional integrity of the person "divided man against himself" and thereby "isolated him from nature, including his own nature." The psyche, shattered and paralyzed by this double severance, became increasingly unable to believe in either psyche or nature, subject or object, and so became increasingly unable to attain a philosophical or theological comprehension of existence. Poe, our representative cousin, "was a religious man whose Christianity, for reasons that nobody knows anything about, got short-circuited; he lived among fragments of provincial theologies, in the midst of which 'coordination,' for a man of his intensity, was difficult if not impossible.... The failure resulted in a hypertrophy of the three classical faculties: feeling, will and intellect."[14]

Each faculty should perform its defined function within the human personality, but when the faculties are freed of those constraining functions, each tends to assert itself more and more absolutely and to insist on achievement of the absolute. At the same time, since the internal divisions undermine a stable relationship between the ego and external reality, the final result is a "subjectivism which denies the sensible world." When our powers are not "bound to the human scale, their projection becomes god-like, and man become an angel" – in Jacques Maritain's image, an "angel inhabiting a machine." With this split between disembodied spirit and mechanical matter, the autonomous, or would-be autonomous, mind demands total knowledge and absolute vision; the would-be autonomous will demands essential possession of the desired object; the would-be autonomous passions are pitched in higher and higher paroxysms toward final frenzy or final ecstasy. Risking all, the disordered psyche presses beyond the bounds of nature. Marlowe's Faust dramatizes an archetype which the Romantic and post-Romantic mind knew all too well: witness Goethe, Byron, Poe, Melville.

Tate's own writings, as he was only too painfully aware, manifest the fatal split. His poems express the modern rage for order and zeal for the absolute, and his images exhibit the derangement of the senses that Rimbaud urged and the synesthetic sensibility that he shared with Symbolistes from Poe and Valéry to Eliot and Stevens and Crane. But his prose pronounced such efforts as foredoomed because they remove language "from the grammar of a possible world" and posit the bold but false notion that "language can be reality, or by incantation can create a reality."[15] It is no accident that Tate cited Eliot's 1948 essay "From Poe to Valéry" at the beginning of "The Angelic Imagination." Those essays serve their authors as a critique of, and a strategic rejection of, the Symboliste aesthetic which informed their earlier work (and, Tate noted, informed the work of Stevens and Crane). And the grounds of rejection were the same: the Symboliste imagination was not symbolic but angelic, and the unnaturalness of the enterprise made the would-be Lucifer satanic.

Tate called Poe "the forlorn demon" and made this epithet the title of a 1953 collection of his essays. The angelic imagination denies the body which it occupies and which, denied, becomes a corpse. All the necrophilia of Poe's work – the dying, the dead, the buried alive, the walking dead, the returned dead – is not merely the claptrap of Gothic fiction but the fantasies of a spooked mind. For Poe claimed that the most exalted emotion is love for a dead woman, because it represents the aspiration of the angelic imagination to possess the spirit of the mortal body. And yet, of course, the body, in being denied, becomes an obsessive concern: a fevered, self-haunted, self-haunting cadaver from which the consciousness cannot break free. The result, says Tate, is "a nightmare of paranoia, schizophrenia, necrophilism, and vampirism."

Overreaching for the absolute wreaks destruction and self-destruction. If the disoriented sensibility looks out, it is to feed vampirically on deadened matter; if it looks in, it is to drown narcissistically in its own turbid deeps. Consciousness has no way out of its trap back into life; "sensation locks us into the self, feeding upon the disintegration of its objects and absorbing them into the void of the ego." Consequently, "everything in Poe is dead"; "if a writer ambiguously exalts the 'spirit' over the 'body,' and the spirit must live wholly upon another spirit, some version of the vampire legend is likely to issue as the symbolic situation"; "the hyperaesthetic egoist has put all men into his void:

he is alone in the world, and thus dead to it." Think of "The Fall of the House of Usher" or "Ligeia": narcissism and vampirism are twin manifestations of the same disease. And not just Poe's peculiar sickness; the serious whimsy of the last sentence of "Our Cousin, Mr. Poe" (1949, the year after Eliot's Poe piece) gives away the source of Tate's fascination: "He is so close to me that I am sometimes tempted to enter the mists of pre-American genealogy to find out whether he may not actually be my cousin."[16]

If Poe foreshadowed the psychological crisis of the modern American poet, then Hart Crane, Tate's friend, who had influenced him strongly during their association in the 1920s, fulfilled the prophecy. Tate begins his essay on Crane with the flat admission: "in our age the disintegration of our intellectual systems is accomplished." The line of descent is clear: from Poe to the French Symbolistes to Crane, the "spiritual heir" especially of Rimbaud, and Crane's attempt to balance Rimbaud with the democratic robustness of Whitman seemed to Tate to offer no adequate philosophical or moral antidote. Tate's polemical poem "False Nightmare" depicts Whitman as a narcissistic onanist, and the combination of Whitman and Rimbaud in Crane only compounds the nightmare.[17]

The dilemma which was to bring Crane, born with Tate into the twentieth century in the concluding year of the previous century, to his suicide in 1932, recapitulates the "more general" and "historical problem of romanticism." For by the time of Crane's (and Tate's) generation "the disorder is original and fundamental. That is the special quality of his mind that belongs peculiarly to our own time." Because of "the locked-in sensibility, the insulated egoism," "every poem is the thrust of that sensibility into the world," and because his sensibility is dislocated from itself and from the world, it engages external reality not in relation but in "collision." Seen from Crane's own angelic point of view,

> he is the blameless victim of a world whose impurity violates the moment of intensity, which would otherwise be enduring and perfect. He is betrayed not by a defect of his nature, but by the external world; he asks of nature, perfection – requiring only of himself, intensity. The persistent, and persistently defeated, pursuit of a natural absolute places Crane at the center of his age.[18]

Although in Tate's estimation Crane wrote "some of the best poetry of our generation," his significance to Tate also lies in the fact that Crane lived out to the last extremity a fate that could have been Tate's as well. For Tate, as for Crane's other admiring friend and critic Yvor Winters, born a year after them in 1900, Crane is the symptomatic Modernist:

> He falls back upon the intensity of consciousness, rather than the clarity, for his center of vision. And that is romanticism.
> His world had no center, and the thrust into sensation is responsible for the fragmentary quality of his most ambitious work. The thrust took two directions – the blind assertion of the will, and the blind desire for self-destruction. The poet did not face his first problem, which is to define the limits of his personality and to objectify its moral implications in an appropriate symbol-

ism. Crane could only assert a quality of will against the world, and at each successive failure of the will he turned upon himself. In the failure of understanding – and understanding, for Dante, was a way of love – the romantic modern poet of the age of science attempts to impose his will upon experience and to possess the world.

The final decadence of the Romantic philosophy and aesthetic is the disintegrated psyche capable of overcoming paralysis only in violence: vampirism to others and drowning in itself. The sequence of American poets from Poe to Dickinson to Crane demonstrates the "incapacity" of the individual consciousness in isolation "to live within the limitations of the human condition." After writing about Crane in 1932 and 1937, Tate returned to the subject in 1952, reiterating his rueful conviction that Crane represents "our twentieth-century poet as hero" – but as tragic hero.[19]

3

The obsession with angelism links Tate's prose and verse. He was obsessed with Poe and Crane because his was an angelic imagination. Tate designated "the experience of 'solipsism' " as his theme, and he called an essay "Narcissus as Narcissus" because it presented his own convoluted New critical exposition of his own "Ode to the Confederate Dead" as a dramatization of the narcissistic psyche.[20]

The poems present that twilit state of mind, moving from or suspended between day and dark, and the avatars of Narcissus and Dracula stalk the twilight, their specters eerily fading in and out of one another. Thus Tate's Alice penetrates the looking glass in an "incest of spirit," self-absorbed and self-consumed in her "bodiless flesh of fire." The lovers in "Shadow and Shade" are disembodied, shadows paling to shades. They are mortal, and so dying, and so dead; sexual possession is death, and vice versa:

> I took her hand, I shut her eyes
> And all her shadow cleft with shade,
> Shadow was crushed beyond disguise
> But, being fear, was unafraid.
>
> I asked fair shadow at my side:
> What more shall fiery shade require?
> We lay long in the immense tide
> Of shade and shadowy desire
>
> And saw the dusk assail the wall,
> The black surge, mounting, crash the stone!
> Companion of this lust, we fall,
> I said, lest we should die alone.

(73)

The mock "Pastoral" finds the couple in a similar state of suspension, the woman awaiting nightfall in sexual frustration while the man is rapt in abstracted passion:

> She, her head back, waited
> Barbarous the stalking tide;
> He, nor balked nor sated
>
> But plunged into the wide
> Area of mental ire,
> Lay at her wandering side.
>
>   (89–90)

The early "To a Romantic" warns Robert Penn Warren (whose underlying Romanticism set him off from others in the Vanderbilt group from the beginning):

> You hold your eager head
> Too high in the air, you walk
> As if the sleepy dead
> Had never fallen to drowse
> From the sublimest talk
> Of many a vehement house.
> Your head so turned turns eyes
> Into the vagrant West;
> Fixing an iron mood
> In an Ozymandias' breast
> And because your clamorous blood
> Beats an impermanent rest
> You think the dead arise
> Westward and fabulous:
> The dead are those whose lies
> Were doors to a narrow house.
>
>   (7)

For the angelic mind will never enter upon the West of the heart's desire. And when it realizes that is is yoked to a corruptible and corrupting flesh, angel turns demon, or more accurately vampire, as in the last line of "Jubilo":

> Then for the Day of Jubilo
> The patient bares his arm at dawn
> To suck the blood's transfusing glow
> And then when all the blood is gone
>   (For the Day of Jubilo)
>
> Salt serum stays his arteries
> Sly tide threading the ribs of sand,
> Till his lost being dries, and cries
> For that unspeakable salt land
>   Beyond the Day of Jubilo.
>
>   (102)

Tate's poems are filled with ghosts, monsters, and zombies. For example, there is the barely alive woman in "Inside and Outside," and the Poe-like and Ransom-like girl married to Death in "The Robber Bridegroom," and the apparitional figures in "A Dream" and "A Vision." In "The Twelve" the

apostles, lost after Jesus' disappearance, are called "the twelve living dead."
"The Oath" opens with a room at dusk:

> It was near evening, the room was cold
> Half dark; Uncle Ben's brass bullet-mould
> And powder-horn and Major Bogan's face
> Above the fire in the half-light plainly said:
> There's naught to kill but the animated dead.
> . . . .
> I thought I heard the dark pounding its head
> On a rock, crying: *Who are the dead?*
>
> (43)

The second of the "Sonnets of the Blood," written to his brother after their
mother's death, says: "Our property in fire is death in life / Flawing the rocky
fundament with strife." In these poems the "death in life" of the sons is
connected with the devouring presence of the mother, and in "Mother and
Son," a narrative poem which states the archetype so powerfully that it
deserves full quotation, the mother is again the vampire:

> Now all day long the man who is not dead
> Hastens the dark with inattentive eyes,
> The woman with white hand and erect head
> Stares at the covers, leans for the son's replies
> At last to her importunate womanhood –
> Her hand of death laid on the living bed;
> So lives the fierce compositor of blood.
>
> She waits; he lies upon the bed of sin
> Where greed, avarice, anger writhed and slept
> Till to their silence they were gathered in:
> There, fallen with time, his tall and bitter kin
> Once fired the passions that were never kept
> In the permanent heart, and there his mother lay
> To bear him on the impenetrable day.
>
> The falcon mother cannot will her hand
> Up to the bed, nor break the manacle
> His exile sets upon her harsh command
> That he should say the time is beautiful –
> Transfigured by her own possessing light:
> The sick man craves the impalpable night.
>
> Loosed betwixt eye and lid, the swimming beams
> Of memory, blind school of cuttlefish,
> Rise to the air, plunge to the cold streams –
> Rising and plunging the half-forgotten wish
> To tear his heart out in a slow disgrace
> And freeze the hue of terror to her face.
>
> Hate, misery, and fear beat off his heart
> To the dry fury of the woman's mind;
> The son, prone in his autumn, moves apart

A seed blown upon a returning wind.
O child, be vigilant till towards the south
On the flowered wall all the sweet afternoon,
The reaching sun, swift as the cottonmouth,
Strikes at the black crucifix on her breast
Where the cold dusk comes suddenly to rest –
Mortality will speak the victor soon!

The dreary flies, lazy and casual,
Stick to the ceiling, buzz along the wall.
O heart, the spider shuffles from the mould
Weaving, between the pinks and grapes, his pall.
The bright wallpaper, imperishably old,
Uncurls and flutters, it will never fall.

(34–35)

The family bed is the scene of birth, copulation, and death. There the "falcon mother" and "sick man" are locked in a mutually defeating battle, all of whose passions are as disembodied as "the dry fury of the woman's mind." The son sees his weakness as his only weapon; by tearing "his heart out in a slow disgrace," he can "freeze the hue of terror to her face." In this engagement between vampirism and self-destruction, the victor is the one who survives – in defeat.

Whenever consciousness, for whatever reason, fails to enter into a sustaining relationship with the world, it recoils narcissistically on itself. "Aeneas at Washington" is in ambiguous straits. Aeneas' westward voyage from Troy ended not in Italy but in the New World, and the poem is a web of contrasts: between the classical and the contemporary, between Aeneas as the man of action and Aeneas as an impotent Gerontion, between the civilization which Aeneas left in flames and the barbarous land to which he had led his people, between Rome, founded by Aeneas, and Washington, the modern Rome. At the beginning of the monologue, Aeneas describes himself in terms as Confederate as Trojan:

I myself saw furious with blood
Neoptolemus, at his side the black Atridae,
Hecuba and the hundred daughters, Priam
Cut down, his filth drenching the holy fires.
In that extremity I bore me well,
A true gentleman, valorous in arms,
Disinterested and honourable.

The South liked to think of itself as Roman, but the sharper contrast here lies between an agrarian Troy ("hemp ripening / And tawny corn, the thickening Blue Grass / All lying rich forever in the green sun") and the "wet mire" of the raw and half-built city of Rome – Washington. Aeneas' nostalgia for the lost Troy and revulsion at his crude lot turn him into a narcissist whose "singular passion / Abides its object and consumes desire / In the circling shadow of its appetite."

In "False Nightmare"[21] Whitman is the antithesis of Aeneas, a narcissist who embodies the crass materialism of the new land and the modern age. In this shrill polemic, Whitman's egoistic individualism makes him the voice of capitalistic exploitation and profit, his large cadences shrunk here to rhyming doggerel:

> "I have the yawp barbaric
> Of piety and pelf
> (Who now reads Herrick?)
>
> "And contradict myself –
> No matter, the verse is large.
> My five-and-ten cent shelf
>
> "The continent is: my targe
> Bigger than Greece. The shock
> Of Me exceeds its marge –

The rape of the land is rendered barren by the rapist's sterile self-regard, so much so that it is less a rape than onanism. Whitman's sexual hucksterism leaves him without posterity; his only child, his nation-son, repeats his onanism and squanders his seed:

> "I have no woman child;
> Onan-Amurikee
> My son, alone, beguiled
>
> By my complacency
> In priggery to slay
> My blind posterity . . ."

"The Meaning of Life: A Monologue" poses a shocking and appalling choice: either destructive action or self-destructive passivity. Although as a boy the poet shrank from men who "shot at one another for luck," now "I know at thirty-three that one must shoot / As often as one gets the rare chance." Why? Because even if one's acts take their toll in injury to others, that guilty responsibility is preferable to the nullity of disengagement. Such angelic narcissism is a negative "kind of lust" that

> feeds on itself
> Unspoken to, unspeaking; subterranean
> As a black river full of eyeless fish
> Heavy with spawn; with a passion for time.
> Longer than the arteries of a cave.

Lost in the watery labyrinth of the solipsistic mind, the blind fish bloat with undeliverable spawn. The terrible moral of this "monologue" is that, given the choice between feeding on one's self and risking a deadly shot, "one must shoot / As often as one gets the rare chance." The terrible irony is that the speaker can speak so categorically because he knows the alternative only too well. His living death is a nightmare swarming with eyeless fish.

"Last Days of Alice" again presents the alternatives of narcissism and violent action, but persists, beyond the acceptance of guilty violence with which "The Meaning of Life" ended, to a desperate prayer for gracious deliverance:

> – We too back to the world shall never pass
> Through the shattered door, a dumb shade-harried crowd
> Being all infinite, function depth and mass
> Without figure, a mathematical shroud
>
> Hurled at the air – blessed without sin!
> O God of our flesh, return us to Your wrath,
> Let us be evil could we enter in
> Your grace, and falter on the stony path!
>
> (39)

Alice's utter isolation on the other side of the looking glass is a result of her narcissism. She saw only herself in the mirror, which seemed "the All-Alice of the world's entity." Out of "love for herself" she "pouted to join her two in a sweet one" but merely "plunged through the glass alone." In the "deep suspension of the looking glass" all motion and action are paralyzed; she hangs in her own vacuous infinity. Here her angelism is complete: beyond the fleshly sphere her body grows "mammoth but not fat," as she "stares at the drowsy cubes of human dust." "Being all infinite, function depth and mass / Without figure, a mathematical shroud / Hurled at the air," she is consumed by a "perfect lust / For vacancy"; abstract mind "turned absent-minded" in an anesthetized body, she "gazes learnedly down her airy nose / At nothing, nothing thinking all the day." What would be passion in a body goes here unrealized and unexpressed: "abstract rage," "the spoiled cruelty she had meant to say," "incest of spirit, theorem of desire,...empty as the bodiless flesh of fire." The second to last stanza sees Alice as the mirror image of us all: "We too back to the world shall never pass." One could say that the "perfect lust / For vacancy" is "blessed" in that it is "without sin," but, as in "The Meaning of Life," sinless vacuity is worse than the pains and risks of human destiny:

> O God of our flesh, return us to Your wrath,
> Let us be evil could we enter in
> Your grace, and falter on the stony path!

Unlike the previous poem, this one moves into another psychological dimension, which can be felt in the elevation of tone and quickening of pace in these last lines. A different voice breaks into the "All-Alice of the world's entity," or rather breaks out of it, to the Incarnational world in which action, even evil action, activates immanent grace inaccessible to narcissistic inertia. The paradox of free will is that our sins can become the means of our redemption. "Last Days of Alice," dated 1931, makes the same point that Eliot had made the year before in the essay on Baudelaire: "so far as we are human, what we do must be either evil or good; so far as we do evil or good, we are human; and it is better, in a paradoxical way, to do evil than to do nothing: at least, we exist."[22]

Almost twenty years before his conversion, Tate published this plea to the

Incarnate God to grace mortal, sinful flesh. But the ninth "Sonnet of the Blood," published in the same year as "Alice," still yokes narcissism and vampirism as the double symptom of the spiritual sickness: "spiders, eating their loves, hide in the night / At last, drowsy with self-devouring shame?" (53). "The Twelve" (again in 1931) are the apostles; the poem shows them after the Messiah's death lost in a waste land which, unlike the end of the Eliot poem, offers no prospect of relief. The "twelve living dead"

> lie in the sand by the dry rock
> Seeing nothing – the sand, the tree, rocks
> Without number – and turn away the face
> To the mind's briefer and more desert place.
>
> (44)

"Winter Mask" (1942) and "Seasons of the Soul" (1944) both depict self-damnation: an inferno of "self-inflicted woe" Tate calls it in "Seasons." "Winter Mask" offers two symbolic "scenes of hell / Two human bestiaries" of narcissim and vampirism:

> The poisoned rat in the wall
> Cuts through the wall like a knife,
> Then blind, drying, and small
> And driven to cold water,
> Dies of the water of life:
> Both damned in eternal ice,
> The traitor become the boor
> Who had led his friend to slaughter,
> Now bites his head – not nice,
> The food that he lives for.
>
> (111–112)

Then the "Mask" concludes:

> I asked the master Yeats
> Whose great style could not tell
> Why it is man hates
> His own salvation,
> Prefers the way to hell,
> And finds his last safety
> In the self-made curse that bore
> Him towards damnation:
> The drowned undrowned by the sea,
> The sea worth living for.
>
> (113)

Robert Lowell, who was much closer to Tate in temperament and sensibility than Ransom was, characterized Tate's verse as registering "the resonance of desperation, or rather the formal resonance of desperation." In an essay called "Religion and the Intellectuals" Tate reflected on this same point in 1950, the year of his conversion to Catholicism:

> As I look back upon my verse over more than twenty-five years, I see plainly
> that its main theme is man suffering from unbelief; I cannot for a moment
> suppose that this man is some other than myself. [Man's] disasters are
> probably the result of his failure to possess and be possessed by a controlling
> sense of the presence of redemptive powers in his experience.

"The Man of Letters in the Modern World," written a couple of years later, is
filled with the urgent sense that men "have got to communicate through love"
because "communication that is not also communion is incomplete." And
communion is religious: man "loves his neighbor, as well as the man he has
never seen, only through the love of God." Ransom commented that Tate's
conversion was the sort of "bold decision" that distinguished Tate from
himself.[23]

An archetypal reading of Tate's poetry would suggest that he was so
obsessed with the shadow – a paralyzing quandary of fascination and revulsion
– that he was stymied in engaging his sexual or spiritual nature creatively
through the agency of the anima, and so blocked from any satisfying realization of the potentialities of the self. But the few poems published since the 1950
conversion suggest an almost willed shift from the contortions of the angelic
imagination toward the disciplined convergence of the symbolic imagination.
It may be significant that there is so little poetry from this period, but the three
major poems are all written in strict imitation of Dante's *terza rima* (in contrast
to Eliot's unrhymed imitation in "Little Gidding"). It seems symptomatic that
these three pieces of a projected spiritual autobiography remain disconnected
fragments rather than a completed narrative like *The Divine Comedy*. Still, in
their truncated way, they serve something of the function of *Four Quartets* for
Tate's final phase.

"The Maimed Man" (1952) recounts, in a cross between dream and nightmare, the youthful Tate's encounter with a shadow figure – "My secret was
his father; I his tomb" (130) – whose decapitation is a blatant symbol of his
psychological mutilation: "Who could have told if he were live or dead?"
(129). But, like "Alice," his poem persists to prayerful alternatives for the
autobiographical speaker: instead of being the maimed man's "known slave,"
the personhood of Jesus ("let me touch the hem / Of him who spread his
triptych like a fan") (129, 130); and through the Virgin Muse, possible
reconciliation with the "dead Mother" (131). Thereby the "swimmer of
night" might become the "swimmer of noonday" (130–131).

"The Swimmers" (1953) does not progress beyond another shadow confrontation between the boy Tate and the mutilated corpse of a lynched Negro.
But "The Buried Lake," published the same year, seems to represent a move
in a new direction long since projected but unattained, and it is the most explicitly Dantescan. The narrative is framed by petitions to Saint Lucy, the
martyred "Lady of light," associated with both suffering and holy hope. It
was Saint Lucy who transported Dante from the lake at the base of Mount
Purgatory up the slope so that he might make his way through Purgatory to
Beatrice and a vision of Paradise. In the body of the poem, Tate goes down to

the lake – at once psychic matrix and baptismal font – whence images (derived, Tate has said, from three actual dreams) rehearse a progression from infancy to adolescence, wracked by sexual and artistic anxieties. Narcissus-like, the speaker plunges, apparently to his death, into the waters of the buried lake where those eyeless fish lurk. thus far the buried lake recalls Poe more than Dante, an angelic rather than a symbolic world. As before, the speaker thinks: "Better stay dead"; but this occasion is different. Drowning turns into baptism: "down, down below the wave that turned me round, / Head downwards where the Head of God has sped / On the third day." In these lines the baptismal submersion is overlaid with the harrowing of hell, which followed upon the crucifixion in anticipation of the resurrection. So now Narcissus rises reborn to the lighted shore and the shining presence of Lucy, whose gouged eyes reveal her martyr's vision:

> forget that you too lost the day
>
> Yet finding it refound it Lucy-guise
> As I, refinding where two shadows meet,
> Took from the burning umbrage mirroring eyes....
>
> . . . .
>
> Lady coming,
> Lady not going, come Lady come: I greet
> You in the double of our eyes....
>
> (139–140)

The mirror image occurs again, not now as Alice's mirror or Narcissus' pool but as a true "looking-glass" wherein the myriad forms of nature are informed by light. In the final rapturous lines Lucy summons the Dove of the Holy Spirit; the speaker's feminine soul finds confirmation of selfhood in Godhead:

> for I have seen it part
> The palpable air, the air close up above
> And under you, light Lucy, light of heart –
>
> Light choir upon my shoulder, speaking Dove
> The dream is over and the dark expired.
> I knew that I had known enduring love.
>
> (140)

There is nothing else like this moment in all of Tate's writing. Not twilight now but dawn; not nightmare or insomnia but waking; not solipsism but "enduring love." "The Man of Letters in the Modern World," published the year before "The Buried Lake," concludes with these words: "It is the duty of the man of letters to supervise the culture of language, to which the rest of culture is subordinate, and to warn us when our language is ceasing to forward the ends proper to man. The end of social man is communion in time through love, which is beyond time."[24] The passage enunciates the measure by which Tate's achievement as a man of letters can be judged; by his faithful attention as poet and critic to the technique of his craft and by his presentation to his contemporaries of their tormented image illumined by the light of love.

The years after Tate's conversion were restless and difficult, not tranquil or serene,[25] but they were in the end sustained by intimations of enduring illumination. Marriage to Caroline Gordon, a novelist and a Catholic, ended in separation and divorce in the decade after his conversion, and marriage to the poet Isabella Gardner was followed in 1966 by marriage to Helen Heinz, a nurse and a former student of his. As in Eliot's life, this late marriage to a much younger woman brought love and a measure of peace; the anima figure became wife – and in this case, mother. In a sonnet of 1970 the love of wife and baby boy lights a glyph "on my shadowy wall" where he can read "how me God favored, if / I have the favor to know Him at all" (141).

An unspoken fact deepens the dark hope of these lines. The son addressed in "Sonnet" is the survivor of twin boys, whose brother strangled accidentally before he was a year old. Under the title "Father and Sons," Robert Lowell, who lapsed from Catholicism at about the time of Tate's conversion, addressed two poems to his old friend in the wake of this tragedy:

> Things no longer usable for our faith
> go on routinely possible in nature;
> The worst is the child's death.
> .   .   .   .
>
> Your twin crawls for you, ten-month twin. They
>   [your parents] are no longer
> young enough to understand what happened.[26]

But Tate's final lines point to a conclusion different from Lowell's. "Farewell Rehearsed" (1976) consists of three short pieces: for Helen, the surviving boy John, and a younger son, Benjamin. Helen is a psychopomp, as Tate, punning on shade-ghost-air-breath-spirit, implores her after death to "guide me to a land of lucky men, / Even luckier than the land that I had left, / Where love of you was all the air I breathed" (142). And in his sons he finds gracing love extended and confirmed; the old man finds voice for the child. From seventy-seven-year-old father to six-year-old Benjamin:

> Come to me darling little Ben,
> And let's play pinching-bug again.
> I love you as my spirit's leaven
> To teach me how it is in heaven,
> Where all is love; stay by me, son,
> That I may know that love is One.
>   (142)

And to eight-year-old John:

> My darling boy whom I shall never know,
> My son, I love you in my deepest fears,
> I'll love you when my eyes, grown cold as snow,
> Will freeze to hide their moment's joyous tears
> When gazing on your happy little face
> Which I'll take with me to the fount of grace.
>   (142)

The distance between the tensed contortions of vampire and victim in "Mother and Son" and the lucid directness of these late poems tallies Tate's psychological, spiritual – and poetic – journey. He may not have reached Dante's symbolic imagination, but in their resolved paradoxes these final poems show that he had moved past Poe and Crane to a verbal decorum and stoic hope more reminiscent of Ben Jonson. Ransom turned out to be correct in assessing Tate's temperament as suited to the Elizabethan Renaissance. Tate, like Eliot, would have preferred Dante's Italy, but the Renaissance was the last stand before the devolution into Romantic and Modernist angelism.

II

I

In a poem of the 1950s, Robert Lowell had Hart Crane call himself the "Shelley of my age." Behind Lowell's designation of Crane as a fated latter-day Romantic stood, perhaps, his mentor Tate's recent anatomy of the angelic imagination and Matthew Arnold's famous description of Shelley as a "beautiful *and ineffectual* angel, beating in the void his luminous wings in vain."[27] Arnold's image of Shelley's angelism summed up the consequences of the errors of Romanticism for such later "classical" anti-Romantics as Eliot and Tate.

As a Modernist, Crane did not set himself against the Romantic legacy, as did (nominally at least) Eliot and Tate, but instead set himself, with a determination more closely related to Stevens and Williams and, however skeptically, Frost, to formulate the terms whereby the Romantic imagination might be effective within and even against secular, materialistic culture. But Crane could not be stoically satisfied with Frost's notion of the poem as a merely momentary stay against confusion or with Stevens' acceptance of the poem as a supreme fiction. A doomed Romantic like Shelley or Poe, Crane flogged himself toward an ultimate and unattainable ecstatic intensity. The obsessiveness of Crane's demand for a continuous imaginative vision – at once self-aggrandizing and self-defeating – made him a courageous hero to friends like Waldo Frank and, later, to critics like R. W. B. Lewis and Sherman Paul, but made him a tragic warning to friends like Tate and Winters.

The only mention of Shelley in Crane's published correspondence occurs in a 1921 list of his special poets.[28] Besides Renaissance and Symboliste favorites, he included several Romantics: Poe, Whitman, Keats, Shelley. One important name is misleadingly absent. For there are more references to Blake than there are even to Whitman in the letters, and it is Blake, rather than Whitman or Shelley, who is invoked as the seer in Crane's two most important critical essays, "General Aims and Theories" and "Modern Poetry."

There can be no question that Crane's consuming obsession was to be a seer like Shelley or Whitman or Blake. Experience, he wrote, was "the effort to describe God," and in 1930, the year of the publication of *The Bridge*, he defined the prophetic function: "poetic prophecy in the case of the seer has nothing to do with factual prediction or with futurity. It is a peculiar type of perception, capable of apprehending some absolute and timeless concept of the imagination with astounding clarity and conviction."[29] Crane's words call to mind again Whitman's description of the prophet as "one whose mind bubbles up and pours forth as a fountain, from divine, inner spontaneities revealing God."[30] But where Whitman sees the prophet as speaking for and revealing God, Crane sees the prophet as speaking for and revealing the imagination. The difference is crucial. In fact, it points to the difference between Romanticism and Symbolisme, or rather, to the evolution of Symbolisme from a decadent Romanticism. With the disintegration of the Neoplatonic synthesis of subject and object which was the epistemological basis of Romanticism, the subjective consciousness lost its sense of vital connection with and participation in an objective order, so that the introverted individual was set adrift in his illusory perceptions and impressions. The development of Symbolisme in France and its far-reaching and long-lasting impact on poetry in English (particularly following Symons' *The Symbolist Movement in Literature* at the turn of the century) mark a shift from the Romantic location of the individual in the cosmos to the exploration of internal states recorded and even created in the act of language.

Eliot reviewed that development in his 1948 essay "From Poe to Valéry" as testimony to his own exorcism of vestigial Symboliste influences from his later poetry. But Crane was a purer Symboliste than Eliot. He could say with Stevens, as not even the early Eliot would, "God and the imagination are one."[31] And it is noteworthy that whereas Eliot drew principally upon the tragic irony and wit of Baudelaire and Laforgue to voice his own self-conscious experience of disillusioned impotence, Crane looked principally to Rimbaud. Admittedly there is verbal evidence of Laforgue's and Eliot's influence in such early Crane pieces as "Pastorale" and "In Shadow," but just as Blake was Crane's Romantic, so Rimbaud was his Symboliste – the Rimbaud of *Illuminations*, hell-bent on being a seer in a dislocated and fractured world.

In fact, it was less Rimbaud's tone and themes that Crane adopted than his technique for provoking a visionary state. Tate observed that Crane "more or less identified himself with Rimbaud.... But he didn't read all of Rimbaud by any means. Rimbaud's awfully difficult and Hart's French was limited."[32] Crane's Rimbaud was the young would-be visionary who asserted: "I want to be a poet, and I am working to make myself a *seer....* To arrive at the unknown through the disordering of *all the senses*, that's the point."[33] John Untermecker's biography underscores Crane's adoption of "Rimbaud's prescription for concocting poetic language: to build poetry through a systematic derangement of the senses. Rimbaud tried drugs. Crane, more conservative, settled on wine – though he could in lucky moments, as all his friends have attested, grow drunk on language alone."[34] Emerson had warned the would-be Dionysian poet that no mere narcotic could effect true spiritual vision, but a century after the apogee of Romanticism, Crane convinced himself that, *faute de mieux*, he had no other choice.

Crane told a disapproving Yvor Winters in 1927 that the reason for the constriction in the range of his poetry was that he sought a "true record of such moments of 'illumination' as are occasionally possible," in which "certain sensations" seem "suitable to – or intense enough – for verse." Earlier, in 1922, he had given his friend Gorham Munson an account of the sort of ecstasy he was ceaselessly seeking in his life and in his poems:

> At times, dear Gorham, I feel an enormous power in me – that seems almost supernatural. If this power is not too dissipated in aggravation and discouragement I may amount to something sometime. I can say this now with perfect equanimity because I am notoriously drunk and the Victrola is still going with that glorious "Bolero." Did I tell you of that thrilling experience this last winter in the dentist's chair when under the influence of aether and amnesia my mind spiraled to a kind of seventh heaven of consciousness and egoistic dance among the seven spheres – and something like an objective voice kept saying to me – "You have the higher consciousness – you have the higher consciousness. This is something that very few have. This is what is called genius"? A happiness, ecstatic such as I have known only twice in "inspirations" came over me. I felt the two worlds. And at once. As the bore went into my tooth I was able to follow its every revolution as detached as a spectator at a funeral. O Gorham, I have known moments in eternity.

The words "vision" and "new consciousness" ring throughout the letters to close friends, always associated with the hermetic imagination whose inchoate energies assume form as language.[35] Moreover, the form "organic" to such sensations and perceptions could not be the logic of reason but, following the derangement of the senses, the "logic of metaphor." To Harriet Monroe's inability to follow "At Melville's Tomb," his unyielding reply showed that he knew what he was doing:

> My poem may well be elliptical and actually obscure in the ordering of its content, but in your criticism of this very possible deficiency you have stated your objections in terms that allow me, at least for the moment, the privilege of claiming your ideas and ideals as theoretically, at least, quite outside the issues of my own aspirations. To put it more plainly, as a poet I may very possibly be more interested in the so-called illogical impingements of the connotations of words on the consciousness (and their combinations and interplay in metaphor on this basis) than I am interested in the preservation of their logically rigid significations at the cost of limiting my subject matter and perceptions involved in the poem.

For a Symboliste like Crane, signification derived less from extralinguistic referentiality than from the elaboration of a self-referential semiotic code of sounds and symbols. As Crane put it, "in manipulating the more imponderable phenomena of psychic motives, pure emotional crystallizations, etc., I have had to rely...on these dynamics of inferential mention," and "the terms of expression employed are often selected less for their logical (literal) significance than for their associational meanings" – that is to say, their "harmonious relationship to each other in the context of [the poet's] organization of them."[36]

Language seeks to become a closed syntagmatic system of infrasuggestiveness within which elements establish a pitch and tonality within the harmonics of the whole. Where Imagism defined itself through analogies with the visual arts, Symbolisme found deeper affinities with music, which organized the resonance of pitch and tone in the sequential system of the musical bar and the melodic line. Like Stevens, Crane came to rely on the modulations of the iambic cadences and the array of sound effects – rhyme, alliteration, assonance, onomatopoeia – for internal harmonic structure, relation, and coherence.

A Romantic poem typically sought to evoke an antecedent experience of the Absolute, but a Symboliste poem typically sought to evoke – on the page, in the ear, in what Stevens called the "delicatest ear of the mind" – a quasi-absolute experience. Subject sought to absolutize itself as poem. Crane was disarmingly clear about his methods and intentions:

> It may not be possible to say that there is, strictly speaking, any "absolute" experience. But it seems evident that certain aesthetic experience (and this may for a time engross the total faculties of the spectator) can be called absolute, inasmuch as it approximates a formally convincing statement of a conception or apprehension of life that gains our unquestioning assent, and under the conditions of which our imagination is unable to suggest a further detail consistent with the design of the aesthetic whole.

Such a perfectly self-contained and self-defined poem "is at least a stab at a truth, and to such an extent may be differentiated...and called 'absolute.' Its evocation will not be toward decoration or amusement, but rather toward a state of consciousness, an 'innocence' (Blake) or absolute beauty." The ideal poem is, then, not "about" anything other than itself. "I try to make my poems experience," Crane said; language is the supreme experience, and the verbal shimmer constellates a unique state of consciousness as a "single, new *word*, never before spoken, and impossible to actually articulate." If "poetry, in so far as the metaphysics of any absolute knowledge extends, is simply the concrete *evidence* of the *experience* of a recognition (*knowledge* if you like)," the poem becomes both "perception and thing perceived, according as it approaches a significant articulation or not." The articulation is itself "the real connective experience, the very 'sign manifest' on which rests the assumption of a godhead."[37]

If pronouncements like these sound at first like Williams' position in *Spring and All*, a closer examination suggests why Williams and Crane had little sympathy with each other's work. In fact, they ranged themselves on opposite sides of the dialectical split through which Romanticism flowed into Modernism. The psychology and aesthetic of Romanticism rested on the correspondence between subject and object through the agency of the Spirit, animating both. As that essential connection became harder and harder to attain and maintain, the focus of perception became increasingly unstable, veering back and forth in the void widening between subject and object. Symbolisme came to represent, in this volatile situation, the tendency to turn inward and assert the primacy of consciousness, and Imagism came to represent the counterreaction of turning outward to assert the primacy of the phenomenal world. In the one case, the psyche objectifies its patterns as art; in the other, the psyche creates art out of its encounter with the phenomena of experience. In the one case, the poem works through blurred and multivalent suggestiveness; in the other, through a clean-edged and precise delineation. In the one case, the poem coheres as metaphor; in the other, as image. Imagist language, however subsistent as an art object, validates itself through its referentiality; Symboliste language, however colorful and resonant, validates itself through its syntagmatic self-referentiality.

In practice, the allegiance to subject or object was, of course, not so categorical as these formulations make out. On the one side, Stevens kept reminding himself that the Symboliste ought never to lose all sense of "things as they are," and on the other, Pound allowed that the "thing" directly presented by the Imagist might sometimes be a state of mind. Nevertheless, the underlying Symboliste and Imagist tendencies do represent the significant split in the psychology of the imagination within Modernism. Symons' *The Symbolist Movement in Literature* was a key document for the *fin de siècle*, and in 1912 Pound found contemporary poetry, even that of Yeats, so freighted with decadent Romanticism that he preferred to link his new Imagist aesthetic with attempts by realist novelists like Flaubert and James and Ford to charge precise language with energy.

Both Imagism and Symbolisme are Modernist rather than Romantic because Romanticism validates subject and object – and the poem which records their convergence – in the authority of Spirit, whereas Modernism validates subject (Symbolisme) or object (Imagism) in the authority and integrity of the artwork. Language, like the post-Impressionist's and the Cubist's applied pigment, authenticated itself in its aesthetic contrivance. Comprehended thus, the continuity and discontinuity between Romanticism and Modernism both come clear at last. Moreover, the new poets themselves recognized the divergence, perhaps incompatibility, of Symbolisme and Imagism as the polarity in terms of which they would define themselves as poets.

Crane saw it in his two new friends: Tate, following Eliot, spoke for the Symboliste line, and the Winters of 1926 and 1927 aligned himself with Williams' Imagism. Temperamentally Crane inclined to the Symbolisme of Tate and Eliot.[38] Tate's "Introduction" to *White Buildings* (1927) pointed to Crane's opposition to Imagist epistemology and devices: "A series of Imagist poems is a series of worlds. The poems of Hart Crane are facets of a single vision; they refer to a central imagination, a single evaluating power, which is at once the motive of the poetry and the form of its realisation."[39] At about the same time that Crane was resisting Winters' efforts to push Williams on him, he was setting his strain of absolute poetry, derived, he said, from Donne, Blake, Baudelaire, and Rimbaud, against what he called the impressionist, really the Imagist, method:

I may succeed in defining it better by contrasting it with the impressionistic method. The impressionist is interesting as far as he goes – but his goal has been reached when he has succeeded in projecting certain selected factual details into his reader's consciousness. He is really not interested in the *causes* (metaphysical) of his materials, their emotional derivations or their utmost spiritual consequences. A kind of retinal registration is enough, along with a certain psychological stimulation.

Consequently, whereas "the impressionist [or Imagist] creates with the eye and for the readiest surface of the consciousness," the Symboliste tries, by contrast, "to go *through* the combined materials of the poem, using our 'real' world somewhat as a spring-board, and to give the poem *as a whole* an orbit or predetermined direction of its own."[40]

Crane cited "Possessions"[41] as an instance of the absolutist aims of the "logic of metaphor":

> Witness now this trust! the rain
> That steals softly direction
> And the key, ready to hand – sifting
> One moment in sacrifice (the direst)
> Through a thousand nights the flesh
> Assaults outright for bolts that linger
> Hidden, – O undirected as the sky
> That through its black foam has no eyes
> For this fixed stone of lust...
>
> Accumulate such moments to an hour:
> Account the total of this trembling tabulation.
> I know the screen, the distant flying taps
> And stabbing medley that sways –
> And the mercy, feminine, that stays
> As though prepared.
>
> And I, entering, take up the stone
> As quiet as you can make a man...
> In Bleecker Street, still trenchant in a void,
> Wounded by apprehensions out of speech,
> I hold it up against a disk of light –
> I, turning, turning on smoked forking spires,
> The city's stubborn lives, desires.
>
> Tossed on these horns, who bleeding dies,
> Lacks all but piteous admissions to be spilt
> Upon the page whose blind sum finally burns
> Record of rage and partial appetites.
> The pure possession, the inclusive cloud
> Whose heart is fire shall come, – the white wind rase
> All but bright stones wherein our smiling plays.

(18)

On first reading, the poem appears virtually impenetrable, hermetically sealed in its dense verbal texture. A second or third reading at least indicates that the "trust" postulated for witness in the first line is only specified (and then vaguely) in the final three lines, and that the origin and development of the poem lie in the tension between (on the one hand) a "thousand nights" of lust, blurred as the rainfall and blind as the night sky and yet "fixed" in the flesh's compulsive search for "direction / And the key," and (on the other hand) "One moment" of "sacrifice (the direst)" and "pure possession," "wherein our smiling plays." The poem moves from hortatory imperatives ("witness," "accumulate," "account") to first-person verbs recounting the speaker's anguish and purgation to a concluding declaration that uses the plural pronoun "our" for the first time to project a union that transfigures lust. The tension is played out in the numerous sets of opposition: "trust," "lust"; "direction," "undirected"; "key," "bolt"; "sifting," "fixed"; "black foam," "white wind"; "sways," "stays"; "hold it up," "rase"; "horns," "heart"; "partial appetites," "pure possession"; "rase," "plays"; and so on.

Beyond these reiterated oppositions, the recurring image of the stone affords the best "key" to the narrative "direction" of the poem. In the first verse paragraph the obscuring rain, seemingly as "undirected" as the heedless sky, sifts one supremely sacrificial moment through a succession of nights alike only in that the flesh in all of its "assaults" is seeking release from "this fixed stone of lust." The second verse paragraph places the poet amid the "stabbing," shifting rain ("sways" echoes "sifting") but begins to admit another possibility. If such special moments might accumulate to an hour, then the sum "total" would reveal a maternal mercy prepared to offer staying solace. "Entering" upon such a possibility, the poet, "wounded" and "trenchant" (probably misused to mean, etymologically "cut," as a reiteration of "stabbing") on yet another night on Bleecker Street, initiates an action: he holds up the stone of lust, like a priest elevating the sacrament, "against a disk of light." His sexual and spiritual suffering ("turning on smoked forking spires," "tossed on these horns," bleeding, blindness) inexplicably gives way before his sacrificial act of trust to an affirmation of the possibility of shared love: the stone of lust is transubstantiated into the "bright stones wherein our smiling plays." The accounting sheet of those thousand nights finally consumes its own "record of rage and partial appetites"; the flames of lust will burn to a pure incandescence. The plurals of the last lines ("stones" rather than "stone," "our" rather than "I," echoing the enchanted "hour" longed for earlier) indicate the companionship of the lovers' childlike play. Though the future tense of the verb leaves the present still expectant, Crane meant it to anticipate fulfillment with assurance.

Such a delineation of the metaphoric strands – light and dark, accounts and sums, sight and blindness, flux and fixity, carnality and purity – does not adequately render or substitute for the effect of the poem. Even Crane had to admit:

> In manipulating the more imponderable phenomena of psychic motives, pure emotional crystallizations, etc., I have had to rely even more on these dynamics of inferential mention, and I am doubtless still very unconscious of

having committed myself to what seems nothing but obscurities to some minds. A poem like "Possessions" really cannot be technically explained. It must rely (even to a large extent with myself) on its organic impact on the imagination to successfully imply its meaning.[42]

The aspiration to an absolute suggestiveness informs most of the best poems in *White Buildings*. For example, there is no question that the third of the love sequence called *Voyages* is an extraordinary feat of metaphoric and auditory resonance:

Infinite consanguinity it bears –
This tendered theme of you that light
Retrieves from sea plains where the sky
Resigns a breast that every wave enthrones;
While ribboned water lanes I wind
Are laved and scattered with no stroke
Wide from your side, whereto this hour
The sea lifts, also, reliquary hands.

And so, admitted through black swollen gates
That must arrest all distance otherwise, –
Past whirling pillars and lithe pediments,
Light wrestling there incessantly with light,
Star kissing star through wave on wave unto
Your body rocking!
                    and where death, if shed,
Presumes no carnage, but this single change, –
Upon the steep floor flung from dawn to dawn
The silken skilled transmemberment of song;

Permit me voyage, love, into your hands...

(36)

The problem with a poem like this one, which sacrifices extension to intension, referentiality to syntagm, is illustrated by the fact that two of Crane's most admiring exegetes come to contradictory readings of the poem. R. W. B. Lewis takes "Voyages III" as the climax of the love affair recounted in the sequence, whereas Sherman Paul concludes, "The consummation so fervently sought in 'Voyages II' is never achieved....Both poems, occasioned by the lover's absence, involve the visionary enactment of consummation....In these poems, the poem itself is the agency of love."[43]

Many of Crane's poems come closer even than Tate's to attaining Tate's ideal: "The poem is its own knower, neither poet nor reader knowing anything that the poem says apart from the words of the poem."[44] Still, that attainment, remarkable as it was recognized to be in the poems which comprise *White Buildings*, did not satisfy Crane. Symbolisme could never be enough; he wanted to be a full-blown Romantic. Rimbaud supplied the epigraph for *White Buildings*, but Crane wanted to be not the Rimbaud of his age but its Shelley – or, better still, its Blake or Whitman – assimilating the fragments of experience into a holistic vision.

"Recitative" uses the image which became the title of Crane's first of two volumes published during his lifetime, and that poem is an exhortation to achieve a unitive vision in a broken, benighted world: "darkness, like an ape's face, falls away, / And gradually white buildings answer day" (25). The direction of the poem is characteristic; Crane confronts the shadow in order to overcome the breach between them. In fact, the poet's recitative addresses the other (his lover as shadow? the shadow aspect of himself?) in a series of imperative directions as the images of division – "Janus-faced," "twin shadowed halves," "breaking," "cleft," "brother in the half," "fragment smile," "shivered against lust," "alternating bells" – are pressed toward the "single stride" and "equal pride" of the final rhyme. That "one crucial sign" is, in its etymology, the sign of the cross in which oppositions intersect. In the fifth stanza and in the seventh and last stanza, "I" and "you" become (more emphatically than in "Possessions") "us," "alike," and "equal."

Crane's characteristic presentation of the city in "Recitative" illustrates the difference between Symboliste and Imagist epistemology and the reasons why he would turn from Rimbaud to Whitman:

> Let the same nameless gulf beleaguer us –
> Alike suspend us from atrocious sums
> Built floor by floor on shafts of steel that grant
> The plummet heart, like Absalom, no stream.
>
> The highest tower, – let her ribs palisade
> Wrenched gold of Nineveh; – yet leave the tower.
> The bridge swings over salvage, beyond wharves;
> A wind abides the ensign of your will...
>
> (25)

Absalom? Nineveh? The skyscraper grants the heart no stream? Unlike the imagery in Whitman and Williams, in Sheeler's and Demuth's Precisionist paintings, skyscraper and bridge and wharves are not, and are not meant to refer to, features of an actual cityscape. They are elements in an internalized cityscape expressive of a psychic state. No matter how stylized and analytically presented Williams' and Sheeler's images may sometimes be, no matter how intent they are on composing self-contained artworks, there is no doubt that their artworks derive from their encounters with a world of objects outside themselves and are meant to refer us back to that phenomenal world. The "white buildings," the skyscraper tower, the swinging bridge of "Recitative" adumbrate the capacity of metaphor to rise above oppositions and seize them in a verbal apprehension of paradoxical unity. The last sentence of Crane's "General Aims and Theories" makes the point: "Language has built towers and bridges, but itself is inevitably as fluid as always."[45]

2

Actually, the two parts of that sentence present the dilemma which *White Buildings* presented and *The Bridge* was meant to overcome. Can "the logic of metaphor" span oppositions and construct a solid significance, line by line and stanza by stanza? Or does it "inevitably" dissipate itself in a stream of private associations? Is language the river or the bridge towering over it? Crane could neither evade nor accept the split between subject and object of which Symbolisme is a consequence and manifestation. Stevens suavely composed verse measures to negotiate the split, but Crane's more vehement Romanticism balked at the *poésie pure* of *White Buildings* and cried out for an objectified vision, verified in the experience of a phenomenal world beyond the creative expressiveness of the imagination. In short, he wanted a symbolic rather than an angelic or Symboliste imagination. Even Sherman Paul admits, "Growth – poetic growth – beyond the confining and finally empty enclosures of the self; the risk of being: this is Crane's problem."[46]

Moreover, Crane agreed with Tate that such a symbolic imagination, such an objectified vision of self and world, depended upon a metaphysical conviction or a theological premise: "Any true expression must rest on some faith in something"; "The romantic attitude must at least have the background of an age of faith"; "It is fallacious to assume that either [Dante or Milton] could have written important religious verse without the fully developed and articulated religious dogmas that each was heir to."[47] Crane protested his philosophical innocence to a Winters now increasingly turning from Imagist to Renaissance poetry and from science to philosophy: "If you knew how little of a metaphysician I am.... I am an utter ignoramus in that whole subject, have never read Kant, Descartes or other doctors."[48] Nevertheless, Crane had read enough of Plato to confirm his own intuition that the multifarious flux of phenomenal existence cohered in the subsuming and absolute One: "The true idea of God is the only thing that can give happiness – and that is the identification of yourself with *all of life*."[49]

Crane's need, then, was to verify self and language in a reality beyond self and outside of language: in nature, in the conditions of urban living, in the ultimate reality of Godhead. For Eliot and Tate, both of whom manifested for Crane an intimidating assurance and authority, the fatal Romantic error, which opened the way for Symboliste solipsism, lay in making the weak individual with his limited consciousness, rather than the collective consciousness with its institutionalized structures, the vehicle of divine relevation. Crane set out to dispute the point by writing a Symboliste poetry of affirmation, like Rimbaud's visionary writings, to counter the Symboliste poetry of negation in Poe and Baudelaire, Eliot and Tate.

"The poetry of negation" and "the vocabulary of damnations and prostrations" were powerfully persuasive – "alas," Crane lamented, "too dangerously so for one of my mind." Precisely against that inclination in himself he turned his will, and in 1922, the year in which *The Waste Land* seemed to elevate the disillusionment of the lost generation to epic and tragic heights, Crane undertook in the longest and most ambitious poem of *White Buildings*, "For the Marriage of Faustus and Helen," a "metaphysical attempt of my own."[50] By "metaphysical" Crane followed Eliot in suggesting several associated meanings as the poetic goal: the resolution of paradoxes on the verbal and metaphorical levels, as in Donne and Herbert, expressive of a sensibility unified in its apprehension of matter and spirit. Indeed, in manic moods, Crane hoped to succeed where Eliot fell short, for "Eliot ignores certain spiritual events and possibilities as real and powerful now as, say, in the time of Blake."[51] Eliot knew better than to try to mix Donne and Blake, but Crane's title proclaimed, against the "dying fall" of Eliot's rhetoric, the hierogamy of the poet-mage and the personification of Platonic Beauty amid the rush and blare of urban life and the havoc of World War I.

Crane's friends responded enthusiastically to the poem, but he knew that he had not found the adequate symbol or convincingly fused the past and the present, the subject and the object, the universal and the particular. Consequently, with "Faustus and Helen" barely complete in February 1923, there came the first reference to a "new longish poem under the title of *The Bridge* which carries on further the tendencies manifest in 'F and H.'"[52] In the earlier effort, "I was really building a bridge between so-called classic experience and many divergent realities of our seething, confused cosmos of today, which has no formulated mythology yet for classic poetic reference or for religious exploitation." His miscalculation in "Faustus and Helen," he felt, lay in repeating Eliot's strategy of invoking the myths of the "decayed" past in the attempt at an imaginative "reorganization of human evaluations"[53] – instead of seeking a new mythos in modern American reality itself, so as to try, like Emerson and Whitman in their time and Williams in his own, to redeem it from materialism.

Crane's aesthetic dissatisfaction with the early poetry is summed up in the dedication of *White Buildings*, despite the Rimbaud epigraph, to Waldo Frank. Even before Crane met Frank in 1922, Frank's rhapsodic *Our America* (1919, with an expanded edition in 1923) had been for Crane "a revelation, for it suggested a way in which industrial America...might be somehow transformed into a better world...by the artist's involvement with it."[54] Through the influence of Frank, Crane was able to write, just a month after his first mention of *The Bridge*, "I begin to feel myself directly connected with Whitman." His "symphonic" epic, then, "concerns a mystical synthesis of 'America'" under the subsuming symbol of the Brooklyn Bridge, because the Roeblings' engineering feat demonstrated the power of the mind over nature. In joining opposing shores, the Bridge is a more imposing symbol of the machine age than Whitman's ferry, at once massively monumental and alive with traffic. In Crane's imagination the bridge encompasses space and time; its roadbed thrusts across to Manhattan and beyond to span the whole continent geographically and historically, hung by cables from stone towers that lift earth to sky and locate motion in eternity. To the imagination this feat in stone and steel "is an act of faith besides being a communication."[55]

Crane's heroic purpose, then, was to construct a bridge in his own medium, piling his metaphors and projecting his lines on the coordinates of geography and history; its "mystic portent" would authenticate subject in object, psychological identity in extrinsic reality. *The Bridge* would be no mere Stevensian fiction or Rimbaudian illumination but an "epic of the modern consciousness," the "Myth of America."[56] As Whitman had outfaced Poe, so he would outface Eliot and Tate.

Portentously – ominously, as it turned out – the first section of *The Bridge* to be completed became the conclusion of the published poem. In "the ecstatic and climactic" lines which came to be called "Atlantis," the real bridge is dissolved in a dizzying blur of metaphors whose Symboliste atmospherics outstrip paraphrase. All of the motion is "upward...up...upborne" – an ascent toward disembodied infinity. The body of the poem would constitute an ascent to this Symboliste climax – but, in the process of composition, would constitute a descent into time and space in order to give the symbol sufficient specific gravity to function as the historical and geographical synthesis of America. The success of his ambitious project, and indeed Crane's poetic future, hung on the effort to find a historical and topographical grounding of reference for psychological and spiritual intimations.

No major American poem of this century, except *The Cantos*, has split critical judgment so polemically. Crane's peers Winters and Tate, whose respect he needed badly, reviewed the poem with demurrals that confirmed his worst fears, and the essays each wrote after Crane's death mourned him as if to exorcise his Romantic-Symboliste shadow from their own psyches. In Tate's judgment, though Crane might delude himself that Eliot's pessimism was only "a point of departure toward an almost complete reverse of direction," in fact his "whole career is a vindication of Eliot's major premise – that the integrity of the individual consciousness has broken down."[57] Winters' indictment of the poem's intellectual, moral, and poetic incoherence – an essay called "The Significance of *The Bridge*, by Hart Crane" – constitutes one of Winters' principal position papers. In this reading, Crane lacked the psychological and philosophical coherence to predicate an ego identity in relation to a habitable world, and so to sustain the symbolic imagination in the creation of a poetic structure. The result is, in R. P. Blackmur's words, "the distraught but exciting splendor of a great failure."[58]

Crane's psychic states in his seven years of fitful and interrupted labor on the poem swung between mania and depression. At the peak of the creative outburst in 1926 which produced most of the poem, Crane wrote boastfully to his mother: "In the last ten days I've written over ten pages of *The Bridge* – highly concentrated stuff...more than I ever crammed into that period of time before. I can foresee that everything will be brightly finished by next May..., and I can make a magnificent bow to that magnificent structure, the Brooklyn Bridge....For the poem will be magnificent."[59] But this creative period came three fevered years after the original idea, and the poem would not be published until 1930 in a form that disappointed Crane. During those extended sloughs of despond between ecstatic creativity, Crane faced his demonic doubts. Though "the very idea of a bridge is...a form peculiarly dependent upon...spiritual convictions," in those dark times it seemed that "the symbols of reality necessary to articulate the span – may not exist where you expected them....By which I mean that however great their subjective significance to me is concerned – these forms, materials, dynamics are simply non-existent in the world." If so, then however deceptively "I may amuse and delight and flatter myself...[,] I am only evading a recognition and playing Don Quixote in an immorally conscious way." His whole gamble assumed that "the validity of a work of art is situated in contemporary reality[,]...that his intuitions were salutary and that his vision either sowed or epitomized 'experience' (in the Blakeian sense)."[60] These self-recriminations to Waldo Frank in 1926 fall just a month before the supreme poetic eruption of his career, but the subsidence of that energy left him more disconsolate than before: "I now find myself baulked by doubt at the validity of practically every metaphor I coin."[61]

Obviously, Crane could undercut the presumptions of his "romantic attitude" and angelic imagination as damningly as Tate or Blackmur or Winters, and his seeming concurrence with the New Critical censure of his project fixed for decades the judgment of *The Bridge* as a magnificent but predictable ruin of the Romantic aspiration, like Keats' "Hyperion" or Shelley's "The Triumph of Life." But more recently, Lewis and Paul have argued that Crane should not be taken at his doubting word and that instead the poem must be read and judged afresh on its own terms – terms which, however abhorrent to the conservatism of Eliot and Tate and Winters, reconstituted the Romantic imagination in a Modernist, and specifically Symboliste, aesthetic. In this view, the quandary of the subjective consciousness alienated from an objective world and absolute values can be resolved if "the poet turns the interior world inside out and finds in the work of poetry itself the values of security." Lewis found Crane's effort so successful that "among modern poems in English, *The Bridge* is the religious poem par excellence."[62] Paul located the failure in Crane's critics: "how could Allen Tate, Yvor Winters, and R. P. Blackmur...have been so unaware of the merits of the *poem* and the tough genius of its maker? How could critics so well versed in Eliot's work find it so difficult to make formal sense of *The Bridge?*" Paul's book-length explication of the poem sets out to vindicate Crane's Symboliste aesthetic: "the overreaching and incoherence that Tate found in Crane's poetry – particularly in *The Bridge* – follow from Tate's failure to appreciate or grant the nature of the 'logic of metaphor.'"[63]

The archetypal reading which follows complements and in the end qualifies the readings of Lewis and Paul by integrating the psychological function of the poem into our sense of its exfoliation. In evaluating the success or failure of *The Bridge*, critics have discussed its techniques and structure in terms of its historical and religious intentions but have not sufficiently taken into account the psychological dimension. Like Pound and Whitman, Crane thought of an epic as a poem with history, but like them too he intended his poem to be an "epic of modern consciousness." In one letter, Crane went so far as to say that the assimilation of memory and history "in the subconscious" projected the epic as the "structure of my dreams."[64] An archetypal reading excavates that personal and internal structure of Crane's epic; at this level, *The Bridge* is Crane's attempt at a "Song of Myself."

The autobiographical and psychic circumstances out of which it arose had much in common with Whitman's situation and very little in common with Pound's. Behind Crane's Whitmanian attempt at "a mystical synthesis of 'America'" lay the equally Whitmanian need to forge a personal synthesis from the neuroses and afflictions of domestic tragedy, though Crane's filiality was even more personally damaging than Whitman's. The psychological terms of Crane's life were set largely by the protracted and vicious antagonism between his parents, which extended beyond their marital years of quarrels and reunions through their divorce and remarriages into the last decade of their only child's life. He always felt himself a son alienated from, dependent on, and bound to a neurasthenic, possessive mother and a tightfisted, harshly judging father, neither of whom could win or lose their fierce competition for him.

Crane's letters to his parents leave no doubt about his being shredded in the emotional crossfire. In 1917 he described himself to his father as "one whose fatal weakness is to love two unfortunate people"; in 1919 he was driven to tell his mother: "I don't want to fling accusations, etc., at anybody, but I think it's time you realized that for the last eight years my youth has been a rather bloody battleground for yours and father's sex life and troubles." Neither physical maturity nor the attempt at separation from both of them brought release. In 1922: "I am quite disrupted. Family affairs and 'fusses' have been my destruction since I was eight years old when my father and mother began to quarrel." Again in 1926, with most of his poem finished: "Nothing but illness and mental disorder in my family. . . . It means tortures and immolations which are hard to conceive, impossible to describe. There seems to be no place left in the world for love or the innocence of a single spontaneous act."[65] The violence of his words registers pain beyond mere self-pity. In "Quaker Hill," the last section of *The Bridge* to be written, he asks that the historical figures of the poem ("slain Iroquois" and "scalped Yankees") serve as psychopomps and "guide / Me farther" into himself, so that he can finally "shoulder the curse of sundered parentage, / Wait for the postman driving from Birch Hill / With birthright by blackmail" (93).

Crane's excursions into American history and geography, like Whitman's, stemmed from a psychological need and served, in turn, a psychological function. Without denying the validity of the poem as historical myth, an archetypal reading would at the same time view the epic as psychodrama and specifically in this instance would see that the historical figures in *The Bridge* function also as symbolic factors in Crane's attempt to come to terms with the mother and father archetypes. At this level, the poem becomes an imaginative strategy to secure release from the overbearing mother and confirmation from the opprobrious father, so that the poet's own masculine and feminine aspects can coalesce in a sexual and spiritual identity.

"Proem: To Brooklyn Bridge" (43–44) projects the simultaneous historical and psychological levels of the poem. This epic invocation is addressed not to a god but to the numinous Bridge (accorded the personal pronoun "Thee") as the concretion of spirit in matter – or the concretion in matter of the aspiration of the human spirit to exceed the limitations of matter. The first formulation suggests an incarnational descent, the second a Neoplatonic and gnostic ascent; the first is (in Tate's terms) symbolic, the second angelic. Together they comprise the central tension in the proem. In a genuine religious or mystical experience, descent and ascent should meet; the way up and the way down are one and the same. Crane undertook *The Bridge* as a test of whether his was a genuinely symbolic imagination or only an angelic or Symboliste imagination. It is not melodramatic to say that his life and work hung on the outcome.

The "Proem" invests the feat of engineering design and construction (from the start, the Bridge was hailed as a wonder of the technological sublime) with imaginative and religious significance: "O harp and altar, of the fury fused." When he was writing the "Proem," Crane seems not to have known Joseph Stella's Futurist paintings apotheosizing the Bridge, but when he became aware of them shortly before publication of the poem, he wrote to Stella, marveling at their congruent efforts and inquiring about using several paintings to illustrate the poem.

By the grace of metaphor, the cables breathe and become "choiring strings," and the traffic lights are seen as an "immaculate sigh of stars, / Beading thy path." At this center of a microcosm teeming with Futurist vectors and arcs of energy, the divine and the human, nature and city, meet. One axis is vertical, restlessly rising and falling between sky and earth; the other is a horizontal thrust, so that the Bridge's arch over the East River extends, by implication, back over the sea to the first explorers and forward with the pioneers across "the prairies' dreaming sod." The spatial grid reconciles motion and location: "Liberty's" Statue presides over "chained" bay waters; the Bridge's span is "unfractioned," "implicitly thy freedom staying thee!" The ominous possibilities of the scene are admitted: the plummeting elevators, the bedlamite's suicidal plunge from the parapets, the sun's rays raking down between skyscrapers as "a rip-tooth of the sky's acetylene." But the direction of the poem intimates an apocalyptic resolution: "Only in darkness is thy shadow clear." The visionary outcasts of the city (prophet, pariah, lover) find visible in the Bridge the source and satisfaction of their longing. Thus curves negotiate between the crossed axes; the wheeling, dipping gulls of the first lines anticipate the suspension cables of the last: "Unto us lowliest sometime sweep, descend / And of the curveship lend a myth to God." Preferring to identify himself with the prophet, pariah, and lover rather than with the bedlamite, Crane launches his psychological trajectory through history (time) and geography (space) to connect with the vision of "Atlantis" at the far end of the poem, a trajectory suspended from the coiled strands of metaphorical rhetoric sweeping up to and down from a remarkable and sustained period of imaginative elevation in 1926.

As Lewis put it, the poem's "subject was hope, and its content a journey toward hope," and for that very reason it was "not an epic on the Vergilian model which Hart Crane sometimes invoked, but on the Romantic model: namely, what [M. H.] Abrams called 'an apocalypse of imagination.'"[66] Crane's hope was that the apocalypse toward which he moved would reveal not only the immanent Deity but an emergent identity, that the poem would lend a myth to Self in lending a myth to God. A previously cited sentence from one of the letters, written as the poem was first taking shape in his mind, identifies God and an image of Self reminiscent of the Whitmanian Cosmic Man: "the true idea of God is the only thing that can give happiness, – and that is the identification of yourself with *all of life.*"[67]

"Ave Maria" (47–50), the opening section of the poem, is a soliloquy of Christopher Columbus, the archetypal American explorer (as he was to many of our artists and poets). Columbus speaks from the apex of his achievement, rounding toward the Old World's shores with word of the New. He has bridged God's "teeming span," "vaulting the sea" (as the end of "Proem" had foretold). For Crane, as for Joel Barlow and Washington Irving and Whitman, Columbus' journey beyond the farthest horizon against all material odds constitutes a triumph of the spirit, and his capacity for such heroic action resides in the unwavering sense of selfhood which made him, in Whitman's phrases, a "true son of God" ("Passage to India") and "a breath of Deity" ("A Thought of Columbus"). But Columbus' masculine character depends on his relation to the feminine. There are two prayers in the soliloquy; the "Te Deum" to the Father with which it ends is preceded by the "Ave Maria" to the "Madre Maria." The Virgin is maternal vessel of Incarnation, joining nature and Godhead; through her issued the divine epiphany in history – reiterated here and now in Columbus. His phrase "yield thy God's, thy Virgin's charity" links mother and father; he is son of both.

But what of Crane? He assumes Columbus' role as voyager in "Powhatan's Daughter" (51–68), by far the longest section of *The Bridge*, developed through five subsections. "Harbor Dawn" finds the poet rising in contemporary Manhattan from a fantasized female lover, who serves as inspiration for the pioneering trek back in time and out across the continent in search of Pocahontas, the American earth mother. In "Rip Van Winkle," the first section of "Powhatan's Daughter," historical figures from a childhood textbook mingle with autobiographical glimpses of Crane's father (in the phallic-aggressive act of stripping a branch to whip him) and his mother (in the erotically disturbing act of bestowing a chill kiss on him after her return from church services). Rip is the first of several surrogate bachelor fathers on this quest for the lover-mother. Irving's Rip spanned historical epochs, and now he hops the subway with the poet to head west under the East River.

In "The River" the train becomes the Twentieth Century Limited, its forward propulsion paradoxically bearing the protagonist back in time, past the contemporary chatter and the clatter of commercial slogans, across the Appalachian spring to the Mississippi heartland, where he discovers the maternal spirit of the place in the company of the "ancient men" who are her children. Crane becomes the initiate, like the young Rip in his fateful meeting with the old men of the mountains, as the aged Rip of the previous section fades into the hoboes and railsquatters of the road gang, who may look like "blind fists of nothing, humpty-dumpty clods" but who really "touch something like a key perhaps" in their tactile knowledge of the Pocahontas body of the American land. Through them Crane is initiated into the mystery of nature and of the maternal archetype; in imagination he "knew her body there, / Time like a serpent down her shoulder, dark, / And space, an eaglet's wing laid on her hair." In his fantasy of the historical Pocahontas as the mother-lover, Crane feels healed of his lifelong dependence on and dread of the feminine. And as in Whitman, deliverance comes in surrender. Borne with his male companions down the Mississippi, he comes to understand that, despite history's record of the authority of independent men, they all in the end "feed the River timelessly"; she "drinks the farthest dale."

The Mississippi turns out to be, for Crane, not the Father but the Mother of Waters. The majestic meters of the concluding quatrains mark her supremacy: "What are you, lost within this tideless spell? / You are the father's father, and the stream – / A liquid theme that floating niggers swell." As female flow, the river swallows patriarchal history, sliding over "De Soto's bones," "down, down" to a climax of debouchment in the mother sea:

> All fades but one thin skyline 'round...Ahead
> No embrace opens but the stinging sea;
> The River lifts itself from its long bed,
>
> Poised wholly on its dream, a mustard glow
> Tortured with history, its one will – flow!
> – The Passion spreads in wide tongues, choked and slow
> Meeting the Gulf, hosannas silently below.
>
> (61)

What Crane comes to experience in "The River" is the child's and the old man's rapture of subsidence in the mother: the subsidence of birth and death. Heretofore his survival and manhood seemed to require terrified resistance to her devouring power, but the newly experienced passion of capitulation caries over into the quatrains of "The Dance," the climactic section of "Powhatan's Daughter," in which the poet imaginatively achieves his manhood in an ecstasy of death, accepting the hegemony of the mother-lover over her lover-sons. The historical regression from the white man to the red man in the course of these quatrains is paralleled by a psychological breakthrough to the unconscious, whereby Crane moves past infantile and adolescent dependence to identification with Maquokeeta, heroic Sachem and husband of Pocahontas. The moment of identification is of profound psychological as well as historical significance. In Crane's fantasy, his approach to his bride Pocahontas releases over the landscape a storm dance tumescent with phallic aggressiveness: "twanges of lightning," "red fangs and splay tongues,"

"Sprout, horn! / Spark, tooth!" "pulsant bone," "flame cataracts." But the wedding dance turns into a death dance in which potency expends itself to impotence; in becoming Pocahontas' mate, he undergoes Maquokeeta's fate: "Know, Maquokeeta, greeting; know death's best; / – Fall, Sachem, strictly as the tamarack!" Maquokeeta-Crane plays a double role in the dance: "liege" in the sense of both lord and vassal, not just medicine man dancing "out the siege" but also victim at the stake: "And buzzard-circleted, screamed from the stake; I could not pick the arrows from my side." Pocahontas the bride is glimpsed briefly as a grieving wife during the death dance but becomes, apparently without a recollection of the loss, wife and mother to the white sons and lovers who "sprint up the hill groins like a tide." Maquokeeta's fall is matched by her ascendancy: "And see'st thy bride immortal in the maize!"; "she is virgin to the last of men." His fate is to be blent "with all that's consummate and free"; his consummation is a release into the cyclic round of time and space.

Does this myth of male descent anticipate – or contradict – the myth of transcendence toward which the poem has been aimed? Does the maternal archetype complement or undermine the image of the Bridge as harbinger of God and Self? These are crucial questions for the outcome of the poem, and while it may be too early in the sequence to tell, it is noteworthy that Crane empathizes not with the new husband of Pocahontas but with the slain Maquokeeta. The final lines of "The Dance" are:

> We danced, O Brave, we danced beyond their farms,
> In cobalt closures made our vows...
> Now is the strong prayer folded in thine arms,
> The serpent with the eagle in the boughs.
>
> (65)

Moreover, the concluding section of "Powhatan's Daughter" is puzzling in its irresolution. After the historical and psychological regression of "The River" and "The Dance," "Indiana" carries the historical perspective forward to the nineteenth century. The feminine "Indiana" recalls Pocahontas; the title puns as well on the Indian territory now become a midwestern state, and the salute between the itinerant squaw and the pioneer farm woman marks the transition from red to white matriarch. But beyond such thematic developments, critics have complained about the abrupt slackening of imaginative energy after "The River" and "The Dance."

A waning of creative energy might well ensue from the elegy for the lover-son in "The River" and "The Dance," especially since "Indiana" shifts the focus to the mourning mother. However, the important thing to note in archetypal terms is the cause of maternal mourning. The pioneer mother who speaks here is bereft not because of her son's death but, on the contrary, because of his departure from her to strike out on a life of his own. However unsatisfactorily, therefore, "Indiana" represents Crane's belated attempt to end "Powhatan's Daughter" not with the capitulation of the son to the mother, masochistically celebrated in "The River" and "The Dance," but instead with his counterblow for independence.

Crane's original plan for this section had in fact been for a father to bid farewell to his seafaring son. But by the time Crane came back to "Powhatan's Daughter" in 1929 to finish it for publication, he was still reeling from his bitter and final break with his mother, and switched the speaker from the father to this weary, pitiable widow clinging to her departing son. According to Sherman Paul, Crane intentionally distilled his mother's tone and voice into the speaker's.[68] In contrast to "The Dance," then, the son faces life, not death, and instead the mother faces death: "I'm standing still, I'm old, I'm half of stone! / Oh, hold me in those eyes' engaging blue." The subdued tone of "Indiana," then, registers the mother's unresigned sadness that her son has become her "Prodigal." But what is missing is the son's voice, and in its absence the mother's distress reflects as well the son's voiceless ambivalence that he has become her "Prodigal." As her monologue indicates, the son is as much fatherless as he has now made himself motherless. In the context of the poem, his hope will lie in his proving himself a son of Columbus. "Indiana" implies a new departure for Cathay or Atlantis, but it fails to take on sufficient dramatic power and direction precisely because the sailor son remains an anonymous phantom. At this crucial point in the poem we need – and miss – the strong cadences of a voice like Columbus'.

"Cutty Sark" (71–74), although written three years earlier than "Indiana," continues in the sequence the wavering note of uncertainty and nostalgia. Crane's chance encounter with a boozy old salt in a waterfront bar confronts him with an avatar of the sailor son near the end of his voyaging. His "shark tooth" ironically echoes Maquokeeta, but even more he recalls old Rip and the old "hobo-trekkers." At this stage of alcoholic impotence he is the antithesis of Columbus; he can offer the poet heroic but nostalgic dreams but no paternal wisdom and no energizing willpower. His allegiance to the sea and to vessels like "Atlantis Rose" indicates his bondage to the mother sea without the mariner's mastery; the surrogate father has become a sentimental Bowery drunk. As Crane walks home across the Brooklyn Bridge in the muzzy dawn, he daydreams of bygone days he never knew, when Cutty Sark was not just a brand of whiskey but queen of the clipper ships. The epigraph from Melville is elegiac: "O, the navies, old and oaken, / O, the Temeraire no more!" The only feminine references are to the "Atlantis Rose," also long gone, and to the Statue of Liberty, whose torch has expired.

The surrogate fathers encountered thus far in the poem – Columbus, Van Winkle, the hoboes, even the old salt – have served, for all their limitations, to propel Crane in the quest, and now the return to Brooklyn after the journey that began in "Harbor Dawn" brings the poem to midpoint and introduces at last the figure of Whitman, translated to the twentieth century. "Cape Hatteras" (77–84) is filled with lines and phrases from *Leaves of Grass*, and the bard is apostrophized as bridge builder:

> Our Meistersinger, thou set breath in steel;
> And it was thou who on the boldest heel

Stood up and flung the span on even wing
Of that great Bridge, our Myth, whereof I sing!

(83)

Just as Waldo Frank claimed, Whitman's chants lend a myth to God and Self and an ideal America; his spirit arches above the "red, eternal flesh of Pocahontas." He combines the functions of calamus-comrade and wise father; through him Crane hopes to claim his personal and national and poetic identity.

Crane knows that his task will be harder, both personally and culturally, than that of earlier daredevils who harnessed nature to their wills. Columbus sought the fabled passage to India by sail, and Whitman's "Passage to India," echoed repeatedly in "Cape Hatteras," hailed the Suez Canal, the transatlantic cable, and the transcontinental railroad as portents of further conquests of time and space. Now in "Cape Hatteras" Crane takes on the full challenge of affirming to Eliot and the post–World War I generation a mystique of the Machine Age. Its place is pivotal in the poem if Crane is to demonstrate (historically) the visionary impulse and its potential in technological progress and (psychologically) the breaking of the mother's possessiveness through assimilation of the father's potency.

The opening lines of "Cape Hatteras" trace a "change / Of energy" as its source passes from unconscious nature to the hand of the human inventor. At the beginning, Nature continues to be imbued with male ambivalence toward the female; she is "hushed" and "surcharged with sweetness," yet eruptively combusting "at the astral core." Within a few lines, however, her power is seized by new masters of energy, who seek to avoid death in the mother by inventing the mechanical means to transcend earth: "Seeing himself an atom in a shroud – / Man hears himself an engine in a cloud!" The Great Navigator's contemporary emanation is the "Corsair of the typhoon," the "Falcon-Ace" in the pilot's seat, the "Skygak."

"Modern Poetry," written a year after "Cape Hatteras" in 1930, glosses this section of The Bridge: "unless poetry can absorb the machine," it "has failed of its full contemporary function." The extravagant rhetoric and compounded metaphors of "Cape Hatteras" are Crane's efforts to apotheosize the dynamo and combustion engine and industrial plant. For many critics, Crane's language does not transfigure the machine so much as disguise it in metaphorical excrescence. Even Lewis defends the disputed lines as deliberately bad; they seem to him "brilliantly successful" as "of course a *very deliberate and conscious self-parody*."[69]

But far from parody, these passages are noteworthy as the most extreme and successful attempt at Futurist poetry in America. Crane was trying to find the verbal equivalent of the Futurist canvases of the Italian Balla and the American Stella in rendering mechanical speed and energy as exponents of the modern spirit:

The nasal whine of power whips a new universe...
Where spouting pillars spoor the evening sky,
Under the looming stacks of the gigantic power house

Stars prick the eyes with sharp ammoniac proverbs,
New verities, new inklings in the velvet hummed
Of dynamos, where hearing's leash is strummed...
Power's script, – wound, bobbin-bound, refined –
Is stropped to the slap of belts on booming spools, spurred
Into the bulging bouillon, harnessed jelly of the stars.

(78–79)

The near hysteria in these verses expresses more than the anxieties of Crane's unraveling life in 1929; it expresses as well Crane's ambivalence about the power of the machine. Whitman voiced a common nineteenth-century complacence in hailing technology in poems like "Song of the Exposition" and "Passage to India," but could that affirmation be made after World War I? Crane's contemporaries Sheeler and Demuth painted machines with immaculate and radiant precision. But for Crane they were genuinely sublime, as threatening as they were exhilarating. Were we victims of our own mastery of nature? The celebration of the Wright brothers' tremendous achievement at Cape Hatteras leaps forward to the air battles over France. The rhetoric of the early passages in this section, testing the limits of verbal control, builds to and breaks apart in the description of the splintering plane crash on the beach.

But with everything apparently lost in the wreckage, Crane calls on Whitman, the poetic voyager-father-alter ego, to bear him beyond tragedy. "Modern Poetry" said that the seer must have the "spontaneity and gusto" to "convert" such experiences "into positive terms."[70] To that end, Crane wills himself up as Whitman: "O Walt! – Ascensions of thee hover in me now / As thou at junctions elegiac, there, of speed / With vast eternity, dost wield the rebound seed!" The final lesson of the smashed plane is not the male hubris humbled to mother earth, but instead another flight undertaken on the wings of Whitman. The direction is "upward," "beyond," "past," "outward" along "that span of consciousness thou's named / The Open Road." In the blur of imagery at the section's end, the Road and the Bridge become the rainbow which has sealed God's renewed covenant since Genesis: "And see! the rainbow's arch – how shimmeringly stands / Above the Cape's ghoul-mound, O joyous seer!" Probably Crane's belated reconciliation with his father in 1929 after his rejection of his mother contributed to the writing of "Cape Hatteras." In any case, the section ends with the two poets – father and son, older comrade and protégé – striding into the future hand in hand.

The typical curve of Whitman's great poems – it is true of "Song of Myself" as well as of the elegies – traces a descent to the shadow area followed by an ascent to a mystical resolution. "Cape Hatteras" came as a last affirmation in Crane's career. After 1929 his only completed poem of lasting significance bore the emblematic title "The Broken Tower." And when "Cape Hatteras" assumed its place in the sequence of The Bridge, the previously written sections that come after it provide no adequate link between the Whitman section and "Atlantis." The red man's myth was the maternal cycles of Pocahontas, and the paternal Whitman seemed to accept the white man's myth of the Bridge. But just at the point in the poem when Crane clasps Whitman's hand for a fresh ascent, continuity falters. Whitman had helped to launch the poem with the writing of "Atlantis" and "Ave Maria," and in 1929 Crane reinvoked Whitman to bless the poem that he by then feared was wrecked beyond completion.

"Three Songs" (85–90) follows "Cape Hatteras," although they were written in 1926 during the burst which also produced most of "Powhatan's Daughter," and the discontinuities in tone and manner after "Cape Hatteras" raise the question of whether Crane was not correct in wondering, as he sometimes did, whether "Three Songs" belonged in *The Bridge* at all. But whatever the poem's structural discontinuities, Lewis pointed out the archetypal connection of "Three Songs" with "Powhatan's Daughter" and with the poet's effort to displace the possessive mother and find himself in union with an alternative, benevolent manifestation of the feminine: "'Three Songs' expresses the poet's intensifying effort to find in some actual female the representation of his divine beloved. [But] the poet is confronted only by degradations of his 'cosmic' love."[71] The missing anima-muse, sought since "Harbor Dawn," was identified with Pocahontas – mistakenly, it turned out, since the bride proved instead to be the devouring mother. And now, in the contemporary world to which Whitman commits him, he finds no adequate exponent of the anima-muse-bride either.

The three women are introduced early in the first lyric: Eve, Magdalene, Mary. The Eve of "Southern Cross" presents an ambivalent attraction. On the one hand, she is "simian Venus, homeless Eve, unwedded, stumbling gardenless...to answer all within one grave." The Southern Cross, the sign of God as contradiction, views her as lascivious temptation and negation. Yet, on the other hand, that negation holds the secret of God's ultimate otherness: "I wanted you, nameless Woman of the South,...It is / God – your namelessness." But the poem remains unresolved ("No wraith.... Yes, Eve, wraith") and ends in images of collapse and drowning. The other two songs demonstrate the unresolved contradiction. The Magdalene of "National Winter Garden" presents woman as whore-mother: the stripteaser to whose "belly" each man "comes back to die alone" and be lugged "back lifeward." "Virginia" presents woman as inaccessible virgin: Rapunzel in the Grain Exchange and Mary in her pseudo-Gothic niche in the Woolworth Building's tower.

The descent quickens in "Quaker Hill" (91–94). The epigraphs from two American female artists take off from the dichotomies of "Three Songs." Emily Dickinson is the type of the nineteenth-century virginal recluse, whereas Isadora Duncan's public performances of modern dances in which the body strove to be vessel of spirit only led her to conclude sadly: "I see only the ideal. But no ideals have ever been fully successful on this earth." Quaker Hill, an upstate New York resort town near Patterson, where Crane had lived with the Tates and to which he often returned for respite from the city's hard living, is here made to exemplify the decline of American idealism from the Quakers to Victorian affluence to jazz-age, country-club materialism.

Like many of his contemporaries, including Waldo Frank, Crane was disturbed by Oswald Spengler's *Decline of the West* (1918), and that large cultural argument provided the context for his familial anxieties. So in "Quaker Hill," the historical question "Where are my kinsmen and the patriarch race?" precipitates an autobiographical response. The rupture with his mother and the tentative rapprochement with his father came perhaps too late in 1929; he still had not "shoulder[ed] the curse of sundered parentage" and assumed his "birthright." Submerging his own dilemma in the larger cultural dilemma, Crane invokes fellow artists for stoic courage in defeat: Dickinson and Duncan, Whitman's elegies (the "throbbing throat" of the whippoorwill), Stevens' "Sunday Morning" ("So, must we from the hawk's far stemming view, / Must we descend..."). Their resistance to the descending spiral is the art that in uttering their anguish ("the stilly note / Of pain that Emily, that Isadora knew!") "shields love from despair" and holds up the ideal against the reality that violates it.

The subway trip that began in "Van Winkle" has become, by the return in "The Tunnel" (95–101), an underground shadow realm presided over by the ravaged and demonic shade of Poe. The inferno is not medieval, as Dante's was, but urban and industrial, as Blake's was, and the subway becomes the symbolic condition of a psychological hell: "hades in the brain," the "chasms of the brain," "interborough fissures of the mind."

"The Tunnel" is the penultimate section of *The Bridge*, and there is almost no preparation or anticipation of the inversion of its infernal state of mind to the paradisal state of "Atlantis" except the lines from Blake's "Morning" prefatory to "The Tunnel": "To find the Western path / Right thro' the Gates of Wrath." The allusion to the Passage to India recalls Columbus and Whitman, and the verses suggest hell is really only purgatory preparatory to the apocalyptic dawn in "Atlantis." By the end of the nightmare subway ride back under the East River, however, Blake's words have receded, and the reader is suddenly and unexpectedly catapulted into the vision of the Bridge, to which the poem has all along been willed.

The superscription from Plato – "Music is then the knowledge of that which relates to love in harmony and system" – anticipates the extreme and deliberately heightened musicality of "Atlantis" (103–108). The thrust is unswervingly up now; the swelling music moves to abstraction, and the diaphanous veils of metaphor disembody the "granite and steel" into a Platonic idea. The spellbinding rhetoric presents the Bridge not as Whitmanian symbol or Williamsesque image but as Symboliste sound and metaphor. In this stanza the massive cables virtually disappear in the "blinding" whirl of words:

> Forever Deity's glittering Pledge, O Thou
> Whose canticle fresh chemistry assigns
> To wrapt inception and beatitude, –
> Always through blinding cables, to our joy,
> Of thy white seizure springs the prophecy:
> Always through spiring cordage, pyramids

Of silver sequel, Deity's young name
Kinetic of white choiring wings...ascends.

(107)

Images and references from the earlier sections of the poem are swept up into an ethereal synthesis, and the last stanza is a crescendo in every word and image of which the rest of the poem resonates:

So to thine Everpresence, beyond time,
Like spears ensanguined of one tolling star
That bleeds infinity – the orphic strings,
Sidereal phalanxes, leap and converge:
– One Song, one Bridge of Fire! Is it Cathay,
Now pity steeps the grass and rainbows ring
The serpent with the eagle in the leaves...?
Whispers antiphonal in azure swing.

(107–108)

The glorious rhetoric carries the poem to its conclusion. But the problem for Crane was that his construction remained a feat of Symboliste language. As a poem *The Bridge* is, despite certain discontinuities in the last third, a magnificent achievement, just as he promised his mother, but as an attempt to flesh out his angelism and ground the symbolic imagination in the data of his life and his American circumstances, *The Bridge* left Crane bitterly disappointed. Reading the sections of *The Bridge* not as in the published order but in the organic order in which they were written, as we do read *The Cantos* and *Paterson*, discloses a significantly different "poem" – and the causes of Crane's despair in 1930.

The Bridge was first conceived in February 1923, upon the completion of "Faustus and Helen," as a poem of much the same length, and Crane sketched out verses that later went into "Van Winkle" and early versions of what became "Atlantis." During three years of gestation the epic potentialities burgeoned in Crane's mind, and in the winter of 1926, living with the Tates outside New York City, he continued to tinker with "Atlantis" and began the Columbus section. When tensions with the Tates precipitated his abrupt departure during the spring, he retreated to his grandmother's (now his mother's) Caribbean house on the Isle of Pines, frazzled and dubious about his ability to carry the project through. Then, in the miraculous weeks of July-August 1926, a frenzy of creativity produced, in roughly the following order, completed versions of "Atlantis" and "Ave Maria," "Proem," "The Dance," "Cutty Sark," "Three Songs," "The Tunnel," and the beginnings of "Harbor Dawn" and "The River," to be completed the following summer. By September 1927 he was able to describe *The Bridge* to his patron, Otto Kahn, with all sections in place except for "Cape Hatteras," "Indiana," and "Quaker Hill." Those sections were not written until the later months of 1929, with difficulty and under the pressure of publishing deadlines. The limited edition from the Black Sun Press appeared in February 1930; and the commercial edition from Liveright, in April 1930. Therefore, although the writing of *The*

Bridge was Crane's anxiety-fraught obsession for seven years, most of the poem came in a single remarkable burst of inspiration, with the most ecstatic sections leading the way: "Atlantis," "Ave Maria," "Proem," and "The Dance." He went on to fill out "Powhatan's Daughter" and squeeze out the remaining sections, but the historical and psychosexual complications which the poem presented and which "The Dance" pointedly raised signaled the prevailingly downward course of the later sections. It is not surprising, then, that when Crane put the last pieces into their assigned places in 1929 and released the poem for publication, he was still worried that the poem had not achieved adequate form and articulation.

As a published artifact, the sections of the poem, like the Brooklyn Bridge itself, sweep down and up from the high point at the beginning ("Proem" and "Ave Maria"), middle ("The Dance" and "Cape Hatteras"), and end ("Atlantis"). From the poet's point of view, however, the poem seemed to graph a quickening disintegration: an ecstatic conception, an orgiastic outburst after several years of stalling, and final gasps under the pressure of publishing rather than under the pressure of inspiration. The creative process during which the artifact was rearranged cut a crazy, zigzag course not unlike the plunge of the doomed airplane that came to Crane at the end of the process:

> down whizzing
>
> Zodiacs, dashed
>
> (now nearing fast the Cape!)
>
> down gravitation's
>
> vortex into crashed
>
> ....dispersion...into mashed and shapeless debris....
>
> By Hatteras bunched the beached heap of high bravery!
>
> (81)

Was Crane thinking of his poetic venture in these lines? Perhaps not. He wanted to believe that *The Bridge*, in its curveship, would lend a myth to God and Self, so that "Deity's young name," hypothesized in "Atlantis," spelled the poet's identity too. But the Northwest Passage through Blake's Gates of Wrath led not, as he had hoped, to a "mystical synthesis of 'America,'" like Whitman's "Song of Myself" and "Calamus," but to a historical and psychological landscape from which he had to escape back to the original abstraction of Atlantis, an "imagined land," as Stevens said in "Mrs. Alfred Uruguay." If the rhetoric seems more hyperbolic and inflated than Crane hoped, the reason is that the "logic of metaphor" and the harmony of music must incant what the tests of experience and of history have not substantiated. Just at the point when Crane needs to have us feel the ideal manifest in the Bridge, Isadora Duncan's haunting words come back: "No ideals have ever been fully successful on earth."

Even Lewis' ringing defense conceded that "the emergent subject of *The Bridge* was not the actual or even the latent greatness of an actual and contemporary America" but rather a "hope reconstituted on the ground of the imagination"; "The thing hoped for was the creation *in poetry* of a new world."[72] The linguistic and literary references in "Atlantis" to the "multitudinous Verb," the "Psalm of Cathay," the "white, pervasive Paradigm," the "One Song" all intimate that it is not the Bridge as poem but the poem as bridge which was to formulate the "Word that will not die." And so, ironically, the accuracy of Lewis' praise specifies the failure of Crane's intention. To the Whitmanian Frank, just a couple of weeks before his creative eruption on the Isle of Pines, he voiced the fear that haunted the enterprise: if the symbols "necessary to articulate the span" cannot be tallied and verified in an objective and historical reality, if "however great their significance to me is concerned these forms, materials, dynamics are simply non-existent in the world," then "I am only evading a recognition and playing Don Quixote in an immorally conscious way."[73] Unlike Stevens, Crane could not, or would not, live in an "imagined land."

In effect, Lewis and Paul praise Crane for writing the poem he did not want to write and for apotheosizing imagination on terms he was seeking to supersede. Paul, therefore, is only partially correct in saying that "Crane's sensibility, aesthetics, and poetry are decidedly modern, for they are characterized by distrust of absolutes (intellectual orders or systems) and respect for experience. . . . The 'confusion' in Crane's work is not inadvertent, as Tate and others believe, but deliberate."[74] Crane's sensibility and his aesthetic, as a matter of fact, wavered uncertainly between Modernism and Romanticism; his compromise was Symboliste. He wanted to believe in absolutes but could not. Consequently, he settled for converting the nuances of relativity into a poetry whose synesthetic "logic" pushed those nuances toward a verbal cohesiveness beyond mere accident. He wanted a statement of the Absolute and settled for a quasi-absolute statement. He wanted a visionary language of things and settled for a language whose vision was intrinsic to the reflexiveness of language itself. Crane knew that if words did not mirror some reality other than themselves, even other than the imagination, they were mirrors facing mirrors, and the poet was, as Tate saw, Alice through the looking glass. Exactly because he was as aware as Tate of the demonic snare of angelism, *The Bridge* seeks to break the closed circuit of his psyche and locate his imagination in his America. Therefore, when Paul asserts that Crane's "poem is not to be judged by anything external to it," that "its form is organic in the primary sense of self-originating and its 'truth' is nothing absolute but the coherence of meanings generated by its language,"[75] he is describing a poem, however great, quite opposite to the one Crane wanted and needed to write.

Crane's career, therefore, illuminates both the continuity and the incompatibility between Romanticism and Modernism. He was adapting a Modernist technique, developed in Symbolisme and its successor, Surrealism, for an increasingly ambiguous epistemology, in the attempt to articulate a Romantic vision of "one arc synoptic of all tides below" (105). *The Bridge* was, in a sense, a self-contradiction from the start; Crane's Modernist masterpiece is a Romantic failure. Frost and Stevens were, in their own ways, as skeptical of absolutes as Crane, but they faced up to the consequences of their skepticism. They could not claim a clarification which was anything but provisional and transitory precisely because it was only aesthetic: the poem as "fiction," as "temporary stay against confusion." Frost's question about "what to make of a diminished thing" resigned him to limits that Crane refused to accept.

As a literary symptom of the solipsistic skepticism of the post-Romantic Modernism, Symbolisme, in its exaltation of the hermetic imagination, induced a powerful influence and strong reactions. Eliot, Tate, and Winters found Symbolisme attractive because it expressed their psychic states, yet for that reason each in turn felt compelled to resist its solipsism by reconstituting a philosophic and literary tradition that antedated Modernism: Eliot and Tate in a notion of Christian Humanism, the unchurched Winters in a notion of Humanism that still based itself in medieval scholasticism and the English Renaissance. Crane's epistemological mistake, if we can call it that, was to rely on Symboliste assumptions and techniques to spring the imagination from the trap Symbolisme represented.

Just as Paul said, the logic of metaphor "builds the poem from the inside out" and thus "creates the field of meaning upon which its coherence depends"; and on that basis, Paul hailed *The Bridge* as one of the major achievements of the Modernist experiment:

> When we recall such early Crane poems as "Porphyro in Akron" and "The Bridge of Estabar," even "For the Marriage of Faustus and Helen," we realize better the difficult resolution of modernist allegiance Crane achieved in *The Bridge*. To be reminded by it so often of Williams is a measure of the distance Crane had come as well as an indication of his particular modernity. We think of *The Bridge* less in relation to *The Waste Land* than to *Paterson*, and chiefly for the reason that both offer us a myth of the imagination, and one that is inalienable from place.[76]

Paul's encomium, however, passes over Crane's expressed intentions for *The Bridge*, intentions that place it between *The Waste Land* and *Paterson*. What makes Williams and Crane and the Eliot of *The Waste Land* Modernist is their attempt at a quasi-absolute and autotelic imaginative creation. But Paul's remarks overlook the fact that Williams and Crane derived from different aspects of Modernism and thus personify a fundamental and clarifying distinction in the development of Modernist poetry.

For that reason, Crane rightly felt a closer affinity to Tate and Eliot than to Williams. Crane did not read Williams with much sympathy, nor would he give Williams serious attention even when pressed to do so by the young, still Modernist Winters. And Williams was equally – and just as understandably – uninterested in and dismissive of Crane's work. For although Imagism and Symbolisme were both Modernist in claiming an integral autonomy for the art object, the two movements saw and said in opposite ways, and these divergent inclinations set up a dialectic within poetic Modernism as it defined itself against, yet in essential issues out of, Romanticism.

As empiricism and skepticism drove a wedge into the Romantic synthesis of subject and object, poets had to align themselves with one side of the split or the other; Symbolisme and Imagism epitomize that division in Modernist aesthetics. Symbolisme turned from the natural symbolism of the Romantics to the registration of subtle internal states in the nuances of words. Arthur Symons' *Symbolist Movement in Literature* (1908) conveniently sums up the connection between the French Symbolistes, aesthetes like Pater and Santayana, and the *fin de siècle* Yeats just a few years before Eliot would write "Prufrock" and "Rhapsody on a Windy Night" and not too long before Stevens would write "Sunday Morning" and "Domination of Black."

But also just a few years before Pound's arrival in London would generate another poetic response to the epistemological dilemma. In 1915, during those years when Pound was thinking out the attitudes which would influence so many later poets, he made the distinction which marks off the Symboliste tendency from the Imagist tendency:

> The Image can be of two sorts. It can arise within the mind. It is then "subjective." External causes play upon the mind, perhaps; if so they are drawn into the mind, fused, transmitted, and emerge in an Image unlike themselves. Secondly, the Image can be objective. Emotion seizing up some external scene or action carries it intact to the mind; and that vortex purges it of all save the essential or dominant or dramatic qualities, and it emerges like the external original.[77]

An individual poet, of course, will at times use both kinds, and Pound even allowed for the subjective Image in Imagism. But the prevailing inclination toward the subjective or the objective Image is what separates the early Eliot from the early Pound, what contrasts Crane and Williams, what differentiates the Symboliste from the Imagist epistemology and technique.

Imagism, in this large and inclusive sense, extended its influence as Pound and Williams extended theirs, and it thereby shaped Objectivist verse in the 1930s and Projective verse in the 1950s. Reacting against the introversion of Symbolisme, Imagism assumed the integrity of the world and turned the imagination out to a peopled landscape, not on the basis of Christian theology (as in the symbolic imagination of Dante) or even explicitly on the basis of Romantic metaphysics (as in the symbolic imagination of Coleridge and Emerson) but on the basis of the human responsibility for the imaginative comprehension of experience. "The verb is 'see,' not 'walk on,'" Pound persisted in saying even at the end of *The Cantos*; "there are only / eyes in all heads, / to be looked out of" sang Charles Olson's Maximus.[78] The Romantic tended to make the poem secondary and inferior to the experience, but the Imagist was Modernist in contending that subject comprehends object most definitively in the aesthetic creation. By completing the encounter between subject and object, the poem became itself an object of experience. Such Imagist attitudes rooted Pound in the Mediterranean landscape, Williams in Rutherford, Charles Reznikoff in Manhattan, Olson in Gloucester as the ground of their poetry.

What the ground of experience offered such poets was not metaphors but images, not the inert material for lively figures, as with the Symboliste, but the vital data of experience. Thinking back to the Imagists, George Oppen underscored the point for his fellow Objectivists:

> It is possible to find a metaphor for anything, an analogue: but the image is encountered, not found; it is an account to the poet's perception, of the act of perception; it is a test of sincerity, a test of conviction, the rare poetic qualities of truthfulness.[79]

There are, of course, other kinds of sincerity and truthfulness which Oppen ignores, but the distinction is crucial. Carl Rakosi wrote that "by being rhetorical or elliptical" the poet evades direct presentation of the experience; "he may make something good, or even better, but the fact remains that he did not retain the integrity of his original impulse."[80]

Hart Crane's notion of the psychology of creation and his resulting sense of the function of form and language associate him, in the Symboliste line of development, with Stevens and Tate and Eliot before the *Quartets*, rather than with the old-fashioned, skeptical naturalism of Frost and Ransom or with the Imagist gestalt of Pound and Williams and H. D. He tried to identify himself with Whitman, in preference to any of his contemporaries, but in fact the poetic stance of *The Bridge* has more in common with *The Waste Land* and, for that matter, with *Notes Towards a Supreme Fiction* than with *Paterson* and *The Cantos*.

The first part of this century followed in the wake of the Romantic zeitgeist and its disintegration, and Modernist experimentation is a manifestation of that philosophic, psychological, and aesthetic ferment. Tate claimed somewhat dolefully that the perfect literary situation arose when the shared values and attitudes that govern and pattern a culture have lost their automatic collective cohesiveness so that they have to be tested, reconstituted, or replaced by the individual consciousness in its own experience and expression. If so, then despite the political upheavals and intellectual crises that seemed to make the artist's function more and more threatened and marginal, the poets who came to a sense of themselves between, say, 1910 and 1920 were in certain ways, whether they knew it or not, in a favored situation as poets. They had to locate themselves in relation to the decadent Romanticism and the emergent Modernism, whether of the Symboliste or the Imagist inclination. The very incoherence of their situation constituted their peculiar historical opportunity, necessitated the drive toward coherence which gave their artistic experimentation its originality and diversity. For sustained achievement, the work of this generation of American poets matches that of the great periods of Western culture, and in English poetry matches, with its own idiosyncratic splendor, that of the Renaissance and Romanticism.

Coda

Yvor Winters and Robinson Jeffers: The Janus-Face of Anti-Modernism

I

During the second and third decades of the twentieth century, the chief poetic talent of the United States took certain new directions, directions that appear to me in the main regrettable. The writers between Robinson and Frost, on the one hand, and Allen Tate and Howard Baker on the other, who remained relatively traditional in manner were with few exceptions minor or negligible; the more interesting writers, as I shall endeavor to show in these pages, were misguided.

That characteristically emphatic and contentious statement[1] opens Yvor Winters' essay "The Experimental School in American Poetry," which became a chapter in his book-length "study of American experimental poetry," *Primitivism and Decadence*, which in turn became part of his monumental attack on the regrettable and dangerous consequences of Romanticism and Modernism, *In Defense of Reason*. Deploying offense as the best defense, Winters launched the forays which made him during the 1930s, 1940s, and 1950s a deadly antagonist of Romanticism and Modernism.

The mature Winters would have liked us to pass over or forget his poetic origins, for he began his career as an experimentalist under the spell of Rimbaud and Williams. However, his intellectual, moral, and aesthetic position shifted in the year or so after he came to Stanford University as a graduate student in 1927. And after he began teaching there the next year, he waged the good fight against both Romanticism and Modernism – in the literary journals and in his correspondence with friends and enemies – from his western fastness far from the bustle of New York and Boston and Chicago, not to mention London and Paris. He almost never ventured into the hostile territory of the eastern establishment and never went abroad. The relative isolation of Stanford, California, at the time suited his temperament and strategy, and he wore as a badge of honor what others took to be quirky and self-righteous eccentricity. He chose to be out of it.

Not far down the coast from Stanford, a little north of Big Sur and just above Point Lobos, named for the sea lions in its coves, Robinson Jeffers had begun after World War I to build Tor House and Hawk Tower with stones rolled up the promontory above Carmel Beach, whence he fronted the Pacific and brooded on the bad turn that the twentieth century and its poetry had taken. Jeffers too seldom traveled east and in some ways was, literarily, more out of it than Winters. He sought no engagement with the enemy, avoided reviewing books and issuing critical statements, had no correspondence with the exemplars of American Modernism, regarded the wars of the journals with an aloofness as cultivated as Winters' embattlement.

Nevertheless, statements like "Poetry, Gongorism and a Thousand Years,"[2] wrung from Jeffers after the Broadway success of his version of *Medea* for the *New York Times Magazine* of January 18, 1948, left no doubt about his dismissive indictment of Modernism. Gongora, a seventeenth-century Spaniard, is presented as the precursor of the Modernist because he used his "remarkable talents" to invent a "strange poetic idiom, a jargon of dislocated constructions and far-fetched metaphors, self-conscious singularity, studious obscurity." But whereas Winters lashed out in defense of reason, Jeffers did so in defense of instinct: "The more extreme tendencies of modernist verse – and shall I say also of painting and sculpture? – are diseases of like nature, later forms of Gongorism; doctrinaire corruptions of instinct." For Jeffers, a great poet of the twentieth century would flee contemporary culture and

> . . . break sharply away from the directions that are fashionable in contemporary poetic literature. [He] would turn away from the self-consciousness and naive learnedness, the undergraduate irony, unnatural metaphors, hiatuses and labored obscurity that are too prevalent in contemporary verse. His poetry would be natural and direct. He would have something new and important to say, and just for that reason he would wish to say it clearly.

So, both Jeffers and Winters seemed (especially from the viewpoint of New York or London or Paris) deliberately eccentric in their western isolation, at the same time that from their own perspectives each rightly recognized the other as adversary. In fact, although they would have hated being paired, together they comprise the Janus-face of anti-Modernism. Kenneth Rexroth, from his central position in the next generation of California poets, recognized Winters as Jeffers' "only serious rival to the title of 'California's leading poet,'"[3] and if that geographic designation marked them as provincials in the eyes of eastern and expatriate establishment, they prized their distance from the centers of fad and fashion. These two Californians were programmatically anti-Modernist, but from programmatic positions so antagonistic to each other that their antagonism raises again the issues of Romanticism and Modernism discussed in the previous chapters and clarifies them through inverse contrasts, as a negative can sometimes clarify a photograph. In the historical argument of this book, Winters' and Jeffers' opposition to each other in opposition to Modernism offers an incisive coda to, and critque of, the Modernist dialectic with Romanticism – and thereby identifies these dissenters, like it or not, as key participants in their literary epoch.

II

Winters made no distinction between Romanticism and Modernism. Together they comprised the "theory of literature and human nature" which has dominated "western civilization for about two and a half centuries," with results that have proved "disastrous in literature" and "dangerous in other departments of human life." He was able to sum up his brief with a debater's graphic succinctness:

> The Romantic theory assumes that literature is mainly or even purely an emotional experience, that man is naturally good, that man's impulses are trustworthy, that the rational faculty is unreliable to the point of being dangerous or evil. The Romantic theory of human nature teaches that if man will rely upon his impulses, he will achieve the good life. When this notion is combined, as it frequently is, with a pantheistic philosophy or religion, it commonly teaches that through surrender to impulse man will not only achieve the good life but will achieve also a kind of mystical union with the Divinity: this, for example, is the doctrine of Emerson.[4]

Emerson became Winters' *bête noire*, not just because he was the most influential American Romantic but also because his ministerial benignity disguised and popularized the demonism inherent in his message of inspired self-reliance. In Winters' rapid-fire logic, "immediate inspiration amounts to the same thing as unrevised reactions to stimuli; unrevised reactions are mechanical; man in a state of perfection is an automaton; an automatic man is insane. Hence, Emerson's perfect man is a madman." For Winters, Emerson masked the shadow face of Poe, just as Whitman masked the shadow face of Crane:

> The doctrine of Emerson and Whitman, if really put into practice, should naturally lead to suicide; in the first place, if the impulses are indulged systematically and passionately, they can lead only to madness; in the second place, death...is not only a release from suffering but is also and inevitably the way to beatitude.[5]

Just as Winters saw Modernism as a philosophic and literary extension of Romanticism, he also tended to ignore the distinctions between Imagism and Symbolisme (the dialectical positions within poetic Modernism) and to condemn both as Modernist manifestations:

> The associationist doctrines [which corrupted psychology and philosophy after the Renaissance] taught that all ideas arise from sensory perceptions, and gradually it came to be thought that all ideas could be expressed in terms of sensory perceptions, but this effort, as in Pound's *Cantos* or in much of Williams ("no ideas but in things"), was doomed to failure. The result is very often a situation in which the poet offers us, or seems to offer us, sense-perceptions for their own sake, or for the sake of whatever vague feelings they may evoke.[6]

Winters saw the dynamic of Modernist poetry in terms of Imagism ("sense-perceptions for their own sake") and Symbolisme ("whatever vague feelings they may evoke"), but from his perspective these "eccentrics...are all motivated by the same ideas about poetry and human nature which destroyed the poetry of the eighteenth and nineteenth centuries: they are nominalists, relativists, associationists, sentimentalists, and denigrators of the rational mind."[7]

Like Eliot, Winters found himself withdrawing past the eighteenth and nineteenth centuries to the Renaissance for his literary models and intellectual affinities; and like Eliot, he rejected the secular Humanism of Irving Babbitt as a specious remedy for Rousseauvian Romanticism. In fact, though Winters presumed Eliot's conversion to be illusory and continued to consider him a Romantic Modernist, Winters' own unecclesiastical conversion was transpiring during the very years which brought Eliot to his public profession as a classicist, royalist, and Anglo-Catholic. As a result, Winters took up his position as an unchurched but explicitly "theistic"[8] Humanist at the same time that Eliot declared himself a Christian Humanist, and both took sixteenth- and seventeenth-century England as their ground of reference.

Winters' early Modernist poetry reveals why he withdrew from Modernism with such vigilant vehemence. *Ash-Wednesday* and *Four Quartets* offer Eliot's own critique of "Gerontion" and *The Waste Land*, but whereas Eliot allowed his early poems to stand as the context for his later development, Winters preferred to bury his early vulnerability to Modernism. He included only a few of the pieces from his first three books of poems in his *Collected Poems* (1952, revised 1960). He did consent to republish *The Early Poems* (1966) shortly before his death, but only reluctantly in order to preclude an unauthorized edition "with no indication of what I had considered my best work." In fact, Winters' "Introduction" claims a double victory over the Modernists by proclaiming the early work "as very good of its kind, quite as good as any of the 'experimental' work of this century," but nonetheless "inferior to my later work."[9]

The early poems indicate that Winters served his apprenticeship under Pound and Williams rather than Eliot. *The Immobile Wind* (1921), *The Magpie's Shadow* (1922), and *The Bare Hills* (1927) develop Winters' distinctive kind of Imagism in the landscape of New Mexico. A poem like "April" presents finely rendered sense impressions with Williamsesque enjambments reminiscent of "The Red Wheelbarrow":

> The little goat
> crops
> new grass lying down
> leaps up eight inches
> into air and
> lands on four feet.
> Not a tremor –
> solid in the
> spring and serious
> he walks away.[10]

What's more, poems like "Two Songs of Advent," which opens *The Immobile Wind*, express a Romantic-mystical identification with nature:

I

On the desert, between pale mountains, our cries –
Far whispers creeping through an ancient shell.

II

Coyote, on delicate mocking feet,
Hovers down the canyon, among the mountains,
His voice running wild in the wind's valleys.

Listen! Listen! for I enter now your thought.

(21)

Through his reading of translations of Japanese and American Indian poetry, Winters was able to concentrate his impressions into one-line images organized into a sequence according to the seasonal cycles. The following excerpts from *The Magpie's Shadow* indicate his active and intense psychological identification with a landscape vibrant with inhuman and transhuman energies:

Myself
Pale mornings, and
I rise.

Winter Echo
Thin air! My mind is gone.

The Hunter
Run! In the magpie's shadow.

Spring
I walk out the world's door.

May
Oh, evening in my hair!

(47–49)

The Whitmanian rush of empathy is paced out and spaced out in Williams-esque moments of perception and Poundian haiku, and indeed the concentration on the moment's Imagistic phrase suggests a ferocity of identification that matches anything in Williams, Pound, or, for that matter, Whitman. These poems leave no doubt that Winters had experienced and expressed the essence of Romanticism and Imagism.

The title of Winters' first important essay, "The Testament of a Stone," published in 1924, attests to the nature mysticism of the early poetry, and its subtitle, "Being Notes on the Mechanics of the Poetic Image," relates it to early Imagist criticism. At this stage, Winters defines a poem as "a stasis in a world of flux and indecision, a permanent gateway to waking oblivion, which is the only infinity and the only rest." Winters means something more intense here than Frost's sense of the poem as a "momentary stay against confusion," something more akin to Keats's rapt wondering, on hearing the nightingale's song, "Do I wake or sleep?": an ecstasy in which the brain is actively receptive, verbalizing with the nerve ends and the antennae of sense organs. Because images provide the aesthetic source and focus for "waking oblivion," the essay derogates as "antiimages" "generalities and concepts," "intellectual correlations that are not evident to the simple senses."[11]

But *The Bare Hills* (1927) began to show another aspect of Winters' Modernism. Winters' need to insist in *The Magpie's Shadow* upon an Imagistic negative capability is only a measure (the same had been true of Keats) of how strong was the counterimpulse to explore the Symboliste convolutions of consciousness. During the early 1920s, he learned to read French and became intoxicated with the French Symbolistes, first Rimbaud and then Baudelaire. *The Magpie's Shadow* has an epigraph from Rimbaud, but the Symboliste influence is not strongly felt until *The Bare Hills*, where the alchemy of the quicksilver mind produces synesthetic effects like these lines from "Quod Tegit Omnia":

> Earth darkens and is beaded
> with a sweat of bushes and
> the bear comes forth;
> the mind, stored with
> magnificence, proceeds into
> the mystery of Time, now
> certain of its choice of
> passion but uncertain of the
> passion's end.
>
> (77)

And a Laforguian Prufrock might be speaking the concluding lines from "The Rows of Cold Trees":

> It was the dumb decision of the
> madness of my youth that left me with
> this cold eye for the fact; that keeps me
> quiet, walking toward a
> stinging end: I am alone,
> and, like the alligator cleaving timeless mud,
> among the blessed who have Latin names.
>
> (98)

Modernist influences persist into the first section of *The Proof* (1930). The remarkable "Song of the Trees" combines the Symboliste synesthesia of the first two lines with the Imagist ecstasy of the rest:

> Belief is blind! Bees scream!
> Gongs! Thronged with light!
>   And I take
> into light, hold light,
> in light I live, I,
> pooled and broken here,
> to watch, to wake above you.
>   Sun,

no seeming, but savage
simplicity, breaks running
for an aeon, stops, shuddering, here.

(135)

It is the consuming intensity of these early experiences that makes them threatening to ego consciousness, and the threat, sometimes only latent but increasingly ominous, presents itself, on the one hand, as the Imagist's mindless capitulation to brute nature (as when the poet's complex human awareness feels itself disintegrate beneath the sun's savage simplicity or yields to the coyote's feral howling) and, on the other hand, as the Symboliste's narcissistic withdrawal into that labyrinthine human awareness where conflicting impressions and blind passions numb and dismember the trapped identity. Winters knew all too well the lures and perils of these disastrous alternatives and named them in the title of his first critical book: Imagistic primitivism on the one hand, Symboliste decadence on the other. The later poems in *The Proof* inaugurate Winters' response to the double threat of primitivism and decadence. They employ the conventions of meter, rhyme, and stanzas to demonstrate the resistance of consciousness to subversion by physical sensation or the unconscious.

Even Winters' most sympathetic critics have seen the psychological causes of Winters' *volte-face* dramatized in the autobiographical short story "The Brink of Darkness" (1932), the only piece of fiction Winters published.[12] Alone (except for his airdale dogs) in the house of his recently dead landlady, the autobiographical narrator feels himself yielding to possession by a conviction of encroaching dissolution: physical death and madness. These twin obsessions finally become personified in the apparition of a demonic shadow image of himself "who gains power over one only in proportion as one recognizes and fears him." He feels himself the victim of "a deliberate and malevolent invasion, an invasion utilizing and augmenting to appalling and shadowy proportions all the most elusive accidents of my life." The fear that the world of light to which his Romantic susceptibility succumbed in "Song of the Trees" was really, to recall Frost's phrase, a "design of darkness to appall" propels Winters' persona-narrator to the point of psychotic derangement: "It was as if there were darkness evenly underlying the brightness of the air, underlying everything, as if I might slip into it at any instant, and as if I held myself where I was by an act of the will from moment to moment."

The narrator is summoned from the brink of the abyss by the necessity to attend to his wounded airdales. The dogs had fled to the surrounding woods, and the first to return is a bitch, her head, mouth, and body bristling hideously and bloodily with the quills of the porcupine she had fought with and tried to bite. The reversion of the domestic animal to the wilderness makes the dog into the figure of the narrator's id, his affinity with the irrational and instinctual violence of physical and unconscious existence. In saving her, he saves himself from his fatal attraction to nature and feeling – that is to say, to death and madness. He draws out the quills, one by excruciating one, and the gruesome ministrations become an "immersion in the brute blood of the bitch" which is at once an exorcism of demons and a baptism into a different psychological and moral existence, vigilant against the dark encroachment of nature and the unconscious. The story is unique in Winters' work; there is nothing remotely like it elsewhere in his published writings. But he allowed the story to stand as powerful and unimpeachable testimony to the fact that, once having lived the nightmare through and wakened to the logic of its illogic, he set the patriarchal mind and will against his susceptibility to dissolution in the material, maternal chaos. The last words of the story are: "I would never return."

The assertion of reason against the threats of death and madness became the consequent, the obsessive, theme of the *Collected Poems*. The sonnet "To William Dinsmore Briggs Conducting His Seminar" salutes Winters' Stanford mentor in the abstract, Latinate diction and discursive, Latinate syntax characteristic of the poet's later style:

> Amid the walls' insensate white, some crime
> Is redefined above the sunken mass
> Of crumbled years; logic reclaims the crass,
> Frees from historic dross the invidious mime.
> Your fingers spin the pages into Time;
> And in between, moments of darkness pass
> Like undiscovered instants in the glass,
> Amid the image, where the demons climb.
>
> Climb and regard and mean, yet not emerge.
> And in the godless thin electric glare
> I watch your face spun momently along
> Till the dark moments close and wrinkles verge
> On the definitive and final stare:
> And that hard book will now contain this wrong.[13]

Language mediates between the unillusioned intelligence and its field of activity: the "crime" of temporal experience, the "invidious mime" of art. In making mental and verbal discriminations which order those complications into a coordinated and subordinated syntax lies the chance to bring "moments of darkness" to the light of comprehension by framing them in the mirror of mind and art. The "hard book" of the concluding line is not just the work under discussion in the seminar but the critical scrutiny and judgment which Briggs personifies: art is in that sense critical, and both art and criticism "contain this wrong," allow the demons to "climb and regard and mean, yet not emerge."

Form, therefore, is the aim and achievement of the human mind and will: "not something outside the poet" (as the Romantic might claim) or "something 'aesthetic,' and superimposed upon his moral content" (as the Modernist might claim) but, rather, "essentially a part, in fact it may be the decisive part, of the moral content." Winters honors Briggs when the turning of the sonnet demonstrates a "correlation between the control evinced within a poem and the control within the poet behind it."[14]

The three stanzas of couplets in "The Slow Pacific Swell" perform the same function, and it will be instructive to keep this poem in mind when we turn to Jeffers' evocations of the Pacific coastline. Here again Winters links nature and the unconscious as the irrational chaos without and within:

> Far out of sight forever stands the sea,
> Bounding the land with pale tranquillity.
> When a small child, I watched it from a hill
> At thirty miles or more. The vision still
> Lies in the eye, soft blue and far away:
> The rain has washed the dust from April day;
> Paint-brush and lupine lie against the ground;
> The wind above the hill-top has the sound
> Of distant water in unbroken sky;
> Dark and precise the little steamers ply –
> Firm in direction they seem not to stir.
> That is illusion. The artificer
> Of quiet, distance holds me in a vise
> And holds the ocean steady to my eyes.
>
> Once when I rounded Flattery, the sea
> Hove its loose weight like sand to tangle me
> Upon the washing deck, to crush the hull;
> Subsiding, dragged flesh at the bone. The skull
> Felt the retreating wash of dreaming hair.
> Half drenched in dissolution, I lay bare.
> I scarcely pulled myself erect; I came
> Back slowly, slowly knew myself the same.
> That was the ocean. From the ship we saw
> Gray whales for miles: the long sweep of the jaw,
> The blunt head plunging clean above the wave.
> And one rose in a tent of sea and gave
> A darkening shudder; water fell away;
> The whale stood shining, and then sank in spray.
>
> A landsman, I. The sea is but a sound.
> I would be near it on a shady mound,
> And hear the steady rushing of the deep
> While I lay stinging in the sand with sleep.
> I have lived inland long. The land is numb.
> It stands beneath the feet, and one may come
> Walking securely, till the sea extends
> Its limber margin, and precision ends.
> By night a chaos of commingling power,
> The whole Pacific hovers hour by hour.
> The slow Pacific swell stirs on the sand,
> Sleeping to sink away, withdrawing land,
> Heaving and wrinkled in the moon, and blind;
> Or gathers seaward, ebbing out of mind.

(60–61)

Winters' sea poem calls to mind others we have read, each typical of its poet: "The Idea of Order at Key West" and "Once by the Pacific," "The Helmsman" and "The Run to the Sea," the Dionysian Canto 2 and "The Dry Salvages" and "Voyages." Winters is, characteristically, less overtly concerned with aesthetics than Stevens, less explicitly teleological than Frost, not mythological like H. D. or cyclic like Williams, not Dionysian like Pound or incarnational like Eliot, and not at all erotically ecstatic like Crane. In terms of Winters' anti-Romanticism, "The Slow Pacific Swell" stands as a conflation of "Tintern Abbey" and "Peele Castle," an inversion of Whitman's sea elegies, with their lulling dissolution in the mother sea. Here the child's ignorant illusion of the sea's tranquil steadiness (first stanza) is shattered by the experience of almost drowning in the violent waters from which monsters break in awesome power (second stanza), so that he is ever after a landsman by determination (third stanza).

As always with sea voyages, this one risks mind as well as body. The poem is as much about mental crack-up as it is about shipwreck – perhaps more so, and words and phrases like "out of sight," "vision," "illusion," "dreaming hair," and "ebbing out of mind" keep the reader aware of the psychological dimension of the poem.

For, as in "The Brink of Darkness," the affinity between nature and the unconscious puts consciousness at jeopardy from within as well as without. Like Ransom, Winters faced the equilibrist's dilemma: "Earth and mind are not one, / But they are so entwined" (122). Physical and psychological survival requires consciousness either to hold nature and the unconscious at a standoff (as the first line to follow suggests) or, better still, if it were possible, to subordinate them (as the second line suggests): "Wisdom and wilderness are here at poise, / Ocean and forest are the mind's device" (121). In either case, there is no more of that early exultation in the surrender of consciousness to nature and instinct: "Thin air! My mind is gone" (*Early Poems*, p. 48).

So the shaping of language into form is the rational mind's device for taming nature and the unconscious into wisdom; its literally lifesaving function is not the enactment of experience, as the Romantics and Modernists would have it, but the conforming of experience to normative values – in other words, not language as gestalt or symbol but language as judgment. Winters came to call his sort of "absolutist," "moralistic"[15] poetry "post-Symbolist." The designation indicated Winters' choice of the conceptual Symbolistes over the perceptual Imagists, but the "post" prefix specified a redirection toward rational discrimination, moral judgment, and verbal denotation that countervened and superseded the contrary Symboliste tendencies. The post-Symbolist aesthetic brought Winters full circle from his earlier notion, in "The Testament of a Stone," of the poem as a "gateway to waking oblivion." Now he considered a poem not an object of experience or an experienced object, as did the Imagists and Symbolistes, but a strategically distanced reflection on experience.

Poetry should aim at making an intellectual statement – not the "direct presentation" of the Imagists or the ambiguous indirection of the Symbolistes.

When words are used as ideograms for things or as correlatives for emotional states, their denotative and conceptual purity is corrupted with sense impressions and emotional associations and to that extent is subverted from the effort to master the mindlessness of nature and of instinct. Yes, language inescapably shares in our corrupted and fallen human estate, but all the more scrupulously should sense impressions and emotional associations be submitted to the criterion of "rational understanding." Like that of other poets, Winters' distinguishing linguistic sense was determined by his epistemology, and he summed up the subjection of feeling to thought and will with typical declarative terseness in the "Foreword" written for *In Defense of Reason*:

> The poem is a statement in words about a human experience. Words are primarily conceptual, but through use and because human experience is not purely conceptual, they have acquired connotations of feeling. The poet makes his statement in such a way as to employ both concept and connotation as efficiently as possible. The poem is good in so far as it makes a defensible rational statement about a given human experience (the experience need not be real but must be in some sense possible) and at the same time communicates the emotion which ought to be motivated by that rational understanding of that experience.[16]

In that programmatic "Foreword," Winters distinguished the "theory of literature which I defend" from other theories: first, from the merely "didactic," which could be more properly relegated to the field of religion and ethics; second, from the "hedonistic," which included Poe and the French Symbolistes and contemporaries like Eliot and Stevens; and third, from the "romantic," which stemmed in America from Emerson and included the theories of primitivists like Whitman and Jeffers and Imagists like Williams. Winters' polemical rage could heat his defense of reason to such intemperate statements as this: "The basis of Evil is in emotion; Good rests in the power of rational selection in action, as a preliminary to which the emotion in any situation must be as far as possible eliminated, and, in so far as it cannot be eliminated, understood."[17] Against the primitivism of Imagism and the decadence of Symbolisme, an embattled Winters raised a standard of reason so pristine that its vehement defense fell prey to the taint of the passion it thought it denied. Winters blamed Emerson and Whitman for the absolutizing of emotion that corrupted the modern mind and killed Hart Crane, without ever realizing that his fear of feeling had led him into an angelism of pure mind as absolute and irrational as Crane's angelism of pure feeling:

> If we were all to emulate Hart Crane, the result would be disastrous to literature and to civilization; it is necessary to understand the limitations of Hart Crane, which are of the utmost seriousness; but when we understand those limitations, we are in a position to profit by his virtues with impunity, and his virtues are sometimes very great. If we are not aware of his limitations but are sufficiently sensitive to guess in some fashion at his virtues, he may easily take possession of us wholly. This difficulty indicates the function of criticism.[18]

Although the growing tendency in Winters' criticism toward rigid and categorical pronouncements makes some of the late essays read like unconscious parodies, statements like the ones previously cited must be understood as acts of projection. That is to say, Winters' accusations and renunciations are launched with such vehemence because they are aimed, first and foremost, at Winters himself; it is the Hart Crane in him who must be exorcised to avoid the Symboliste's fate. The primitivism in nature and himself which much of his early poetry expressed was lived out in his only short story to the brink of madness and death, and though his poems thereafter sought to mediate the dark threat, the best of them belie what sometimes sounds in the criticism like an equally dangerous severance of head from heart. Though Winters' students and disciples view his poetry and his criticism as consistently of a piece, it is also possible to read in Winters' career the thwarting of the poet by the embattled and cranky critic; all but a handful of his poems had been written by 1943. Nevertheless, to the very end (and a couple of his best and most moving poems came in the 1950s), the poems acknowledged that it is the tangled entwinement of earth and mind which exacts the difficult moral judgment of language.

It is easy to see how Winters' seeming paranoia made it easy, sometimes too easy, to dismiss him as a crank. The intensity of his early commitment to Williams' Imagism required him to comment on Williams for the rest of his life, and his last comment is his most intemperate:

> William Carlos Williams..., in his view of life and poetry, was an uncompromising romantic. It is surprising, in light of this fact, that he appears to have been a devoted husband, father, and physician, eminently virtuous and practical in these capacities, and often naively shocked by the behavior of some of his bohemian acquaintances who held the same ideas but acted upon them. He was a thorough bore in print except on a few occasions. He believed in the surrender to emotion and to instinct as the only way to wisdom and to art.... Williams' artist would have no need for ideas and no awareness of them; in fact, he would display no signs of consciousness whatever....it is foolish to think of Williams as a great poet; the bulk of his work is not even readable. He is not even an anti-intellectual poet in any intelligible sense of the term, for [he] did not know what the intellect is. He was a foolish and ignorant man, but at moments a fine stylist.[19]

The passage confirms Winters' continuing personal need to exorcise his profound susceptibility to Williams' influence – that is to say, to the influence of Romanticism and Modernism. But unfortunately and paradoxically, the effect of such posturing has been self-defeating because it has deflected attention from the substance of his critique of Romanticism and Modernism and from his considerable achievements as a poet, including the experimental work of the 1920s. It has taken a number of years since his death in 1968 to deconstruct the polemics and see Winters for what he was: a man whose resistance to the temper of the age bespoke both the intelligence and the passion of his involvement in its most volatile issues.

III

Not surprisingly, neither Winters nor Jeffers sought a meeting, though only a hundred or so miles of coastline highway separated them. Winters rejected Jeffers without hesitation as a more primitive instance than Williams of the Romantic's intellectual, moral, and aesthetic deficiencies. In fact, because during the 1920s and 1930s Jeffers enjoyed a popularity unusual among poets, he became a particular target for Winters' attack. In his reviews of Jeffers' books, Winters dismissed him as devoid of intellectual purpose, ethical principles, and aesthetic form; at one point, he sneered that Jeffers' Inhumanist position left him but one "simple and mechanical" solution – "namely, suicide, a device to which he has, I believe, never resorted." "The Experimental School in American Poetry" in *Primitivism and Decadence* begins its anatomy of poetic methods with an analysis of the method of repetition, the simplest and crudest of all, and, after citing repetition as the "chief method of Whitman," Winters immediately takes up Jeffers as its leading contemporary exemplar.[20] His remarks are an abridged version of his earlier review of *Dear Judas*, and the attack in Winters' subsequent reviews never wavered or relented:

> Self-repetition has been the inevitable effect of anti-intellectualist doctrine on all of its supporters...if life is denied, the only theme is the rather sterile and monotonous one of the denial. Similarly, those poets who flee from form, which is infinitely variable,...can achieve only the uniformity of chaos; and those individuals who endeavor to escape morality, which is personal form and controlled direction,...achieve nothing save the uniformity of mechanism. [Jeffers'] aims are badly thought out and are essentially trivial.[21]

And again: "The book [in this instance, *Thurso's Landing*] is composed almost wholly of trash."[22]

With characteristic aloofness, Jeffers never replied directly to Winters' attack or even seemed to take notice. There is no mention of Winters in his *Selected Letters*, and his belated, indirect response in "Poetry, Gongorism and a Thousand Years" would have seemed to Winters merely a concession rather than a refutation of his point:

> Poetry is not a civilizer, rather the reverse, for great poetry appeals to the most primitive instincts. It is not necessarily a moralizer; it does not necessarily improve one's character; it does not even teach good manners. It is a beautiful work of nature, like an eagle or a high sunrise.[23]

Unlike Winters, Jeffers resolved for the most part not to traffic with either advocates or adversaries of the Modernist camp. Detachment was more dignified and freed him to consolidate his own position. The poetry would be his best witness in the short as well as the long run. Jeffers' correspondence is significant for what it does not say as much as for what it says. The published letters contain not even a reference to Williams, H. D., Moore, Stevens, Ransom, Tate, or Crane. There are two passing references each to Eliot, Pound, and Frost, polite replies to Edwin Arlington Robinson and Sara

Teasdale, and some letters to Mark Van Doren. But Jeffers' closest literary friendship was with his fellow Californian George Sterling, during the two years before Sterling's suicide in 1926. What drew Jeffers to Sterling was less the geographic connection than his distance from Modernist poetics. When Sterling worried about the conventionality of his technique, Jeffers wrote back assuringly: "The sun of blank verse hasn't set, certainly not, has the sun of the hexameter?"[24]

In fact, the literary preferences expressed in the letters establish how much of a Romantic Jeffers was. "English poetry has more significance for me than American. That is, poetry of the past – certainly not of the present."[25] The letter cites the influence of Shelley, Wordsworth, Yeats, Milton, Tennyson, Swinburne, and Rossetti. As for American Romantics: "Emerson's a great and good man. We've only had two great men yet in American literature. – Poe is the other"; "Poe captured me when I was very young. . . . Emerson interested me; Whitman never did." No mention of Dickinson at all, and as for Thoreau, an anti-establishment isolato like himself: "I am ashamed to say that I never read anything of Thoreau's."[26]

The odd note in Jeffers' acknowledgment of Romantic forebears is his emphatic disclaimer about Whitman. Una Jeffers wrote with underscorings: "*R. J. says he owes less to W. W. than to most other poets of his era and sees no reason to link W. W. and R. J.*"[27] But such denials convinced no one. Both admirers and enemies saw the relation between Jeffers and Whitman, though it was in many respects a shadow relationship, and Winters was correct in linking them as Romantic prophets of a mystique of physical instinct whose method was repetition; this affinity of naturalistic mysticism in both poets produced their oracular directness and clarity of emphasis, their paratactic syntax of parallelism and repetition, the cumulative rhythms of their long and irregular unrhymed lines. Like Whitman, Jeffers associated the aesthetic emotion with "the bodily senses" and verse rhythm with material rhythms: "physics, biology, the beat of the blood, the tidal environments of life to which life is formed."[28]

No doubt Jeffers found himself repelled, as were Pound and Williams, by Whitman's optimism, the philosophic and political idealism, the seemingly easy and all-embracing democratic camaraderie. Like Winters, Jeffers was a Calvinist; however, as we shall see, Jeffers took the Calvinist counterstrain within Romanticism itself, which impelled Byron to dissent from Wordsworth and Poe from Emerson, and made that pessimistic Calvinist determinism part of his distinctive kind of pantheism.

Perhaps, as William Everson, Jeffers' best critic and only poetic disciple, claims, Whitman's free verse appeared "too disingenuously obvious, too transparently *available*, for [Jeffers'] classical formation, his reserved aristocratic instinct."[29] Jeffers preferred to think of his philosophical differences with Whitman (he said that he balanced his Romanticism with Lucretius' materialistic naturalism) as allowing a prosody governed by older conventions: Old Testament verses, the Anglo-Saxon and Germanic alliterative line with its marking of stresses instead of feet, and, most important, classical quantitative measures.[30] Still, Jeffers' gauge was flexible enough to accommodate Whitman: "I can't propose any rule, it is a matter of ear and rhythmic sense." Right from the start, a reviewer of *Roan Stallion, Tamar and Other Poems* made the connection: "Nothing since Whitman has had as vigorous a beat as these rough lyrics."[31] And Everson's study of Jeffers' versification concludes that "more than any other American, [Jeffers] was able to profit by [Whitman's] exhilarating innovations" while "masking [their] abiding presence under his...own prosodic system."[32]

Among his contemporaries, Jeffers, with his Irish roots, considered Yeats a great poet, but Yeats is the poet who most obviously bridged the nineteenth and twentieth centuries and personified the transition, and connection, between Romanticism and Modernism. Jeffers' roots were in the nineteenth century, and a remark to his friend Albert Bender indicates how far removed his sensibility was from the contemporary ferment: "There is no more admirable figure in American literature to-day than Edwin Markham, no one I'd rather meet or hear speaking."[33] If as late as 1927 Jeffers considered the author of "The Man with the Hoe" a literary "giant," what indeed could he possibly make of the stirrings in the literary centers of New York, London, Paris? He was not unaware of what had been going on there. His letters and prefaces record his ideological disaffection, but it was a disaffection of informed choice.

When the publisher insisted that Jeffers provide an "Introduction" to the Modern Library edition of *Roan Stallion, Tamar and Other Poems*, the two books that had made him a literary sensation à la Byron, he took the occasion to define his originality against that of his contemporaries:

> The more advanced contemporary poets were attaining it [originality] by going farther and farther along the way that perhaps Mallarmé's aging dream had shown them, divorcing poetry from reason and ideas, bringing it nearer to music, finally to astonish the world with what would look like pure nonsense and would be pure poetry. No doubt these lucky writers were imitating each other, instead of imitating Shelley and Milton as I had done.[34]

But the irony of the word "lucky" here is borne out by Jeffers' conviction that Mallarmé's Symboliste direction led to an empty verbal echo chamber:

> Mallarmé and his followers, renouncing intelligibility in order to concentrate the music of poetry, had turned off the road into a narrowing lane. Their successors could only make further renunciations; ideas had gone, now meter had gone, imagery would have to go; then recognizable emotions would have to go; perhaps at last even words might have to go or give up their meaning, nothing to be left but musical syllables. Every advance required the elimination of some aspect of reality, and what could it profit me to know the direction of modern poetry if I did not like the direction?[35]

But was there no direction to try other than Symboliste abstraction of feeling from physical reality into the convolutions of language and perhaps even only of musical sound? What about the Imagist commitment to presentation of the thing? "Someone must be setting the pace, going farther than anyone had dared to go before. Ezra Pound perhaps?" The Imagist direction seemed more likely than the Symboliste, but no, its scope was too restricted and its tone too refined, its aesthetic too formalist and Modernist, its self-consciousness undermining its dealings with nature: "I wish I liked [Pound's] work better, but indeed I have read very little of it."[36]

Jeffers dated the sudden emergence of his original voice and manner from the rather tepid Romanticism and conventional meters of *Flagons and Apples* (1912) and *Californians* (1916) by two related events that transformed his life: his marriage to Una Call Kuster in 1913 and their settling the next year – for the rest of their lives, as it turned out – on the Carmel coast:

> Here was life purged of its ephemeral accretions. . .contemporary life that was also permanent life; and not shut from the modern world but conscious of it and related to it; capable of expressing its spirit, but unencumbered by the mass of poetically irrelevant details and complexities that make a civilization.

This submission of the assertive ego to marriage located in cyclic time and in native place quickened a conversion from which he worked out his pantheist sense of nature and a philosophy of human nature that he sometimes called "human naturalism" and came in later years to call "Inhumanism." And Una, he reiterated again and again, was ever the anima-muse, the *genius loci*: "My nature is cold and undiscriminating; she excited and focused it, gave it eyes and nerves and sympathies. She never saw any of my poems until they were finished and typed, yet by her presence and conversation she has co-authored every one of them."[37]

It is worth noting, in the context of Winters' charge of anti-intellectualism, that Jeffers' emphasis on the instinctual source and appeal of poetry assumed rather than precluded a philosophic and religious stance, which he alternately elaborated in long narrative and dramatic poems and in shorter lyrics that were by turn descriptive, meditative, and political. This 1951 response to an inquiry from the American Humanist Association provides a succinct recapitulation of his beliefs:

> The word Humanism refers primarily to the Renaissance interest in art and literature rather than in theological doctrine [Winters was such a Humanist]; and personally I am content to leave it there. "Naturalistic Humanism" – in the modern sense – is no doubt a better philosophical attitude than many others; but the emphasis seems wrong; "human naturalism" would seem to me more satisfactory, with but little accent on the "human." Man is a part of nature, but a nearly infinitesimal part; the human race will cease after a while and leave no trace, but the great splendors of nature will go on. Meanwhile most of our time and energy are necessarily spent on human affairs; that can't be prevented, though I think it should be minimized; but for philosophy, which is an endless research for truth, and for contemplation, which can be a sort of worship, I would suggest that the immense beauty of the earth and the outer universe, the divine "nature of things," is a more

rewarding object. Certainly it is more ennobling. It is a source of strength; the other [i.e., humanistic individualism] of distraction.[38]

The label "naturalistic humanism" put the noun's emphasis on the wrong term for Jeffers and suggested something more like Emerson's self-reliant Transcendentalism; "human naturalism" seemed closer to his pantheism, which grounded itself in biology and physics rather than metaphysics. Like Frost he vociferously proclaimed himself a Western materialist-realist in opposition to the subjective idealism of the Orient: "the Indian feeling that the world is illusory and the soul – the *I* – makes it, is very foreign to me."[39] The early "Credo" makes an important statement about the cosmological and epistemological difference. Where the Oriental tends to think of all seemingly material phenomena, even the vast Pacific, as insubstantial phantasms of consciousness, Jeffers affirms the transhuman endurance – by the measure of human time, the eternity – of material things:

> Multitude stands in my mind but I think that the ocean in the bone vault is only
> The bone vault's ocean: out there is the ocean's;
> The water is the water, the cliff is the rock, come shocks and flashes of reality. The mind
> Passes, the eye closes, the spirit is a passage:
> The beauty of things was born before eyes and sufficient to itself; the heart-breaking beauty
> Will remain when there is no heart to break for it.[40]

It is also clear from his statement to the American Humanist Association that despite Winters' charges of amorality, Jeffers' pantheism had moral implications and effects. Inhumanism did not obviate moral responsibility. Jeffers acknowledged that unlike animals, which are by nature amoral, conscious humans bear the moral burden for their lives and dealings with others, and so in nature humans are the only species capable of morality – and thus vulnerable to immorality. The narrative and dramatic poems examine, in terms of the violent lives of the characters, the tragic consequences of the ego-centered failure to live up to that idiosyncratic responsibility. The responsibility and the failure define the tragic human estate.

Jeffers' Calvinist sensibility came in part from his minister father, who had taught theology at a Presbyterian seminary, but the son preferred to understand original sin in terms of biological accident or evolutionary error rather than Calvinist doctrine. Morality, and so immorality, are peculiarly but merely human manifestations. The drama of Jeffers' writings stems from his fixation on the fact that our species's unique evolution of consciousness has endowed us with mind and will, but mind and will are depraved by the egotism which is a condition and consequence of consciousness.

On the other hand, ego consciousness is fortunately limited to our species, so that the rest of material existence remains inviolate and impervious to human morality or immorality. "Birds and Fishes," one of Jeffers' last poems,

almost makes the mistake of attributing greed and malice to the feeding of
seabirds on fishes but then recovers to find in the violence of the scene a
manifestation of the "beauty of God":

> Every October millions of little fish come along the shore,
> Coasting this granite edge of the continent
> On their lawful occasions: but what a festival for the sea-fowl.
> What a witches' sabbath of wings
> Hides the dark water. The heavy pelicans shout "Haw!" like Job's friend's
> warhorse
> And dive from the high air, the cormorants
> Slip their long black bodies under the water and hunt like wolves
> Through the green half-light. Screaming, the gulls watch,
> Wild with envy and malice, cursing and snatching. What a hysterical greed!
> What a filling of pouches! the mob
> Hysteria is nearly human – these decent birds! – as if they were finding
> Gold in the street. It is better than gold,
> It can be eaten: and which one in all this fury of wild-fowl pities the fish?
> No one certainly. Justice and mercy
> Are human dreams, they do not concern the birds nor the fish nor eternal
> God.
> However – look again before you go.
> The wings and the wild hungers, the wave-worn skerries, the bright quick
> minnows
> Living in terror to die in torment –
> Man's fate and theirs – and the island rocks and immense ocean beyond, and
> Lobos
> Darkening above the bay: they are beautiful?
> That is their quality: not mercy, not mind, not goodness, but the beauty of
> God.[41]

For Jeffers, then, as for Emerson, original sin consisted in a fall into ego
consciousness, which sets mind against nature and individuals against one
another. The melodramatic violence and sexuality of the California narratives
and the adaptations of Greek plays (which brought Jeffers his fame and comprise the larger part of his writing) enact the psychic and moral dislocations
which drive egotistic human beings to destruction and self-destruction. These
longer works reflect Jeffers' readings in Jung and particularly in Freud,
whose ego psychology offered scientific, secular confirmation of his Calvinist determinism. But where for Emerson, as for Jung, consciousness also
opened the possibility of a triumph beyond tragedy by enabling reintegra-
tion of ego into selfhood, Jeffers was, like Freud, more dubious about that
possibility, but unlike Freud, he pointed the way out of the conundrum by
a regression from ego consciousness. The late poem "Carmel Point" concludes:

> Meanwhile the image of pristine beauty
> Lives in the very grain of the granite,
> Safe as the endless ocean that climbs our cliff. – As for us:

> We must uncenter our minds from ourselves;
> We must unhumanize our views a little, and become confident
> As the rock and ocean we were made from.[42]

Consequently, despite Jeffers' Inhumanist pessimism about the human condition, and despite his acid retort to moralistic critics like Winters that art need not necessarily improve one's character, he considered the effect of poetry, even of his violent melodramas, to be cathartic and therapeutic for himself and his audience; his poetry carries us, or at least directs us, out of ourselves by enacting the aberrant human tragedy to the point of oblivion in divine nature. To George Sterling he explained his intention in *The Tower Beyond Tragedy*, a version of the Agamemnon plays: "My idea was to present as a part of the action, the culminating part, that liberation which the witness is supposed to feel – to let one of the agonists be freed, as the audience is expected to be, from passion and the other birthmarks of humanity. Therefore *beyond* tragedy – tragedy and what results."[43]

But Jeffers had read Jung as well as Freud, and he responded to Jung's effort to move beyond the ego psychology of Freud by proposing a theory of archetypes as psychic instincts toward an integrated participation in the cosmos. In the early love lyric "Divinely Superfluous Beauty," which is placed close to the tragic title narrative of the *Tamar* volume, the erotic and ecstatic love between Jeffers and Una cracks their ego isolation, and their rooted union paradoxically releases them into the land and sea and air of their sublime place:

> The storm-dances of gulls, the barking games of seals,
> Over and under the ocean...
> Divinely superfluous beauty
> Rules the game, presides over destinies, makes trees grow
> And hills tower, waves fall.
> The incredible beauty of joy
> Stars with fire the joining of lips, O let our loves too
> Be joined, there is not a maiden
> Burns and thirsts for love
> More than my blood for you, by the shore of seals while the wings
> Weave like a web in the air
> Divinely superfluous beauty.[44]

Though the marriage was a life bond, its stormy course taught Jeffers, if he needed the lesson, that such harmonious moments of ego loss are rare. Nevertheless, they are the moments toward which and by which life is directed. Jeffers knew that the fall into consciousness could be willed away only through suicide: a choice he consistently rejected as cowardly (though Winters taunted him with inconsistency in this regard). Instead, he assumed the uniquely human responsibility of consciousness and brought to the encounter with "divinely superfluous beauty" the comprehension unique to consciousness. Only humans can encompass subject and object in the very surrender of subject to object. Jeffers agreed with the Keatsian paradox that the climax of consciousness comes with the negative capability which extinguishes ego in otherness. The highest function of poetry, then, is the articulation of ego-negating moments in preparation for the final quenching of consciousness in biological death.

Una's death in 1950 diminished life and poetry, just as Jeffers foresaw it would, but the rapturous anticipation of unconsciousness in nature produced some powerful lyrics in his remaining years. "Vulture" is a final testament to pantheistic death and resurrection:

> I had walked since dawn and lay down to rest on a bare hillside
> Above the ocean. I saw through half-shut eyelids a vulture wheeling high up in heaven,
> And presently it passed again, but lower and nearer, its orbit narrowing, I understood then
> That I was under inspection. I lay death still and heard the flight-feathers
> Whistle above me and make their circle and come nearer.
> I could see the naked red head between the great wings
> Bear downward staring. I said, "My dear bird, we are wasting time here.
> These old bones will still work; they are not for you." But how beautiful he looked, gliding down
> On those great sails; how beautiful he looked, veering away in the sea-light over the precipice. I tell you solemnly
> That I was sorry to have disappointed him. To be eaten by that beak and become part of him, to share those wings and those eyes –
> What a sublime end of one's body, what an enskyment, what a life after death.[45]

The desultory pace of the opening description of the wheeling vulture quickens with "But how beautiful he looked," and the poet's sudden and horrifying desire to serve as carrion for the beautiful, powerful bird of prey reaches the limit of consciousness and articulation in his "enskyment" in the blood and sinew of the barbaric bird. Across the continent from Paumanok, Jeffers the Romantic Inhumanist found himself in a place much like that of Whitman the Romantic individualist at the end of "Song of Myself":

> The spotted hawk swoops by and accuses me, he complains of my gab and my loitering.
> I too am not a bit tamed, I too am untranslatable,
> I sound my barbaric yawp over the roofs of the world.
> . . . .
> I bequeath myself to the dirt to grow from the grass I love,
> If you want me again look for me under your boot-soles.

Jeffers explained the epistemology of his "sensuous mysticism" (that is, of his experience of the divinity of nature) in terms of a correspondence between subject and object, human and inhuman and transhuman, which would have been familiar to Emerson and Whitman, Coleridge and Keats. One letter admits that although the human attribution of a transcendent correspondence with brute nature may be a "delusion," the possibility that it may instead be "mystical certainty" makes life and poetry interdependent:

I did not in my verses intend a distinction between aesthetic experience and what you call sensual mysticism. The intention in poetry is not primarily analytical; in my experience the two feelings were wound together, and so I expressed them. . . .

When I wrote "beauty is thy human name" I was trying to express the feeling, which still remains with me, that this human and in itself subjective sense of beauty is occasioned by some corresponding quality or temper or arrangement in the object. Why else should a quite neutral thing – a wave of the sea or a hill against the sky – be somehow lovely and loveworthy, and become more so the more it is realized by contemplation? . . . The feeling of deep earnestness and nobility in natural objects and in the universe: – these are human qualities, not mineral or vegetable, but it seems to me I would not impute them into the objects unless there were something in not-man that corresponds to these qualities in man. This may be called delusion, or it may be called mystical certainty, there is no external proof either way; and it is probably not essential to the religious attitude we are discussing, though with me it is part of it.[46]

American Romanticism had lost a lot of baggage on the way west. The collapse of Romantic idealism after Whitman left Jeffers *in extremis*, but his greatness came when he was inspired at land's end to reach down and recover "mystical certainty" in the tidal currents and the quick of the stone on his own Lucretian, Calvinist, Darwinian, Freudian, Jungian ground.

So Jeffers did not abdicate the responsibilities of consciousness after all, as Winters accused him of doing, but he did construe them in terms opposite to Winters'. Jeffers bent consciousness to release rather than to thwart, to realize rather than to correct, the instinctual life of nature and the unconscious. Where Winters rejected Modernism for its Romantic abdication of consciousness, Jeffers rejected Modernism for its assertion of consciousness, its abdication of unconsciousness. In other words, Winters rejected Modernism for its Romanticism; Jeffers, for its anti-Romanticism. Both were right – and wrong. The dialogue between Winters and Jeffers demonstrates again that the way in which the tenets of Romanticism and Modernism slip into and out of each other is the elusive key to reading the ideology of the literary epoch.

IV

In the topography of American poetry, the long way from Paumanok to Point Lobos led through Paterson, and along the way, Romanticism and Modernism, Symbolisme and Imagism crisscrossed. The crossings, marking connection as well as divergence, map different epistemologies for the poetic process and different ontologies for the poem.

What linked Williams in one direction to Whitman and in the other to Jeffers is the same factor that distinguished them all from the Symbolistes in France and the United States, namely, a prevailingly perceptual rather than conceptual notion of art. Pound's distinction provides a useful formula for apprehending the elusive dialectic between Romanticism and Modernism and within each.[47] The perceptual artist, says Pound, is the subject "*receiving* impressions" from the phenomena of the objective world, recognizing significance in, and deriving meaning from, those encounters, submitting identity and art to the shaping influence of circumstances and forces outside of the observing, responding individual. In contrast to the artist toward whom "perception moves," Pound sees the other kind of artist "as directing a certain fluid force against circumstance, as *conceiving* instead of merely reflecting and observing." The conceptual artist employs mind and will and imagination to confer significance on the inchoate impressions of external objects by imposing on the medium an invented aesthetic coherence. In the perceptual mode, art presents the subjectifying of objective reality; in the conceptual mode, art presents the objectifying of subjective reality.

The Romantic response to Cartesian rationalism, which had dangerously intensified the split between subject and object as the ideological force of theological and philosophic syntheses waned in Western culture, was to subsume subject and object in a metaphysics of the imagination. The initial thrust of Romanticism at the turn of the nineteenth century was predominantly perceptual: the individual had sight and insight; in mystical or at least intuitive moments, subjects could apprehend the reality of objects, both their phenomenal and their noumenal reality, intimating the absolute in the contingent. But such moments of coherence were difficult for the individual to reach and construe, much less to sustain. So the psychological instability of those isolated peak moments impelled Romanticism, from the start, to hover and hesitate, even to retreat from the perceptual to the conceptual pole. Symbolisme developed out of Romanticism by midcentury and anticipated the skeptical alienation of Modernism.

The Modernist response to the collapse of Romantic idealism was to strip the imagination of metaphysical prerogatives and reconstitute it as the supreme faculty of human consciousness capable of de-creating and re-creating the disorder of nature and the psyche into the conceptual, invented forms of art. But now the volatile ambiguity between subject and object in the creative process allowed the conceptual artist sometimes to hanker after the verities of the perceptual and even to wonder whether art might not be in apposition rather than opposition to nature, so that the autotelic art object still bore some intrinsic relation to the extrinsic object. The transition marked the shift between early and late Eliot, even between early and late Stevens. In the heyday of High Modernism, Imagism set out to propose an alternative to Symbolisme in an effort to recover something of the integrity and meaningfulness of the thing, and the evolution of Pound's poetry, and of H. D.'s and Williams', reveals the Romanticism persisting in and through Modernist experimentation.

For his own generation of poets after World War II, William Everson made an epistemological distinction which echoes Pound's contrast between the perceptual and the conceptual artist: "one kind of poet or artist [the conceptual] creates a world of his own making, while another [the perceptual] stands witness to a world beyond the world of his making."[48] The development of American poetry in the second half of this century deserves its own detailed account, but it is indicative of the pertinence and persistence of the dialectic between Romanticism and Modernism that the terms most descriptive of the movements and developments of the past fifty years are "Postmodernism" and "Neoromanticism."

I call the period under study in this book "The American Poetic Renaissance" for a number of reasons. To begin with, I want to allude to F. O. Matthiessen's study of mid-nineteenth-century Romanticism as the "American Renaissance" and thus bring the Romantic period in our poetry into dialogue with the Modernist. In contrast to that earlier burst of American literary and cultural expression, art during the first half of the twentieth century displayed range and virtuosity on an international scale that suggest more of the luster of a Renaissance, and without question a generation of Americans extraordinary in the whole history of poetry dominated that period. As vigorously as anyone, the expatriate Pound hoped and worked for a Renaissance in America and in the West, and if history turned out to be tragically different from his hopes, the aesthetic achievements of his generation are no less remarkable for that. In fact, they are all the more remarkable.

"Renaissance" is always a Janus-faced word; it looks backward as well as forward. The Modernists took on the twentieth century with bravery and gusto and (in Stevens' word) nobility, impelled by a sense that the exhaustion of the Romantic ideology had precipitated the immense psychological and cultural crisis which overshadowed them. The source of their brave nobility was a conviction that they defended and asserted against the rising clamor that it had no philosophic or theological or historical justification: the conviction shared by the Imagists and Symbolistes alike that their technical mastery of the medium would summon and demonstrate a power of imagination adequate to the task of wringing order out of the confusion around them. Against cultural disintegration and social unheaval they pitted the individual will, and they claimed heroic prerogatives for the creative imagination unarmed with philosophic and theological absolutes.

The Postmodernists of the second half of this century – a descendant of Williams' like Robert Creeley, of Stevens' like John Ashbery, of Pound's like Ed Dorn – view such ambitions as deluded by an egotism as vaunting as that of the Romantics, and they have been unable and unwilling to make such empowering claims for the imagination despite ever graver threats of nuclear war and institutionalized oppression and psychological instability. But it seems to me too easy to conclude censoriously that the Modernists' failure to save the world from catastrophe by art proves the presumptuousness of their ambitions and ideals. The fact that the legacy of this remarkable generation of poets is for the most part personal and aesthetic rather than political and philosophic defines the ideological terms and cultural limitations of their venture. Philosophically, they were left with the remnants of an individualist ideology that were increasingly difficult to shore up, much less to justify on intellectual or emotional grounds; politically, they were blinkered by assumptions of race, class, and gender that made them, with rare exceptions, heedless of the plight of the majority of humankind, suffering from the tragedies and outrages of history in more basic ways than relatively privileged artists were called upon to endure. Nevertheless, their abiding belief in the moral and psychological function of art, a conviction that the Romantics passed on and the Postmodernists find more and more dubious, challenged and sustained them through their own doubts and self-doubts, and their efforts to substantiate that belief as a hope for human survival made for the splendor of the coherence, however idiosyncratic and flawed, that they wrought against daunting odds.

Notes

Introduction

1   "Syllabus of a Course of Six Lectures on Modern French Literature" by T. Stearns Eliot, M.A. (Harvard), is reproduced in A. D. Moody, *Thomas Stearns Eliot: Poet* (Cambridge: Cambridge University Press, 1980), pp. 41–49.
2   *Women of Trachis* (New York: New Directions, 1957), p. 50.
3   *The Collected Poems of Wallace Stevens* (New York: Alfred A. Knopf, 1954), p. 130; *The Necessary Angel: Essays on Reality and the Imagination* (New York: Alfred A. Knopf, 1951), p. 34.

Chapter 1: Robert Frost and John Crowe Ransom

1   *The World's Body* (New York: Charles Scribner's Sons, 1936), p. 55.
2   Thomas Daniel Young, *Gentleman in a Dustcoat: A Biography of John Crowe Ransom* (Baton Rouge: Louisiana State University Press, 1976), pp. 282, 115, 133, 181.
3   Young, p. 288.
4   *Selected Essays of John Crowe Ransom*, ed. Thomas Daniel Young and John Hindle (Baton Rouge: Louisiana State University Press, 1984), p. 31. This essay first appeared in *Fugitive* 4 (June 1925), 63–64. Subsequent notes in this chapter refer to this volume as *Selected Essays*.
5   "Poetry of 1900–1950," *Kenyon Review*, XIII (Summer 1951), 452–453.
6   *Selected Essays*, p. 31.
7   *The Poetry of Robert Frost*, ed. Edward Connery Latham (New York: Holt, Rinehart & Winston, 1969), p. 348. Subsequent notes in this chapter refer to this volume as *Poetry*.
8   *Selected Prose of Robert Frost*, ed. Hyde Cox and Edward Connery Latham (New York: Holt, Rinehart & Winston, 1966), p. 115. Subsequent notes in this chapter refer to this volume as *Selected Prose*.
9   *Poetry*, p. 122.
10 *Selected Prose*, p. 112.
11 *Poetry*, pp. 435–436.
12 *Selected Prose*, p. 118.
13 *Poetry*, p. 421.
14 *Selected Letters of Robert Frost*, ed. Lawrance Thompson (New York: Holt,

Rinehart & Winston, 1964), p. 226. Subsequent notes in this chapter refer to this volume as *Selected Letters*.

15 *Poetry*, p. 250.
16 *Selected Prose*, p. 67.
17 *Poetry*, p. 385.
18 *Poetry*, p. 282.
19 *Poetry*, pp. 376−377.
20 *Selected Prose*, p. 65; *Selected Letters*, pp. 299, 361, 385−386.
21 *Selected Prose*, p. 91.
22 *Poetry*, p. 302.
23 *Poetry*, p. 212.
24 *Poetry*, p. 225.
25 *Selected Letters*, pp. 530−531.
26 *Selected Letters*, p. 462.
27 *Selected Letters*, p. 462.
28 *Selected Letters*, p. 584; *Selected Prose*, p. 118.
29 *Selected Letters*, pp. 324−325.
30 *Selected Prose*, p. 65.
31 *Selected Letters*, pp. 79, 88.
32 *Selected Prose*, pp. 59−60.
33 *Selected Letters*, pp. 79, 80−81, 83−84, 110, 111, 140, 151, 192; *Selected Prose*, p. 18.
34 *Selected Prose*, pp. 112−113, 114.
35 *Selected Prose*, pp. 24−25, 36−37, 61; John Ciardi, "Robert Frost: Master Conversationalist at Work," *Saturday Review*, XLII, 12 (March 21, 1959), 18−20.
36 *Selected Prose*, pp. 18, 41, 60, 20, 24; *Selected Letters*, pp. 199, 493; Ciardi, p. 20; *Poetry*, pp. 119−120.
37 *Selected Letters*, p. 465; *Selected Prose*, pp. 106−107, 20.
38 *Poetry*, p. 441.
39 *Selected Prose*, pp. 18, 19, 20.
40 *Selected Prose*, p. 116.
41 *Interviews with Robert Frost*, ed. Edward Connery Latham (New York: Holt, Rinehart & Winston, 1966), p. 176; *Selected Letters*, p. 361.
42 *Selected Letters*, pp. 228, 105−106; *Selected Prose*, p. 102.
43 *Poetry*, pp. 422−424.
44 *Poetry*, p. 348.
45 *Poetry*, p. 5.
46 *Poetry*, pp. 224−225.
47 *Poetry*, p. 245.
48 *Poetry*, pp. 297, 264−265, 119.
49 *Poetry*, p. 251.
50 *Poetry*, p. 296; *The Poems of Emily Dickinson*, ed. Thomas H. Johnson (Cambridge, Mass.: Harvard University Press, 1955), II, 493.
51 *Poetry*, pp. 101−102.
52 *Poetry*, p. 331.
53 *Poetry*, pp. 443−444.
54 *Poetry*, p. 334.
55 *Poetry*, p. 403.
56 *The Old Man and the Sea* (New York: Charles Scribner's Sons, 1952), pp. 58, 60, 82−83.

57 *Poetry*, pp. 241–242.
58 *Poetry*, pp. 377–379.
59 *Poetry*, pp. 257–260.
60 *Selected Prose*, p. 107.
61 *Poetry*, p. 470.
62 Two useful studies are Louise Cowan, *The Fugitive Group: A Literary History* (Baton Rouge: Louisiana State University Press, 1959), and John L. Stewart, *The Burden of Time: The Fugitives and Agrarians* (Princeton, N.J.: Princeton University Press, 1965).
63 Quoted in George Hemphill, *Allen Tate* (Minneapolis: University of Minnesota Press, 1964), p. 17.
64 "In Amicitia," *Sewanee Review*, LXVII, 4 (Autumn 1969), 534.
65 *The World's Body*, p. ix.
66 *The World's Body*, p. x.
67 *Poems and Essays* (New York: Vintage, 1955), pp. 148–149.
68 Previously unpublished letter, quoted in *The Burden of Time*, p. 223.
69 *Selected Poems*, 3rd ed. (New York: Alfred A. Knopf, 1969), p. 140.
70 Previously unpublished letter, quoted in *The Burden of Time*, p. 224.
71 *Selected Poems*, p. 12.
72 *Selected Poems*, p. 85.
73 *Selected Poems*, pp. 30–31.
74 *Selected Poems*, pp. 63–64.
75 *The World's Body*, p. 347.
76 *Selected Poems*, p. 121.
77 *Selected Poems*, p. 146.
78 *Selected Poems*, pp. 77–78.
79 *Selected Essays*, p. 31.
80 *Selected Poems*, pp. 91–92.
81 *The World's Body*, pp. vii, xi, 329.
82 *The World's Body*, pp. 342–345.
83 *The New Criticism* (Norfolk, Conn.: New Directions, 1941), pp. xi, 281.
84 *Beating the Bushes: Selected Essays 1941–1970* (New York: New Directions, 1972), pp. 1–46.
85 *Poems and Essays*, pp. 79, 157, 99.
86 *Poems and Essays*, pp. 99–101.
87 *Poems and Essays*, p. 101.
88 *Poems and Essays*, p. 184.
89 *Poems and Essays*, p. 169.
90 *Poems and Essays*, p. 182; "In Amicitia," p. 538.
91 *Poems and Essays*, p. 166.
92 *The World's Body*, p. xi.
93 *The New Criticism*, p. 281.
94 *The World's Body*, p. 348.
95 *Beating the Bushes*, pp. 175–176.

Chapter 2: Wallace Stevens

1 *The Letters of Wallace Stevens*, ed. Holly Stevens (New York: Alfred A. Knopf, 1966), pp. 22, 24, 27, 30, 49, 50; henceforth cited as *Letters*.

2 Wallace Stevens, *Opus Posthumous*, ed. Samuel French Morse (New York: Alfred A. Knopf, 1957), p. 172; *Letters*, p. 122.

3 *The Collected Poems of Wallace Stevens* (New York: Alfred A. Knopf, 1954), p. 66.

4 *Collected Poems*, pp. 66–70.

5 *Collected Poems*, pp. 25–27.

6 *Collected Poems*, pp. 204–205.

7 Wallace Stevens, *The Necessary Angel: Essays on Reality and the Imagination* (New York: Alfred A. Knopf, 1951), p. 142.

8 *Letters*, pp. 237, 831, 834.

9 *Collected Poems*, p. 59.

10 *Letters*, p. 430.

11 *Opus Posthumous*, p. 163.

12 *Letters*, p. 288.

13 *Selected Prose of Robert Frost*, ed. Hyde Cox and Edward Connery Latham (New York: Holt, Rinehart & Winston, 1966), p. 59; T. S. Eliot, *To Criticize the Critic* (New York: Farrar, Straus & Giroux, 1965), p. 39.

14 *Opus Posthumous*, p. 171; *The Necessary Angel*, pp. 32, 33; *Collected Poems*, p. 176.

15 *Collected Poems*, p. 12.

16 *Collected Poems*, pp. 198, 199.

17 *Collected Poems*, pp. 8–9.

18 *The Poetry of Robert Frost*, ed. Edward Connery Latham (New York: Holt, Rinehart & Winston, 1969), p. 250.

19 *Opus Posthumous*, pp. 162, 170, 167.

20 *The Necessary Angel*, pp. 151–152.

21 *Collected Poems*, pp. 98–102.

22 *Collected Poems*, p. 322.

23 *Letters*, pp. 391, 290, 413, 473, 539.

24 *Letters*, pp. 391, 598; *Opus Posthumous*, p. 178.

25 *Letters*, pp. 122–123.

26 *Collected Poems*, p. 53.

27 *Collected Poems*, p. 54.

28 *Letters*, p. 263; *The Necessary Angel*, p. 32.

29 *Collected Poems*, p. 497.

30 *Collected Poems*, p. 433.

31 *Letters*, p. 710.

32 *The Necessary Angel*, p. 24.

33 *The Necessary Angel*, p. 30.

34 *Collected Poems*, pp. 128–130.

35 *Collected Poems*, pp. 222, 215.

36 *Collected Poems*, p. 87.

37 *The Necessary Angel*, p. 52.

38 *Collected Poems*, pp. 248–250.

39 *Letters*, p. 352.

40 *Collected Poems*, pp. 388–389.

41 *Collected Poems*, pp. 442–443.

42 *Collected Poems*, p. 524.

43 *Collected Poems*, p. 209.

44 *Collected Poems*, pp. 403–404.

45 *Letters*, pp. 143–144.

46   *Collected Poems*, p. 397.

47   *Letters*, p. 293.

48   *Collected Poems*, p. 16.

49   *Letters*, p. 463.

50   *The Necessary Angel*, p. 96.

51   *The Necessary Angel*, p. 72.

52   *Opus Posthumous*, p. 173; *Letters*, p. 435.

53   *The Necessary Angel*, pp. 173–174.

54   *The Necessary Angel*, pp. 81–82.

55   *The Necessary Angel*, p. 31.

56   *Opus Posthumous*, pp. 116–117, 89.

57   *Opus Posthumous*, pp. 117–118; *The Palm at the End of the Mind: Selected Poems and a Play*, ed. Holly Stevens (New York: Alfred A. Knopf, 1971), p. 398.

58   *Letters*, p. 228.

59   *Letters*, p. 589.

60   *Letters*, p. 716.

61   *Letters*, p. 768.

62   Paul Mariani, *William Carlos Williams: A New World Naked* (New York: McGraw-Hill, 1981), pp. 498–499; *Selected Letters of William Carlos Williams*, ed. John C. Thirlwall (New York: McDowell, Obolensky, 1957), p. 229.

63   *The Autobiography of William Carlos Williams* (New York: Random House, 1951), p. xii.

64   Mariani, pp. 630–631.

65   *Spring and All* in *Imaginations*, ed. Webster Schott (New York: New Directions, 1970), pp. 90–91.

66   *Imaginations*, pp. 89, 93.

67   *Imaginations*, pp. 110, 111, 105, 121.

68   *Imaginations*, p. 112.

69   *Imaginations*, pp. 105, 107, 112.

70   *The Necessary Angel: Essays on Reality and the Imagination* (New York: Alfred A. Knopf, 1951), pp. 57–58.

71   *The Necessary Angel*, pp. 175, 161, 26, 36.

72   *The Necessary Angel*, pp. 54, 136, 36, 153, 30.

73   *The Necessary Angel*, pp. 164, 175.

74   *Imaginations*, pp. 27, 15.

75   *Letters*, pp. 271, 245.

76   *Selected Letters of William Carlos Williams*, p. 305.

77   *Letters*, pp. 589, 592; Mariani, p. 630.

78   *Imaginations*, p. 15.

79   Mariani, p. 499.

80   *Letters*, p. 803.

81   *Letters*, pp. 800–801.

82   Mariani, p. 498.

83   *Opus Posthmous*, ed. Samuel French Morse (New York: Alfred A. Knopf, 1957), pp. 254, 255, 256.

84   *Opus Posthumous*, p. 256.

85   *Opus Posthumous*, p. 251.

86   *Opus Posthumous*, p. 258.

87   *Imaginations*, p. 102.
88   *Imaginations*, pp. 101, 105, 111, 91.
89   *Imaginations*, pp. 115–116.
90   *The Necessary Angel*, p. 96.
91   *The Necessary Angel*, p. 138.
92   *The Necessary Angel*, pp. 136, 140, 141, 151.
93   *The Necessary Angel*, pp. 57–58, 32.
94   *Collected Poems*, p. 18.
95   *Collected Poems*, p. 534.
96   *Imaginations*, pp. 95–96.
97   *Collected Poems*, pp. 339–346.
98   The *Collected Later Poems of William Carlos Williams* (New York: New Directions, 1950, 1963), pp. 113–115; Mariani, p. 824.
99   *Collected Later Poems*, p. 114; *Collected Poems*, pp. 343–344.
100 *Collected Poems*, p. 524.

Chapter 3: T. S. Eliot

1   Ezra Pound, "For T. S. E." in *T. S. Eliot: The Man and His Work*, ed. Allen Tate (New York: Delacorte Press, 1966), p. 89.
2   *The Idea of a Christian Society*, first published in 1939, in *Christianity and Culture* (New York: Harcourt, Brace, 1960), p. 19.
3   Hugh Kenner, *The Invisible Poet: T. S. Eliot* (New York: McDowell, Obolensky, 1959).
4   Grover Smith, Jr., *T. S. Eliot's Poetry and Plays: A Study in Sources and Meaning* (Chicago: University of Chicago Press, 1956), p. 7.
5   The manuscript notebook and folder are among the Quinn papers in the Berg Collection of the New York Public Library. For a description, see Lyndall Gordon, *Eliot's Early Years* (Oxford: Oxford University Press, 1977), pp. 22–23. I consulted the unpublished notebook and folder, but Valerie Eliot will not permit direct quotation from unpublished poems before there is a published edition.
6   *Collected Poems 1909–1962* (New York: Harcourt, Brace & World, 1963), p. 25. Henceforth in the notes of this chapter this volume will be identified as *Collected Poems*.
7   Gordon, p. 102.
8   Gordon, pp. 23, 24, 33–34, 38–39.
9   *Poems Written in Early Youth* (New York: Farrar, Straus & Giroux, 1967), p. 20.
10   *Ara Vos Prec* (London: Ovid Press, 1920), p. 30. The text is reprinted in full in James E. Miller, Jr., *T. S. Eliot's Personal Waste Land: Exorcism of the Demons* (University Park: Pennsylvania State University Press, 1977), pp. 48–49. For more information on the "Ode," cf. Smith, p. 37; T. S. Matthews, *Great Tom: Notes Towards the Definition of T. S. Eliot* (New York: Harper & Row, 1974), p. 44.
11   *Poems Written in Early Youth*, p. 22.
12   *Poems Written in Early Youth*, p. 23.
13   Gordon, pp. 58, 72–80. For other accounts of Eliot's marriage, see Robert Sencourt, *T. S. Eliot: A Memoir* (New York: Dodd, Mead, 1971), pp. 49–63, and Matthews, pp. 40–55.
14   Gordon, pp. 61–62.

15 *Poems Written in Early Youth*, pp. 28–30.
16 Gordon, p. 2; Charlotte Eliot, *William Greenleaf Eliot: Minister, Educator, Philanthropist* (Boston and New York: Houghton Mifflin, 1904), pp. ix–x.
17 *Easter Songs* (Boston: James H. West Co., 1899).
18 *Savonarola: A Dramatic Poem* (London: R. Cobden-Sanderson, 1926).
19 Gordon, p. 27.
20 *Poems Written in Early Youth*, p. 26.
21 *Collected Poems*, pp. 3–7.
22 *Collected Poems*, pp. 8–12.
23 Gordon, p. 26.
24 *Collected Poems*, p. 23.
25 Sencourt, pp. 57–62; Matthews, pp. 46–47.
26 *Collected Poems*, pp. 14, 16–18, 20, 21, 22.
27 *Selected Essays* (New York: Harcourt, Brace, 1950), pp. 4–5, 135, 136, 137.
28 *On Poetry and Poets* (New York: Farrar, Straus & Giroux, 1957), p. 295; *To Criticize the Critic* (New York: Farrar, Straus & Giroux, 1965), pp. 22, 126.
29 *To Criticize the Critic*, pp. 55, 126.
30 *Collected Poems*, p. 19.
31 *Collected Poems*, p. 24.
32 Irvin Ehrenpreis, "Mr. Eliot's Martyrdom," *New York Review of Books*, XXV, 1 (Feb. 9, 1978), 3.
33 Smith, pp. 44–45.
34 Gordon, pp. 40, 54, 71; Matthews, pp. 22, 37.
35 Gordon, p. 79; Matthews, p. 48.
36 Gordon, p. 72; Matthews, p. 49.
37 *Collected Poems*, pp. 45–46.
38 *Collected Poems*, pp. 47–48.
39 *Collected Poems*, pp. 49–50.
40 *Selected Essays*, p. 376.
41 Quoted in F. O. Matthiessen, *The Achievement of T. S. Eliot* (New York: Oxford University Press, 1935), p. 24.
42 *To Criticize the Critic*, p. 44; Gordon, pp. 2, 5, 8.
43 Gordon, pp. 126, 133.
44 *On Poetry and Poets*, p. 243.
45 *Notes Towards a Definition of Culture*, first published in 1948, in *Christianity and Culture*, pp. 155; *Selected Essays*, p. 357.
46 *To Criticize the Critic*, p. 52.
47 *Writers at Work: The Paris Review Interviews, Second Series*, ed. Van Wyck Brooks (New York: Viking Press, 1963), p. 110.
48 *To Criticize the Critic*, pp. 27–42. For Eliot on the provinciality of nineteenth-century American letters, see *To Criticize the Critic*, pp. 51–53, 59–60.
49 *Selected Essays*, pp. 368, 433; *The Idea of a Christian Society* in *Christianity and Culture*, p. 72.
50 *Selected Essays*, pp. 381, 433, 437–438; Gordon, p. 71.
51 *Selected Essays*, pp. 4, 5, 12.
52 *Selected Essays*, pp. 6–7, 15.
53 *To Criticize the Critic*, p. 44.
54 *Selected Essays*, p. 402.
55 *Selected Essays*, pp. 246–247, 249, 303, 309–310; *The Use of Poetry and the Use of*

Criticism (London: Faber & Faber, 1933), p. 84; *On Poetry and Poets*, p. 173.

56 Cf. John D. Margolis, *T. S. Eliot's Intellectual Development 1922–1939* (Chicago: University of Chicago Press, 1972), pp. 53–67.

57 Margolis, p. 12; *Selected Essays*, pp. 15–18, 329–330, 401, 423.

58 *Selected Essays*, pp. 1, 7, 9, 11; *On Poetry and Poets*, p. 299.

59 *Selected Essays*, pp. 13, 19; *The Sacred Wood* (London: Methuen, 1920, reprinted 1960), p. 7; *To Criticize the Critic*, pp. 34, 39; Archibald MacLeish, *Collected Poems 1917–1952* (Boston: Houghton, Mifflin, 1952), p. 41.

60 *Selected Essays*, pp. 124–125, 132–136.

61 *Selected Essays*, pp. 9, 7–8, 10.

62 *To Criticize the Critic*, p. 41; *Selected Essays*, p. 392.

63 *The Use of Poetry and the Use of Criticism*, p. 25; *Selected Essays*, p. 28.

64 *Selected Essays*, pp. 11, 96; *The Sacred Wood*, pp. ix–x; *On Poetry and Poets*, pp. 125, 212, 220.

65 *On Poetry and Poets*, pp. 9, 222; *Selected Essays*, pp. 3, 13, 22.

66 See, for example, *On Poetry and Poets*, pp. 3, 17–18, 117; *To Criticize the Critic*, pp. 16, 19, 20, 33–34.

67 Margolis, pp. 42–43; *Selected Essays*, pp. 7–8, 10–11, 117; *On Poetry and Poets*, p. 9.

68 I am grateful to a 1978 Ph.D. dissertation written by one of my students, Katherine Kampmann Namphy, for enlightening me on the philosophic basis of Eliot's key critical concepts such as feeling, objective correlative, impersonality, and so on. *Selected Essays*, p. 8; *On Poetry and Poets*, pp. 276, 93; *The Use of Poetry and the Use of Criticism*, p. 138.

69 *The Use of Poetry and the Use of Criticism*, pp. 118–119; *On Poetry and Poets*, p. 32.

70 *On Poetry and Poets*, pp. 106–107.

71 Matthiessen, p. 8; *Selected Essays*, p. 6.

72 *The Use of Poetry and the Use of Criticism*, pp. 144–145.

73 *To Criticize the Critic*, p. 132.

74 *On Poetry and Poets*, pp. 277–278.

75 *Selected Essays*, p. 10.

76 *Selected Essays*, p. 96.

77 *Selected Essays*, p. 117; *On Poetry and Poets*, pp. 83, 299.

78 Allen Tate, "Postscript by the Guest Editor," *T. S. Eliot: The Man and His Work*, ed. Allen Tate (New York: Delacorte Press, 1966), p. 391. Robert Lowell commented, in a conversation with me, on the fact that Eliot's major poems came from crises of one kind or another in the poet's life.

79 *The Waste Land: A Facsimile and Transcript of the Original Drafts*, ed. Valerie Eliot (New York: Harcourt Brace Jovanovich, 1971), p. 1.

80 Smith, p. 306.

81 *Collected Poems*, pp. 29–31.

82 *Collected Poems*, pp. 53–76.

83 *The Waste Land: A Facsimile and Transcript*, pp. 10–13.

84 *The Waste Land: A Facsimile and Transcript*, pp. 12–13; Gordon, p. 96.

85 *The Waste Land: A Facsimile and Transcript*, pp. 12–15.

86 *The Waste Land: A Facsimile and Transcript*, pp. 38–41, 44–47.

87 I am very grateful for this connection to my colleague at Stanford, Jay Fliegelman.

88 *Collected Poems*, pp. 79–82.

89 *Collected Poems*, pp. 85–94.

90 These lines are from "At Easter-Tide," the first poem in Charlotte Eliot's *Easter Songs*, (1899).

91 *Collected Poems*, pp. 99–108.

92 Smith, p. 132.

93 *Collected Poems*, pp. 125–129.

94 *Collected Poems*, pp. 175–209.

95 Matthews, pp. 139–151; Gordon, pp. 55–59.

96 *Selected Essays*, pp. 234–235.

97 *Selected Essays*, p. 235.

98 Mircea Eliade, *Cosmos and History: The Myth of the Eternal Return* (New York: Harper Torchbooks, 1959; published originally in French in 1949).

99 *Lord Weary's Castle* (New York: Harcourt, Brace, 1946), p. 5.

100 *On Poetry and Poets*, p. 297.

101 *The Use of Poetry and the Use of Criticism*, pp. 152–153.

102 *Writers at Work*, pp. 104–105.

103 *On Poetry and Poets*, pp. 75–95; E. Martin Browne, "T. S. Eliot in the Theatre: The Director's Memories," in *T. S. Eliot: The Man and His Work*, pp. 116–132.

104 *Collected Poems*, pp. 111–124.

105 *The Use of Poetry and the Use of Criticism*, p. 153.

106 *Collected Poems*, pp. 147–171.

107 *Murder in the Cathedral* (New York: Harcourt, Brace, 1935).

108 *The Family Reunion* (New York: Harcourt, Brace, 1939).

109 *On Poetry and Poets*, pp. 90–91.

110 *The Cocktail Party* (New York: Harcourt, Brace, 1950).

111 *The Confidential Clerk* (New York: Harcourt, Brace, 1954).

112 *The Elder Statesman* (New York: Farrar, Straus & Cudahy, 1959).

113 Browne, p. 132.

114 For accounts of Eliot's marriage to Valerie Fletcher, see Sencourt, pp. 210–221; Matthews, pp. 159–161; Gordon, pp. 80–81; Peter Ackroyd, *T. S. Eliot* (London: Hamish Hamilton, 1984), pp. 319–324.

115 *Collected Poems*, p. 221.

116 *T. S. Eliot: The Man and His Work*, p. 115; reprinted in C. Day-Lewis, *The Whispering Roots* (London: Jonathan Cape, 1970), p. 58.

117 *T. S. Eliot: The Man and His Work*, p. 89.

118 *Selected Essays*, p. 235.

Chapter 4: Ezra Pound

1 Noel Stock, *The Life of Ezra Pound* (New York: Pantheon, 1970), pp. 12, 19.

2 *Personae: The Collected Shorter Poems of Ezra Pound* (New York: New Directions, 1926), p. 89.

3 *Selected Prose 1909–1965*, ed. William Cookson (New York: New Directions, 1973), pp. 145–146.

4 *Collected Early Poems of Ezra Pound*, ed. Michael John King (New York: New Directions, 1976), p. 185.

5 *Collected Early Poems*, pp. 269–270, 271.

6 *Collected Early Poems*, p. 287.

7   *The Cantos* (New York: New Directions, 1972), p. 24. Henceforth page references for passages from *The Cantos* will be cited in parentheses in the text.

8   *Personae*, p. 235.

9   *Personae*, pp. 92-93.

10   The verses cited can be found in *Collected Early Poems*, pp. 27, 42-43, 44.

11   *Gaudier-Brzeska: A Memoir* (New York: New Directions, 1960), p. 98.

12   *Literary Essays of Ezra Pound*, ed. T. S. Eliot (New York: New Directions, 1954), p. 3.

13   *Literary Essays*, p. 4.

14   *Personae*, p. 109.

15   *Gaudier-Brzeska*, p. 89.

16   *The ABC of Reading* (New York: New Directions, reissued 1951), p. 52.

17   *Selected Prose*, p. 101.

18   Cf. T. E. Hulme, *Speculations: Essays on Humanism and the Philosophy of Art*, ed. Herbert Read (London: Kegan Paul, Trench, Trubner, 1924), and *Further Speculations*, ed. Sam Hynes (Minneapolis: University of Minnesota Press, 1955).

19   *Gaudier-Brzeska*, pp. 89-90, 105-106.

20   Remy de Gourmont, *The Natural Philosophy of Love*, tr. Ezra Pound (New York: Rarity Press, 1931), p. 170.

21   William E. Wees, *Vorticism and the English Avant-Garde* (Toronto: University of Toronto Press, 1972), p. 191; *Gaudier-Brzeska*, pp. 89, 92; Donald Davie, *Pound* (Glasgow: Collins, 1975), pp. 62-74.

22   *The Chinese Written Character as a Medium for Poetry* (San Francisco: City Lights Books, 1968), pp. 6, 7, 8, 9, 10, 12, 19-21.

23   *The Chinese Written Character*, pp. 17, 22.

24   *The Chinese Written Character*, pp. 22-23.

25   *The Chinese Written Character*, p. 3.

26   Hugh Kenner, *The Pound Era* (Berkeley and Los Angeles: University of California Press, 1971), pp. 105, 230-231.

27   *Selected Prose*, p. 33.

28   *The Spirit of Romance* (New York: New Directions, 1952), pp. 154, 92-93.

29   *Literary Essays*, p. 49.

30   *Selected Prose*, p. 53; *Writers at Work: The Paris Review Interviews (Second Series)*, ed. Van Wyck Brooks (New York: Viking, 1963), p. 48.

31   *Selected Prose*, p. 53.

32   *The ABC of Reading*, p. 75.

33   *The Chinese Written Character*, p. 31; *Pavannes and Divisions* (New York: Alfred A. Knopf, 1918), p. 258; *Gaudier-Brzeska*, p. 94.

34   *Guide to Kulchur* (New York: New Directions, 1935), p. 51.

35   Stock, p. 184.

36   Stock, p. 12; *Literary Essays*, p. 49.

37   Emerson's remark comes from "The Poet" from *Essays: Second Series*; Whitman's remark comes from the section on "Death of Thomas Carlyle" in *Specimen Days*.

38   *Selected Prose*, p. 23.

39   *The Odyssey*, tr. Robert Fitzgerald (New York: Doubleday, 1961), p. 199.

40   Daniel Pearlman, *The Barb of Time: On the Unity of Ezra Pound's Cantos* (New York: Oxford University Press, 1969), pp. 43-45.

41   Hugh Kenner's pioneering study, *The Poetry of Ezra Pound* (London: Faber & Faber, 1951), is an explication of the ideogramic method.

42 Joseph Campbell, *The Hero with a Thousand Faces* (New York: Bollingen Foundation, 1949), pp. 337, 261; *The Chinese Written Character*, pp. 22, 23; *Collected Early Poems*, p. 322.

43 The phrases from Emerson are taken from the following essays: "Poetry and Imagination" in *Letters and Social Aims*; "Beauty" in *The Conduct of Life*; and "The Poet" in *Essays: Second Series*.

44 "Poetry and Imagination"; *Selected Prose*, pp. 47–48.

45 Campbell, p. 261.

46 Campbell, p. 259.

47 C. G. Jung, *Two Essays on Analytical Psychology*, *The Collected Works of C. G. Jung* (New York: Pantheon, 1966), Vol. VII, p. 95.

48 *Guide to Kulchur*, pp. 347, 44; *Literary Essays*, p. 154.

49 Mircea Eliade, *Cosmos and History: The Myth of the Eternal Return* (New York: Harper Torchbooks, 1959), also published under the title *The Myth of the Eternal Return: Archetypes and Repetitions* (New York: Pantheon, 1954).

50 See, for example, Neumann's discussion of the artist's matriarchal consciousness in *The Archetypal World of Henry Moore* (New York: Pantheon, 1959).

51 Kenner, *The Pound Era*, p. 143.

52 *Guide to Kulchur*, pp. 159, 194.

53 *Guide to Kulchur*, p. 160.

54 See Sharon Meyer Libera, "Casting the Gods Back Into the NOUS: Two Neoplatonists and the Cantos of Ezra Pound," *Paideuma*, II, 3, 368–369.

55 Cited in Pearlman, p. 96.

56 *Guide to Kulchur*, p. 301.

57 *Guide to Kulchur*, pp. 159, 352.

58 *The Letters of Ezra Pound 1907–1914*, ed. D. D. Paige (New York: Harcourt Brace & World, 1950), p. 191.

59 "Studies in Anality" appears on pp. 179–304 of *Life Against Death: The Psychoanalytic Meaning of History* (Middletown, Conn.: Wesleyan University Press, 1959).

60 Ezra Pound, *Impact: Essays on Ignorance and the Decline of American Civilization*, ed. Noel Stock (Chicago: Henry Regnery, 1960), p. 144; *Selected Prose*, p. 265.

61 *Selected Prose*, p. 3; *Guide to Kulchur*, p. 156.

62 Donald Davie, *Ezra Pound: Poet as Sculptor* (New York: Oxford University Press, 1964), pp. 127–131. *Stones of Rimini* (1934) has been reissued: New York: Schocken Books, 1969.

63 *Selected Prose*, p. 32.

64 *Selected Prose*, p. 270.

65 *Guide to Kulchur*, p. 223.

66 Confucius, *The Great Digest and The Unwobbling Pivot*, tr. Ezra Pound (New York: New Directions, 1951), p. 187. See also *The Pound Era*, p. 458.

67 *Literary Essays*, pp. 149, 158–159.

68 *Guide to Kulchur*, p. 77.

69 *Literary Essays*, pp. 160, 161; *Guide to Kulchur*, p. 77.

70 *Literary Essays*, pp. 177, 159; *Sailing After Knowledge*, p. 124.

71 *Selected Prose*, p. 55.

72 *Selected Prose*, p. 70.

73 Walt Whitman, *The Correspondence*, ed. Edwin Haviland Miller (New York: New York University Press, 1969), Vol. IV, p. 70.

74 For a discussion of the psychological significance of this archetypal image, see the chapter "The Lady of the Beasts" in Erich Neumann, *The Great Mother: An Analysis of the Archetype*, tr. Ralph Manheim (Princeton, N.J.: Princeton University Press, 1955), Bollingen Series Vol. XLVII, pp. 268–280.

75 *The Great Mother*, pp. 305, 35.

76 *The Great Mother*, p. 273.

77 *The Spirit of Romance*, pp. 94–95.

78 Pearlman, p. 172.

79 *The Great Digest and The Unwobbling Pivot*, p. 20; *The Barb of Time*, pp. 193–210, 304–311.

80 *Guide to Kulchur*, p. 135.

81 *Guide to Kulchur*, p. 32; *The Great Digest and the Unwobbling Pivot*, p. 189.

82 *Jefferson and/or Mussolini* (New York: Liveright, 1935), p. 19.

83 Mary de Rachewiltz, in an unpublished lecture entitled "John Adams and Ezra Pound," delivered at Stanford University on April 13, 1976.

84 Stock, pp. 375, 369, 372–373, 359.

85 *The Letters of Ezra Pound*, p. 180; *The Life of Ezra Pound*, pp. 376, 373–374.

86 For a discussion of this passage from Eliot's *After Strange Gods*, see George Dekker, *Sailing After Knowledge*, pp. 8–14.

87 Pearlman, p. 284.

88 *The Great Digest and The Unwobbling Pivot*, p. 10.

89 Cf. Kenner, *The Pound Era*, pp. 145–162.

90 *Literary Essays*, pp. 154–155.

91 *The ABC of Reading*, p. 52.

92 *Guide to Kulchur*, p. 152.

93 For an account of Pound's ordeal in Washington with the courts and the asylum by his lawyer, see Julian Cornell, *The Trial of Ezra Pound* (New York: John Day, 1966).

94 Stock, p. 439.

95 Thomas Grieve, "Annotations to the Chinese in *Section: Rock-Drill*," *Paideuma*, IV, 2 and 3 (Fall–Winter 1975), 379–380, 382.

96 James Neault, "Apollonius of Tyana," *Paideuma*, IV, 1 (Spring 1975), 171; James Wilhelm, *The Later Cantos of Ezra Pound* (New York: Walker and Co., 1977), pp. 62, 101.

97 *Writers at Work: Second Series*, p. 58.

98 *Writers at Work: Second Series*, p. 59.

99 *Hermetic Definition* (New York: New Directions, 1972), p. 17.

100 Allen Ginsberg, "Allen Verbatim," *Paideuma*, III, 2, 268.

101 *Guide to Kulchur*, p. 295.

102 *Selected Prose*, p. 123.

Chapter 5: H. D.

1 *The Complete Poetic Works of Amy Lowell*, ed. Louis Untermeyer (Boston: Houghton Mifflin, 1955), p. 459.

2 Wallace Stevens, "The Figure of the Youth as Virile Poet," in *The Necessary Angel: Essays on Reality and the Imagination* (New York: Alfred A. Knopf, 1951), p. 52.

3 Adrienne Rich, "Snapshots of a Daughter-in-Law," in *Snapshots of a Daughter-in-Law: Poems 1953–1962* (New York: Harper & Row, 1963), p. 26. See also Rich,

"When We Dead Awaken: Writing as Re-vision," in *On Lies, Secrets, & Silence* (New York: Norton, 1979), pp. 33–49.

4 *Letters to Mothers* (New York: Harper & Bros., 1845; first published 1838), pp. vii, viii, 16.

5 "Preface" to *Select Poems* (Philadelphia: A. Hart, 1850), p. 9.

6 *Select Poems*, pp. 234–235.

7 Cf. "Emily Dickinson and the Deerslayer: The Dilemma of the Woman Poet in America," in *Shakespeare's Sisters: Feminist Essays on Women Poets*, ed. Sandra Gilbert and Susan Gubar (Bloomington: Indiana University Press, 1979), pp. 122–134. See also *The Tenth Muse: The Psyche of the American Poet* (Cambridge, Mass.: Harvard University Press, 1975), pp. 255ff.

8 Poem 199, *The Poems of Emily Dickinson*, ed. Thomas H. Johnson (Cambridge, Mass.: Harvard University Press, 1955), Vol. I, p. 142.

9 Quoted by Robert Duncan in the "Rites of Participation" chapter of his *H. D. Book* in *Caterpillar*, I, 2 (January 1968), 142–143.

10 *The Complete Poems of Marianne Moore* (New York: Macmillan and Viking, 1981), p. 62.

11 *The Complete Poems of Marianne Moore*, p. 134.

12 *The Complete Poems of Marianne Moore*, p. 220.

13 Gilbert Sorrentino, "AN OCTOPUS/of ice," in *Something Said* (San Francisco: North Point, 1984), pp. 163, 166.

14 Adrienne Rich, "A Note on Nora Jaffe," *Caterpillar* I, 2 (January 1968), 106.

15 Robert Duncan, Part II, Chapter 7 of *The H. D. Book*, *Credences II*, II, 2 (July 1975), 63.

16 Robert Duncan, Part II, Chapter 4 of *The H. D. Book*, *Caterpillar 7*, II, 2 (April 1969), 40–41.

17 Ezra Pound, "A Retrospect," *Literary Essays* (New York: New Directions, 1954), p. 4; *Gaudier-Brzeska: A Memoir* (New York: New Directions, 1970), p. 89.

18 *Complete Poetic Works*, p. 477.

19 *Collected Poems 1912–1944*, ed. Louis L. Martz (New York: New Directions, 1983), p. 55.

20 *Collected Earlier Poems* (New York: New Directions, 1951), p. 87.

21 Part I, Chapter I of *The H. D. Book*, *Coyote's Journal 5–6*, pp. 14, 16, 11.

22 Joseph N. Riddel, "H. D. and the Poetics of Spiritual Realism," *Contemporary Literature*, X, 4 (Autumn 1969, A Special Number on H. D.), 449–453.

23 "Norman Holmes Pearson: An Interview," *Contemporary Literature*, X, 4 (Autumn 1969), 437.

24 Robert Duncan, Part II, Chapter 4 of *The H. D. Book*, *Caterpillar 7*, II, 2 (April 1969), 28.

25 *Coyote's Journal 5–6*, pp. 14, 16, 11.

26 Robert Duncan, Part I, Chapter 3 of *The H. D. Book*, *TriQuarterly*, 12 (Spring 1968), 70; Denise Levertov, "H. D.: An Appreciation," *Poetry*, C, 3 (June 1962), 186.

27 Thomas Burnett Swann, *The Classical World of H. D.* (Lincoln: University of Nebraska Press, 1962).

28 *Collected Poems*, pp. 28–29.

29 *Collected Poems*, pp. 19–20, 10–11.

30 *Collected Poems*, p. 23.

31 *Collected Poems*, pp. 9, 5.

32 *Collected Poems*, pp. 6, 9, 26.
33 Bryher, *The Heart to Artemis* (New York: Harcourt, Brace & World, 1962), p. 186; *Collected Poems*, pp. 12–13.
34 *Collected Poems*, pp. 24–25.
35 *Collected Poems*, pp. 5, 14, 21, 36.
36 *Collected Poems*, pp. 51–55.
37 *Tribute to Freud*, "Foreword" by Norman Holmes Pearson, "Introduction" by Kenneth Fields (Boston: David R. Godine, 1974), p. 44.
38 *Tribute to Freud*, pp. 91, 93.
39 *Tribute to Freud*, pp. 6, 71. The remark about Freud and Jung appears in an unpublished journal entitled *Compassionate Friendship* and dated Feb. 18, 1955–Sept. 21, 1955, now in the Beinecke Library, Yale University.
40 The remark about James comes from a letter, dated Sept. 15, 1922, to John Cournos, from the H. D. correspondence with Cournos in the Houghton Library, Harvard University.
41 *Palimpsest* (Carbondale: Southern Illinois University Press, 1968). Subsequent page references for quotations are indicated in parentheses in the text.
42 *The Heart to Artemis*, pp. 186–187.
43 *Hedylus* (Boston: Houghton Mifflin, 1928; Redding, Conn.: Black Swan Press, 1980). Page references for quotations given in parentheses in the text are from the 1980 reprint.
44 *Hilda Doolittle* (New York: Twayne, 1967), p. 89.
45 *Tribute to Freud*, pp. 19, 25.
46 *Tribute to Freud*, pp. 34, 27.
47 *Tribute to Freud*, p. 121.
48 *Tribute to Freud*, pp. 33, 28, 29.
49 *Tribute to Freud*, pp. 31–34.
50 *Tribute to Freud*, pp. 31–32.
51 *Bid Me to Live (A Madrigal)* (New York: Grove, 1960). Subsequent page references for direct quotations are given in parentheses in the text.
52 *Compassionate Friendship*, p. 60.
53 Eric W. White, *Images of H. D.* and H. D., from *The Mystery* (London: Enitharmon Press, 1976), p. 18.
54 *The Poems of Emily Dickinson*, Vol. I, pp. 122, 277; Vol. II, pp. 393–394.
55 *Compassionate Friendship*, p. 54.
56 *Tribute to Freud*, pp. 141–142, 149–150.
57 *Hippolytus Temporizes* (Boston: Houghton Mifflin, 1927). Page references for direct quotations are given in parentheses in the text.
58 *Collected Poems*, p. 291.
59 In "The Argument" that precedes the text of *Hippolytus Temporizes*.
60 *Tribute to Freud*, p. 170.
61 *The Autobiography of William Carlos Williams* (New York: Random House, 1951), p. 219. Robert McAlmon and Kay Boyle, *Being Geniuses Together 1920–1930* (New York: Doubleday, 1968), pp. 61–62.
62 For a discussion of H. D.'s sexuality, see Susan Friedman and Rachel Blau Duplessis, "'I Had Two Loves Separate': The Sexualities of H. D.'s *Her*," *Montemora* 8 (New York: Montemora Foundation, 1981), pp. 7–30.
63 Bryher, *The Days of Mars: A Memoir 1940–1946* (New York: Harcourt Brace Jovanovich, 1972), p. 79.

64   *Trilogy* (New York: New Directions, 1973). Page references for direct quotations are given in parentheses in the text.

65   Part I, Chapters 3 and 4 of *The H. D. Book*, *TriQuarterly 12* (Spring 1968), 97.

66   Norman Holmes Pearson, "Foreword" to *Hermetic Definition* (New York: New Directions, 1972), p. v.

67   *Hermetic Definition*, p. v.

68   *Hermetic Definition*, p. vi. The typescript of *Majic Ring* is at the Beinecke Library, Yale University. See also the typescript of *Compassionate Friendship* there, pp. 47, 78, 79, 81, and *Notes on Recent Writing*, pp. 14, 18, 22–23.

69   *Tribute to Freud*, pp. 87–90, 64–66, 101.

70   "The Dream," from *The Gift*, *Contemporary Literature*, X, 4 (Autumn 1969), 618.

71   *Tribute to Freud*, p. 109. Susan Friedman has an extensive commentary on H. D.'s involvement with the occult in *Psyche Reborn: The Emergence of H. D.* (Bloomington: Indiana University Press, 1981), pp. 157–207.

72   *Tribute to Freud*, pp. 145, 13–14.

73   *Tribute to Freud*, pp. 102–103.

74   *Tribute to Freud*, pp. 44–56.

75   Norman Holmes Pearson, "Foreword" to *Trilogy*, pp. vi–vii.

76   *Trilogy*, p. vii.

77   *Trilogy*, p. ix.

78   *Trilogy*, p. ix.

79   *Trilogy*, p. ix.

80   *Tribute to Freud*, p. 56.

81   *Tribute to Freud*, p. 44.

82   *Tribute to Freud*, p. 146.

83   *Tribute to Freud*, p. 123.

84   Part I, Chapter 2 of *The H. D. Book*, *Coyote's Journal 8*, 27.

85   Marilyn R. Farwell, "Adrienne Rich and an Organic Feminist Criticism," *College English*, XXXIX, 2 (October 1977), 191–203.

86   "Poetry and Experience: Statement at a Poetry Reading," in *Adrienne Rich's Poetry*, ed. Barbara Charlesworth Gelpi and Albert Gelpi (New York: Norton, 1975), p. 89.

87   "H. D.: An Appreciation," *Poetry*, C, 3 (June 1962), 183–184.

88   *Notes on Recent Writing*, p. 22.

89   *Helen in Egypt* (New York: Grove Press, 1961; New York: New Directions, 1974). Since the New Directions edition is in print and available, whereas the Grove Press edition is not, page references given in parentheses in the text come from the New Directions edition.

90   The first quotation comes from the typescript of an unpublished journal, dated Feb. 18, 1955–Sept. 21, 1955, and entitled *Compassionate Friendship*, in the H. D. Archive at the Beinecke Library, Yale University, p. 17. The second comes from the "Hirslanden Notebooks," Book III, p. 28, also at the Beinecke Library.

91   *HERmione* (New York: New Directions, 1981), pp. 82, 173, 131.

92   *Compassionate Friendship*, pp. 79, 35.

93   *End to Torment: A Memoir of Ezra Pound, with the Poems from "Hilda's Book" by Ezra Pound* (New York: New Directions, 1979), p. 11; *Compassionate Friendship*, p. 111.

94   "Hirslanden Notebooks," Book III, pp. 7, 26, 24.

95   "Hirslanden Notebooks," Book III, p. 27; Book I, p. 4.

 96 *End to Torment*, pp. 73, 71, 84, 81.
 97 *Compassionate Friendship*, pp. 65, 17, 46.
 98 *Collected Poems 1909–1962* (New York: Harcourt Brace & World, 1963), pp. 177, 209; *The Poetry of Robert Frost*, ed. Edward Connery Latham (New York: Holt, Rinehart & Winston, 1969), p. 379; *Pictures from Breughel and Other Poems* (New York: New Directions, 1962), p. 132; *The Cantos* (New York: New Directions, 1972), p. 803; *Women of Trachis* (New York: New Directions, 1957), p. 50.
 99 *Compassionate Friendship*, pp. 12–13.
100 Letter to John Cournos, dated Feb. 5, 1929, from the collection of H. D. correspondence with John Cournos, in the Houghton Library, Harvard University.
101 "Hirslanden Notebooks," Book III, p. 27; *Compassionate Friendship*, p. 29.
102 *Newsweek*, LV, 18 (May 2, 1960), 92.
103 The sequence appears in *Hermetic Definition* with two other sequences from her last years, "Sagesse" and "Winter Love." Page references for direct quotations are indicated in parentheses in the text.
104 Norman Holmes Pearson, p. 445.
105 *Compassionate Friendship*, p. 29.
106 "Among School Children," in *The Collected Poems of W. B. Yeats* (New York: Macmillan, 1956), p. 214.
107 *The Great Mother: An Analysis of the Archetype*, tr. Ralph Manheim (Princeton, N.J.: Princeton University Press), 1955.

        Chapter 6: William Carlos Williams

  1 *The Letters of Wallace Stevens*, ed. Holly Stevens (New York: Alfred A. Knopf, 1966), p. 592; see also pp. 588–589; *Selected Essays of William Carlos Williams* (New York: Random House, 1954; reissued New York: New Directions, 1969), p. 12. The latter volume will henceforth be identified in the notes as *Selected Essays*.
  2 Quoted in Mike Weaver, *William Carlos Williams: The American Background* (Cambridge: Cambridge University Press, 1971), p. 164.
  3 *Selected Essays*, p. 205; *The Selected Letters of William Carlos Williams*, ed. John C. Thirwall (New York: McDowell, Obolensky, 1957), pp. 220–221. The latter volume will henceforth be identified in the notes as *Selected Letters*.
  4 *Selected Essays*, p. 201; *The Autobiography of William Carlos Williams* (New York: Random House, 1951; reissued New York: New Directions, 1967), p. xi. The latter volume will henceforth be identified in the notes as *Autobiography*.
  5 *Autobiography*, pp. 158, 137.
  6 *Autobiography*, p. 55. For a discussion of Williams' relations with his parents, see the two following biographies: Reed Whittemore, *William Carlos Williams: Poet from Jersey* (Boston: Houghton Mifflin, 1975), and Paul Mariani, *William Carlos Williams: A New World Naked* (New York: McGraw-Hill, 1982).
  7 *Autobiography*, pp. 49, 166, 51, 91, 107.
  8 *Autobiography*, p. 91.
  9 *Autobiography*, pp. 91–92.
 10 "Preface," *Selected Essays*, n.p.
 11 *Autobiography*, pp. 166–167, 14.
 12 *Autobiography*, pp. 44–45; "Preface," *Selected Essays*, n.p.
 13 *Autobiography*, pp. 4–5, 224, 91.

14 *I Wanted to Write a Poem*, ed. Edith Heal (Boston: Beacon Press, 1958), p. 14.

15 *I Wanted to Write a Poem*, p. 16; *Interviews with William Carlos Williams: "Speaking Straight Ahead,"* ed. Linda Welshimer Wagner (New York: New Directions, 1976), p. 76. This volume will henceforth be identified in the notes as *Interviews*.

16 *Autobiography*, pp. 9–10, 222–223.

17 *I Wanted to Write a Poem*, p. 1.

18 *Autobiography*, pp. 11, 55.

19 *Selected Essays*, pp. 259.

20 Weaver, pp. 25, 21.

21 *Autobiography*, p. 55; *Selected Essays*, p. 13.

22 *Selected Essays*, pp. 259, 246.

23 *Collected Earlier Poems of William Carlos Williams* (New York: New Directions, 1951), p. 34. Henceforth this volume will be identified in the notes as *Collected Early Poems*.

24 *Selected Essays*, pp. 303–304, 243.

25 *Selected Essays*, p. 259; *I Wanted to Write a Poem*, pp. 5–6, 8.

26 *Selected Essays*, p. 250.

27 *Selected Essays*, pp. 268, 269, 281; *The Embodiment of Knowledge*, ed. Ron Loewinsohn (New York: New Directions, 1974), p. 105; Benjamin Sankey, *A Companion to William Carlos Williams' Paterson* (Berkeley and Los Angeles: University of California Press, 1971), p. 169.

28 Weaver, p. 39.

29 *Selected Letters*, pp. 194, 219; *Interviews*, p. 55.

30 *I Wanted to Write a Poem*, p. 37.

31 *Spring and All*, reprinted in *Imaginations*, ed. Webster Schott (New York: New Directions, 1970), pp. 89–91, 93, 95. All further citations of *Spring and All* refer to this edition. The poems from the volume are also reprinted in *The Collected Earlier Poems*, pp. 241–287.

32 *Selected Essays*, pp. 72–73; see also pp. 55, 69–71.

33 *Selected Letters*, p. 224; Weaver, pp. 33–34.

34 *Selected Essays*, pp. 32, 33–34, 132, 68; *Autobiography*, p. 138.

35 *Selected Letters*, pp. 186, 146; *Selected Essays*, pp. 71, 231.

36 *Imaginations*, pp. 100, 102.

37 *Imaginations*, p. 105.

38 *Selected Letters*, pp. 238–239; *Selected Essays*, p. 256.

39 *Autobiography*, pp. 264–265.

40 *The Cantos* (New York: New Directions, 1972), p. 797; *Selected Essays*, pp. 213, 196, 256–257.

41 *Selected Essays*, pp. 104, 123; *Selected Letters*, p. 226.

42 *Selected Essays*, p. 238.

43 *Imaginations*, pp. 100, 105.

44 *Autobiography*, pp. xiii–xiv.

45 Eileen Simpson, *Poets in Their Youth* (New York: Random House, 1982), p. 103.

46 Weaver; Bram Djikstra, *The Hieroglyphics of a New Speech: Cubism, Stieglitz, and the Early Poetry of William Carlos Williams* (Princeton, N.J.: Princeton University Press, 1969).

47 *Interviews*, p. 53; Mariani, p. 726.

48 M. M. Bakhtin, *The Dialogic Imagination*, ed. Michael Holdquist and tr. Caryl Emerson and Michael Holdquist (Austin: University of Texas Press, 1981), pp. 84–85, 243.

49 *Imaginations*, pp. 107, 110–112, 121, 129.
50 *Imaginations*, pp. 116–117, 120, 129, 133, 134, 117, 138.
51 *Imaginations*, p. 93.
52 *Interviews*, p. 71.
53 *Selected Letters*, p. 132.
54 *Selected Essays*, pp. 275, 273, 278.
55 *Imaginations*, pp. 95–96, or *Collected Earlier Poems*, pp. 241–242.
56 *Imaginations*, p. 96, or *Collected Earlier Poems*, p. 242.
57 *Imaginations*, pp. 98–99, or *Collected Earlier Poems*, p. 243.
58 *Imaginations*, pp. 107–109, or *Collected Earlier Poems*, pp. 249–250.
59 *Imaginations*, p. 138, or *Collected Earlier Poems*, p. 277.
60 *Collected Earlier Poems*, p. 99.
61 *Collected Earlier Poems*, pp. 93–94.
62 *Collected Earlier Poems*, p. 136.
63 *William Carlos Williams: A Collection of Critical Essays*, p. 173.
64 *Interviews*, pp. 55, 56, 41, 40.
65 *Collected Earlier Poems*, p. 407.
66 *Profile of William Carlos Williams*, ed. Jerome Mazzaro (Columbus, Ohio: Charles E. Merrill, 1971), p. 72; *Selected Letters*, p. 214.
67 *Profile of William Carlos Williams*, p. 77.
68 *Collected Earlier Poems*, pp. 3–12.
69 *I Wanted to Write a Poem*, pp. 25–26.
70 Bakhtin, p. 251.
71 *Interviews*, p. 76. The 1926 "Paterson" can be found in *The Collected Earlier Poems*, pp. 233–235.
72 *The Embodiment of Knowledge*, p. 90; *Autobiography*, p. 391.
73 *I Wanted to Write a Poem*, pp. 71–73; Weaver, pp. 8–16. Weaver published excerpts from Ward's poem on pp. 165–200.
74 *Selected Letters*, p. 253.
75 *Selected Letters*, pp. 163, 230, 234–235.
76 *Selected Letters*, p. 175.
77 *Selected Letters*, pp. 257–258, 265; *Profile of William Carlos Williams*, pp. 62–63, 72.
78 Walter Scott Peterson, *An Approach to Paterson* (New Haven, Conn.: Yale University Press, 1967); Joel Conarroe, *William Carlos Williams' Paterson: Language and Landscape* (Philadelphia: University of Pennsylvania Press, 1970); Weaver; Sankey; Margaret Glynne Lloyd, *William Carlos Williams' Paterson: A Critical Reappraisal* (Rutherford, N.J.: Fairleigh Dickinson University Press, 1980).
79 All quotations from *Paterson* come from the reset text of the single-volume edition (New York: New Directions, 1963), and page numbers in the chapter are given after the quotations.
80 Conarroe, pp. 10–16.
81 *Selected Letters*, p. 333; *Selected Essays*, p. 206.
82 Sankey, p. 37.
83 Quoted in Sherman Paul, *The Music of Survival: A Biography of a Poem by William Carlos Williams* (Urbana: University of Illinois Press, 1968), p. 117.
84 Sankey, p. 71.
85 Sankey, p. 101.

86 Sankey, p. 133.

87 Sankey, pp. 179, 180.

88 Weaver, pp. 103–114.

89 *I Wanted to Write a Poem*, p. 22.

90 Sankey, p. 211.

91 *Autobiography*, p. 392.

92 Sankey, p. 201.

93 *Selected Letters*, p. 286.

94 *Profile of William Carlos Williams*, pp. 68, 70.

95 Paul, p. 39.

96 *Profile of William Carlos Williams*, pp. 77–78.

97 John C. Thirwall, "The Genesis of the Epic *Paterson*," *Today's Japan*, IV (March 1959), 70, quoted in Conarroe, p. 98.

98 *The Collected Poems of T. S. Eliot 1909–1962* (New York: Harcourt, Brace & World, 1963), pp. 177, 178; *The Cantos* (New Directions, 1972), pp. 13, 797.

99 *Selected Essays*, pp. 108, 283; *Selected Letters*, pp. 176–177.

100 Charles Olson, *Selected Writings*, ed. Robert Creeley (New York: New Directions, 1951), p. 82; *Selected Letters*, p. 326.

101 *Pictures from Brueghel and Other Poems* (New York: New Directions, 1962), pp. 108–120.

102 *Selected Letters*, p. 329.

103 *Selected Essays*, pp. 283, 286, 287; *Selected Letters*, pp. 332, 335–336; *Interviews*, pp. 45, 68.

104 *Selected Essays*, pp. 337, 340; *Selected Letters*, p. 332.

105 *Selected Letters*, pp. 326–327.

106 Weaver, p. 83; *Interviews*, p. 67.

107 *I Wanted to Write a Poem*, pp. 80–82, 88–89.

108 Weaver, pp. 85–86.

109 *William Carlos Williams: A Collection of Critical Essays*, p. 172.

110 *Pictures from Brueghel*, p. 86.

111 *Pictures from Brueghel*, pp. 129–132.

Chapter 7: Allen Tate and Hart Crane

1 John Crowe Ransom, "In Amicitia," *The Sewanee Review*, LXVII (Autumn 1959), 529.

2 *Essays of Four Decades* (Chicago: Swallow Press, 1968), p. 531. Henceforth this volume will be identified in the notes as *Essays*.

3 *Essays*, pp. 3, 14.

4 *Essays*, pp. 64, 67.

5 *Essays*, pp. 511, 349, 351.

6 Robert Lowell, "Visiting the Tates," *The Sewanee Review*, LXVII (Autumn 1959), 558, 559; *Essays*, p. 57.

7 *Essays*, p. 595.

8 *Collected Poems 1919–1976* (New York: Farrar, Straus & Giroux, 1977). Page references to extended passages cited are indicated in parentheses in the text.

9 *Essays*, pp. 292, 295.

10 *Essays*, pp. 533, 545, 577, 578, 586, 592.

11   Quoted in John L. Stewart, *The Burden of Time: The Fugitives and Agrarians* (Princeton N.J.: Princeton University Press, 1965), pp. 332–333.

12   *Essays*, p. 538.

13   *Essays*, pp. 427, 438.

14   *Essays*, pp. 428, 429, 402, 405, 45.

15   *Essays*, pp. 410, 412, 405, 406.

16   *Essays*, pp. 403, 391–396, 398, 400.

17   *Essays*, p. 310.

18   *Essays*, pp. 310, 314, 319, 320.

19   *Essays*, pp. 319–322, 327–328.

20   *Essays*, pp. 595–596.

21   Tate did not include "False Nightmare" in *Collected Poems 1919–1976*, but the poem appears in *Poems* (New York: Charles Scribner's Sons, 1960) on pp. 56–58 and in *The Swimmers and Other Selected Poems* (New York: Charles Scribner's Sons, 1970) on pp. 61–62.

22   T. S. Eliot, *Selected Essays* (New York: Harcourt, Brace, 1950), p. 380.

23   Lowell, p. 559; Allen Tate, "Religion and the Intellectuals," *Sewanee Review*, XVII (March 1950), 250–251; *Essays*, pp. 385–386; Ransom, p. 537.

24   *Essays*, p. 16.

25   Radcliffe Squires, *Allen Tate: A Literary Biography* (New York: Pegasus, 1971), pp. 188–193.

26   *Notebook* (New York: Farrar, Straus & Giroux, 1970), p. 253.

27   *Life Studies* (New York: Farrar, Straus & Cudahy, 1959), p. 55; *Poetry and Criticism of Matthew Arnold*, ed. A. Dwight Culler (Boston: Houghton Mifflin, 1961), p. 380.

28   *The Letters of Hart Crane*, ed. Brom Weber (Berkeley and Los Angeles: University of California Press, 1965), p. 67. Henceforth references to this volume will be identified in notes as *Letters*.

29   John Unterecker, *Voyager: A Life of Hart Crane* (New York: Farrar, Straus & Giroux, 1969), p. 362; *The Complete Poems and Selected Letters and Prose of Hart Crane* (New York: Liveright, 1966), p. 263. Henceforth references to this volume will be identified in notes as *Complete Poems*.

30   From "The Death of Thomas Carlyle" in *Specimen Days*.

31   *The Collected Poems of Wallace Stevens* (New York: Alfred A. Knopf, 1954), p. 524.

32   Unterecker, p. 240.

33   *Illuminations*, tr. Louise Varese (New York: New Directions, 1957), p. xxvii.

34   Unterecker, p. 242.

35   *Letters*, pp. 301–302, 91–92, 127, 138.

36   *Complete Poems*, pp. 234, 220–221; *Letters*, p. 238.

37   *Complete Poems*, pp. 219–221; Unterecker, p. 362; *Letters*, p. 237.

38   Edmund S. de Chasca, *John Gould Fletcher and Imagism* (Columbia: University of Missouri Press, 1978), pp. 112–113, 119–190; Thomas Parkinson, *Hart Crane and Yvor Winters: Their Literary Correspondence* (Berkeley and Los Angeles: University of California Press, 1978), p. 9.

39   *Collected Poems of Hart Crane*, ed. Waldo Frank (New York: Liveright, 1946), p. xiv.

40   *Complete Poems*, p. 220.

41   The texts of Crane's poems were taken from *The Poems of Hart Crane*, ed. Marc

Simon (New York: Liveright, 1986), and the page references are given in parentheses in this chapter.

42 *Complete Poems*, p. 222.
43 R. W. B. Lewis, *The Poetry of Hart Crane: A Critical Study* (Princeton, N.J.: Princeton University Press, 1967), pp. 161–165; Sherman Paul, *Hart's Bridge* (Urbana: University of Illinois Press, 1972), pp. 149–152.
44 *Essays*, p. 595.
45 *Complete Poems*, p. 223.
46 Paul, p. 27.
47 *Letters*, pp. 264, 260; *Complete Poems*, p. 263.
48 *Letters*, p. 301.
49 *Letters*, p. 140.
50 *Letters*, pp. 89, 87.
51 *Letters*, p. 115.
52 *Letters*, p. 118.
53 *Complete Poems*, pp. 217, 218.
54 Unterecker, pp. 153–154.
55 *Letters*, pp. 128, 125, 124, 261.
56 *Letters*, pp. 125, 308, 305.
57 *Letters*, p. 114; *Essays*, p. 321.
58 *Form and Value in Modern Poetry* (New York: Anchor, 1957), p. 285.
59 *Letters*, pp. 269–270.
60 *Letters*, pp. 260–261.
61 *Letters*, p. 323.
62 Lewis, p. 267.
63 Paul, pp. 10, 298, 284.
64 *Letters*, pp. 308, 124, 242, 232.
65 *Letters*, pp. 8, 18, 108, 279–280.
66 Lewis, pp. 229, 231.
67 *Letters*, p. 140.
68 Paul, pp. 223–224.
69 Lewis, p. 331; *Complete Poems*, p. 261.
70 *Complete Poems*, p. 262.
71 Lewis, p. 340.
72 Lewis, p. 231.
73 *Letters*, p. 261.
74 Paul, p. 290.
75 Paul, p. 296.
76 Paul, pp. 298, 302.
77 Ezra Pound, *Selected Prose 1909–1965*, ed. William Cookson (New York: New Directions, 1976), pp. 374–375.
78 *The Cantos* (New York: New Directions, 1972), p. 796; Olson, *Selected Writings*, ed. Robert Creeley (New York: New Directions, 1966), p. 238.
79 George Oppen, "The Mind's Own Place," *Montemora*, 1 (Fall 1975), 133; reprinted from *Kulchur*, 10 (1963).
80 *The Contemporary Writer: Interviews with Sixteen Novelists and Poets*, ed. L. S. Dembo and Cyrena N. Pondrom (Madison: University of Wisconsin Press, 1972), pp. 199–200.

Coda: Yvor Winters and Robinson Jeffers

1   *In Defense of Reason* (Denver: Alan Swallow, 1947), p. 30.
2   "Poetry, Gongorism and a Thousand Years" is reprinted in Melba Berry Bennett, *The Stone Mason of Tor House: The Life and Work of Robinson Jeffers* (Los Angeles: Ward Ritchie Press, 1966), pp. 202−207. The passages quoted in this paragraph appear on pp. 203−204.
3   Quoted in Brother Antoninus (William Everson), *Robinson Jeffers: Fragments of an Older Fury* (Berkeley: Oyez, 1968), p. 114.
4   *In Defense of Reason*, pp. 8−9.
5   *In Defense of Reason*, pp. 54−55, 590.
6   *Forms of Discovery: Critical and Historical Essays on the Forms of the Short Poem in English* (Chicago: Alan Swallow, 1967), p. 251.
7   *Forms of Discovery*, p. 323.
8   *In Defense of Reason*, p. 14.
9   *The Early Poems of Yvor Winters 1920−1928* (Denver: Alan Swallow, 1966), pp. 7−8.
10   *The Early Poems*, p. 86. Subsequent page references to *The Early Poems* are given in parentheses after the quoted passages.
11   Dick Davis, *Wisdom and Wilderness: The Achievement of Yvor Winters* (Athens: University of Georgia Press, 1983), pp. 46−47.
12   "The Brink of Darkness" first appeared in the July−September 1932 issue of *Hound and Horn* and was reprinted in *Anchor in the Sea: An Anthology of Psychological Fiction*, ed. Alan Swallow (Denver: Alan Swallow, 1947), in the British *Collected Poems of Yvor Winters* (Manchester: Carcanet Press, 1978), and in *Mirror and Mirage: Fiction by Nineteen*, ed. Albert J. Guerard (Stanford, Calif.: Stanford Alumni Association, 1980).
13   *Collected Poems* (Denver: Alan Swallow, 1960), p. 47. Subsequent page references to the *Collected Poems* are given in parentheses after the quoted passages.
14   *In Defense of Reason*, p. 22.
15   *In Defense of Reason*, pp. 3, 11.
16   *In Defense of Reason*, p. 11.
17   *The Uncollected Essays and Reviews of Yvor Winters*, ed. Francis Murphy (Chicago: Swallow Press, 1973), p. 221; *In Defense of Reason*, p. 3.
18   *In Defense of Reason*, pp. 12−13.
19   *Forms of Discovery*, pp. 318−319.
20   *In Defense of Reason*, pp. 30−35.
21   *Uncollected Essays and Reviews*, pp. 68−69.
22   *Uncollected Essays and Reviews*, p. 123.
23   Quoted in *The Stone Mason of Tor House*, p. 205.
24   *The Selected Letters of Robinson Jeffers 1897−1962*, ed. Ann. N. Ridgeway (Baltimore: Johns Hopkins University Press, 1968), p. 35.
25   *Selected Letters*, pp. 200−201.
26   *Selected Letters*, pp. 7, 201, 209.
27   Quoted in Everson, p. 37.
28   Quoted in Bennett, p. 151.
29   Everson, p. 37.
30   For Jeffers' comment about Lucretius, see *Selected Letters*, p. 201. For comments on prosody, see *Selected Letters*, pp. 28, 151−152, 173, 174, 206.
31   Quoted in Bennett, p. 111.

32 *Selected Letters*, p. 173; Everson, p. 37.

33 *Selected Letters*, p. 111.

34 *Roan Stallion, Tamar and Other Poems* (New York: Modern Library, 1935), p. viii.

35 *Roan Stallion, Tamar and Other Poems*, p. ix.

36 *Roan Stallion, Tamar and Other Poems*, p. viii; *Selected Letters*, p. 369.

37 "Foreword" to *The Selected Poetry of Robinson Jeffers* (New York: Random House, 1938), pp. xv–xvi.

38 *Selected Letters*, p. 342.

39 *Selected Letters*, p. 184.

40 *Roan Stallion, Tamar and Other Poems*, p. 295.

41 *The Beginning and the End and Other Poems* (New York: Random House, 1963), pp. 73–74.

42 *Hungerfield and Other Poems* (New York: Random House, 1954), p. 97.

43 *Selected Letters*, p. 35.

44 *Roan Stallion, Tamar and Other Poems*, p. 220.

45 *The Beginning and the End*, p. 62.

46 *Selected Letters*, pp. 262–263.

47 *Gaudier-Brzeska: A Memoir* (New York: New Directions, 1970; first published in 1916), pp. 89–90.

48 *Earth Poetry: Selected Essays and Interviews 1950–1977* (Berkeley: Oyez, 1980), p. 36.

Index